NINETEENTH CENTURY ART
A CRITICAL HISTORY

NINETEENTH
A CRITICAL

With 369 illustrations, 51 in color

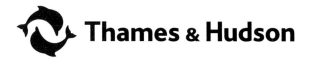

Thames & Hudson

STEPHEN F. EISENMAN

CENTURY ART
HISTORY

THOMAS CROW

BRIAN LUKACHER

LINDA NOCHLIN

FRANCES K. POHL

ACKNOWLEDGMENTS

A number of individuals have generously assisted in the completion of this book: the contributing authors—Thomas Crow, Brian Lukacher, Frances Pohl, and Linda Nochlin—have been unstinting with their time, their helpful criticisms, and their kindness. I am very grateful to them. David Craven has offered encouragement at crucial stages of the composition of the book; he alone knows how many of the ideas about method are indebted to him, and how well or poorly they have been represented. Eric Frank, my colleague and friend at Occidental College, has been generous in helping me identify the art historical and iconographical sources for a number of the works discussed. Abigail Solomon-Godeau has been a smart and stimulating debater about matters that concern women and Paul Gauguin. As my live-in editor and interlocutor of first resort, Mary Weismantel has by her efforts both preserved my collaborators' regard for me and propelled forward the entire effort. I cannot adequately thank her for her intelligence, companionship, loyalty, and love. Finally, I would like to thank the people who taught me about nineteenth-century art at the State University of New York at Albany, the Williams College Graduate Program in Art History, and Princeton University—Robert Kinsman, George Heard Hamilton, Daniel Robbins, Albert Boime, and Thomas Crow.

In the captions to the illustrations, measurements are in inches (centimeters in parentheses), height before width, unless otherwise indicated.

First published in the United States of America in 1994 by Thames & Hudson Inc.,
500 Fifth Avenue, New York, New York 10110

thamesandhudsonusa.com

Reprinted 2001

Library of Congress Catalog Card Number 93-61271

ISBN: 0-500-23675-5 (hardback)
0-500-27753-2 (paperback)

Printed and bound in Slovenia by Mladinska Knjiga

CONTENTS

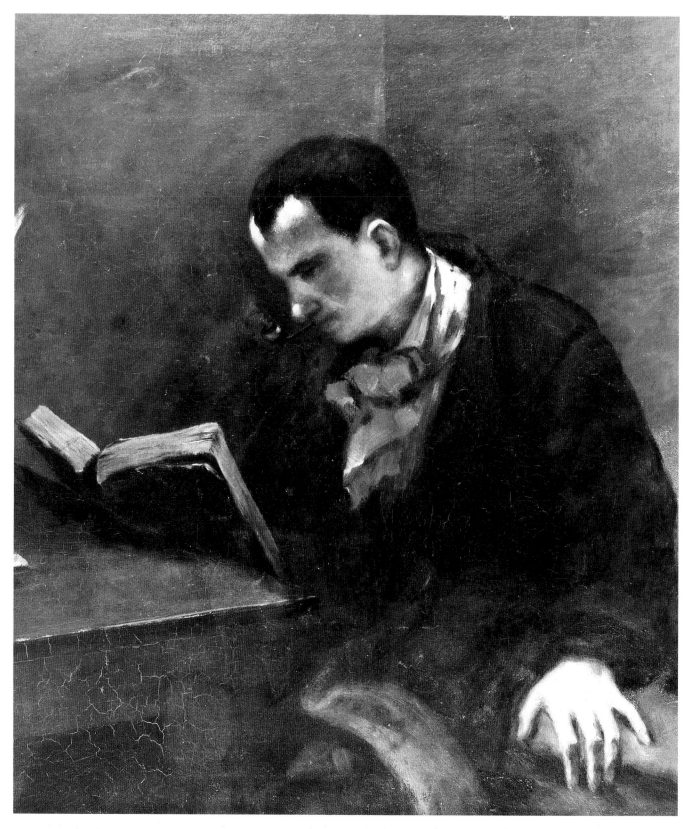

GUSTAVE COURBET *Portrait of Baudelaire* ca. 1848. 20⅞ × 24 (53 × 61). Detail

INTRODUCTION: CRITICAL ART AND HISTORY

THE ART DISCUSSED IN THIS BOOK WAS MADE IN Europe and North America during a period of rapid and profound social and political transformation. The close of that epoch of change—now almost a hundred years distant—did not, of course, end the drama of modernization. In fact, far from slowing down, the dynamic of change begun in the nineteenth century was accelerated in the twentieth. Soon the terms "imperialism," "assembly line," and "mass culture" entered the modern European and American lexicons, supplanting an earlier vocabulary that included "nation," "industry," and "the popular." Yet if actions and words were shifting their arenas and changing their meanings, the basic facts of crisis and everlasting uncertainty remained the same. Indeed, if the history and culture of the nineteenth century are compelling today, it is largely because the twentieth century accepted and embraced their legacy of political and cultural revolution. The rudiments of that historical legacy are generally familiar but bear retelling.

The end of the eighteenth century marked the final dissolution of feudalism in Europe, a primarily agricultural and rigidly hierarchical productive and social order that had survived for seven centuries. In the place of feudalism, there now stood a capitalist and bourgeois economic and social edifice. This epochal reconfiguration of European economy and society—long in coming but no less dramatic in the end for its gradual preparation—was marked by outbreaks of revolution in Europe and the Americas. Beginning in 1776, and continuing for a generation, wars of colonial independence—inspired by Enlightenment principles of political consent and social contract—were waged and won in the Americas, the Caribbean, and Mexico. These victories in turn rebounded in the core nations of Europe, accelerating already existing demands for social justice, economic equality, and political enfranchisement. By the middle of the nineteenth century, the social upheaval that had begun with the bloody dispatch of the French Bourbon monarchs in 1793—the event that appears in retrospect as the exclamation point at the end of the feudal sentence—was becoming more mature, democratic, and inclusive. In 1848, the increasingly self-cognizant working classes of France, Germany, Austria, Italy, and England rose up in arms (or in the latter case organized themselves into a political movement) to combat the vestigial aristocratic, and the new bourgeois, elites who maintained economic and political dominance. (Quick successes were soon followed by profound failures to transform the economic and political status quo.) A decade and a half later, the slave plantation system of agriculture in the southern United States was overturned by women and men driven at times by moral outrage and at others by economic calculation.

By the last quarter of the century, change itself had become entrenched in the politics and culture of the West. Economic cycles of boom and bust followed close upon each other, new agricultural and industrial technologies transformed countryside and city alike, and the efforts of women to achieve emancipation began to rival in intensity the ongoing class and ethnic struggles. In the United States, the genocide of Native Americans was nearly completed by 1890 (the year of the Wounded Knee Massacre), even while large numbers of new European and Asian immigrants arrived at Atlantic and Pacific harbors. As the twentieth century dawned, the restlessness and violence that had characterized a revolutionary century was becoming internationalized. The new age of imperialism that reached its apogee in the decade before 1914 accomplished the dividing of the non-European world into colonies for the benefit of a half-dozen Western states, yet notably failed to secure either peace or generalized prosperity. Indeed, imperialism soon generated its own antinomies: vastly destructive wars between the imperialist nations were fought, broad (though fragile) alliances were forged among oppressed European and non-European peoples, and metropolitan bourgeois culture itself was on the point of being dethroned.

The nineteenth century was thus punctuated at its beginning, middle, and end by revolutions—political, industrial, and cultural—and by the less violent struggles of workers, women, and indigenous peoples for freedom and equality. The visual arts of the epoch were also indelibly marked by restiveness, change, and insurgency; they too were shaped and figured by the irruption of classes and interests formerly excluded from the domain of national culture. (The insight into a link between the ethics, politics, and material life of a society and its art, we shall soon see, was an achievement of the age.) No longer the reliably pliant vehicle of entrenched elites, art was often now the contradictory, unpredictable, and critical voice of diverse individuals, subcultures, and interest groups.

The prints, drawings, and paintings of the English William Blake and the Spanish Francisco Goya, for example, offer clear instances of the responsiveness of artists to the cultural crises of the early nineteenth century. In Blake's illustrated poetic books such as *America* (1793) and *Europe* (1794), he lamented the failure of his native country to embrace the revolutionary upwellings in the United States and France. In Goya's series of etchings called *Los Caprichos* (1799), he condemned the prevailing ignorance and prejudice of the Spanish monarchy and clergy, and espoused the emancipatory principles of the French Enlightenment. Yet more than simply proclaiming the value of democratic and Enlightenment ideals, Blake and Goya found ways to embody revolution in the forms and subjects of their art. Each represented the political and social crises of their day in the language of solar and Manichean metaphors: Light erases Darkness, Day combats Night, God confronts Satan, Master opposes Slave, Orc (Blake's personification of desire) battles Urizen (his figure of reason), Truth (Goya's preferred allegory) tries to vanquish Ignorance. Perhaps most remarkable of all, however, is the fact that Blake and Goya represent their themes and protagonists dialectically—that is, they describe them as various and mutable. Neither light nor dark, reason nor unreason, neither God nor the devil are singular and eternal; like the dawning revolutionary age itself, they are multiple and protean, contingent upon the political and social perspectives of the spectator.

William Blake and Francisco Goya were surely exceptional, among nineteenth-century artists, for their radicalism and political perspicacity. Yet even conservative figures, such as the arch-Classicist J. A. D. Ingres, often manifested an active, critical engagement with the facts of modern social change. Ingres's *The Apotheosis of Homer* (1827), for example, appears

to represent Classicism as a timeless canon of physical beauty and formal perfection passed down, generation to generation, from archaic Greece to the Christian Middle Ages, to modern, enlightened France. Yet a close examination of the picture suggests that it represents at the same time the cultural and ethical divide increasingly felt to exist between the past and the present.

Exhibited in 1827 at the Salon Carré of the Louvre palace (the most prestigious venue in Paris for the display of works of art), *The Apotheosis* depicts the blind Homer, enthroned before an Ionic temple and crowned with laurel by a winged Victory (or Fame). At his feet, in postures that recall the figures of *Day* and *Night* from Michelangelo's Tomb of Giuliano de' Medici, are seated allegorical representations of *The Iliad* (beside a sword) and *The Odyssey* (with an oar resting on her lap). To Homer's immediate right are the three great tragedians Aeschylus, Sophocles, and Euripides, and to his left the poet Pindar (offering the lyre) and the sculptor Phidias (with left arm extended, holding a mallet). Ranged around and below these Greeks are other ancient and modern luminaries indebted to Homer: Apelles leads Raphael by the hand, Virgil guides Dante, Molière (holding the mask of drama) stands beside Racine, and Shakespeare accompanies Poussin (in the left foreground, pointing to Homer). Omitted from the picture, but everywhere implicit, is Ingres (he included himself in a preliminary version), who as recent Academician and proud recipient of the *Légion d'honneur*, saw himself as the honored heir to Poussin, Raphael, and, especially, the Greeks. In 1818, Ingres proclaimed: "In matters of Art, I have not changed. Age and reflection have, I hope, strengthened my taste, without diminishing its ardor. I still worship Raphael, his century, and above all the divine Greeks." For Ingres, therefore, ancient Greece represented both the childhood of Europe—the origin of European culture from the fourteenth through nineteenth centuries— and the full swell of a maturity that could never be superseded.

Commissioned for the ceiling of the newly decorated room of Egyptian antiquities in the Louvre, *The Apotheosis of Homer* proclaims Classicism an indisputable canon guaranteeing a stable cultural foundation for the present. The painting suggests that present French and European culture is the culmination of a continuous line of development beginning in archaic Greece, and passing through the Roman empire, the Christian Middle Ages, the Renaissance, the time of Louis XIV, and the present age of Charles X. The painter and critic Etienne Delécluze described the static and retrospective aspects of the *Apotheosis* in his Salon review for the 1828 *Journal des débats* when he praised Ingres for dispensing with the pretension of artistic originality in his painting and instead graciously accepting the formal "archetypes" provided by all the great personages he represents. Delécluze writes:

63

The individual originality of these men is incontestable, but what placed them beyond all comparisons were the era and circumstances under which they lived. Homer found himself at the ideal point for giving life to mythological traditions; Dante for fixing the poetic theology born in the fifth century; Shakespeare for transfusing the ideas of the south into northern brains; Phidias for clothing symbolic idols with man's image; and Michelangelo for *incarnating* the Middle Ages. But once all these great combinations have been fashioned and fixed, all that can be done is to modify the archetypes indefinitely.

This subtle crafting and modification of the Classical corpus of "archetypes," according to Delécluze, was Ingres's achievement. Yet this was in fact an achievement more of a negative than of a positive kind: it involved the erasure of historic and artistic difference and dissonance and the substitution of a bland and conflict-free Classicism. Banished from the Classical tradition in Ingres's painting are the irrational pessimism of Euripides, the devastating loneliness of Dante (as he leaves behind his guide Virgil on the threshold of Paradise), the alienation of Hamlet, and the stunning anticlassicism of the aged Michelangelo; what remains is only costume, cliché, and hollow splendor. In thus purging from the Classical past and present all that gave it complexity and vitality, Ingres's *Apotheosis* comes to resemble an attack upon, more than an homage to, the legacy of Homer, and it should not surprise us that most critics of the painting found it objectionable.

Indeed, if we now look again at the *Apotheosis of Homer*, we notice how much more it resembles a crude pastiche than an ideal paradigm of Classicism. Figures are ranked in rigid bands echoing the horizontal and vertical steps in the foreground and columns in the background; they hold hands but fail to interact or engage the viewer, despite the grotesquely abbreviated *repoussoirs* in the extreme foreground. Can there be any other explanation for the flatness, awkwardness, and stiltedness of the picture than that Ingres was recording—poignantly, reluctantly, perhaps even helplessly—the breakdown in the authority of the Classical tradition in the modern world?

Delécluze himself half understood the problematical nature of *The Apotheosis* when he described its painter's technique as "submitting less to the laws of linear perspective than to laws of a perspective that one could call *chronological* . . . in giving more relief to the modern figures and gradually weakening his colors as he reaches the semi-fantasy figures of Orpheus and Linus, who are on the furthest plane of the picture." In the hands of Ingres, the ancient world is one of blindness, shadows, and loss; the great monuments of Greek antiquity are destroyed—the Athena Parthenos, the Colossus, the

entire *oeuvre* of Apelles—and there are no comparable modern works to take their place. Indeed, the further you enter the modern world, as the art historian Norman Bryson has written, elaborating Delécluze, "the more the nobility and generality of countenance evident in such figures as Phidias and Apelles gives way to the ironical peering and sardonic expressions, at their nadir in the busy scribbling and sarcastic 'smile of reason' of Voltaire [at the lower right corner]." Bryson's word for this representation of absence or loss is "desire," but the passivity of the term seems to me misleading; I am more persuaded that what is at work is an active, restless, and critical intelligence. Ingres saw and felt (however much he may have lamented) the weakness and febrility of the Classicism of his day and could not avoid depicting it. Precisely such a knowledge of cultural crisis and change—featured in the art of conservatives such as Ingres as much as in the work of radicals such as Blake and Goya, or later in the century Gustave Courbet—is the distinguishing trait of the most salient art of the nineteenth century; this is the art I am calling *critical*.

Taking our cue from the art of the period itself, therefore, the authors of this book intend to consider it critically. Although this approach has been adopted in many of the monographs that inform the writing of this volume, it has not previously been used in surveys of nineteenth-century art. The authors of most earlier surveys, beginning with Richard Muther (1907) and Léonce Bénédite (1910), and extending to Rosenblum/Janson (1984) and Lorenz Eitner (1988), were empiricists in the sense that they based their research methods upon the model of investigations in the natural sciences. They proceeded by induction, collecting art historical data—artists' names and biographies, anecdotes, titles of artworks, genres and subjects, key dates, stylistic developments, and the documented responses of patrons, critics, and the public— and then assembled them into "long chains of deductive reasoning," in the words of empiricism's parent, Descartes, in the confidence that "there can be nothing so remote that we cannot reach it, nor so recondite that we cannot discover it." Even Fritz Novotny's idiosyncratic volume for the Pelican History of Art (1960) generally conforms to this model. Although he frames his chronological survey (1780–1880) with references to the "spiritualization" of art in the hands of the philosopher Kant and the painter Cézanne, he nevertheless speaks of his own approach in empiricist terms: his book entails, he says, the study of the "laws which govern the development of art" and its "prevailing lines of development." Indeed for Novotny, scholarly (scientific) method and subject matter are perfectly merged, since he sees the nineteenth century as "defined [by] the study of the external appearance of nature. [It is] the century of Naturalism."

Empiricism has dominated studies of nineteenth-century

art but has rarely been explicitly acknowledged as a methodology. An exception to this silence is John Rewald, who honestly champions it in his popular and indispensable *History of Impressionism* (1946; 4th revised edition, 1973). In his introduction, Rewald approvingly cites the words of the nineteenth-century French political historian Fustel de Coulanges: "History is not an art, it is pure science. . . . Like all science, it consists in stating the facts, in analyzing them, in drawing them together and in bringing out their connections. The historian's only skill should consist in deducing from the documents all that is in them and in adding nothing they do not contain."

In a manner not dissimilar to Rewald, Robert Rosenblum in the introduction to his and H. W. Janson's *Nineteenth-Century Art* (1984; *Art of the Nineteenth Century*, English edition), rejects "the purist tyranny of abstract and absolutist systems," insisting that "art historians should be as flexible, various, and comprehensive as possible in their approaches, and be willing to consider anything from the history of technology to the abiding mysteries of genius and psychology as potentially illuminating their ever more vast subject." True to their words, Rosenblum and Janson are certainly more catholic than their predecessors in their near encyclopedic inclusion of diverse artists outside the established canon and in their wideranging discussions of the many sources and documents of art history. Among the relevant themes for study cited in his introduction, Rosenblum lists the Bible, opera, ballet, tuberculosis, syphilis, prostitution, and photography. Yet, however open-minded the authors are, their overall goal and achievement is similar to that of survey authors that came before: it is to construct a more or less unified art historical mechanism that functions noiselessly and without friction, and in which contradiction and superfluity is as nearly as possible eliminated. Like earlier writers, too, all these authors remain deeply committed to a micrological analysis, seeing in the details of artists' lives and commissions, as the Frankfurt School social theorist Max Horkheimer in 1937 described the harvest of empiricism, "a sum-total of facts [which] is there and must be accepted," instead of the conscious and unconscious "activities of society as a whole." Empiricism thus acts as a kind of sieve which holds back from view the large social, economic, and political forces determining art production, while permitting the small formal, biographical, and patronage factors to pass before the scholarly gaze.

The empiricist attitude maintains a traditional Cartesian separation of facts from values, an approach which goes against much recent scientific and theoretical investigation. Rarely, indeed, have as many critics and researchers—from the fields of literature and philosophy to jurisprudence and physics—joined their voices together as they now have in questioning what they see as the myth of an interest-free science and scholarship. Art history itself, especially art history of the nineteenth century (with the notable exception of its basic survey texts), has been significantly transformed in the last two decades by this new attitude. The discipline has been especially redefined in the light of the revival of structural linguistics in the late 1960's and the emergence of its various critical successors. Previous scholarly confidence in the role of the artist or author as the isolated genius inventor— a modernist fiction—and in the view of the critic or historian as a dispassionate observer is today questioned if not wholly rejected. Marxist philosophy has also played a signal role in overturning the formerly prevailing confidence that art history could be told as a straightforward, descriptive narrative independent of the interests, politics, gender, or ideology of artists, audiences, and critics.

The word "ideology," which re-emerged as a term of cultural criticism during the student movement in the 1960's, has already been used several times in this introduction; it requires brief elaboration. By ideology is meant the characteristic bodies of knowledge, belief, imagery, and expression that are created by a particular social class at a given moment in history. Ideologies arise largely unbeknownst to their subjects as a set of workaday assumptions or commonsense notions about the world. They provide their possessors with a coherent image of their lived relation to social reality, and are thus an effective (because surreptitious) instrument for the domination of one class or group by another. Ideologies both follow from economic and political power, and are an instrument for achieving that control. "The ideas of the ruling class," wrote Karl Marx and Friedrich Engels (the first to theorize ideology), "are in every epoch the ruling ideas." The mid-twentieth-century political theorist Louis Althusser offered a brief but compelling example of one of the ideologies that arose at the dawn of the nineteenth century but which is still vital to class stability today:

> [According to] the ideology of *freedom*, the bourgeoisie lives in a direct fashion its relation to its conditions of existence: that is to say, it comprehends its real relation (to the laws of a liberal capitalist economy), but *incorporates* it into an imaginary relation (the idea that all people are free, including "free" workers).

By this (somewhat tendentious) example of the way in which the ideology of freedom masks the severely circumscribed liberties of workers in a liberal capitalist economy, it can be seen that ideology *per se* is powerful precisely because it is both an imaginary representation of social and material relations and an actual lived relation to reality. Ideologies are thus like mimetic works of art in their dualism of illusory and real; they represent reality in a conventional and an historically contingent fashion. They are what is filtered out of an art history which is solely concerned with detail and objectivity. Althusser's use of the term ideology, however, was polemical and often mechanistic; as a Structuralist Marxist, he rejected altogether any link between imaginative representation and material truth, and he denied the existence of human autonomy or individual volition.

An art history that acknowledges ideological forces need not be as doctrinaire as Althusser. Indeed, the best recent art historical scholarship—whether Marxist, Structuralist, Post-Structuralist, or Feminist—has been both empirical and critical; it has implicitly argued for a simultaneous consideration of observable facts and material conditions, and their expression in class and gender ideology. In all cases, however, and regardless of the specific critical perspective of the author, a passive attitude of scientific dispassion is seen to be an impossibility since it is assumed that the situation of spectators affects their perspective.

The discussion above has summarized a few of the tenets of a new critical as opposed to a purely empirical art history. Yet even if these recent scholarly transformations had not taken the firm hold that they have, the need for a broader and more critical approach to nineteenth-century art should have been apparent empirically through close attention to the material itself. For if the nineteenth century saw the first flowering of the application of empiricism in the humanities, it also first divined and theorized the critical interconnections between seeing and knowing and between vision and society. From Hegel to Marx, from Carlyle to Ruskin, from Baudelaire to Bergson, nineteenth-century authors and critics explored the links between perception and history. The most complete discussion of the question is found in the writings of Marx, effectively summarized by Horkheimer when he wrote:

> It is not only in clothing and appearance, in outward form and emotional makeup that humans are the product of history. Even the way they see and hear is inseparable from the social life-process as it has evolved over the millennia. The facts which our senses present to us are socially preformed . . . through the historical character of the object perceived and through the historical character of the perceiving organ.

The description by Marx of the historical character of perception in his *Economic and Philosophic Manuscripts of 1844* is more complex. He wrote that the transformation of the alien, objective world into a subjective world of consoling "human reality" depends upon the state of development of the human senses:

> Just as music alone awakens in people the sense of music, and just as the most beautiful music has no sense for the unmusical ear . . . for this reason the *senses* of the social

person are *other* than those of the non-social person. Only through the objectively unfolded richness of people's essential being is the richness of subjective *human* sensibility (a musical ear, an eye for beauty of form . . .) either cultivated or brought into being. For not only the five senses but also the so-called mental senses—the practical senses (will, love, etc.)—in a word, *human sense*—the humanness of the senses—come to be by virtue of *humanized* nature. The *forming* of the five senses is a labor of the entire history of the world down to the present.

Marx's point is that while humans by their nature as humans have senses and perceptions, these are rude and unformed in the absence of their specific development and cultivation, which only occurs historically. Moreover, all the senses are differently developed according to the nature of the particular society in which the person lives: a capitalist society in which the *sense of having* dominates is clearly different in its sensual or perceptual capacities from a feudal or Communist society which does not subscribe to the concept of private property. And finally, Marx stands his argument about the impact of society upon the human senses on its feet by arguing that the cultivation of the senses—whether in the form of art, music, or literature—in its turn plays a significant role in the historical unfolding of a society. Giving material form to our sensual instincts or capacities, both theoretically and practically, "is required," he writes, "to make people's *sense human*, as well as to create the *human sense* corresponding to the entire wealth of human and natural substance." (I shall return later to this question of the active or formative role of art in the making of modern society.)

A similar if somewhat narrower formulation of the link between history and material culture, or between art and ideology, was achieved a decade after Marx by the moralist and esthetician John Ruskin. An important figure in the revival of the arts in mid-century Britain and in its medieval revivalism, Ruskin wrote in his essay "On the Nature of Gothic and the Function of the Workman therein" (1853) that: "The art of any country is the exponent of its social and political virtues. The art or general productive and formative energy of any country, is an exact exponent of its ethical life. You can have a noble art only from noble persons, associated under laws fitted to their time and circumstances." Ruskin's observation led him to compose a body of art history and criticism that is at once finely tuned to the subtlest formal nuances of the works of architecture, painting, or sculpture under his purview and unabashedly partisan in its championing of those works that conformed to his moral and ethical opinions. A closer consideration of Ruskin reveals that the two sides of his critical practise are both informed by his appreciation of art as a form of labor. Ruskin's insight was later summarized in a sentence by his student, the author, designer, and political activist William Morris: "Yet the essence of what Ruskin then taught us was simple enough, like all great discoveries. It was really nothing more recondite than this, that the art of any epoch must of necessity be the expression of its social life, and that the social life of the Middle Ages allowed the workman freedom of individual expression, which on the other hand our social life forbids him."

At about the same time that Marx, a German, was writing his essay concerned with the historical character of the senses, and the Englishman Ruskin was publishing his radical view that every age had its own unique vision and art corresponding to its peculiar ethical and social life, a French poet and journalist was suggesting much the same thing. It was Charles Baudelaire who provocatively argued that artists and writers be resolutely of their own time; it was he who established the model of the critic who is profoundly and passionately engaged with his subject and his epoch. Jettisoning any notion of Classical "archetypes," as found for example in Delécluze, and setting the tone for future critical encomiums to modernity, he wrote at the conclusion of his review of the 1845 Paris Salon exhibition: "The true painter we're looking for will be the one who can snatch from the life of today its epic quality, and make us feel how great and poetic we are in our cravats and our patent-leather boots. Next year let's hope that the true seekers may grant us the extraordinary delight of celebrating the advent of the *new*!"

With this essay, and others that followed, Baudelaire, as well as such later nineteenth-century critical thinkers as Morris and Stéphane Mallarmé, discovered that vision itself, as well as the artistic forms that are its sensual embodiment, is not given for all time, but is contingent upon a host of changing, historical factors. Thus empiricism, born in the early Enlightenment and maturing alongside positive science in the nineteenth century, had already begun to shrink in stature beneath the wilting gaze of nineteenth-century critical consciousness. As a method of understanding the world that was dependent upon a stationary observer and controlled experiments, it could not withstand the social and political revolutions that jolted the century.

The critical method employed in this survey of nineteenth-century art therefore receives much of its authority from the nineteenth century itself. To claim more than this, however, would be to fall victim to the very empiricism—the myth that the scholar is society's unbiased memory—that is being criticized. Remembrance, like history, exists in the present even as it records the past; just as memories are aroused by recent events, so history is stirred by contemporary life. Although based upon empirical research, this book thus rejects the interest-free claims of empiricism in favor of an

approach that recognizes and highlights the ideological links between present and past. The effect of this recognition can be to bring the past closer and make the present, in a sense, more distant. In turn, this simultaneous familiarization and alienation has two functions: first, it is to heighten our understanding of the human choices and cultural contingencies that shaped past art, and secondly, it is to assist in the achievement of a more objective or "distanced" reckoning with the contradictions and potentialities of our present culture. The art historican, situated in contemporary culture and ideology, cannot easily separate these two operations; indeed, the one informs the other.

Only the course of subsequent events and developments, often dozens of years later, makes certain earlier moments, artists, and monuments historical. Thus an art history that seeks to understand causes cannot be content to let the historical record speak for itself. The uniqueness of, for example, the revolutionary paintings of J.-L. David or Goya cannot be understood by the facts of patronage or the circumstances of exhibition alone. Without a reckoning with the larger ideological sea-change, apparent only in distant retrospect, of which these artists are the pioneers, the extraordinariness of, say, David's *Brutus* (1789) or Goya's *Courtyard with Lunatics* (1793–4) may be seen only as the result of psychological anomaly or even denied altogether. By the same token, the contradictions that marked later art movements, such as Impressionism nearly a century after, are unobservable without a critical cognizance of the movement's subsequent history: in the case of Impressionism, this legacy includes its ubiquity in museum exhibitions, scholarly publications, and advertising. Impressionism, we shall discover, was in its subject matter and forms both a radical challenge to official, academic conventions and an expression of the highest aspirations of an enlightened bourgeoisie who increasingly dominated the French political and economic arena. The very duality, however, is only understood by considering the contradictory development of modern popular culture and leisure—a subject clearly outside the limited chronological frame of the Impressionist movement proper.

Similarly, an art history that attends only to primary sources and documents is at least inadequate if not in a literal sense impossible. Equally dubious, however, is the status of a "Social History of Modern Art" that seeks to include comprehensively, as the scholar of nineteenth-century art Albert Boime has written, "the 'Salieris' [as opposed to the Mozarts] of the art world, the so-called mediocrities who have been ranked according to what only can be considered an arbitrary and even capricious standard." Although the democratic sentiment is admirable, and Boime's research enormous, the method in fact purports to a breadth it cannot possibly achieve: if the entirety of an epoch's cultural

10
80

production is equally worthy of study, how can the project ever have boundaries? How can the writer avoid the historicist nightmare (a terror, we shall see, frequent among the nineteenth-century revivalists) of simply re-presenting the entirety of the historical record—unchanged, undistilled, and endless? In addition, Boime would abjure the responsibility to which the art historian, of all scholars, is asked most of all to attend: the discrimination of major from minor, primary from secondary, instrumental from incidental, and critical from accommodating.

By this relative indifference to formal quality, the social historian of art is guilty of throwing out the baby with the bathwater. Boime is right, of course, to criticize the pretension of generations of scholars and artists who claimed that their work was beyond material or, indeed, pecuniary influence. In fact, the work of connoisseurship and all of its accoutrements—the *catalogue raisonné*, the searching for provenance or pedigree, the formal analysis that reads like stocktaking—is accurately described as the proper domain of commercial art dealers and auction houses rather than of independent scholars. But in dismissing judgments of artistic formal significance as merely "arbitrary" and "capricious," Boime for one is reverting to the neopositivist (or empiricist) position of dichotomizing content (seen as primary) from form (secondary). Boime himself undercuts this view in his introduction to the first volume of *A Social History of Modern Art* (1988) when he describes visual art as "essentially a language of signs that transmits ideas." Since all languages are by definition social constructions, the formal language of art too must be imbued with social content. Far from merely reproducing pre-existing ideas, then, artistic form is an essential determinant of just what is expressed, and thereby plays a formative material role, as Marx wrote in 1844, in the evolution of society and history. No mere obedient servant (even less, passive mirror) of ideology, artworks are one instrument with which humanity makes and remakes itself. In this way, formally innovative works of visual art may in fact be judged more significant than conservative ones because they

played a greater role in bringing about (or, at least, compellingly addressing) historical change.

By contesting visual received ideas, as well as art's institutionalized relation to its public, formally or technically advanced modern art was alienated from the prevailing ideology of society in such as way as also to challenge the existing social orders. This survey of nineteenth-century art, therefore, is focused mainly upon canonical modernist works—mostly paintings made in France—in the belief that this "canon" represents just such a body of formally advanced and politically alienated works. The "modern tradition," to cite the useful oxymoron, alone among nineteenth-century artistic traditions retains the potential to embrace and represent conflicts and contradictions still forceful today. Indeed, what is most extraordinary about the art under review here is the degree to which the same contentious political and artistic questions it addressed continue to reverberate in our own day; these issues include the debates over the value of local versus national, and popular versus elite cultures, the question of the existence of a "canon" of great authors and artists, and concerns with the artistic representation of sexuality, social class, gender, and ethnicity. Nineteenth-century artists also confronted for the first time in the history of art the emergence of techniques for the mass-reproduction and distribution of their works as well as the vexing question of the politics of public exhibition and museum display. In addition, the critical modernist project they initiated was intimately engaged with the forms and imagery of mass and non-European culture—for example, with magazine illustration and Native American Mandan hide paintings.

It is of course possible to insist too strongly on the commonalities between art issues past and present, but the constellations are often convincing. Indeed, we believe that if our texts raise contemporary political questions concerning representation, whether of class, gender, ethnicity, or sexuality, they will have succeeded in more closely approaching a nineteenth-century art in which there emerged a new historical and critical consciousness of society and culture.

CLASSICISM AND ROMANTICISM

· 1 ·

PATRIOTISM AND VIRTUE: DAVID TO THE YOUNG INGRES

THOMAS CROW

THE CULT OF CIVIC VIRTUE

IN 1781, NO ONE IN FRANCE HAD THE SLIGHTEST IDEA that a revolution would begin before the decade was out, an upheaval of every social institution which would not spare the traditional fine arts. But artists were ready in advance to overturn old norms and customs of art-making. Over the next eight years, the French public would confront a novel idea of the artist's vocation: no longer the dutiful servant of the state and the church who defines success in terms of official favor, the new-model artist (invariably assumed to be male) vaunts his independence from the dictates of royal patrons and postures of conformity; he speaks over the heads of insiders and bureaucrats to make contact with the large audience who thronged the spaces of the public exhibitions, the so-called Salons, which took place in the old palace of the Louvre every two years. By virtue of this appeal, the perceived character of this audience begins to change. Where it had been a floating and passive crowd, it becomes the embodiment of active public opinion, a palpable force with a role—even a dominant one—in determining the success of painting or sculpture.

This new common ground between artist and audience can be defined by two terms: patriotism and virtue. To understand them, however, it is necessary to reconstruct their specific power and use in the period. Patriotism did not carry the chauvinistic overtones which encumber the word today; nor did virtue connote a priggish or self-satisfied private morality. Devotion to the nation, to *la patrie*, represented a universalized allegiance to one's fellow citizens and to the idea of the general welfare, usually at odds with obedience to the dictates of the state and accepted social custom. The duty of the artist was to set an example of individual emancipation, to break free, at least subjectively, from government patrons who represented only a self-seeking minority. Nor was one's art to be slavishly adjusted to the contingent habits and costume of one's country; to mirror one's compatriots as one found them would be merely to reproduce and endorse all the defects of an unequal society. An ideal was therefore required, and the republics of ancient Greece and Rome were called on to provide a counter-example to a corrupt present. An artist who could live up to these demands would thereby demonstrate a civic virtue worthy of comparison with the self-denying heroes of antiquity.

The philosophical and political debates of the 1760's and '70's had separated the inheritance of Classical antiquity from its normal role of providing symbols of authority and rule. In the previous century, Louis XIV had customarily been likened both to Alexander the Great and the sun god Apollo; Classicism was a catalog of pomp and magnificence. But in these years approaching the Revolution, Classical culture was more likely to call to mind a toughened citizen-soldier or a stoic philosopher living in voluntary poverty with whom an ordinary Frenchman with some education might identify. The very words patriotism and virtue summed up this change.

This growing gap between the Classical tradition and the needs of the ruling order created a new space in which painters could operate. The artist who recognized this first and exploited it with the greatest power was Jacques-Louis David (1748–1825). In 1781, he was 33 years old, still considered a young and relatively untried artist. He had undergone the lengthy and laborious training required of any ambitious aspiring painter, which included years of long sessions devoted to drawing from prints, then from plaster casts of ancient sculpture, and finally from the live model. This sequence of study elevated the inheritance of Classical art over the direct evidence of living nature, which the young student could only approach once he had thoroughly absorbed an idealizing abstraction. All of David's formal artistic education

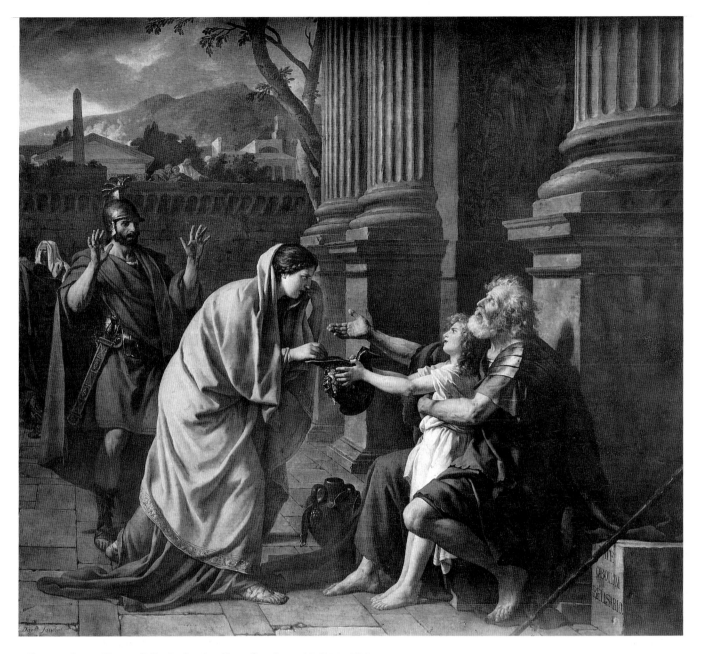

1 JACQUES-LOUIS DAVID *Belisarius Begging Alms* 1781. 9'5⅛ × 10'2⅞ (287.3 × 312.1)

took place within the Royal Academy of Painting and Sculpture, which had been established under Louis XIV to organize and perpetuate a clear hierarchy of ambition and honor among artists. Only those painters capable of producing complex narrative compositions on Classical themes ('history paintings' as they were called) could aspire to the highest rewards that the state could offer.

The culmination of a successful youthful career, which David reached at the age of 26, was the Rome Prize. This gave the winner a scholarship period, lasting three years or longer, at the French Academy in Rome. There the best young artists were given their final induction into the great tradition, now surrounded at first hand by the remains of ancient art and the exemplary classicizing art of the Italian Renaissance. David had extended his stay for nearly six years, and when he returned in 1781 he seemed more than ready to take his place in the normal succession of history painters, one whose first loyalty would be to the established traditions of the Academy and its duty to embellish the aura of the monarchy.

His first painting for the Salon, however, began to probe the potential of traditionally Classical subject matter to exploit the new dissenting constructions of patriotism. He produced a

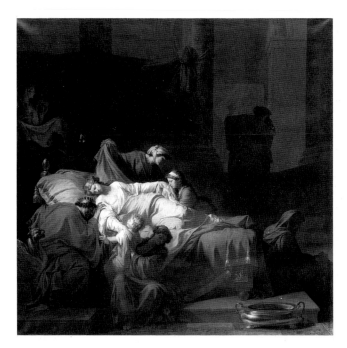

2 **PIERRE PEYRON** *The Death of Alcestis* 1785. 10′8 × 10′6 (327 × 325)

officials who believed that reform was necessary in order to put the French monarchy back on secure social foundations. The character of Belisarius thus provided David with a means to put his feet in two camps at once: both that of dissenting patriots outside the corridors of power and that of a small group of reforming bureaucrats who were themselves isolated and on the defensive within the government. David needed to appeal to this latter group, as it happened to include the administrator responsible for the Academy and the visual arts. David obligingly put his stress on emotions of pity and sentimental regret, his hero's misery and its contrast with an exalted former state constituting a mute appeal for a renewal of lapsed royal benevolence—and nothing more incendiary.

A CALL TO ORDER

The success of the *Belisarius* with both camps demonstrated how the Salon exhibitions, with their free and open access to everyone, could put vivid images of the virtue of the ancients into public circulation. The reduction of a complex story to a few figures and eloquently simple gestures was itself viewed as a reproach to the profusion of subsidiary figures and ornament in older academic art, which seemed more about the vanity of display than the communication of moral truth. In terms of David's career, it had the effect of securing the first of a regular succession of state commissions for large-scale narrative paintings: he had arrived as a history painter.

With that arrival came a large number of students attracted by his synthesis of daring political allusion with impeccable command of the Classical tradition. While aspiring artists received their formal training in drawing at the Academy, they acquired their practical instruction in making paintings in the studio of an individual master. David had served his apprenticeship with the most rigorous Classicist of the older generation, Joseph-Marie Vien. With his own students, he took devotion to the example of the ancients beyond strictly artistic concerns to include the philosophical and practical organization of studio life as a whole. In contrast to the authoritarian hierarchy observed by other masters, David encouraged a far more open, egalitarian atmosphere. At a time when most young artists abandoned formal education in their early 'teens, he laid down the requirement that all of his students know Latin and thus have independent access to Classical learning. His studio, rather than the hidebound Academy, would provide their primary locus of intellectual discussion and moral identity. Together they began to act on the belief that modern French artists could behave as had the artists of the Greeks, who (so it was argued) were granted creative liberty and thus were inspired to express the ideals of their communities in perfected physical form.

1 large canvas on the theme of the blind Belisarius begging for alms. This character was the actual Roman general largely responsible for the Emperor Justinian's extensive conquests. According to legend, Belisarius became the victim of jealous intrigue at court. Falsely believing him guilty of treason, the Emperor ordered that he be blinded and dispossessed. In David's painting, an old soldier who had served in his victorious campaigns recognizes the fallen leader in his pitifully dependent condition. The painting amplifies this veteran's shock of recognition through the contrast between the magnificent triumphal arch, redolent of glory and rule, with the fall from glory enacted in a beggar's abject acceptance of charity from a passing woman.

The theme of Belisarius was not just any item from the catalog of ancient virtue. The writer Jean-François Marmontel had published a novel with that title in 1767, in which the exiled general is made to deliver lengthy monologues denouncing the social evils that his creator believed were eroding the vitality of the French state: official religious intolerance, a parasitical nobility, the reign of luxury over civic virtue, and the domination of favoritism over merit. Eventually, the sanity of his message induces the mighty again to seek his counsel: Justinian himself comes in secret, in the company of his heir Tiberius, to listen to his once and ever-faithful general, who can no longer see him.

This hopeful parable of the ruler coming to his senses was not ungrounded in political reality. Marmontel's embattled novel had attracted the support of certain embattled state

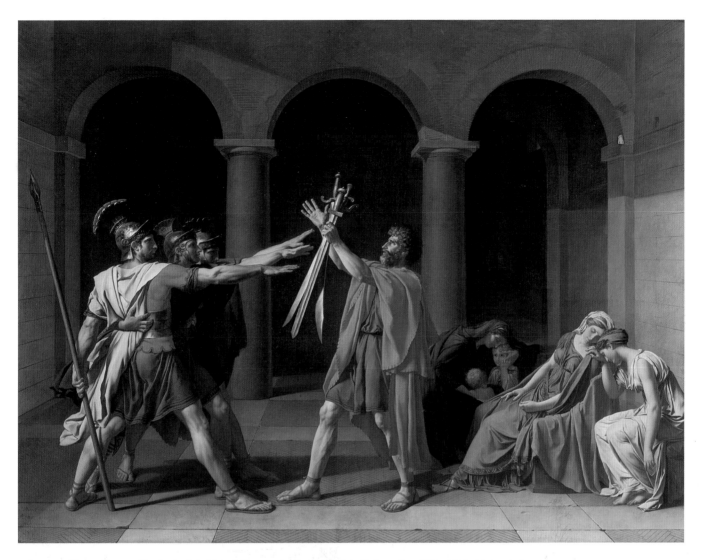

3 **JACQUES-LOUIS DAVID** *The Oath of the Horatii Between the Hands of Their Father* 1785. 10′9⅞ × 13′11¼ (329.9 × 424.8)

In a short time, David's studio began to preempt the functions of the Academy. When his most favored apprentice, Jean-Germain Drouais (1763–88), came to compete for the Rome Prize in 1784, both master and pupil treated the result as a foregone conclusion. When Drouais was predictably successful, they effectively declared themselves independent of the state by financing the journey from their own resources. The bond between them was so tight that David accompanied him to Rome and remained for nearly a year. Two other students also made the trip, so that something of the same close-knit studio environment could be transferred to Italy.

During his time in Rome, he completed, with Drouais's assiduous assistance, the work that would give him his breakthrough to dominance over French painting for the rest

3 of his long life: *The Oath of the Horatii Between the Hands of Their Father* (1785). His subject matter came indirectly from the seventeenth-century tragedy *Horace* by Pierre Corneille, a touchstone of Classical drama known by any educated French person in the way that *Hamlet* or *Macbeth* would be known in the English-speaking world. The narrative of the play concerns the triplet champions of early Rome, summoned to settle the war with neighboring Alba by combat with that city's champions, their own cousins, the likewise triplet Curiatii. In the tangled ties of kinship that gave Corneille his tragic material, the wife of the youngest Horatius, the only warrior of the six to survive, was sister to the Curiatii, while his own sister, Camilla, was betrothed to one of his victims. She became one in her turn when Horatius finds her mourning her beloved and kills her on the spot.

As fixed in a surviving preparatory drawing, the subject which had been assigned David was the father of the clan successfully defending his son before the Roman people for

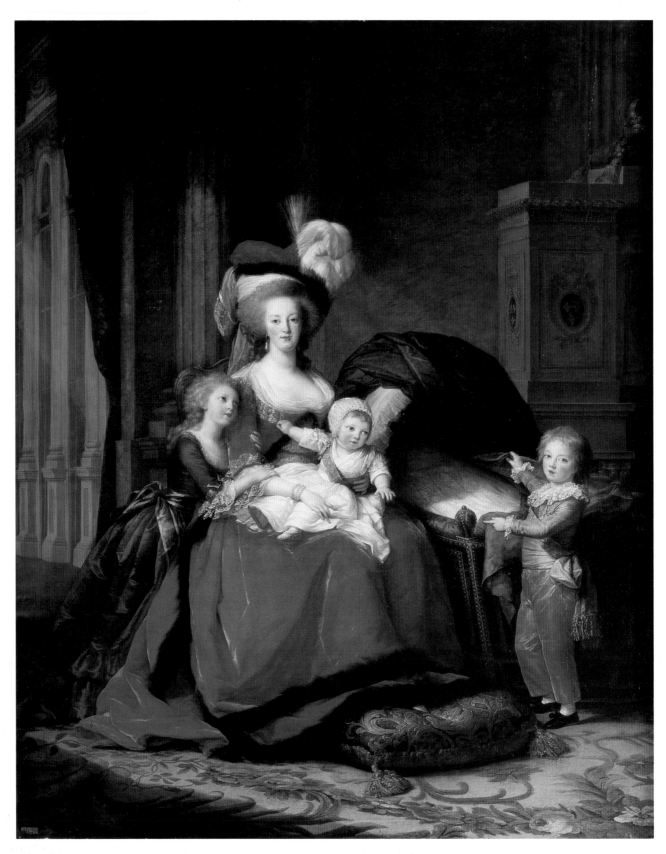

4 ELISABETH-LOUISE VIGÉE-LEBRUN *Marie-Antoinette With Her Children* 1787. 9'¼ × 84⅝ (275 × 215)

the latter crime. This is a free adaptation of Corneille's final scene, where the elder Horatius pleads for his son's pardon before the king of Rome. But the final composition does not depict the event described in his commission. The defense of the murderous victor is forgotten; the new subject is a pledge by the three sons to triumph or die for the honor of Rome, an event imagined by the artist to have occurred before the fateful combat (this oath appears nowhere in the play or in any of Corneille's ancient sources). In order to equal the visual impact of any other painting in the Salon, he enlarged without permission the previously agreed dimensions of the canvas by fifty percent.

Thus David was also taking over responsibility for setting the scale and subjects for his paintings, despite their being paid for by the state. This went hand in hand with calculated defiance at the level of style. His invention of the oath-taking allowed him to distill the complexities of the story into a striking unity, an almost primitively elemental configuration of bodies. It would demonstrate how much strength history painting could gain from an austerity of means that seemed at one with the stoicism of these early Romans. At the same time, David took advantage of the inherent problem faced by history painters in communicating to the Salon audience from the heights of the room (all large canvases were hung near the distant ceiling, as can be seen in contemporary engravings). Like no one else's painting, it would beam its narrative across the spaces of the crammed exhibition, and leave its starkly calligraphic configuration of male bodies as a permanent image in the memory of its viewers.

The abrupt transitions and dialectical sharpness of the new painting, its austere and declamatory voice, stood in pointed contrast to the intricately embellished pictorial rhetoric of his
2 academic colleagues. An example would be *The Death of Alcestis,* shown in the same Salon by his principal rival Pierre Peyron (1744–1814), whose theme, taken from the drama of Euripides, is a wife's self-sacrifice so that her husband might live. David's innovations made Peyron's compactly interwoven grouping of figures, emerging from a darkened, softening atmosphere, seem a thing of the past, too subtle and self-involved to make an impact in the civic arena. That David retained a similar mode of composition in his self-contained group of female figures, but exclusively there, made the contrast all the more emphatic.

David's withdrawal from Paris and his gathering of the independent forces of his studio helped strengthen his resolve to overturn the accepted conventions of narrative in painting. The impact of the painting is inseparable from its violations of his audience's habitual expectations as to how such a scene should be organized. It implicitly rejected the developed compositional skills of generations of academic painters. To press all of the figures into the same foreground plane, to join the male and female groups with no mediating transitions or mutual recognition between them, to offer no release into deep space beyond the starkly symmetrical colonnade—by every contemporary standard, these were all daring and dissonant simplifications.

It was through this rhetoric of style that David's painting spoke most forcefully to feelings of patriotic discontent with the established cultural order. In the eyes of its admirers, its harsh notes and impatience with compositional subtleties elevated the mind and moved private emotions away from center stage; the pride and inflexibility of the early Romans, so foreign to modern mores and so telling a reproach to them, had come alive on canvas.

THE ENTERPRISE OF WOMEN

The initiatives of David and his group depended on a large and secure level of state subsidy for history painting, the sheer scale of which left room for dissenting gestures. Such support had been in place for no longer than a decade. Previously official sponsorship of the highest genre had been more often a matter of lip service rather than actual funds; artists relied on income from private commissions for portraits and decorative works. From 1775 onwards, however, the ambitious male talents of the new generation were drawn into the production of highminded (and usually mediocre) public paintings, and this left a vacuum in the other genres of art. Almost instantly a cohort of talented women came to the fore. The year 1783 saw the admission of two women to the Academy (there were places for only four)—Adélaïde Labille-Guiard (1749–1803) and Elisabeth-Louise Vigée-Lebrun (1755–1842). In terms of both quality and patronage at the highest levels, they would go on to dominate portraiture during this final decade of the Old Régime—including portraits of the royal family, which were 4 virtually equivalent in status to Classical history paintings.

The latter artist, 28 years old at the time of her reception, had the easier path to recognition. Her father, Louis Vigée, had been a portraitist and teacher in the lesser Academy of Saint Luke (the survivor of the old artists' guild). By the age of 15, her precocious talent was attracting well-born and wealthy clients, and in 1779 she sealed what would be a continuing relationship with the young Queen Marie-Antoinette. She married a successful art dealer, J.-B.-P. Lebrun, and conducted herself as a significant figure in society, presiding over her own soirées and attracting regulars from the upper spheres of Parisian culture and state administration. The reigning tone was one of elegant simplicity on antique models.

Vigée-Lebrun and David maintained a wary social relationship; the latter's education and style made him a natural colleague, but his patriotic commitments occasionally caused

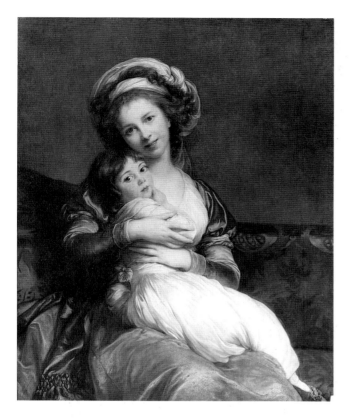

5 ELISABETH-LOUISE VIGÉE-LEBRUN *Portrait of the Artist With Her Daughter* 1789. 41⅜ × 33 (105 × 84)

him to recoil from her cozy alliance with the royal house. Her portraits indeed served as a medium for the incorporation of certain Enlightenment attitudes into the style and self-image of the ruling elite. She moved the genre away from conventional attitudes and costume intended to convey rank and station, toward a cultivated disdain for affectation and a corresponding emphasis on individual feeling. Her self-portrait with her daughter (1789) set a kind of standard in this new pursuit of innocent candor. In it she defines herself in terms other than those of her energetic professional prowess. The clothes are simple and unpretentious; they belong to no precise social location but serve to suggest an imaginative community of grace and feeling; the natural freshness of skin is at one with the natural spontaneity of the embrace.

The compression and intertwining of the two figures into a compact oval at the same time represents a survival of one of the favorite devices of Rococo decorative artists from the early decades of the century: a familiar old form is made to perform a new duty. And Vigée-Lebrun's version of the natural is characterized throughout by a reassuring consistency and absence of the unexpected. Having already demonstrated that sort of reliable performance early in her career, she was handed one of the most important and most delicate public commissions of the 1780's.

This was not a didactic history painting, but a state portrait of the Queen with her children. By the middle years of the decade, Marie-Antoinette had become a focus for popular resentment against state policies and the government's endless crisis of indebtedness. A tide of published political dissent took delighted advantage of her reputation for unprincipled extravagance and scandalous public behavior, particularly in the company of her rakish and reactionary brother-in-law, the Comte d'Artois. Vigée-Lebrun's portrait displays the traditional pomp of regal portraiture, provided by the setting in the Versailles Palace with the magnificence of the Hall of Mirrors visible to the left. The Queen's pose is properly upright, and the artist has arranged the group into the solid pyramid ordained by the most sanctified academic teaching. That seriousness of bearing and self-presentation was crucial in the intended effect of the painting, in that the King's foreign wife was widely seen to have distracted the amiably simple monarch from his paternal devotion to the nation.

The portrait's stress on her role as mother was meant to answer further charges that she had failed in her conjugal duties. The studied precariousness of the baby's seat in her lap, flanked by gestures of loving emotion from the older children, was designed to show the Queen as not only having grown into her role as mother to the royal heirs but as being a good mother in the natural, nurturing manner celebrated by the eighteenth-century cult of sensibility. It was no fault of the artist's competence in rendering this balancing act that the state, out of fear of a negative public response, withheld the portrait from the official opening of the Salon of 1787. Any positive benefit was annulled in the general ridicule, and the empty space in the hanging was quickly equated with the looming fiscal deficit. Vigée-Lebrun herself left France at the first outbreak of the Revolution and found an eager clientele at princely courts throughout Europe.

The career of Labille-Guiard followed a substantially different course from that of her more luminous rival, and it demonstrates the widening options that opened up (albeit grudgingly and briefly) to women artists during this decade. She was six years older and had received her most important training from a history painter, F.-A. Vincent, rather than a specialist in the portrait genre. She achieved a rank not unlike Vigée-Lebrun's, in 1785 becoming portraitist to Mesdames, the King's unmarried aunts, but her sense of vocation displayed a greater intellectual and professional gravity.

This she projected with confidence and conviction in the self-portrait which she submitted to the Salon of 1785. At over six feet in height, the canvas presents her on a queenly scale of her own. Instead of any comforting domesticity, she advertises herself as already a teacher and master of her genre: two attentive students hover behind her chair. The setting is

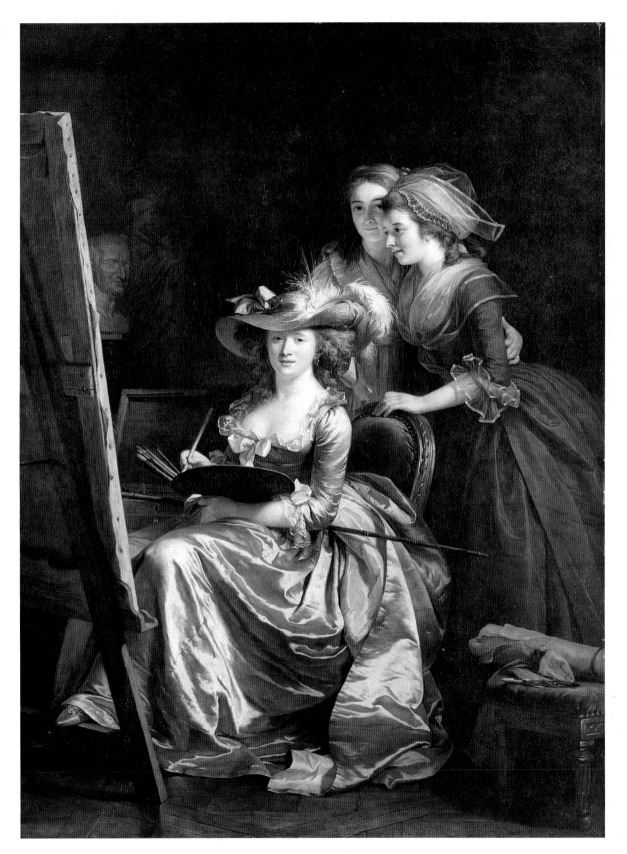

6 ADÉLAÏDE LABILLE-GUIARD *Self-Portrait With Two Pupils* 1785. 83 × 59½ (210.8 × 151.1)

unabashedly a place of work, as the prosaic stretcher bars and tacked canvas make plain. A sculpted bust of her father in the severe Roman mode (from an actual work by Pajou) looks on, but no living male intrudes on the studio's enterprise. This would have been a point of some importance to the artist, since both she and Vigée-Lebrun were subject to the slander that men had actually produced their paintings, a back-handed but galling tribute from a sexist culture. Labille-Guiard's link to Vincent remained intimate—they would marry in 1790—so she was especially vulnerable to this reflex suspicion. The finery of her dress and hat, perhaps incongruous to modern-day eyes, would have been deemed an expected and correct outward sign of status and accomplishment. At the same time she encourages a worthy simplicity in the dress of her students.

This self-portrait stands as a reminder that enlightened pedagogy as a feature of the artist's new intellectual independence was not necessarily limited to the erudite pursuits of male Classicists. Labille-Guiard herself took a sympathetic part in the coming Revolution and painted one of the few known portraits of Robespierre.

THE CIRCLE OF MEN

After his return from Rome, David was some time in reorganizing the collective work in his own studio. A combination of injury, illness, and indecision prevented him from making a start on an equivalent successor to the *Horatii*, though he had a royal commission in hand. In the end, he capitalized on new friendships in order to keep his name before the public at a lower cost to his time and resources but with little or no lessening of impact.

Early in 1786, a wealthy young jurist named Trudaine de la Sablière, a scion of one of the country's most distinguished families of royal administrators, presented himself as the patron of David's *Socrates at the Moment of Grasping the Hemlock* (1787). He paid more than handsomely for the honor of commissioning it: 7000 livres to begin with, according to one report, augmented to 10,000 livres in the end as an expression of his delight with the results (this for a cabinet-sized picture when the state was paying only 6000 livres for a full-scale historical canvas like the *Horatii*).

The story comes from the writings of Plato, who had been a student of the martyred philosopher, and more recently from a retelling of the suicide by the French *philosophe* Denis Diderot. Despite its stark prison-setting and theme of self-sacrifice, the *Socrates* calls into question the tendency to classify all of David's history paintings of the 1780's under the heading of an austere and militant virtue. His formal choices were made within a rhetorical conception of painting, one in

which style was less the mark of an artist's unique personality and more a considered adjustment to the demands of the subject matter and the occasion. This smaller canvas, offered as an emblem of personal friendship, called for a more harmonious and interwoven compositional order.

In philosophical terms, it is a more complex theme than the tale of the *Horatii*, emblematizing subtle constitutional and moral questions in place of Corneille's broadly brushed nationalist legend. It catches the ambivalence Trudaine would display toward any expansion of the principle of free expression to incorporate popular participation in political life (he would go to the guillotine in 1794 for that reluctance). The suicide of Socrates is the result of a prior and more fundamental renunciation of political action under conditions of democratic sovereignty: from the moment of his indictment forward, he accepts without resistance the judgment of the democratic assembly the better to reject the legitimacy of the authority behind it. What more fitting purchaser to have than the man who would go on to translate the American *Federalist Papers* into French, including James Madison's strictures against unrestrained factions and the potential "tyranny of the majority" in democratic legislatures?

The treatment of the male body is also changed from the strained austerity of the *Horatii* in a way that corresponds to masculine bonds in Greek society and in Platonic thought. The figure of the anonymous cupbearer—in its scale, placement, color, and sensual attractiveness—functions as a balancing element of the composition equal in weight to the figure of Socrates himself, a Ganymede assisting at the passage to immortality. In Plato's account of the suicide, the jailor bearing the poison is only a minor, anonymous presence, but this prominence given to the physical for its own sake evokes another facet of Plato, one in which the contemplation of the beautiful male body is enlisted for the purposes of enlightenment. The speeches of the participants in Plato's *Symposium* describe the contemplation of the beautiful male adolescent by the mature citizen as a potential means to lead the mind upward from the realm of the sensual to an understanding of universal good. Though Socrates is allowed his "philosophical" refusal of the sexual seductiveness of Alcibiades, there is a great deal of humorous carousing and delicious reminiscence of erotic feeling on the part of the wealthy Athenians present. And in the end the sexual abstinence of Socrates is meaningful only because of the palpable desire stimulated by the proximity of the beautiful male beloved. In David's painting, Socrates reaches for the cup and for the boy in the same gesture.

Later, in his monumental history painting *Leonidas at Thermopylae* (1814), David would put on display his understanding of the central place held by same-sex *eros* in the warrior culture of ancient Greece. The *Socrates* likewise is

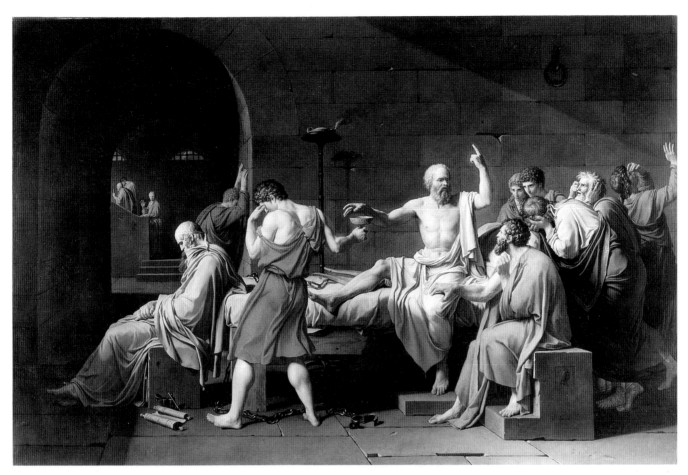

7 JACQUES-LOUIS DAVID *Socrates at the Moment of Grasping the Hemlock* 1787. 51⅛ × 77⅛ (129.9 × 195.9)

meant to be a Greek painting, not a Roman one, imbued with a sophisticated scholar's appreciation of "Greek love." Trudaine was the center of a circle famous for both its intellectual sophistication and its lavish entertainments; it was a milieu in which the serious pursuit of political wisdom was bound up with the cultivation of a lightly carried erudition amid multiple temptations of the table and the bed. David plainly enjoyed the attention of this company, and his painting is a tribute to and document of one ideal of leisured, disinterested masculine fellowship, which had many points in common with Plato's. And the beauty of the *Socrates* is how many of these points it manages to touch within such a compactly legible image.

A VIOLENT PATRIMONY

Despite the distractions of such erudite and worldly company, David's most important bonds remained the working relationships of the studio. A new arrival, the twenty-year-old

Anne-Louis Girodet (1767–1824), painted a number of the background figures in the *Socrates,* and other talented students were in the wings. But David's aspirations for his group—and for many observers the hope of French painting—were centered on the distant Drouais, who was engaged in his own struggle to assert his independence against the constraints imposed by the French authorities in Rome. In practical terms, however, a lone student isolated in a foreign environment was dependent on the Academy, and his earliest Roman painting conformed to the first of its requirements: a painted study of the male nude to be submitted to the judgment of the academic elders back in Paris. Barred by entrenched authority from devoting his talents to the highest genre of narrative historical painting, he set about elevating this obligation to the same exalted plane.

Drouais's *Dying Athlete,* completed in 1785, transformed 8 the balanced studio pose on which it is based into a tense internal drama. As depicted, the wound is all but invisible, but the entire body is organized to mark the spasm of pain that energizes the figure. Although the body as a whole seems fully drawn out along its continuous lower contour, it is in fact twisted unnaturally at the center along a harshly incised transition. Its languid extension is violated at the center of the torso in a contraction that reads as an involuntary one of pain. The raking light further throws that area into shadow so that the body is divided by zones of light and dark as well as by its disposition in space. The light is the zone of control; despite the wrenching pain, the warrior's reaction to it is limited to the dark zone; he resists and contains it so thoroughly that the overall composure of his figure is undisturbed. The effort it costs the warrior is registered in the contrast of the supporting right hand with the left. What had been no more than the model's fatiguing effort to maintain the pose, becomes an inner determination to hold the body upright to the end, to refuse collapse into unconsciousness.

This is the mark of the hero, and it is meant to enlarge the aura of heroism beyond exploits of the fictional warrior to take in the suffering artist's achievement as well. After Drouais, it would became a pattern for young artists to use the single male figure as a primary focus for their early ambitions and self-definition as artists. They would develop its potential as a carrier of complex meaning far beyond anything their elders had attempted at the same stage of life. But Drouais was also impatient to test himself directly against his master's example. With David's encouragement, he worked in secret, neglecting his obligatory student work in order to throw himself into a project beyond his years and station, one plainly intended for the public arena of Paris.

The subject which they chose together was a moment in the life of Caius Marius, a general and consul of the late Roman Republic. This episode comes in fact from the decline of Marius's career into corruption and tyranny. Under a sentence of death by the Roman Senate, he faces down his executioner by the sheer force of his presence; in the next moment the soldier drops his sword and flees. The malign side of the "hero" is not, however, immediately apparent, resembling as he does the severe but benevolent patriarch of the *Horatii*. Its minimalist pairing of two soldierly male characters extended David's Corneillian esthetic—the dialectical sharpness, abrupt transitions, self-aggrandizing utter-

8 JEAN-GERMAIN DROUAIS *The Dying Athlete* 1785. 49¼ × 71¾ (125 × 182)

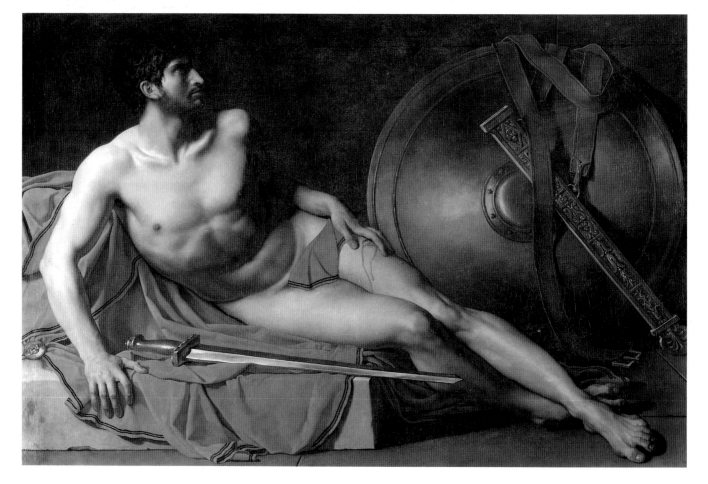

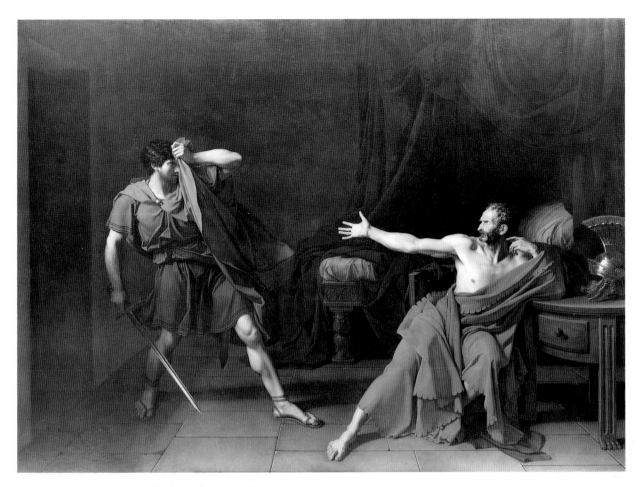

9 **JEAN-GERMAIN DROUAIS** *Marius at Minturnae* 1786. 9′ × 12′2 (274.3 × 370.8)

ance, and single-minded stress on pride and inflexibility in the mores of ancient Rome—to a degree that eliminated even David's small allowances for prevailing taste.

But the *Marius* (1786) at the same time reveals something of the tense emotional and psychological interplay between the two artists. It is figured most of all in the cloak with which the young soldier shields his face, which Drouais uses as a device to turn his painting diametrically against its model in the *Horatii*. The theme of the latter painting was one of solidarity between the generations, the authority of the father passing to his sons along with the swords: David's heroes were engaged in rapt attention to the tense point of contact between them, and the vision of the spectator was vicariously engaged with the same intensity. But when that same spectator puts himself or herself in the place of either protagonist in the *Marius*, the effect is blindness and isolation. The deceptively noble face of Marius was one that Drouais refused to contemplate; he put an abyss, a cancellation of vision, between that implacable visage and himself.

This simultaneous affirmation and denial, vision and blindness, left unresolved at the heart of the painting, and all the visible signs of the strain involved in controling the refractory materials that went into its making, worked in the end to its advantage. Despite its moral ambiguities, the impression it conveys of a bristling, barely contained energy could readily be understood as the sign of virtue condemned to perpetual struggle in an unjust society. When the *Marius* was put on display in the Drouais family home in the early spring of 1787, public response was wildly enthusiastic. The painting was capable of creating the excitement of a Salon triumph without the necessity of a Salon. Thomas Jefferson joined the stream of spectators and came away overwhelmed by the experience: "It fixed me like a statue a quarter of an hour, or half an hour, I do not know which, for I lost all ideas of time, even the consciousness of my existence." The intensity of the painting, which is in large part a result of its unresolvable contradictions of meaning, temporarily banished rational reflection from at least one spectator otherwise eminently capable of it.

Drouais never had the opportunity to overcome this anxiety

of influence in a comparable painting, not could he fulfill the hopes of his Parisian admirers. Early in 1788 he died of smallpox while still in Rome. His death at the age of 26 was widely ascribed to his zealous overwork in pursuit of ideal artistic virtue; David was inconsolable. Those unrealized expectations and the circumstances of his death were romanticized into legend that had a powerful effect on several generations of young artists who followed him. Like him, they would want success early and on terms guaranteed not by training and experience but by special inner qualities which set the artist apart from the routine existence and dulled perceptions of others. It would henceforth be the burden of the modern artist perpetually to be called on to demonstrate that exalted state.

TRAGEDY AND THE REPUBLIC OF EQUALS

There was an unintended coincidence between David's grief over the loss of a virtual son and the theme of the painting he was preparing for the Salon of 1789, and this surely made his engagement with the subject even more intense. In his *Lictors Returning to Brutus the Bodies of His Sons*, the hero is the founder of the Roman Republic, Junius Brutus (namesake of Caesar's assassin), as he might have received the beheaded corpses of his two male heirs, executed at his own order for treason against the new political order. It was through the blood ties of their mother, who was related to the expelled king, that the two sons had been enlisted in the plot to restore the monarchy. Under the law that Brutus had himself brought into being, a sentence of death was mandatory, and the law obliged him to deliver it and to witness the execution.

Like the *Horatii*, the painting concerns the rigor of a father who must contemplate the sacrifice of his male offspring for the good of the country. But where their end in the former is heroic, here it is ignominious. And David exploits an even starker syntax of disassociation in order to call the categories of male heroism into question. The immobile central actor vacates the center of the composition and sits in a shadowy corner; other key elements of the action are likewise scattered to the sides of the canvas, most conspicuously the grief-stricken female nurse at the far right. One great gap occupies the center; across it, the opposition between male and female, between clenched angularity and supple, curvilinear form, verges on disassociation. Meaningful connections are made not so much in the actions and expressions depicted, but rather in the mind of the viewer, which is activated by the gaps and silences between separate and distinct elements. The formal dismemberment of both composition and surface becomes not only means but metaphor, for the dismember-

ment of Brutus' sons is the unseen event which defines all of the living figures, and the dismemberment of the family unit—glossed over in the *Horatii*—is its consequence.

By virtue of its disruptions of normative order in technique and composition, the painting can be decidedly ambivalent about the costs of the hero's political resolve. The grieving women as a group (who alone catch the light), the unheard protest of Brutus' wife (whose outstretched hand stabilizes the entire composition), are treated with as much if not greater sympathy. The painting allows room for both halves of the Greek historian Plutarch's famous judgment on his action, that it "cannot be sufficiently condemned or sufficiently praised," that Brutus' character was at one and the same time "that of a god and that of a savage beast," which is to say, simultaneously above and below the human community. It encompasses a truly tragic recognition that the social body can come into being only by means of a temporary transgression of the condition of humanity itself; and as the existence of society violates the continuum of nature, so nature will have its revenge.

David's *Brutus* may be the closest the art of painting has ever come to rendering tragedy in its own, pictorial terms rather than merely illustrating those of the stage. At the same time, however, it questions one of the fundamental assumptions of tragic drama going back to Aristotle: that great passions are the property of the well-born. The nurse, isolated at the far edge of the composition in her own private world of sorrow, is the chief formal and thematic counterweight to Brutus himself. The tension visible in her jawline, neck, and shoulder, the lean and austere grandeur invested in her body, oppose the smooth, uninflected rendering of Brutus' wife, making the response of the noble matron seem somehow histrionic and inadequate by comparison.

The power of that figure becomes even more striking in the light of evidence that it was not painted by David but by a new recruit to the studio, François Gérard (1770–1837). Likewise, as crucial a detail as the head of Brutus may have been painted by Girodet. In any event, the two young painters had been drawn into an intimate collaboration parallel to that between David and Drouais on the *Horatii*. It is today an old-fashioned expression to refer to the students or followers of an artist as constituting a "school." But it is important to restore the basic meaning of the word in this instance: no less than the circle of Trudaine, David's studio had become a place of collective learning and experiment within the Classical tradition, but with the added pressure and risk of a high-stakes project to be accomplished and tested in public. And the practical character of their interaction generated a different kind of art, an interrogation of the idea of civic virtue which is a world away from the comfortable philosophical pieties of the *Socrates*.

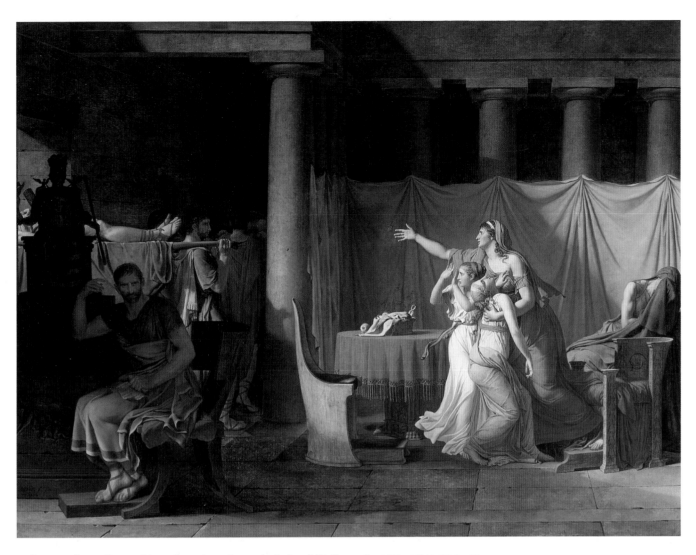

10 JACQUES-LOUIS DAVID *Lictors Returning to Brutus the Bodies of His Sons* 1789. 10'7⅛ × 13'10¼ (322.9 × 422)

These were lessons to which Girodet in particular was attending—the concentration of bodily eloquence within contours of a compact geometric simplicity, the evocation of inexpressible sorrow and loss through absence and a drastic reduction of pictorial incident. Through his aristocratic family he gained a commission, unusual for such a young artist, to paint a large-scale work (11½ feet in height) on the subject of the Virgin with the dead Christ. In so doing, he was responding to the other major event of the 1789 exhibition, which had seen something of a revival (temporary of course) in large-scale religious painting. Twenty-one canvases, more than half of those in the "historical" category, had been commissioned by the state or by various church bodies on Christian subjects. A *Lamentation of Christ* by Jean-Baptiste Regnault, a state commission intended for the main altar of the chapel at Fontainebleau, received the largest share of attention before the late arrival of the *Brutus*. Enthusiastic

admirers in the press found much to praise in the contrast between the shadowed background with its suggestive mystery and the vividness of the foreground group of figures with its startling juxtapositions of color and unsettling naturalism in the treatment of Christ's body.

Girodet's painting was on a directly analogous subject and was almost as large. His conception both pays homage to Regnault, his master's rival, and challenges him in the Davidian terms of austere rhetorical grandeur. The shift in subject from the public scene of deposition and lamentation to the private mourning of the Virgin allows him to reduce the elements of the story to a laconic minimum. Like Drouais's *Marius*, it plays its two highlighted figures, marked by vividly saturated hues, against a large field of indistinct gloom penetrated by a narrow beam of illumination. For both fledgling history painters, this device allowed them to avoid the complications that come with a large complement of

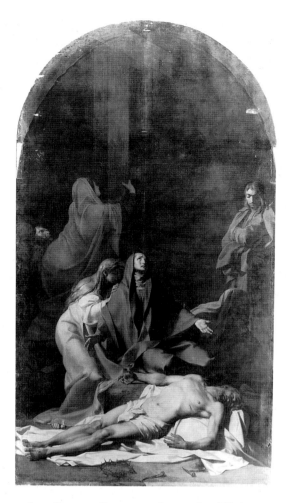

11 JEAN-BAPTISTE REGNAULT *Lamentation of Christ* 1789. 13'11⅜ × 91¾ (425 × 233)

had been. In a Classical manner, Girodet boldly carves his signature in a fictive inscription at the foot of the sarcophagus, proudly appending his age of 22.

FIGURES OF REVOLUTIONARY VIRTUE

The curtailment of religious painting was but one effect of the changes in the French art world set off by the taking of the Bastille in 1789. David and the painters in his circle were sympathetically engaged with the Revolution from the start, but decisive changes in their art were slow in coming. Reform-minded artists in Paris put their initial energies into a drive for egalitarian reorganization of the Academy, including open access to the Salons. The first important artistic innovation would take place in Italy rather than France, generated out of the momentum established in David's studio in 1789.

Girodet, having won his Rome Prize, left Paris in 1790 determined to extend the independent identity he had staked out in his *Pietà*. In order to live up to the ideal of precocious genius, he had to contend not only with David's powerful influence on him, but with Drouais's example as well. The intransigent attitude he displayed in Rome, his expressions of contempt for the Academy and its teaching, followed the path

12 ANNE-LOUIS GIRODET *Pietà* 1789. 11' × 92¼ (335 × 235)

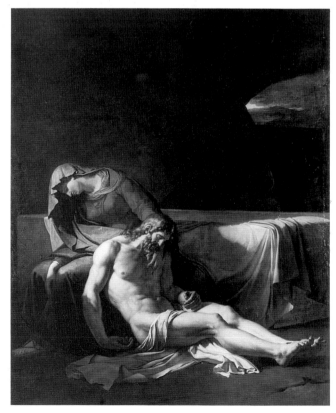

figures and at the same time gain the instant sense of gravity and profundity conveyed by darkness and isolation. Even more than Regnault, he has forsworn obvious Christian symbols; there are virtually none in the painting. The accessories are Classical or natural: shroud, sarcophagus, cavern, dawn. Girodet has fused the bodies of Virgin and Christ into one continuous outline, a union of life and death expressed in basic bodily terms. And the open expression of sorrow in Regnault's Virgin is transformed into a veiled inclination of the head, the eyes in shadow, the neck conforming to an oppressive horizontal line, in a direct echo of the veiled form of Brutus' grieving servant.

But for all of the painting's indebtedness to rhetorical ideas present in the *Brutus*, the moody gloom and quiet of Girodet's *Pietà* represented a marked departure from what anyone would have expected of the Davidian group. It was a precocious and risky painting, particularly in its effective manipulation of a vast area of virtually featureless painted surface, and was as impressive in its way as Drouais's *Marius*

10

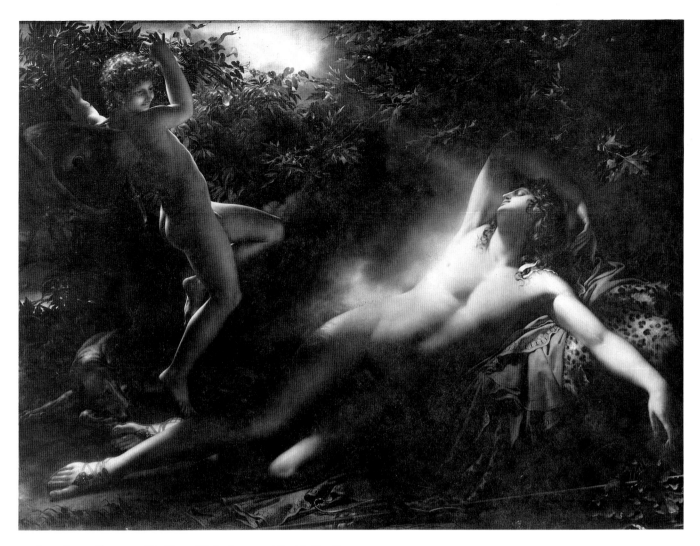

13 ANNE-LOUIS GIRODET *The Sleep of Endymion* 1791. 19⅛ × 24½ (49 × 62)

laid down by his late colleague. And like Drouais, he had to manifest that resistance while meeting the requirement that he paint the male nude. How then was he to imitate Drouais's example of independence and his transformation of the academic nude into an emblem of that independence without falling into a dependent imitation of his predecessor?

He found his subject in a realm of mythology far removed from the vigilantly martial world of David's and Drouais's Roman heroes. His painting, completed in 1791, depicts Endymion, the beautiful boy with whom the moon goddess Selene fell into desperate infatuation. In some accounts she put him into perpetual sleep so that he would always be available to her nocturnal visits. Girodet has rendered her as immaterial moonlight, whose passage through the overhanging branches is facilitated by a smiling figure with the combined traits of Eros and Zephyr.

He stated repeatedly, in letters written during and

immediately after his work on the picture, that this was to be a work owing absolutely nothing to David's example and that he would spare no effort necessary to achieve this independence. It is difficult to cite a prior instance in which that very modern form of youthful rebellion is expressed so vividly and insistently by an artist. And he evolved its form through what amounts to a systematic reversal of almost every one of the salient traits of Drouais's prototype in the *Dying Athlete*. The athlete had been tense, maximally alert, disfigured and suffering, yet ready with his weapons. Endymion, by contrast, is drained of tension, never conscious, physically flawless and in a perpetual state of bliss, with weapons discarded in the foreground. The hard daylight delineated the body of the athlete with an unnatural clarity; the soft moonlight envelops the body of Endymion with a diffuse but entirely natural obscurity.

More than Girodet realized, his painting reached beyond

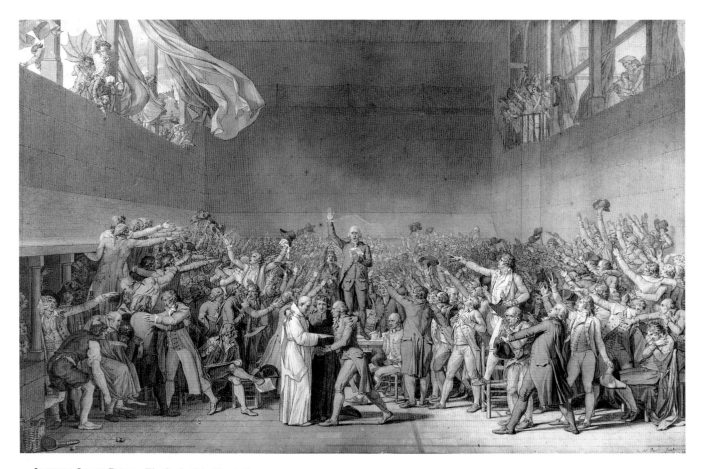

14 JACQUES-LOUIS DAVID *The Oath of the Tennis Court* 1791. 26 × 41⅜ (66 × 105)

the *Brutus* back to the philosophical world of David's
7 *Socrates*. Its apparent androgyny is more precisely the
narrowing of a total ideal of human beauty into an exclusively
male realm, a move which pays homage not only to the
homoerotic bias of ancient Greek culture but also to the bonds
of exclusively masculine fellowship within the studio itself.
Girodet had set out to prove that the internal complexity of
potential appropriate to the hero could be articulated even
without Drouais's intercutting between the poles of grandeur
and beauty, that it could be accommodated entirely within the
latter category. The result is a body that is removed from life
yet never decays; that is subject to perpetual repetitions of
sensual pleasure yet is never exhausted by them; that is trained
like an athlete of antiquity for war yet remains forever
untouched by violence, knowing death only in the midst of
ecstatic animation of the nerves, muscles, blood, and skin.

As he was completing the *Endymion,* Girodet was also
becoming an active participant in the Revolutionary process.
He would go on to lead Republican artists in violent clashes
with the Vatican. So it is difficult to draw obvious connections
between political and esthetic commitments. The younger
artist's preoccupation with ideal mythology markedly con-

trasts with David's simultaneous immersion of his art into the
flow of living history back in Paris. In 1791, in the first Salon
of the Revolution, his master showed a highly finished
drawing which predicted a new kind of history painting. This
was the *Oath of the Tennis Court,* celebrating the moment 14
during the Estates General of 1789 when the delegates of the
Third Estate pledged themselves to remain in permanent
assembly until they had achieved a constitution: they would
"die rather than disperse until France was free." To capture
the moment David conceived a vastly multiplied oath of the
Horatii, which now bound the assembled representatives of
the nation to a new foundation of civic order.

The source of the commission was not the state, but an
unofficial political body calling itself the "Society of the
Friends of the Constitution," more commonly known, after
the old monastery in which it held its meetings, as the
Jacobins. Its commission to the artist was organized as an
expression of the national will: the gargantuan final picture,
with its life-sized foreground figures, was to be paid for by
three thousand subscribers, who would receive a print of the
image in return. The canvas was to hang in the National
Assembly itself, to hold before the nation's legislators both the

foundation of their authority and an ideal model of the general will in operation.

Both act and image hark back to the antique models of patriotic fervor and self-sacrifice which David had figured so vividly in his earlier work. But this literal bonding of art and the primal moment of Revolutionary public life proved to be less a way forward than a cul-de-sac for history painting. The lesson of David's experience is that when the artist forsakes the distance of metaphor, the actual public sphere will perpetually escape representation. This was the fate of the Tennis Court project. To finish it would have required an impossibly stable political consensus. After the King tried to flee France to join the external enemies of the Revolution, the Jacobins split into antagonist monarchist and republican factions (the more radical group retaining the name); the dream of accord emblematized in the *Oath of the Tennis Court* had vanished. Amid the growing factional struggles, perpetual economic crisis, and panic induced by military attacks on France, today's hero was likely to become tomorrow's traitor. This process of historical change would not stand still to accommodate the atemporal and time-consuming medium of painting. By 1792 David had all but abandoned his canvas with only a few of the central figures sketched in the nude. His pupil Gérard won a state competition with a similar project to memorialize the effective moment of the monarchy's downfall, *10 August 1792*, but likewise never moved to the stage of working it up on canvas.

FIGURES OF REVOLUTIONARY DEATH

The vicissitudes of these projects were part of a general upheaval affecting virtually every aspect of conceiving, making, and viewing art. Both the practical and esthetic ambitions of painters and sculptors had been formed for generations within stable governing institutions that took responsibility for training, advancement, housing, and—for the most favored artists—assuring a livelihood. That tradition and those institutions were suddenly overturned, and by 1792 a new Republican government was instructing young artists to despise everything for which the old order had stood. The church, long a source of patronage, was under siege. A puritanical austerity in private life was encouraged and increasingly enforced as a sign of civic virtue, while a succession of revolutionary regimes asked artists to invent forms for philosophical and ideological messages wholly new to public art. Unfortunately, those regimes lacked the will and money to pay for what they required, and artists were forced back on their own resources in the midst of a shattered economy.

Some artists and craftworkers found employment in a novel and enormous enterprise of symbol-making: the creation of the great Revolutionary festivals, with their myriad floats, costumes, temporary architecture, and sculptural props. David, as he was drawn into the radical political leadership, took on the role of supervising this entire apparatus as the organization of political pageants and ceremonies turned into a year-round industry. But he would eventually return to painting at the behest of his political allies, and in doing so came to affirm the value of his pupil Girodet's concentration on the eloquent male body.

Early in 1793, following the King's execution, a royalist soldier had murdered a deputy, Lepelletier de Saint-Fargeau, who had voted for the death sentence. David was called upon to paint a memorial to the political martyr and produced a 15 rather conventional image of the Classical hero on his deathbed reminiscent of his own fallen *Hector* from 1783 (and gave over most of the actual painting to Gérard). That summer another, more incendiary assassination took place. The extreme populist writer and deputy Jean-Paul Marat was attacked in his bath by a counter-Revolutionary zealot named Charlotte Corday. Marat was the hero of the organized *sans-culottes*, the movement of artisans and workers in the poor neighborhoods of the city. A major symbolic tribute was required, and David again was summoned to produce a painting to stand in for the lost martyr. But the Revolutionary leadership, of which the artist was a part, was worried about the demands of the popular movement and its propensity to spontaneous violence. The Terror was about to begin, but in their view terror had to be strictly controlled from above.

David put that ambivalence into paint. In his *Marat at His* 16 *Last Breath*, the martyr is the saintly "Friend of the People." The papers on the edge of his rude writing stand show that he had been dispatching some money to a soldier's widow when surprised by his killer (whose own false letter requesting an audience he still holds). His nudity could be read as both a metaphorical and actual mark of heroic stature, in that he typically carried on his duties through the pain of an excruciating skin disease, which he could soothe only by immersion in a medicinal bath. While the subject's passion for equality and fraternity is plain, he is past all action and the image is meant to console its viewer far more than incite him or her to a rage for vengeance.

Marat's pose, the instruments of violence, the inscriptions, the plain wood of the upright box, the insistently perpendicular compositional order, all conjure up Christ's sacrifice without leaving the factual realm of secular history. For guidance in this delicate task, he called on the absent Girodet's experiment in religious painting from 1790, in which his pupil had already diminished overt Christian trappings in favor of atmosphere and the body's own eloquence. Amid numerous borrowings, the most obvious sign of David's reliance on

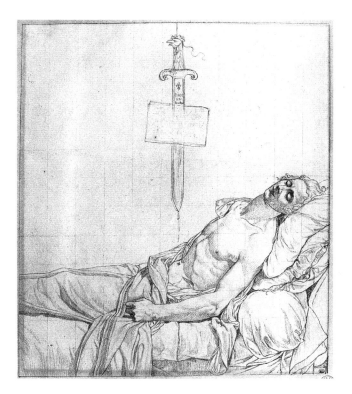

Girodet's *Pietà* is the tracing of the contour along the head and shoulders of the Virgin into the line of the sarcophagus; in a startling transposition, this has become almost precisely the line of Marat's head and body as it emerges above the bath— the key division of the composition between a lower zone full of incident and an upper zone of shadowy, meditative stillness. 12

For the third of his Revolutionary martyr portraits, the *Death of Bara* (1793), David returned to the Classical canon to imagine a boy-victim of the counter-Revolution as an unblemished, eerily beautiful ephebe, suffering but without visible wounds, dreaming more than dying, near to but not within the fury of combat. The regard of the artist, with which we are invited to identify, appears to have scandalously little to do with civic virtue or battlefield heroism, despite the charge to the painter. The sensuality of the body seems to go beyond a youthful beauty appropriate to its age and innocence, and commentators have assumed with near unanimity that the painting suffers from an overbalancing from public to private preoccupations. 17

But his response first of all must be understood in terms of

15 ANATOLE DEVOSGE after **JACQUES-LOUIS DAVID** *The Death of Lepelletier de Saint-Fargeau* 1793. 18½ × 15¾ (46.7 × 40)

16 JACQUES-LOUIS DAVID *Marat at His Last Breath* 1793. 63¾ × 49⅛ (160.7 × 124.8)

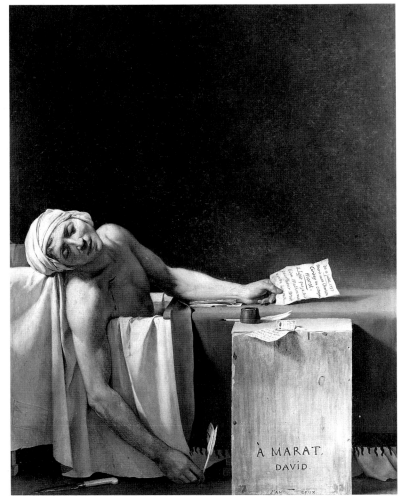

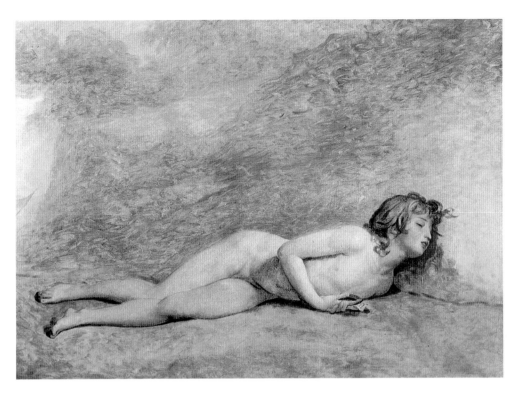

17 JACQUES-LOUIS DAVID *The Death of Bara* 1793. 46½ × 61 (118 × 155)

the special circumstances of the 1793 commission. The young Joseph Bara, who had actually died in ambiguous circumstances, was a contrived martyr. How was David to move from the celebration of mature victims—Lepelletier and Marat— who were significant historical actors, known personally to the artist, to the representation of an unknown boy? How was he to ennoble what was at best a trivially unlucky act of bravado? How was he to find a fresh form for the abstract stereotypes of outraged innocence and the sacrifice of youth with which he was forced to work, following Robespierre's unreal dictum that "the French alone have thirteen-year-old heroes?"

Once again, when faced with a demanding and unconventional assignment, he looked to the work of his students. In this instance, he was responding to the nude academic study as transformed by his own followers, the late Drouais and Girodet in particular. In their hands, it had become a privileged emblem of virtue and self-sacrifice in youth, and their vision of physical perfection carried with it a statement of anti-authoritarian originality in style and conception.

If David had needed a vivid reminder of this potential, he received one in the summer of 1793 when Girodet's *Endymion* was finally seen, to great success, in the Paris Salon. His pupil's inspired interplay of conceptual oppositions in the realm of abstract and ageless beauty would have corresponded to the difficult combination of ideas, and conditions bound up

in the Bara commission. It had made concrete the longstanding ideological association between the physical perfection achieved by the ancients and their free society of equal, active citizens. Though this is not to say that the translation was entirely successful or that the *Bara* could be said to have functioned as a legible icon of utopian virtue. In fact one can see in it a collapse of this intimate dialogue within the inherited rhetorical codes of Classical art.

Certain aspects of the painting have undeniable power: the nervous scumbling applied simultaneously to the body and its setting continued David's recent ventures into extreme gestural freedom in the remarkable Revolutionary-period portraits of Madame Chalgrin and Madame Pastoret. Here it permitted him to appropriate, by means of a maximally porous rather than maximally sealed technique, Girodet's atmospheric unity of figure and ground. But when it came to the suppression of the genitals—imperative in view of the mandate that David represent outraged innocence—the result was less happy. The overall illumination and blond light deprived David of Girodet's device of veiling shadow; his response was to take the boy's body and break it in two, simultaneously to figure its suffering and to downplay its sex. The body is twisted unnaturally at its center, subjected to a wrenching discontinuity, which marks the body's violation, the bayonet wound to the midsection that killed the boy. This

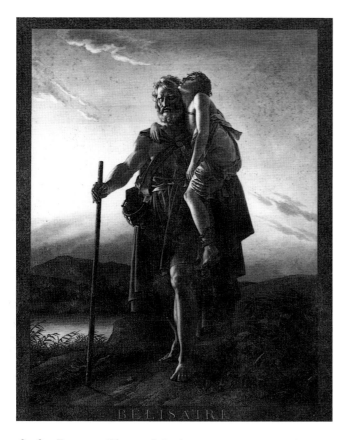

18 after FRANÇOIS GÉRARD *Belisarius* 1795. 18⅜ × 13½ (46.5 × 34.5)

device, along with the shadowed abdomen, directly recalls the
8   abrupt inner displacement of Drouais's *Athlete,* which David
superimposed over the undisturbed imaginary wholeness of
the *Endymion.* Much of the strangeness of the image is derived
from the clash of these two incompatible bodies in one.

LEAVING TERROR BEHIND

There was no opportunity for a public response to David's
Bara because Robespierre's government was overturned in
the summer of 1794, one day before the scheduled festival in
honor of the child-martyr. This Thermidorian Reaction (so-
called because of the month in the Revolutionary calendar in
which it took place), ended the period of radical change, and
republican France entered a five-year phase of indecisive
collegial government. David, as a close associate of the fallen
Jacobin leader, had narrowly escaped the same sentence of
death. As it was, he was sent to prison and remained in
confinement for more than a year. Gaining his full freedom
late in 1795, David soon recovered his lost position and large
teaching studio, but his circle would no longer be the
dominant nexus of practice it had been before Thermidor.

Without David to provide a center, the various components

that had gone into the collective work of the old studio split
apart. Without the critical spirit of the 1780's or the political
commitment of the early '90's, these dispersed elements came
to express narrower, more obvious and usually more
conservative interests. In the Salon of 1795, the first under the   18
new order, the great consensus success was a new *Belisarius* by
Gérard. This painting (now lost) harked back to the pathetic
qualities of David's own version of 1781, but exaggerated that   1
pathos by imagining that the blind outcast's young guide had
been killed by a snake; Belisarius is left without aid, carrying
the boy's corpse through a deserted wilderness.

Gérard was painting for the Salon because he, and all of his
generation of young artists, had seen their career interrupted
by war in Europe. The French Academy in Rome had been
sacked by pious Romans early in 1793 (Girodet had narrowly
escaped the scene with his life) and had remained closed ever
since. The Revolutionary reforms of the exhibition system
meant that painters who would normally have been continuing their studies in Italy were free to make precocious careers
in Paris. The ineffectual efforts of the government to sustain a
program of public commissions meant that the artist's
professional survival depended upon early public recognition.

This state of affairs encouraged a volatile, speculative
approach to subject matter and style. The success of Gérard's
Belisarius encouraged a number of young artists to produce
their own similar elderly victims. As that success was seen as a
matter of emotional effect rather than reflection on history and
virtue, the identity of the outcast could be altered at will.
Fulchran-Jean Harriet gave the theme a turn into the
landscape sublime in 1796, offering an *Oedipus at Colonus* in   19
which Belisarius' dead guide is replaced by an unconscious
Antigone. Despite its source in the tragedy of Sophocles, the
harsh, windswept environment is unrelieved by the presence
of Theseus (the hero of the Athenian polis) or any other sign of
the blinded exile's final reconciliation with civic culture.

In David's *Brutus,* the sorrow of any individual actor is only
one element in a larger complex of causes and effects
addressed to the viewer's active understanding; emotional
responses are elicited—and deepened—through cognitive
apprehension of the inevitability of that suffering. In these
paintings of the 1790's, by contrast, individual pain and loss
are isolated and exploited for sheer intensity of effect. This
cult of emotion savored for its own sake revealed its
compatibility with the politics of reaction in the painting that
enjoyed the most enthusiastic response in the 1799 Salon.
Pierre-Narcisse Guérin (1774–1833), seven years younger
than Girodet, was the first artist of the period to come to
prominence who had not studied with David. He had received
his training in Regnault's studio and won the Rome Prize in
1797. Still unable to travel to Italy, he set to work on a *Return*   20
of Belisarius to his Family for the Salon. The subject

corresponds exactly to a passage in Marmontel's Enlightenment novel, the same text on which David had drawn for his public debut in 1781. But Guérin went further than had Gérard in suppressing the earnestly political implications of his source, to the point of effacing the identity of Belisarius altogether. After the painting had been completed, he altered the identity of his hero by the simple measure of restoring his sight and inventing a new name and personal history out of whole cloth.

Now the subject was one Marcus Sextus, proscribed by the dictator Sulla during the civil wars of the late Roman Republic. After the fall of his persecutor, he returns home to find his wife dead and family shattered. Public response to this fable in 1799 was overwhelming; crowds surrounded it; visitors attached poems to its frame; art students decorated it with laurel garlands. The allegory was patent to everyone: for Sulla, read Robespierre; for Marcus Sextus, read the moderate émigrés who had fled the Revolution but were beginning to return under the more lenient and conciliatory regime that came after Thermidor. In order that nothing cloud that meaning, the artist avoided choosing a hero whose complex character and fate would be well known from literature and artistic precedent. Here there were no troubling ambiguities; the concept was simple and designed for a predictable effect.

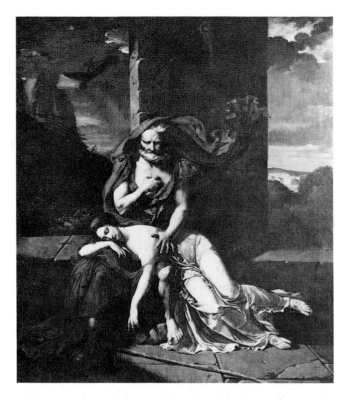

19 FULCHRAN-JEAN HARRIET *Oedipus at Colonus* 1796. $61\frac{1}{2} \times 52\frac{3}{8}$ (156 × 133)

20 PIERRE-NARCISSE GUÉRIN
The Return of Marcus Sextus 1799.
$85\frac{1}{2} \times 95\frac{1}{2}$ (217 × 243)

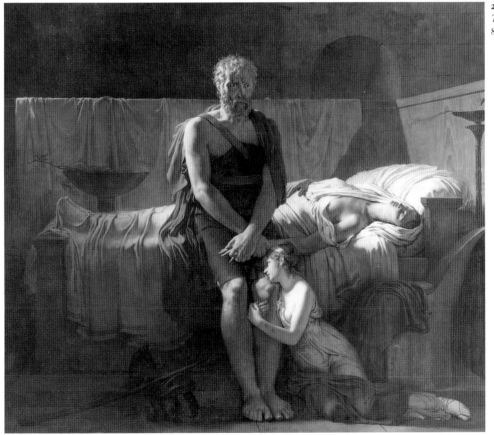

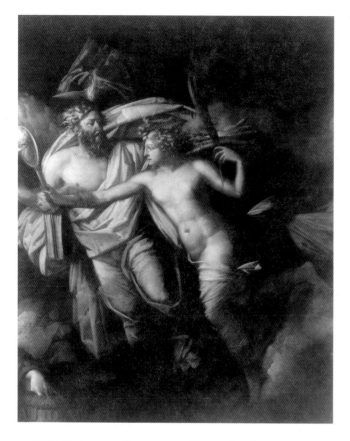

21 PHILIPPE-AUGUSTE HENNEQUIN *Allegory of 10 August* 1799. 88¼ × 68⅞ (224 × 175). Detail

In stylistic terms, Guérin's painting was a recycling of David's signature devices from the previous decade (David was heard to say that Guérin "had been listening outside my door"), with something of a Girodet-style nocturne thrown in for melancholy effect. But in moral and intellectual terms, it was a violation of what had been the most deeply held beliefs within David's circle about the responsibility of history painting to interrogate and translate the complex inherited specifics of its themes.

But to see the Directory period as leading to a simple victory of reaction would be misleading, despite Guérin's conspicuous triumph. Even in that Salon, the jury awarded the first medal to Philippe-Auguste Hennequin (1762–1833),

21 an unreconstructed Jacobin, for his massive *Allegory of 10 August*. This canvas (now sadly mutilated) memorialized the insurrection which brought about the final overthrow of the monarchy as "The Triumph of the French People," and transferred the symbolic language of the Revolutionary festivals into the medium of painting. That artist went on to

22 have a similar success in 1800 with his *Remorse of Orestes*, a mythological narrative that was an equally transparent

allegory of the persecutions suffered by those still loyal to the patriotic cause.

Hennequin, who was of Drouais's generation, had remained something of an outsider throughout his career. After a brief, unhappy time in David's studio, he made his own way to Rome, was caught up in the Revolution in Lyon, and was imprisoned in 1795 for his part in the ultra-leftist "Conspiracy of Equals" led by Gracchus Babeuf. Only on his release in 1797 did he begin his career as an exhibiting artist in the Paris Salon. Both of his prize-winning canvases demonstrated that his loyalty to a learned Classicism as the natural expression of popular democracy was as dogged as his Jacobinism. At the same time his irregular training manifests itself in a naive awkwardness in drawing and a tendency toward labored handling and an undisciplined accumulation of figures and incidents. In the densely packed, agitated composition of the *Orestes*, the technical shortcomings worked much more to his advantage in conveying the terrifying impasse of its hero. Orestes suffers the torments of the Furies because he has fulfilled his divine obligation to avenge the murder of his father; in that his mother was the murderer, he has nevertheless committed a crime abhorrent to the human community. As an allegory of the persecutions suffered by the followers of Babeuf (and by leftist democrats in general), it uses the complexity of its tragic source in a way that contrasts with Guérin's avoidance of any known referent that might complicate his message. Hennequin makes his complaint, to be sure, but shares with his viewer a recognition that necessity never removes the moral stigma of murder.

That Hennequin could enjoy success with such defiance of political orthodoxy—and even normal standards of competence—is a sign of the disarray and fragmentation that characterized culture in this period. Any previous honors an artist might have received could not guarantee continued recognition and support. Intense competition brought about splits between former close friends such as Girodet and Gérard. The former's arduous return from Italy—plagued by delays, malaria and dangers from enemies of France—consumed more than two years. Finally reaching Paris in 1795, he found himself unable to capitalize on the high reputation that his *Endymion* had prepared for him. Wealthy speculators and military contractors were now in a position to command and direct the work of artists for whom little public support was forthcoming. There was as a result a corresponding license in matters of painterly style that rendered moot the freedom and individual distinction that Girodet had struggled so hard to attain within official structures. In fact, the cultivation of originality had largely passed from the culture of art into the fashions of an extravagant, youth-conscious and apolitical elite. Gérard proved himself far more adaptable in recording the carefully constructed images of its leading

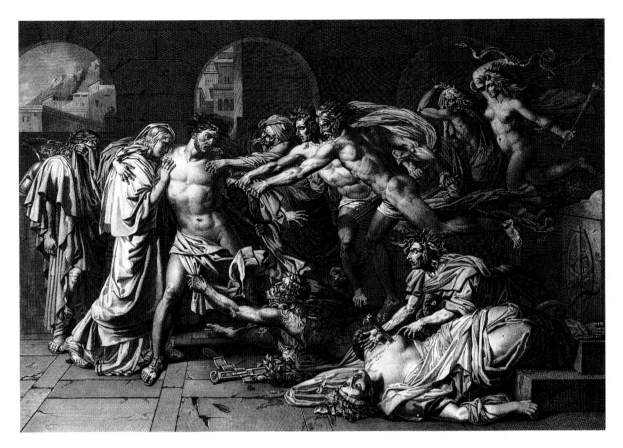

22 after PHILIPPE-AUGUSTE HENNEQUIN *The Remorse of Orestes* 1800. 15⅜ × 22¼ (39 × 56.5)

figures, as in his portrait of Madame Récamier (1805). The style was for dress and coiffure after the antique, but this was Classicism exploited for its elegant simplicity and flattering eroticism, not for its association with civic virtue.

Public life was marked by a willed forgetting of the rigors and austerities of Robespierre's Republic of Virtue. The resentful Girodet was forced to witness the superficial appearance of his *Endymion* establish a corresponding fashion in history painting. His rival Gérard led the way in capturing the *Endymion's* sealed envelope of flesh and delivering it to a strain of precious eroticism that sought a place beyond the vicissitudes of political orthodoxy. The latter's *Cupid and Psyche* was the center of attention in the Salon of 1798. Its landscape setting is outside of time; the bodies exhibit the immunity to temporal corruption appropriate to mythical beings. The innocent Psyche is about to feel the first kiss of an *invisible* Cupid, and the erudite viewer is meant to take pleasure in this metaphysical conceit, while the frozen stillness and all of the hovering on the edge of physical contact and of awakening carnal desire amount to a heightening of the sexual tension inherent in the subject.

Girodet's contribution to the same exhibition clashed with his old companion's recourse to mythological refinement. In perhaps the last of the great Revolutionary portraits, fully comparable to David's *Marat*, he depicted Jean-Baptiste Belley, representative to the French National Assembly from the colony of Saint-Dominique (present-day Haiti). It would be better to say that this is a double portrait contrasting the living and the dead, the African and the European, the force of action and the force of ideas. Belley leans against a splendid commemorative bust of Abbé Raynal, the great Enlightenment advocate of political reform, which the artist has imaginatively erected on a hilltop of the Caribbean island. Raynal's liberationist ideas and his arguments against colonial exploitation had prepared the ground for Belley's decisive intervention in the Assembly in 1794, when he won approval for the abolition of slavery in the colonies and full citizenship for blacks.

The Belley painting celebrates a heroic triumph of Enlightenment ideas and the principle of equality. The rhetorical antitheses of the paired portraits raise its ambitions to the intellectual and moral standing of history painting. But unlike the *Marat*, Girodet's work was a willful, individual exercise, and a lonely one. It found no echo even within the

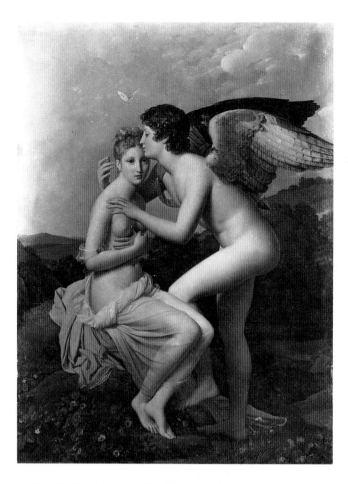

23 FRANÇOIS GÉRARD *Cupid and Psyche* 1798. 73¼ × 52 (186 × 132)

1826) were a crucial instrument in the separation of the Classical tradition from political and moral reflection on the present. That artist's illustrations of Homer's *Iliad* and *Odyssey*, produced for Roman patrons during the 1790's, were distinguished by an austere reduction of pictorial description to the play of contour and two-dimensional pattern. Neither he nor his English sponsors saw Classicism as bound up with the recovery of republican liberties in the present; his imagery belongs to a realm before history even begins. And the admirers of the abstract intelligence of his designs tended to view all subsequent compromise with empirical experience as a corruption of the pure origins of the tradition.

Gérard showed conspicuous attention to this esthetic current in the *Cupid and Psyche*. Constance Charpentier (1767–1849) was one emergent artist who was able to take its potential further. She, along with a number of other women, had taken advantage of a Revolutionary loosening of the rules in artistic instruction to develop skills in the allegorical realm of history painting. In the past, they would have been barred from the study of the model and so from academic training. Before 1789, David had unsuccessfully fought against that restriction, but in the new environment, Charpentier had been able to study with him and with Gérard, establishing herself as a regular exhibitor in the Salon. In a work entitled *Melancholy*, which met with an enthusiastic public reception in 1801, she found a striking way to translate Flaxman's graphic linearism into painting. She accomplished this by building the work out of two opposed conventions of illusion and by a manifest inconsistency of illumination. The single, dejected female figure, garbed in a simple Greek gown, is saturated with light to the point that internal modelling and details are suppressed. The startling and unreal contrast with the darkly atmospheric forest setting concentrates all of the pictorial stress onto the contours of the figure. That boundary between light and dark is the passage which effects an

reconstituted studio of David. There the shift away from contemporary history had taken an even more exaggerated turn toward an archaizing Classical culture and the simplified graphic conventions of Greek vase painting, Pompeiian frescos, and early Renaissance art. The graphic innovations of the English sculptor and draftsman John Flaxman (1755–

24 JOHN FLAXMAN, "The Fight for the Body of Patroclus," from *Illustrations to Homer's "Iliad"* 1793. 6⅝ × 13 (16.8 × 33.6)

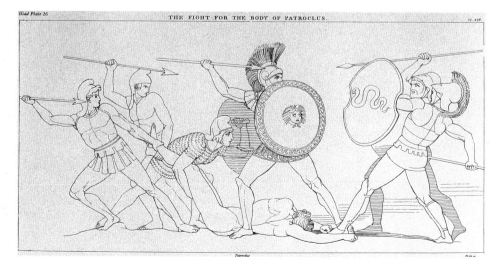

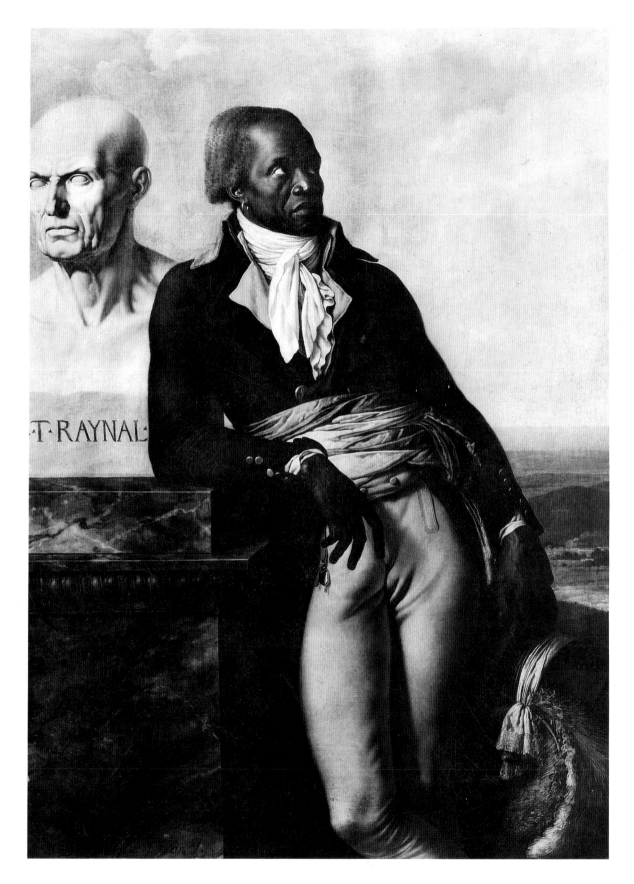

25 ANNE-LOUIS GIRODET *Portrait of Jean-Baptiste Belley* 1797. 63 × 45 (160 × 114.3)

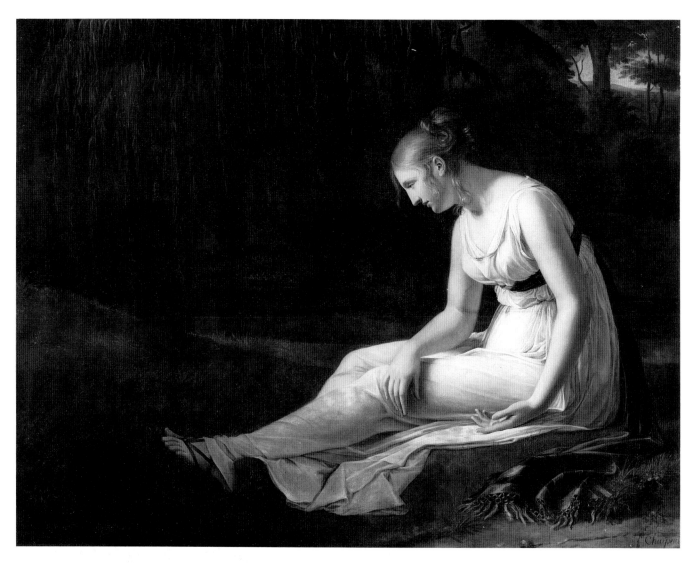

26 **CONSTANCE CHARPENTIER** *Melancholy* 1801. 52 × 66 (132 × 167.6)

ingenious reconciliation between a subjective poetics of
ambiguity and the control of Classical rationalism (bringing
up to date the Enlightenment equation between nature and
the forms of ancient art). As a viewer, one is given the vague
background in which to indulge in reverie oneself; at the same
time the figure provides a surrogate with which one can
identify, but less as a full-bodied presence than as an
interruption in the field of dreaming. It bends physical form
toward signifying the essentially mental condition of melancholic reverie.

In the same year, a painting appeared from one of the new
27 male Davidians, Jean Broc's (ca. 1780–ca. 1850) *Death of
Hyacinth in the Arms of Apollo,* that likewise manipulated light
to suppress plasticity in pictorial illusion. Its mythic source,
best known from the Latin poet Ovid, recounts the jealousy of
the wind Zephyr: filled with unrequited passion for Apollo's

boy lover, he causes the god's discus to swerve and kill the
beautiful Hyacinth. Broc's concentration on ideal adolescent
nudity continued what Gérard had begun three years earlier
in the *Cupid and Psyche,* and he adopts the same low viewpoint
that reduces the background to simple bands of meadow and
sky in a poetic never-never land. But the backlighting has the
effect of reducing even further the weight and surface texture
of flesh: the edges of the bodies are drawn with light rather
than the dark tones that normally indicate the recession and
disappearance of three-dimensional form.

This is a device already exploited by Girodet in the figure of
Zephyr who hovers over Endymion; Broc went further by 13
making it the governing logic of his entire composition. It gave
him the means to solve the same conceptual problem faced by
Charpentier, that is, how to make the obdurately empirical
medium of oil painting approximate the elemental simplicity

of the decoration on Greek ceramics or of Flaxman's drawings. The rippling sequence of fingers on Apollo's right hand, joined to the faces of the lovers in double profile, is a passage of conspicuous virtuosity in this regard. In terms of the painting's theme, reversal as a formal procedure underscored a frankness in celebrating the reversal of normative heterosexuality. It transforms the Platonism of David's *Socrates*—that same-sex desire among males is a path to mental concentration and knowledge of abstract truth—into its own anti-naturalistic visual idiom.

The proponents of these ideas formed something of a self-contained sect within the studio (variously called the Primitives, Meditators, or the Bearded Ones) and did not share in the sort of collaboration and trust enjoyed by the first generation of pupils. Their cultivation of virtue was an inwardly directed and exclusive affair. David, on the other hand, never wavered from his commitment to public art and a public role for the artist; even while in prison he was preparing sketches for his next great history painting. But at the same time he was as attentive as Gérard had been to the ideological force of this newly purified, Hellenic Classicism.

The result was a massive canvas, completed in 1799, the *Intervention of the Sabine Women*. It was very much David's intention that this subject be distinguished from the better-known rape of the Sabines, famously depicted by Poussin and Rubens among countless others. That prior event was the

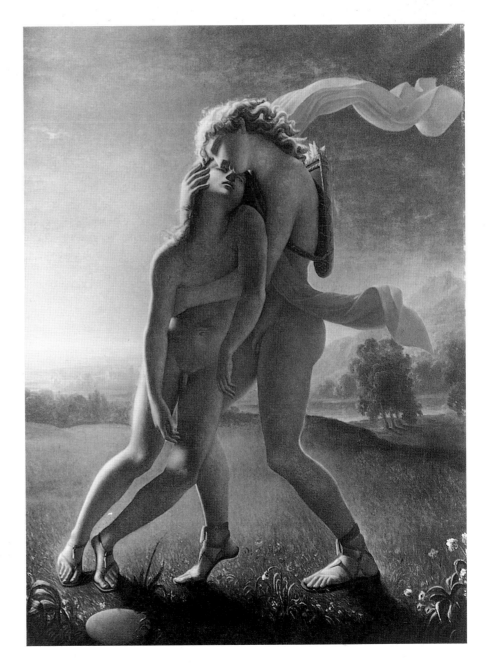

27 JEAN BROC *The Death of Hyacinth in the Arms of Apollo* 1801. 70 × 49½ (177.8 × 125.7)

28

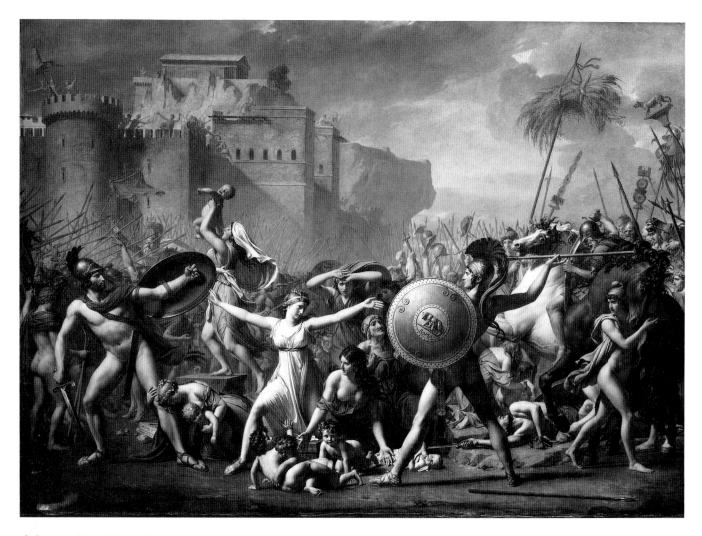

28 JACQUES-LOUIS DAVID *The Intervention of the Sabine Women* 1799. 12'8 × 17'¾ (386 × 520)

beginning of the narrative trajectory which David captured near its end. The early Romans, a rough and exclusively male lot, needed women in order to perpetuate their community; to this end they employed a ruse to steal the wives of their neighbors. It is three years before the Sabine men are able to mount a successful counter-attack, and in that time marriages have been established between the Romans and their captives and a new generation has been born. As the two armies meet and their respective leaders—Romulus for the Romans and Tatius for the Sabines—prepare for single combat, the women throw themselves into the midst of battle, pleading for reconciliation between the two states. At the center is Hersilia, wife of Romulus himself.

In a pointed reversal of the value system which governs the *Horatii* and *Brutus,* the existence of irreconcilably divided loyalties here guarantees a happy ending. The *Sabines* was conceived at David's most desperate hour as a bid for rehabilitation, and it was designed for maximum public

appeal. He saturated the scene with screams, shouts, and confusion, making the spectator's experience approximate that of spectacular melodrama. In place of tragic parsimony of incident, the composition offers profusion of detailed illustration and tempts one's attention toward a deep landscape setting. The most sentimentally affecting element of the story, the children deliberately placed in harm's way, stare directly out at the spectator.

All of this finally is in keeping with the premeditated message of the painting and its essentially strategic conception: none of the copious incident and detail serves to alter the conclusion one is to draw from Hersilia's plea for peace between Romulus and Tatius. The message of harmony is given in advance; everything else in the composition is there as illustration of its necessity. In its most radical phase, the new French Republic had come to be personified as a woman; Hersilia is that personification resurrected as an ideal mother of healing and nurturing, clad all in white.

3, 10

The suspended conflict appears all the more as a suspension of history itself by virtue of David's startling decision to depict his warriors in the nude. While this was believed to conform to an ancient Greek practice, it had no historical pertinence to a Roman subject. But he took the step, late in the compositional development of the painting, to appropriate the idealizing Hellenism being promoted by his students. The design of the principal triad of figures could be a vignette from Flaxman. The effect of its paradoxical delicacy and formalized balance is to remove the memory of actual conflict and violence to a safer realm of myth.

David's mode of exhibiting the painting achieved a further gathering of power to himself. His response to the lack of state funds for the support of art was to ignore the Salon of 1799 altogether and arrange an independent showing of the work in his own space, charging an admission fee to every visitor. Owing to this isolation and personal control over its display, David for the first time was able to present one of his large-scale paintings at eye-level rather than at the top of a crowded Salon hanging. He further exploited these new circumstances by placing a standing mirror opposite the painting. The spectators were invited to use the reflection in order to achieve a distanced, totalizing view of the narrative; at the same time they would see themselves as participants in the action behind them. This is the first of more than one trick he would later play with mirrors in his private exhibitions in an effort to mystify and spectacularize the act of viewing. Having designed a work that maximized the potential for such effects and that reinforced rather than tested the beliefs of its audience, he made the next logical move in financially speculating on the successful appeal of his strategies. He was handsomely repaid for his effort: the painting stayed on view for five years and financed the purchase of a substantial country house and land. The entrepreneurial artist of the nineteenth century was well and truly launched.

THE SUBLIME OF AUTHORITARIANISM

A month before the opening of David's exhibition of the *Sabines* in the last month of 1799, the constitutional government had fallen in the coup of 18 Brumaire. Emerging as leader of a new regime was the charismatic young general Napoleon Bonaparte. Careful at this point to preserve republican forms, his faction came up with the title of First Consul; it evoked the chief executive office of the Roman Republic, one first occupied by Brutus. Napoleon was no stranger to David: he had visited the artist's studio in 1797 and given a mighty impression as an exemplar of martial virtue. On assuming power, he made an immediate effort to bind David to the new government as its official painter. The first

successful product of that alliance was the portrait (1800) of the general, calmly seated on a rearing charger, crossing the Alps over the Saint-Bernard Pass. The actual crossing was a more prosaic affair on the back of a donkey, but plainly the rhetorical requirements of leadership were to prevail over accuracy: carved in the stone are the names of Hannibal and Charlemagne, who had followed the same route to Italian conquests. The setting of natural sublimity of course does more than serve historical commemoration: as in Harriet's *Oedipus*, the wild terrain and turbulent weather are meant to lend action and drama of an irrational kind to the sheer presence of the main actor.

At the same time, however, the wind-blown cloak and broken clouds remain superficial effects laid over an obdurately stable and Classical substructure. Even the perilous slopes and shafts of light arrange themselves in a rigid X-shaped armature which fixes Napoleon firmly in his seat. Soon the republican painter discovered that his deeper moral and artistic preoccupations were at odds with the Bonapartist vision of public art. By 1802, David had begun work on a major new historical canvas. The subject was Leonidas at Thermopylae, the hero being the leader of that small band of Spartans who held off the entire Persian army at a narrow pass, but at the cost of every Greek soldier. He chose the

29 JACQUES-LOUIS DAVID *Napoleon at the Saint-Bernard Pass* 1800. 8′10⅝ × 7′7¼ (270.8 × 231.8)

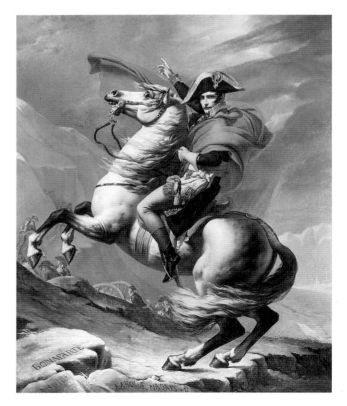

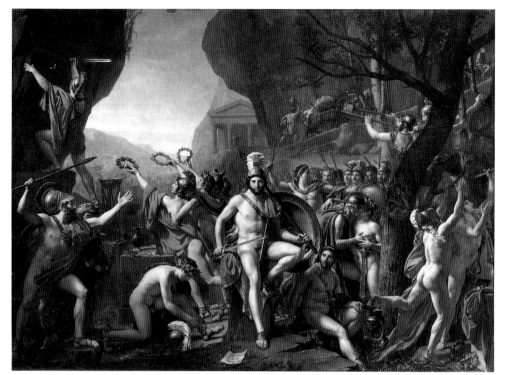

30 JACQUES-LOUIS DAVID
Leonidas at Thermopylae
1814. 12'11¼ × 17'5 (395.6 × 530.9)

moment of reflection and preparation before the battle, and continued the pre-Revolutionary line of ancient leaders who sacrificed everything for virtue and the welfare of the community. Napoleon, on seeing the picture in preparation, dismissed the entire idea as a painting of losers. David suspended work on the *Leonidas* for a decade and soon was diverted into the wearying and esthetically thankless task of glorifying the new Emperor's rite of coronation in 1804. The outcome was an overbearingly enormous canvas enumerating every dignitary present at the pompous ceremony in Notre-Dame (and though he made a study of the arrogant self-crowning itself, David ended by shifting his moment away from any suggestion of usurpation to the aftermath when the freshly Imperial Bonaparte turned to crown his consort Josephine).

This was painting as duty, and it was performed as such. It returns to a conception of rhetorical elevation as copious magnificence in the accumulation of ornaments and witnesses to glory. But much Napoleonic painting was conceived without this sort of clear brief. As political legitimacy devolved into the charisma of one man, painters were presented with a qualitatively new situation. Although he was convinced that art mattered, the ruler himself could not be exactly sure of what he wanted until he saw it. His identity and self-image—general to statesman, Consul to Emperor—were continually subject to change. Artists' initiatives were bound to take on a speculative character, and speculation could as easily turn out wrong as right.

Gérard, typically, was first to take advantage of the Consul's known enthusiasm for the *Ossian* poems. These were claimed as the rediscovered epic cycle of an ancient Celtic bard of that name, though they had actually been produced a half-century earlier by the Scottish writer James Macpherson. Because invented to eighteenth-century requirements, true believers could take the Ossianic as more pure and primitive even than the poetry of archaic Greece, and the *primitifs* of David's studio put them on a level with the works of Homer and Hesiod. Even those who doubted the announced provenance of the verse appreciated it precisely for its modernity: its evocations of a dark and primal northern world inhabited by heroes and spirits corresponded to a growing cult of subjectivity and irrationalism. In a painting destined for Bonaparte's country retreat at Malmaison, Gérard makes his Ossian a blind and bereft old man, conjuring from his lyre the memories of lost parents and children, who surround him as ghostly spirits in a moonlit miasma. With the wild setting, eerie nocturnal lighting, and subject matter of fevered imaginings in an elderly survivor, Gérard distilled the developments of the 1790's into a cloudy fantasy unconstrained by Classical logic or structure.

Girodet had a good claim to being the most experimental painter in his generation, and his rivalry with Gérard was intense. He seized on the First Consul's decorating plans for Malmaison as a chance to rehabilitate his career as a history painter, seeking at the same time to surpass his old friend and studio-mate in the Ossianic stakes. Not content with replicat-

31

ing the other-worldly setting and mood of the poems, he sought to incorporate Napoleon's contemporary concerns into the invented mythology. In his 1802 painting, French commanders, killed in recent campaigns, arrive in a Valhalla presided over by the blind Celtic bard and packed to the breaking point with ghosts and spirits. The upper zone is dominated by elements of overt allegory after Hennequin (if more suavely handled) in the floating personification of republican liberty and the victory of a Gallic cock over an Austrian eagle. These are only the beginning of a catalog of allegorical correspondences to persons and recent political events, ingeniously conceived but nearly impossible to decipher without the guidance of a detailed inventory. In a further burst of conspicuous invention, Girodet conceived the entire atmosphere and lighting of the scene according to his understanding of electric luminosity, using recent discoveries of science as a spectacularly vivid equivalent to the afterlife.

All of Girodet's prodigious natural ability was on show in the painting, which deploys the resources of illusionism to construct a dense tissue of physical impossibilities. The packed accumulation of figures is relieved by a translucent delicacy in their rendering: "figures of crystal," in the words of David, who praised his old pupil's originality to his face, but dismissed it to others as outlandish and undisciplined. Contemporary evidence suggests that Gérard's more straight-forward illustration of strictly Ossianic themes found greater favor both in public and with the First Consul. Two former adherents of the Davidian *primitifs*, the twin brothers Franque, would later adopt the same arrangement as a

31 FRANÇOIS GÉRARD *Ossian* 1801. 72⅝ × 76½ (184.5 × 194.5)

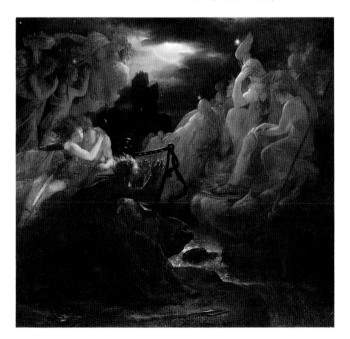

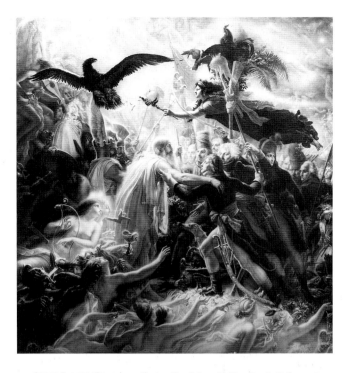

32 ANNE-LOUIS GIRODET *Ossian Receiving the Napoleonic Officers* 1802. 37 × 73½ (93.9 × 186.7)

formula to depict Napoleon himself being beckoned by spirits in a dream to return from Egypt in 1799 and save France by assuming power.

The setback may well have been beneficial to Girodet in that he turned away for a time from political subject matter and from appeals to the ruler's immediate interests. For the Salon of 1806, he prepared an immense *Deluge*, a terrifying emotional drama in a turbulent and darkly primitive world. In contrast to his *Ossian Receiving the Napoleonic Officers*, he reduced the drama to a configuration of elemental simplicity and unmistakable meaning. This subject, centered on the burden of a strong young father, struggling to support a parent, a spouse and a child simultaneously, had become a popular one in the immediately preceding period. Regnault had shown a small canvas on the subject alongside his *Lamentation* in 1789; there the man carries his father on his back and is therefore unable to seize hold of his wife and son as the current sweeps them away. Contemporary viewers were prepared to overlook the curiously sluggish current, and it became one of his most popular works: he eventually painted several replicas to meet demand from collectors. Not for the first time, of course, Girodet took cues from the success of this artist and pushed the same material toward a more extreme and ambitious statement.

Regnault's conception of the scene, in that it stresses the emotion of irretrievable loss, fits within the category of sentimental subjects, and its compact dimensions are those of

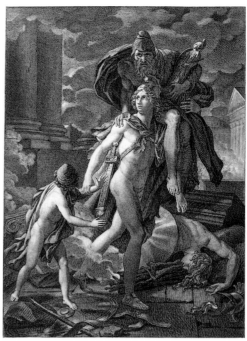

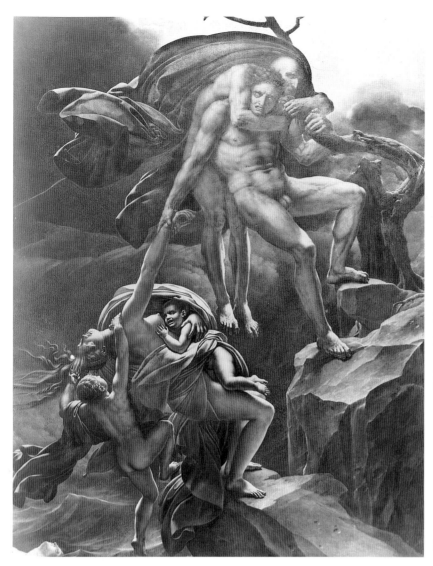

34 JACQUES-LOUIS DAVID and FRANÇOIS GÉRARD *Aeneas Carrying Anchises From the Ruins of Troy* late 1790s. 9⅝ × 6⅛ (24.5 × 15.5)

33 ANNE-LOUIS GIRODET *The Deluge* 1806. 14'1¾ × 11'2¼ (431 × 341)

a cabinet picture. Girodet, by contrast, wanted to maximize both the drama and the physical impact of terror in a canvas of outsized, aggressively public scale. The size of his figures is grander than life. He stacked them vertically, which corresponds to the perilous fall along the cliff face and allows the canvas to tower over the spectator. So that the scene would conform to the requirements of high drama, he chose a moment when his central male figure has not yet lost his grip on the wife and child. The aged father has become the very embodiment of dead weight, already inert and corpse-like, clutching a futile bag of gold; he exerts monstrous strength from a withered body that seems beyond age. Thanks to this death grip of the past, the frail support of the vital younger generations is about to fail, and all the characters are poised on the brink of oblivion in the rushing torrent.

Consistent with his public ambition, Girodet took advantage of an established Classical prototype—the motif of the Trojan hero Aeneas carrying his father and leading his son

from the burning ruins of the city, precisely as rendered by Gérard for a series of printed illustrations to Virgil's *Aeneid* in **34** the later 1790's (in which both he and David had also collaborated). But Girodet has reversed the meaning of the motif from one of filial devotion to one of fatal conflict of obligations. If one defines expressive dissonance in any art form in terms of departure from a settled sense of harmony, then this painting is maximally dissonant within the conventions of history painting. The artist has stretched the internal contrast of age and youth virtually to the breaking point—just as the man's arm is being pulled to its limits. The terrified expressions defy every Classical norm of composure, a quality heroic actors had been assumed always to exhibit even in extreme pain. Muscles bulge and tendons strain. An outsized, funereal cloak swirls in a freakish whirlwind.

To compare the *Deluge* to David's conception of the Spartan leader Leonidas is to see how thoroughly Girodet had **30** seized and transformed the conventions of heroic nudity. For

David, the hero gathers and contains his strength within himself in order to exert it at will; for Girodet, the hero, such as he remains, is a victim, his strength arrayed as a conduit across which uncontrollable, nonhuman forces exert themselves: among these is the sexual desire which binds him to his mate and to the next generation. The larger community, with its veneration of constraining authority and wealth, is a threat to his survival. But this is less a motif of youthful rebellion than a figure for the finality of human isolation. At this point Girodet had finally set his art against the rationalist, communitarian precepts of his formation in David's circle. This was recognized by conservatives in the fine-arts division of the Institute, the umbrella cultural organization under Napoleon's Empire, who despised the Jacobin associations that still clung to the Classical canon. In a competition to select the best works of art produced during the first decade of Bonapartist rule, the jury preferred the *Deluge* to David's *Sabines*.

DREAMS BEYOND HISTORY

In the same year that Girodet exhibited the *Deluge*, an artist of the next generation made his own dramatic bid for official favor. Repeating the former's own tactics in 1802, J.-A.-D. Ingres (1780–1867) sought to appeal directly to the self-regard of Napoleon and to distinguish himself from the competition by a conspicuous display of esthetic originality. The painting 35 was *Napoleon on the Imperial Throne* (1806). In its conception, Ingres sought to actualize in esthetic terms the kind of pedigree which David had etched into the rock of the Saint-Bernard Pass, one extending back through the Emperor Charlemagne and the origins of Frankish kingship to Roman antiquity. As Bonaparte had clothed his usurpation of absolute power in ancient formalities, so Ingres proceeded to represent his body within pictorial conventions appropriate to ancient times. The painstaking precision of detail, which gives the symbolic accessories a weight equal to the man, was likened at the time to the manner of Flemish "primitives" like the Van Eycks. The hieratic frontal pose is arranged in the manner of Byzantine and early medieval ivory carvings of quasi-divine rulers. The Emperor's face is mask-like and displays a waxen pallor; the figure as a whole is imprisoned within a rigid geometry that finds its ultimate point of reference in ancient renderings of the colossal statue of Zeus, sculpted by Phidias from gold and ivory as the cult image at Olympia.

Ingres had been a pupil in David's studio during the late 36 1790's. His winning Rome Prize painting of 1801, *The Ambassadors of Agamemnon Visiting Achilles*, had displayed a striking command of the rhetorical distinctions basic to the Davidian project. At the beginning of the epic, the greatest warrior among the Greek army at Troy withdrew from the war after a petty argument with his commander. Both Achilles and his companion Patroclus display the languidly ephebic grace appropriate to noble bodies that have withdrawn from the fray and are therefore free to manifest the homoerotic attraction that binds them in comradeship. Patroclus, the transitional figure and the first to reenter the battle, playfully sports the helmet of Achilles, an anticipation of the disguise that will lead to his death at Hector's hands. The entreating warriors, driven by the Trojan forces to the very brink of defeat, display the hardened musculature and indented contours of bodies marked in strife. Such competition paintings had to be completed in a matter of weeks with no models or preparatory drawings permitted in the cell-like individual studios. As a consequence, few could stand up to exacting judgment; but Ingres's entry achieved a deservedly high reputation. Not only did it contend successfully with the

35 JEAN-AUGUSTE-DOMINIQUE INGRES *Napoleon on the Imperial Throne* 1806. 8'8⅝ × 63 (265.7 × 160)

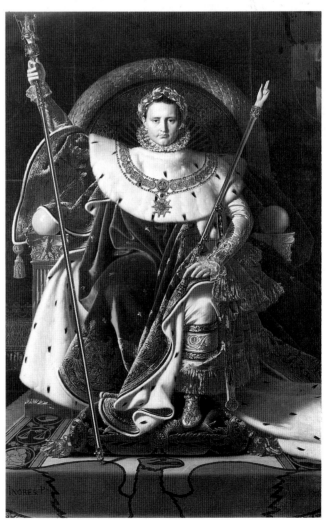

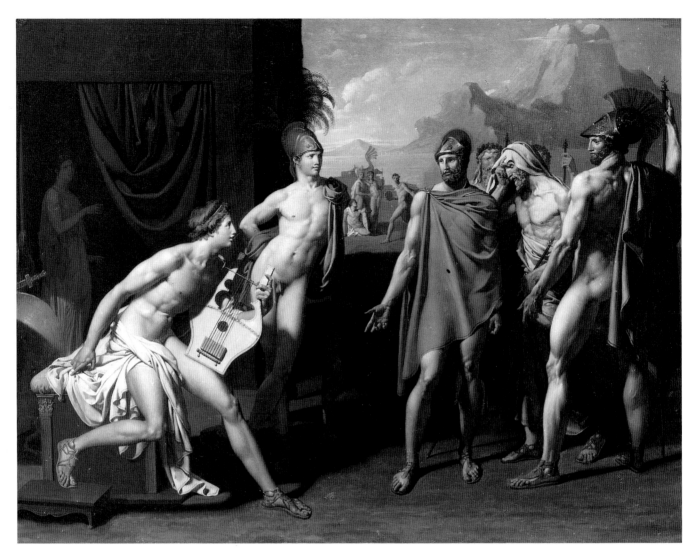

36 JEAN-AUGUSTE-DOMINIQUE INGRES *The Ambassadors of Agamemnon Visiting Achilles* 1801. 43¼ × 61 (109.9 × 154.9)

24 authority of Flaxman's Homeric engravings, the English artist himself saw and praised the result.

By the middle of the decade, Ingres had extended the rhetorical conception of form in a new direction: over the repertoire of body types derived from antique models, he imposed a set of distinctions derived from the historical change in artistic styles over time, including nonclassical ones. According to this logic, if one were treating subject matter from a particular period or evoking ideas associated with it, one would adopt the manner of its art. The pastiche of styles in his enthroned Napoleon was a demonstration of this approach. It did not find immediate favor, earning the young Ingres a stubborn reputation as an eccentric medieval revivalist. Bonaparte's negative reaction completed the parallel with Girodet in 1802: the Emperor found the naked archaism of his claim on power embarrassing when projected with such scrupulous fidelity by the powers of art.

Conveniently this setback coincided with the reopening of the French Academy in Rome, and Ingres was able belatedly to take up the scholarship he had won five years before (and he contrived to remain in Italy for the next fifteen years). His first painting of the nude, to be sent back for inspection in Paris, extracted the Classical prototype from beneath the Bonapartist trappings and expanded it into an overwhelming totem of masculine power. The subject matter of his *Jupiter and Thetis* 37 (1811) concerns the divine intervention that lay behind the desperate entreaties of the Greek warriors to the reluctant Achilles. The latter's divine mother is shown supplicating the chief of the gods to strengthen the Trojans and teach the Greeks a lesson for Agamemnon's high-handed mistreatment of her son. The jealous Juno looks on and plots her revenge.

The common source in the Olympian Zeus makes a pair of Ingres's enthroned Napoleon and his Jupiter. They illustrate the double-sidedness of artists' subservience to an absolute

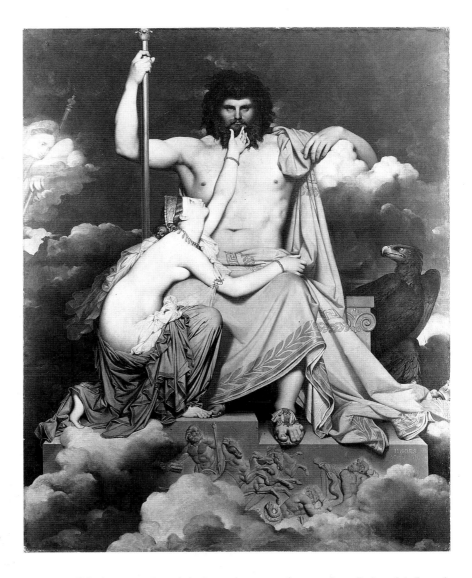

37 JEAN-AUGUSTE-DOMINIQUE INGRES *Jupiter and Thetis* 1811. 11′4⅝ × 8′5¼ (347 × 257.2)

authority. The dependent adoration of a dominant political figure easily transmutes itself into a personal fantasy of power and domination, and both are equally aspects of isolation and vulnerability. In this case, as so often, that domination is exercised over a woman, a diminutive figure who is turned into an impossibly sinuous and compliant emblem of submission. Ingres's imagination of untrameled strength, encouraged by the cult of the First Consul/Emperor, helped remove the rational constraints on the linear Classicism of the period. Because its approach to the human figure devalued inner substance in favor of pliable outline, it offered little resistance to the compulsions of private desires. The emphasis on silhouette in the figure of Thetis differs markedly from that 26 achieved by Charpentier in her figure of Melancholy, in that it is not a product of the signifying structure of the painting as a whole; rather it proceeds from exaggeration and distortion, and the suppression of internal anatomy is just that, a diminishing of the body's structural resistance to the artist's command.

Certainly Ingres's personal expansion of pictorial rhetoric into self-conscious archaism was an ingenious extension of the practises within which his education had taken place. But historical circumstances were such that, in contrast with David's sharpening of Classical rhetoric in the *Horatii*, it did 3 not trigger a new collective dialog. Nor could any painter have accomplished this. As individual artists became more detached and competitive, career patterns began to show the strains of maintaining an entire tradition by means of the frail emotional and intellectual resources of any single individual. Girodet's technical innovations in the *Endymion* had probably 13 had the greatest individual impact on the art of the next decade, but his own art veered erratically and unpredictably between styles and themes. The baffled responses of his audience left him feeling bitter and misunderstood. Ingres, on the other hand, dealt with the erosion of community and stable benchmarks of Classical practise by refusing the very principle of development and change. He would obsessively return to favorite motifs and compositions, seizing any opportunity to try out small refinements in replicas and repetitions in other media. In one famous instance of this, he inserted the torso and head of his anonymous nude study of 1808, the so-called *Vapinçon Bather*, almost without alteration into the midst of his crowded *Turkish Bath*, painted more than 50 years later, by which time the context from which it took its meaning had changed enormously.

Girodet and Ingres were among the most committed Classicists of the early Empire, yet the art of both remains remarkable for its highly subjective and idiosyncratic character, its insistent revelation of the irreducible creative personality. That these are traits which have come to define Romanticism in art should be enough to underscore the point that the greater part of the Romantic legacy was in fact engendered within the project of later Classicism by artists who were determined to remain faithful to its traditions, indeed, who could not imagine a serious art outside of those traditions. Both artists cultivated an exactingly polished technique in finishing the surfaces of their paintings, building up glazes so as to banish as far as possible individual gestural imprints in the paint. A "licked" finish would become one of the clichés of conformist academicism later in the century, but in the cases of its two originators, their obsessiveness with a sealed surface reads as a holding action, a determined imposition of an impersonal discipline over the involuntary exposure of the self.

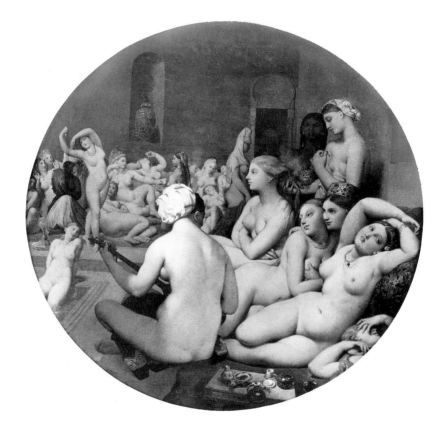

38 JEAN-AUGUSTE-DOMINIQUE INGRES *The Turkish Bath* 1862.
Diameter 42½ (108)

· 2 ·

CLASSICISM IN CRISIS: GROS TO DELACROIX

THOMAS CROW

FORCE OF ARMS

THE ROMANTIC STYLE IN THE USUAL SENSE OF THE term—energetic brushwork, linear order giving way to the impact of color, elevation of contemporary and exotic subject matter to epic intensity—arrived in the first decade of the nineteenth century. But it was as much a product of the translations and distortions of the Classical inheritance as was the art of Girodet and Ingres. Its chief innovator, Antoine-Jean Gros (1771–1835), was likewise a student of David and loyal to Davidian values all of his life. The most distinctive achievements of his career were attained against that loyalty under the pressure of political contingencies.

In age Gros fits between Girodet and Ingres, and this had a decisive impact on his formation. Girodet had been among the last of the Old-Régime students to have at least the better part of the normal period of training in Rome. Ingres was able belatedly to enjoy his after the French Empire had consolidated control of Italy. Gros's time came just at the point when Rome was closed to the French in 1793. He did manage to travel to Italy, spending time in Florence and in Genoa while those cities remained friendly territory (in the latter, he spent time with a weary Girodet recuperating on his long journey back to France). There was plenty to see and absorb, but he was denied the crucial opportunity to hone his drawing in a supportive institutional environment amid the monuments of Rome. In order to remain safely in Italian territory for as long as he did he needed protection, and the Bonaparte brothers looked after him; for a time in the late 1790's, he held a noncombatant's post with the army that left him ample time to practise his art (from this Gros has latterly acquired an exaggerated reputation as a soldier-artist).

That myth of Gros's early life would, however, have followed naturally from the painting with which he established his reputation on returning to Paris in 1801. The new Consulate decided to undertake a program of large-scale painting glorifying the successes of the French army and to that end proposed a competition in 1801 for paintings to commemorate the victory of a small party of 500 French against massed Arab cavalry numbering 6000 at the Battle of Nazareth two years before. Gros's sketch, to the consternation of many critics, took the prize. What they could not grasp was the absence of a clear center to the composition and to the depicted action. General Junot himself is well to the rear, shown in individual combat with a Mameluke horseman rather than in overall command of the operation. The entire composition is made up of such vignettes, the unifying principle of the painting coming from strong notes of color repeated at intervals and rhythmic interlacing of the episodes achieved through surface handling of the paint.

The absence of a more solid underlying structure was not simply Gros's choice; it proceeded in part from the government's lacking any precise account of the battle. In place of a coherent verbal overview, it provided some anecdotes of individual acts of bravery, more often by common soldiers than by officers. This sort of record conformed to a mode of celebrating French victories that had persisted from the more democratic phase of the Revolution: the success of republican arms was attributed to the commitment of the citizen soldier fighting out of patriotic devotion rather than coercion or greed. Within this propagandistic mode, Junot's valor would be equal to that of the anonymous soldiers in the foreground, and so Gros faithfully rendered it. He augmented these with two scenes of his own invention designed to proclaim a basic humanity and idealism underlying the French adventures abroad: a vignette of Arabs about to decapitate a helpless European was contrasted to one of a French soldier protecting a surrendering captive from being shot.

39

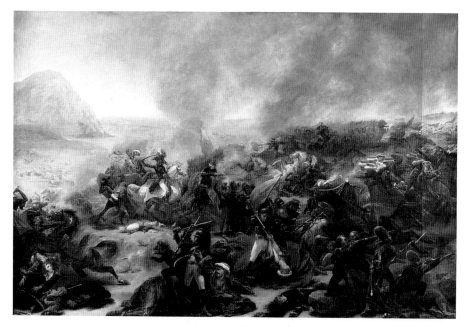

39 ANTOINE-JEAN GROS *The Battle of Nazareth* 1801. 53¼ × 76¾ (135 × 195)

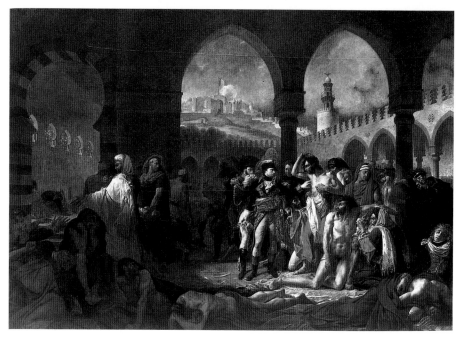

40 ANTOINE-JEAN GROS *Napoleon in the Plague House at Jaffa* 1804. 17′5½ × 23′7½ (532.1 × 720)

The inventive artistic solution he devised for knitting all of this together had the further effect of conveying, through rapid gestural notation and the liberation of color, an exciting sense of the fury and confusion of battle. It was important too that this novel category—heroic history painting of a contemporary event—not be confused with the meticulous description deployed by traditional painters of battles, an approach which had always placed their efforts among the lower genres. Had Gros more deeply internalized the routines of Classical drawing, he might well have lacked the necessary flexibility and improvisatory flair to deal with this complicated brief. As it was, his success put him in a commanding position to respond to escalating demands for contemporary reportage in history painting.

The commission for a full-scale version of the Nazareth subject never in fact materialized. As it looked back to the Directory's citizen army ideal, it was out of step with the Bonapartist cult, according to which French victories were guaranteed by the charismatic command of one individual. Three years later Gros made good this discrepancy with *Napoleon in the Plague House at Jaffa* (1804). The actual conquest of the Palestinian city was again the success of another general, so this time there was no question of the painting dealing with the battle itself. Instead Gros exploited an outbreak of plague which spread from the city's Arab defenders to the victorious French. Bonaparte is shown fearlessly touching the sore of one of his suffering soldiers while his aide anxiously holds a handkerchief to his face. The ostensible subject matter is eminently rational: fear was thought to advance the spread of the disease, and the general is here by personal example attempting to arrest the idea of inevitable contagion and death. But the effect in the painting is irrational: the sick among the French seem almost to rise by magic to make contact with their leader. Dominating the foreground, by contrast, are the shadowed figures of those dead and dying deprived of that touch. The ordinary soldier is now powerless. To the extent that heroic nudity had been a bearer of republican ideals, Gros reversed its normal meanings in transforming it into a sign of dependent helplessness, nowhere more emphatically than in the grotesquely outsized soldier on his knees in the foreground, who looks away from his attentive Arab physician toward his diminutive, tightly clothed commander.

As in the *Battle of Nazareth*, Gros has exploited animated surface and punctuation with vivid color to convey the exotic locale and the horrific sensory impact of the plague house. A good deal more control was required, however, in that this painting was required to return to a traditionally hierarchical arrangement with the hero at its center. The contemporaneity of the scene, its unfamiliar aspect and profusion of picturesque detail should not obscure the fact that Gros met this challenge by appropriating a touchstone of the modern Classical tradition—David's *Brutus*.

The crucial device by which his teacher's painting articulated the irresolvable conflict between public duty and private devotion had been the great divide in the composition, the formal interruption that split the civic from the domestic sphere. The two were pried apart in such a way that enormous tension remained between them: the engaged viewer would find no settled position for his or her sympathies; the meaning of the work consisted in his or her mental reenactment of the conflict. Gros deployed his architecture and divided his figures in order to reproduce almost exactly David's compositional scheme. The Arab doctors at the left, with their desperate charges, occupy the same position as the grouping of Brutus with the procession bearing the corpses (down to a repetition of the litter-bearer's sidelong glance). Bonaparte and his men, bathed in light, correspondingly reproduce the clustering of Brutus's wife and daughters with their ascending pattern of bare limbs. And the delirious French soldier at the far right introduces a darker note of isolation and blindness directly analogous to David's (and Gérard's) grieving nurse.

But the utter transformation in the meaning and use of this powerful scheme is the most revealing sign of the impact of absolutist priorities on history painting. There is no tension between the divided parts of Gros's composition; the viewer is not challenged by simultaneous appeals to two sides of his or her moral character. The split rather represents a reassuring division between European Enlightenment, in the person of the conqueror, and the darkness of the Oriental vanquished, who are inured to death and impassive in its presence. On the ruin of David's critical examination of republican virtue, Gros constructed an immutable division out of Christian eschatology, in which the radiant presence of Christ in Limbo is contrasted to an Arab Hell (the seated figure in the left-hand corner, the stand-in for Brutus, mimics representations of the cannibalistic Ugolino from Dante's *Inferno*). This conflation of conquest and redemption was all the more useful in view of the disturbing reports that the French, on Napoleon's order, had themselves visited a hellish massacre on the surviving, unarmed defenders of the city.

AN IMPERIAL ANTIQUITY

Ambitious painting under the empire has perhaps been misleadingly typified by such propagandistic and questionable glorifications of Napoleon. A comparative stability and freedom of movement on the Continent, which came in the wake of French conquests, allowed for more pacific develop-

41 ANTONIO CANOVA *Perseus* 1801. Height 86⅝ (220)

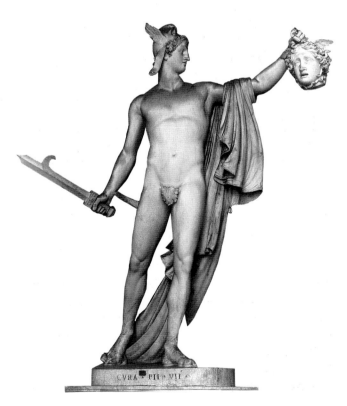

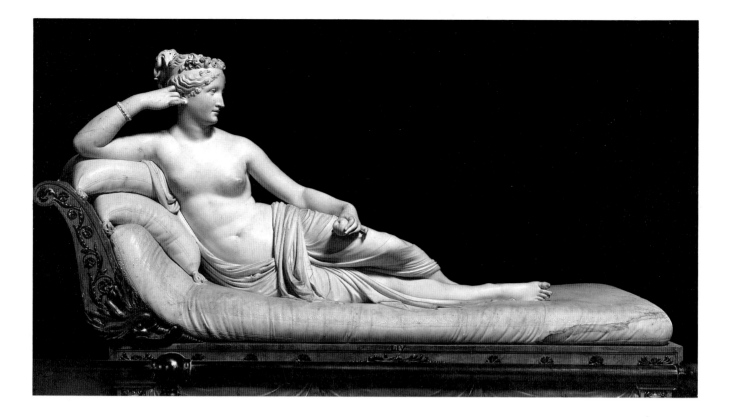

42 ANTONIO CANOVA *Pauline Borghese as Venus* 1808. Length 79 (200.7)

43 ANTONIO CANOVA *Magdalene* 1796. Height 37 (94)

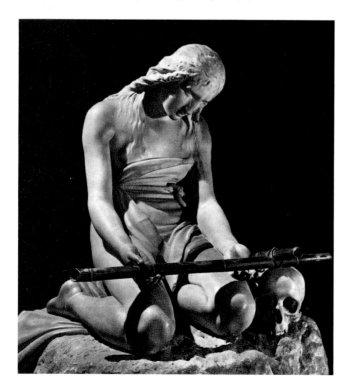

ments as well. Patrons from across Europe competed for the talents of the French Classicists, and the most favored manner was the precious, mythological Classicism that had been incubated under the Directory.

One patron in particular, Giovanni Battista Sommariva, led this current of taste and thematic interest. After 1806, he was resident in Paris and known under various titles, including Marquis de Sommariva, though he had begun his career as a barber's assistant in norther Italy. Subsequently trained as a lawyer, he arrived in Milan in 1796 just at the moment when the victorious General Bonaparte had arrived and begun his organization of a French puppet republic in the region. The upstart lawyer astutely and unscrupulously negotiated a path through the shifting tides of war, retreating to France when fortune dictated. By the turn of the century, he was Napoleon's surrogate in Milan and in that capacity amassed an enormous fortune, a showplace villa on Lake Como, and a commensurate number of bitter enemies.

Even before his definitive fall from power, Sommariva was deliberately attempting to gain prestige and rehabilitate his unsavory *parvenu's* reputation by enlightened patronage of art. His first instrument in this regard was the immensely influential sculptor Antonio Canova (1757–1822). This artist, of Venetian origins, had come to prominence in the same Roman milieu which supported Flaxman in the 1790's. As a native-born Catholic, he was in line for the sort of sculptural commissions to which his English contemporary could never

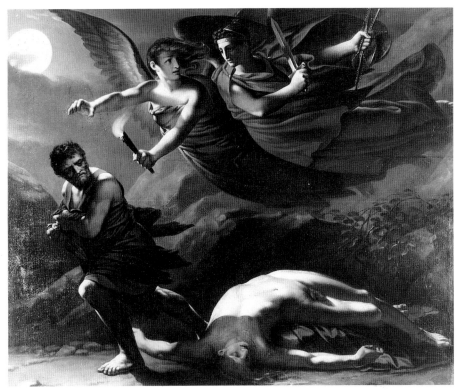

44 PIERRE-PAUL PRUD'HON *Crime Pursued by Vengeance and Justice* 1808. 96 × 9'7 (244 × 292)

aspire. These included the monumental papal tombs that consolidated his position as the preeminent official sculptor of the age. His prestige had originally been established, however, with smaller compositions on Classical themes which manifest an esthetic analogous to the purified linearism of Flaxman's
41 Homer. The *Perseus* (1801), a mid-career work, demonstrates his paradoxical ability to communicate a sculptural idea through the abstract element of line rather than through plastic volume and mass. Viewed directly from the front or the rear, the high information-content conveyed by the indented profile contrasts with the comparatively lower level of articulation in the polished surface of the stone. This internal contrast allowed Canova to combine a strong intellectual clarity with subtle and luxurious refinement in his tactile values.

The combination came to appeal enormously to the Bonaparte family. The Emperor's sister, Princess Pauline Borghese, had been married into Italian nobility as part of their legitimation as the new pan-European dynasty. It was the client herself who requested that she be represented as
42 Venus Victorious, and in his portrait (1808) Canova obligingly imagined her as simultaneously displaying the dignified pose of a patrician Roman matron and the careless nudity of a goddess for whom mortal opinion is nothing. In public, it would have been cause for scandal, but its intended audience was limited to those whose sophistication in such matters could be assumed. Only some guests of the Borghese family

were conducted to see the work, their visits customarily taking place at night in the dramatic illumination and deep shadow of torchlight. Canova himself favored this same theatrical device in displaying his work to prospective clients. The fashion for nocturnal viewing by artificial light represented yet another avenue by which sculpture was assimilated to modes of illusion more characteristic of two-dimensional representation, but in this case the effect was further from Flaxman's 24
linearism and closer to the chiaroscuro of Girodet's *Endymion*. 13

A group of Canovas formed the core of Sommariva's collection, and he gave similar dramatic emphasis to their display. These he housed first at his Italian villa, which he transformed into a shrine to classicizing art, then in an imposing Parisian townhouse, where they provided fresh stimulus to mythological fantasy art. His proudest possession
among these was a single figure of the penitent Magdalen 43
(1796), in which the sensuality of the revealed body is reclaimed for orthodox piety only by the artist's Classical economy of means. This particular sculpture—perhaps improbably to our eyes—was one of the most acclaimed works of art of the early nineteenth century. The novelist Stendhal was one of its most ardent admirers, and it brought its owner tremendous prestige. For its installation, Sommariva had a special shrine constructed where it was surrounded by violet furnishings and lit by a single alabaster lamp.

Canova's art made a direct impact on the work of the
French artist Pierre-Paul Prud'hon (1758–1823) in his *Crime* 44

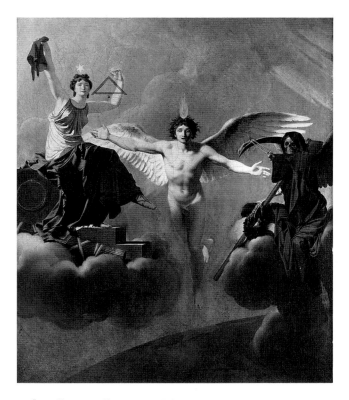

45 JEAN-BAPTISTE REGNAULT *Liberty or Death* 1795. 23⅝ × 19¼ (60 × 49)

rhetorical preoccupations. He developed a characteristic manner, highly individual for the times, which deemphasized dialectical clarity in favor of a calculatedly hazy merging of objects with their atmosphere (he painted first in monochrome, then introduced color in selected areas, overlaying the whole with a series of translucent glazes). As in the Rococo fantasies of Boucher in the previous century, this emphasis on surface lent itself to fantasies of freedom from the constraints of gravity.

Two such mythological subjects, both personifying the wind, were among the best-known of his paintings—*Psyche Carried by Zephyrs to Cupid's Domain* (also 1808) and the single *Zephyr* (1814), shown as a playful preadolescent momentarily suspended just above his reflection in a glassy pond. Both returned to themes made fashionable by the Davidians under the Directory, his unorthodox technique giving them a new currency, and both were commissioned by Sommariva. As with Canova, this collector was conspicuously signaling the affinity of his taste and of his person with the Bonaparte family, Prud'hon having painted portraits of the Emperor, the Empress, and Napoleon's son and heir, the ill-fated King of Rome, over the course of the Imperial period. His portrait of the Empress Josephine (1805), turns away from the pomp of her recent coronation (memorialized in the

46

47

44 *Pursued by Vengeance and Justice* (1808), an allegorical subject painted for the principal chamber of the Napoleonic criminal court. The fleeing figure is modeled after a sculpture by the Italian. The other elements come from a comparable repertoire: the airborne deities follow the pattern of one of Flaxman's outlines, and the nude male victim, divided by shadow and brilliant moonlight, is a flexed, upended tribute to
13 *Endymion.* All of this the artist melded together in a general twilight which underscores its message of menace, threat, and retribution. That effect was markedly different from the allegories of clarity and light which had characterized Republican official art. In that an exemplary effort in the
45 earlier mode, Regnault's *Liberty or Death,* had been conceived at the height of the Terror, it could be argued that Prud'hon's conception exhibits a greater realism about state power. At the same time, however, it drains any vision of idealism and impartiality from the conduct of justice and replaces those standards with an imaginary regime marked by violent sensuality.

The Empire years represented a great rehabilitation for Prud'hon, who was older than Girodet and Gérard, a contemporary of Hennequin whose career had likewise followed an unorthodox and uneven pattern. Supported by a provincial fellowship in Rome, he had remained defiantly outside the Davidian circle and resisted its esthetic and

46 PIERRE-PAUL PRUD'HON *Psyche Carried by Zephyrs to Cupid's Domain* 1808. 76¾ × 61⅞ (195 × 157)

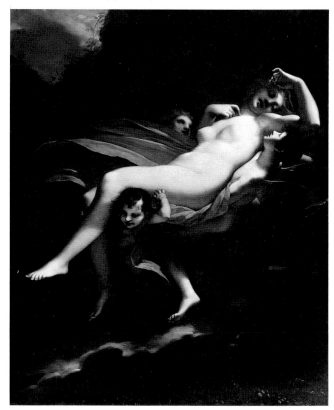

gargantuan canvas by David) to a contemplative pose among the woodland surroundings of her park at Malmaison. The strong illumination of the sitter, with its emphatic, Canova-like contour, exteriorizes the state of mental reflection in the contrastingly dark and undefined setting, which extends far beyond the confines of the frame. Prud'hon transformed Constance Charpentier's abstract personification of psychological depth into one aspect of the new iconography of rulership. In 1814, he predictably produced a commensurate likeness of Sommariva himself, exhibited in the same Salon as the *Zephyr*, which shows him suspending his attention to a well-thumbed book amid twilit parkland, flanked by two of his Canovas which seem to emerge from the shadows as totemic emanations of Nature herself.

Other collectors, domestic and foreign, pursued the same artists and supported the same sensibility. Prince Yusupoff, a high Russian nobleman, commissioned Guérin in 1811 to paint a replica of a picture, *Aurora and Cephalus*, that the artist had supplied to Sommariva the year before, and a matching pendant on the subject of Iris and Morpheus as well. The pair, both of which show a beautifully unconscious mortal male subject to a goddess's infatuation, amounts to an elaborate homage to the continuing authority of Girodet's *Endymion* under the culture of the Empire. The destination of the paintings demonstrate how completely Girodet's Revolutionary utopianism had been divorced from the image of human perfection with which it had been associated in the 1790's. Guérin's mechanical handling of the clouds and the celestial illumination shows the degree to which the singularity and daring of his model had been reduced to conformist formulae.

At this point, however, Girodet himself would have been the last to object to the embrace of his signature esthetic by such patrons. He had grown firmly and cantankerously conservative since the turn of the nineteenth century. From the time of his miscalculated Ossianic painting for Malmaison, he would go on avidly courting those in power. Sommariva had garnered wide public acclaim when he arranged for the inclusion of Canova's *Magdalene* in the Salon of 1808; for the same exhibition Girodet produced a painting which played on the sensibility so expertly orchestrated by the Italian collector. He drew his subject from the novel *Atala* by the neo-Catholic writer Châteaubriand, a phenomenally popular fantasy about Christian converts in America: the scene is the aftermath of the suicide by the violated heroine of the title, who has honored a Christian childhood pledge to preserve her virginity or die. His stilled and brooding treatment of this morbidly sensational subject, structured around the contrast between the ideal beauty of Atala and the exotic male physicality of her bereaved lover Chactas, made it the one unalloyed public success of Girodet's mature career.

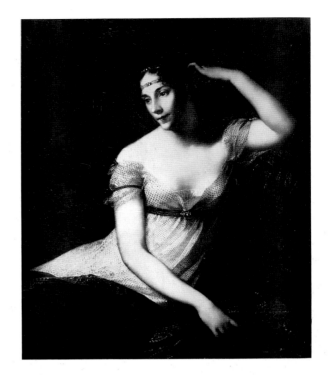

47 PIERRE-PAUL PRUD'HON *Portrait of Empress Josephine* 1805. 96 × 70½ (244 × 179)

48 PIERRE-NARCISSE GUÉRIN *Aurora and Cephalus* 1811. 8′4¼ × 73¼ (254.5 × 186)

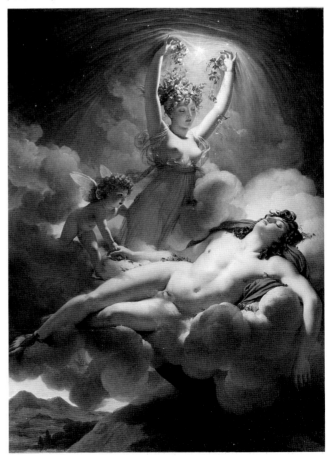

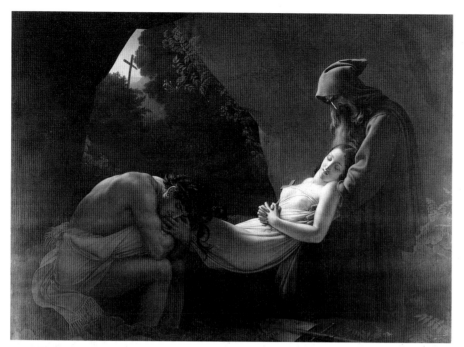

49 ANNE-LOUIS GIRODET *Atala at the Tomb* 1808. $77\frac{1}{2} \times 8'6\frac{3}{8}$ (197 × 260)

50 CHARLES LANDON after ANNE-LOUIS GIRODET *Pygmalion and Galatea* 1819. $5\frac{1}{8} \times 3\frac{3}{4}$ (13 × 9.5)

This may be precisely because it was far from his most original or inventive work.

Sommariva naturally courted him, but the result of their collaboration was probably the least happy of any of the collector's initiatives. In 1812 he commissioned Girodet to treat one of the central myths of artistic creation, the story of the sculptor Pygmalion who falls in love with his own creation and successfully entreats Aphrodite to bring the statue to life. True to his previous instincts, Girodet sought to introduce an effect of stunning originality which would go beyond all previous approaches to the subject: the marble statue would be captured at the precise instant when an electric spark of life coursed through previously inanimate matter.

The story itself recalls that of Endymion by means of a symmetrical reversal of its terms: there a divine being was smitten by love for a mortal and had both robbed him of consciousness and given him an unchanging, eternal beauty (like a work of art); in the Pygmalion myth a mortal is smitten by an image of undying beauty and brings about its divine transformation into mortal flesh and human awareness. As it happened, however, the fashioning of the painting entailed an altogether unwelcome reversal of the sureness and facility that had graced his youthful masterpiece. Working largely at night under lamplight, isolated from daytime visitors, he was said to have entirely effaced the painting three times over a period of six years. Where the *Endymion* still carries extraordinary power by virtue of the seamless, uninflected surface of paint in which the illusion is embedded, the surface of the *Pygmalion* is clotted and uneven, bearing witness to indecision and obsessive, dissatisfied reworking (its protracted gestation

surely lies behind Balzac's famous story of the *Unknown Masterpiece* of 1831, in which the fictional master Frenhofer futilely attempts to give the painted image of a woman the ultimate illusion of life, effacing a magnificent likeness through obsessively dissatisfied reworking). Girodet's concentration of the spectacular effects of metamorphosis came at

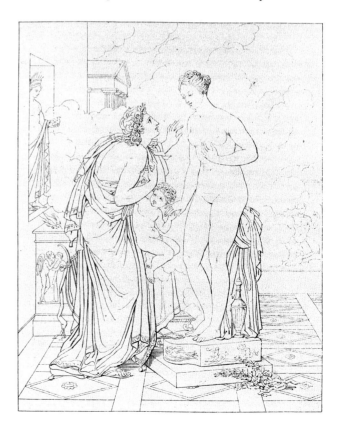

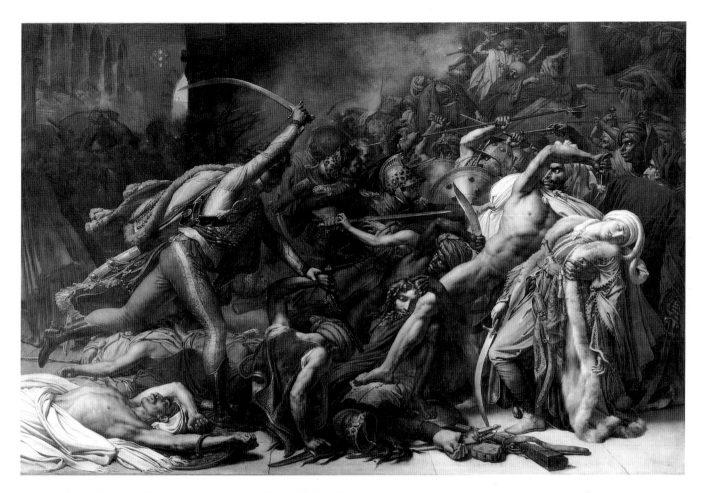

51 **ANNE-LOUIS GIRODET** *The Revolt at Cairo* 1810. 11′8⅛ × 16′4⅞ (356 × 500)

the expense of any equivalent attention to the action, which remains stiff and insipid by comparison to all of his previous work. His failure to find adequate form for his subject turned its theme of the ultimate creative act into a bitterly ironic commentary on the artist's declining powers.

THE ARTIST HERO IN THE FACE OF EMPIRE

The implicit negative judgment contained in the failure of Girodet's *Pygmalion* was not of course on its maker alone. It summed up the condition of Classicism, once shared social metaphors had been withdrawn from the visual repertoire of antiquity. The artist himself, in the years just prior to beginning Sommariva's commission, had completed what was perhaps the most confident and inventive painting of his
51 entire later career, the *Revolt at Cairo,* for the Salon of 1810. In it he found an appropriate object for the idiosyncratic skills which had betrayed him in the *Ossian.* The subject was an event of twelve years before, during the same Middle Eastern

campaigns that had supplied Gros with his early subject matter. Girodet isolates one concentrated scene of quasi-anonymous struggle, choosing the moment when a rebellious Arab onslaught is just being turned. In the foreground, a single French officer appears single-handedly to be forcing back an insurgent phalanx of claustrophobic density. That imbalance conforms to the ethnocentric patriotism of Gros's *Plague House at Jaffa,* but Girodet's characterization of Arab 40 resistance does not reproduce his colleague's ascription of resignation and passivity to the colonized. At the right side of the composition is a magnificently defined rebel whose stance precisely parallels that of the charging European. It is the Arab who exhibits heroic nudity, which allows exertion in extreme peril to be manifested sensually in every anatomical detail. What is more, this leader of resistance finds sufficient strength to support a fallen comrade.

Underneath the tumult of the action, one can make out the basic planar grid of Classical composition, and Girodet has answered the demands of a traditional painting of action—where the hero must be tested against a worthy opponent—as much as he has answered the demands of propaganda.

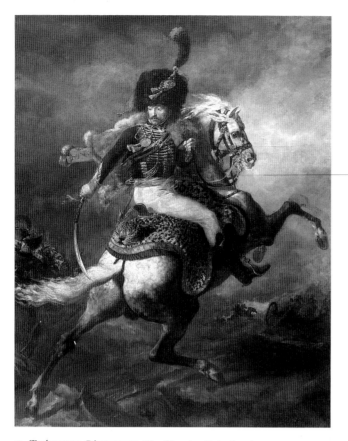

52 THÉODORE GÉRICAULT *The Charging Light Cavalryman (chasseur)*
1812. 11′5½ × 8′8¼ (349 × 266)

Without there being any known dissenting intentions on the part of the artist, that overriding allegiance to tradition upset the normal ethnic hierarchies of Napoleonic battle painting. The private, contemplative themes encouraged by new patrons like Sommariva represented by contrast a narrowed and comparatively impoverished version of the Classical tradition; for Girodet it meant having little to draw upon but a futile recollection of past youthful glory.

During the second decade of the nineteenth century, the most convincing revival of the larger ambitions of Davidian Classicism likewise came from the exploitation of marginal possibilities allowed within contemporary Imperial subject matter. Its author, Théodore Géricault (1791–1824), was an unconventional outsider in the increasingly professionalized ranks of younger artists. He has come down to us as the first great Romantic, and of his startling singularity as an artist and personality there can be no dispute. But singularity is itself a quality that must be put together from bits and pieces of already existing models. And the more one knows about the ambitious young artists who came immediately before him, the less idiosyncratic Géricault's impulses seem. One can begin to see him constructing his own autobiography, re-

enacting the myths of artistic individuality current in his own time. In an environment awash with mercenary temptations, he managed convincingly to revive the Revolutionary ideal of the independent, public-minded artist, impatient for glory and indifferent to merely monetary rewards.

Under the Empire, the biography of Drouais was increasingly taken to exemplify this ideal. His legend falsely condensed the objective circumstances of a precocious career into an enduring mythology of a miraculously singular talent sweeping all before it. And Géricault, who possessed similar financial and social advantages but none of Drouais's professional pedigree, formed his ambitions in the shape of that legend in 1812 and 1814. He believed in it to the point of rejecting any sustained application to learning his craft; during brief stints in the studios of Carle Vernet and Guérin, he attempted to substitute spontaneity and bravura for soundness in drawing and composition (to the point that he acquired the nickname of 'pastry cook' among his fellow students). Despite such uncertain preparation, he nonetheless chose to put his name before the public in 1812 with a heroic single figure, one that would manifest, in unexpected ways, ambitions for psychological and narrative complexity of a kind normally encountered in multifigured narrative *machines*.

At the age of 21 and using his own resources entirely, he prepared a canvas of monumental dimensions for the Salon of 1812. *The Charging Light Cavalryman (chasseur)* is both 52 portrait and battle painting: it differed from previous Imperial equestrian portraits in that its announced subject (a lieutenant Dieudonné) was unknown and effectively an anonymous individual; it differed from previous descriptions of French military heroics in its very Classical investment of heroism as a potential within an isolated figure. The development of his sketches passes a crucial point when the direction of the rearing horse is changed from leftward to rightward, while the gesture and attention of the rider, if not actually his seat, remain directed toward the left as before. This uses the body, movement, and even the expression of the horse to convey an internal complication within the action and thoughts of the rider.

This is realized in the final painting with enormous assurance, but it should be recognized that the eloquence and complexity of his body is only implied, translated into external surface equivalents spread outwardly in two dimensions. An energetic and unfinished application of paint instills the excitement of the theme across the physical surface of the canvas. Every directional form leads one's attention away from the torso of the figure, which lacks any effective volume, any capacity for action within itself. This necessitates perpetual distraction and displacement toward outthrust extremities, ornaments, and turbulent, luminous atmosphere.

It might be argued in reply that the elaborate modern

uniform itself prevents exposure of the body and that the nature of the subject matter prevents anything approaching the expressive nudity of Classicism. But the rider's tight sleeves and breeches only reveal how two-dimensional and pattern-like Géricault's understanding of the figure remains, neither modeling nor contour conveying strength in the grip of his legs or the sweep of his sword arm. The signs of strength that work effectively are isolated ones displaced to the ends of limbs: the boot in the stirrup and the clenched fist around the reins. It comes as no surprise to learn that the painting was worked out largely through color sketches without preparatory drawing. Worries over drawing would probably have prevented the painting ever being realized at all.

Works of startling genius can come about through compensation for deficiencies and the overcoming of self-imposed difficulties. In this instance, the imbedded weakness in the work is an inescapable mark of the social on the singular identity of the artist, that is, the mark of those existing identities to which he must somehow answer if he is to complete his own. Because Géricault was not yet ready to match the example of a Drouais on its own terms, the heroic body that was its emblem is registered in the *Light Cavalryman* as an absence, a non-body which generates the painting's spectacular compensatory invention by its very unrepresentability.

The year 1814 saw the first fall of Napoleon from power in France and a temporary return of the Bourbons before their definitive restoration after Waterloo in 1815. It was decided that a Salon would hastily be held to mark the return of monarchist culture, but it had to be exceptionally open in order to obtain an adequate number of works. Géricault took advantage of the opportunity to double his representation in the exhibition by including the *Light Cavalryman* along with whatever new work he could prepare in time. Again his bid for **53** renewed attention was a monumental single figure, *The Wounded Heavy Cavalryman*, which he plainly intended as a pendant to the earlier work. The object would be to deepen the effect of the new painting (and give the old an enhanced resonance and timeliness) by setting up a quasinarrative interplay of antithesis between them: light versus heavy, active versus passive, mounted versus earthbound, vigorous versus debilitated. Gravity rules in the second painting, in contrast to the first where the horse and its passenger had been connected to the earth by only one spindly, springing limb. The most obvious of these antitheses has always dominated commentary, that is, the one provided by Napoleon's intervening reversal of fortune in the snows of Russia. While Géricault doubtless made room for that reading, it was just one part of a grandly rhetorical construction of opposed qualities between the two paintings, and this had more to do with enlisting the modern single figure to do the sort of

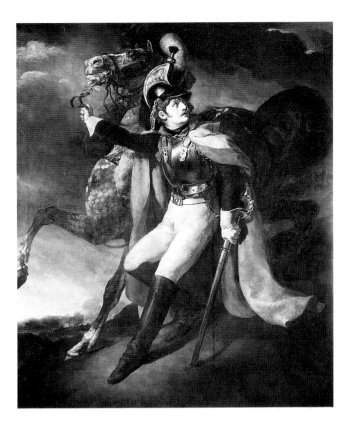

53 THÉODORE GÉRICAULT *The Wounded Heavy Cavalryman (cuirassier)* 1814. 11′9 × 9′7¾ (358 × 294)

meaningful work normally reserved for the complex internal narratives of Classical history painting.

For purposes of balance between the paintings, the addition of a mount was necessary. And the soldier's need simultaneously to keep his feet and to maintain his grip on the animal in turn justifies the dramatic contrapposto of his pose. Much has been made of the horse's strange, occluded foreshortening—the result of a restricted format—as the painting's most serious failing. But this seems less serious than Géricault's failure to articulate the key areas of muscular exertion necessary to complete the action. And these again are passages where the costume permits the closest approach to the nude. The thighs of the figure are massive without their underlying structure being sufficiently defined; they cannot convey the strength required to keep those heels planted in the ground and the body braced against the descent and the horse's panicky movements. Worse is the flaccid, perfunctory shape of the right arm, which offers no discernible sense of how sufficient force is being applied to the grip on the bridle.

These failings of execution are overwhelmed in the end by extraordinary passages elsewhere, the daring expansiveness of the painting's conception, and its complex dialectic with its predecessor. Géricault's early proclivity for undertaking major Salon canvases at the last possible moment made their

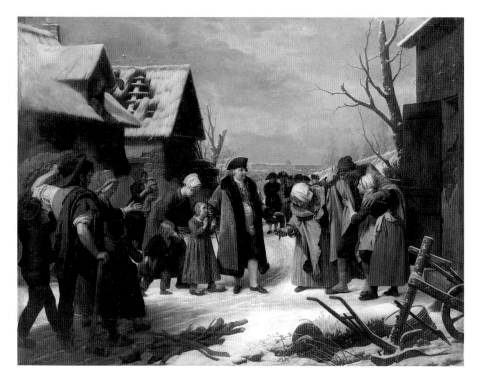

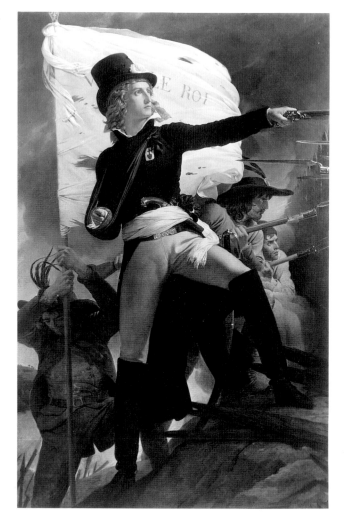

54 LOUIS HERSENT *Louis XVI Distributing Alms to the Poor* 1817. 70 × 90¼ (178 × 229)

55 PIERRE-NARCISSE GUÉRIN *Henri de Rochejaquelein* 1817. 85 × 56 (216 × 142)

impact all the more startling but their conspicuous short-cuts unavoidable. The pressure and the ambitious scale gave him his schooling, painful though it was. Having been refused the honor of a state purchase of either canvas, he could do nothing but return them to his studio and later, unable to bear the sight of them, have them rolled and put away.

RETURN FROM THE WRECKAGE

In 1816, in the wake of this experience, Géricault made a concerted attempt to win the Rome Prize and retroactively acquire the traditional formation he had denied himself as a young student. After a predictable failure to gain the final round in the competition, he again fell back on his own resources, making the rounds of Florence, Rome, and Naples, throwing himself into a new discipline of Classical drawing and command of the nude.

On his return to Paris the following year, he felt himself ready to compete on the supreme level of multi-figured narrative. But the range of available options had altered considerably since his departure. The restoration of the Bourbon monarchy was by now firmly established, enforced by the allied armies of Europe. A correspondingly conventional iconography of praise for royalty and the counter-Revolution was now in place. Among those who eagerly responded was Louis Hersent (1777–1860), a contemporary of Guérin's and likewise an ex-student of Regnault. This artist had early turned away from the Classicism of his training for

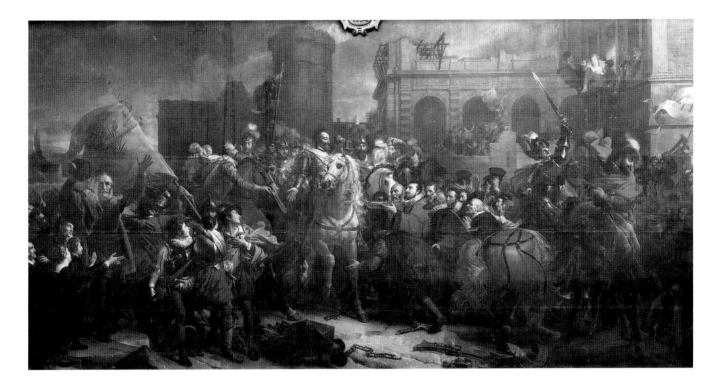

56 FRANÇOIS GÉRARD *Entry of Henri IV into Paris* 1817. 16'7⅞ × 31'4¼ (510 × 958)

more picturesque subject matter. To honor the new King, Louis XVIII, he turned to the sentimental mode of eighteenth-century genre painting to depict Louis XVI (older brother of the reigning monarch) distributing alms to the poor during the harsh winter of 1788. Conservative commentators waxed lyrically about the old King's habit of secretly performing such charitable acts in the neighborhood of Versailles and compared the figure in Hersent's maudlin composition to those of beneficent rulers of antiquity— Trajan, Titus, and Marcus Aurelius.

Géricault also saw the genre of the heroic single figure in battle preempted by the regime to celebrate the leaders of the ultra-Catholic and Royalist resistance to the Revolution in the Vendée region of the west of France. Some half-dozen artists were given these commissions in 1816. The enterprising Guérin was one of the first to complete his, a portrait of Henri de Rochejaquelein (1817), which he showed in the Salon of the following year. It is striking to see the ease with which Republican conventions of celebrating individual courage in the thick of battle were turned to opposite ends through the substitution of different iconographical props: the white flag of Royalism, the sacred heart pinned to the chest. This particular Vendéen 'general' was the most aristocratic of the group, which included individuals who had been little more than opportunistic bandits. He had died in 1794, murdered— according to his apologists—by duplicitous Republicans to whom he had offered clemency. Guérin lends to his pose and

features the practiced beauty and composure of the young Classical warrior, the better to underscore the themes of self-sacrifice and inborn nobility.

The ease with which such opportunistic transformations could be effected did as much as anything to drain the moral authority from the Davidian figural canon. Even for artists steeped in its tradition, other stylistic options were equally accessible. Gérard greeted the returning Bourbons with a vast historical canvas (1817) depicting the seventeenth-century monarch Henry IV being met by the civic leaders of Paris in an atmosphere of popular celebration. Henry IV was the founder of the Bourbon dynasty, and even during the Revolution he had been held up as the virtuous monarch, solicitous of the welfare of the people, from whose example subsequent rulers had disastrously departed. His accession to the throne, symbolized in his acceptance by Paris, put an end to a terrible period of protracted civil war. Gérard's choice was thus in some ways more canny than Hersent's, in that the historical precedent was more exact and powerful, while it allowed the new regime to exploit a current of criticism once directed against the monarchy. He also exploited the possibilities of historicism, as opened up by Ingres, but without any of the latter's tendency toward preciousness and esotericism. *The Entry of Henry IV* expertly recalls the teeming magnificence, the multiplied subsidiary characters, the rich costume, detail, and color of Peter Paul Rubens and other masters of pomp and circumstance from the founding age of Absolutism.

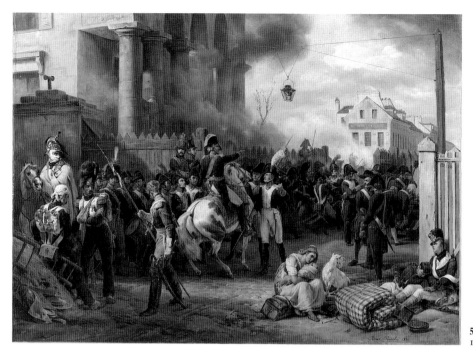

57 HORACE VERNET *City Gate at Clichy*
1822. 38⅜ × 51⅜ (97.5 × 130.5)

Gérard had renewed his longstanding rivalry with Girodet, each now vying to be named to the revived Old-Régime office of First Painter to the King. It was a contest in which the former easily prevailed, untroubled as he was by any concern to restore the authority of Classical form from within its core mythology. His *Henry IV* set a pattern for a stylistically eclectic approach to historical drama, emphasizing costume and spectacular effects, which a group of younger artists would carry through the 1820's. It was this group (much less than Géricault or Eugène Delacroix) that contemporaries would designate as 'Romantics', and it included avowedly liberal painters like Ary Scheffer and Horace Vernet (1789–1863) as well as uncomplaining Royalists. The young Vernet, a friend of Géricault, would apply this approach to a celebration of the Imperial army's resistance to the Allies at the gates of Paris and the military successes of the Revolutionary forces (*The City Gate at Clichy* and *The Battle of Jemappes*, both 1822).

57   Vernet's studio became a social center for young, disaffected ex-officers and artists, bored and antagonistic to the Restoration (he himself painted a group portrait of the studio, full of in-jokes and putting the practise of art no higher than fencing and riding). Géricault found a natural home there, but he lacked its insouciance about artistic matters. Having begun as something of a dilettante in the acquisition of technical skills, he sought now, perhaps alone in his generation, to reinvest formal values with the moral import they had carried under the Republic.

He now possessed a command of Classical drawing that was doubly remarkable in an artist who remained essentially self-taught. The question, given the depressing examples around

him, was what kind of subject matter would carry his exalted ambition. His drawings from Rome demonstrate that his interest in pictorial action and drama easily carried over into a personal fascination with violence and victimization. Back in Paris, he was first attracted to newspaper accounts of the murder of a liberal official in the provinces, a certain Fualdès, which carried bizarre details of secret conspiracy, transvestism, and ritual murder. He took his meditations no further than a series of drawings, having subsequently found a subject in which horrific suffering was redeemed by far clearer public significance: the shipwreck in 1816 off the West African coast of the frigate *Medusa*.

58–9
62

In its essentials, the story of the survivors of the disaster would not have seemed a vehicle for Géricault's new ambitions for Classical grandeur. The incompetently commanded flagship of a small fleet had run aground in the notorious shallows of the Arguin bank. The commander of the vessel was a returned émigré aristocrat who had spurned the advice of the experienced naval officers under him. As the privileged commandeered the inadequate lifeboats, a large raft was lashed together from the masts and spars. Some 150 seamen and soldiers were forced to crowd together on this precarious, openwork platform; there was no room for them to do anything but stand and the structure was so overloaded that the water came to their waists.

As soon as the officers in the boats (which also carried the cruelly impatient governor of Senegal) realized that towing the raft was slowing their own progress to a crawl, they cut the line, leaving its occupants to their fate. The castaways were then struck from without by a storm and from within by a

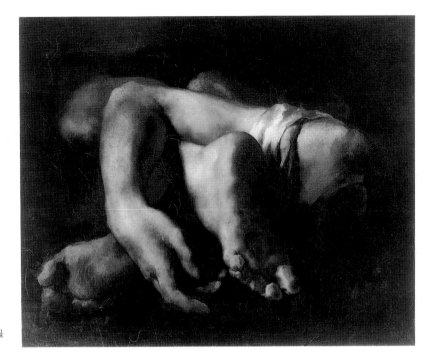

58 THÉODORE GÉRICAULT *Severed Limbs* 1818. 20½ × 25⅛ (52 × 64)

horrific episode of despairing delirium in which factions among the enlisted men violently attacked the officers with the intention of breaking up the raft and committing collective suicide. The latter killed and wounded large numbers of the mutineers. The fighting, along with accidental or voluntary surrender to the waves, reduced their number to less than thirty within six days of the abandonment.

The living soon began to eat the flesh of the corpses which remained on the raft. A group of the hardiest and most lucid, including the ship's surgeon Savigny, augmented this horror by organizing deliberate killings of those nearest death in order to stretch the pitiful provisions. Through these

expedients, fifteen survived for another week. At virtually the last possible moment, an accidental pass by a search vessel brought the raft in sight, and the blackened, emaciated survivors were taken to the primitive French capital in Senegal. Five more died there; only ten were ever to reach France.

The details of the story only became known because a confidential report written by Savigny to explain his conduct was leaked to the press by elements within government opposed to the Minister of the Marine, and particularly to his policy of excluding experienced Imperial officers from service. The wounded naval administration concentrated its

59 THÉODORE GÉRICAULT *Despair and Cannibalism on the Raft of the Medusa* 1818. 11 × 15 (28 × 38)

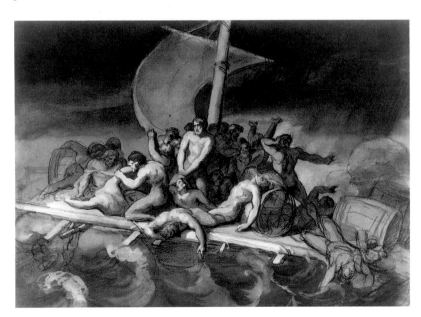

revenge on the bearer of the news, who then went public with a book on the disaster (written with Corréard, another survivor more recently returned from Africa) to vindicate himself. Their cause found ready support in the circle around Vernet, where the same grievances toward the Restoration were keenly felt. Géricault's seizing on the subject combined an attraction to the events in themselves and a commitment to Savigny's and Corréard's account of their actions.

Their version of events was far from unchallengeable, and both the governor of Senegal and the naval authorities had been quick to seize on the grim fact of cannibalism and Savigny's particular responsibility for the deliberate policy of murder which had allowed him and his confederates to survive (the lone woman on board, the canteen attendant, had suffered a broken thigh and was among those killed). Géricault famously immersed himself in every detail of the castaways' ordeal; he was said to have visited hospitals to see dying men at first hand and painted his eerily evocative studies 58 of severed heads and limbs as a counterpart to the charnel-house of dismembered bodies which the raft had become. He completed full compositional studies of the two episodes of greatest horror, the mayhem of the mutiny and the subse-59 quent cannibalism. But in the end the demands of his artistic ambition—to equal the clarified grandeur of Davidian historical painting on his own terms—exactly coincided with the moral vindication of the raft survivors. Compromising facts and events are sacrificed in the interests of a purified compact of common humanity, redeemed by suffering and achieving salvation through its own unaided powers. He chose 62 the moment of the first, agonizing sighting of the rescue ship, when no one knew if they had been seen in return and the group is galvanized into one last collective action in order to attract its attention; it is as if the dependent plague victims of 40 Gros's *Plague House at Jaffa* had suddenly found the inner resources to take over their own redemption.

It is crucial to recognize that the painting (1819) communicates its subject matter as an idea rather than anything resembling reportage. Were it remotely true to the facts, the bodies would be starved and disfigured by sun poisoning, sores and open wounds. Instead Géricault seized the opportunity to display all of the impressive command of the athletic male nude that he had achieved since departing for Rome—and he could do this on a scale that was larger than life, a notoriously difficult challenge to draftsmanship. He added figures, including three blacks, to answer the needs of his composition. The unconscious youth, cradled in the arms of a middle-aged protector, is a beautiful Athenian ephebe out of Girodet, Broc, or Guérin. The finished painting is a complex hybrid of the hyper-traditional (a centralized pyramidal arrangement of nude figures) and the unexpected (building it on a pitching sea with a cast of contemporary, semi-

anonymous victims). But perhaps its most startling paradox is the degree to which this grand narrative involving many figures continued at the same time in the same problematic of the isolated hero which had preoccupied the artist in his first public paintings.

His catastrophic indecision over the hanging of the painting in the Salon of 1819 was a direct manifestation of its double character: finding that the organizers had placed it low on the wall, he chose instead to have it elevated over the portal of the vast exhibition space in the Louvre. But even as he stayed to watch his painting being hoisted into position, he recognized that he had made a grievous error. The elevated position was the one he automatically felt to be appropriate for an imposing historical composition: the highest genre of painting was defined by expansiveness of effect and breadth of comprehension; its decorum normally demanded a certain distance of viewing so that its totality would be legible and local detail reduced to suitably subordinate importance. The bodies in the *Raft* are painted with all the imposing generality demanded by tradition, but Géricault and his friends were right to see the painting's force drain away as it was removed from an intimate proximity to the viewer. The direction of the artist's compositional decisions had been to push the figures forward into the viewer's presence, until bodies seem to spill out of pictorial space altogether. Without crucial details being immediately present, as they are today in its low hanging in the Louvre, contact with the drama was lost.

One such detail, which can stand for all, is the extended hand of the unconscious youth in the lower left. Like everything in the painting, it is twice as large as life; this has the effect of making it seem twice as close as one expects it to be, however near to the painting one stands. The paradox of the *Raft* is that its colossal size both creates and demands an intimacy of approach that is normally the province of an easel painting. The tender pathos of that open palm is so involving in its emotional invitation that, once it is accepted, any disinterested vantage point outside the composition disappears. The chain of mingled bodies, uniting the races of Europe and Africa, becomes the equivalent of one single body in a state of transformation; its internal quickening proceeds from the group of moribund figures at the left across and upward through rekindled alertness at the center onto the ecstatic vitality of the frantic signaling at the pinnacle of the group. The only figure which is obviously beyond reviving lies on an opposing diagonal to this unified movement, which distributes the physical and moral awakening of one body over the variations of nineteen individuals. This collective body has a brain—the four cooler heads clustered around the mast—but its salvation is overwhelmingly an affair of nerves, sinews, and blood. In this way Géricault, in his production as a public artist, remained a painter of the heroic single figure.

Through the *Raft's* inspired anomalies of theme and scale, he managed to recast historical drama in its terms, pushing painting to an extreme of gigantism in order to generate a paradoxical intimacy with one generalized, eloquent body.

PUNISHMENTS OF THE DAMNED

By the time the *Raft* went on display, the scandal had done its work: the captain had been disgraced, the governor and minister had been removed. A new law opened up military ranks to those who had served under the Empire: the King himself had recognized that exclusionary policies were harming the state. Géricault believed that his celebration of the catalyst for reform would be honored by state purchase. He failed in this aim, though the painting was in fact (contrary to legend) rated quite highly by the Academy and awarded a medal. Still, there was no possible private destination for such a work in France and his disappointment was profound.

Ill health, mental and physical, aggravated by horse-riding injuries would cause Géricault's early death in 1824 at the age of 33. Although he planned new historical compositions (now on openly liberal themes like the evils of the slave trade), his limited energies permitted work only on a more modest scale. But even here his innovations were immense, commensurate with those of his Salon painting. A sojourn in England, where he successfully showed the *Raft* in a paying exhibition, led to remarkable experiments in drawing and printmaking. Taking up the new medium of lithography, he produced prints for a wider market, documenting scenes of common life—labor, sports, disability and alcoholism, the indigent poor, a public hanging. And in his primary medium, he manifested similarly

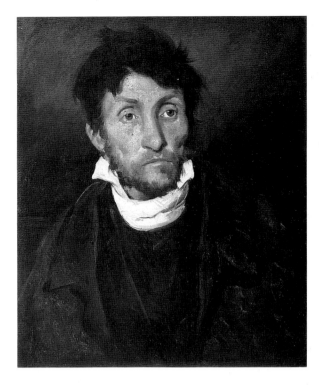

broad sympathies in five of the most remarkable exercises in portraiture ever painted.

These have come down to us as his "portraits of the insane," and there may have been as many as ten of them. They were discovered almost a half century after the artist's death, and any original data concerning their motivation and purpose has been lost; all one knows of their dating is that they came after the *Raft*. There is some evidence that suggests Géricault underwent psychiatric treatment himself within advanced medical circles where new, humane forms of

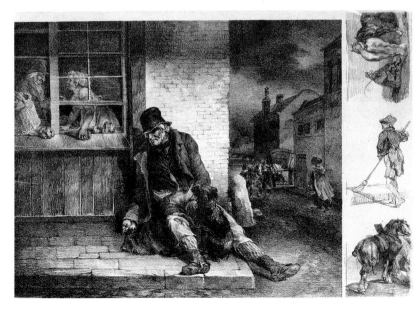

60 **THÉODORE GÉRICAULT** *Pity the Sorrows of the Poor Old Man* 1821. 12½ × 14⅞ (31.7 × 37.6)

61 **THÉODORE GÉRICAULT** *Portrait of an Insane Man* 1822–3. 24 × 19¾ (61.2 × 50.2)

treatment had been pioneered. French psychiatry in this period had developed the modern therapeutic approach in which mental illness is seen as continuous with normal life; one line of argument even presented the insane as a kind of modern aristocracy in whom the Revolution's democratic emancipation of individual thought and feeling had simply reached an insupportable extreme.

Géricault's surviving portraits display a sympathetic objectivity which is at least congruent with this new scientific attitude. According to late nineteenth-century testimony, each represents a particular psychological malady, 'a monomania' in contemporary parlance. Each sufferer is depicted according to the portrait conventions of the time, particularly the plain dignity in dress and technique which David had developed in his portraits (and self-portraits) of the Revolutionary period. Géricault conveys the underlying texture of muscle, fat, and bone in each face with startling economy and with a mobile technique which he is able to vary to surprising effect from subject to subject.

For the viewer, each is an occasion for the simultaneous discovery of an individuated person and of the uncertain traces of impersonal, objective conditions; each prompts reflection on the degree to which knowledge of other selves always entails the unstable convergence of the two. In their way they answer the same demands for elevation and complication in the single figure which Géricault had pursued in his public art. Reversing the *Raft's* passage through the colossal to arrive at the intimate, each portrait begins within a confined and homely approach to one isolated figure but deploys its plain-spoken manufacture and modestly suspended judgment to prompt in the viewer mental events commensurate in scale with those elicited by the most sweeping narrative.

The paintings pursue one latent implication of the *Raft's* construction of heroism, that is, the heroic subject may not necessarily be an effective actor in the world; heroism may well be manifested in resistance to forces which overwhelm isolated and vulnerable individuals. One's approach to such subjects is through a simultaneous diagnosis of the threatening conditions and identification with the extreme states of mind induced by confrontation with a hostile external world. The most innovative project in historical painting of the 1820's, that of the young Eugène Delacroix (1798–1863), would move toward the latter of these two poles.

Géricault and Delacroix had between them something of the same tense combination of filiation and rivalry that had existed within the circle of David. The latter had lost his father in infancy and his mother in adolescence. He shared Géricault's background in the upper bourgeoisie (his legal father Charles had been an important diplomat) and also took his early training in Guérin's studio. The two became

acquainted there in 1817, and Delacroix posed for one of the slumped boys in the left foreground of the *Raft*. When the older artist received a state commission for a Sacred Heart of Jesus, he surreptitiously passed it on to his grateful protégé. But the ambition of the younger very quickly surpassed such routine works. He pressed himself to complete a major painting for the Salon of 1822 in place of competing for the Grand Prix de Rome. The result was a strikingly original exercise on a literary theme, the *Bark of Dante and Virgil*, 66 depicting the passage of the two poets across the marshes surrounding the fifth circle of hell.

His first Salon entry demonstrated that he would absorb his Italian culture outside the normal institutional channels. Where Géricault had only postponed his pilgrimage to Italy, Delacroix would forgo the passage that once had been deemed essential in the development of any ambitious painter (he would later travel to the exotic territory of North Africa, following French colonial expansion, as a kind of substitute). The considerable intellectual and technical demands of the highest genre had, nevertheless, to be met in other ways. His recourse to the *Divine Comedy* marks one solution: cultivation of the most advanced literary taste, which in this period was elevating alternative poetic traditions over the legacy of French Classicism: Dante, Shakespeare, Goethe, Byron over Racine and Voltaire. Delacroix would illustrate all of these foreign writers during the 1820's.

Searching for the means to make a painting of such literary sources, however, he turned to a more local and immediate mode: Géricault's *Raft*. Indeed almost all of his major work of this decade can be read as a meditation on one or another aspect of that work, which concentrated and filtered for him virtually the entire previous tradition of historical painting. In spite of Dante's description of passing over a calm and misty slough, Delacroix chose to show the vessel threatened by a turbulent sea. He exploits the *Inferno* to recall the predictable equation of the *Medusa* survivors' suffering and sins with the punishments of hell (as Géricault himself had quoted Dante's cannibalistic Ugolino in the vignette of the older man cradling the nude adolescent). The damned souls clinging to the bark call directly to mind the bodies on the fringe of the raft, and one exhibits a mindless, devouring hunger. On that platform of bodies, Delacroix has constructed a compositional pyramid capped by the poet's beckoning gesture toward a distant horizon.

If the painting lacks the *Raft's* movement into depth, this can perhaps be explained by the differences in stages of technical competence between the two artists. In its summary application of paint, compression of space, and emphasis of surface pattern, Delacroix's *Dante and Virgil* exhibits some of the same traits as Géricault's *Charging Light Cavalryman*. 52 Where confident command of drawing is lacking, there is a

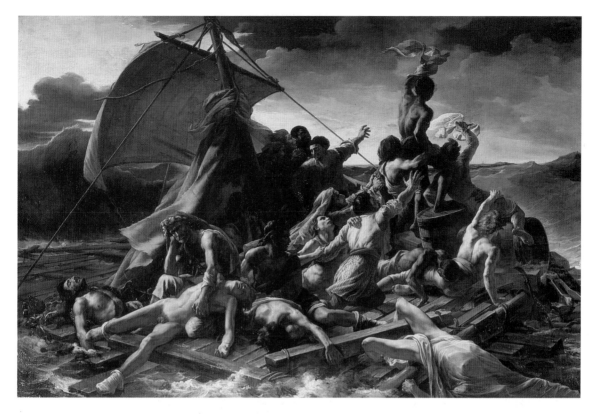

62 THÉODORE GÉRICAULT *The Raft of the Medusa* 1819. 16′1 × 23′6 (490.2 × 716.3)

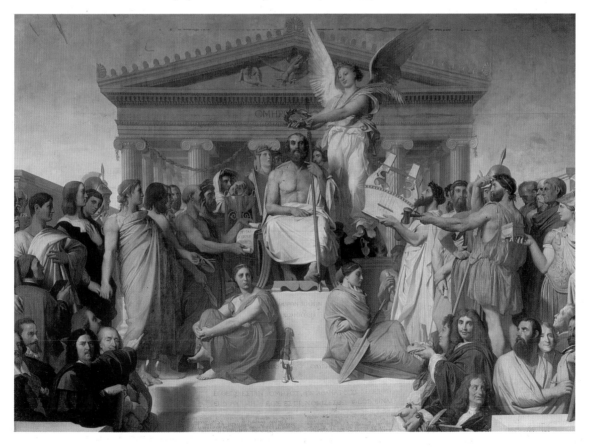

63 JEAN-AUGUSTE-DOMINIQUE INGRES *The Apotheosis of Homer* 1827. 12′8 × 16′11 (386 × 515.6)

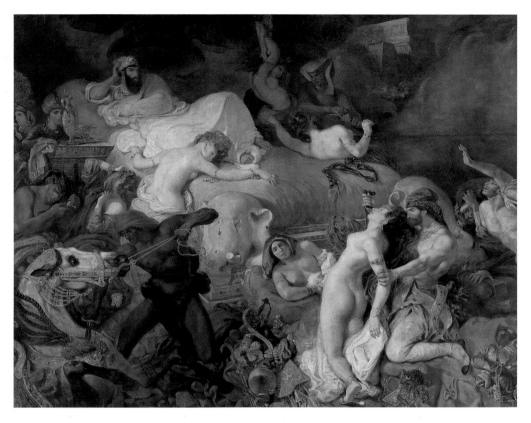

64 EUGÈNE DELACROIX *The Death of Sardanapalus* 1827. 12′11½ × 16′3 (395 × 495)

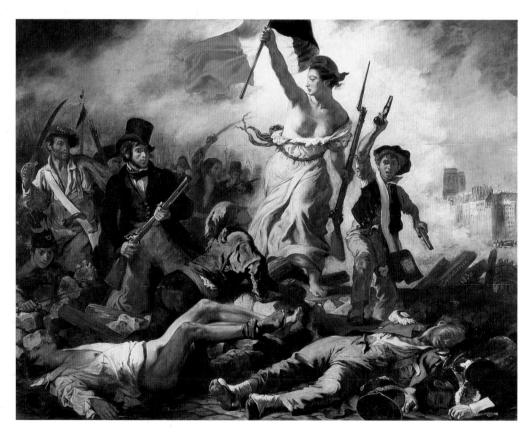

65 EUGÈNE DELACROIX *The 28th of July: Liberty Leading the People* 1830. 8′6¾ × 10′8 (260 × 325.1)

corresponding effort to compensate through emphasis on texture and the multiplication of arresting incidents and effects across the surface. Unlike his mentor, however, Delacroix would essentially remain at this stage and forge a consistent pictorial idiom out of it, one capable of organizing the most complex narrative structures.

In coming to understand this art, which has come down to us as the essence of Romanticism, it is important to see the ways in which Delacroix's practice represents the logical outcome of developments reaching back into the 1790's and beyond. Gérard and Guérin established the model of precocious Salon success when the Rome Academy was closed by war and the Revolutionary exhibitions removed the old restrictions on entry. Their ability to capitalize on that opportunity, dignified by the Davidian notion of the artist as self-creating exemplar of virtue, helped remove the old artisanal associations from an artistic career. This is turn made painting seem an attractive and feasible venture to a quasi-aristocratic amateur like the young Géricault. And as the normal routines of training and socialization played a minimal part in his development, the next step was to move permanently outside of the confining discipline embodied in the Rome-Prize procedure, with its controlled stages of progress, humiliating submission to repeated judgment, and years of subservient conformity.

As Géricault had quickly recognized, there was a considerable price to be paid for such abstinence, but it was one Delacroix was willing to assume. The artist would have few learned routines on which to rely, a diminished fund of concrete knowledge once so patiently, even subliminally absorbed over years of artistic exercise among the monuments of Italy. No ambitious painter could as yet forgo traditional demands for high erudition and elevation of thought, but these qualities would now depend upon the inevitably limited intellectual resources that any single individual could command. And there was a corresponding pressure for immediate results, and this meant rapid, cost-effective execution. The credentials of this new-model artist were not secured by any institution: they had to be tested and proven in every public outing. Each major painting was a speculative exercise in which it was imperative that public attention be seized with some effective combination of the familiar and the strikingly novel.

66 Delacroix's *Dante and Virgil* fulfilled nearly all of these requirements in a canvas of relatively modest dimensions. For the Salon of 1824, he moved to capitalize on its public success

67 with a painting on a truly monumental scale, the *Massacre at Scio*. The subject comes from the recent events of the Greek war of independence from the Ottoman Turks, which had begun in 1821 and would go on through most of the decade. It was the struggle that was famously to enlist the English poet

Byron, who perished at Missolonghi in that same year. The Greek cause provided a rallying point for disaffected liberals in France as well, who chafed against the repressive regime of Charles X but who lacked any effective avenues of resistance at home. As the government was constrained to follow the policy of the Holy Alliance in favor of the Turks, liberals were safely able to present themselves as defenders of core Western values against a brutal Oriental despotism.

Some two years before, the population of the island of Chios (the legendary birthplace of Homer and a seat of Hellenic learning) had been subjected to a brutal campaign of retaliatory terror, its towns razed, its inhabitants murdered or sent into slavery. As a subject it was of a piece with the *Raft* as well as with those unrealized projects of Géricault's later years, the victims of the slave trade and the prisoners of the Spanish Inquisition released by democratic insurgents in 1820. In the year of his mentor's death, Delacroix paid him homage—and laid claim to his legacy—with his own crowded scene of collective martyrdom arranged into a canted pyramid of dead and suffering bodies set against the sea's sharp horizon.

The *Massacre at Scio*, however, made plain the difficulties entailed in trying to build so directly on the *Raft of the Medusa* without bringing to the task the same degree of immersion in the subject and lengthy trial and error in achieving a final composition. The principal group rests awkwardly within the vertical format (over 12 feet high), in that Delacroix could not find a way to treat the large upper zone in more than a perfunctory, space-filling way. As the critics of the Salon noted with near unanimity, the painting lacks any focus of effective action, leaving one's attention divided by fragmented vignettes. Most of these, derived from generic iconographies of plague and disaster, do little to evoke the specific outrages of the Turks. One mounted warrior carries a naked woman into captivity and prepares to slay her male defender, but his haughty demeanor, splendid costume, and easy command of a spirited horse fascinate more than repel: this cavalryman seems an orientalized cousin of Géricault's flamboyant 52 *chasseur*.

In its defense, it could be said that the confusions of the painting are the same confusions of philhellene sentiment in France of the period. The stock images to which Delacroix resorted were current in journalistic and literary responses to the massacres. Polemics in favor of the Greeks, along with fashion inspired by eastern Mediterranean dress, frequently digressed into admiring tributes to the beauty of the Turkish physique and costume. Delacroix and his friends simply did not know enough about the people and cause they were celebrating. In the manner of frustrated and disaffected liberals in many later times and places, they substituted imaginary identification with a distant colonial resistance for

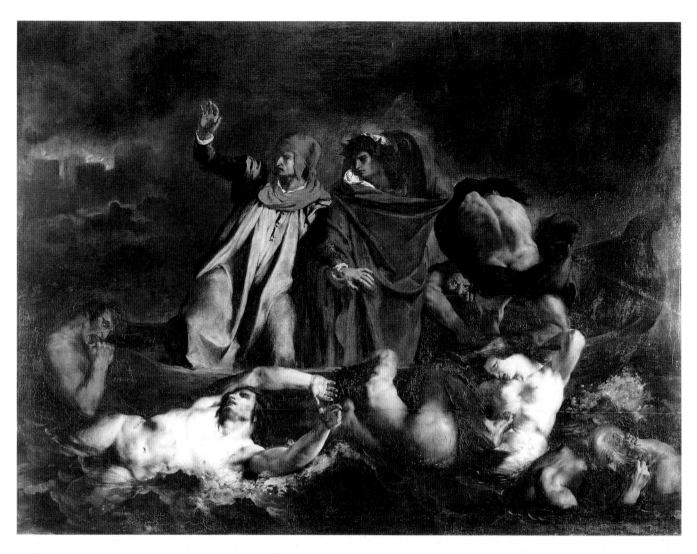

66 EUGÈNE DELACROIX *The Bark of Dante and Virgil* 1822. 74 × 94⅞ (188 × 241)

the struggle they were unable to pursue at home. The painting could not magically provide by itself the coherence lacking on the level of its uncertain political motivation.

SUICIDE OF THE DESPOT

The year of Delacroix's public setback over the *Massacre at Scio* was simultaneously one of belated vindication and Salon success for Ingres, returning from his long sojourn as an expatriate in Italy. He had labored for the previous four years over one large painting commissioned for the cathedral of his home city of Montauban. The subject combined a normal devotional motif, the Virgin and Christ child, with a piece of ultra-Royalist historicism, the vow of Louis XIII (which gives the painting its title). The monarch of the seventeenth century appears in the position normally occupied by an adoring saint. The vow in question was a dedication of the kingdom to the

Virgin in an appeal for divine assistance in defeating the forces of the French Protestants.

The entire picture is in fact an extreme extension of Ingres's well-rehearsed historicist approach, executed with his customarily precise professionalism. Since 1820 he had spent most of his time in Florence, and the central religious motif is an undisguised pastiche of various versions of the motif by its High-Renaissance master, Raphael. As a result, the painting is an unstable concatenation of parts and degrees of fictionality. The Virgin and Child are ostensibly either a vision or an unseen divine presence, but the effect is a rather idolatrous one of a known work of art, a material representation, being addressed and adored. The parted curtains signify an earthly unveiling or the boundary of a theatrical stage set. Reversing the old relation between royal patron and artist, divine right is shown seeking its confirmation in the blessing of a painter's genius.

68

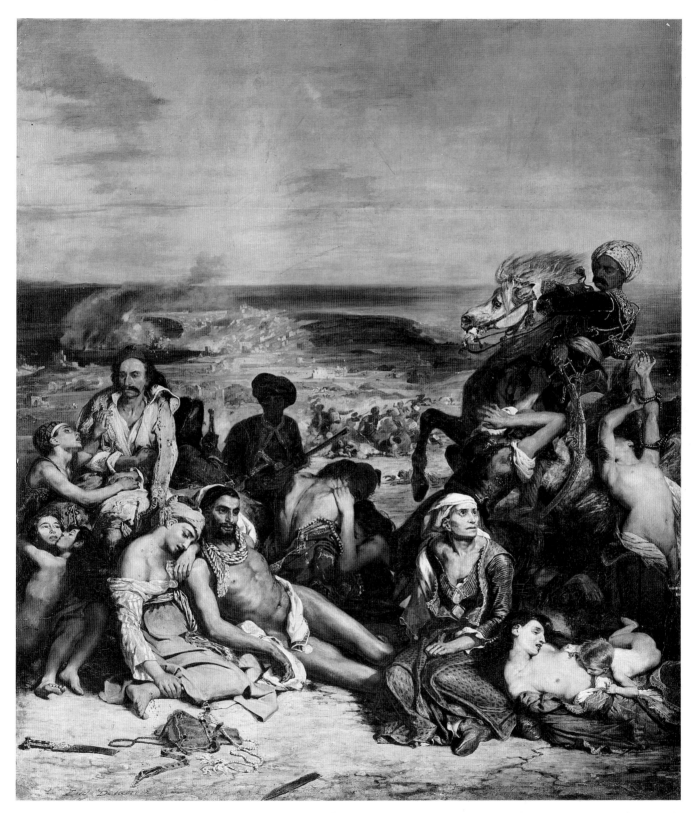

67 EUGÈNE DELACROIX *The Massacre at Scio* 1824. 13′8¼ × 11′7⅜ (417.2 × 354)

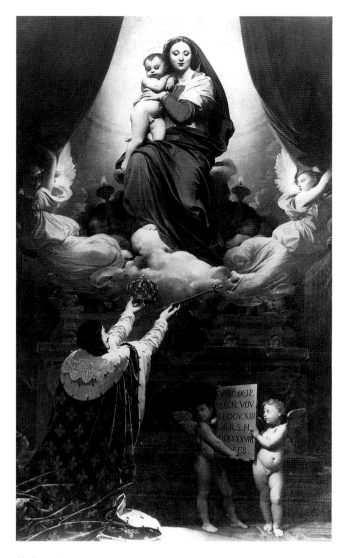

68 Jean-Auguste-Dominique Ingres *The Vow of Louis XIII* 1824. 13′9¾ × 8′8⅛ (421 × 264.5)

None of this stood in the way of the painting receiving the warmest official welcome. There is a painting by François-Joseph Heim showing Charles X distributing prizes at the Salon of 1824: Ingres's *Vow* is tellingly placed directly above the figure of the King. As Gérard had understood with his *Entry of Henry IV*, the outward forms of the restored Bourbon dynasty, propped up by foreign powers, would necessarily be a theatrical show of past moments of glory. The artists who tried most assiduously to meet the needs of the regime in the end produced the most profound exposure of its shallowness and artificiality. Where Ingres had missed the mark with Napoleon, who believed that he had created a new synthesis of ancient and modern forms of state power, his instincts were precisely right for the Restoration. He moved on to his monumental allegory for the new royal museum, the *Apotheosis of Homer*, which famously fossilizes a rigid cultural genealogy leading back through the French Classicism of Louis XIV, High Renaissance, and Periclean Athens to reach its pure source in the archaic origins of Greek culture.

Commentators of the time, continuing the habits of Revolutionary esthetics, tried to place a frame of moral and political significance around artists' stylistic choices. One such construction has persisted into many present-day accounts, pitting the backward-looking conservatism of Ingres's manner against the liberating quality of Delacroix's gestural colorism. But the latter could just as easily be turned to the support of the prevailing social order. One of the great official successes of the Salon of 1827 was Eugène Devéria's (1805–65) *Birth of Henry IV*, in which royal pageantry is rendered with conspicuously open brushwork, high-keyed color, and profuse invention in its details. This work pushed to a conclusion the infantilization of royal power which Ingres had begun in 1817 with *Henry IV Playing With His Children*, a small cabinet picture executed in the delicate manner of a Flemish miniature.

Devéria's success, which brought a rain of prizes and commissions his way, made him for a time the recognized leader of the 'Romantic' school. This confirmed many Republicans in their view that rapid, gestural technique and the stress on color over line represented a craven, unpatriotic acceptance of English styles, in particular that of Thomas Lawrence. Romanticism for them was the signature style of the hated Holy Alliance and a betrayal of the glorious achievements of French painters under the Republic and Empire, which had paralleled the conquests of French arms and elicited admiring imitation by artists across Europe. This was as strong a position as that which linked the new school with opposition to authority (as in the Greek struggle for independence), but it was fatally weakened by the absence of a commanding artistic personality to give it form. Ingres was a living refutation of any necessary connection between Republicanism and Classicism. Even David himself, in exile in Brussels since 1815, devoted himself to portraits and esoteric exercises in Greek mythology. Much of the frustration of this camp came out in the emotional responses to Girodet's death in 1824. An enormous procession gathered for the burial, and Gros stepped forward in tears at the graveside to make an unscheduled apology for having abandoned the true path of correct drawing in favor of the shallow gratifications of color and splashy execution.

From the early 1820's on, Gros attempted to be true to his word, but his born-again devotion to firm contours and antique subjects could not quiet the claims that the Davidian manner was a straitjacket for any modern artist and that any such effort was doomed from the start. The belittling responses to his painting and his own growing feelings of failure ended with his suicide in 1835. Despair over the general artistic impasse of the late Restoration took on powerful imaginative form in the huge painting on the theme of suicide with which Delacroix challenged Ingres and Devéria in 1827—the *Death of Sardanapalus*.

In terms of official and critical responses, the challenge was decidedly unsuccessful. In terms of the artist's ability to render a teeming scene of death and destruction into a coherent statement, it nevertheless represented a great advance over the *Massacre at Scio* of three years before. The link to Byron remains, now in literary rather than biographical terms. The story of the last Assyrian king, committing suicide rather than submit to conquest, was the subject of Byron's verse poem of 1821, which was translated shortly thereafter and performed on stage in Paris. In taking up the theme, Delacroix increased his difficulties by a wholesale magnification of the story's nihilistic implications. Byron's hero is accompanied in death only by a favorite concubine who voluntarily accepts his fate. The painter returns to the ancient legends which portrayed Sardanapalus as a licentious monster; he is shown indolently observing the execution of his orders that the destruction of his possessions and the women of his harem take place before his eyes as the massive pyre is set alight.

His assimilation of Géricault's model is this time secured through a diametric reversal of its meaning: at the peak of the canted pyramid is no longer a lowly black sailor reaching outward to save his companions; instead the occupant is an absolute ruler at the height of arrogance, looking inward to will the death of everyone in his vicinity. The painting's ambiguities of space, which externalize the riot and disorder in the mind of the architect of the scene, are brought into line

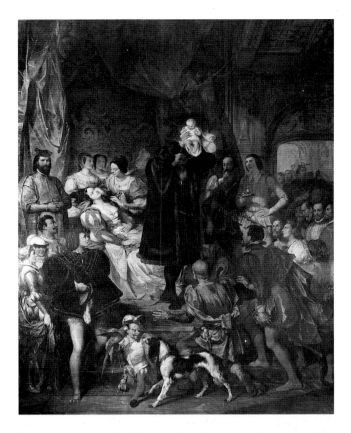

by that strong underlying design (cover up the one visible corner of the bed and the composition collapses into the undisciplined hotchpotch its detractors said it was). The same could be said of the dispersion of eye-catching incident across the entire surface and of the sustained intensity of hue, which artfully conflates blood with fire and enforces an overwhelming feeling of claustrophobic menace. The painting compels

69 EUGÈNE DEVÉRIA *The Birth of Henri IV* 1827. 15'10½ × 12'10⅛ (484 × 392)

70 JEAN-AUGUSTE-DOMINIQUE INGRES *Henri IV Playing With His Children* 1817. 39 × 49¼ (99.1 × 125)

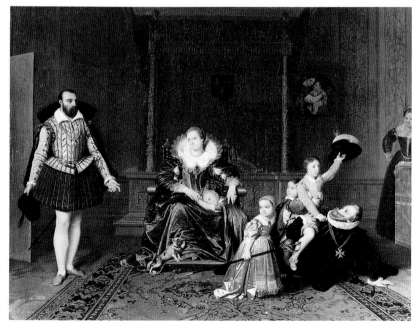

conviction through its abandonment of all compromise with the public values of the Davidian past or the Royalist present: the social compact implodes, and Delacroix comes into his own as a history painter.

In an essay published shortly afterwards, Delacroix wrote of a time in Michelangelo's early career when, so it was believed, neglect by patrons brought him close to giving up. Later in life, he would paint the sculptor in a state of idleness, surrounded by his past creations but with his chisel thrown to the studio floor, and he gave to his painted Michelangelo the traits and the pose he had earlier given to his Sardanapalus, making plain an understanding of the ruler's destructive despair as metaphor for the artist's condition.

His extravagant projection of futility in the *Sardanapalus* was played out most centrally through imaginary violence against women conceived entirely as objects of erotic possession. The regrettably automatic sexism of the time, which made such extreme fantasies acceptable, cannot be set aside. But as complete a statement as this painting was, it represented only a temporary swing in its maker's sense of possibility. Like David in his movement from *Horatii* to *Brutus*, Delacroix was capable of better, even within the masculinist assumptions he would never have questioned. In the same year (1827), he returned to the theme of the Greek struggle, but chose to condense his renewed expression of solidarity into one, monumental figure—an allegorical personification of Greece standing at the site of Missolonghi (where Byron had died), mutely appealing for the help of the West. In 1826 the city had again been the object of a Turkish assault, one so overwhelming that its defenders blew up the walls, destroying it and themselves rather than surrender. This prompted a new wave of Western agitation for the Greek cause, and Delacroix completed the large canvas in only three months.

The terrible collective suicide which ended the siege of Missolonghi made lurid fantasies about ancient despots seem paltry by comparison. With *Greece,* he conceded that representation of such total carnage in the real world was beyond both his ken and the capacities of his art, so he sought another solution within the neglected resources of Western tradition. The turn to explicit allegory allowed him to reintegrate the body of the oriental woman as heroic emblem. As in Girodet's *Revolt at Cairo*, an anecdotal ascription of nakedness to an exotic victim—while retaining a potentially erotic appeal to some viewers, both male and female—cannot help conveying the connotations of moral superiority indelibly linked to the ideal nude. The disordered clothing, a conventional sign of distress, discloses the breast of an inviolable goddess; the male victim by contrast appears only as a stain of blood and a severed limb.

For any French observer, such a figure would also have brought directly to mind "Marianne," the female symbol of the Republic adopted by the Jacobins in the immediate wake of Louis XVI's overthrow in 1792. This cast a partisan Republican light on the aspirations of the Greeks. The Ottoman forces appear only in a curiously flattened Egyptian soldier at some illegible distance to the rear. Haste may explain this lapse of convincing illusion, but it may well be a case of Delacroix experimenting with an overtly artificial, allegorical approach at the level of form, a way of building cognitive complexity into a painting that ran with rather than against the uncertainty of his draftsmanship. The two figures together, for all of their incongruity, forecast directly his response when upheaval at home in France ended the Restoration regime.

On July 28, 1830 discontent across the entire social spectrum with the reign of Charles X brought on violent insurrection in the streets of Paris. That moment of revolt, which so vividly recalled the great "days" of the 1789 Revolution, was quickly left behind when the deposed King's cousin, Louis-Philippe, was installed at the head of what came to be called the July Monarchy. Delacroix did not finish his painting in honor of the revolt until 1831. He was no radical and would personally have had no argument with moderate constitutional monarchy. But the demands of his artistic allegiances and skills caused him to produce a painting, *The 28th of July: Liberty Leading the People*, quite at odds with the comfortable status quo.

The first of these allegiances is of course the unrealized public potential of the *Raft of the Medusa. Liberty's* barricade, heaving up in the foreground, is the raft itself turned ninety degrees to the right so that the bodies tumble off its leading rather than its trailing edge. Géricault's sprawling barelegged corpse is shifted more or less intact from the lower right corner to the lower left, precisely marking the way he transposed his model. The straining pyramid of figures now pushes toward the viewer rather than toward a distant horizon.

The most pressing question would have been what to place at the peak of the rising. Géricault had selected a black man, bare to the waist, who could serve simultaneously as an emblem of the African locale and as a condensed personification of all oppression and every desire for emancipation from intolerable conditions. The anonymity of the figure, turned away from the viewer's regard, the magnificent description of the nude torso, along with its ethnic exoticism, made it a key device in universalizing the import of the subject. Delacroix turned to his immediately previous personification of the same urgent demands: a change in headgear to the Phrygian cap of the great Revolution (the mark of a freed slave in antiquity) and *Greece* becomes Marianne, emerged from the long darkness of royal tyranny to fight for France. In that she is a woman, she completes the

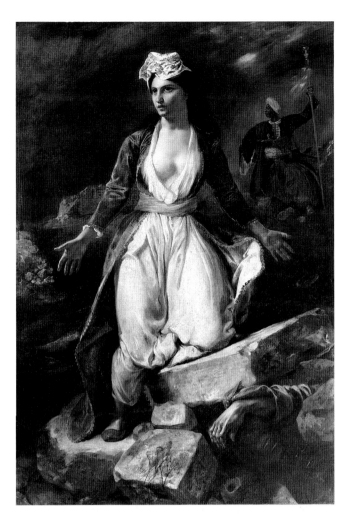

71 EUGÈNE DELACROIX *Greece on the Ruins of Missolonghi* 1827.
83⅞ × 56 (213 × 142)

whole of humanity; in that she can be nude, she represents a natural condition of humankind, suffocated by oppression but revealed again in revolt.

To some at the time, *Liberty* seemed to be merely a robust plebeian—sun-browned, barefoot, and careless of all modesty—who would naturally have leapt into the fray. She is indeed this character to a sufficient degree that she belongs with the surrounding sociological enumeration of male types engaged in the struggle, all ages and classes represented among the living and dead. She calls up certain colorful contemporary accounts of working-class women who rallied their compatriots on the barricades. If she were the least bit more idealized, more evidently a part of the order of symbol, the painting would revert to a curious juxtaposition of reportage with arbitrary allegorical accompaniment.

But the body of *Liberty* hovers between actual physicality and a different kind of pictorial order altogether. Her leading arm is a dark silhouette deprived of persuasive foreshortening, defined by its difference from the white expanse of the tricolor flag behind; it exists as an interruption of the continuity of that abstract sign. Her head turns unnaturally to present a similarly flattened outline to the viewer. In a way that is directly reminiscent of inner transformation from mortal body to goddess in Canova's allegorical portrait of Pauline Borghese, the figure stands simultaneously as a sculptural presence and as a mental abstraction. Delacroix makes Woman the link between matter and understanding, the medium of passage from fact to meaning and back again. The discreet departures from a naturalistic norm are sufficient to impose a governing conceptual order on the disparate collection of bodies and actions surrounding her, that order carrying with it the ethic of purposeful civic virtue embedded in the legacy of Revolutionary Classicism. The imprint of that legacy may have been reduced to a trace, but that it could work so effectively is a sign of its continuing power. That the conceptual artifice of Classicism could function only when treated with such extreme discretion was just as clear a sign that it was at the point of being lost as a resource for art.

In fact, a crisis in Classicism was evident in other national cultures as well during the first quarter of the nineteenth century. In Spain and England (states in which the grip of antiquity had never been as powerful as in France), Francisco Goya and William Blake among others set different unifying myths against the legacy of Greece and Rome. In the case of Goya the chief rhetoric employed was *Majism,* a subcultural style and tradition derived from the Spanish *pueblo*; in the case of Blake it was chiliasm, borrowed from English radical and millenarian sects. These two artists' contributions to what appears to have been a widespread Western movement of cultural nonconformism and political insurgency—Romanticism—must now be considered in detail.

· 3 ·

THE TENSIONS OF
ENLIGHTENMENT: GOYA

THE WORK OF FRANCISCO GOYA (1746–1828) expresses most vividly the revolution in art that occurred during the three decades following the political upheavals of 1789. Goya was indeed the archetypical artist of his age, whose alternatively triumphant and tormented life and art reveal both the dizzying freedoms and brutal coerciveness inaugurated by Enlightenment and revolution. Shaken and divided by the conflicting demands of patrons, by loyalty to the Spanish elite and *pueblo* alike, and by the shattering of previously secure divisions between public art and private desires, Goya, it could be argued, was paradigmatic in ushering in the epoch called Romanticism, which was, some argue, the first cultural expression of the modern age.

Just as an examination of Goya's complex genius may therefore shed light on the cultural crises that marked his age and influenced our own, so a consideration of the political turmoil of Goya's Spain can illuminate aspects of his art and the new global order that then emerged. A critical history of Goya in his times must therefore include consideration of the artist's life as well as the following developments: *nationalism,* which arose as the justification for, and the defense against, Imperial war; *guerilla* armies, formed in Spain to fight the invading armies of Napoleon in the name of the nation; and the *pueblo* (the people) who emerged as significant actors in the drama of historical change and *modernization*. All of these phenomena are the product of the struggles between Napoleonic France and its southern neighbor. No artist other than Goya was so intimately involved in these complex world-historical matters; no other man or woman suffered and expressed them so intensely or so conspicuously, yet survived and, in a sense, transcended them.

An introduction to the psychological and historical complexity of Goya's life and art is provided by a glance at two self-portraits from his 1799 collection of satirical etchings and aquatints called *Los Caprichos (The Capriccios)*, an album of 80 prints originally conceived in 1797: *Caprichos 1,* Frontispiece; and *Caprichos 43*, "El sueño de la razón produce monstruos" (The sleep of reason produces monsters"). The Frontispiece self-portrait reveals a cynical and disdainful artist, prosperous and wary, with doughy cheeks, puffy eyelids, and sharp eyes; he seems fully convinced of his own superiority and of the value of his many indictments of sin, stupidity, and corruption contained in the eighty ensuing plates. "The author's . . . intention," Goya wrote on the margin of a sheet containing a study for *Caprichos 43*, "is to banish harmful beliefs commonly held, and with this work of *caprichos* to perpetuate the solid testimony of truth." The Goya of *Capricho 1* is thus assertive, self-satisfied and confidently up-to-date. He is *ilustrado* (enlightened) Goya, *afrancesado* (Francophile) Goya, and elitist Goya; he is no fool and will just as surely suffer none.

The Goya of "El sueño," however, is very different. Recalling the distraught Brutus in David's painting of 1789 (see p. 26), the artist here is melancholic and frightened, unstable and lacking confidence; he has suffered the breakdown of his own reason and, perhaps, expects others to experience the same. The atmosphere of Goya's print is dark with foreboding: resting his head and arms on a pedestal or work table, the artist is accompanied by a cat (predatory symbol of the night) near his left shoulder, and surrounded by a swarm of mocking owls (symbols of folly) and bats (symbols of ignorance). The diagonal of Goya's body and crossed legs point toward an overlarge lynx—another creature of the night—whose crossed paws mimic the posture and hands of the artist. Unlike him, however, the lynx will remain on vigilant guard against the monsters of greed and stupidity.

Placed at the beginning of the second part of the *Caprichos*, "El sueño" thus functions as a suitable introduction to a

72—3

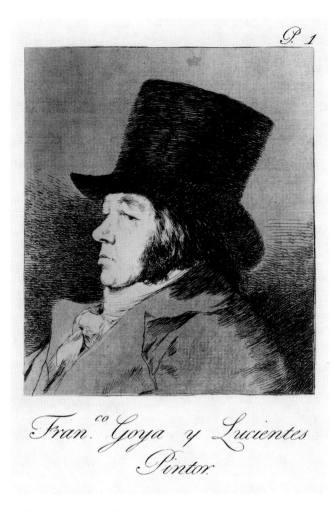

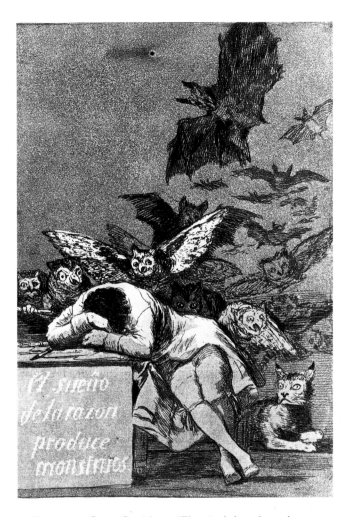

72 FRANCISCO GOYA *Caprichos 1* frontispiece, 1799. 8⅝ × 6 (21.9 × 15.2)

73 FRANCISCO GOYA *Caprichos 43* "El sueño de la razón produce monstruos" (The sleep of reason produces monsters") 1799. 8½ × 6 (21.6 × 15.2)

number of plates which mock lust, folly, and ignorance in the form of witches and demons, such as *Caprichos 68,* "Linda maestra!" ("A fine teacher!"). Yet it is by no means clear that the cloud of monsters that darkens Goya's self-portrait is that of popular ignorance, soon to be dispersed by the artist's satiric pen and sunlit powers of reason. Just as likely is it that Goya is reflecting upon the distressing antipodes of his own mind and upon the janus-face of Enlightenment itself. For in fact, the very creation of art in an age of Reason entailed a dangerous flirtation with madness. More than any previous period in history, the Enlightenment was a time when artists questioned the received ideas of absolutist politics and hierarchized religion, embracing in their stead new subject matter painted in innovative new styles. Desiring, however, to maintain the former emotional impact and historical stature of their work, artists were now required to exercise to the utmost their powers of independent invention and imagination—in effect to draw their art directly from their own psychic

wellsprings. Where the violent or erotic narratives from ancient history and religion—the penitent Magdalen, the beheading of John the Baptist, the Bath of Diana, David with the head of Goliath—once served the purpose of safely channeling libidinal desire toward a socially sanctioned outlet, these same stories were now valued only insofar as they exposed the emotional depths of their human protagonists. Without the measured psychic release that these once revered narratives provided, the violence and eroticism that are part and parcel of the creative process (and which exist as the mirror of Enlightenment itself) were now liable to pour forth in a flood. The price to be paid for this artistic *genio* (genius), therefore, could be high indeed; in times of war, civic strife, or emotional distress, it could include madness. In the "Sleep of Reason," Goya announces that he is prepared to pay this price. Imagination, he claims, is wed to Nightmare; Science, he fears, resurrects Ignorance; Reason itself engenders Monsters. Goya's artistic vision in the *Caprichos* and his

84

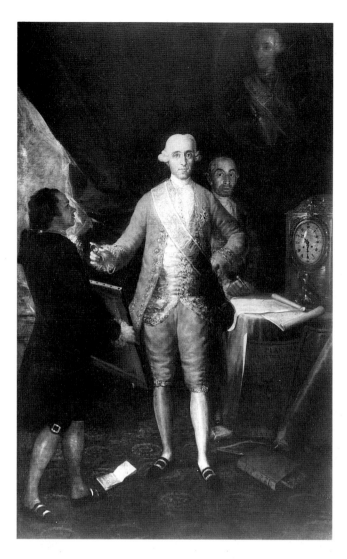

74 FRANCISCO GOYA *Conde de Floridablanca* 1783.
81½ × 42 (207 × 106.7)

75 FRANCISCO GOYA *Charles IV and His Family*
1801. 9'2¼ × 11'¼ (280 × 335.9)

subsequent art was dark, we shall discover, but prescient in its imagining of the modern century's union of Enlightenment and barbarism.

Goya was born near Saragossa in Aragón, Spain, some 75 miles from the French border; his father was a goldsmith and his mother a minor aristocrat. (These three facts of the artist's birth—proximity to enlightened France, and filial ties to both craftspersons and nobles—would fix the unique trajectory of his life and career.) After studying painting in Saragossa and Madrid, Goya traveled to Italy in 1770, remaining there for a little more than a year. His activities during this time are not fully known, though it is fairly certain that he spent at least several months in Rome, studying Classical statuary, as well as works by such Baroque masters as Domenichino and Reni. Back in Saragossa by mid-1771, Goya remained there (executing a few local religious commissions) until 1774, when he was summoned to Madrid by the Neoclassical painter Anton Raphaël Mengs to create designs for the Royal Tapestry Factory. For another two decades, Goya would continue to receive (what he increasingly saw as onerous) commissions for tapestry cartoons, while his career as a court portraitist and a religious painter blossomed. Among his important portraits from this time are *Conde de Floridablanca* 74 (1783) and *The Family of the Infanta Don Luis* (1784); both are bold and innovative. Each possesses a dramatic *chiaroscuro* and a surprising informality, recalling at once the lighting of Jacob Van Honthorst and the composition of William Hogarth. Another artistic influence must immediately be mentioned, however: it was clearly Velázquez who presided over Goya's art historical pantheon. Goya's inclusion of

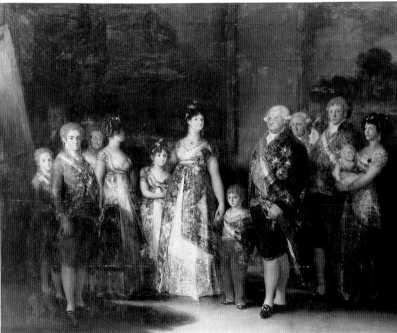

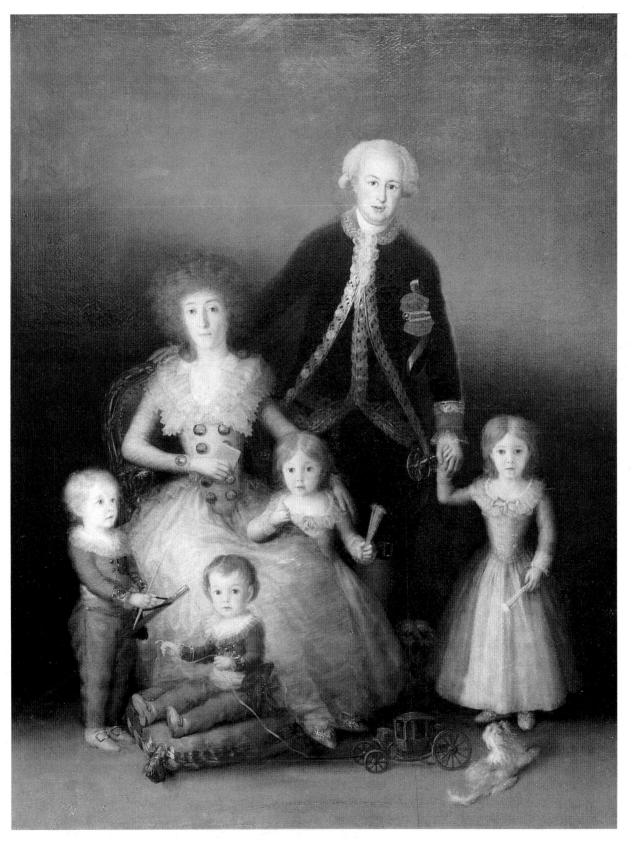

76 FRANCISCO GOYA *The Family of the Duque de Osuna* 1788. 88⅞ × 68½ (225.7 × 174)

himself in both of the above portraits—as well, of course, as in the later *Charles IV and His Family* (1801)—his embrace of spatial and compositional ambiguity, and most of all his psychological incisiveness, all remind us of Velázquez, the great master of the Spanish Baroque.

In recognition of Goya's talents as church and palace decorator and portraitist, he was appointed to the post of Pintor del Rey (Painter to the King) in 1786. Soon after, he painted *The Family of the Duque de Osuna* (1788), the very picture of the enlightened, noble Spanish family. Patron of the arts, sciences, and letters, president of the Madrid Economic Society, member of the Spanish Royal Academy and generous host of a *tertulia* (salon) attended by the most renowned artistic and intellectual *ilustrados* of Madrid, the Duque is seen posing informally beside the Duquesa and their children. Standing in an indeterminate space, he lists gently to one side, supported on his right by the back of his wife's carved-gilt armchair and balanced on his left by the hand of his eldest daughter. The obvious affective ties between the parents and children, and the fact that the two boys at the lower left are shown at play, reveal that the Duque and Duquesa were in fact advocates of the new French and Swiss pedagogical ideals which emphasized the special innocence of childhood and the important role of parents in the education of their children. The Osuna library is known to have contained the works of Rousseau, Voltaire, and the French Encyclopedists, and their friends included the satirist Ramón de la Cruz and the poet and dramatist Leandro Fernández Moratin, whose didactic works were thoroughly *afrancesado,* or French in inspiration. Indeed, the latter's mocking commentary on the proceedings of the 1610 witchcraft trial at Logroño (an important literary source for several works of Goya) was probably inspired by Voltaire's mockery of the Inquisition in *Candide* (1759).

By the end of the decade of the 1780's, the successful Goya was receiving more commissions than he could handle, including portraits for the new king, Charles IV, and his queen, María Luisa. He received as well additional tapestry and Church commissions, honors, titles, and wealth. After his appointment by Charles III to the post of Pintor del Rey, he proudly boasted to his friend Zapater, "Martin, boy, now I'm King's Painter with 15,000 *reales*!" Just three years later, in April 1789, he was promoted to the post of Pintor de Cámera (Court Painter) to Charles IV. In the following year he was elected to the Real Academia de Bellas Artes de San Carlos (Royal Academy of Fine Arts of San Carlos, one of the most progressive art academies in Europe) and made an honorary member of the prestigious and enlightened Real Sociedad Aragonesa (Royal Society of Aragon). Goya's rise to fame and fortune, spurred by his own vaulting ambition as well as by a talent that rivaled his much-admired Velázquez, seemed unending. His friendships with Floridablanca, the Osunas, and with the newly influential Gaspar Melchor de Jovellanos (author of a report on Spanish agriculture that became a veritable handbook for liberal reformers), among others, seemed to ensure that the artist's horizons would remain forever cloudless. Yet at this very moment, Goya's career was disrupted by the storms of the French Revolution.

In Spain the shock of 1789 and its aftermath essentially halted the pace of Enlightenment that had been accelerating since the beginning of the reign of Charles III (1759–88). The aim of the Reform King and his Prime Ministers, beginning with the Marquis of Esquilache (1759–66), was to modernize a country whose power and worldwide influence had fallen far behind that of its European rivals to the north. The population of Spain would need to be expanded, agriculture and the economy revived according to the new free-trade and agronomic principles of the French physiocrats, cities cleansed and rebuilt, and the power of the Church—especially its Holy Office of the Inquisition—curbed if not destroyed. Progress in each of these areas was often halting or slow; more than once the Holy Office aroused sufficient popular opposition to prevent important reforms. Yet despite these setbacks, and despite the extreme numerical inferiority of the *ilustrados* compared with the bloated population of the "useless classes" (nobility, clergy, and state bureaucracy), Enlightenment had made serious inroads in Spain by the time Charles III's reign ended: economic societies were formed, educational scholarships permitted ambitious students to study in France and England, and the proportion of the "unproductive classes" in the population was reduced by royal decrees and expropriations.

The extent of Spanish reform, however, like that of Bourbon France, was limited by royal dependence on the very classes whose power and wealth were to be curbed. The nobility and clergy were hardly likely to support modernizing themselves out of existence, and it is likely that Caroline reforms had reached their outer limits when the Revolution in France essentially put a stop to the whole enterprise. Reform, in any case, was one thing, revolution clearly another: even at its most farsighted, popular democracy had never been part of the Spanish Bourbon plan, nor the seizure of church properties, nor a Declaration of the Rights of Man and Citizen, nor the regicide. Each succeeding French revolutionary event or initiative caused the Spanish monarchy and nobility to recoil; by late 1792 it was clear that the Spanish Enlightenment would have to be postponed. The former flood-tide of French publications would now be dammed at the border, French residents of Spain would be silenced, Spanish students in France would become exiles, and the Jesuit order and Inquisition would once more be given their head, all in an effort to extinguish the spread of the revolutionary *incendio.*

Spanish foreign and domestic policy was now in turmoil as valued allies became enemies and enemies friends; the longstanding treaty with France was in shreds and a hasty (and temporary) marriage of convenience was made with England. In the midst of the scramble in 1792, the 25-year-old Emmanuel Godoy—the King's favorite and the Queen's lover—was named First Secretary of State to the royal office. The king had chosen Godoy precisely for his youth and loyalty to the crown, but the selection shocked the conservative clergy as well as the enlightened reformers who saw in the appointment a return to the corruption and perversity that had marked the years of Spanish decadence. At the same time, the *afrancesados* were reeling from many other blows. Those *ilustrados* or *luces* (lights) who had once received royal support or sanction for their reformist ideas, now shrank from public view or switched sides. By early 1793, Spain and France were at war, and the *afrancesados* were torn between national loyalty and allegiance to the international torch of Enlightenment; Goya suffered in kind, and from 1792 to 1793 barely survived a grave illness which, when it was over, shook his confidence and mental stability and left him permanently deaf. For the next three decades Spain would be pitched forward and back in a torrent of revolution and reaction, international and civil war, military coups and popular insurgencies, and mad quests for a mythic national essence that could somehow give meaning to it all. Goya, born of the *pueblo* but now inextricably linked to the *ilustrados,* would witness and represent this paroxysm of national schizophrenia and violence.

As the *ilustrados* retreated in the face of attacks from church and crown, popular resentment toward new enlightened Spain began to gather strength as well. The *luces* had always been only a small fraction of a population that remained overwhelmingly poor and peasant; their proposals for "land reform" on the whole meant enclosure and capitalization of formerly common lands, and their ideas of democracy did not generally entail universal suffrage or radical redistribution of wealth. To the Spanish *pueblo*, therefore, the Enlightenment was largely an unwanted *afrancesado* affair that threatened to undermine the traditional and (marginally) sustaining life and culture that had been developed over the centuries. Thus an odd alliance was made between the *pueblo* and the forces of traditional conservatism—the crown, the clergy, and the entrenched civil servants—against the *ilustrados* who had sought to reform the organization of the state, its economy, and its educational system in the name of the very same *pueblo*. In Spain nationalism was at war with modernization.

The conservative union described above was inherently unstable (and the crises and violence it spawned would extend into the late twentieth century), but its effects were seen at all class levels and in all forms of cultural production. Thus, for

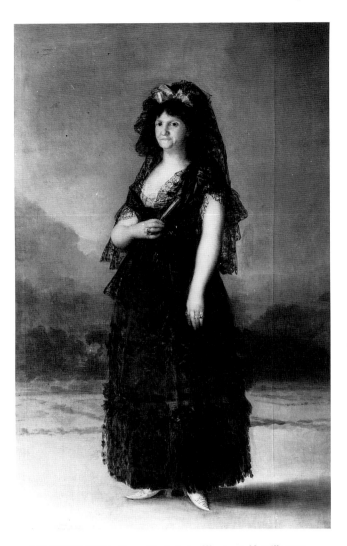

77 FRANCISCO GOYA *Queen María Luisa Wearing a Mantilla* 1799. 82¾ × 51⅛ (210 × 130)

example, in the decade before and the two decades after the outbreak of war with France, there occurred a great revival of Spanish popular culture, with its theater of *duende* (ghosts or spirits), monsters and grotesques, and its legends of rebellious bandits, smugglers, bullfighters, and other *picaro* (rogue) types. Equally popular was the cult of the *majas* and *majos.* These proletarian aristocrats, or plebeian nobles, with their distinctive manners and dress, were quickly imitated by all strata of Spanish society, including the "true" aristocrats, who admired them for their presumed embodiment of the pure Castilian blood and spirit. Goya often depicted the hereditary nobility in the guise of *majas* and *majos*, including the artist's lover, the Duquesa de Alba, and the unknown model for the *Naked* and *Clothed Majas* (ca. 1798–1805), and even the Queen herself in *Queen María Luisa Wearing a Mantilla* (1799). The French Ambassador to Spain, J. F. de Bourgoing, offered a vivid description of the *majas* and *majos* in his 1788 account of his travels on the peninsula:

78–9
77

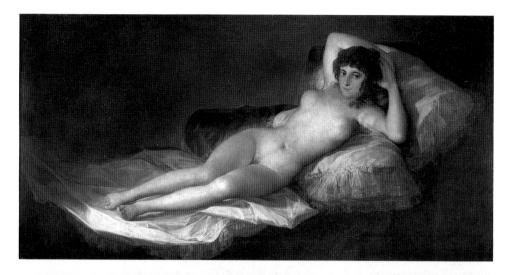

78 FRANCISCO GOYA *Naked Maja*
ca. 1798–1805. 37⅛ × 74¼ (94.9 × 189.9)

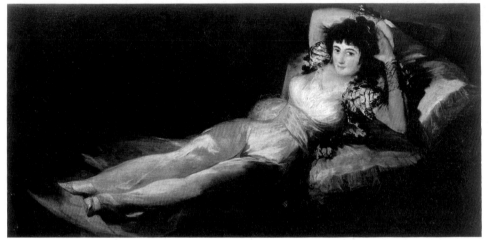

79 FRANCISCO GOYA *Clothed Maja*
ca. 1798–1805. 37⅛ × 74¼ (94.9 × 189.9)

The Majos are beaux of the lower class, or rather bullies whose grave and frigid pomposity is announced by their whole exterior. . . . Their countenance, half concealed under a brown stiff bonnet, called *Montera*, bears the character of threatening severity, or of wrath, which seems to brave persons the most proper to awe them into respect, and which is not softened even in the presence of their mistress. . . . The Majas, on their parts . . . seem to make a study of effrontery. The licentiousness of their manners appears in their attitudes, actions and expressions; and when lewdness in their persons is clothed with every wanton form, all the epithets which admiration can inspire are lavished upon them. This is the disagreeable side of the picture. But if the spectator goes with a disposition, not very scrupulous, to the representations in which the Majas figure, when he becomes familiarized to manners very little conformable to the virtues of the sex, and the means of inspiring ours with favorable sentiments, he sees in each of them the most seducing priestess that ever presided at the altars of Venus. Their impudent affectation is no more than

a poignant allurement, which introduces into the senses a delirium that the wisest can scarcely guard against, and which, if it inspires not love, at least promises much pleasure.

Bourgoing's focus upon the bewitching eroticism of *Majism* was a rehearsal for the racist and sexist ideology of Orientalism that would soon erupt across Romantic Europe. Just as significantly, it clearly reveals the degree to which the aristocracy of both France and Spain underestimated the democratic and insurgent potential of their nations' working-class subcultures. As the art historian Francis Klingender has observed:

Majism, the frivolous imitation of the real majas and majos by the smart set, is a symptom of the *encanaillement* [keeping of bad company] of the court aristocracy who would have been wiser to conceal their degradation. When on the edge of the abyss the aristocracy has a curious habit of destroying its moral defenses by toying with the ideology of the enemy. Blind to the implications of the bourgeois

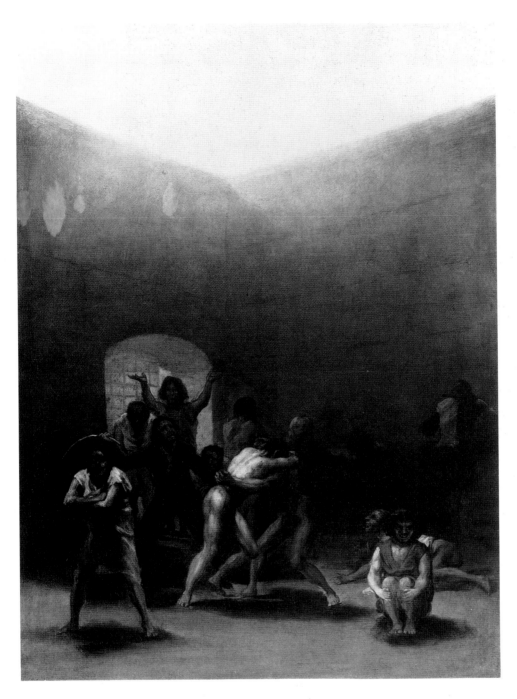

80 **FRANCISCO GOYA** *Courtyard with Lunatics* 1793–4. $17\frac{1}{4} \times 12\frac{7}{8}$ (43.8 × 32.7)

cult of nature, the French nobility applauded the milk-maid fashion of Marie Antoinette, and the Spanish grandees were similarly heedless of the democratic roots of majism, when they perverted its moral freedom.

Soon, the *majas* and *majos* of Spain, the *sans-culottes* of France and the "free-born Englishmen" of Britain would wage *guerilla* wars (literally "little wars"), erect barricades or lead the clamor for a new democratic charter. *Majism* was thus

among the first of the subcultural styles that would play a powerful role in the drama of nineteenth-century culture and revolution and in the imaginations of the epoch's most talented artists. Like such later phenomena as *flaneurie* (see p. 239), *Majism* was a fashion of dress and a style of life, and however ultimately contradictory its political filiations, it helped organize people into collectives able to act (for a time) with a single purpose. For artists such as Goya, without fixed class identity, and increasingly without the economic or ideological security supplied by reliable religious and political patronage, subcultural style was a powerful attraction. Goya's frequent representation of *Majism*, in his portraits as well as in his tapestry cartoons (*The Picnic*, ca. 1778), thus represents more than a simple keeping abreast of fashion; it indicates a political and psychological identification with groups and individuals who exist on the margins of the ruling society.

78–9   Goya's *Naked* and *Clothed Majas* express more than the predominating aristocratic and exploitative vision of working-class sexuality as a species of exoticism. Indeed, painted for Godoy, the two *Majas* positively trumpet the *encanaillement* that was the eventual undoing of the upstart Prime Minister and putative nobleman. By its peculiar anatomical geography, the *Naked Maja* especially, ironically celebrates that "perversion [of] its moral freedom," as Klingender termed it, which marked the aristocratic reception of *Majism*. The model for the painting is unknown, but her face possesses a uniqueness as pronounced as her body's ordinariness. In fact, the key to the picture's irony lies in this lack of fit between head and body, an absence marked by the vague treatment of neck, shoulders, and hair. With her pubic region located directly in the center of the painting, she is an expression of that perfect and vulgar metonymy that substitutes an organ for a complete human being. Like the women in paintings by François Boucher and J.-H. Fragonard, she is given over completely and shamelessly to spectatorial consumption. Yet unlike them, as André Malraux has written, "she calls attention to the least physiological aspects of her sex, her personality." In Goya's *Naked Maja*, the masculinist objectification of female sexuality, and its psychological antidote, has "progressed" as far as it ever would in the nineteenth century. Later in France Gustave Courbet, Edouard Manet, and Paul Cézanne would all look back in fright and admiration at Goya's achievement, finding there just that unique combination of physical and psychological, or real and allegorical, that expressed the temper of modern life and sexual exchange.

To claim to see irony, or at least allegory, in what appears to be an exercise in pornography may seem to be overreading, but it must be remembered that at the very moment these paintings were conceived, Goya was lampooning Godoy and the epicurean excesses of the nobility in his drawings in the *Sanlúcar Album A* and *Madrid Album B* (1796–7), as well as in the *Caprichos*. Ultimately, the question of Goya's intentions here, like the question of specific parodic intent in the famous
75   portrait of *Charles IV and His Family*, is probably unknowable, both because of the lack of relevant documents on the subject and because of the inherent difficulty of ever fully discerning artistic intention itself. Some things, however, can be asserted with confidence: as the decade closed, and the new century dawned, Francisco Goya represented with increasing frequency the *pueblo* as well as the grotesque and marginal figures of Spanish popular culture—the *duende*, the witch, the monster, the donkey, and the *majas* and *majos*. As at once a man of the *pueblo* whose tastes ran to bullfighting and street festivals, and a man of the *ilustrados* eager, for example, to master and practice his French, Goya was clearly divided in his attitude toward refulgent nationalism (*costumbrismo*) and rationalism. Indeed, his shifting allegiance to both "popular" and enlightened Spain is compellingly revealed in an extraordinary sequence of works that begins with the   80
Courtyard with Lunatics (1793–4), includes *The Witches'*   83
Sabbath (1797–8) and the *Caprichos,* and culminates in the
Executions of the Third of May, 1808 (1814) and the *Disas-*   82
ters of War.   89–93

THE IMAGE OF THE *PUEBLO*: THE LATER ART OF FRANCISCO GOYA

Consideration of *Courtyard with Lunatics* must begin with an account of Goya's nearly contemporaneous physical and mental breakdown. A few weeks after France's declaration of war on Spain in March 1793, Goya's illness was discussed in a letter between his friends Martínez and Zapater: "the noise in his head and the deafness have not improved, but his vision is much better and he is no longer suffering from the disorders that made him lose his balance." The exact nature of Goya's illness is unknown, but the conclusion that it was at least worsened by the virulent political environment seems unavoidable. Now in self-imposed exile in Cadiz, Goya gradually recovered sufficient strength to return to his work and to Madrid, and by January 1794 had nearly completed a set of eleven small pictures painted on tin. Intending to submit the works to judges of the Academia de San Fernando, Goya wrote to his friend at the Academia, Bernardo de Iriarte: "In order to distract my mind, mortified by reflection on my misfortunes, and in order to recoup some of the expenses they have occasioned, I executed a series of cabinet pictures in which I have managed to make observations that commissioned works ordinarily do not allow, and in which fantasy and invention have no place." These eleven pictures of "fantasy and invention" inaugurate Goya's second career.

The works that have so far been identified with this group, of which *Courtyard with Lunatics* is certainly one, mark a profound change in Goya's art. Dark, dramatic, sometimes terrifying, Goya's new vision seems a century removed from the still Rococo refinement and wit of the tapestry designs and portraits created only a few years earlier. No longer merely *representing* the world of popular carnival, fantasy or nightmare, Goya has discovered instead how to create pictorial equivalences of these realms. "It was the discovery," Malraux has written, "of the very meaning of style; and at the same

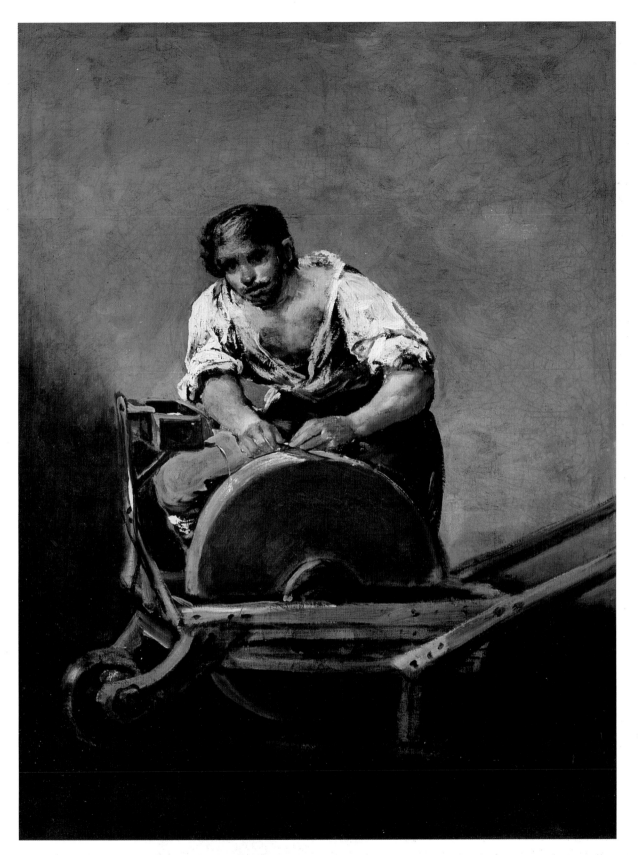

81 Francisco Goya *The Knife Grinder* ca. 1808–12. 25⅝ × 19⅝ (65 × 50)

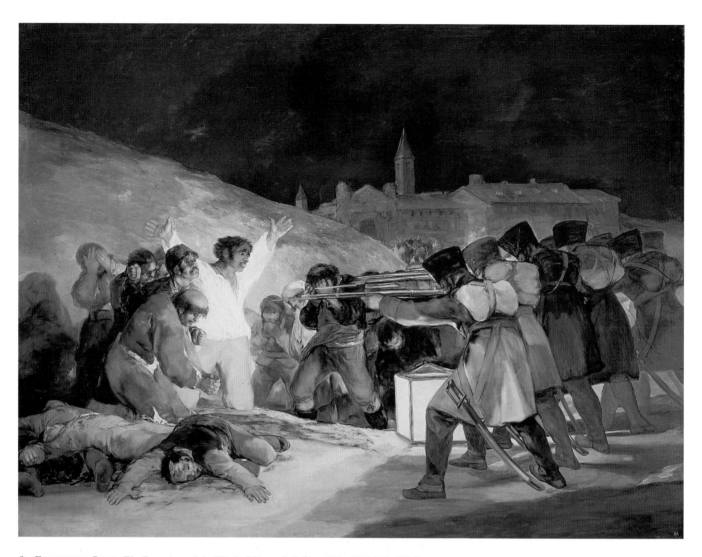

82 FRANCISCO GOYA *The Executions of the Third of May, 1808* 1814. 8'8¼ × 11'3⅞ (266 × 344.8)

time, of the peculiar strength of painting, of the power of a broken line or the bringing together of a red and a black over and above the demands of the object represented.'' *Courtyard* does not offer an operatic representation of madness, as we find in the *Carceri* (prisons) engravings of the Italian G. B. Piranesi, or a conversation-piece madness as we discover in Hogarth's engraving of ''The Madhouse'' for *A Rake's Progress* (both of which were probably seen by Goya in the collection of Martínez), but instead an imaginary and horrifying vision of the loneliness, fear, and *anomie* engendered by mental illness and social alienation. Occupying the foreground of a courtyard sealed off by heavy masonry blocks and an iron gate at the rear, a dozen ''patients'' and a single warden sit, stare, posture, implore, grimace, wrestle, or discipline themselves. The top of the picture is evaporated by sunlight, rendering all the more monstrous the nightmarish scene below.

There can be little doubt that Goya intended his picture as an indictment of the widespread punitive treatment of insanity. Until the reforms instigated by E. J. Georget in France and Samuel Tuke in England in the late 1810's, the insane had generally been confined with criminals, the sick, and the indigent in vast warehouse asylums such as Salt-pêtrière in Paris, and the hospital of Bethlehem (Bedlam) in London. Inmates at these institutions usually received no treatment whatsoever, but were put in iron manacles or subjected to physical punishment and back-breaking labor. The purpose of this irrational-seeming generalized confinement was in equal parts economic and political. During periods when labor was in short supply, asylums provided a large ready pool of workers whose gross exploitation had the added advantage of depressing the salaries of those on the outside; during periods when labor was abundant, asylums absorbed great numbers of the unemployed, keeping them subdued and under watch. The political, or ideological, purpose of confinement is perhaps harder to pinpoint precisely, but the philosopher Michel Foucault has plausibly argued that it was intended for the chastisement of the "immorality of the unreasonable" and for fending off the revolutionary threat—represented by madness—of absolute political and personal freedom.

Indeed, to an enlightened generation that extolled the virtues of *liberté*, the reform of prisons and asylums was an essential goal. The subject was common in the writings of Beccaria, Voltaire, and Condorcet, among others, and was surely a frequent topic for discussion in the enlightened *tertulia* in which Goya moved. Condemnation of brutality toward prisoners—criminals and the insane—was explicitly the subject of a number of Goya's later paintings and drawings as well as the subject of works by the English artists Francis Wheatley and George Romney and the French Théodore Géricault. Goya's small painting, in which the light of reason above is shown exposing or disinfecting the brutality of prejudice below, thus seems fully consistent with *afrancesado*

73 ideology. Yet like *Capricho 43*, "The Sleep of Reason," there is in *Courtyard with Lunatics* an oppressive sense of foreboding and despair, especially in the standing and seated figures in the left and right foreground; there is also a sense of sadism, as if Goya and we were among those spectators at Bethlehem or Charenton who paid a penny or a *sous* for the privilege of watching the mad behave like animals in a menagerie the better to reassure us of our own reason. Goya was probably just such a witness at Saragossa, where he claimed in a letter to Iriarte to have watched the above performance. How uncertain of his own reason must Goya have been to watch such a scene! How he must have recoiled at his own pleasure to paint such a picture!

Goya's growing ambivalence toward Enlightenment and attraction to the dark Spain of popular culture and super-
83 stition is equally apparent in *The Witches' Sabbath* and
84 *Caprichos 68*, "A Fine Teacher!" Both are coarse, vulgar, and grotesque in subject and execution and thus a far cry from the refinement and wit that are the usual tokens of Enlightenment culture. Both are at once satires and celebrations of the new popular penchant for witchcraft and the licentiousness it betokened. *The Witches' Sabbath* (1797–8) is one of six paintings on the subject of witchcraft commissioned by the Duquesa de Osuna for the bedroom of her country house. In the center of the small canvas appears a seated he-goat or devil crowned with vine leaves. Encircled by young and old witches, he conducts his service with raised cloven hooves while receiving offerings of live children from the two witches on the right, and dead children from the witches on the left. The light from a crescent moon at the upper left casts a phosphorescent blue pall over the macabre landscape, while a

half dozen circling bats are seen in silhouette. Goya's painting may have been derived from a discussion of witchcraft in Moratín's satiric account of the seventeenth-century *auto da fé* (execution of the judgment of the Inquisition) of Lograño, but numerous other popular sources were available. Particularly relevant here was the widespread and longstanding association of witchcraft with female sexual freedom, a tradition summarized by Moratín when he wrote: "The he-goat was a very respectable personality in Antiquity, and much esteemed by women for his fine *prendas* [jewels or endowments]." The beast's bountifulness is in fact revealed by his long horns and by the visual pun created by the agitated yellow shawl at his loins. Created during a brief interlude of relative self-confidence among the *ilustrados*, Goya's satirical painting indulges the artist's broad *pueblo* humor while also, perhaps, alluding to a decadent regime overseen by a cuckold for a king and a gigolo for a Prime Minister. Such self-assured wit and irony would become rare for Goya in the new century; it would gradually be replaced by helpless negation and gall.

The condemnation of sexual license and corruption apparent in *The Witches' Sabbath* and the five other paintings created in 1797–8 for the Duquesa de Osuna, becomes more rancorous and more complex in *Los Caprichos*. On February 6, 1799 there appeared the following notice in the *Diario de Madrid*, announcing the publication of a "collection of prints of extravagant subjects, invented and etched by Francisco Goya:"

> The author is convinced that censuring human errors and vices—although it seems the preserve of oratory and poetry—may also be a worthy object of painting. As subjects appropriate to his work, he has selected from the multitude of stupidities and errors common to every civil society, and from the ordinary obfuscations and lies condoned by custom, ignorance or self interest, those he has deemed most fit to furnish material for ridicule, and at the same time to exercise the author's imagination.

Despite the artist's disclaimer, it is clear that these *Caprichos*, which went on sale on February 19 at the modest cost of 4 *reales* each, were specifically intended to ridicule the cupidity, licentiousness, and superstition of modern Spain and not simply "every civil society." Indeed, Goya's contemporaries embraced the work both as a kind of *roman à clef*, in which the ruling troika—Godoy, María Luisa, and the King—among others, were particularly lampooned, and as a broader indictment of official corruption, *Majism*, witchcraft, and a rampant Inquisition. The Duque and Duquesa de Osuna were smart to purchase four sets before publication; just two days after their appearance, the albums were withdrawn from sale, probably because of a threat from the Holy Office.

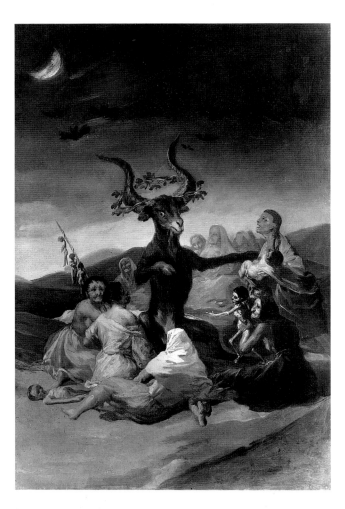

83 FRANCISCO GOYA *The Witches' Sabbath* 1797–8. $17\frac{3}{8} \times 12\frac{1}{4}$ (44 × 31)

Los Caprichos, we have already seen, is at least superficially
the product of *ilustrado* ideology. *Caprichos 50,* "Los Chinchillas" ("The Chinchillas"), depicts two figures being
spoon-fed by a third. The two have closed eyes, padlocks over
their ears and are wrapped in coats which resemble noble coats
of arms; the reclining figure at the bottom clutches a rosary,
while the one at the right grips a sword as he is fed by the
middle figure with blindfold and donkey's ears. This latter
jackass obtains his delicious gruel from the great two-handled
cauldron in the center of the print. As with many of Goya's
Caprichos, "The Chinchillas" is both allegorical and literary:
in the former sense, it is awkward and unnaturalistic, recalling
the plates in such iconographic encyclopedias as the famous
Iconologia (1593) of Cesare Ripa; in the latter sense, it has an
anecdotal character that suggests a larger narrative context.
Indeed, the specific literary origin of *Caprichos 50* is found in a
popular comedy of manners by José de Cañizares that
satirized the ignorance and pomposity of its noble protagonist,
Lucas de Chinchilla. In his print, as in the play, Goya

expresses the view that nobles who are preoccupied with their
own aristocratic genealogy (symbolized by their oversized
coats of arms) are blind (eyes closed) and deaf (ears padlocked)
to understanding, accepting only the food of Ignorance
(represented with blindfold and donkey ears). One contemporary explanation of "The Chinchillas" ran as follows:
"Fools that pride themselves on their nobility surrender to
indolence and superstition, and they seal off their understanding with padlocks whilst they are grossly fed by Ignorance."
Despite its ready readability, however, Goya's image is not a
straightforward allegory of the value of Enlightenment over
Ignorance or aristocratic decadence; as with his *Courtyard*
painting and "The Sleep of Reason," "Los Chinchillas"
appears to embrace aspects of the very darkness and
superstition it otherwise condemns: the disturbing face of
Ignorance who wields his spoon like a dagger, the grotesquely
pastiched bodies of the "nobles," and finally the oppressive
weight created by the aquatinting of the upper half of the
plate, all suggest the nightmare world of unreason—of the
madhouse—more than the enlightened satiric theatre of
Cañizares. In Goya's *Caprichos,* in other words, it is often
hard to determine whether the artist deplores or delights in his
disturbing subject matter.

A similar ambiguity is apparent in an earlier print in the
series, *Caprichos 10,* "El amor y la muerte" ("Love and
Death") which ridicules the exaggerated pride and bravado of
Majism. A mortally wounded *majo,* sword at his feet, collapses
in the embrace of his lover. Their faces are pressed together in
pain and anguish, as a dark cloud above seems poised to
descend upon and envelop them; all the chivalric romance of
dueling has been chilled in the cold night of death. Here as
elsewhere in the *Caprichos,* Goya ridicules the foolishness or
self-destructiveness of the popular classes in a clear expression
of *ilustrado* ideology. Yet it must at the same time be noted
that however critical he is of them, it is the *pueblo,* and not the
elites of Spain, that have now become Goya's preoccupation.
Moreover, for all the bourgeois moralizing in "Love and
Death," the man and woman are depicted with extraordinary
sympathy and pathos. The same sympathy is found in
Caprichos 42, "Tu que no puedes" ("You who cannot"), in
which two members of the *pueblo* are burdened by asses
perched on their back, and in *Caprichos 52,* "Lo que puede un
sastre!" ("What a tailor can achieve!"), in which a pious crowd
kneels in worship before a tree that is draped to resemble a
cowled monk. This latter image mocks popular belief in
miracles and witchcraft, but the focus is clearly on the
reverence and awe of the kneeling woman in the foreground; it
is her psychology that is compelling, just as it is the *maja's*
expression of mourning in "Love and Death" that provides
the image its drama and conviction. In the hands of Goya, the
pueblo make their first heroic appearance in the visual record

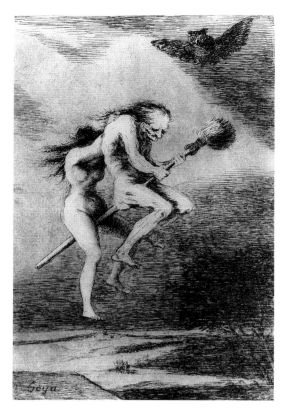

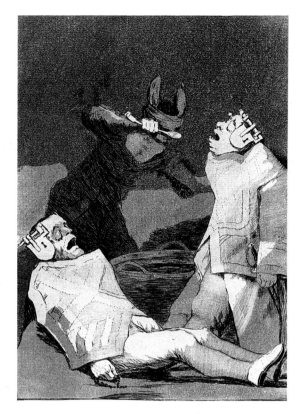

84 FRANCISCO GOYA *Caprichos 68* "Linda maestra!" ("A fine teacher")
1799. 8⅜ × 5⅞ (21.3 × 15)

85 FRANCISCO GOYA *Caprichos 50* "Los Chincillas" ("The Chincillas")
1799. 8¼ × 5⅞ (20.8 × 15.1)

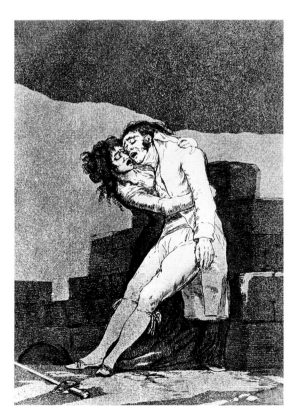

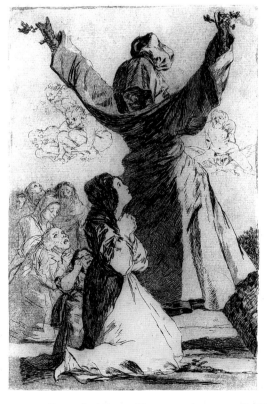

86 FRANCISCO GOYA *Caprichos 10* "El amor y la muerte" ("Love and
Death") 1799. 8½ × 6 (21.8 × 15.3)

87 FRANCISCO GOYA *Caprichos 52* "Lo que puede un sastre!" ("What a
tailor can achieve!") 1799. 8½ × 6 (21.7 × 15.2)

of European culture: they are not types, but individuals, and thus are not consistent, but contradictory, not passive but active—indeed at times revolutionary.

Goya's embrace of the *pueblo*—suggested in the tapestry cartoons and witchcraft paintings but first clearly revealed by the *Caprichos*—soon after became a dominant theme in his art. This orientation, it must be acknowledged however, was the result of economic circumstance as well as political conviction and emotional temperament: after 1801, the artist's public and private sources of patronage began to dry up. Goya's close ties with the court were largely severed after the completion of the portrait of the family of Charles IV, perhaps because of dissatisfaction with the portrait, but more likely because of a renewed campaign against the *ilustrados*. The liberal prime minister Urquijo was deposed and jailed in 1801 at the same time that the great *ilustrado* Jovellanos himself was exiled and then imprisoned. Other shocks soon followed: in 1802, the Duquesa de Alba died suddenly, followed a year later by Goya's great friend Zapater. By 1805, Goya's distance from his former noble patrons was increased still further by virtue of his son's marriage into a prominent family of Saragossa merchants, and by his own friendship with Leocadia Zorilla, an articulate and fierce opponent of absolutism who would later become Goya's companion. From this moment on, Goya depicted the Spanish bourgeoisie (a rare and threatened species in Spain), and increasingly the *pueblo*. In great canvases such as *The Water Carrier* and *The Knife Grinder* (ca. 1808–12), and especially in the almost innumerable drawings and prints, Goya portrayed proletarians, beggars, prisoners and their victimizers—the hereditary nobility, soldiers, and clergy. In the last two decades of his life, Goya would focus upon the *pueblo* while recording his private reflections and fears concerning the horror of the War of Spanish Independence (1808–14) and its destructive aftermath.

The Goya of the *Disasters of War* (ca. 1810–20), the *Executions of the Third of May, 1808* (1814), and the "Black Paintings" (ca. 1820–23) is very different from the artist who once painted tapestry cartoons and portraits. Whereas the earlier artist was a public figure who recorded, however presciently, the appearance of the leading men and women of his time, the later artist was a private man who represented the unknown and unheralded *pueblo*; whereas the earlier painter drew upon an existing vocabulary of religious, political, and moral verities, the later painter had no such secure foundations; and finally, whereas the earlier Goya directed his art to an audience he knew and whose expectations he could predict, the later Goya painted, drew, and etched for no audience of whom he could be certain, or for one from which he had more reason to expect punishment than reward. Isolated and vulnerable, independent and experimental—it may be said, in short, that the later Goya experienced and represented the

alienation which the Romantics and indeed all modern artists would both suffer and enjoy. For perhaps the first time in history, a major public artist—Goya had been designated First Court Painter in 1799—withdrew to the confines of his own insights and imagination in order to create an essentially private art intended to please or succor himself alone. When his art was exhibited, we shall see, it was largely ignored or disdained; Goya's greatest renown would be achieved after his death.

We have noted some of the political and cultural transformations that created the conditions for Goya's alienation—the conflict in Spain between Enlightenment and traditional culture, the ideological struggle among aristocratic, bourgeois, and popular classes over the question of national identity, or "Spanishness," the economic and political turmoil generated by the Revolution in France, and the slow demise of an artistic tradition based upon shared beliefs and standards of excellence. Yet, until 1808, Goya remained a more or less passive, more or less aloof, observer and recorder of this turmoil and these events. His art, we have seen, was insightful, complex, and perhaps even keenly dialectical, but it was still generally the dispassionate product of that cynical regard seen in the frontispiece self-portrait from the 72 *Caprichos*. After 1808, however, the Goya of the arched brow and curled lip was no more; like David in France after 1792, or Courbet in 1870–71, Goya was now a participant in, and a victim of, the earthquake of war and revolution. The public artist and the private man could now no longer be separated.

In 1808, widespread revulsion for the corrupt court of Charles IV and especially for the intrigues of his minister Godoy, led to the abdication of the King and the crowning of his son, Ferdinand VII. In 1807 Napoleon, in pursuit of his policy of isolating England from the rest of Europe, had seized the opportunity to occupy the Iberian Peninsula and in May 1808 placed his brother Joseph Bonaparte on the throne of Spain. Appealing to *ilustrado* and *pueblo* alike, the new French monarch immediately proclaimed a policy of national regeneration, modernization, secularization, and Enlightenment. Distrustful, however, of such *afrancesado* reforms when put forward under successive Caroline regimes, the plebeians of Madrid and elsewhere were certainly not going to accept the dictates of the hated French invaders. Thus, on May 2 and 3, 1808, the *madrileños* rose up in arms against the French and their mercenaries in defense of Ferdinand VII and Spanish independence. Within days the uprising in the city was crushed, but the war had migrated across the countryside in a bloody and confused *guerilla* conflict that would last for six years until the surrender of Joseph Bonaparte and the restoration of the Spanish monarchy.

Goya's great *Executions of the Third of May, 1808*, like its 82 companion *The Second of May*, was paid for by the Crown and 88

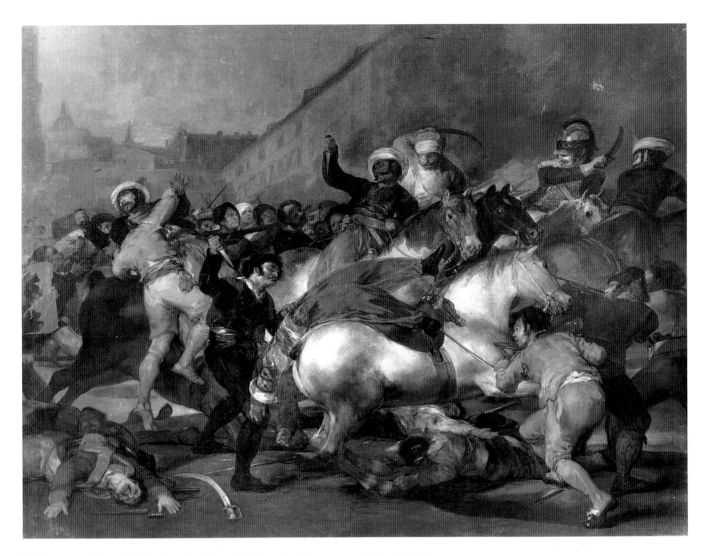

88 FRANCISCO GOYA *The Uprising of the Second of May, 1808* 1814. 8′9 × 11′4⅛ (266.7 × 345.8)

painted in 1814. It was intended as a testimonial to the courage and suffering of the Spanish *pueblo*. Amid a huddle of people and bodies, a man in white with arms outstretched is faced by a phalanx of executioners. His eyes show fear and resignation as he awaits the same bloody end as befell those of the *pueblo* sprawled obscenely in the dirt in front of him. Although he has company, he is alone this night on the hill of Príncipe Pío on the outskirts of Madrid; like Christ on the hill of Golgotha, he bears the stigmata and is illuminated in death by an unearthly light. The colors and light in the picture are coarse and garish as Goya continues to experiment with "the very meaning of style," with the metaphorical relationship between, for example, paint and blood, darkness and fear, illumination and pathos. All of the artist's subtle skills of composition, coloring, and characterization are marshaled here in order to expose and consecrate the martyrdom of the *pueblo* at the hands of faceless and pitiless French centurions.

In evaluating the meaning of Goya's *Executions*, it must be remembered that it was painted in 1814 after the restoration of Ferdinand VII and the arrest, expulsion or imprisonment of the Spanish *afrancesados* and *liberales*, many of whom counted among the artist's friends. Goya himself had tried to flee Spain in 1812 and two years later was hauled before the restored Inquisition to explain his "obscene" *Naked* and *Clothed* 78–9 *Majas* and to undergo a lengthy "purification." His request to the Council of Regency early in 1814 for an allowance to paint the *Second* and *Third of May* was therefore clearly an effort to get back in official good graces by painting pictures that could provide a dramatic justification for the recently concluded war, and sanction for the restored regime of Ferdinand. In order to regain his good name and position, Goya would represent the nightmarish chaos of the previous six years as a coherent battle of the *pueblo* against atheist invaders in the name of Church and King.

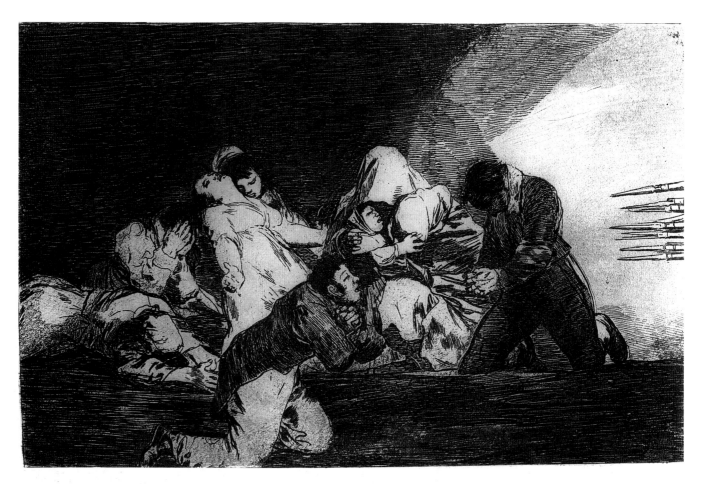

89 FRANCISCO GOYA *The Disasters of War 26* "No se puede mirar" ("One can't look") ca. 1810–20. $5\frac{5}{8} \times 8\frac{1}{4}$ (14.4 × 21)

The story of the War of Spanish Independence was not, of course, so simple, but neither were Goya's pictures very convincing as propaganda. The initial uprising of the *pueblo* was anti-elite as well as anti-imperialist, and the conflict became quickly fragmented and radicalized. *Guerilla* bands and *juntas* of "right" and "left" were formed in efforts either to repel "godless" *liberales* or to install a new secular and popular democratic constitution. A liberal constitution was indeed passed by a Cadiz government in exile in 1812, but in the context of national civil war, it had little significance or effect; it was quickly overturned when Ferdinand returned to power. Thus Goya's *Executions of the Third of May*, for all its realistic horror, was an effort to provide a mythic integrity to the Spanish war by exalting the heroism and sacrifice of the *pueblo*. In this function, it may be compared with David's *Intervention of the Sabine Women*, painted at the conclusion of another extended period of civil conflict and international war and likewise intended to unify an audience behind an undemocratic regime. Yet unlike David's, Goya's painting did not bring its author wealth and renewed acclaim. Goya's *Executions* was perhaps too frank in its representation of

national sacrifice, too sincere in its pathos, too literal in its equivalence of flesh, blood, and paint. Indeed, the *pueblo* themselves embodied the contradictoriness of Goya's enterprise: though they welcomed in 1814 the restoration of the rule of Church and Crown (chanting in the streets of Madrid, it is said, "Long live our chains!"), the same *pueblo* was often a source of profound social radicalization. Perhaps the *pueblo* and the war itself (like the U.S. war against Vietnam) were thus simply inconducive to heroic and propagandist representation. In any case, upon its completion, the picture was quickly secreted in the Prado basement, not to be seen or even acknowledged for two generations.

If *The Executions of the Third of May, 1808* was Goya's public, righteously indignant response to French imperialism, the *Disasters of War* was his private, ambivalent response. Drawn and engraved between 1810 and about 1820, these plates could not be published in Goya's lifetime due to their emotional intensity and political and moral ambiguity; except for a small number of artist's proofs, the *Disasters* only appeared in 1863, some thirty-five years after Goya's death. When they were conceived in 1808, however, they were

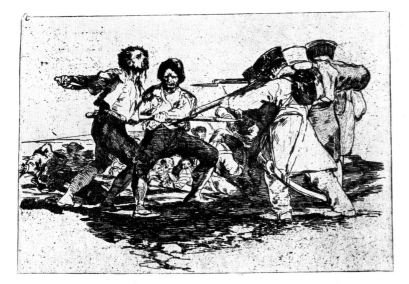

90 **FRANCISCO GOYA** *The Disasters of War 2* "Con razon ó sin ella" ("Whether Right or Wrong") ca. 1810–20. 6⅛ × 8 (15.5 × 20.5)

91 **FRANCISCO GOYA** *The Disasters of War 79* "Murió la verdad" ("Truth is dead") ca. 1810–20. 7 × 8⅝ (17.5 × 22)

92 **FRANCISCO GOYA** *The Disasters of War 80* "Si reucitariá?" ("If she were to rise again?") ca. 1810–20. 7 × 8⅝ (17.5 × 22)

93 **FRANCISCO GOYA** *The Disasters of War 84* "La seguridad de un reo no exige tormento" ("The custody of a criminal does not call for torture") ca. 1810–20. 4½ × 3⅜ (11.5 × 8.5)

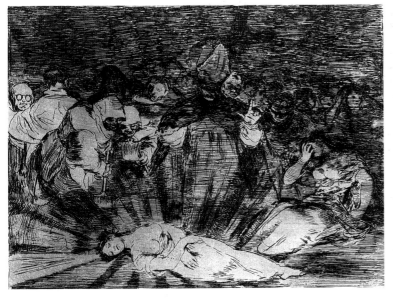

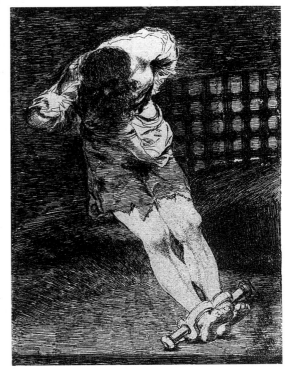

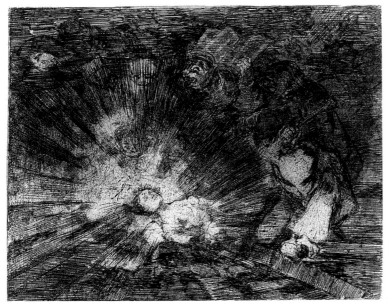

intended, like the *Executions,* to be a public display of patriotism and nationalist zeal. Their genesis is as follows: within months of the outbreak of hostilities, Goya was called upon by General Palafox to travel to his native Saragossa "to see and examine," the artist wrote, "the ruins of that city in order to illustrate the glories of its citizens, from which I cannot excuse myself as I am so much interested in the glory of my native land." Goya thus accepted the commission, made the hazardous journey to Saragossa, and began to make the oil sketches and drawings that served as preparation for the prints he called *The Terrible results of the bloody war in Spain against Bonaparte. And other emphatic caprichos,* but which are known today as the *Disasters of War.* Far from representing heroic resolve and singularity of purpose, however, these prints express revulsion at the horror and brutality of war. They expose the savagery of the *pueblo* as well as the French and condemn the Spain of the restoration as much as the regime of Bonaparte.

The 82 plates of the *The Disasters* may be generally divided into three groups which depict: the victims and horrors of war (plates 2–47), famine, death, and burial (plates 48–64), and "*caprichos enfáticos*" (literally, "emphatic capriccios," plates 65–80), that is, nightmares and scenes of corrupt clerics, monsters, and grotesques. Most of *The Disasters* were completed by 1814, but a few, especially from the third group, were probably made during the period of monarchical reaction and Inquisitorial virulence after 1814 but before the liberal coup of 1820. Among the prints of the first group are
90 *Disasters 2,* "Con razón ó sin ella" ("Whether right or wrong") and *Disasters 3,* "Lo mismo" ("The same"), both of which, significantly, show the Spanish attacking the French
89 with axes, pikes, knives, and even teeth. *Disasters 26,* "No se puede mirar" ("One can't look"), undoubtedly a model for *The Executions of the Third of May, 1808,* reverses the brutality and shows the French pitilessly slaughtering the *pueblo;* it also offers a particularly vivid example of Goya's use of brief captions both to illuminate and undermine the meaning of his images. Spanish men, women, and children are gathered in a cave in order to be shot. They beg, crawl, cover their faces, and turn their backs to the executioners *at whom they cannot bear to look.* Their killers are visible to us only by the ends of their rifle barrels and bayonets jutting in from the right margin; *they cannot be seen.* Are such horrors as these appropriate subjects for art, suitable vehicles for esthetic pleasure; *should one look at them? "One can't look"* and yet one *must see* the brutality and senselessness of war. *Disasters 28 and 29* again reverse the polarity of horror and show the *pueblo* torturing and killing a single victim, a bourgeois who is probably also an *afrancesado,* and thus a "traitor" to Spain. And so the horrors compound in image after image— shootings, stabbings, famine, rape, and death.

Among the plates from the final group of "*caprichos enfáticos*" are the bleak *Disasters 79 and 80,* "Murió la verdad"   91–2 ("Truth is dead") and "Si reucitaría?" ("If she were to rise again?"). These depict the burial of a young woman (perhaps an allegory of the Constitution) by a rabble of grotesque clerics, and the same woman, unburied, perhaps in a state of decomposition. In the first print, her body emits strong beams of light, emblem of reason and truth; in the second, her light is dimmed along with her youth and beauty. Probably conceived in 1819, during the bleak nadir of the *ilustrados* and *liberales,* these plates express the pathos and alienation of one who has seen the collapse of Reason and yet who remains condemned forever to hope. The very last images that Goya intended for his *Disasters* (though not included in the posthumous edition of 1863), reveal a similarly poignant dialectic. They show chained and tortured prisoners, recalling the world of *Courtyard with Lunatics* and the *Caprichos.* Like these earlier works, *Disaster 84,* "The custody of a criminal does not call for   93 torture," expresses the reforming zeal of the *ilustrado;* yet unlike them, there is no irony, or satire, or even the prayer of Enlightenment. The prisoner is slumped and manacled, crushed between the margins of this small plate as between prison walls. Goya undoubtedly saw or heard of such tortures during the period of Spanish guerilla war and French "counter insurgency" between 1810 and 1814. He would see or hear of them again in 1814–15, and again during the period of White Terror unleashed against popular radicalism and the *liberales* after the second restoration of Ferdinand in 1823–4. Fearing such a fate for himself, the aged artist left Spain for France in 1825 and died there, in relative peace, three years later. The reason Goya's despair was so great was that he had seen the barbarism of Enlightenment itself in the person of Napoleon as well as the defeat of Enlightenment by Spain.

The works of Goya's last decade are not uniformly bleak. They include several portraits, religious paintings, the robust and experimental *Bordeaux Milkmaid* (1825–7), and a small number of lithographs, a new medium for the artist. Most remarkable and perplexing, however, are the so-called "Black Paintings" created to decorate the walls of two rooms of his suburban Madrid residence, the Quinta del Sordo (Deaf Man's House) between 1820 and 1823. Painted during a brief constitutionalist interlude, these frescos (now transferred to canvas) cannot, however, be considered confident celebrations of revived truth and reason. They are primarily grotesque or macabre, and any allegorical or satiric content they may possess is extremely recondite, and was so to its earliest viewers. *Saturn Devouring His Children* and *The*   94 *Sabbath* may, like the *Caprichos,* allude to the violence and superstition of the Inquisition, but now without the spirit of reform. Nightmarish and even lurid, these are private images, lacking public purpose, lacking even an audience apart from the artist himself, his son, his companion Leocadia, and the few surviving friends courageous enough to visit the home of an ancient *ilustrado* reprobate. Given the dark emotional timbre of these fourteen paintings, the question must arise: is Goya any longer an artist of the Enlightenment?

The "Black Paintings", like the late *Disasters,* were created by Goya for himself during an epoch when reason slept. Disdaining public meanings, conventional forms, and scrutable iconography, Goya appears to have lost, or anyway abandoned, his reason in the "Black Paintings". They are painted with unprecedented boldness and breadth and are alternately sober and shrill in their coloration. Yet there is a logic to these and to the other, less disturbed late works of Goya, such as the *Milkmaid* or the many drawings of the French popular classes from *Album G* (1824–6). The historian Gwyn Williams detected it when he wrote: "As for the grotesque, the maniacal, the occult, the witchery, they are precisely the product of the sleep of *human* reason; they are *human* nightmares. *That these monsters are human is, indeed, the point.*" Goya's very focus upon the grotesque is an expression of his continued fascination with ordinary people, with the Spanish *pueblo,* and (after 1825) with the French *menu peuple* in all its complexity. For Goya, as for other artists since Breugel, the grotesque and the popular define and occupy a world opposed to order, rationality, the ideal, and the aristocratic. Yet unlike the popular grotesques of earlier artists, Goya's are not decorative or picturesque. They are defined, we have seen, by their contradictoriness, that is by their combined brutality and nobility, their unreason and virtue, their blindness and vision; they offer the artist and the viewer no comforting homilies about loyalty or truth, but then, neither are they as frozen or static as the project of Enlightenment had become. Although they are primarily vehicles of a profound artistic pessimism and alienation, Goya's *pueblo* reveal a new direction in the history of art—a proclaimed unity of purpose and perspective among artists and the insane, the alienated, the dissident, and the popular. This perspective, belonging to the radical, the nonconformist

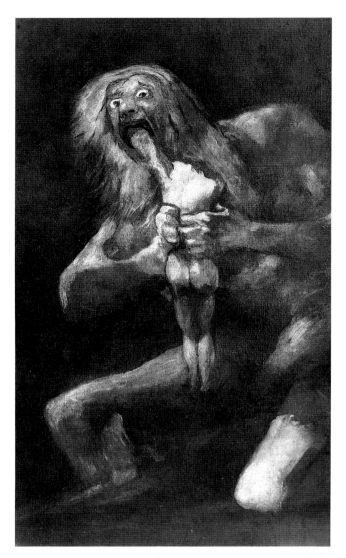

94 FRANCISCO GOYA *Saturn Devouring His Children* ca. 1820. 57⅛ × 32⅝ (145 × 82.9)

and the socially or culturally marginal, was championed in France by Géricault and Delacroix; in England it would be represented principally by William Blake, to whom we shall now turn.

VISIONARY HISTORY PAINTING: BLAKE AND HIS CONTEMPORARIES

BRIAN LUKACHER

BLAKE'S REVOLUTION

WHILE DAVID AND GOYA WERE ALTERNATELY advancing and reprehending the ideologies of Enlightenment, Revolution, and Empire during the course of their artistic careers, the English poet, printmaker, and painter William Blake (1757–1827) was producing a highly imaginative and hermetic art that was no less responsive to the impact of these same historical forces and events in Britain. Unlike his French and Spanish counterparts, however, Blake dwelt for the most part on the margins of artistic activity in his country, effectively cut off from the preeminent fine arts institutions and the most respected avenues of patronage in late Georgian London. If David and Goya took on celebrated and visible roles—sometimes dangerously so—as their nations' premier artists during times of pronounced political and social upheaval, Blake's situation was quite different, as best summed up by his own admission, "I am hid." Blake's proclaimed devotion to creative and spiritual self-definition through mystical revelation, in opposition to any and all authoritarian standards (artistic, religious, or social), makes him exemplary of an alienated, countercultural Romanticism, a notion that certainly seems overburdened with later twentieth-century values and misconceptions but that is nevertheless borne out by the specific conditions of Blake's life and art. Undoubtedly, "Blake" has become a kind of cultural palimpsest for the social and psychological utopias of our own century: how else could he be claimed by some as a visionary, and conveniently heterogeneous, precursor to Karl Marx and Carl Jung? For our purposes, Blake's contribution to the visual arts around 1800 proves most vital to understanding the fate of history painting and the question of national cultural identity in English Romantic art.

To appreciate Blake's predicament as an artist "hidden" from, and yet directly engaged with, the esthetics and politics of his day, our attention will be focused on his self-sponsored, one-man exhibition of 1809, an occasion that marked Blake's most decisive effort to solicit the attention of a public audience. Exhibiting sixteen of his "Poetical and Historical Inventions" at his brother's London residence (also the site of the family hosiery shop, an unusual art venue), Blake promoted his self-appointed calling as the artistic reformer of Britain in the midst of the Napoleonic Wars. In some verses written around the time of the exhibition, he imagined an angelic annunciation instructing him, "'Descend thou upon Earth/ Renew the Arts on Britain's Shore,/ And France shall fall down & adore./ With Works of Art their Armies meet,/ And War shall sink beneath thy feet.'" Blake's pacifist hope for the political efficacy of his art was, paradoxically, cast as a nationalist appeal for patronage and recognition, something made clear in the published "Advertisement" and *Descriptive Catalogue* for his exhibition. Resentful that his art had been dismissed, if acknowledged at all, as little more than "a Madman's Scrawls" (his words), Blake looked forward to the eventual redemption of his artistic stature: an esoteric engraver who had struggled within an artisan subculture of radicals and mystics was ready to assume his position as an empowered history painter assuaging and redirecting the misguided energies of war-torn empires.

Blake's career began in the 1770's as an engraver of antiquarian and reproductive fine art prints, his lifelong work in commercial engraving serving as an intermittent source of income that did little to save him and his wife, Catherine Boucher, from abject poverty (friends and infrequent patrons would express their surprise at the physical squalor and economic deprivation of the Blakes' living conditions). Blake received brief instruction in life drawing at the recently established Royal Academy of Arts (chartered by King

George III in 1768) and submitted watercolors of historical and biblical subjects to the annual Academy exhibitions. Throughout his career, however, he would remain an adversarial outcast of the Academy, condemning its restrictive, and yet at times overly eclectic, pedagogy and exhibition policy, and especially its hypocritical failure to encourage a genuinely progressive English school of historical art. Blake's faith in the supremacy of history painting and, more generally, in idealist esthetics was nonetheless dependent on the propounded artistic principles of the Academy. Typically for Blake, indicting or negating a system of thought or an institution of power also entailed incorporating and redefining its values within the imaginative program of his own art and beliefs, whether it be the rational empiricism of Enlightenment philosophy, the self-contradicting authority of constitutional monarchy, or the emergence of industrial capitalism, all of which were to be the subject of scathing commentary in his pictures and writings.

It was during the early 1790's that Blake developed a unique approach to producing his illuminated books of poetry. Experimenting with the technique of relief etching, he printed the handwritten scripts of his poetic sagas graphically embellished with decorative, emblematic, and narrative motifs. The visual imagery, far from simply illustrating or supplementing the poetry, could simultaneously amplify and contradict the content of the verse, the dynamic between word and image often undermining epistemological assumptions about the very processes of reading, seeing, and interpreting. Figurative elements sometimes occupied separate plates or were integrated into the design of the text. The books of poetry were printed in small numbers and hand-colored, often with Catherine Boucher responsible for the tinting. A medieval craft esthetic was thereby conflated with reproductive printing techniques, Blake seeking to reconcile the autographic singularity of his illuminations with their intended multiplication.

Blake's poetic books from this period can best be characterized as spiritual allegories of revolutionary politics. Creating their own mythic personifications of human desires, habits of mind, and world views, designated by primitivizing, onomatopoeic names such as Orc, Los, and Urizen, Blake's writings often seem like a strangely invented form of biblical science fiction, though the abiding influence of Miltonic and Ossianic verse is ever at hand. The demiurgic struggles recounted in his poetry appear to transpire in either a cosmic or cellular void, or, geographically speaking, in an English nation poised ominously on the brink of eschatological destruction. In lamenting and exhorting over the cycles of oppression and liberation and of persecution and resistance under which his mythic characters labor, Blake's "Giant forms," as he would call them, perform epic psychodramas of contemporary history, centering on England's failure to embrace the revolutionary fervor of America and France. Blake was in frequent contact with the radical, intellectual circle of the publisher Joseph Johnson, which included the political and feminist republicans Thomas Paine and Mary Wollstonecraft. These associations, along with his social and professional roots in the urban artisan milieu that was the wellspring of English Jacobinism during the 1790's, affirm Blake's radical political credentials. His poetic books *America* (1793) and *Europe* (1794), both subtitled "A Prophecy," chart the travails of political liberty against the despotic, royalist authority of church and state, the contest clothed in seemingly obscure imagery of god-like powers battling over the soul of Albion (Blake's figure for the humanity of England). Blake's writings during the 1790's register with some urgency the emergence and repression of social and political protest among the English Jacobin movements that had found inspiration, and later disillusionment, in the French Revolution and the establishment of the Republic. With England's declaration of war against France in 1793, and with Prime Minister William Pitt's repressive policies against any organized expressions of social dissent, the country became increasingly embroiled in a climate of political paranoia, spurred on by invasion scares, grain shortages, and government censorship. As the decade closed, the rise of Napoleon ensured that the nationalism and militarism required for the defense of England would continue to preempt or suppress any calls for revolutionary reform. Much of Blake's art and poetry addresses the English Revolution that would never come to pass.

BODY POLITICS AND RELIGIOUS MYSTICISM

Blake's hopeful testimony to this nascent English revolutionary impulse is seen in one of his most renowned images, the color print known as *Albion Rose* (ca. 1794–5). The first sketches for the human figure date back to around 1780, and it is thought that the concept of the picture commemorates Blake's experience of the Gordon Riots of that year—anti-Catholic and anticolonial war protests in London that ignited into widespread mob violence; Blake was among the crowd that stormed and burned Newgate Prison, an episode made famous in Dickens's historical novel *Barnaby Rudge* (1841). The youthful male nude of Albion seen alighting on a sloping summit gives us the essentials of Blake's visual language: the human figure employed as a corporeal sign of spiritual, intellectual, and political positions. The balletic, self-exalting presentation of the body in *Albion Rose*—derived, while also diverging, from Renaissance proportion diagrams of the Vitruvian Man, as well as from Neoclassical engravings of

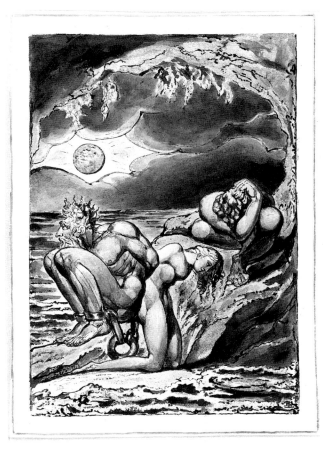

95 **WILLIAM BLAKE** frontispiece to *Visions of the Daughters of Albion*
1793. 6⅝ × 4¾ (17 × 12)

sculptural antiquities excavated at Herculaneum—is comple-
mented by the glorious burst of colored light that surrounds
the figure. Arms extended and hair aflame, the body of Albion
is posed in triumphant frontality. Blake attenuates and
simplifies the anatomical structure of the human form, its
modeling kept to a minimum with the contour lines strongly
demarcating the figure within its prismatic aureole. This
linear definition of the refulgent body is counterpointed to the
mottled darkness of the hillside and the eclipsed black of night
seen in the lower portion of the print. Although Blake
espoused an unswerving Neoclassical purity of line in artistic
execution, the coloristic explosions in his work—often
signifying a perceptual and sensual materialism against which
Blake declaimed—are vital to his pictorial designs and their
dialectical play of esthetic (and implicitly ethical and metaphysical) contraries.

The figure of Albion is not simply a Neoclassical exercise in
antique heroic nudity. Albion is nothing less than the body of
England, obviously divested of the outward signs of social
class and historical identity: refined yet elemental, chaste yet
sexualized, and ennobling yet leveling, in a state of what Blake

would call "Naked Beauty Displayed." Like most of Blake's
nudes, Albion seems a knowing contradiction, a disembodied
embodiment. He is of the flesh and plainly physical, but he
also functions as an ethereal blueprint for some regenerated
model of a utopian humanity, Christ-like and Apollonian all at
once. In *America* (1793), Blake envisioned the infectious,
liberating impact of the American Revolution on the British
people, "Leprosy London's Spirit" cured and reawakened as
"a naked multitude." Elsewhere in the poem, he writes of a
dawning freedom: "The morning comes, the night decays . . . /
Let the slave grinding at the mill run out into the field,/ Let
him look up into the heavens and laugh in the bright air." This
transition from oppressive darkness to revealed radiance,
from imprisoned labor to pantheistic release, in turn recalls
Paine's solar metaphor for political freedom in his *The Rights
of Man* (1791): "But such is the irresistible nature of truth,
that all it asks, and all it wants is the liberty of appearing. The
sun needs no inscription to distinguish him from darkness."
The self-illuminating figure of Albion, likewise, announces
this resplendent visibility of liberty. Using the most canonical
feature of Classical humanist art—the idealized nude—Blake
fashioned a revolutionary icon, a pictorial entreaty for social
and spiritual transformation; as he would implore his readers
in the preface to his later poem *Milton* (1804–08), "Rouze up,
O Young Men of the New Age!"

Much more common, however, in Blake's art of the 1790's
was the imagery of subjugation and enslavement. In the
solemn and tormented frontispiece to his poem *Visions of the*   95
Daughters of Albion (1793), Blake delineates the constricted
body language of mental and physical bondage. The female
protagonist of the poem, Oothoon, is seen manacled to her
slave-master/rapist, while her jealous and inhibited lover
cowers and withdraws into himself on the cavernous ledge
above the enchained figures. The poem, broadly speaking,
intertwines abolitionist and quasi-feminist arguments against
sexual and economic exploitation, denouncing the trade in
flesh that commodifies both "the swarthy children of the sun"
and "the virgin joys of life." The social and moral perversion
of freedom is translated, visually, by Blake into the physical
constraints of his bound figures—these miniaturized variations on Michelangelesque nudes that typified his figurative
style. The agonized subjection of the figures is conveyed not
only through their poses and gestures—opposing, for example, the taut frenzy of the male with the bowed resignation
of the female—but also through their formal definition, with
the lineaments of their anatomies harshly and schematically
rendered, their massive bodies contained and reduced to
compact diagrams of human despair. In keeping with Blake's
aversion to the conventions of pictorial illusionism, the bleak
landscape setting in this design is expressively metaphoric,
rather than objectively descriptive. The grotto entrance

frames a disconsolate vista of sea, clouds, and darkened sun, the realm of nature treated as flat patterns of unnaturalistic color shades, resisting any logical sense of graduated spatial recession. This mental landscape inverts into a skull-like, anthropomorphic profile that only reinforces the malevolent plight of the incapacitated titans. Concurrent with these mythic abstractions of oppression were Blake's more documentary, engraved illustrations of the inhumane actuality of contemporary slavery that he prepared for Captain John Stedman's book entitled *Narrative of a Five Years' Expedition against the Revolted Negroes of Surinam, in Guiana, on the Wild Coast of South America* (1796). Based on Stedman's eyewitness drawings that recorded the varieties of torture and punishment meted out to rebellious slaves by their colonial masters, Blake's engravings, like the one depicting a black man bound and hung by his torso to a gallows, are unflinching in their portrayal of the repressive violence connected with the traffic in slavery. The slaves are often shown, as in this plate, with expressions of stoic restraint, their quiet fortitude meant to elicit civilized compassion for their unendurable physical suffering, while also making them seem all the more impervious—almost inhumanly so—to the brutal circumstances of their punishment. Suspended hopelessly between the grim skeletal remains of past victims and the distant slave ship visible in the harbor, the tortured slave is made to objectify the perpetuation of death that was necessarily synonymous with the perpetuation of slavery itself.

96

Blake's preoccupation with the conflicting powers of revolution and oppression was inseparable from his Christian religious mysticism. He embraced, assimilated, and critiqued eighteenth-century mystical systems with habitual regularity, ranging from the apocalyptic hermeneutics of the Swedish mystic Emmanuel Swedenborg to the Neoplatonic scholarship of the English mystic Thomas Taylor. Using self-induced trances as a source of artistic inspiration, experimenting occasionally with an antinomian lifestyle as a way of recapturing prelapsarian bliss (William and Catherine had been espied nude, emulating Adam and Eve, in their cottage garden), and frequently entertaining visitations from the spirit world (often from his deceased brother and fellow artist Robert or from more celebrated guests like Dante and Milton), Blake had constant recourse to the otherworldly in his struggles against the prevailing structures of society and art. These nonconformist religious and mystical tendencies in his work and temperament make him all the more fascinating and compelling to some, and all the more irrelevant and trying to others.

With his art consistently cast in terms of "visions" and "prophecies," Blake was participating in a widespread millennial anxiety that swept through significant segments of English society during the closing decades of the eighteenth

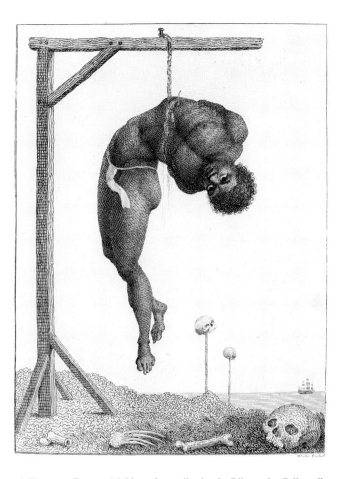

96 WILLIAM BLAKE "A Negro hung alive by the Ribs to the Gallows," from John G. Stedman *Narrative of a Five Years' Expedition against the Revolted Negroes of Surinam, in Guiana, on the Wild Coast of South America* 1796. $7 \times 5\frac{1}{8}$ (18 × 13.5)

century. As the historian E. P. Thompson observed in analyzing the concomitant rise of religious enthusiasm and political radicalism that marked the English reaction to the French Revolution, "Chiliasm touched Blake with its breath; it walked abroad . . . among the Jacobins and Dissenters of artisan London." With the century perilously waning and with revolutionary events on the Continent inciting political and social discord within England, contemporary history appeared to promise the impending fulfillment of biblical, apocalyptic scenarios, especially in the collective imagination of the ever growing, religious nonconformist sects and their self-styled prophets. One such prophet, Richard Brothers, the "Prince of the Hebrews" who foretold the imminent collapse of all monarchies, along with the destruction of London, "the modern Babylon", was even arrested for seditious treason in 1795 and confined to a lunatic asylum where he drew up published plans for London's promised resurrection as the New Jerusalem, the influence of which may be detected on Blake's own later poetic epic *Jerusalem, The Emanation of the Great Albion* (1804–20). The proliferation of these chiliastic

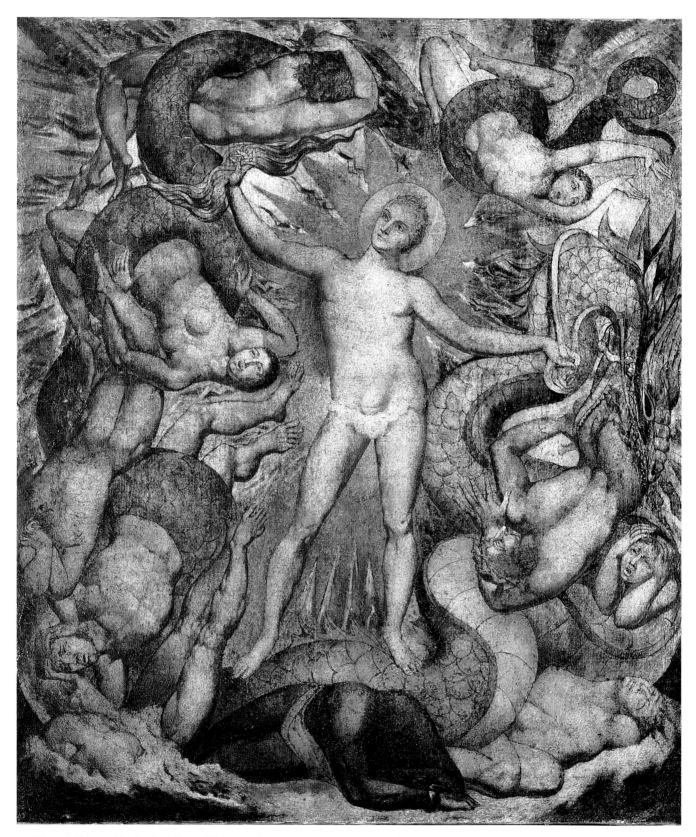

97 **WILLIAM BLAKE** *The Spiritual Form of Nelson Guiding Leviathan, in whose wreathings are infolded the Nations of the Earth* 1809. 30 × 24⅝ (76.2 × 62.5)

predictions of historical destruction and spiritual renewal during this period was deeply symptomatic of both social disenchantment and political disenfranchisement, to which the increasingly obscurantist and prophetic quality of Blake's imagery bears striking witness. Those modern scholars most attuned to the social formation and historical specificity of Blake's work, particularly Jacob Bronowski and David Erdman, have noted that by 1800 Blake's imaginative religiosity brought with it a certain degree of political quietism that was in part necessitated by the conservative nationalism dominating social and political discourse in England.

BLAKE'S PUBLIC ART

As noted earlier, Blake's 1809 exhibition was to have signalled his galvanizing re-emergence from the obscurity of his early career. Although Blake's "Advertisement" and *Descriptive Catalogue* for the exhibition often evince a dutiful patriotism in his solicitous claims for public attention, Blake does not shy away from his more typically invective commentary on the suffering of art in "a corrupt state of Society." He referred to the works he exhibited as "Experiment Pictures," primarily because they were executed in tempera on canvas, a new medium for Blake that he also described as "fresco painting" and that he saw as a pointed challenge to what in his estimation was the commercial and esthetic vanity of oil painting (unfortunately, the surviving tempera pictures from the exhibition have themselves badly deteriorated). These experiment pictures were meant to serve as mere models for gargantuan frescos that Blake hoped would be commissioned by the government for the adornment of national monuments. Representative of these delusively ambitious frescos was the

97 first picture listed in the catalog: *The spiritual form of Nelson guiding Leviathan, in whose wreathings are infolded the Nations of the Earth.* Admiral Lord Nelson, the British naval commander who died at the Battle of Trafalgar in 1805, was certainly a topical and popular hero in the public consciousness during the Napoleonic Wars, and contemporary artists were quick to capitalize on the nationalist cultural craze for commemorative military monuments, most of which were endlessly planned and debated by governmental committees and in the art press, but were rarely ever built. Even before the death of Nelson, John Flaxman had proposed plans for an allegorical naval monument with an imposing statue of Britannia to be set within a sepulchral precinct on Greenwich Hill, dedicated to public commemoration in honor of England's naval triumphs against the French. The designs for

98 this antique-inspired, megalomaniacal project—characteristic of Flaxman's severe and reductive graphic style that would prove so influential among European artists—were engraved

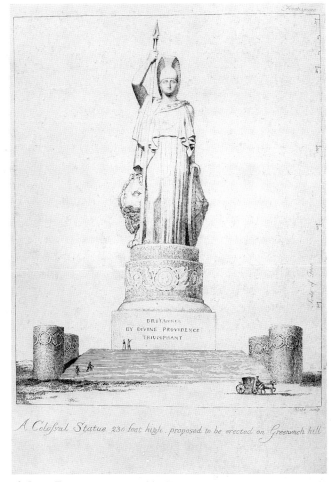

98 JOHN FLAXMAN, engraved by WILLIAM BLAKE "Design for the Monument to British Naval Victories with a Statue of Britannia," 1799. 8¼ × 5¾ (21 × 14.6)

by Blake in 1799. Flaxman's scheme reflected the Neoclassical obsession with designing vast, memorializing public spaces where spectacles of national power could be celebrated in a modernized Greco-Roman ambience. Blake's own dream, ten years later, of having his modestly scaled pictures monumentalized and venerated as a public art of national import conformed to the prevalent cultural politics that called for the artistic aggrandizement of British contemporary history. Blake was hardly insensitive, however, to the compromising logic that would render the purposefulness of art entirely subservient to nationalist and imperialist causes; as he wrote in 1810, "Let us teach Buonaparte, & whomsoever it may concern, That it is not the Arts that follow and attend upon Empire, but Empire that attends upon & follows the Arts." In another draft of this statement, Blake would substitute "Englishmen" for "Buonaparte."

Blake's divided attitude toward the strained allegiance between art and empire is apparent in his allegorical interpretation of Nelson. As befits his "spiritual form," he is clothed only in a loincloth and a halo, the mortal hero now deified within a mandala-like pattern of highly abstracted rays of light. The naval warrior's aloof and calm expression, and the almost automatistic ease with which he lassoes the interminable sea monster that encircles him, makes him seem divinely oblivious to the futile struggle of the women and men trapped within the serpentine coils (one figure with sword in hand, just beneath Nelson's left arm, is already caught in the dragon's maw). As a terrifying image of dominion and conquest, the picture is especially attentive to these dread casualties ("the Nations of the Earth") that have fallen under Nelson's imperial sway. At the base of the composition, the figure of an expired slave is prominently shown, liberated from the stranglehold of the sea serpent, but only to be left as a lifeless castaway on the narrow shore of freedom. The leviathan referred to in the picture's title alludes both to the biblical leviathan, a monstrous opponent to divine will, as well as to Thomas Hobbes's famous political trope for the corrupting power of the ship of state. As Nelson's beastly agent of war, the leviathan has, at very best, ambivalent connotations for the maritime supremacy of Britain. Blake's Nelson harks back to his revolutionary prototype, the nude Albion; but in this later picture, the physical freedom of the human form is not so certain, the body of Nelson appearing much less taut and energetic, having now become more encumbered and restricted by its supernatural task. One must wonder whether Nelson guides the leviathan, or whether the sea creature guides, and perhaps even enslaves, the transcendent hero.

The artistic traits of Blake's picture—its claustrophobic anti-illusionism, its denatured and contorted treatment of the human body, and its overall fascination with heroic supernaturalism and ritualized violence—connect his work with the more innovative currents in recent English historical and poetical paintings. Blake saw his art as belonging to an abortive tradition of progressive history painting that, in his opinion, had already fallen victim to the purely commercial vicissitudes afflicting art patronage in England.

BLAKE AND CONTEMPORARY ENGLISH ART OF THE SUBLIME

Foremost among Blake's contemporary artistic heroes was the Irish-born painter James Barry (1741–1806). Barry had received early encouragement and support from such prominent and influential men as the Conservative statesman and esthetician Edmund Burke and the founding President and leading portraitist of the Royal Academy, Sir Joshua Reynolds. Although Barry rose quickly through the ranks of the Academy to become its Professor of Painting in 1782, he carried on a rancorous crusade against the Royal Academy's,

and by extension English society's and the state's, failure to promote "public taste" for history painting; in his view, private interest and social and political factionalism had destroyed the civic ideal of a truly public art representative of egalitarian values (he had even turned down an invitation to become America's national history painter). His hectoring criticism of the Royal Academy led to his expulsion in 1799. Although he found other institutional sponsorship that allowed him to pursue his ambitious painting cycles of historical and allegorical subjects, Barry's career ended in poverty and disillusionment, making him the unquestioned martyr to the lost cause of history painting in England—so much so that Blake planned to write "Barry, an Epic Poem."

In his effort to promote a distinctly national school of history painting, Barry, along with other artists of the period, often turned to Shakespearean and Miltonic themes for inspiration. His *King Lear Weeping Over the Body of Cordelia* 101 (1786–7) depicts a Shakespearean scene that was significantly censored and rewritten for late eighteenth-century stagings of the play: the grim pathos of Lear cradling the body of his only faithful daughter, with the corpses of the other conspiratorial daughters close at hand, was deemed too transgressive for Georgian theatre audiences. For Barry, the deranged fury of an aged king cursing over his internecine family implied political questions about the stability of monarchical power and its potentially irrational conflict of private and public passions. Lear and his male entourage of mourners dominate the foreground stage of Barry's picture, the monumental figures divulging a profound range of emotional reactions to the spectacle of their despairing king. Lear himself, with his windswept mane of white hair and prophet-like grandiloquence (critics of the day complained of his Semitic mien), would provide a figurative and psychological model for many of Blake's looming patriarchs and domineering gods, as well as for later artistic renditions of the Gaelic bard Ossian and his mythic heroes that were so popular among painters from David's *atelier*. The landscape background of Barry's composition, offering visual escape from the massive array of *dramatis personae,* is most notable for its inclusion of primitive Druid trilithon temples, evoking the ancient history and religious civilization of Britain. Barry's *Lear* was part of a commercial enterprise known as "the Shakespeare Gallery," a project underwritten by the London publisher and alderman John Boydell who had commissioned most of Britain's leading artists to paint Shakespearean episodes for public exhibition, the pictures later to be engraved in large stocks for public sale. Since history painting was not receiving direct encouragement through royal patronage, these speculative financial ventures submitted the future of British narrative art to the uncertain and variable forces of the marketplace.

Barry was also an accomplished printmaker whose

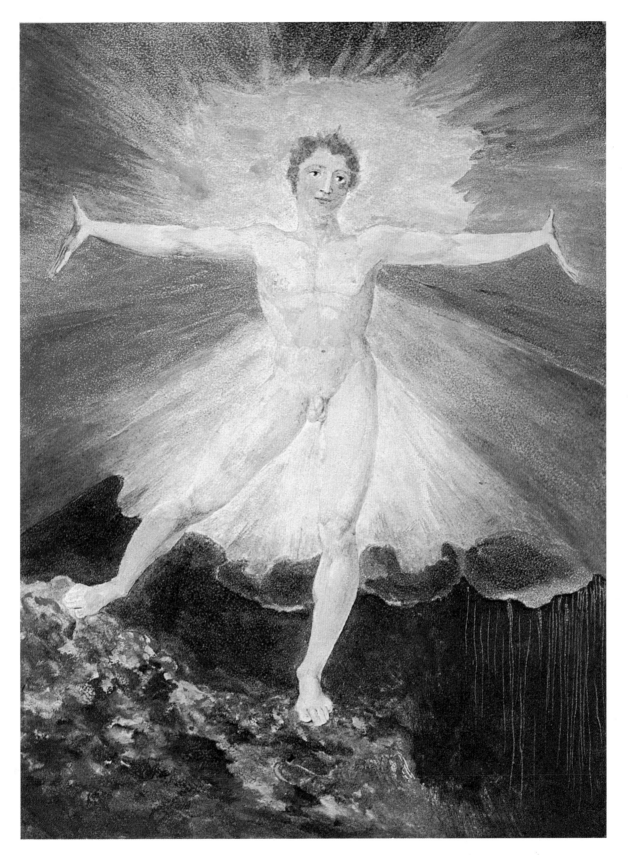

99 **WILLIAM BLAKE** *Albion Rose* ca. 1794–5. $10\frac{5}{8} \times 7\frac{7}{8}$ (27.1 × 20.1)

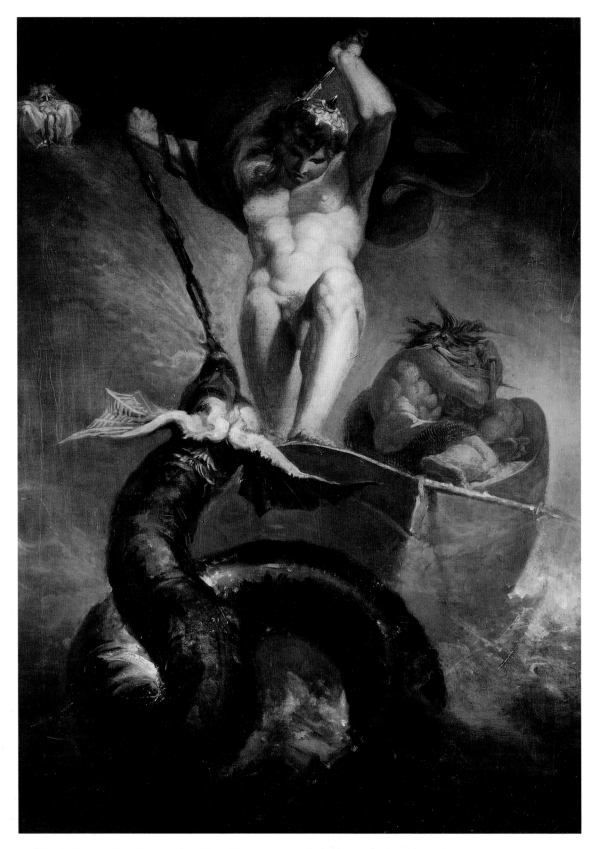

100 HENRY FUSELI *Thor Battering the Midguard Serpent* 1790. 51½ × 36¼ (131 × 92)

illustrations of Miltonic subjects demonstrated, often better than in his paintings, a heroic figure style that had earned Blake's admiration. Barry's etching *Satan and His Legions Hurling Defiance Toward Heaven* (ca. 1792) was most emphatically a visual essay in the sublime. Edmund Burke had formulated the esthetics of the sublime in a treatise from his student days, *A Philosophical Inquiry into . . . the Sublime and the Beautiful* (1756). Here the sublime was defined as a pleasure of terror, esthetically mediated of course, in which the imagination revels in thoughts of fear, privation, and subjection, all the while identifying with obverse conditions—states of sensory and psychological overstimulation and illusions of omnipotent power. For Burke, Milton's *Paradise Lost* was the creative work that exemplified the sublime, particularly the passage in which the fallen Satan rises out of the fiery lake of Chaos to curse the heavens—the precise episode illustrated in Barry's etching. In fact, Barry's composition responds to Burke's stipulation in the *Inquiry* that only poetic, not pictorial, images could most compellingly inspire these sublime affections. Barry's Satan is seen rousing his warriors and directing their rebellious attention upward to the celestial realm, the eerie light from the infernal depths below creating rich patterns of chiaroscuro that accentuate the vigorous modeling of the figures. The visuality of the sublime is conceived by Barry as a masculine realm of physical strength in which the swelling and extended bodies of the fallen angels, congested along the precipice of a flaming abyss, strain to break through the very boundaries of the image. The insurgent theme of the Miltonic illustration operates on many levels: the pictorial assault on the poetic sublime, the radical Barry challenging the conservative Burke (and the entire artistic and social establishment for that matter), and the suppressed energies of political revolt finding an irresistible embodiment in the dark heroism of Satan. Burke himself had originally associated this scene from Milton with, in his words, "the ruin of monarchs, and the revolutions of kingdoms."

Along with Barry, it was the Swiss-born painter Henry Fuseli (1741–1825) with whom Blake most closely identified as a fellow, underappreciated artist whose excessive imagination seemed to contest, while also appealing to, the mercantile art culture of late eighteenth-century London. Fuseli's intellectual background was remarkable: he emerged from the literary and philosophical circles of the Sturm und Drang (storm and stress) movement in Zurich and Berlin; by 1770, he had translated Winckelmann's art historical writings on Greek art into English, consulted with and written a critical commentary on Rousseau and his moral philosophy, and finally turned to painting as a professional pursuit on the encouraging advice of Reynolds. After an eight-year Roman sojourn, Fuseli settled in England in 1780 where he estab-

lished his dual career as a painter of occult, mythological, and poetical subjects and also as a prolific literary reviewer. Among his closest colleagues could be counted the influential theorist of physiognomic science J. C. Lavater, the Liverpool art collector, banker, and abolitionist William Roscoe, and the revolutionary feminist and political activist Mary Wollstonecraft (she had reportedly become infatuated with Fuseli and wanted him to join her on a tour of Republican France in 1792).

At once admired and scorned for his cynical libertinism—he was renowned for his colorful blaspheming and overbearing manner—Fuseli enjoyed testing the limits of artistic decorum. His pictures consistently fix upon the human figure *in extremis*, as seen in the second version of his most celebrated and scandalous painting, *The Nightmare* (1790), a work that visualized the disturbing torments of a sleeping woman. Drawing from traditional folklore about demonic visitations and the supernatural carnality of dreaming, as well as from eighteenth-century medical theories on the psychophysiology of human sleep, Fuseli depicted the nocturnal intrusion of a grimacing incubus and his electrified, spectral nightmare into a woman's bedchamber. The dreaming woman is shown supine and vulnerable, surmounted by the peculiarly fetal-looking fiend that is meant to serve as a vengeful personification of *her* desires; the psychical disables the somatic, resulting in the occult rape fantasy of the female protagonist. It is of course more accurate to say that the fantasy is Fuseli's, the dreaming delirium of this implied sexual violation posited as internal to the feminine so as to mask the demonic projection of masculine desire: that is, under Fuseli's stage direction, the dreaming woman victimizes herself. As though part of a Sadean reenactment of a spooky Nativity scene, the virginal victim gives birth to the gnomic offspring of her libidinal impulses, the visual displacement of suggestive sexual imagery discernible in the vaginal parting of the curtains and in the phallic end of the bolster that supports the dreamer's body (the upper torso revealingly thrown back in poised abandon). Although the first version of *The Nightmare* (1781) may have employed this imagery of supernatural persecution in veiled allusion to the diminished status of Britannia after the war with the American colonies and in the wake of the civil disorder of the Gordon Riots, Fuseli maintained a lifelong obsession with the feminine realm of dreams, and with what he referred to as (paraphrasing Shakespeare) "the undistinguished space of women's will." His famous aphoristic remark about having to endure "the epoch of viragos" betrays obvious misgivings about the progressive advocacy for women's rights in the Wollstonecraft circle. In his later private, graphic erotica from about 1810, however, Fuseli was prone to inverting the terms of sexual domination, the scenario in these drawings often involving a

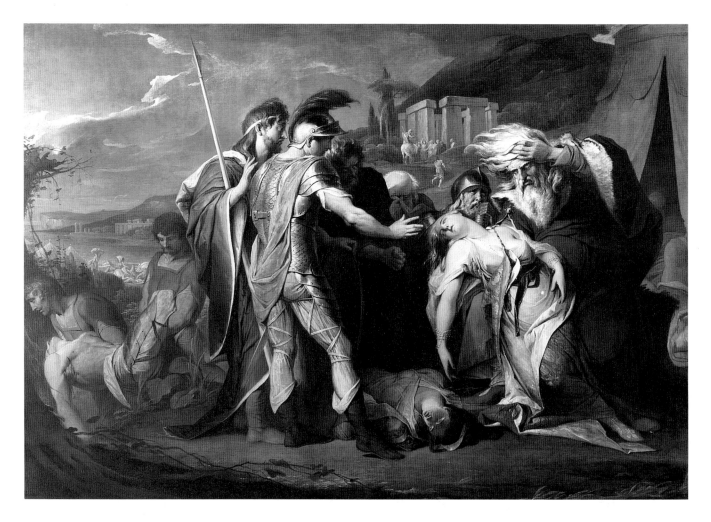

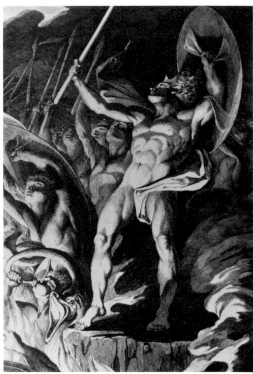

101 **JAMES BARRY** *King Lear Weeping Over the Body of Cordelia*
1786–7. 8'10 × 12'½ (269 × 367)

102 **JAMES BARRY** *Satan and His Legions Hurling Defiance Toward the Vault of Heaven* ca. 1792–4. 29⅞ × 19⅞ (74.6 × 50.4)

restrained Promethean male being sexually suffocated by a muscular grouping of ornately coiffed courtesans. The feminine is seemingly liberated from the oppressive breeding of dreams, but only to minister to the masochistic fantasies of the artist. 104

Fuseli's credo that "the forms of virtue are erect, the forms of pleasure undulate," can properly be taken as the guiding principle behind his more heroic species of history paintings. Blake's image of Nelson subduing a serpentine monster is in many ways a hieratic reworking of the conquering male nude that dominated Fuseli's forceful Diploma painting for the Royal Academy, *Thor Battering the Midguard Serpent* (1790). 100 Along with subjects from Milton and Shakespeare, Fuseli favored epic myths from Nordic legend and the *Nibelungenlied*—this new emphasis on the Northern European mythic canon in accordance with current speculations on the cultural geography of nations espoused by the German philosopher of history J. G. Herder (who had praised Fuseli in 1774 as "a genius like a mountain torrent"). Inspired by the strained and expressive exaggeration of human anatomies in late Michelangelo and in Giulio Romano, Fuseli's figure of Thor is most assuredly a concerted study in "erect virtue." With the masculine body shown flexed and towering (Fuseli was fond of low vantage points and drastic foreshortening), Thor remains highly sexualized in his supreme moment of physical exertion. His genitals at the center of the picture are barely kept from view by the shadow of his projecting leg; but this pronounced swathe of shadow also connects his sex to the bloody head of the sea serpent that he has just snared from out of the misty waters. The subsidiary figures of the massive,

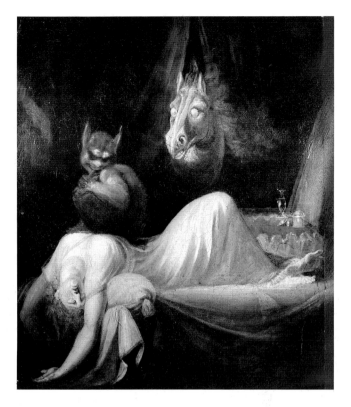

103 HENRY FUSELI *The Nightmare* 1790. 30 × 24⅞ (76 × 63)

104 HENRY FUSELI *Symplegma (Man and Three Women)* ca. 1810. 7½ × 9⅝ (18.9 × 24.5)

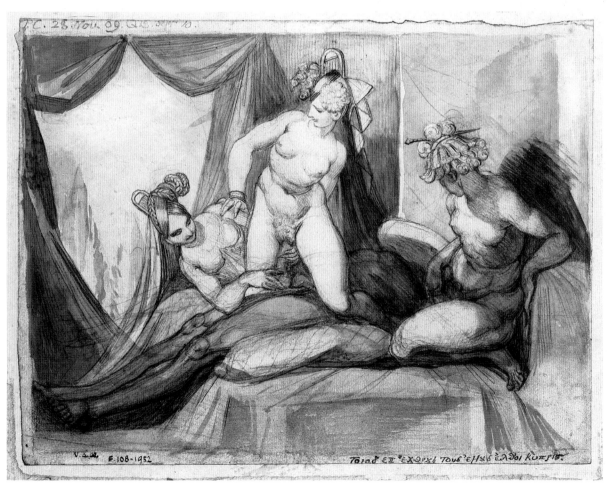

aged boatman, shrinking away in fear, and the ancient god Wotan observing the struggle from on high—perched like a more feeble version of the incubus in the upper corner of the picture—only serve to swell the superhuman scale and fearless heroism of Thor. As a youthful deity with power over the elements of nature and the cultivation of land, Thor held more plebeian and popular associations than most of the more noble and venerable gods from the Eddic pantheon. In characterizing the revolutionary tremblings of Europe in late 1789, Fuseli almost seemed to be anticipating the visual impact of his figure of Thor, as when he wrote of "an age pregnant with the most gigantic efforts of character . . . whilst an unexampled vigour seems to vibrate from pole to pole through the human mind, and to challenge the general sympathy."

But Fuseli was generally reluctant to grant any direct social or moral function to modern English art, his own or anyone else's. In his role as Professor of Painting at the Royal Academy (a position he assumed in 1801), he asserted, with fierce candor, that the very existence of academies and public exhibitions "were and are symptoms of Art in distress and . . . the decay of Taste." His epic male figures exploding out of shadowy voids were insistent reminders of the absence of heroic grandeur in contemporary society and culture: futile challenges to what Fuseli derided as "that Micromania which infects the public taste" (by which he meant the diffuse esthetic interests of private patronage and commercial collecting habits that militated against the creation of "great works"). The Romantic poet and philosopher Samual Taylor Coleridge came closest to recognizing the contradictory sexual politics and cultural pessimism of Fuseli's own great works when he judged them finally to be an art of "vigorous impotence."

PROPHECY AND PREHISTORY

97 Blake's more utopian effort to redeem contemporary society through his eternalizing icons of modern history like *Spiritual Form of Nelson* ironically brought his art in close alliance with that most transient and unelevated type of visual culture, political caricature. Although Blake once chastised a prospective patron's artistic taste by remarking "I can perceive that your Eye is perverted by Caricature prints," the overwrought conjunction of modern history and cosmic allegory in many of his own pictures from the 1809 exhibition was not dissimilar to the teeming fantastical imagery produced during this period by the brilliant caricaturist James Gillray (1757–1815). Gillray received instruction in drawing at the Royal Academy and was well versed in both Old Master and contemporary art. By the 1790's he had become a prolific caricaturist for the

Tory (conservative, royalist) Party, even though the vehemently anti-Jacobin themes of his prints did not reflect his own political beliefs. While Blake's 1809 exhibition was dismissed by a reviewer from the liberal journal *The Examiner* as the work of "an unfortunate lunatic," it was Gillray who actually spent his final years debilitated by insanity. In his crowded and complex etching *Phaeton Alarm'd!* (1808), 105 Gillray casts the Tory spokesman and propagandist George Canning as the new Phaeton, the "Sun of Anti-Jacobinism," coursing through the heavens above the war-torn earth (aflame and surmounted by a tiny Napoleon), his path beset by astrological personifications of his political opponents. The mythical, God-like defender of the Tory government is challenged by the monstrous clutter of Whig parliamentarians whose cartoonish portraits remain distinctly legible, even through their exceedingly grotesque armature. Blake's Nelson could easily claim Gillray's Canning as a fellow luminary from the nationalist firmament (the recently deceased Pitt, who is portrayed as the Tory father figure of Apollo in the lower left shadow of the Gillray print, was also given his "Spiritual Form" by Blake in a companion picture to the Nelson painting for the 1809 exhibit). Gillray's parodic and allusive appropriation of myth and allegory was an obvious strike against the pretense and hyperbole of history painting.

In mythologizing the daily politics of England, Gillray's prints often explicitly lampooned the imagery of high art at the Royal Academy, showing that the moral and esthetic exclusivity of history painting could be brought unceremoniously to the print culture of the streets. His *Phaeton Alarm'd!* knowingly refashioned the apocalyptic uproar of Benjamin West's *The Destruction of the Old Beast and False* 106 *Prophet*, exhibited at the Royal Academy in 1804. West's painting belonged to an official commission for a series of religious history paintings that were to decorate the royal chapel at Windsor Castle. The ambitious project went awry when West, an American expatriate who succeeded Reynolds as President of the Royal Academy, fell out of royal favor, presumably because George III suspected him, and politicized factions within the Academy, of "democratick" sympathies. Many of the works from this planned cycle illustrated passages from the Book of Revelation, a point of contention with the King who criticized West's propensity for what he called "Bedlamite scenes from Revelations" (itself a revealing comment in the light of George III's own bouts of madness). West's apocalyptic spectacles nevertheless proved extremely popular with exhibition audiences in both London and Paris. In the religious painting cribbed by Gillray, West practised his own more typical style of academic eclecticism, the triumphant stampede of equestrian Christian warriors treated in gleaming, Neoclassical profile, while the vanquished armies of the false prophets and the lionheaded demonic adversaries

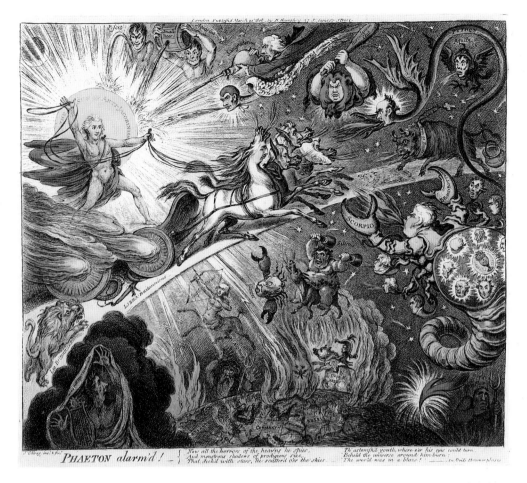

105 JAMES GILLRAY *Phaeton Alarm'd!* 1808. 13 × 14½ (33 × 36.8)

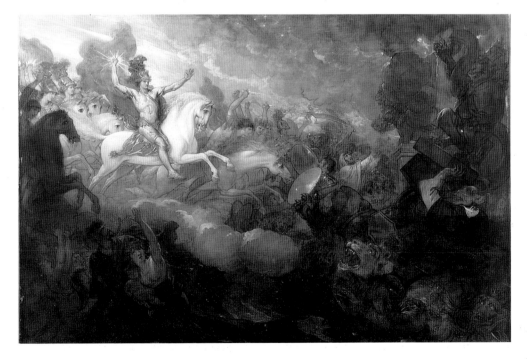

106 BENJAMIN WEST *The Destruction of the Old Beast and False Prophet* 1804. 39 × 56½ (99 × 143.5)

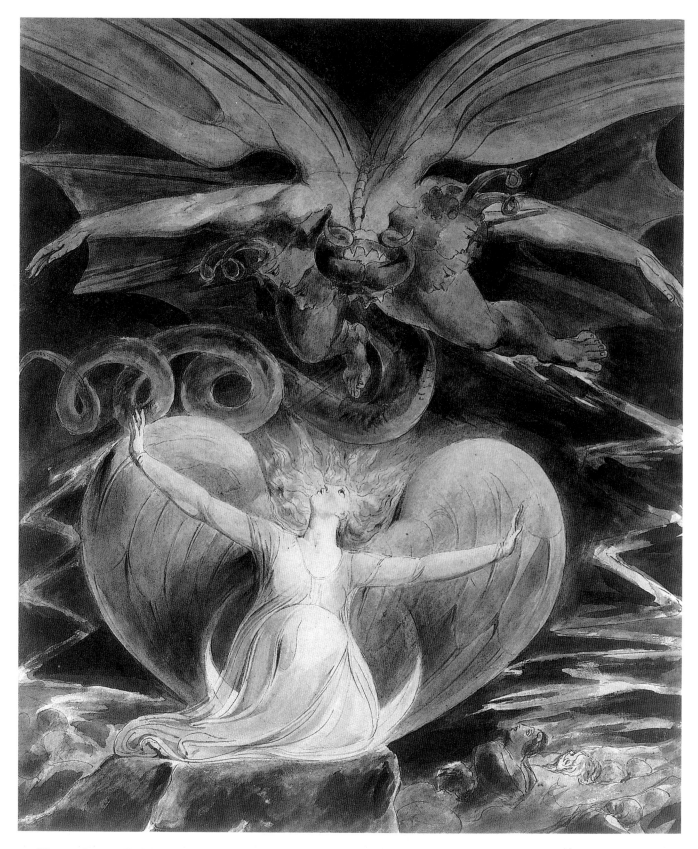

107 WILLIAM BLAKE *The Great Red Dragon and the Woman Clothed With the Sun: "The Devil is Come Down"* ca. 1805. $16\frac{1}{8} \times 13\frac{1}{4}$ (40.8 × 33.7)

of God, seen retreating into tenebrous chasms and windswept clouds, are indebted to Rubens and the trappings of Baroque allegory. The appeal of West's pictures of this kind lay not in their learned artistic accomplishment, but rather in their contemporary historical and millennarian overtones: with the resumption of the Napoleonic Wars after the Treaty of Amiens and with the recent turning of the century, such apocalyptic paintings were redolent of widespread fears for the future survival of England and the fate of Europe.

Despite the dichotomy between the artistic careers of West (the professionally prominent academicist) and Blake (the insular engraver and poet), their art shared in the nationalist, religious fervor of these early years of the nineteenth century. While West was exhibiting his epic *machines* of biblical destruction, Blake was also illustrating the Book of Revelation for a group of scriptural paintings that had been commissioned by his only steady patron, Thomas Butts (a government munitions clerk whose politics and occupation were strikingly antithetical to those of Blake). Eschewing the yards of canvas and cast of thousands required by West, Blake's apocalyptic designs have a figurative conciseness, gestural eloquence, and compositional equipoise that allowed him to translate the religious mystery and copious allegory of the Book of Revelation into terse visual epigrams. These

107   qualities are most evident in his stunning watercolor *The Great Red Dragon and the Woman Clothed with the Sun: "The Devil is Come Down"* (ca. 1805), a work that could also be

103   described as an eschatological refrain of Fuseli's *Nightmare*. Roughly contemporary with Blake's spiritualization of Nelson for the 1809 exhibition was West's own project for a

108   monumental painting of *The Apotheosis of Nelson* (1807), a design replete with architectural and sculptural surrounds that were to have made the entire ensemble into a secular altarpiece commemorating British maritime power and the religion of nationhood. Although West was most renowned for his grand-manner history paintings of contemporary events, especially death scenes of prominent military and political figures, here he invents a composite allegory in which Nelson's draped corpse is being conveyed heavenward by gigantic and mournful figures of Neptune, Britannia, and Victory. Ponderous, erudite, and reverential, the painting may be seen as the more official version of the visionary national artform that Blake was trying to expand upon with the 1809 exhibition.

Blake sought to legitimize the conception of his own works by comparing them not to the acclaimed, patriotic art of West but to, as he wrote in his *Descriptive Catalogue*, "compositions of a mythological cast, similar to those Apotheoses of Persian, Hindoo, and Egyptian Antiquity." Inspired by late eighteenth-century mythographic and antiquarian speculations on the origins of art and religion, Blake asserted that through

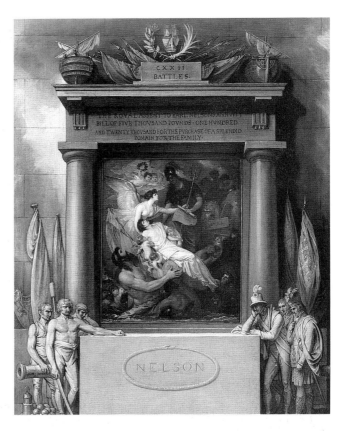

108 BENJAMIN WEST, design for *The Apotheosis of Nelson* 1807. 39½ × 29 (100.3 × 73.8)

his own mental travels ("taken in vision") he had seen the lost sacred art of the Jews that had adorned the palaces, temples, and city walls of the ancient world, and that these originary instances of public monumental sculpture and painting formed the basis for all subsequent artistic traditions, whether Greco-Roman or "Asiatick." The auratic and archaizing character of *Spiritual Form of Nelson* was indebted to   97
eighteenth-century engravings of Indian antiquities, as seen, for example, in the illustrations of relief sculptures from the   109
Shiva Temple at Elephanta that appeared in Baron d'Hancarville's comparative study of ancient art and myth, *Researches on the Origin, Spirit, and Progress of the Arts of Greece; . . . on the Antique Monuments of India, Persia, the Rest of Asia, and Egypt* (1785), a study which purported to reveal the primacy of sexual and occult symbolism to the cultural and mythic forms of earliest civilizations worldwide. Blake's catalog commentary also spoke of reviving mythological and recondite meaning in modern art and posited a syncretic theory of artistic tradition encompassing "the finest specimens of Ancient Sculpture and Painting and Architecture, Gothic, Grecian, Hindoo, and Egyptian." In preparing his later engraving (ca. 1820) of the *Laocoön*, Blake summarily rewrote   110
the history of art by reattributing the Hellenistic sculpture—a

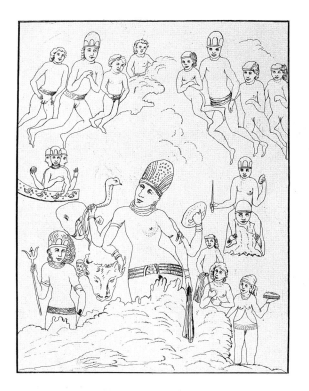

109 BARON D'HANCARVILLE *Researches on the Origin, Spirit and Progress of the Arts of Greece; . . . on the Antique Monuments of India, Persia, the Rest of Asia and Egypt* volume 1, plate 10, 1785. 6 × 8 (15 × 20.5)

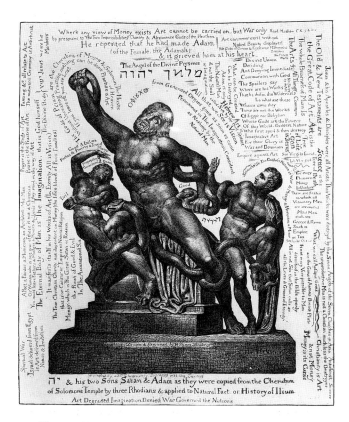

110 WILLIAM BLAKE *Laocoön* ca. 1820. 10⅞ × 8⅜ (25.2 × 21.2)

paradigmatic artwork that had been central to the German Enlightenment esthetic debates of Winckelmann and Lessing—as a copy of a lost original from the Temple of Solomon. With its array of inscribed mottos lamenting the corruption of art by war and money, this reproductive print of a fundamental piece of ancient statuary is transformed into a didactic proclamation about the divine origins and modern plight of art. Although Blake saw the panoply of ancient world art as unified by "a spiritual agency," it was one that remained tied to a Judeo-Christian origin. The antiquarian fantasy of incorporating all of world culture within a renewed English art of national grandeur cannot be divorced from the imperialist fantasy that is the subject of Blake's picture—the transfigured Nelson (culled from both Shiva and *Laocoön*, construed as both protective demi-god of Albion and militaristic Antichrist) enfolding the nations of the earth within its primordial serpent.

Mythic accounts of national origins and exotic dreams of colonial encounters were much in evidence at Blake's 1809 exhibition. Paintings (now lost) of "savage girls" aboard a missionary vessel and of the Sanskrit scholar Charles Wilkins among Indian Brahmins could be seen along with *The Ancient Britons*, a picture whose catalog entry included Blake's account of Druidic and Arthurian legend given as proof that Albion and the English nation had originally descended from the lost continent of Atlantis and from the lost tribe of Israel. The national identity of Blake's England could only be redeemed by virtue of its visionary prehistory and its colonizing future—the more conjectural, global, and syncretic, the better. Thus, while scorning the veristic and documentary demands of contemporary history painting, Blake would argue that "the history of all times and places is nothing else but improbabilities and impossibilities." Prefiguring the dilemma surrounding later manifestations of primitivism and mysticism in nineteenth-century art, Blake's work was at once critical of and constituted by its own historical experience, announcing itself as both powerless and transcendent, victimized and prophetic.

Writing a few months before his death, Blake acknowledged his own inability, or rather unwillingness, to participate fully in the creation of a nationalist culture. He commented yet again on the longstanding opposition of "Englishmen" to his standard of "Republican Art," an opposition that was not in the least overcome by the nationalist strains of his 1809 exhibition. Intent on disassociating himself from any illusion of social and cultural unanimity within England and from the generic defining of its national identity, Blake looked back over his lifetime and concluded: "since the French Revolution Englishmen are all Intermeasurable One by Another, Certainly a happy state of Agreement to which I for One do not Agree."

· 5 ·

NATURE HISTORICIZED: CONSTABLE, TURNER, AND ROMANTIC LANDSCAPE PAINTING

BRIAN LUKACHER

LANDSCAPE INSTINCTS AND THE PICTURESQUE

"THERE DOES NOT EXIST, AS FAR AS I KNOW, IN THE world a single example of a good historical picture; . . . the production of it is a task which the closing nineteenth century may propose to itself." This comment by John Ruskin, from the third volume of his treatise *Modern Painters* (1856), might easily be mistaken as being in the spirit of a lament. But the failure of history painting, and the dim possibility of its successful revival in the remaining decades of the century, was not an issue of overriding concern for Ruskin. As the most prolific and profound commentator on art and society during the Victorian epoch, Ruskin was both identifying and facilitating the eclipse of historical painting by landscape painting, in effect signaling one of the more important transformations in nineteenth-century artistic practise. His monumental *Modern Painters,* whose five volumes spanned 1843 to 1860, was devoted to the study of what its author called "the landscape instinct," an instinct that Ruskin justifiably believed had come to prevail over modern cultural life and that had determined much of the character of the Romantic imagination earlier in the century, whether in literature or painting.

Although the raison d'être for *Modern Painters* was to put forth a passionate defense of the lifework of England's leading and most controversial landscape artist, J. M. W. Turner, the scope of Ruskin's study eventually encompassed not only an entire history of European landscape art but also an inquiry into the scientific and spiritual conditions of the human perception of nature, and of the primary interrelationship between natural environment and social development. Ruskin took surprisingly little solace in his assertion that human sensitivity to landscape had reached its apogee in the nineteenth century. The predominance of this landscape instinct was to him symptomatic of the current degeneration of humanity, of what he described in his chapters "Of Modern Landscape" and "The Moral of Landscape" as "the present crisis of civilization." Responsible for the making of this crisis were Ruskin's *bêtes noires* of modern society: faithlessness bred by the scientific objectification of nature; untoward faith in the redemptive promise of technology and utilitarian reform; and moral insensibility brought on by excessive, material self-interest in an industrializing world. With space and time vanquished by such modern inventions as the railroad and the telegraph, the refuge humanity needed to find in the natural world was itself no longer guaranteed. In the nineteenth-century search for, and seeming conquest of, the landscape, Ruskin detected, in his words, "the elements of progress and decline being strangely mingled in the modern mind." Although his own merging of social criticism and landscape esthetics is frequently qualified as being an anxiously Victorian misreading of Romanticism, Ruskin recognized that the Romantic experience of nature (the landscape encounter as a presentiment for spiritual and psychological reflection) also had an inescapably social dimension, one in which the Romantic landscape could be revealed as an ideologically contested site of material progress and historical struggle.

In English art criticism, the national preference for landscape painting over history painting had been remarked upon well before the time of Ruskin's *Modern Painters.* Writing in 1807, an anonymous critic for *The Literary Panorama* applauded the emergent, native taste for landscape art, but in doing so, also felt compelled to make some distinctions based on the academic hierarchy of the genres: "The landscape scenery of our island is distinguished by its own features, and these afford scope for the sublimest efforts of art. History Painting has not been the *forte* of this country. It is a branch of art not suddenly brought to perfection. Our artists seldom allow due time to their works; they seldom ripen them by perseverence and study. What their mental conceptions suggest they execute instantly; but instant execution is no friend to historical excellence." By inference, this writer argues that the genre of landscape painting was more conducive to the capricious, instantaneous habits of English artists, habits which were themselves due in part to the absence of an established academic tradition and to the commercial vagaries of artistic taste (both of these factors were often cited by art critics of the day as the chief inhibitions to the British cultivation of history painting). Landscape painting accommodated the impulsive mental freedom that is here deemed characteristic of artistic traits in England, while also allowing the country's painters to perform a public service by displaying the indigenous esthetic wealth of the national scenery.

Although this unsigned critic spoke of the English recovery of nature in terms of "the sublimest efforts of art," the most popular terminology for the esthetic claims of landscape at this time revolved around the notion of the *picturesque*. Made fashionable during the late eighteenth century by the published travelogs of the Reverend William Gilpin, the picturesque esthetic encouraged discerning tourists to evaluate and classify the scenic qualities of topographic locales according to pictorial modes of landscape painting. English scenery could be exoticized (and acculturated) in the eye and mind of the picturesque tourist by virtue of its passing resemblance to the seventeenth-century landscape art of Claude Lorrain and Salvator Rosa, the picturesque imagination often seeking to reconcile the contrasting styles and moods of these Italianate models (the pastoral serenity of the former with the rugged violence of the latter). The tourist well versed in the playful formalism and classifying criteria of the picturesque could take visual possession of a prospect and thereby entertain an illusory dominion over nature: the land transformed into a landscape through the refining and all-encompassing act of perception. As Gilpin advised his readers, "the province of the picturesque eye is to survey nature; not to anatomize matter. It throws its glances around in a broad-cast stile. It comprehends an extensive tract at each grand sweep."

From its initial project of cultivating the visual semantics of nature-seeking tourists (both from the landed gentry and the burgeoning middle classes), the picturesque esthetic soon became the subject of tireless polemical debate among art theorists, associationist philosophers, and landscape designers. With the Napoleonic Wars, the English countryside became the locus of conflicting interests: on the one hand, there was an economic imperative for increasing agricultural yield through accelerated enclosure of common land and scientific agrarian reform, and on the other, a cultural imperative for promoting rural England as a picturesque landscape park of ever varying visual pleasure, particularly so since travel to the Continent had to be drastically curtailed during wartime. Gilpin and other landscape estheticians insisted that the picturesque vista had to be kept free of scenes of rural labor and industrial production—those very sources of economic growth and national strength on which England depended. The resistance of picturesque sightseeing and landscape design to the agrarian demands and social relations of the countryside was itself the subject of satirical comment, as witnessed in the novels of Jane Austen and the caricatures of Thomas Rowlandson. As late as 1834, the art critic Anna Jameson recounted her somewhat uncomfortable experience of trying to elicit the esthetic interests of "an independent English yeoman"; after describing the picturesque beauty of the surrounding landscape, her admiring remarks about the scenery met with this riposte from the farmer, "'*Picturesque!*' he repeated with some contempt; 'I don't know what *you* call picturesque, but *I* say, give me a soil, that when you turn it up, you have something for your pains.'" Judging from this anecdote, the cult of the picturesque, of such popular appeal precisely because it appeared to democratize the elitist cultural pretensions of landscape appreciation, could not overcome the social divisions of class, profession, and gender.

The picturesque, whether touching on the formalist connoisseurship of the landscape or on the social engineering of life within the landscape, was often restrictive in its task. Treatises on the picturesque invariably employed illustrative plates to demonstrate, through contrast and comparison, its modifying esthetic principles. In Gilpin's summa *Three Essays: On Picturesque Beauty, On Picturesque Travel, and On Sketching* (1792), two landscape etchings are set opposite one another. The first shows a symmetrical, unmodulated composition, embodying the maternal, orderly protectiveness of nature that Burke had designated earlier in the century as "the beautiful." The second shows Gilpin's picturesque re-arrangement of these primary landscape features: the terrain and foliage now seen with irregular outlines and variegated surfaces, a serpentine path directing the eye through the interlocking, receding passages of the scenery, and two shadowy figures plotted in the foreground—perhaps travelers in "pursuit of the object" (to quote Gilpin)—who are in turn echoed compositionally by the paired outcropping of ruins on the distant promontory above them. Here one finds the kind of permutational interplay between the natural and the artificial that was so central to arguments about the picturesque. As the

111–1

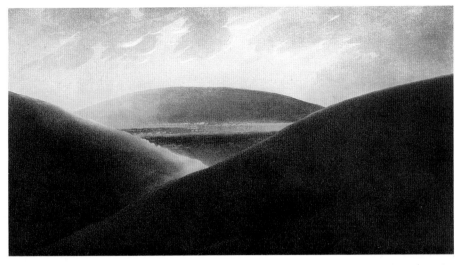

111 WILLIAM GILPIN, plate from *Three Essays: On Picturesque Beauty, On Picturesque Travel, and On Sketching* 1792. 6⅛ × 9 (15.5 × 22.5)

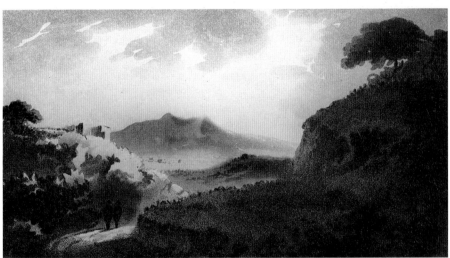

112 WILLIAM GILPIN, plate from *Three Essays: On Picturesque Beauty, On Picturesque Travel, and On Sketching* 1792. 6⅛ × 9 (15.5 × 22.5)

literary historian Martin Price has observed, "The drama of the picturesque is readily cast into the form of the energies of art wrestling with the materials of nature, or the alternative form of the genius of nature and time overcoming the upstart achievements of a fragile, but assertive art."

Within this picturesque contest between nature and art, and between land and landscape, the outward signs of social diversity were not particularly welcome. Even the most pragmatic and professionally active of picturesque landscape gardeners, Humphry Repton (1752–1818), was sometimes troubled by the unsightly impingements of rustic life in his own designs for estate parks and villages. More so than most landscape gardeners swept up by the picturesque tide, Repton attempted to reconcile the social and economic requirements of a property with its scenic potential; consequently, he spoke of "humanizing as well as animating beautiful scenery." Although his writings on the theory of landscape gardening often expressed disdain for the picturesque as a faddish weathervane of taste favored by "successful sons of

commerce," Repton's proposals for the improvement of landed estates rarely strayed far from a domesticated picturesque idiom. In preparing his garden designs for prospective clients, Repton would also utilize "before" and "after" scenes of the same landscape, his elaborate watercolor drawings equipped with flaps and overlays that would help dramatize the transformation of the view at hand. He made use of this device in the 1816 design for his own garden prospect in Hare Street, Essex. Repton amends the prosaic character of the village scene by distancing and obscuring its unseemly details. The village green, once a common for grazing livestock, is appropriated by Repton for his private garden preserve, its curving, hedged boundary replacing the rigid linearity of the fence along his property that had barely kept crippled vagrants at bay (the loitering figure in Repton's "before" improvement episode most probably identifiable as an indigent war veteran). Flowering shrubs and arboreal trestles protect the eye from the distractions of passing stagecoaches and local shopkeeping. The picturesque garden functions as a

113–14

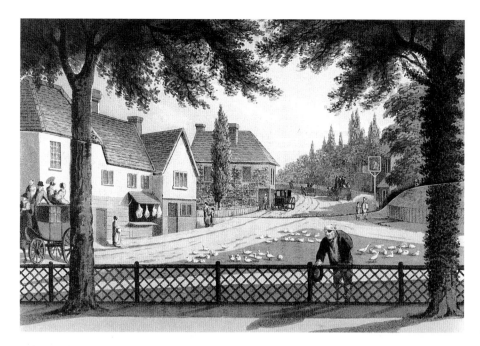

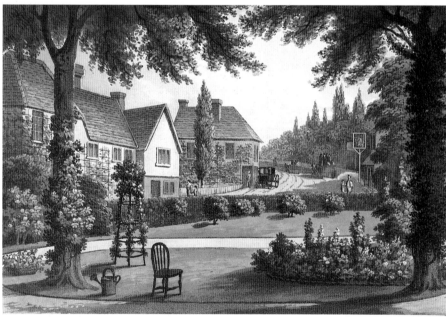

series of projecting screens that removes the social actuality of village life from view. Even after eradicating these eyesores from his garden vista (one is tempted to say, "dehumanizing" rather than "humanizing" it), Repton could still write of an affection for "the cheerful village, the high road, and that constant moving scene which I would not exchange for any of the lonely parks I have improved for others."

RUINS AND CITIES

The late eighteenth-century vogue for the picturesque also encouraged many landscape artists, amateur and professional alike, to specialize in topographic watercolor painting, a medium that lent itself to both formulaic compositional techniques and innovative experiments in landscape sketching out-of-doors. For the most advanced landscape watercolorists of this period, the tenets of the picturesque were to be quickly mastered, and just as quickly superseded, a development that is best exemplified by the work of Thomas Girtin (1775–1802). Girtin's modest career began, typically enough for the landscape artists of his generation, in architectural drafting and in the coloring of topographic engravings of Gothic antiquities and country seats. During the mid-1790's, he was employed by Dr. Thomas Monro, a physician and an

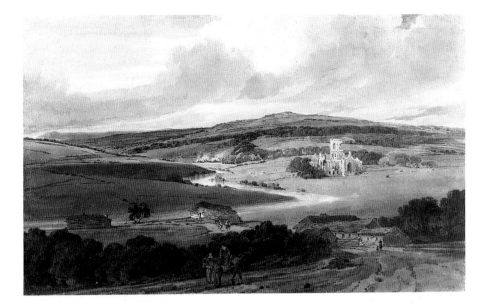

115 THOMAS GIRTIN *Kirkstall Abbey* 1800.
12 × 20 (30.5 × 50.8)

unscrupulous proprietor of lunatic asylums, who also oversaw an informal landscape drawing academy that convened in his London townhouse. In 1799, Girtin was at the center of the Sketching Society, a group of watercolor painters who pursued not only picturesque motifs culled from tours of Wales and the Lake District, but also historical landscape subjects from Ossianic legend and other poetical sources. Censured by some for his republican political sympathies and dissolute lifestyle, Girtin was widely recognized at the time of his premature death as the most promising landscape painter

115 of the English school. His watercolor of *Kirkstall Abbey* (1800) epitomizes the picturesque topography of ruins that pervaded much of the landscape imagery in the outpouring of prints and drawings during this period. Girtin's vista strands the ruined abbey in the middle distance of a predominantly umber landscape, the jagged outline of the bleached architectural structure distinguished from the undulating sweep of the valley (the ruins remain cushioned somewhat within a darker copse of trees). Picturesque devices are evident in the formal correspondence between the cloud masses and the interspersed areas of foliage, and also in the serpentine path of the river that directs the excursion of the eye through the landscape. However, Girtin's watercolor diverges from accepted notions of the picturesque in its conspicuous inclusion of the mundane and unromantic aspects of rural life: rustic laborers straggling along the muddy road in the foreground, with the cob and timber farm buildings (not conforming to the picturesque taste for quaintly ramshackle cottages) that only serve to accentuate, and even render more ironical, the faded grandeur connoted by the medieval ruins. In the distance, at the visible terminus of the river's winding, smoke is seen rising from the terrain, an indication of human labor operative within the landscape (whether it be from firing

kilns or from the burning and clearing of brush). The landscape of rural utility at first may seem at odds with the landscape of antiquarian and philosophic meditation. But this apparent incongruity is more purposeful than not—the historical remnants of Britain's national past, rife with poetical and esthetic associations for the cultivated viewer, alongside the purely external traces (figures and buildings) of the workaday demands of rural Britain. The landscape is conceived as nostalgic and retrospective, as well as unreflectively present and productive.

Girtin also applied his considerable talents as an architectural draftsman and a landscapist to a relatively novel form of early nineteenth-century visual culture—the panorama. In 1802, his "Eidometropolis," a panoramic view of the London 116 cityscape, opened to great critical acclaim. Although panoramas, dioramas, and other kinds of mechanized scenic exhibits and light shows were initially received as exclusive entertainments of fashionable society, these visual spectacles became increasingly popular within the emergent urban mass culture of the period. Panoramas were often devoted to sensational kinds of subjects: dramatic scenes of terrifying natural phenomena (volcanos, waterfalls, and similarly uncontrollable sublimities) and of exotic places connected with the British Empire and its military conquests within an expanding global arena. Through the panoramic recreation of these elemental and remote landscapes, the city could, in a sense, contain and incorporate nature within its metropolitan domain. Interfusing the procedures of both science and art, and technology and culture (thereby adumbrating the later development of photography and cinema), the panorama and related visual media also remained fixed upon the specularity of the evergrowing metropolis. The modern city and its cosmopolitan populace required a naturalized and heightened

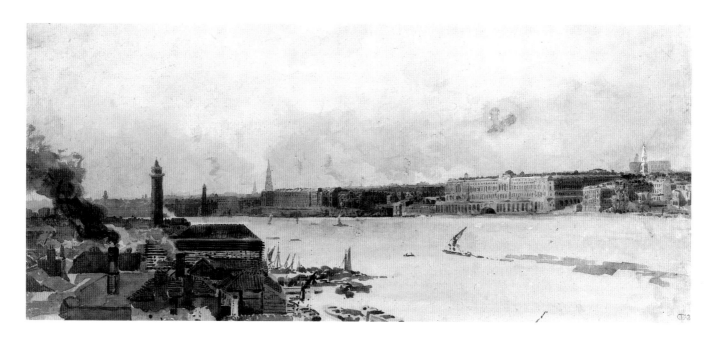

vision of itself. As the early twentieth-century philosopher and critic Walter Benjamin remarked on the widespread appeal of the panoramic urban vista (paraphrasing an earlier discussion from Marx): "The city dweller, whose political superiority over the country is expressed in many ways in the course of the [nineteenth] century, attempts to introduce the countryside into the city. In the panoramas the city dilates to become landscape."

116 The "Eidometropolis" was primarily a river view of the city, with its circular survey of London following the embankment of the Thames, the commercial artery signifying Britain's maritime prowess. Girtin's original oil painting, now lost, measured 108 feet in its circumference and was admired both for its wealth of topographic and anecdotal detail and its subtle observation of atmospheric effects. One of the surviving watercolor sketches for the panorama affords a view of the Adelphi Terrace (a prominent residential development where Girtin had worked at Dr. Monro's) and Somerset House (the site of the Royal Academy), landmarks attesting to the civic and cultural identity of late Georgian London. But the point of view taken from the south bank, visible in the left foreground, also encompasses the rapidly developing industrial quarters of the city, with its nearby clutter of foundries, breweries, and quays. Girtin's nuanced watercolor technique, especially in the complex overlapping of rooflines and fuming smoke and vapor as well as in the abbreviated calligraphy used to notate the passing skiffs and their wake on the Thames, worked effectively in capturing the breadth of the urban vista. Even in the finished panorama, where one would generally expect to find a highly delineated visual register, Girtin was credited with sustaining a more diffused, atmospheric style that was deemed all the more appropriate to the urban/

industrial landscape; as a contemporary reviewer wrote: "the view appears through a sort of misty medium arising from the fires of the forges, manufacturers, &c."

Girtin's dual engagement with picturesque scenes of rusticity and ruin and with the panoramic spectacle of the metropolis points to the almost indivisible relation of the countryside to the city in the social and cultural fashioning of nineteenth-century landscape esthetics. The seeming dichotomy of the rural and the urban in the pictorial and literary production of landscape imagery was perhaps more dialectical than oppositional. Nevertheless, the prevailing ideology of an urban perspective on the natural world, in which nature and the rural landscape are construed as a cultural resource offering moral respite from what one early-nineteenth century commentator called "the guilt and fever of a city life," would inform much of the artistically progressive, though often socially regressive, landscape painting of the century, from the British watercolor school to French Impressionism.

CONSTABLE'S RUSTIC NATURALISM

Writing from London in 1802, the aspiring landscape painter John Constable (1776–1837) would complain: "Panorama painting seems all the rage . . . [but] great principles are neither expected nor looked for in this mode of describing nature." Throughout his artistic career as the most innovative exponent of a rustic, naturalist landscape art, Constable was often troubled by the theorizing of "great principles" in painting. His many opinions on the function of landscape art (recorded in his voluminous correspondence and in a series of lectures he delivered late in his life) are in some ways most

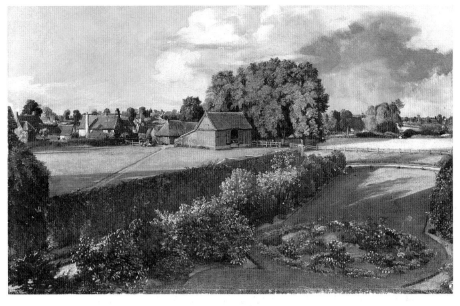

116 (*left*) THOMAS GIRTIN *Somerset House* watercolor for "Eidometropolis," 1802. 9⅝ × 21¼ (24.4 × 54)

117 JOHN CONSTABLE *Golding Constable's Flower Garden* 1815. 13 × 20 (33 × 50.8)

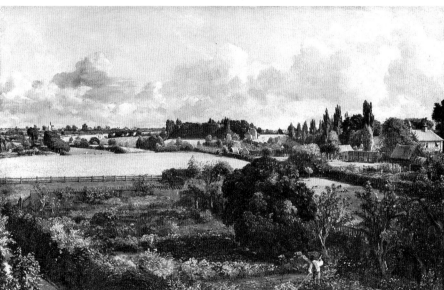

118 JOHN CONSTABLE *Golding Constable's Kitchen Garden* 1815. 13 × 20 (33 × 50.8)

remarkable for their self-contradicting claims. On one hand, he could bluntly pronounce: "In such an age as this, painting should be *understood,* not looked on with blind wonder, nor considered only as a poetic aspiration, but as a pursuit, legitimate, scientific, mechanical." And on the other, he could wax poetic about his own attachment to his native landscape of the Stour Valley as being the very wellspring of his art (this is the most oft-quoted passage from Constable's writings): "Still I should paint my own places best; painting is but another word for feeling, and I associate 'my careless boyhood' with all that lies on the banks of the Stour; those scenes made me painter . . . I am fond of being an egotist in whatever relates to painting." Constable's landscape painting would seek to negotiate a rapprochement between the antipodes of science and sentiment, between a vision of nature that was objectifying and transparent and yet also subjective and solipsistic. Constable's art is most instructive and compelling because of its very effort to overcome any disparity between this positing of landscape as an apprehensible form of knowledge with undiluted truth content and also as an expressive recollection of a fantasized, autochthonous union of self and nature.

This admixture of observational detachment and personal investiture is often recognized as being fundamental to the achievement of Constable's landscape painting. From 1809 onward, Constable decided to restrict himself to a regional landscape art focused on the canals, fields, mills, and cottages surrounding and including his father's property near East Bergholt in Suffolk, East Anglia. If, in his decision to pursue 117–18 an artistic career, Constable had resisted his familial obligations to take over the milling and farming business, he could at least repossess this patrimony, repeatedly, through representing it. The landscapes portrayed in his art were not simply disinterested objects of picturesque beauty redolent of a vaguely updated pastoralism. Instead, the lay of the land and the stretches of scenery were inscribed by memory and personal history, in which a socio-economic, and even psychological, identification with the landscape served as a virtual precondition for the artistic knowledge of "nature." Constable's self-imposed exile within the countryside of his father's property (an exile not abroad, but at home), and the optical and emotional alertness to the local particularity of that landscape, is best documented in his pair of small paintings from 1815 depicting his father's gardens, fields, and rural outbuildings. Painted from the upstairs window of the family house, Constable's site-specific orientation to the landscape and the sweeping embrace of the vista are indebted to the unprincipled principles of panorama painting that the artist had disparaged earlier during his student years in London. In the rural setting of this more personal landscape, the mere task of describing nature was redeemed and made pure, undemanding of any overarching esthetic formulae. Constable would often write, in self-heroizing terms, of his own dedicated search for a natural, incorrupt vision of landscape; disavowing artistic precedent and pronounced stylistic idiom, the painter advocated a guileless sincerity and dogged faithfulness in establishing an unmediated rapport with nature.

In the views rendered from his family's estate house, the illusion of this undeclamatory naturalness of vision was predicated in great part on the highly cultivated and controlled character of the agricultural landscape that was being described. With their attention to the patterning and demarcation of the agrarian property, these paintings maintain a casual orderliness in their presentation of the landscape: the parterres, hedgerows, fences, and paths that subdivide the diagonal wedges and the horizontal bands of the scenery attest to the proprietary pleasure taken in surveying and recording these prospects. Visually, the paintings reconcile acute clarity with atmospheric diffusion of detail; brushwork is at once incredibly descriptive of specific landscape features and yet also broadly textured and summary in its indication of such motifs as livestock, windmills, and distant gates and rooflines. The irregular geometry of the landscape is set against the more transient, though no less closely observed, effects of atmosphere and light: the deepening shadows that lengthen across the well-kept lawns and gardens, and the amassing clouds that are captured with a meteorological precision and yet are also made to respond compositionally to the density and outline of the trees and foliage on the ground below.

Conforming very much to a georgic conception of landscape, these pictures point to a contradition that runs throughout Constable's art in its pictorial treatment of the human labor that was necessarily required to secure the productive balance and imagined harmony of nature and society celebrated and promoted in this kind of imagery; as the literary historian John Barrell has commented: "No painter offers us a more civilised landscape than Constable, but the existence of the men who have civilised it has for the most part to be inferred from the image of what their effort has achieved." These pictures of the family property are not without considerable human incident: harvesters, gardeners, and threshers are present, but only just. Reduced to distant highlights or chromatic accents within the landscape, the laborers are deftly integrated into the painted fabric of Constable's well-ordered vision of nature. Just as these figures are shown tending the property that is not theirs, Constable's landscape in turn tends to them, almost suppressing the human presence as a mere visual cipher amid the productivity of the natural world.

During the 1820's, Constable worked to create a monumental version of the naturalist landscape of a rural society that was legitimized, at least in the artist's mind, by its associative connections with his own past. Although his artistic inspiration lay in the Stour Valley, Constable's artistic career was centered in London. Intent on commanding greater respect from the Royal Academy and from those art critics who guardedly commended his art for its "portraiture" of nature, Constable began exhibiting largescale pictures (the so-called "six-footers") of the agrarian and waterway landscapes of his home county of Suffolk. Ranging in mood and format from the epically placid *The Hay Wain (Landscape: Noon)* (1821) to the disquieting turbulence of *Dedham Vale* (1828), these exhibition landscapes sought to shore up an image of rural England during a period when social relations in the countryside were being strained by economic depression and civil unrest on the part of the agrarian working class. As much as Constable presumed to be unconcerned with the social actuality of the rural scene (the effects of nature were absorbing enough), his six-footers nevertheless betray an ambivalent awareness about the difficult task of sustaining some quasi-empirical mythology of rural England. Just before sending *The Hay Wain* to the Royal Academy exhibition, Constable lamented, almost as if to anticipate and rationalize the urban insensitivity to his Stour Valley landscapes: "Londoners, with all their ingenuity as artists, know nothing of the feelings of country life, the essence of landscape." The vivid optical immediacy of *The Hay Wain* implied an effort to render perception itself more unsullied and refreshed through its intensification of both the intangible atmospheric effects of light and shadow and the more palpable textures of moisture, plantlife, and earth. The painting's mood tends toward

117–18

119
121

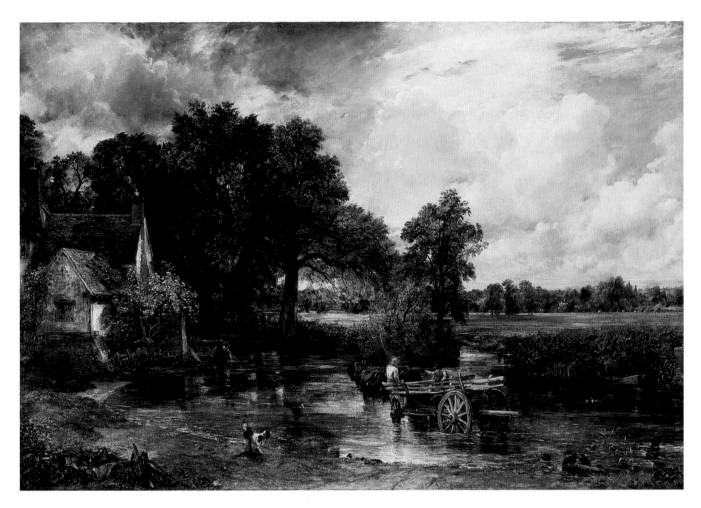

119 JOHN CONSTABLE *The Hay Wain (Landscape: Noon)* 1821. 51¼ × 73 (130.5 × 185.5)

bucolic lassitude, seizing a moment of routine uneventfulness that is compromised somewhat by the activated paint surface of the landscape, especially in the glistening foliage, the tremulous reflections in the stream, and the thickening clouds (hence the appeal of Constable's facture to French Romantic painters and critics when this picture was shown in the Paris Salon of 1824). If *The Hay Wain* makes wonderful work of perceptual attentiveness, it shows rural labor as almost sluggishly and unselfconsciously performed. One wonders if the wagon stalled by Willy Lott's cottage (a neighboring resident of the Constables' property renowned for his having never ventured far from the environs of his shaded habitat) will ever emerge out of the watery mire and return to the sunlit harvest meadow glimpsed in the distance, where another wagon is seen already burdened with hay and ready to depart for the barn. This, then, is Constable's feeling for country life, where the inevitable cycle of rural labor becomes synonymous with habitual indolence, and where seeing and representing the landscape is made to seem more demanding than harvesting it.

CONSTABLE AND THE RUIN OF ENGLAND

The outbreaks of Luddite insurrection and rural arson in East Anglia, and the failing market prices during the post-Napoleonic War years that undermined the economic status of rural gentry like Constable's family, seem like unthinkably remote social nightmares when looking at *The Hay Wain*. Such was the function, whether consciously or unconsciously, of Constable's six-footers. The incommensurability between the landscape imagery and the social experience of the countryside can nevertheless be discerned in Constable's ambitious exhibition paintings of the 1820's. The tremendous 1828 exhibit of *Dedham Vale* (Constable referred to the picture as "perhaps my best") rehearses yet another of the artist's "native scenes" which he had first painted in 1802, this Wordsworthian recurrence of a familiar landscape over a temporal span of one's life indicative of the painter's more reflexive inquiry into his own comprehension of the natural world. With its Claudian proscenium of framing foliage and its serpentine river view measured out and broken at key

121

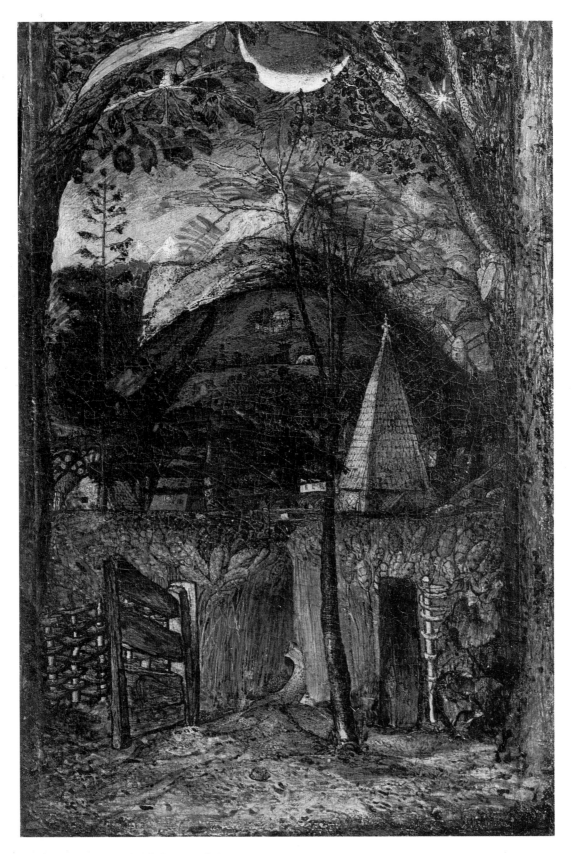

120 **Samuel Palmer** *A Hilly Scene* ca. 1826. 8⅛ × 5¼ (20.6 × 13.3)

recessional junctures by the topographic landmarks of mills, cottages, and bridge, and further on, of the church tower standing guard over the village, the painting tentatively retains many of the picturesque principles of design that Constable had hoped to disinherit through his development of an artless, unaffected naturalism. The moral and social iconography of the landscape, its cherishing vista of a faithful, hard-working agricultural community, is complicated by the foreground ridge of darkness wherein the figures of a vagrant mother and her child can be discerned, their makeshift encampment within the tangled thicket of trees and underbrush in poignant contrast to the well-tended vista of fields and village stretching off into the distant valley. Here is a rare instance in which Constable admits a scene of rural poverty into his landscape, albeit obscuring it within the shadowy recesses of the overgrown furrow. One might be led to think that this pathetic intrusion is meant to be overlooked, the eye diverted easily into the expansive valley beyond. But it is also hidden so as to be revealed. Reluctant to sentimentalize excessively over the ordeals of pauperism, Constable perhaps saw this foreground passage as a primitivist episode in the formation of rural England that finds its fulfillment or resolution in the unfolding landscape of the Stour Valley.

Later, in 1836, while lecturing on the history and theory of landscape painting, Constable recounted an anecdote that provides an interesting gloss on the problematic foreground of *Dedham Vale*. Describing a drawing he had made of a beautiful tree in Hampstead (he feminized the landscape motif as "this young lady"), Constable digressed: "some time afterwards, I saw, to my grief, that a wretched board had been nailed to her side, on which was written in large letters, 'All vagrants and beggars will be dealt with according to law.' The tree seemed to have felt the disgrace, for even then some of the top branches had withered . . . In another year one half became paralyzed, and not long after the other shared the same fate, and this beautiful creature was cut down to a stump, just high enough to hold the board." In *Dedham Vale*, the blasted and tortured tree to the left and the slender, though no less involuted, coulisse of trees on the right mimic and gesture in empathetic response to the "disgrace" of the figurative scene that they surround. Without literally bearing the cruel and demeaning signs of impoverished homelessness, the trees are made to suffer and feel for that which society cannot. Constable once admitted to loving trees more than people. And so his trees in *Dedham Vale* are burdened with a compassion for a human plight that the artist would otherwise seem predisposed to conceal or repress. Constable often spoke of equating nature with "moral feeling" and "moral awareness"; nature redresses, at least at the level of expressive sentiment and natural metaphor, the social ills of humanity, a strategy that conveniently insulates any moral conflict

suggested by the presence of the vagrant figures from its more truly social origin.

The stylistic temper of *Dedham Vale* predicts the more foreboding and abstracting qualities of Constable's later art. The drastic mood-swing in Constable's work during the late 1820's toward a solemn and yet agitated expression of landscape is usually ascribed to his psychological despondency of mourning (his wife had died in late 1828), his ongoing professional estrangement from the artistic establishment (his belated election as a Royal Academician in 1829 did little to alleviate the resentment he felt toward the London artworld), and his social alienation from an agrarian setting that could no longer offer shelter from the divisive forces of political protest and class conflict (throughout the '20's Constable increasingly voiced unhappiness with the changing face of the social landscape of the countryside, culminating with his rare outburst of political paranoia over the national debate of the Great Reform Bill of 1831–2). The pretense to a descriptive naturalism gave way to a more urgently and vigorously executed painting style in which the effects of chiaroscuro and the tactile manipulation of pigment were both drastically deepened. Straying from the by now exhausted topography of the Stour Valley, the pictures broached more heroic and symbolic strains of ruin and storm imagery, as seen in the exhibition oil painting *Hadleigh Castle, Mouth of the Thames—Morning After a Stormy Night* (1829) and his watercolor and mezzotint *Old Sarum* (1832). Instead of the cultivated agrarian scenery that had dominated Constable's art, these works dwell on nature's blighting of human history, the ruined tower of Hadleigh Castle with its vertical wound of shadow answered by the diagonal shafts of sunlight flooding across the Thames estuary and the distant coastline. The sentinel-like ruin has its private and public connotations—a cathartic remnant of recollected desire and a feudal, and perhaps futile, reminder of an historical past when power and authority were more watchful and protective of England. Although the surface of the finished painting is not as anxiously marked as its large oil sketch, the animated rendering of forms, both inert and shifting in the moldering ruins and the scudding clouds, is taken to new extremes. In a letter of 1830, Constable even worried that his distinctive painting style had become too expressively mannered, "a species of self-worship," as he phrased it. The fluctuating visibility of nature in *Hadleigh Castle* conveys the mutable emotiveness of the picture, ranging from despairing to hopeful, from negational to exhilarated.

Similarly, the watercolor of *Old Sarum* speaks of both endurance and loss, the more programmatic aspect of the picture explicated in the accompanying text to the print in which Constable comments on the significant historical associations of the vanished city: here, according to the artist,

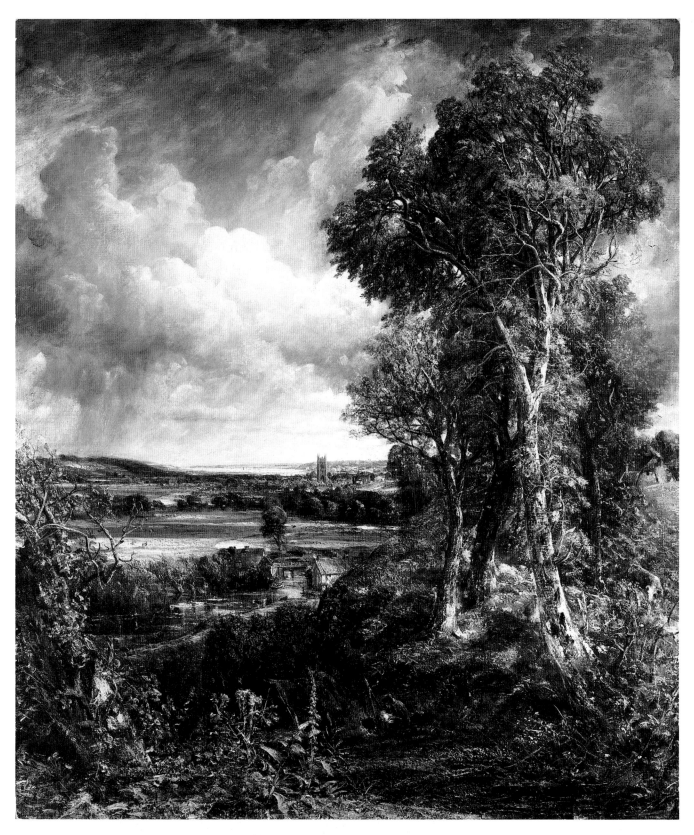

121 **JOHN CONSTABLE** *Dedham Vale* 1828. 57⅛ × 48 (145 × 122)

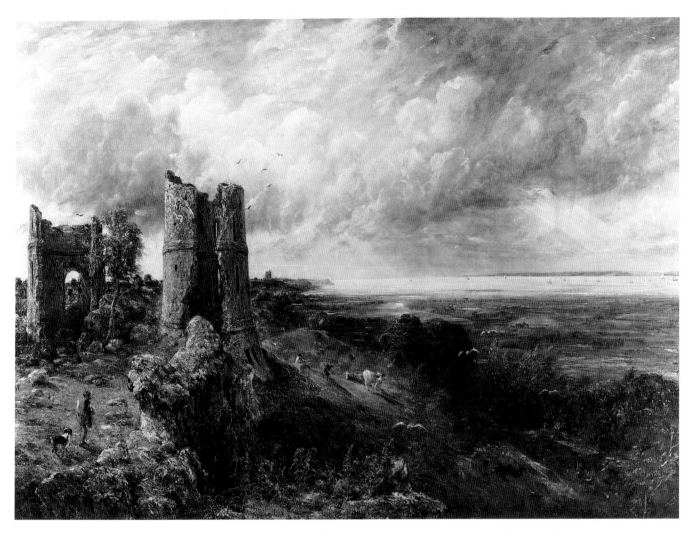

122 JOHN CONSTABLE *Hadleigh Castle, Mouth of the Thames—Morning After a Stormy Night* 1829. 48 × 64¾ (122 × 161.9)

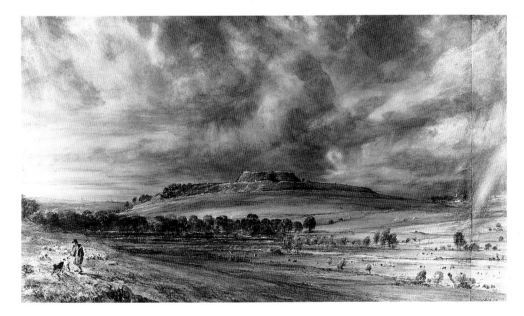

123 JOHN CONSTABLE *Old Sarum* 1832. 11⅞ × 19⅛ (30.1 × 48.6)

was the originary site of parliamentary law and feudal civil order, its monumental battlements reclaimed by the landscape only to serve eventually as the counterpastoral haunt of a solitary shepherd. Fearful of the assault on Tory Anglicanism signaled by the Reform Bill crisis and its democratizing mission for parliamentary reform, Constable sees the active ruination of the present-day government reflected in the abandoned ruin of the past. The desolate, twilit earthwork in *Old Sarum*—nature and history inextricably united—stands as a kind of retrospective prophecy of what can go wrong in even the most authoritative of times, its apt political contemporaneity recognized by the portraitist Thomas Lawrence, also President of the Royal Academy, who advised Constable to dedicate the plate to the House of Commons (the borough of Old Sarum was also notorious for the very political corruption that the Reform Bill proposed to remedy), an irony probably not appreciated by Constable during his time of political reaction. Toward the close of his career, Constable asserted that landscape was no longer only "the child of history"; his ruin images set out to elaborate this subsumption of history by landscape. The introspective, "egotistical" project of Constable's landscape painting, however, could not help but become implicated in and even disfigured by the fragmenting debates over the political and social destiny of nations.

VISIONARY LANDSCAPES OF PALMER AND MARTIN

For a far more exaggerated conception of the English Romantic landscape as an imaginative refuge from the social struggles of contemporary life, the work of Samuel Palmer (1805–81) is even more telling, though much less involving, than that of Constable. The son of a London antiquarian bookseller and Baptist lay preacher, Palmer fell under the influence of the elderly and neglected William Blake in 1823–24. Along with a small group of young, unknown watercolorists and engravers who declared themselves "the Ancients," Palmer lionized Blake and advanced his idea of art-making as mystical craft and spiritual vocation. Retreating to the village of Shoreham in Kent, this sect of artists transformed the specific locality of the countryside into otherworldly landscapes filtered through literary images of agrarian life from the Psalms and the *Georgics* of Virgil. Untrammeled by the naturalist scientism that Constable had pursued, Palmer subjected what he called "generic Nature" to an imaginative recasting; as he wrote, in a characteristically rapturous letter from Shoreham, of "midsummer scenes, as passed thro' the intense purifying separating transmuting heat of the soul's infabulous alchymy." His compact tempera and watercolor

panel *A Hilly Scene* (ca. 1826) is the outcome of one of these alchemical transmutations, the Shoreham landscape contracted into a prelapsarian vision of supernatural bounty that scorned the agricultural and technological improvements of modern farming. In Palmer's landscape, the dense harvest field threatens to overtake the cottages and village church; with its Gothic nave of framing trees and its symmetrical alignment of neatly quilted hillsides, the composition of nature adheres to a divine ordonnance that pretends to transcend mere human design. The sickle moon and evening star almost touch the nearby awning of foliage, the celestial realm magnified and brought close to earth. Although Blake was relatively uninterested in landscape painting (he once expressed admiration of some foliage sketches by Constable), the influence of his archaizing anti-illusionism is strongly felt in Palmer's Shoreham landscapes of the 1820's. The internal illumination of the tightly contoured landscape motifs, the opalescent and vibrant containment of every form, even the sexualized, anthropomorphic fecundity of the landscape—all show the imprint of Blake on Palmer's miniature abstractions of the natural world.

A landscape like *A Hilly Scene* is almost claustrophobic and exclusionist in its effect. Even though the beholder is invited to enter through the open gate to this Blakean "green and pleasant land," the path through the overscaled field of grain quickly narrows and is compressed by the suffocating richness of the landscape. While Palmer drew inspiration from Blake's visionary pastoralism, his own politics were closer to the self-interested conservatism of Constable than to the radical religious utopianism of his mentor. Just as Constable believed that the Reform Act would deliver governmental power to "the rabble and dregs of the people, and the devil's agents on earth," so Palmer, in an election pamphlet he wrote in 1832 addressing the recent rise of incendiary rural protest, warned of the political enfranchisement of "a crew of savages and a thoughtless rabble." If, in 1826, sequestered in Shoreham reading the scriptures, Palmer could write, "towards evening the dawning of some beautiful imaginings, and then some of those strong thoughts that push the mind . . . on the right road to TRUTH," by 1832, the evenings were not so translucent and inspirational, as Palmer evoked the more ominous night vision of the reform movement: "Their optics are adapted to darkness. And it is now a very dark night in Europe. The radicals are elated." The concentrated fantasy of rural England secured by Palmer in paintings like *Hilly Scene* would not endure much past the early 1830's; the atemporal and misleadingly benign landscapes that emerged from Palmer's condition of visionary blindness could no longer withstand the impact of the darker optic of social discord.

The regressive intimacy of Palmer's landscapes plainly sought to forestall the social dissidence of life and culture in

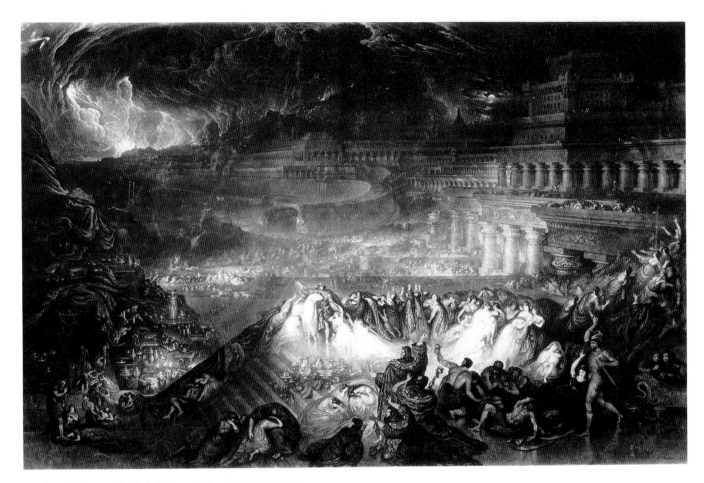

124 JOHN MARTIN *The Fall of Ninevah* 1829. 36 × 26¾ (91.4 × 68)

early nineteenth-century England. The very antithesis to Palmer may be found in the work of the apocalyptic landscapist whose paintings and prints were an unavoidably popular sensation in post-Waterloo England, John Martin (1789–1854). Specializing in historical and poetical landscapes, most often of biblical and Miltonic scenes of cataclysm and destruction, Martin closed the gap between the high art of academic landscape painting and the popular culture of the theatrical nature spectacle. Highminded artists and critics saw his art as vulgar and unrespectable, William Hazlitt, for example, declaring that Martin's work, "has no notion of moral principles . . . [with] this craving after morbid affectation." Constable resentfully belittled Martin's enormous success, and the literary and fine arts press alternately judged his art to be the divine emanations of an untutored genius (Martin's training was as a coach and china painter) or the cheap tricks of a crowd-pleasing entrepreneur (his works were widely replicated both in prints and in dioramas and stage sets). Although the narrative content of his art was drawn from the ancient history of eastern empires and the spiritual prehistory of humanity as described by Milton,

Martin's images were nevertheless supremely modern in character, transposing the social and environmental crises of industrial Britain into primeval and antiquarian arenas of cultural fantasy. As the historian Jules Michelet noted in his journal after arriving in England in 1834, "Bentham, Malthus, and Martin are the true expression of Great Britain: the self-interest, the crowds, the stifling population." Both the appeal and the affront of Martin's art lay in its sublime sublimation of the impact of industrial capital and rampant urbanism into imagery of omnipotent and catastrophic acts of nature and divine justice visited upon long-vanished empires, as in his architectural extravaganza *The Fall of Ninevah* 124 (1829), a mezzotint that Martin's deranged brother, Jonathan (incarcerated for an incendiary assault on York Minster), would knowingly rework as a vision of the conflagration of modern London. In Martin's popularizing historical landscapes, the tribulations of contemporary society (urban growth and its attendant problems of population and disease control as alluded to by Michelet) were displaced into the remotest epochs of sacred and natural history.

One of Martin's more quiescent and reflective landscapes,

though no less concerned with abject destruction at the edge of history, was his watercolor *The Last Man* (ca. 1832). Martin was responding to the literary vogue for this dystopian theme in Romantic poetry and fiction: Byron's "Darkness" (1816), Mary Shelley's novel *The Last Man* (1826), and Thomas Campbell's poem of the same title and date were his sources. Like latter-day science fiction that envisions the ravaging of the earth and civilization by plagues and ecological disasters, this early nineteenth-century topos of the last man bearing witness to the end of historical time and the death of nature played upon all of the social anxieties of the period. It also supplied the Romantic landscapist with the *ne plus ultra* in ruin imagery; the last man, after all, had the tragic pleasure of surveying global ruin, as Mary Shelley's protagonist explained: "Time and experience have placed me on a height from which I can comprehend the past as a whole, and in this way I must describe it . . . The vast annihilation that has swallowed all things—the voiceless solitude of the once busy earth, the lonely state of singleness which hems me in, and mellowing the lurid tints of past anguish with poetic hues, I am able to escape by perceiving and reflecting back the grouping and combined colouring of the past." Martin's watercolor also tints and glazes in this eerie combination of the lurid and the poetical: the miasmic streaks of color washed across the sky, obscuring the pallid sun and pressing down on the parched terrain, the atmosphere itself appearing like the strata of the earth. Deep shadows bleed back into the distance of the mountain and harbor view, the depopulated remains of the architectural landscape receding into the darkness. In the foreground, enormous rock spurs jut over the wasteland, broken by the flowing gorges in the terrain, suspending the viewer over what Campbell referred to in his "Last Man" poem as "the gulf of time." The abyssal depth of these chasms signifies a rupture in time, a visual trope for the proleptic accomplishment of the scene before us. The isolated figure of the last man on the promontory is vaguely Christ-like, though divested of any redemptive promise; he offers this glimpse into the future as a cautionary object of fateful instruction, addressing the viewer with a rhetorical gesture of lamentation. In the depiction of the prominent geological fragments, Martin suggests the petrified movement of earth history, the flow of time embedded in the landscape. Etched into the surface of the earth are waves of human corpses, their skeletal outlines already swept up into the geological current. The natural world services civilization for one last time, as the mass grave of human history.

Despite the fantastical nature of this and other pictures by Martin, the artist was also preoccupied with different branches of scientific inquiry, especially hydraulic engineering and paleontology. Martin invested the fortune amassed from the sale of prints after his epic landscapes and architectural vistas in utopian (and money-losing) schemes for renovating the Thames embankment in London, consolidating the city sewage system and purifying the water supply. These efforts in futuristic urban reform were counterbalanced by his work as an illustrator of natural history, particularly his imaginative reconstructions of extinct dinosaur species based on fossil remains. In *The Last Man*, the stilled waters and abandoned maritime city warn of the contemporary failure to solve the industrial/urban dilemmas of modern England. And when the viewer looks at the profile of projecting rockfaces in Martin's watercolor, the geology assumes a monstrous aspect, as though the gigantic mold of reptilian creatures can be seen reemerging at the end of human history. Prehistory reawakens underfoot at the closure of time, the first and the last bound together in this geological landscape of historical extinction.

TURNER'S MEANINGFUL OBSCURITY

Whether contrastively embodied in Constable's georgic naturalism or in Martin's science fantasy, Romantic landscape painting in England was being developed as an artform of historical reflection. No artist was more deeply involved in this enterprise of advancing the expressive and stylistic range of landscape painting than J. M. W. Turner (1775–1851), the chief rival to both Constable and Martin. Although it was the evangelical Ruskin who most enthusiastically defended and defined the significance of Turner's incomparable contribution to nineteenth-century landscape painting, something of the profound difficulty and internal contradictions of Turner's art are best summarized in an appreciation written by the French philosopher and art theorist Hippolyte Taine in 1862. He immediately alighted upon Turner's dual attachment to discursive meaning and disorienting sensation in his depiction of landscape, especially in the artist's late works:

> By degree the sensation of the eye, the optical effect, appeared to Turner of secondary importance; the emotions and reveries of the speculative and reasoning brain obtained the empire over him. He felt a wish to paint gigantic and philosophic and humanitarian epics . . . His works compose an extraordinary jumble, a wonderful litter in which shapes of every kind are buried. Place a man in a fog, in the midst of a storm, the sun in his eyes, and his head swimming, and depict if you can, his impressions upon canvas—these are the gloomy visions, the vagueness, the delirium of an imagination such as Turner's.

To elevate and make more complex the signifying and narrative possibilities of landscape painting, and yet also to arrive at a new artistic visuality that would transmit the heightened sensory experience of the flux of nature: these two

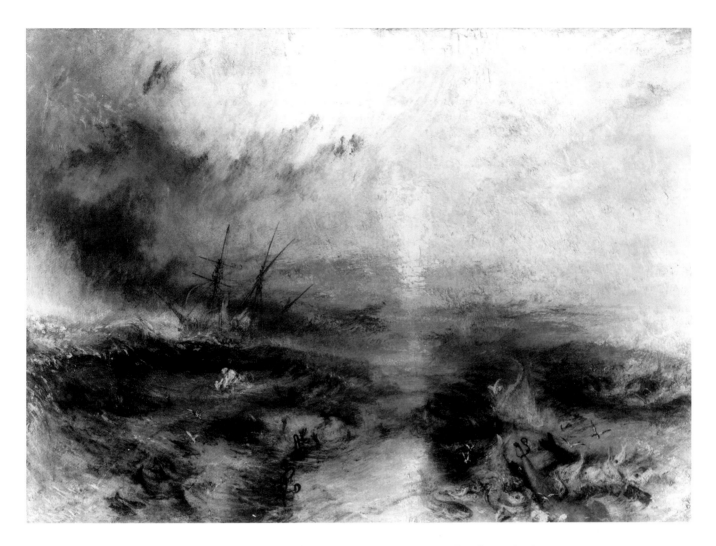

129 JOSEPH MALLORD WILLIAM TURNER *Slavers Throwing Overboard the Dead and Dying—Typhoon Coming On* 1840. 35⅞ × 54¾ (91 × 138)

temporality, an activated visual field of historically transitional viewpoints and occluded atmospheres in which past and present contest one another.

    The late marines and landscapes of Turner, culminating with such extraordinarily radical paintings as *Slavers Throwing Overboard the Dead and Dying—Typhoon Coming On* (1840) and *Rain, Steam, and Speed—The Great Western Railway* (1844), strained the discursive and visual boundaries of landscape painting. In these works the dichotomy between signification and sensation in Turner's art, as recognized by Taine, was most strongly tested. In *Slavers,* Turner's lifelong passion for nautical disaster and blood-red sunsets found its perfect expression in a near contemporary subject of moral outrage and social conscience. Inspired by a late eighteenth-century account of a slave ship that jettisoned its ailing human cargo at sea for the purpose of collecting insurance money (slavers could collect insurance only on those slaves "lost at sea," not those that died from neglect and disease), Turner

once more pits the callous inhumanity of humanity against the vengeful moral authority of nature. Although the abolitionist movement in England had already succeeded on the domestic front, the colonialist slave trade still flourished (British vessels would patrol their waters for Spanish and French slavers), while Chartist agitators began making pointed parallels between the exploitation of child labor in industrial England and the slave-supported plantation system in the tropics and the Americas.

    In Turner's painting, the turbulent ocean is already littered with the manacled bodies of the victims of the slave trade, their hands straining above the sea swells, responded to only by diving gulls and monstrous schools of fish that prey upon the human flesh. In the right foreground waves, Turner draws attention to the torments of a female slave, the treatment of the figure's swelling breast and belly and extended leg meant to appeal to the social and sexual prerogative entertained by the London viewer over these hapless victims, no matter the appropriate guilt and compassion that the painting was also meant to inspire through the inclusion of such horrific details. Like the grotesque, leering fish gathered round to feed upon the body of the slave (critics would compare the figurative elements in Turner's art to the mutational caricatures of Grandville), the viewer can both relish and be repulsed by the spectacle of death enacted in this animalistic, sensualized ocean. Ruskin even evoked the swelling movement of the sea in the picture as being "like the lifting of its [the ocean's] bosom by deep-drawn breath after the torture of the storm"; he displaces repressed sexual horror onto the tormented, maternal sea, perhaps an appropriate rhetorical move since in Turner's painting the body of the sea, and its fierce aquatic progeny, consumes the rejected body of humanity. The upended leg of this slave is echoed formally by the bowsprit of the slave ship in the distant waves, the vessel driven toward the fury of the oncoming typhoon (the wedge of gray–blue foaming mist and the wall of cloud to the left of the ship). Lampooned mercilessly in the contemporary press with a kind of nervously outrageous humor, the picture would gain its more sympathetic and compelling reading from Ruskin. His prose picture of Turner's *Slavers*, in *Modern Painters* (1843), is justifiably famous for its passionate interleaving of form and content, as in this oft-quoted passage:

> Purple and blue, the lurid shadows of the hollow breakers are cast upon the mist of night, which gathers cold and low, advancing like the shadow of death upon the guilty ship as it labours amidst the lightning of the sea, its thin masts written upon the sky in lines of blood, girded with condemnation in that fearful hue which signs the sky with horror, and mixes its flaming flood with the sunlight, and cast far along the desolate heave of the sepulchral waves, incarnadines the multitudinous sea.

Allegorizing as he goes, Ruskin invests each phase describing an element of Turner's seascape with meaning and moral inflection, not that he is very interested in expressing empathy for the disturbing human content of the picture. Blood, death, and guilt are finally part of nature as refracted through Turner's omniscient mastery of the seascape (and Ruskin's secondary mastery of those effects through language). The social and economic conditions that provided the theme of the painting are not Ruskin's real concern. He sees the desperate hands and limbs of the victims only through the gesturing of the waves and the mists, the slaves already dismembered and disembodied, haunting and enveloping the vessel as "ghastly shadow." To Ruskin, the blood-stained sun that splinters the sky and sea, thickening and staining the very pigment of the canvas, effectively takes up the slack for humanity, answering for its profit-driven amorality only with further violence, solemn and frenzied all at once. The retributive function of

nature in *Slavers* has an almost nihilistic futility to it, an idea articulated as well in Turner's verse fragment appended to the picture's title, which closes with the hopeless question, "Hope, Hope, fallacious Hope!/ Where is thy market now?"

This ironical and disjunctive refusal to market hope, to locate fixed meanings or to find moral certitudes within the often destructive dialectic of nature and society, is also evident in Turner's greatest technological landscape, *Rain, Steam, and Speed*. Depicting an engineering wonder of the 1840's, Brunel's Great Western Railway, specifically one of the rail system's new bridges traversing the Thames Valley at Maidenhead, the painting establishes a series of antitheses and correspondences between nature and technology. The topography of the landscape is obscured by the unsettled weather of streaking sun and showers, the commanding form of the railway viaduct imposing its linear geometry upon the once picturesque terrain. With scumbled pigment on the front of its engine car, the train bears down upon its perspectival path with a manic velocity (or at least an illusion of such is given), the coaches of the train rendered as a compressed blur rapidly receding into the mist. Despite the expansiveness of the vista and the plunging spatial depth of the rail trestle, the painting still draws the eye to the surface of the canvas, to its rich textures of pigment with luminous transparencies set opposite deep passages of shadow. The steam engine that now propels this train through the swirling landscape may be taken as a technical model, maybe even a scientific allegory, of natural power, in which fire, water, and mist are recombined to produce locomotive power. While the dark and pronounced forms of the railway isolate it from the fluctuating, atmospheric realm of nature, Turner's painting also shows how this blurring of sight, this animation of space and time, is the result of a new mode of perception facilitated by the motive and propulsive energy of the train. Through the visual metaphor of Turner's artistic medium, nature and machine are strangely analogized.

Within its sweeping effects of light and mist and the insistent dissolution of its forms, the picture veils small representational signs that call into question the historical status of the railway and its technology of travel. A rowboat is seen drifting in the river; a plowman is just visible to the right of the train bridge; and on the bridge itself, a coursing hare outdashes the oncoming train. These may appear to be like comic sleights of hand and eye; but in part because of their graphic fragility and visual tentativeness, these wry pictographs recollect the preindustrial human relations to the natural world, undisruptive and almost passing unnoticed within the technological landscape. Concerned with the mutable fabric of being and being seen, these stray signs reward the viewer with another fallacy of hope: that one

130

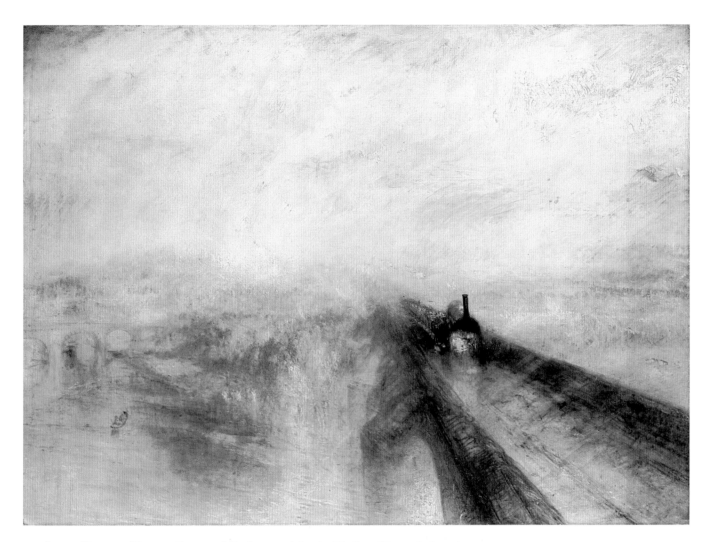

130 JOSEPH MALLORD WILLIAM TURNER *Rain, Steam, and Speed—The Great Western Railway* 1844. 35⅞ × 48 (91 × 122)

should look all the more intently at the landscape when social and industrial change is about to overtake it.

Ruskin did not want to think about this painting; it only showed what a great artist could do with a degraded subject. The critic and novelist W. M. Thackeray, after humorously recommending that the spectator look quickly at the picture before the train vanishes, concluded, "The world has never seen anything like this picture." The Impressionists later guaranteed that the world would see many more of its kind. Turner's *Rain, Steam, and Speed* remains a thoroughly Ruskinian painting in its exploration of the "landscape instinct" and the social imperatives that accompanied and formed it. The Romantic modernity of the picture resides in its contradictory accommodation of "progress and decline" (Ruskin's phrase) that was to be the most representative aspect of the nineteenth-century cultural effort to historicize nature and to socialize the landscape. As the twentieth-century critical theorist Theodor Adorno has observed, almost in an updated spirit of Ruskin's earlier social philosophy of landscape, "In every perception of nature there is actually present the whole of society."

LANDSCAPE ART AND ROMANTIC NATIONALISM IN GERMANY AND AMERICA

The capacity of landscape painting to enfold contradictory ideologies about national and cultural identities in the early nineteenth century was equally significant for Romantic art in Germany and America. The elevation of landscape painting as a spiritually and culturally symbolic artform was fundamental to the shared mission of the German artists Philipp Otto Runge (1777–1810) and Caspar David Friedrich (1774–1840).

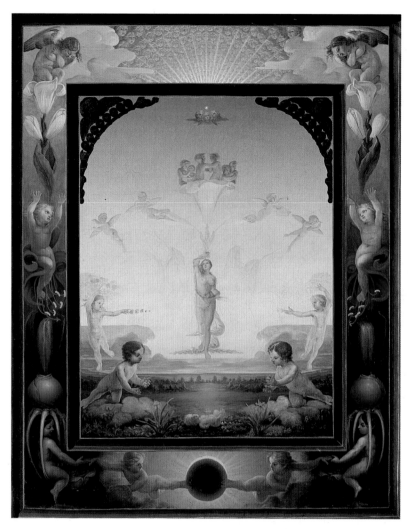

131 PHILIPP OTTO RUNGE *Morning* 1808. $42\frac{7}{8} \times 33\frac{5}{8}$ (108.9 × 85.9)

132 CASPAR DAVID FRIEDRICH *Abbey in the Oak Forest* 1809–10. $39\frac{1}{2} \times 67\frac{3}{8}$ (100.4 × 171)

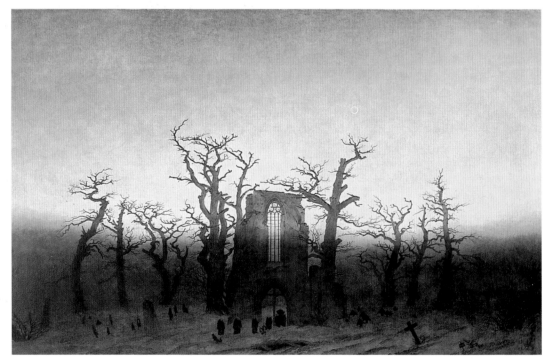

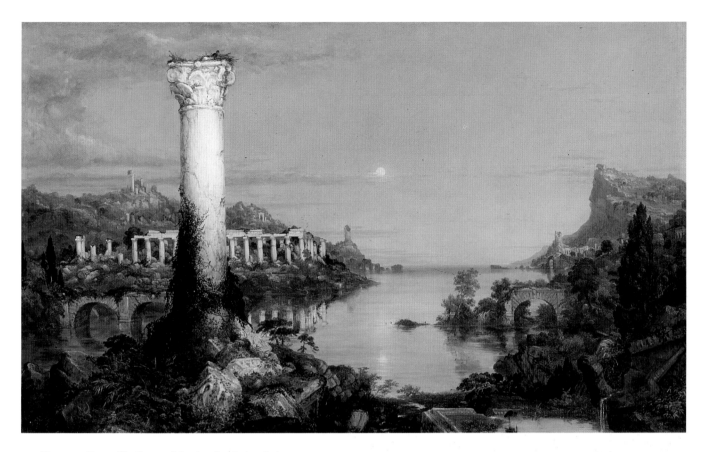

133 THOMAS COLE *The Course of Empire: Desolation* 1836. $39\frac{1}{4} \times 63\frac{1}{4}$ (99.7 × 160.7)

Both artists conceived of landscape painting as *the* art of the future through which a rejuvenated and unified German state could communicate both its sense of heritage and of destiny. Fostering a mystical pantheism in their often ethereal evocation of the natural world, these German Romantic landscapists saw their art as one of highly subjective self-expression—fragmented, unfulfilled, and yearning in both theory and practise; and yet this art was also to serve as a nationalistic fulcrum of collective hope for political and spiritual unity, especially in the wake of the Napoleonic invasion of the German states. Writing of the moribund condition of modern religious and historical art, Runge cautiously predicted in 1802, "Perhaps the time might come when a beautiful art could again arise, and it would be landscape painting."

Runge's Romantic prospectus for this new landscape art is exemplified in his ambitious project known as the *Tageszeit* (*Times of Day*), a cycle of designs allegorizing the temporal rhythms of life (human and natural, material and spiritual). Although begun as a series of linear outline drawings in 1802–03, this unfinished project came closest to fruition in the small version of Runge's painted design for *Morning* (1808). Influenced by the mystical semiotics of natural elements

propounded by the seventeenth-century theosophist Jakob Böhme (whose ideas were being revived in the new *Naturphilosophie* of the Dresden Romantic circle with whom the artist was sometimes affiliated), Runge's *Morning* was to have been read as a kind of hieroglyphic abstraction of a spiritualized natural world, both sacral and decorative in its overall effect. Its iconic symmetry and frame-within-frame device also signaled the status of the image as a 'new-age' altarpiece, one without sectarian limitations, in which the claims of mysticism and science, and of intuitive feeling and empirical insight, were to be harmonized. This light-suffused landscape of a meadow at dawn is attended to, and almost dominated by, figurative genii and spirits, syncretic vestiges of fairy folklore (floral sylphs), pagan myth (the presiding figure of Aurora), and Christian mystery (infant Christ born from the fecund earth). In the borders, Runge intertwines botanical and cosmological motifs, the tendrils and globular minutiae of plantlife merging and interchangeable with eclipsed sundisks and galactic spirals. Overburdened with theoretical systems of color symbolism and numerical proportion, Runge's *Tageszeit* sought to transform landscape painting into a signifying compound of regenerative nature-images infused with occult meaning and instrumental knowledge.

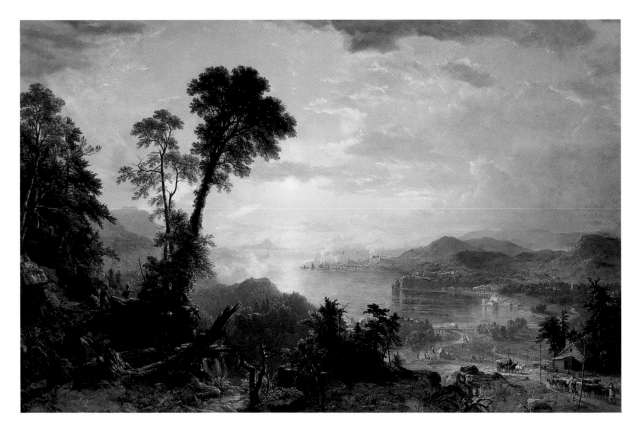

134 **ASHER B. DURAND** *Landscape, Progress* 1853. 48 × 72 (121.9 × 182.9)

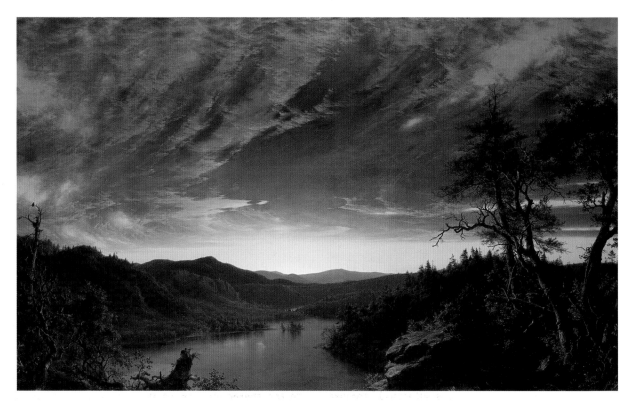

135 **FREDERIC EDWIN CHURCH** *Twilight in the Wilderness* 1860. 40 × 64 (101.5 × 162.6)

Like Runge, Friedrich's symbolic and expressive development of landscape art was profoundly responsive to the Napoleonic occupation of the German states. But while Runge's *Morning* was redolent of a liberating reawakening of nationalist sentiment and pantheistic optimism, Friedrich's art was more often sepulchral and solemnly meditative in sentiment and subject. Although more outwardly descriptive of the natural world than that of Runge, Friedrich's landscapes also sought to go beyond the materiality of nature, to treat the topographic data of landscape in transcendent or immanent terms. As he remarked on the objective of landscape painting: "Art stands as the mediator between nature and humanity. The original is too great, too sublime, for the multitude to grasp." For Friedrich, this central task of "mediation" (a concept primary to the philosophical esthetics of the Jena Romantics) in the artistic rendering of nature inevitably led to a tragic recognition of the impasse between nature and humanity, as well as that between nature and art, between mind and spirit, and even between subject and object. Friedrich's landscapes are often most compelling because of their knowingly acute failure to make visible a pure metaphysics of nature.

The picturesque repertoire of landscape motifs assumes an
132 edgy poignancy in Friedrich's remarkable painting *Abbey in the Oak Forest* (1809–10), due in large part to the haunting stasis of the composition and to the unerring linearity of the painting technique. Here one witnesses a funeral procession of monks amid a snow-covered graveyard, the earthbound religious ritual shrouded in a broad band of fog. Only the ruined Gothic portal and the gesturing oaks reach above the gloom into the atmospheric ellipse of twilit sky. In keeping with mimetic and organic theories of the origins of the Gothic style promoted by Goethe and Hegel, Friedrich's painting draws the parallel between the religious edifice and the natural architecture of the heroic oakyard, both types of monuments rooted to Germanic soil. The broken tracery of the Gothic window also echoes the crescent moon faintly visible in the sky above. The remnants of religious faith are thus reflected in the forms of nature, as though to offer spiritual solace from the ravages of historical decay that otherwise come to determine the estranged mood of the painting. This landscape of interment typifies Friedrich's esthetic of mourning. What is being interred, and mourned, is not only the corpse of a brethren monk, but religion itself (the sanctuary of God is already in ruins), and also the hope for a redeemed German nation (Friedrich was anxiously despondent, more so than usual, over the French occupation). The entombment of spirit, whether of the individual soul or of the collective soul of the fatherland, resonates throughout the whole of nature.

In telling contrast to the predominantly retrospective and commemorative imagery of history and nature in the melan-
cholic art of Friedrich, the emergent school of landscape painters in America, centered around the English-born Thomas Cole (1801–48), contended with, and often propagated, cultural myths about the futurity of the nation and the primeval vastness of the North American wilderness. Even in his early topographic landscapes of the Hudson River Valley and the Catskill Mountains from the 1820's, Cole explored the peculiar paradox of the American landscape as a national symbol of both unspoiled nature and unchecked cultivation. His painting *Sunny Morning on the Hudson River* (1827) is 136 dominated by the looming shadows of the Catskill Mountains, the narrow foreground plateau of the landscape occupied by expressively frail and withered trees and the rocky outcropping of a geological ruin. This curious area of the landscape, while meant to signify a savage, untamed domain of nature, has manifold historical associations: it is distinctly patterned after the Italian landscape style of Salvator Rosa, thereby imparting a European art historical authority to a passage of American topography. More importantly, the altarlike formation of the geology is suggestive of the sanctified status of America as a new "Promised Land"; the biblical providence of the North American landscape, however, entails the supercession of the indigenous Indian culture, and so, this earth sculpture may also be recognized as an Indian antiquity (from Thomas Jefferson onward, American antiquarians and natural historians were fascinated by Indian tumuli and ritual stones). Even when depicting the presumably incorrupt wilderness of the American landscape, Cole alluded to both past and future civilizations. Beyond the sublime obscurity of the mountainscape in this painting, the undulating ribbon of the Hudson River is seen in the distance, sunswept and with vessels on its placid waters. Cole's treatment of this scenery, and the rising popularity of his own art devoted to the region, testifies to the commercial and touristic development of a changing landscape that could no longer sustain its own wilderness status.

Cole's disenchantment with the populist politics of Jacksonian democracy and its expansionist rhetoric of unlimited national growth became increasingly apparent in the 1830's, both in his art and his writings. After a trip to Europe, Cole pursued what he called "a higher style of landscape," by which he meant historical and allegorical landscape painting in emulation of the contemporary works of Turner and Martin. His group of five paintings *The Course of Empire* 133 (1836) surveyed the rise and fall of a civilization from its barbaric hunting and gathering phase through its pastoral, cultivated state and into its seeming apogee as a Greco-Roman style empire of lavish splendor, succeeded, predictably enough, by a scene of the once-flourishing architectural vista swept up in war and violence. The final painting, entitled *Desolation*, envisions nature's reclaiming of the ruin land-

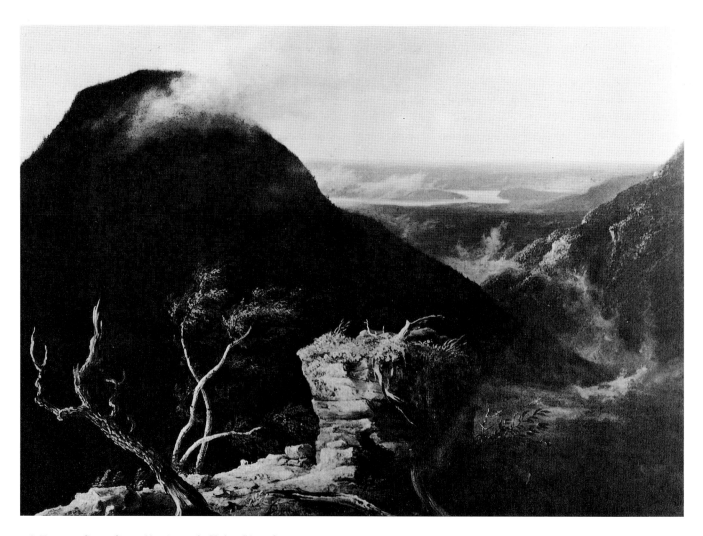

136 THOMAS COLE *Sunny Morning on the Hudson River* 1827. 18¾ × 25¼ (47.6 × 64.1)

scape, an almost welcome episode in the historical cycle proposed by Cole's five-painting set-piece. Influenced by cyclical theories of history postulated in a popular Jacobin treatise on the corruption of civilization and religion, Comte de Volney's *The Ruins of Empire* (1791), and also by philosophical ruin imagery in Byronic verse, Cole's final painting of the series may be interpreted as an image, not of outright despair, but of renewed promise. In his 1836 "Essay on American Scenery," Cole expressed his concern over a much less preferred form of desolation in the modern actuality of the American landscape, in which, as he observed, "the most noble scenes are made desolate . . . desecrated by what is called improvement." Regretful over the expanding settlement of the frontier and the spreading railway lines, Cole was nonetheless resigned that "such is the road society has to travel." The contemporaneity of Cole's pictorial saga on cyclical history is also evident in editorial commentaries on the inexorable bond between the American landscape and the rapid material progress of American society; as a writer for *The Knickerbocker* commented in an 1835 essay, appropriately called "The Downfall of Nations": "What an extent of territory we have yet to people. Our range of forests offers a home to the oppressed. The landscape has been bountiful in her gifts. Metallic ores abound in our mountains and beds of coal have opened their veins to our view, as if in anticipation of the immense destruction which future generations may effect in the pathless landscape."

Cole's successors and students openly addressed this simultaneous despoliation and fulfillment of the American wilderness in their epic landscape paintings. Asher B. Durand's *Landscape, Progress* (1853) and Frederic Church's *Twilight in the Wilderness* (1860) were received as uniquely national landscapes of quintessentially American experience. Durand's painting indulges in a technological pastoralism, in which the broad prospect of an imaginary Hudson River Valley landscape plays host to the modern improvements

134
135

disparaged by Cole: railway viaducts, telegraph poles, steam-ships, and growing communities are safely nestled within the sweeping panorama of the morning landscape. Viewed from a foreground precipice littered with blasted trees (and a Claudian coulisse thrown in for good measure), the landscape is observed by two Indians who look on, obviously not as the beneficiaries of American progress that the painting wishes to exalt, but rather as its few surviving victims. The inclusion of the Indian figures brings an historical aura to the landscape of promise and settlement; they are, quite literally, history. The beholder's point of view is aligned to that of the Indians, but only to give greater distance to the spectacle of national power and its pleasurable integration within the natural order. The fateful note of sentiment sounded for the vanishing Indian race is overcome by, and predicated on, the prospective mastery of the vista in which the viewer is meant to take pride.

Uniting a scientific naturalism with the pictorial theatricality of the sublime, Church's *Twilight in the Wilderness* dispenses entirely with any traces of humanity; neither white man's progress nor the Indian's fading presence disrupts the breathtaking vista of the wilderness landscape. Without sacrificing a clear-eyed empiricism in its delineation of atmosphere, foliage, and mountainous terrain, Church's painting brings a sanctimonious awe to the presentation of nature. Critics of the day were divided over whether a divine hush or an apocalyptic turbulence prevailed over the spirit of the landscape. Just when the viewer has settled into a tranquil moment of contemplation before this pristine landscape, the atmospheric drama of scarlet-tinged clouds, eerily reflected in the centrally receding river, propels the eye into the far reaches of the mountain view. As Cole's most loyal and accomplished student, Church retained a commitment to the allegorical conception of landscape painting. And while not cluttering this landscape with figurative and emblematic elements, Church does include a cruciform assemblage of branches poised at the end of a blasted tree trunk, the shape silhouetted in the foreground against the glowing body of water. Divine providence both guards over and threatens the security of the wilderness scene.

Painted on the eve of the American Civil War, Church's *Twilight in the Wilderness* allegorizes nature as history, the landscape divested of humanity and yet also transformed into a visible sign of national struggle. As if to invite the prepositional slippage in the painting's title, twilight *of* the wilderness, the landscape's immobilizing moment of transience betrays the national mythology of a wilderness esthetic. And in rendering a landscape free of humanity and yet animated with intimations of providential power, Church's vision of the twilit wilderness landscape dims the recognition of the violent and traumatic experience of the American frontier: the twilight, not of nature, but of entire cultures and populations of Native Americans.

New World Frontiers

· 6 ·

OLD WORLD, NEW WORLD: THE ENCOUNTER OF CULTURES ON THE AMERICAN FRONTIER

FRANCES K. POHL

THE BUCKSKIN JACKET AND THE PARKER PEN

IN 1941 THE ANTHROPOLOGIST CLAUDE LÉVI-STRAUSS described a particular encounter in the American room of the New York Public Library: "There, under its neo-classical arcades and between walls paneled with old oak, I sat near an Indian in a feather headdress and a beaded buckskin jacket—who was taking notes with a Parker pen." Lévi-Strauss marveled at these unexpected juxtapositions—the feather headdress and the Neoclassical arcades, the beaded buckskin jacket and the Parker pen, the French anthropologist and the Native American researcher. Earlier in the century the U.S. photographer Edward Curtis responded to similar juxtapositions in a different manner. He retouched his images of tribal peoples in order to remove such "impurities" as suspenders, parasols, and alarm clocks.

The juxtapositions outlined by Lévi-Strauss and brushed away by Curtis have been an integral part of the daily experiences and cultural representations of those who have inhabited the North American continent since the arrival of European settlers in the sixteenth century. To ignore these juxtapositions or brush them away results in a deceptively static and one-sided view of the encounters between these European settlers and the indigenous populations, a view that most often presents Native Americans as having been systematically conquered and their cultures subsequently preserved in a "pristine" state in the museums and private collections of Euro-Americans. While conquering and controlling the indigenous peoples of North America was certainly a central component of the European agenda in the New World, this conquest was never complete. Native

peoples and their cultures continued to exist, to adapt and change, and exert their own influences on the Europeans who came to subdue and record them (the two processes often went hand in hand).

The complexities of these juxtapositions, these encounters between the Old World and the New, need to be kept in mind when looking at nineteenth-century U.S. art. The U.S. in the nineteenth century was not a homogeneous society, but neither was it a collection of separate entities embodying the pristine cultures of Native America, Africa, England, Ireland, Italy, Spain, or China. The anthropologist Eric Wolf has argued that "the world of humankind constitutes a manifold, a totality of interconnected processes." This chapter will investigate certain aspects of this totality of interconnected processes as they manifested themselves in nineteenth-century pictorial representations of encounters between Native Americans and Europeans.

The following pages contain only a few examples of the thousands of such images that appeared in the nineteenth century. The questions raised in these pages, however, can be applied to the larger body of images and can lead to a greater awareness of the central role they played—and continue to play today—in the formation of popular concepts of the U.S. and its peoples. Most of the works in this chapter do not depict "violent" encounters—U.S. soldiers shooting or stabbing Native Americans or vice versa. Rather, I have focused on portraits of Native Americans by white artists or scenes of Native Americans in their villages or in classrooms in order to show that these seemingly non-violent encounters also have a coercive aspect to them, that they reveal a social system that relies on pictorial representations as well as physical force to control or subdue a people. The works by Native American artists also show how Native Americans resisted the extinction of their culture, or its preservation only in museums as collections of static artifacts, by recording their own visions of their changing world.

The pictorial representations of Native Americans and Euro-Americans appeared in many forms—photographs, engravings, lithographs, drawings, paintings, and sculptures. They also appeared in many different places—the home (particularly in the form of popular magazines and sets of stereoscopic photographs), art galleries, community centers (which were often the sites for traveling exhibitions), business establishments, government archives, and public plazas. Just as it is a mistake to think that separate, pristine cultures existed side by side in the U.S. in the nineteenth century, so too is it a mistake to think that popular or commercial art and fine art occupied completely separate spheres. For example, while the venue for the display of each category of objects might differ (the art gallery versus the magazine page), those who worked for popular magazines often drew upon the conventions of fine art in composing their images while fine artists, in turn, often looked to popular culture for inspiration. Indeed, many artists who came into prominence in the fine art world in the U.S. over the century began their careers as commercial artists and often continued to create illustrations for popular magazines after their reputations as fine artists had been established. Some did so for financial reasons, others for political reasons, believing that the work of "fine artists" needed to be made more accessible to a larger, non-artworld audience in order to improve the esthetic and moral fiber of the nation. In addition, the meaning of a particular image depended upon where it appeared and who viewed it. For example, a painting may well have meant one thing when seen by an art critic hanging in a gallery and quite another when seen by a garment worker in engraved form in a magazine. Acknowledging the effect of venue and audience on the meaning of an image results in a fuller understanding of the wideranging and varied impact of pictorial representations in the nineteenth century.

THE MYTH OF THE FRONTIER

According to the historian Richard Slotkin, the oldest and most enduring national myth in the U.S. is the myth of the frontier. Since colonial times, this myth has underpinned the rhetoric of pioneering progress, world mission, and eternal battle against the forces of darkness and subversion. While it began in the materiality of frontier life, it continued long after people had ceased to live in frontier conditions. The historian Frederick Jackson Turner articulated the major elements of the myth of the frontier in an address in 1893 at the World's Columbian Exposition in Chicago. For Turner, the frontier—or the "West"—was synonymous with the U.S. itself. It was here where the successive meetings between savagery and civilization took place and were resolved and where citizens became sturdy and independent. Once the Pacific coast had been reached and the frontier had literally disappeared, it lived on for Turner in the character of the nation, in the ruggedness and inquisitiveness and aggressive individuality that marked the national spirit.

The frontier myth, according to Slotkin, endures to this day as a primary organizing principle of U.S. historical memory because it is able to encode the "lessons of history" in easily graspable stories or catchphrases; history is successfully disguised as archetype. The enemies of the U.S. become the "Indians," the noble or ignoble savages, while the U.S. military dons the persona of the cowboy. These "cowboy and Indian" stories appear throughout the mass media—movies, television, comic books, novels—and are acted out time and again by young children in playgrounds and backyards across the nation. Such is the power of this myth that challenges to its "truthfulness," which were particularly evident during 1992, the year marking the quincentenary of Columbus' arrival in the Americas in 1492, are often labeled "unAmerican." And yet such critical challenges must be undertaken in order to unravel the complex layers of meaning embedded in the tens of thousands of images of the frontier that were produced in the U.S. in the nineteenth century.

While Native Americans were constantly represented as actors on the frontier stage in the nineteenth century, they had earlier been used as the very embodiment of the frontier itself, of that wild land that needed to be tamed and made "productive." This geographic personification—the Native American as the New World—appeared most often in the form of the semi-naked "Indian Queen" with classicized features. This emblematic figure had been used since the arrival of Europeans in the New World to represent this world as a whole—North, Central, and South America—but she also briefly enjoyed the status of a national symbol in the U.S. in the late eighteenth century, when such symbols were being actively sought by the new nation. Such a representation can be found in Augustin Dupré's *The Diplomatic Medal* (1790). 137 Here the figure of Mercury, the winged messenger representing Europe (the Old World), greets the female personification of the U.S., wearing a feathered headdress and skirt (the New World). She is seated beside packaged objects, toward which she gestures with her right hand. In her left hand she holds a horn filled with fruits which she extends toward Mercury. Thus, in exchange for manufactured goods from Europe, the newly formed United States of America would provide food and raw materials. In order more clearly to connect the packaged objects to the left of the female figure with Europe,

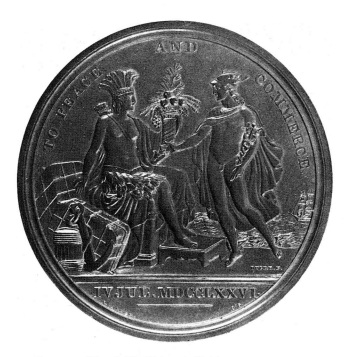

137 AUGUSTIN DUPRÉ *The Diplomatic Medal* 1790. Diameter 2⅝ (6.7)

symbol of the American eagle festooned with a medallion containing the stars and stripes of the new national flag, identify her as a representation of the United States of America. Her association with the indigenous peoples of the New World has also not totally disappeared. It remains in the form of the childlike figure with Native American features who accompanies her. It is this childlike figure who now wears the feathered headdress and skirt worn by the woman in the diplomatic medal. While the female figure in the engraving does retain two token feathers attached to her headband, they are much more elegant than those in the child's headdress.

According to the art historian Barbara Groseclose, this shift from a strong central character bearing Native American referents to an ancillary childlike Native figure parallels the enforced dependency of Native peoples on the U.S. federal government during the nineteenth century. Native physiognomy or clothing now refer to "condition, not geography—race instead of place." This is borne out in the engraving by the placement of the native figure behind the shield and by the figure's adoring gaze in the direction of America. The subservience of this native figure is further evident if we

138 "America," anonymous engraving from *The Four Continents* 1804. 13⅝ × 9⅞ (34.6 × 24.6)

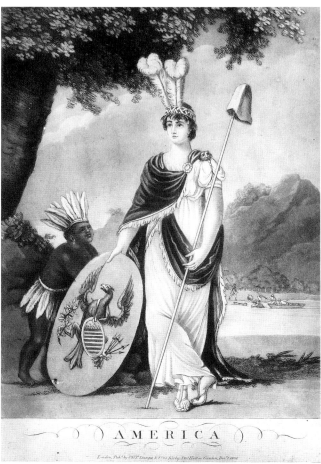

an anchor is placed in the foreground, which corresponds to the ship behind Mercury. And finally, in addition to the commemorative date on the lower portion of the coin—July 4, 1776—which marks this female figure as representing the U.S. rather than the New World as a whole, are the words above the figures—"To Peace and Commerce."

In the early years of the nineteenth century, this "Indian Queen" was replaced by a figure whose "Greekness" received greater emphasis, as in an anonymous engraving, "America," of 1804. The bared breasts and feathered skirt of the figure on the diplomatic medal are replaced by a simple gown reminiscent of the clothing worn by women in ancient Greece. Yet this figure also has a decidedly "contemporary" look to her. The Greek world was a major source for designers of female clothing in the early nineteenth century, particularly in France. "America" also wears an elaborate cloak elegantly draped across her shoulders, and against her left arm rests a long pole with a liberty cap on its top end, a reference to both the American Revolution of 1776 and the French Revolution of 1789. Indeed, one could almost imagine her attending a ball in Paris in honor of Napoleon Bonaparte, whose coronation as Emperor the same year the engraving was produced brought an end, at least for the time being, to the political experiments in revolutionary republican rule brought on by the French Revolution.

While the title of the engraving might suggest that this female figure represents the New World as a whole, the liberty cap and the shield, on which is emblazoned the new U.S.

compare the compositions of the diplomatic medal and the engraving. The relationship between the U.S. and Europe is presented in the medal as an exchange of gifts between equals. Mercury offers the gifts of the powers of Europe to the enthroned Indian Queen, who is both Old World (classicized features) and New World (feathered skirt and headdress). Both are presented within a horizontal composition as mutually interdependent. Both are shown with heads in profile and frontal torsos; both are approximately the same size and on the same level; both are "dignified" by Classical referents. The New World is gendered female and is associated with the land or nature; the Old World is male and will transform the products of nature offered to it by the female figure into products of culture, manufactured goods.

The relationship articulated in the engraving between Euro-Americans and Native Americans—domestic relations as opposed to foreign relations—is one of subservience, not equality. The composition itself is hierarchical. The native figure is located at the base of a triangle whose apex is the head of America. The native figure is half the size of America and leans toward her, gazing upward, while she is erect and gazes off into the distance. The native figure is more closely associated with the land in terms of skin color and costume and is the compositional counterpart of the moose-hunting scene to the right of America (the place occupied by the ship in the medal—again, domestic production versus foreign trade). The native figure is also not clearly gendered; s/he is a child, to be protected by Mother America and by the shield of Euro-American governance.

The decreasing presence of Native Americans as central emblematic representations of the U.S. parallels the increasing classicization of national symbols, and of narrative pictorial representations in general, in the early nineteenth century when national spokespeople promoted the U.S. as a new Greek democracy or Roman republic. In another work of 1804, John Vanderlyn's (1775–1852) painting *The Death of Jane McCrea*, the classicizing elements appear in the physiques and poses of the two Mohawk warriors, who are about to scalp the young colonist Jane McCrea. It was commissioned by Joel Barlow, President Jefferson's envoy to France, who had commemorated the event in his anti-British epic poem *The Columbiad*. The painting is meant to illustrate an incident that allegedly occurred during the American Revolution, when many Mohawks were hired by the British to help defeat the rebellious colonists, rather than constitute, like the engraving "America," an emblematic representation of the nation as a whole. Yet the blond Jane McCrea can also be read as a symbol, this time of colonial women and of the nation at large, for one justification for the decimation of the Native population was the threat they posed to colonial women and, thus, to the nation's future.

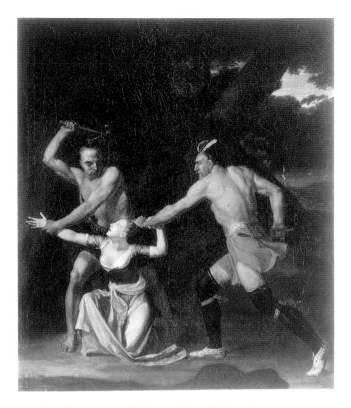

139 JOHN VANDERLYN *The Death of Jane McCrea* 1804. 32½ × 26½ (82.5 × 67.3)

The use of colonial women in this way—as symbols of colonial vulnerability—is particularly evident in narratives documenting the captivity of Europeans among Native Americans which first appeared in written form at the end of the seventeenth century, and in engravings and paintings like Vanderlyn's in the late eighteenth century. By the beginning of the nineteenth century, the captivity narratives which received the most attention were those in which the captor was a Native American man or men and the captive a European woman. These narratives cannot, of course, be read simply as records of the general historical practise of captivity in the seventeenth and eighteenth centuries. They give little indication, for example, that Native American men, women, and children formed the largest body of captives on the British Colonial frontier or that such native captives were treated as cruelly as were those white captives depicted in white-authored captivity narratives. Indeed, the Native American woman who received the greatest attention in art and literature, the early seventeenth-century Powhatan Pocahontas, was presented most often not as a captive (which she was), but as a symbol of the Christian salvation of Native American "savages" and the legitimacy of colonial appropriation of Native land through her various roles as John Smith's savior, the mediator between her people and the colonists at Jamestown, and the Christian wife of the tobacco planter John

Rolfe. This is certainly the case, for example, with John Gadsby Chapman's *The Baptism of Pocahontas* (1837–40), located in the Rotunda of the U.S. Capitol Building in Washington, D.C.

Representations of European captives among Native Americans were, like Chapman's painting, consciously constructed narratives meant to further the interests of the British colonists who produced and/or promoted them. As the anthropologist Pauline Turner Strong has recently pointed out, in the captivity narratives promulgated by colonial clergymen (who often edited or wrote the accounts):

> the figure of the female captive represents the vulnerability of the English colonies in the New World, where they are preyed upon by the brutish and diabolical forces of the wilderness which destroy domestic and civil order and threaten to seduce or devour them. The opposition between a vulnerable female Captive and a male Captor unrestrained in his savagery is fundamental to this interpretation.

Vanderlyn's painting graphically illustrates this opposition between the Native American male as diabolical force and the European female as vulnerable captive. Yet it also reveals the complex play between attraction and repulsion that marked so many paintings of Native Americans by Euro-Americans and that was present in some of the written captivity narratives as well. In the many narratives documenting male captivity that appeared in the early nineteenth century (for example, that of Daniel Boone), the experience of captivity among Native Americans was presented as having toughened the European male, as having made him more virile, more masculine. Of course, the European returns to his own people, who are then able to appreciate the transformation. Yet not everyone returned. In the Reverend John Williams' earlier account of his own captivity and that of his family in 1704, he records that once he and his family were freed, he was unable to "reclaim" his daughter Eunice, who was 7 years old at the time of her capture. Eunice eventually married a Mohawk who had been converted to Catholicism by the French Jesuits and remained in the community of Caughnawaga. She was thus doubly lost—to Catholicism and to a Native American male.

Eunice's story was soon buried, however, among the more numerous accounts of female deliverance from diabolical male Native forces through divine intervention or, as in Vanderlyn's painting, through death at the hands of these same forces. Vanderlyn's Mohawk warriors are not Catholic converts wedded in a Christian ceremony to white women, but fearful savages threatening to "seduce or devour" Jane McCrea. The attraction, or "seductiveness," of the Native male is present in the painting's sexual charge, in the powerful, "manly" physiques of the Native American men

and the almost bared breasts of the supplicant Jane McCrea. These elements, in conjunction with the impending blow from the tomahawk, worked simultaneously to enrage and arouse (in a sexual sense) and strike fear into the hearts of the white viewers, both male and female, who attended Vanderlyn's pay-as-you-enter exhibitions of this painting and others in New York, Baltimore, New Orleans, and other cities across the nation. As if to emphasize the power of the Native men, European manhood is represented by the tiny, ineffectual figure of McCrea's fiancé in the distant right background running vainly toward his loved one.

While Native Americans no longer played an emblematic role as national symbols in the nineteenth century, they still remained closely tied to the land in both literary and pictorial representations, a land that Europeans viewed with covetous eyes. From their arrival in the New World onward, European colonists believed the key to prosperity and a new life lay in the acquisition of greater and greater quantities of land. Yet the land they desired was already occupied, and by a people who held it communally, rather than individually. There was no private property, no individual ownership. Native peoples did not practise European techniques of intensive cultivation or mining, nor did they make the land produce more than was necessary to sustain the tribe. This communal ownership and lack of "productivity" was deemed "uncivilized" by Europeans and even, in the late nineteenth century, "communistic." The taming and "civilizing" of Native Americans and the taming and "civilizing" of the land, accomplished by the forcible removal of the former from the latter, were thus crucial elements in the material establishment of the nation and in the confirmation of the concept of "America" as a country whose very existence depended upon private ownership and the rights of the individual, in particular the right to exploit the land.

For most of the nineteenth century, the richest land yet to be exploited by European colonists and their descendants lay west of the Mississippi River. This was the area most commonly conjured up in people's minds when they heard the term "the West." One highly visible image of this unconquered territory was Emmanuel Leutze's (1816–68) *Westward* 141 *the Course of Empire Takes Its Way (Westward Ho!)*, painted in 1861–2 for the Capitol building in Washington, D.C. Leutze had studied and worked in Dusseldorf between 1841 and 1859 and was contacted in 1854 about a possible commission to decorate the Capitol building. The title of Leutze's work is drawn from a poem by the Irish idealist philosopher Bishop George Berkeley entitled "Verses on the Prospect of Planting Arts and Learning in America" (1752). The poem was inspired by Berkeley's efforts in 1726 to establish an experimental college in Bermuda to convert American Indians to Christianity. Its final stanza reads:

Westward the course of Empire takes its way;
The four first Acts already past,
A fifth shall close the Drama with the day;
Time's noblest offspring is the last.

Housed in the Capitol Building, Leutze's painting articulated the belief of European colonists since the sixteenth century that they had a Christian duty and an inalienable right to expand their territory and influence. This belief was codified in the U.S. in the nineteenth century in the doctrine of Manifest Destiny, which was used to justify the conquest and colonization of the western frontier. In conquering the west, the final New World frontier, Euro-Americans would bring to culmination the progress of civilization.

The sun-bleached bones and burial scene in the center of the painting attest to the hardships that the pioneers endured in crossing the vast continent, whose natural power and beauty is evoked by the towering, snow-capped mountains, the broad expanse of plateau land, and Golden Gate Bay, the port of San Francisco. Yet Leutze chooses to downplay one of the most written-about hardships encountered during the journey across the continent: Indian attacks. The only references to such attacks in the central scene are the bandaged head of the young man in the center foreground and the bow and arrows held by the boy who drives the first team of oxen (the latter is missing from the early oil study). Instead, Leutze places Native Americans in the margins of the composition, caught up among the plant tendrils of the painting's border along with wild animals, which, like Native Americans and the land itself, must be conquered and subdued. Native Americans are thus marginalized, both literally and figuratively, functioning as a framing device for the exploits of the U.S. pioneers.

Also included in the painting's border are roundels containing such figures as Moses, the spies of Eshcol bearing the fruits from Canaan, and Hercules. Yet these Old World figures are not presented as the equals of the Native figures or even as occupying the same world. Rather, they occupy their own separate worlds contained within the leafy borders of the roundels instead of being caught up among the vines like the animals and Native figures. These Old World men serve to reinforce the sanctity and significance of the central scene. Like them, the U.S. settlers are embarked on a momentous journey of discovery marked by trials and tribulations.

THE STAIN ON A PAINTER'S PALETTE: CHARLES BIRD KING AND GEORGE CATLIN

There is one other reference to Native American life in Leutze's painting *Westward the Course of Empire Takes Its Way*. It appears in the medallion portrait of the explorer William Clark in the lower right-hand corner of the oil study. Unlike Daniel Boone in the left-hand portrait, who is dressed in recognizably European clothes, Clark wears a buckskin jacket and animal-fur headdress, clothing that would have been immediately associated with the dress of Native Americans. These medallion portraits were transferred to the vertical frame segments in the final composition. In their place in the lower border were painted symbols of mining, agriculture, and hunting, activities which would transform the land from a state of wilderness into one of civilized productivity.

The practise of white men dressing up as Indians in the nineteenth century was not uncommon. For explorers like Clark, wearing Indian clothes and learning Indian ways was often essential for survival. For white men living in urban centers, dressing up as Indians was often a way to express symbolically a dissatisfaction with the material results of the government's expansionist policies—the decimation of Native peoples and of the forests in which they lived—or with the very idea of Progress itself. This form of dissatisfaction was literally acted out in various plays throughout the nineteenth century, one of the most popular of which was *Metamora: or, The Last of the Wampanoags; An Indian Tragedy in Five Acts* (1828) by John Augustus Stone. Native peoples represented a time of innocence and nobility before the development of urban centers and industrialization. As mentioned earlier, Native life also represented, for many men now caught up in urban professions, a more "manly" environment.

There were certain white men, however, who were not satisfied with simply donning the clothes of Native Americans; they also wanted to re-dress the Native Americans themselves, to define through pictorial representation what it meant to be or to look "Indian." Two such men were the painters Charles Bird King (1785–1862) and George Catlin (1796–1872). The works of King and Catlin can only be understood in the context of the U.S. government's official pronouncements about and actions against Native Americans in the first half of the nineteenth century. In 1803 President Jefferson signed an agreement with France to purchase for $15 million the region of Louisiana, which extended from the Mississippi River to the Rocky Mountains and from the Gulf of Mexico to British North America, thus effectively doubling the size of the U.S. This territory was inhabited, however, by numerous North American tribes. Their removal, therefore, became a central goal of U.S. Indian policy. What could not be settled by treaty or trading was settled by force or by disease. The removal of Native peoples from this territory was facilitated by pronouncements by government officials that Native peoples were already doomed, that their disappearance was inevitable not because of the actions of the U.S. government but because of their inherent inferiority. The popular literature of the period also abounded in stories of the "Last Indian," of noble savages who had to step aside because of the inevitable advance of civilization.

In 1824 the U.S. Secretary of War declared that Indians as a race were approaching extinction, despite the fact that their numbers were still significant. Many artists responded to this claim by hastening to paint what seemed to be the last generation of Native Americans. In 1856 the editor of the art magazine *The Crayon* wrote:

> It seems to us that the Indian has not received justice in American art. . . . It should be held in dutiful remembrance that he is fast passing away from the face of the earth. . . . Absorbed in his quiet dignity, brave, honest, eminently truthful, and always thoroughly in earnest, he stands grandly apart from all other known savage life. As such let him be, for justice sake, sometimes represented.

The government encouraged such representation by commissioning artists like King to paint portraits of many tribal chiefs. King studied in London at the Royal Academy and in the studio of the U.S. expatriate painter Benjamin West before returning to the U.S. in 1812. He set up a studio as a portrait painter in Washington, D.C. in 1819, and between 1821 and 1842 completed approximately 143 portraits of Native Americans. He was able to record the likenesses of Native Americans and thus capture the frontier experience in the comfort of his studio in Washington, D.C. because many Native delegations traveled to the capital in the 1820's and '30's to sign treaties negotiated with the U.S. government which ceded large tracts of land for western expansion. Members of these delegations often sat for their portraits, which were subsequently included in the Department of War collection or sold through private galleries. The portraits thus became part of a series of documents that recorded the "legal" transfer of the ownership of land from Native peoples to the federal government, a transfer that signified the "civilizing" of the "untamed" frontier.

142 One of the earliest of such portraits was King's *Young Omahaw, War Eagle, Little Missouri, and Pawnees*, painted in 1822. While the title of this multiple portrait suggests that this is an image of five different individuals, all bear a striking resemblance to one another. The art historian Julie Schimmel has suggested that the five men were based on the facial features of two Pawnee chiefs, Petalesharro, chief of the Pawnee Loups, and Peskelechaco, chief of the Republican Pawnees. King had painted these two chiefs when they had visited Washington, D.C. with a tribal delegation in 1821. Perhaps in attempting to emphasize the nobility of these individuals, King has sacrificed their individuality, creating a

facial composite that he hoped would draw a sympathetic response from a white audience. This facial type was interpreted by at least one observer, the English traveler William Faux who saw the delegation in Washington, D.C., as that of the ancient Roman. Faux noted that all of the men were "of large stature, very muscular, having fine open countenances, with the real noble Roman nose, dignified in their manners, and peaceful and quiet in their habits." Yet while the Roman noses and the peace medal around the neck of War Eagle reinforce the nobility and "peacefulness" of the five men, the face paint, jewelry, hair styles, and war club (its blade pointed ominously at War Eagle's neck) signify their difference and, ultimately, their savagery. Survival for Native peoples could be assured only through the abandoning of such signs of difference and the subsequent adoption of the signs of civilization—the clothing and habits of Euro-Americans.

While most mid-nineteenth-century viewers of King's multiple portrait would have read the costumes, facial paint, and hairstyles as evidence of a "noble savagery," late twentieth-century scholars have begun to read them, instead, as clues to a complex visual language used by many Native American tribes. The painted facial designs related to certain religious rituals and often signified a personal protective medicine. The way in which a person's buffalo robe was positioned also carried a specific message. Nine message-conveying robe positions are currently known, two of which involve baring one shoulder, which was either a courtship sign or a message of admonition. Hairstyles among the Omaha and Pawnee tribes signified tribal affiliation. The peace medals distributed by government officials were often prized possessions and signs of status. Thus while some contemporary art historians have questioned whether King's portrait contains accurate likenesses of five specific individuals, others have seen it, nevertheless, as providing valuable pieces of an historical puzzle now being reconstructed by contemporary scholars in their attempts to understand the dynamics of nineteenth-century tribal culture, even if only as filtered through the eyes of nineteenth- and twentieth-century Euro-Americans.

In 1830, two years after he was elected president, Andrew Jackson secured the passage of the Indian Removal Bill. By 1838, seventy thousand Native Americans had been forcibly removed from their homes east of the Mississippi to the Plains area west of the river, despite treaties signed earlier guaranteeing these people the right to their lands. Thousands died during this forced march. In the early 1830's the governor of Georgia summarized the general attitude of white negotiators toward treaties with Native peoples:

> Treaties were expedients by which ignorant, intractable, and savage people were induced without bloodshed to yield

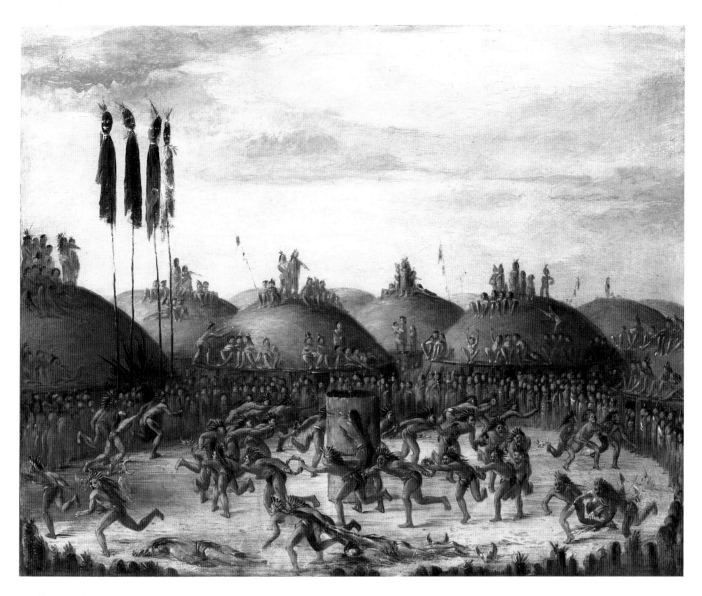

140 GEORGE CATLIN *The Last Race, Part of Okipa Ceremony* (Mandan) 1832. 23⅜ × 28⅛ (58.8 × 71.3)

up what civilized people had the right to possess by virtue of that command of the Creator delivered to man upon his formation—be fruitful, multiply, and replenish the earth, and subdue it.

This religious justification, which formed the moral basis of the ideology of Manifest Destiny, would be called upon time and again in dealings with Native Americans. White Europeans were the chosen people, Native Americans the heathen savages, agents of the devil who had to be converted or destroyed.

Unlike King, George Catlin did not wait in the nation's capital for Native Americans to come to him to have their portraits painted. In 1830 he left his position as a successful portrait painter in Washington, D.C. and Philadelphia for the frontier city of St. Louis. Over the next six years he would make five trips into the territory west of the Mississippi. In 1832 he explained his reasons for wanting to paint Native American life:

I have, for some years past, contemplated the noble races of red men who are now spread over these trackless forests and boundless prairies, melting away at the approach of civilization. Their rights invaded, their morals corrupted, their lands wrested from them, their customs changed, and therefore lost to the world; and they at last sunk into the earth, and the plowshare turning the sod over their graves, and I have flown to their rescue—not of their lives or of their race (for they are doomed and must perish), but to the rescue of their looks and their modes, at which the acquisitive world may hurl their poison and every besom of destruction, and trample them down and crush them to death; yet, phoenixlike, they may rise from the "stain on a painter's palette", and live again upon canvas, and stand forth for centuries yet to come, the living monuments of a noble race.

While Catlin thus sympathized with the plight of Native Americans, he also believed that they were "doomed and must perish." He does not attempt to rescue "their lives or . . . their race" but only "their looks and their modes." Native Americans can survive only as representations constructed through the eyes of a white artist. Catlin engages in what the anthropologist Renato Rosaldo calls "imperialist nostalgia," a yearning for that which one has directly or indirectly participated in destroying, a preservation of "looks and modes" in the face of the "unfortunate but necessary" destruction of a people.

Catlin produced over five hundred scenes of Indian life, including *The Last Race, Part of Okipa Ceremony* (Mandan) in 1832 and *Clermont, First Chief of the Tribe* (Osage) in 1834. He organized many of these paintings, along with costumes and a collection of native objects, into an "Indian Gallery," which toured the U.S. from 1837 to 1840 and then traveled to London and Paris in the 1840's. In 1837, the year the tour started, the Mandan, a tribe whose "looks and modes" Catlin had "rescued," was nearly completely wiped out by a plague of smallpox. Catlin's father wrote to him and commented that this event would greatly increase the value and importance of his son's works for they would, indeed, be one of the few reminders of a once flourishing tribe. The prophecy of the demise of Native Americans seemed to be coming true.

The success of Catlin's "Indian Gallery" in Europe was due in part to the fact that what Catlin presented was an affirmation of an already well established conception of the Native American as "noble savage." The British poet and dramatist John Dryden first used this phrase in 1670 in a play about the New World entitled *The Conquest of Granada*: "I am free as nature first made man, Ere the base laws of servitude began, When wild in the woods the noble savage ran." This concept of "noble savagery" as a desirable condition was again promoted in the eighteenth century by Rousseau, Voltaire, and other French Enlightenment thinkers in their criticisms of what they viewed as corrupt contemporary French morals and practises. While Catlin's images were more particularized than earlier European representations of the generic "noble savage," they still participated in a larger discourse about an "innocence" or "purity" that, while desirable in many ways, was part of a past that, in the end, could not be recreated. The "noble savage," untainted by civilization, was destined to make way for its inevitable arrival.

Thus, despite Catlin's attempts to reproduce on canvas or paper exactly what he saw in front of him, his images of Native American life were filtered, by himself and by the many individuals who viewed his work, through the lens of an "imperialist nostalgia" that celebrated an ideal "noble savage." There were also instances when he intentionally altered a scene or composition. One example of this can be found in the frontispiece to his memoirs, *Letters and Notes . . .*, published in London in 1841. Catlin would like us to believe that this frontispiece records a scene that actually occurred. Beneath the engraving is the caption "The Author painting a Chief at the base of the Rocky Mountains". Yet in Catlin's written description of this scene in the text of the memoirs he states that he painted the second chief of the Mandan tribe, Mah-To-Toh-Pa, indoors with a belt containing a tomahawk and scalping knife and wearing a bear claw necklace, surrounded by women and children. In the frontispiece these specific items have been removed. The scene has been shifted outdoors and two tipis have been located behind the group of figures.

What is the significance of these changes? How do they alter the meaning of the image? Removing some of the chief's symbols of power as a warrior and spiritual leader—the tomahawk, scalping knife, and bear claw necklace—makes him appear less threatening, both to Catlin within the image itself and to the reader of Catlin's memoirs. Moving the scene outdoors allows Catlin to increase the number of figures who are witness to his recording of the features of the Mandan chief. This larger number, which now includes men as well as women and children, attests to the importance of the event and the significance of Catlin's artistic achievements. The expressions of fear and wonder on the faces of the spectators also attest not only to Catlin's own accomplishments as an artist, but also to those of European artistic mimesis in general. Catlin represents his ability to capture the physical likeness of the chief on canvas as an act of magic in the eyes of the Mandan villagers. While he has chosen to render his figures in the reductive graphic style of the Neoclassicist Flaxman, whose drawings of Greek vase figures were often described as "neo-primitive," Catlin's figures are still much more three-dimensional than the elementary stick figures on the sides of the tipi that represent Mandan artistic expression.

Catlin's familiarity with the pictorial art of the Mandan is recorded in his memoirs. In fact, Ma-To-Toh-Pa gave Catlin a replica of his own painted buffalo-skin robe on which he had recorded his military exploits. While the whereabouts of this robe is unknown today, another robe (collected in 1837) closely resembles Catlin's own written and pictorial descriptions of the one he had been given. The horses and human figures are certainly two-dimensional and highly schematic. Yet they are much more sophisticated in their rendering and

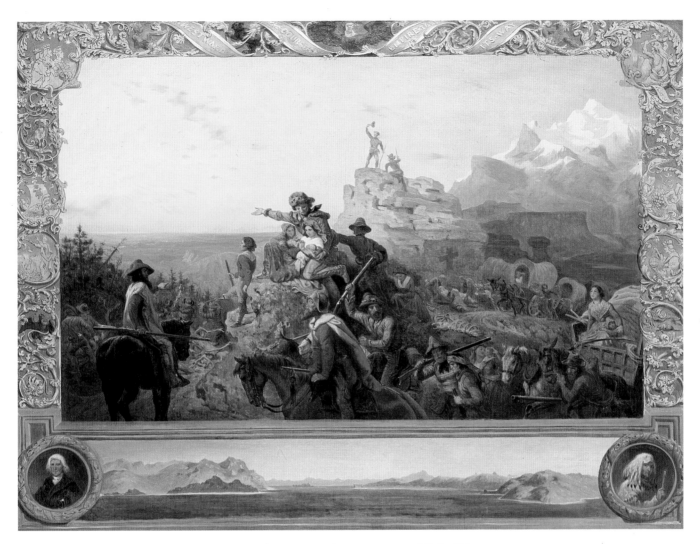

141 EMMANUEL LEUTZE study for *Westward the Course of Empire Takes its Way (Westward Ho!)* 1861. 33¼ × 43⅜ (84.5 × 110.2)

design than the stick figures on the tipi. These stick figures, with their triangular torsos and frontal heads, actually more closely resemble the designs on an earlier Mandan buffalo robe sent to President Jefferson by the explorers Lewis and Clark in 1805. The later Mandan robe reveals an increasing sureness in the handling of human and animal bodies and a greater concern with decorative patterning. Artists in various Plains tribes would continue to develop this narrative artform throughout the nineteenth century and use it as a means of written communication, incorporating knowledge they had gained from observing the work of artists like Catlin while maintaining their own distinctive style and iconography. A major change in materials occurred in the middle of the century with the widespread introduction through trade of paper and new pigments. Some examples of these new works will be discussed below.

The tipis themselves may have been included for compositional reasons. The central tipi not only provides a surface for the display of Native American imagery, but also connects the two major figures in the composition, Catlin and Mah-To-Toh-Pa. The lines marking the sides of the tipi literally run through the heads of the two figures, anchoring them within the pyramidal composition and suggesting a certain equality between them. The easel located between the two figures also echoes the shape of the tipi, reinforcing the comparison between the stick figures located on the sides of the tipi and the mimetic portrait resting on the easel, between the "childlike" record of gun-toting exploits and the European celebration of noble individuality. But the inclusion of the tipis in this particular scene is puzzling in view of the fact Catlin knew quite well that the distinctive architecture of the Mandan was a spherical earth structure, not a bison-hide tipi. These spherical structures are evident in his painting *The Last Race, Part of Okipa Ceremony.* The art historian Kathryn Hight has argued that by locating the Mandan in front of tipis, the dwelling structures of nomadic Plains tribes, rather than in 140

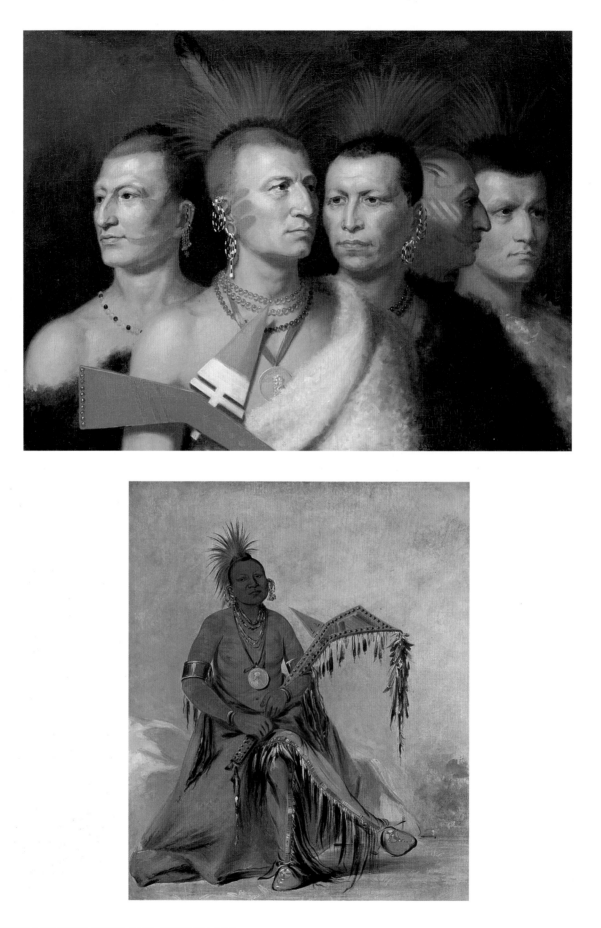

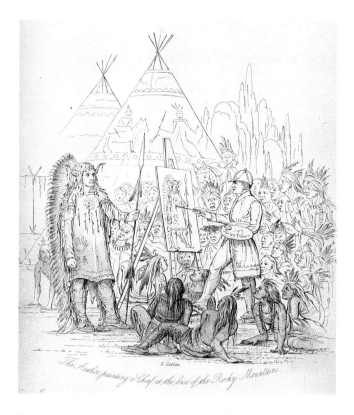

It is interesting to compare this engraving with a later painting based on it, *Catlin Painting the Portrait of Mah-To-Toh-pa—Mandan* (1857–69). In this painting Catlin has removed the tipis and shifted Mah-To-Toh-Pa closer to the center of the painting, increasing the number of Mandan located behind the chief. He has also replaced the European easel of the earlier engraving with a makeshift structure of branches tied together, which replicates the structural framework of the tipi. In addition he leaves the canvas only roughly attached to its frame, suggesting the loosely attached hide coverings of the tipi. Thus, the tipi and easel of the engraving have been collapsed together in the painting.

The effect of these changes is to heighten the presence of the Mandan chief in the composition and the connection between the Mandan and nature, and to locate Catlin the artist more clearly within the Mandan world. The emphasis on Catlin and his talents as a painter of "Indians" was appropriate for the frontispiece of his memoirs. In his Indian Gallery, however, where he claimed to be recreating the "looks and modes" of various Native American tribes, viewers would have been more interested in the physical features and particularities of Mah-To-Toh-Pa and Mandan culture in general and in the surrounding landscape. Yet Catlin is still very much present as artist and creator in this image, and perhaps even more so than in the engraving, for in the painting Catlin presents himself as literally repainting the surfaces of the "Indian" tipi, as redefining the significance of the Mandan chief, and of pictorial representation in general, in Mandan culture.

front of the spherical earth structures of the more sedentary, agricultural Mandan, Catlin participates in the creation of a generalized view of Native Americans, one which erases their differences and particularities (the tipi soon became a sign for "Indian"), even as he claims to be recording these particularities.

142 (*left, above*) CHARLES BIRD KING *Young Omahaw, War Eagle, Little Missouri, and Pawnees* 1822. 36⅛ × 28 (91.8 × 71.1)

143 (*left, below*) GEORGE CATLIN *Clermont, First Chief of the Tribe* (Osage) 1823. 29 × 24 (73.7 × 61)

144 (*above*) GEORGE CATLIN *Letters and Notes* . . . , frontispiece, "The Author painting a Chief at the Base of the Rocky Mountains," 1841. 9½ × 6 (24 × 15)

145 (*right*) MANDAN buffalo robe, collected in 1837. Width 82¾ (210)

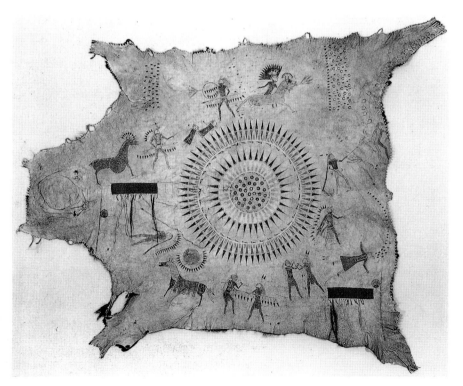

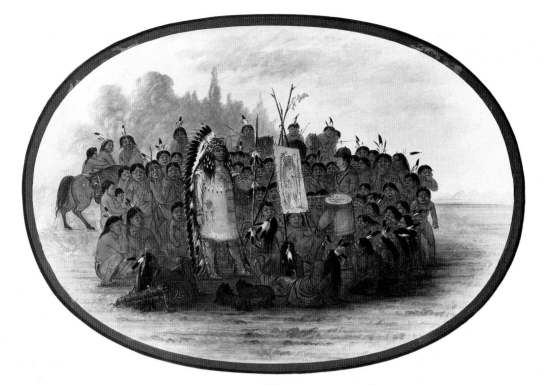

146 GEORGE CATLIN *Catlin Painting the Portrait of Mah-To-Toh-Pa—Mandan* 1857–69. 15⅛ × 23⅞ (39 × 60.6)

ALTERNATIVE REPRESENTATIONS: PHOTOGRAPHY AND LEDGER ART

At the same time that Catlin was drawing on the conventions and tools of easel painting to construct his image of Native Americans, others were utilizing a different medium, one which they claimed was better able accurately to render the faces of the frontier—photography. How these photographic faces differed from the painted faces by Catlin can best be seen by comparing Catlin's *Clermont, First Chief of the Tribe* to Thomas Easterly's *Keokuk, or the Watchful Fox* (1847).

Clermont is seated on a rock, with a loosely painted landscape behind him, an arrangement common in British portrait painting. He is at ease, legs crossed, head slightly tilted, eyes looking off into the distance, the hint of a smile on his face. His skin and clothes are painted a warm red-brown. The viewer's eye wanders freely over Clermont's body, stopping to examine the jewelry or feathers or painted war club cradled in his arms or the peace medal hanging around his neck. There is a sense of complicity between the viewer/painter and the sitter, a willingness on the part of Clermont to expose himself to such scrutiny.

The opposite is true of Easterly's photograph of the Sauk and Fox leader Keokuk. Confrontation replaces complicity. Rigidly posed in a stark interior setting, eyes staring straight ahead, Keokuk forces the viewer to acknowledge the artificiality of the posing process even as the viewer is struck by the immediacy or presence of Keokuk himself. Paintings like Catlin's were able to sentimentalize, to romanticize, and thus to create a comfortable distance between the viewer and the subject. Easterly's photograph, like many mid-nineteenth-century photographs, did not do this. Instead it presented in black and white the impassive, the stony-faced, rendered in sharp detail yet emotionally inaccessible. It captured the underlying hostility embedded in this encounter between white photographer and Native American chief. Keokuk's imprisonment within the photographic frame can be seen as the pictorial counterpart of the real imprisonment of his people on reservations (as I indicated earlier, conquering and recording often go hand in hand). It is little wonder Native Americans saw photography as the work of the devil.

Keokuk was well known for his diplomacy in negotiating with government officials. In 1837 he succeeded in protecting Sauk and Fox claims to their Iowa land holdings against counterclaims by the Sioux. Over a decade earlier, in 1824, he had traveled to Washington, D.C. with a delegation of Sauk and Fox, Iowa and Piankashaw leaders. During this visit his portrait was painted by King. A copy of this portrait, made by King in 1827—*Keokuk, Sac (Watchful Fox)*—reveals King's reliance on the same European portrait tradition that Catlin drew upon in painting Clermont. The same contrasts exist, therefore, between King's painting of Keokuk and Easterly's photograph. In the painting Keokuk is at ease, a slight smile on his face, his gaze directed beyond the picture frame. The

143
147

148

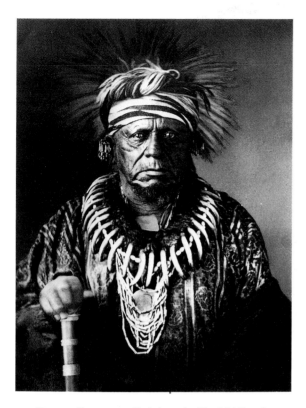

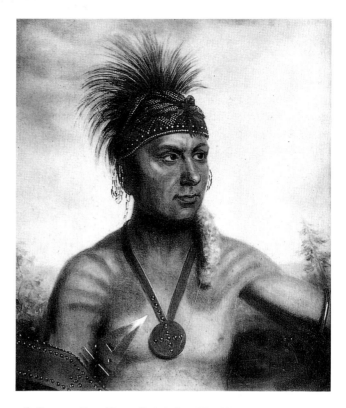

147 THOMAS EASTERLY *Keokuk, or the Watchful Fox* 1847.

148 CHARLES BIRD KING *Keokuk, Sac (Watchful Fox)* 1827. 17½ × 13¾ (44.4 × 34.9)

trees and sky in the background locate the tribal chief in an ill-defined landscape, belying the fact that the portrait was painted in King's studio. Easterly engages in no such illusionism. Keokuk sits in front of a blank backdrop, directly engaging the viewer with his gaze. The bulky figure of the older man also contrasts with the slender, almost boylike body of the young Keokuk. It is difficult to imagine that the painted Keokuk is the same young man that the ethnologist Henry Rowe Schoolcraft, who met him in 1825, described as "like another Coriolanus," "a prince, majestic and frowning. The wild, native pride of man, in the savage state, flushed by success in war, and confident in the strength of his arm, was never so fully depicted to my eyes." While Schoolcraft played upon the savagery of the "noble savage," King chose to emphasize the nobility, downplaying any sense of threat or aggression.

Many of the photographs of Native Americans taken by Easterly and others appeared in sets of stereoscopic photographs sold throughout the latter half of the nineteenth century for viewing in the home. Photographs were also added to official government records of transactions between Native American peoples and government representatives and were translated into illustrations that appeared in popular magazines and novels. Sometimes these photographs provided only general inspirations for such illustrations; other times they

were literally copied. This was also the case with certain paintings and drawings. Sometimes the magazine illustrator utilized general painterly conventions in creating his or her image; other times s/he copied specific paintings or drawings in detail.

Page forty-one of the January 16, 1869 issue of *Harper's Weekly* contains a series of images taken from the worlds of both painting and drawing, and photography. This page is part of a larger article recounting General Custer's surprise attack and victory over the Cheyenne Chief Black Kettle at Washita River, Oklahoma, on November 27, 1868. After killing the chief and 102 of his warriors, Custer and his troops proceeded to the undefended village where all men over 8 years old and many of the women and younger children were also killed. The lodges and winter stores of food and ammunition were then destroyed, leaving those who survived to die a slow death from starvation or exposure to the cold. Custer also destroyed 875 Indian ponies.

The three wood engravings that take up most of the page are meant both to illustrate and justify what came to be known as the Washita River Massacre. The top and bottom images were engraved versions of drawings produced by Theodore R. Davis, a well-known illustrator–reporter on the *Harper's* staff. While Davis had spent six months with Custer out West in 1867, he had been back East for at least a year when the

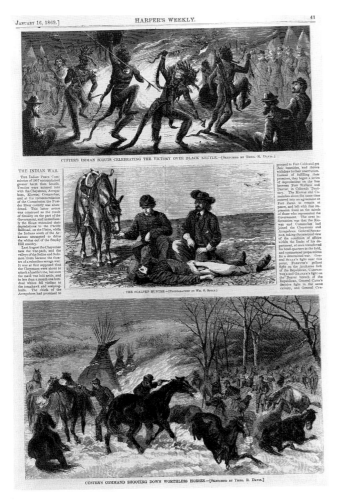

CUSTER'S INDIAN SCOUTS CELEBRATING THE VICTORY OVER BLACK KETTLE.—[SKETCHED BY THEO. R. DAVIS.]

THE INDIAN WAR.

THE SCALPED HUNTER.—[PHOTOGRAPHED BY WM. S. SOULE.]

CUSTER'S COMMAND SHOOTING DOWN WORTHLESS HORSES.—[SKETCHED BY THEO. R. DAVIS.]

149 THEODORE R. DAVIS and WILLIAM S. SOULE, Page 41, *Harper's Weekly*, January 16, 1869.

149   Washita River Massacre occurred. His experience with Custer undoubtedly made him the most logical person to be assigned the task of illustrating the article.

The drawings Davis produced give the impression that he had actually been present at Washita River, an impression that is reinforced by the very fact that they are "sketches," quickly executed, and by the phrase "Sketched by Theo. R. Davis" included in parentheses after the captions for each image. Davis did not portray the actual battle itself, but instead showed two events that happened immediately afterwards. The top engraving is captioned "Custer's Indian Scouts Celebrating the Victory Over Black Kettle." The opposition between the civilized white soldiers and the savage Indian scouts is spelled out in the wild gestures, face paint, and costumes of the group of Osage and Kaw scouts, who perform by firelight, and the impassive faces and poses of the white soldiers who watch. The demonic aspect of the scouts is further reinforced by the tails that form part of their costume. This sketch also suggests that Native Americans, as much as

whites, were responsible for the massacre at Washita River. The U.S. Army took advantage of existing rivalries between tribes and played one tribe off against another, promising land or weapons in exchange for cooperation.

The bottom image shows Custer's soldiers engaged in an activity that the caption describes as "shooting down worthless horses." Again there is an opposition between the wild, terrified horses and the calm soldiers who shoot the horses in the head at close range. Thus, the horses—untamed nature—and Native Americans are equated. This would not be the first time that the destruction of animals was seen as parallel to the destruction of Native Americans. The animal in question, however, was usually the buffalo. Just as the destruction of the Cheyenne horses (certainly not "worthless" to them) was part of the military strategy of the 1868–9 campaign, so too was the destruction of buffalo part of a larger military strategy. "Kill every buffalo you can," advised one army officer. "Every buffalo dead is an Indian gone."

The frantic activity contained in the upper and lower sketches is in sharp contrast to the stasis of the central image. The words in parentheses after the caption "The Scalped Hunter" explain this contrast—"Photographed by Wm. S. Soule." Photographic technology at that time required the subject to remain still for long periods of time—anywhere from five to thirty seconds. Photographs of military ventures, therefore, often included images of burned-out buildings or of corpse-filled battlefields. This is particularly evident in the extensive photographic record of the Civil War that was produced by photographers such as Mathew Brady and Alexander Gardner. While the sketch could capture the action of war, even if only as conceived of in the imagination of the artist, the photograph could clearly capture only its more deadly aftermath.

This wood engraving after a photograph by William Soule contains the one dead person on the magazine page. But this white man did not die as a consequence of the Washita River battle. The source of the photograph is included in the *Harper's* article. The hunter Ralph Morrison was murdered and scalped by Cheyenne warriors less than a mile from Fort Dodge, Iowa, on December 7, 1868. William Soule, stationed at the Fort, "availed himself of the opportunity to benefit science and gratify the curiosity of your readers by taking a counterfeit presentment of the body, literally on the spot." This was, according to the author of the article, "the only picture ever taken on the Plains of the body of a scalped man, photographed from the corpse itself, and within an hour after the deed was done." The author continues:

> The pose of the remains is delineated exactly as left by the savages, the horrible contortion of the ghastly features, the apertures left by the deadly bullet, the reeking scalp, the

wounds, the despoiled pockets of the victim, all are true to life anomalous as the presentment of death may seem.

The gruesome detail of this description serves not only to titillate the reader but also to reinforce the veracity of the visual account. This aspect of truthfulness is further guaranteed by the scientific method used to capture the scene—photography—despite the fact that the written description includes elements not readily visible, or not visible at all ("horrible contortion"), in the engraving. Of course, even if the dead body had been photographed exactly as it had been found, the two figures behind it were obviously posed to create a connection between the dead man and the actions of the soldiers who would avenge his death. The death of one white hunter thus becomes the justification for the Washita River Massacre and its aftermath, as captured in the images at the top and bottom of the page, despite the fact that the hunter was killed ten days after the massacre itself had occurred.

The battles between Native American warriors and the U.S. Army continued throughout the late 1860's and early '70's, with the former suffering increasing numbers of defeats. In the spring of 1875 seventy-two Southern Plains chiefs and warriors were imprisoned at Fort Marion in Saint Augustine, Florida. These leaders of the Cheyenne, Kiowa, Arapaho, Comanche, and Caddo Indians were deemed "dangerous criminals" by the U.S. government for their wartime aggressions and were held in Fort Marion to ensure that their people would adjust more peacefully to the reservation life that had been imposed upon them in the aftermath of the Southern Plains wars.

During their three years of incarceration at Fort Marion, many of these chiefs and warriors filled drawing books with brightly colored images of Plains Indian life. Such drawings on paper were not unique to Fort Marion, but had appeared earlier in the century after the introduction of paper and drawing materials to the Plains Indians by white traders. By the last third of the century this "ledger art," so-called because the paper often came from accountants' ledgers, began to replace the traditional pictorial surface of buffalo-hide robes within tribal culture. The imagery that filled these ledger books continued a long tradition of narrative pictorial art that had developed within Plains tribal culture both before and after the arrival of Europeans. The figures were highly two-dimensional, with clear, dark outlines that were carefully filled in with flat areas of color. The exploits of warriors and hunters were the primary subject matter of these works, which were often taken along on hunts or into battle.

Captain Richard H. Pratt encouraged the artistic efforts of his prisoners by providing them with drawing materials and allowing them to sell their works to the tourists who often visited the fort. There was thus a new audience for the work of these artists—white tourists rather than fellow warriors or tribal members. The effect of both this new situation of imprisonment and this new audience can be seen in the changing subject matter: scenes from daily life at the fort were now added to war and hunting exploits—which led to new representations of the encounter between whites and Native Americans. At least one of the Fort Marion artists, the Cheyenne Howling Wolf, also had extensive contact with European artistic traditions during a trip to Boston for medical treatment, which resulted in certain stylistic changes in his work, notably an increased painterliness that countered the two-dimensionality of his earlier ledger art.

In *Fort Marion Prisoners Dancing for Tourists* (1875–7) the 150 Cheyenne warrior Cohoe presents his own interpretation of the theme of "the savage Indian entertaining civilized Euro-Americans" that had been represented by Davis approximately six years earlier in his *Harper's* sketch. There are striking differences between the two images. While Davis places the viewer at eye level, within the circle of army officers, Cohoe presents a double perspective. The viewer is simultaneously on the same level as the group and above it. The overall feeling is of distance, or removal, as opposed to the inclusiveness of Davis' piece. While Davis creates a sense of three-dimensionality through the use of shading and perspectival conventions, Cohoe emphasizes the two-dimensionality of his image through the use of flat areas of color and clearly outlined figures placed in a space devoid of ground lines or other orientational markers. Davis pays great attention to the costumes of the dancing scouts while Cohoe pays equal attention to the costumes of the white tourists, particularly those of the women. The identities of Cohoe's figures appear, indeed, to lie in their clothing rather than their facial features, for their faces are left completely blank.

Both Davis and Cohoe were creating for white audiences. They were, however, creating from strikingly different positions. The white artist Davis was creating within the conventions of Western art for an employer committed to the sensationalization of information and for an audience eager to experience—vicariously of course—some of the drama of the frontier, an audience that, for the most part, had accepted the distinction between "savage" and "civilized" that is embedded in Davis's image. The Cheyenne prisoner Cohoe, on the other hand, was drawing upon the conventions of Plains Indian hide painting to create images for white tourists who wanted to take with them a souvenir of their trip to what the art historian Janet Berlo describes as an "idealized penal colony, where a miniature but representative society of Plains warriors enacts scaled-down and sanitized simulacra of warfare for their captors' pleasure." The three-dimensionality and mimetic nature of Davis' work read as "real" to the white viewer; the two-dimensionality of Cohoe's work read as

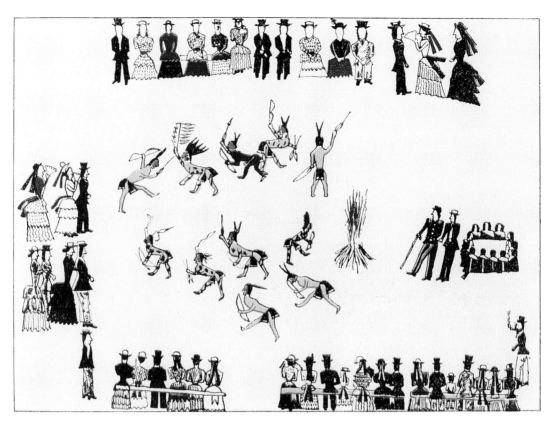

150 COHOE. *Fort Marion Prisoners Dancing for Tourists* 1875–7.

childlike, naive. The tourists who left Fort Marion thus took with them, again in Berlo's words, "a memento of their voyeuristic experience, secure in their privileged insight into 'the Indian Problem' and its solutions."

150   Yet Cohoe's fellow prisoners would have read the image differently. Having experienced, themselves, the indignity of having to don "traditional dress" to perform for tourists, they may well have read the scene as one of humiliation rather than pleasurable entertainment. The two-dimensional style would have signified not "childlikeness," but their own art traditions, while the tourist audience arranged in rigid order around the dancers would have conveyed a sense of the dancers' own entrapment, both literally at Fort Marion and figuratively within a foreign culture. Yet the gaps between the groups of tourists suggest that this entrapment was far from complete. The continuation of their ceremonies and their visual arts traditions, in no matter how compromised a form, undoubtedly functioned as a means of resistance to the imposed white order. Through their ledger drawings the imprisoned chiefs and warriors represented their experiences at Fort Marion not only for themselves and for white tourists, but also for other members of their tribes: the Fort Marion prisoners often sent drawings to their families as "letters" and received similar pictographic responses in return.

The Kiowa artist prisoner Wo-Haw also created an image that spoke to the entrapment of Native Americans within white culture. In *Reading Class at Fort Marion* (1875–7) Wo-Haw depicts, again in the flat, two-dimensional Plains style, a schoolroom scene where nine warriors, in Western suits with hair shorn, attentively watch the female teacher in the center. But this group is also being watched, not by another white teacher or soldier but by the spectral form of a Native American with a feather in his long hair. Here is the ghostly presence of that culture from which these warriors had been forcibly removed, a culture that their white captors wanted them to forget or to replicate only for the amusement of tourists. 151

In the late nineteenth century two solutions had been proposed to the "Indian problem": extermination ("the only good Indian is a dead Indian") and assimilation. The need for a "solution" became even greater after the defeat of Custer on June 25–26, 1876 by the Sioux at the Battle of Little Big Horn in southeast Montana. An article in the September 1876 issue of *Frank Leslie's Popular Monthly* suggested that reservations and the Indian way of life should be abolished and Indians given trousers and shirts instead of blankets. This blueprint for survival was also promoted a decade later by The Friends of the Indians, which included many wealthy philanthropists

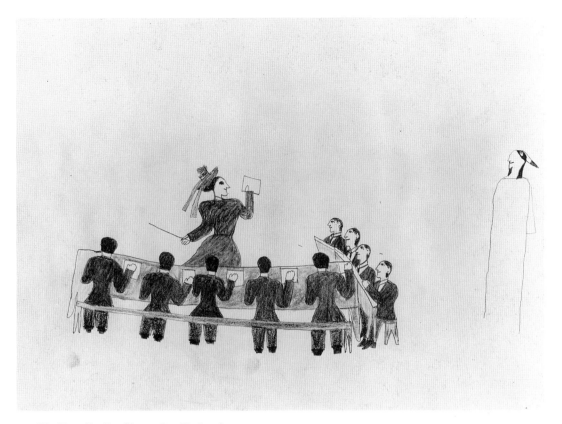

151 WO-HAW *Reading Class at Fort Marion* 1875–7. 8¾ × 11¼ (22.2 × 28.5)

and Protestant clergymen, who felt Native Americans should be given membership in U.S. society in exchange for a repudiation of their Indian ways. The Friends lobbied in support of the Dawes Act, passed by Congress in 1887, which offered an allotment of land and eligibility for full citizenship to every Native American male who willingly cut his ties with his tribe and adopted the habits of "civilized" Euro-American life.

Yet the author of the article in *Frank Leslie's Popular Monthly* also acknowledged that there had been greater success in assimilating Africans and Chinese than there had been in assimilating Indians, primarily because the former had been removed from their homelands and cultures, making their immediate survival in this new country more dependent upon assimilation. But this was not a "new" country for Native Americans, and their sense of entitlement to their ancestral lands and ways of life was strong. Assimilation was successful only after a large percentage of the Native population had been killed, and then only partially successful. The land on which they lived, and continue to live, functioned as a reminder of their culture and their history.

Another image speaks to this process of assimilation, an image captured almost a decade after the final major military encounter between Native Americans and the U.S. military at

Wounded Knee, South Dakota, on December 29, 1890, a battle Native Americans lost. The image in question is a photograph by the Washington, D.C. photographer Frances Benjamin Johnston entitled *Class in American History* (1899– 1900). It was part of a larger series Johnston had been commissioned to execute of the Hampton Institute, a co-educational school for African Americans and Native Americans founded just after the Civil War. The series was shown at the Universal Exposition in Paris in 1900 as part of an exhibit tracing the rapid progress of African Americans since the end of the Civil War. Here again, as in Wo-Haw's drawing, Native Americans in Western European garb with cropped hair, this time accompanied by African Americans, are pictured with a Native American in "traditional" dress. This time the "traditional" Native American is not a ghostly presence—the scientific medium of photography did not traffic in ghosts. He is present in the flesh and blood—but not, however, as evidence of a living culture. Rather, he is presented as "history" and as artifact, a symbol of a noble yet "savage" culture done away with by the forces of "progress" embodied in the print of gunslinging cowboys or U.S. cavalry above the heads of the children and in the very clothes of the children themselves.

Both Wo-Haw and Johnston present, in their images, the

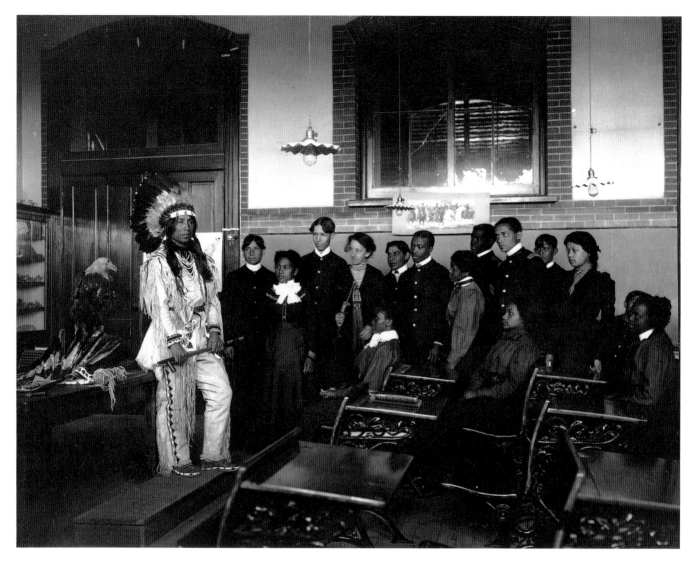

152 FRANCES BENJAMIN JOHNSTON *Class in American History* 1899–1900. 7½ × 9½ (19 × 24.1)

juxtapositions marveled at by the anthropologist Lévi-Strauss and brushed away by the photographer Curtis. They mark the coming together of two worlds that was so crucial a part of the development of visual culture and of a sense of national identity in the U.S. in the nineteenth century. Wo-Haw presents Native American culture as a living presence (albeit a ghostly one) in the daily lives of his people; Johnston presents it as a curiosity, an example of what needs to be left behind as a lived experience, yet, at the same time, kept alive as a memory through endless pictorial representations. This living memory is necessary, according to Slotkin, in order to assuage a national conscience trying to reconcile the near-destruction of a people with the establishment of a democratic nation. Wo-Haw's image, and others like it, however, also need to be brought to the fore in order to remind us now that Native American culture did not die in the nineteenth century, but remained a resilient and dynamic force in Native life. Recognizing this allows us to read the many images of the American frontier critically, not as records of unchallengable facts or truths but as the products of individuals perpetuating or resisting the material and ideological processes of colonization and conquest.

· 7 ·

BLACK AND WHITE IN AMERICA

FRANCES K. POHL

AMERICA AS AN AFRICAN INVENTION

When emmanual leutze's *westward the course of Empire Takes Its Way (Westward Ho!)* appeared in its final form in the Capitol building in Washington, D.C. in December 1862, there were certain significant changes from the oil study of 1861. One of these changes, already mentioned in Chapter 6, was the addition of symbols of mining, hunting, and agriculture. A second change, and perhaps the most important, was the inclusion of an African American man in the center foreground leading a white woman and child on a mule.

The historian Lerone Bennett, Jr. has argued that "it is impossible to understand white America, it is impossible to understand Thomas Jefferson or George Washington or the U.S. Constitution, without some understanding of Africa's gift to the New World. And what that means . . . is that America, contrary to the generally accepted view, is an African as well as a European invention." The presence of large numbers of peoples of African descent on the North American continent since the sixteenth century has had a profound effect on the development of social, political, and economic structures in the U.S. For example, African slave labor made possible the growth of a plantation economy in the South in the seventeenth and eighteenth centuries, while African American wage labor contributed to the expansion of industrialization in the North in the late nineteenth century. And just as colonists from Northern Europe attempted to justify their destruction of Native Americans through the construction of the myth of the "noble savage," so too did these same colonists and their descendants try to justify their enslavement and exploitation of Africans and African Americans through representations of them as inferior to white Europeans. On the one hand, Africans were childlike and in

need of care; on the other, they were savage and in need of disciplining (they were not, however, "doomed to perish" for their labor was central to the country's economy). Pictorial representations of Africans and African Americans played an integral part in the construction and perpetuation of these beliefs and in the defining of a national culture. But they also played an integral part in the challenges to these beliefs and to this definition of national culture, challenges which grew in number and intensity by the middle of the nineteenth century and led to armed conflict between the North and the South. This chapter will look at both kinds of representations, those which attempted to enforce the myth of the child savage, and those which condemned it and offered alternative visions of Africa(n) as America(n).

Leutze received his Capitol commission in June 1861, only a few months after the opening salvo of the Civil War. One of the many causes of this war was disagreement over whether or not slavery should be extended into the new territories. Secretary of War Simon Cameron, who approved Leutze's initial study, was an expansionist opposed to the emigration of African Americans into the western territories. Leutze's inclusion of an African American man in such a prominent position in the final version of his celebration of western expansion indicates that he differed with Cameron on this point (Leutze's pro-abolitionist sentiments were well known). Instead, he suggests that African Americans, like their white counterparts, might experience a new freedom in the West. The inclusion of the African American man as part of a family group on a mule also suggests a parallel between the flight of the Holy Family from persecution at the hands of Herod and the opening up of the West. Leutze therefore provides another gloss on the theme of Manifest Destiny, this time marked by the morally charged arguments of the abolitionist movement.

The Civil War forced a re-evaluation of the image of the

141

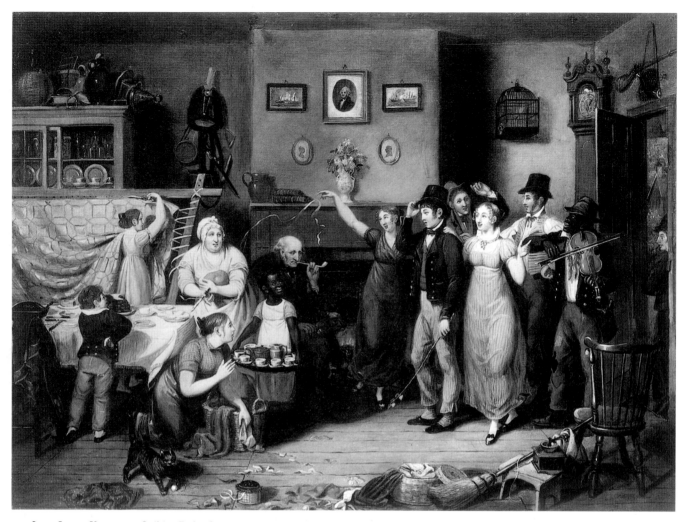

153 JOHN LEWIS KRIMMEL *Quilting Frolic* 1813. 16⅞ × 22⅜ (42.8 × 56.8)

African American in the art and literature of the U.S. Prior to the Civil War the dominant nineteenth-century stereotype of African American men was the high-stepping, banjo-playing "darkie," happy and childlike, who, when not working contentedly in the fields, performed either for his family or for his white owners. African American women were "mammys," protective of their white charges and proud of their place as servant, maid, and nanny within the white household. Enslavement was seen as "good" for Africans, who were inherently "savage" and had to be domesticated through slavery. To free them, therefore, would actually do them a disservice, for they would lose their childlike innocence (which some argued was achieved through enslavement and others claimed was "innate") and revert to savagery.

Such stereotypes appear in John Lewis Krimmel's (1786–1821) painting *Quilting Frolic* (1813). Krimmel was born in Germany and studied with the genre painter Johann Baptist Seele before coming to the U.S. in 1810. He was also an

admirer of the works of the British artists William Hogarth and David Wilkie and, like them, recorded the looks and foibles of the peasant, merchant, and artisanal classes.

Quilting Frolic contains a detailed inventory of the belongings of a middle-income household. The paintings on the wall—a portrait of Washington flanked by two maritime scenes, one of which involves a battle—attest to both the cultured and patriotic character of the household members. Other objects hanging on the walls or resting on the tops of cupboards indicate the social status and lineage of the family. The black servant girl and the black fiddler also mark this family's social status, the girl through her role as a servant and the fiddler through his shabby clothing, which contrasts so markedly with the finery of the white figures next to him. According to the art historian Guy McElroy, Krimmel was also among the first "to utilize physiognomical distortions [toothy grins, oversized lips] as a basic element in the depiction of African-Americans; his comic portrayal was probably meant to establish a good-natured humorous scenario, but it profoundly reinforced developing ideas regarding the humorous, even 'debased' appearance of African-Americans."

While the stereotypical depictions of African Americans produced by Krimmel and others dominated the artworld in the first half of the nineteenth century, such images did not go totally unchallenged, particularly after the establishment of the American Anti-Slavery Society in 1833. Joining African American anti-slavery organizations such as the Free African Society, founded in 1787, and the General Coloured Association, founded in 1826, the American Anti-Slavery Society became one of the key organizations in the U.S. abolitionist movement. Led by both African Americans and whites, it flooded the southern slave-holding states with abolitionist literature and lobbied throughout the U.S. for an end to slavery. It was fueled by the rise of evangelical religion in the 1820's, which called for an end to sinful practises and allowed African Americans to enter its ranks. The early abolitionist movement also revived the charges of political hypocrisy that had been leveled at the rebel revolutionaries by the British at the end of the eighteenth century. How could revolutionaries claim independence in the name of freedom and liberty when they themselves were enslaving a whole race of people? Many artists and writers belonged to, or were inspired by, the efforts of the abolitionist movement and translated its messages into written or painted form.

One such artist was Nathaniel Jocelyn (1796–1881). Initially trained as an engraver, he turned to painting in 1820 and became well-known as a portraitist in the New Haven area of Connecticut, although he returned to engraving at the end of his career after a disastrous studio fire. In 1839 he produced a large oil portrait entitled *Cinque*. It commemorates an event of that year in which Cinque, one of fifty-three men and women captured by Spanish slavers in the Mendi region of Africa, led a rebellion against the slavers on the ship *La Amistad*. The Spanish had transported their slaves to Havana, despite a treaty forbidding slave trading in British waters. The rebellion occurred after the slaves had been sold in Havana and were being transported to Puerto Rico. While Cinque and the others demanded that the ship return to Africa, the crew altered its course at night and managed to bring it ashore on Long Island. U.S. forces arrested the mutineers and freed the crew, but abolitionists defended the cause of the mutineers. After two years of legal proceedings, the Supreme Court ruled the Africans had been illegally seized. Cinque and his compatriots then toured the Northeast, appearing at numerous anti-slavery meetings, before returning to Africa in 1841.

In place of the physiognomical distortions used by Krimmel in his depiction of the black fiddler, Jocelyn has produced a highly individualized, noble portrait of an African

154

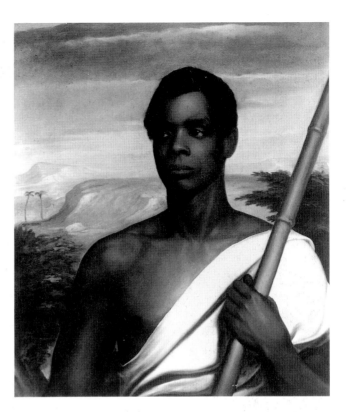

154 NATHANIEL JOCELYN *Cinque* 1839. 30¼ × 25½ (76.8 × 64.8)

man. Jocelyn's abolitionist sympathies played a major role in his decision to depict Cinque in this manner. But he was also undoubtedly influenced by the numerous accounts of Cinque's activities in the popular press that included descriptions of him as "of magnificent physique [and] commanding presence." Phrenologists had also carefully analyzed Cinque's head in an attempt to understand his daring behavior and had reported that the shape of his head indicated "great vigor of body and mind . . . ambition, independence . . . love of liberty." Such inquisitiveness suggests that, despite well-known accounts of numerous slave rebellions on board slave ships, many Euro-Americans still assumed that "ambition," "independence," and the intelligence necessary to plan a successful revolt were anomalies among Africans. Their obsession with his physical features, recorded in Jocelyn's portrait, also suggests that they thought his intelligence could be due to the fact that he did not "look like an African": in other words, he did not look like the stereotype of Africans that had been created by white artists in the U.S.

Jocelyn has also rejected the ragged clothing of Krimmel's fiddler and instead has clothed Cinque in the white toga of ancient Greece and Rome. By utilizing certain conventions from European Neoclassical painting—the pose, the toga—Jocelyn creates a parallel between the struggles for freedom of Cinque and African slaves in general and the struggles of

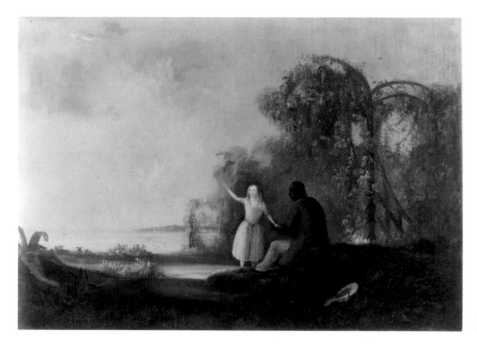

155 ROBERT SCOTT DUNCANSON *Uncle Tom and Little Eva* 1853. 27¼ × 38¼ (69.2 × 97.2)

ancient Greeks and Romans. Cinque is thus re-dressed—his African clothing is removed and the suggestion of "otherness" displaced to the palm trees in the background—in order to make his message more palatable to a white audience accustomed to conceiving of the U.S. as a continuation of the political ideas of democratic Greece and Republican Rome. The reference to Greece also had a more contemporary relevance. The U.S. had supported the Greeks in the Greek War of Independence against the Turks that lasted from 1821 to 1830. Many U.S. politicians and abolitionists viewed this conflict as one between the civilized, heroic Greeks and the barbarous, heathen Turks, who often trafficked in slaves. Jocelyn included at least one reference, however, to the specific contemporary reality of African slaves. Instead of a spear, Cinque holds in his left hand a stalk of cane, a reference to the sugar-cane fields of the Caribbean where Cinque and the other fifty-two African slaves were to have labored.

The abolitionist movement also resulted in growing support for the education of African Americans. A number of African American writers and artists received both the financial and moral backing they needed in order to succeed in their chosen field. One such artist was Robert Scott Duncanson (1821 or 1822–72). Duncanson began his career as a painter of still lifes and "fancy pieces" in Cincinnati, Ohio and, with the help of funds from the Anti-Slavery League and private patrons, was able to make three trips to Europe (1852, 1865, 1870) where he studied European landscape traditions. He subsequently produced a number of landscape paintings with titles such as *Valley Pasture* (1857), *Falls of Minnehaha* (1862) and *Landscape with a View of Vesuvius and Pompeii*

(1871) that reveal the influences of the U.S. landscape painter Thomas Cole and the Europeans Claude Lorrain and J. M. W. Turner.

Duncanson produced only two paintings that dealt directly with African American subjects, one of which was *Uncle Tom and Little Eva* (1853). Located in the foreground of a landscape that combines a luminous harbor scene with an overgrown arbor are the two central characters in Harriet Beecher Stowe's popular abolitionist novel *Uncle Tom's Cabin; or, Life Among the Lowly* (1852). Duncanson's composition was patterned after a wood engraving by Hammatt Billings (1818–74) that appeared in the illustrated edition of the novel (1852), as well as on the coversheet of the popular song *Little Eva; Uncle Tom's Guardian Angel* by John Greenleaf Whittier (1852).

Billings' engraving illustrates a scene at the opening of Chapter 22 at the St. Clare family's summer home, "on a little mossy seat, in an arbor, at the foot of the garden" on the shores of Lake Pontchartrain. It is sunset on a Sunday evening and Little Eva is reading from the Bible to her humble and faithful servant and friend Uncle Tom, who had earlier saved her from drowning. The scene illustrates Little Eva's commitment to educating the family's black servants and, ultimately, to using her inheritance to buy a home in one of the free states so all of the servants could be liberated. It also attests to Little Eva's (and thus Stowe's) belief that both spiritual and physical salvation for African Americans would be found through devotion to the Christian God. The little blond Eva thus represents the best of abolitionist sentiment and Christian love, although she dies shortly after the scene by the lake and

155

156

thus leaves the task of freeing African American slaves to those who have been inspired by her example.

The patronizing tone of both the written passage and the engraving are unmistakable: the blond, white child will lead the old black man out of darkness and ignorance into salvation and light. The passivity and devotion of Uncle Tom was seen by white abolitionists as evidence of his humanity and of the rightness of their efforts to free him. While such portrayals may have been necessary in order for the abolitionist movement to make political headway, they were not whole-heartedly accepted by all African Americans. "Uncle Tom" soon became a derogatory label, used by some African Americans to criticize others who felt their salvation lay in working with, rather than against, white people and their interests. Stowe herself reaffirmed her commitment to the "Uncle Tom" approach to liberation in her second anti-slavery novel, *Dred* (1856), in which she condemns the idea of African Americans achieving freedom through retaliation against whites. The character of the African American rebel in the book is obviously patterned after Nat Turner, the slave who led a rebellion in 1831 in Virginia that resulted in the killing of fifty-five whites before the rebellion was crushed and Turner caught and hanged. Turner's was only the latest in a series of revolts or planned insurrections that had increased the tension between southern plantation owners and their growing slave population.

Duncanson's painting maintains the patronizing tone of the Billings engraving and the Stowe text, suggesting that he shared Stowe's sentiments regarding the "Uncle Tom" approach to the liberation of slaves. He has made the scene more dramatic than the Billings engraving, however, by placing Little Eva in front of Uncle Tom, standing and gesturing toward the setting sun with eyes turned upward. There is a sense of Christlike prophecy in her pose, suggesting her impending death, and an equal sense of religious devotion on the part of Uncle Tom. This interpretation of the scene draws, once again, upon Stowe's text: "[Uncle Tom] loved her as something frail and earthly, yet almost worshipped her as something heavenly and divine. He gazed on her as the Italian sailor gazes on his image of the child Jesus,—with a mixture of reverence and tenderness."

Those, like Nat Turner, who rejected the "Uncle Tom" approach to the problem of slavery advocated open rebellion. Indeed, the rebelliousness of southern slaves had forced the federal government to confront the real possibility that an end to slavery might come about through a massive slave uprising, which might well spread beyond slavery to an attack on the enslavers and the privileged classes in general. While the Civil War is connected in the minds of many to the liberation of African American slaves, it was as much, if not more, about controlling the *way* in which they were to be liberated.

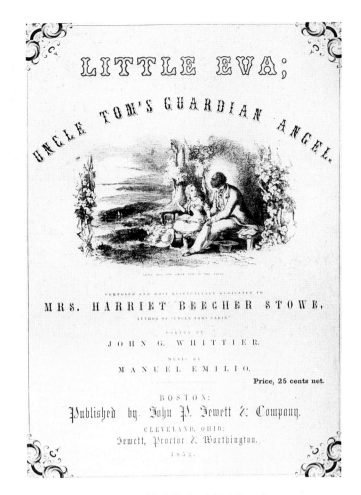

156 HAMMATT BILLINGS *Uncle Tom and Little Eva* 1852. 3½ × 5½ (8.9 × 14)

The possibility of a massive slave revolt was once again brought home to the southern states in 1859. That year, the sixty-year-old white man John Brown led a group of twenty-two men, five of whom were African American, in an attempt to seize the federal arsenal at Harper's Ferry in West Virginia and then set off a revolt of slaves throughout the South. His plan failed and he was executed by the state of Virginia with the approval of the federal government. Many in the South were convinced that northern abolitionists and politicians were behind Brown's actions and that the North was committed not only to depriving them of their property, but also, if necessary, of carrying out their objective through the arming of southern slaves.

The critical reception of two different images produced in 1859 gives an indication of the tensions surrounding the issue of slavery in the U.S. at this time. John Rogers (1829–1904), a Yale-trained engineer who turned to sculpture in the late 1850's, created many small genre scenes which were repro-duced in plaster and sold in great numbers. The first work that Rogers mass-produced and offered for sale on a mail-order

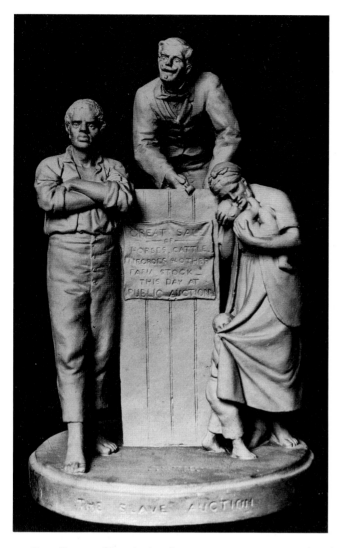

157 **JOHN ROGERS** *Slave Auction* 1859. Height 13¼ (33.7)

more positive response, was Eastman Johnson's (1824–1906) *Negro Life in the South*, later renamed *Old Kentucky Home* 158 after the 1853 Stephen Foster popular song written in black dialect. The painting was exhibited at the National Academy of Design's 1859 spring exhibition and portrays African Americans engaged in a variety of leisure-time activities— playing the banjo, dancing, socializing, playing with children. In style and subject matter it shows the influence of Johnson's studies in Dusseldorf and Holland from 1849 to 1855. While there he had been impressed by the minutely detailed studies of peasant and small-town life that had been recorded by Dutch artists, particularly in the seventeenth century.

The figures are arranged for the most part in discrete groups in front of a ramshackle house. A woman and child look out of the top window at the scene below. But they are not the only ones gazing upon these activities. Stepping through a hole in the fence between the slave quarters and the slave-owners house is a young white girl, dressed in a finery that, as in the Krimmel painting, contrasts sharply with the ragged clothing of the slaves. Her presence is acknowledge by two young girls, one of whose skin is much darker than the other. While the varying shades of skin color contained in the painting could be accounted for by the varying skin colors of West Africans themselves, this variety could also be caused by another avenue of contact that was quite common between male slave-owners and their female slaves—rape. The offspring of such violent encounters were always considered African American, and thus slaves.

The painting was an instant success when it appeared before the public, due to both its style and its content. The scene was painted in painstaking detail, achieved in part through Johnson's use of the backyard and household servants of his father's house in Washington, D.C. as models. This detail engaged viewers and convinced them of the artist's consummate talents. The scene was also noncommital on the issue of slavery. Abolitionists in the North interpreted the scene as a condemnation of the dismal living conditions of southern slaves while slaveholders in the South were con-firmed in their belief that, despite somewhat "uncomfortable" living conditions, southern slaves were basically a happy lot. The contrast between the delapidated slave quarters and the home of the white slave-owners could also be read in two ways—as evidence of the future prospects of a liberated people on the one hand, or as evidence of the peaceful coexistence of master and slave on the other.

AFRICAN AMERICANS AND THE CIVIL WAR

What was the relationship between this image—and the many others like it showing happy, dancing slaves—and the

157 basis was his *Slave Auction* (1859), put on the market only a few weeks after the execution of John Brown. The group includes a white auctioneer in the center, calling for bids, while a slave family is located in front and to the right and left of the podium. The male slave assumes an angry and aggressive stance, arms crossed, a scowl on his face. The woman cradles one child in her arms while another hides behind her skirt. The message of the piece is twofold: slavery is an affront to the dignity and humanity of African Americans, and African American men are not passively going to accept this consignment to slavery. The work did not sell as well as Rogers had expected, prompting him to comment at the end of the year: "I find the times have quite headed me off . . . for the Slave Auction tells such a strong story that none of the stores will receive it to sell for fear of offending their southern customers."

The second work produced in 1859, which received a much

material conditions of slave life in the South? John Little, a freed slave, helps us formulate at least a partial answer:

> They say slaves are happy, because they laugh, and are merry. I myself and three or four others, have received two hundred lashes in the day, and had our feet in fetters; yet, at night we would sing and dance, and make others laugh at the rattling of our chains. Happy men we must have been! We did it to keep down trouble, and to keep our hearts from being completely broken: that is as true as the gospel! Just look at it,—must not we have been very happy? Yet I have done it myself—I have cut capers in chains.

But the singing and dancing could not keep down trouble in the South. After Abraham Lincoln's election to the presidency in the fall of 1860, six southern states seceded from the Union, with five more joining them later. Their goal was to set up a separate, sovereign nation that would allow them to control their agricultural economy, which relied for its success on slave labor. The northern industrial states wanted economic expansion, wage labor, a free market economy and high protective tariffs for manufactured goods, all of which the southern states opposed. Lincoln's main aim during the early months of the war was to preserve the Union, even if it meant assuring the southern states that he would not dismantle the institution of slavery. As late as September 1862, when he issued his preliminary Emancipation Proclamation, he promised to leave slavery intact in the states that came over to the North. The January 1, 1863 Emancipation Proclamation declared slaves free in those areas still fighting the North but said nothing about slaves behind Union lines. But abolitionist forces pushed for a more all-encompassing declaration and, in April 1864, the Senate adopted the Thirteenth Amendment declaring an end to slavery. The House of Representatives followed with a vote of approval in January 1865.

Many of the paintings of African Americans during and immediately after the Civil War focused on the flight of slave families. These images were often based on events artists had witnessed while serving in the army or accompanying Union forces. The treatment of escaped slaves had become a particularly volatile political issue in 1850, the year California applied for statehood. Before this, there were fifteen free states and fifteen slave states. The addition of California threatened to tip the balance in favor of the free states. A compromise was worked out between the North and the South that allowed California to join the Union. One element of this compromise was the Fugitive Slave Act, which called for the forced return of escaped slaves to the South. This Act was further reinforced by the Supreme Court's Dred Scott decision of 1857 which confirmed that a slave's arrival in the free North did not automatically give the slave his or her freedom. Three justices also held that an African American descended from slaves had no rights as a U.S. citizen and therefore no standing in court. It was not until the Civil War and, in particular, the January 1863 Emancipation Proclamation that arrival in the North signified freedom for slaves.

158 EASTMAN JOHNSON *Old Kentucky Home* (*Negro Life in the South*) 1859. 36 × 45 (91.4 × 114.3)

Two examples of images depicting the flight of slaves to the North are Eastman Johnson's *A Ride for Liberty: The Fugitive Slaves* (ca. 1862–3) and Theodor Kaufmann's *On to Liberty* (1867). Johnson's *A Ride for Liberty* is strikingly different from his earlier *Old Kentucky Home*. In place of a meticulously rendered anecdotal scene of slave families contentedly enjoying themselves, one finds a sketchily rendered nighttime scene of flight from danger. The faces of the family on the horse, along with the horse itself, are mere dark silhouettes against a gray, smoke-filled sky. The scene certainly belies the southern claim that slave families were happy with their life on southern plantations. This fleeing family, like the scene in Leutze's *Westward the Course of Empire*, also contains Christian connotations, suggesting a parallel with the flight of Mary, Joseph, and the baby Jesus to Egypt.

Theodor Kaufmann (1814–after 1877) enlisted in the Union Army in 1861 and advocated the Union cause in his writings, lectures, and paintings. German-born, he received his artistic training in Munich and Hamburg before coming to the U.S. in the early 1850's. In his painting *On to Liberty*, Kaufmann creates a dramatic scene of the flight of African American women and children, although it is much more anecdotal in its detailed rendering of costumes and facial features than Johnson's *A Ride for Liberty*. Emerging out of a dark forest, the group of women and children head toward Union lines in the distant right of the painting. While the scene is filled with tension, Kaufmann provides some comic relief in the group of children to the right, the older boy dragging the younger one along by the back of his shirt. He also adds an element of voyeurism to the painting, undoing the blouse of the female slave to the far left so that her breasts are partially revealed. The absence of adult men from the group attests to the fact that adult male slaves were often conscripted by the Confederate Army to work as laborers during the war and thus were less likely to be fleeing with their families.

African Americans were also enlisted in the war effort by the North. There were two categories in which they appeared, the first as "war contraband," or escaped slaves, the second as

159 EASTMAN JOHNSON *A Ride for Liberty: The Fugitive Slaves* ca. 1862–3. 22 × 26¼ (55.8 × 66.6)

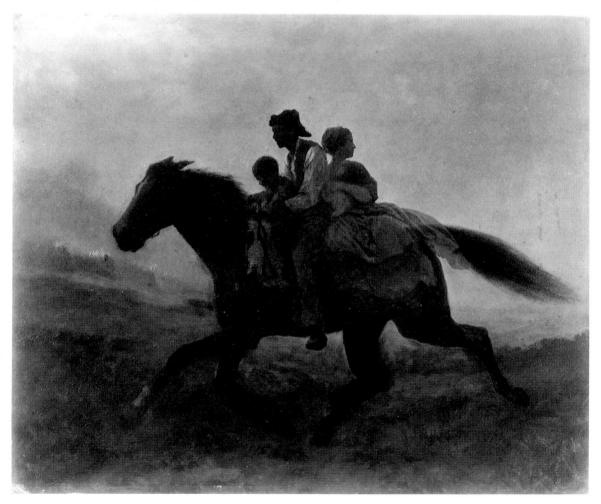

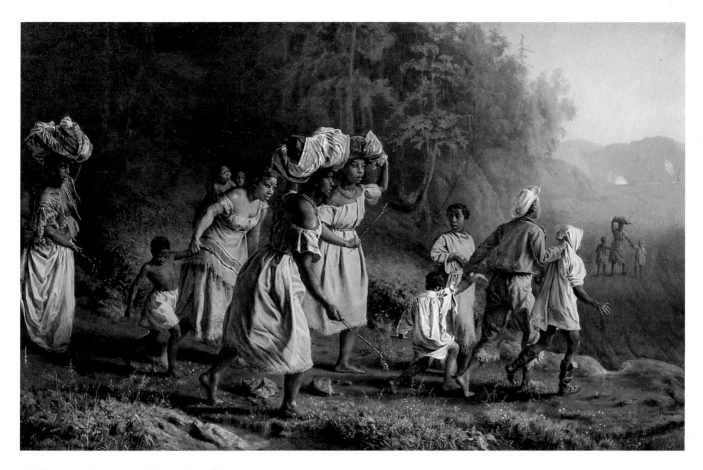

160 THEODOR KAUFMANN *On to Liberty* 1867. 36 × 56 (91.4 × 142.2)

enlisted soldiers. In both capacities they carried out the more menial tasks of the war effort, including cooking for the troops, building roads, driving mule teams, and burying the dead. Until 1864, African American soldiers were also paid less than white soldiers. While the institution of slavery may not have existed in the North, racism certainly did.

The lives of African Americans in the Union Army were portrayed in both photographs and paintings or engravings. As was the case with depictions of Native Americans, photographs tended to portray a starker image of wartime experiences than paintings or engravings. During the war many companies began producing sets of stereo views of the war for the home front audiences. As photographic technology was still unable to depict clearly objects in motion, most of the photographs included scenes of camp life or of the aftermath of war. In many cases each scene in the set was accompanied by a written explanation so that the viewing of these images could constitute an educational experience.

162   *A Group of "Contrabands"* (ca. 1861–5) was produced by the War Photograph and Exhibition Company. It shows a group of African American teamsters or mule drivers lined up in front of a large wagon and a shack which is described as

their home. Their eclectic clothing indicates their contraband status, and their solemnity—if not sullenness—and placement in the middle ground of the composition suggest both a physical and psychological distance between them and the viewer. The image is a far cry from the dancing, banjo-playing slaves of earlier paintings.

Another stereoscopic view, this time produced by Taylor and Huntington Publishers, shows the fate of an African American soldier in the Union Army accused of having "attempted to commit a rape on a white woman" near Petersburg, Virginia. The soldier, whose name was Johnson, was tried by courtmartial, found guilty, and hanged. All this information is included on the back of the image. The photograph, entitled *Execution of a Colored Soldier* (1864),   163 shows the dead soldier hanging from the scaffold, his face covered by a white cloth. Union soldiers rest in the shade of a tree to the right. The descriptive paragraph on the back of the photograph also included the following: "A request was made of the Rebels, under a flag of truce, that we might be permitted to hang Johnson in plain sight of both armies, between the lines. The request was granted, and this is a photograph of him hanging where both armies can plainly see him." The

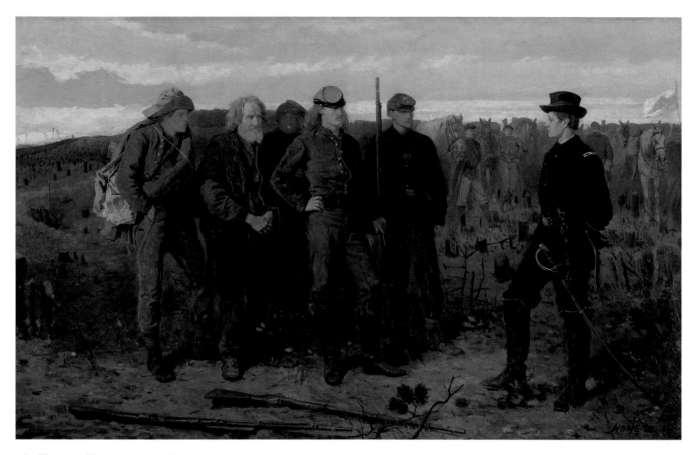

161 WINSLOW HOMER *Prisoners From the Front* **1866.** 24 × 38 (60.9 × 96.5)

educational value of this photograph lay in its assurance that freedom for African Americans would not be achieved at the expense of "white womanhood." While the description suggests that Johnson was fairly tried, few, if any, black men were ever acquitted when charged with a crime against a white person. The public display of his hanging for both armies also suggests that the white men on both sides of the war saw this as an occasion for racist entertainment.

The life of African American men in camp was also captured by the artist Winslow Homer (1836–1910). Homer was born in Boston in 1836 and grew up at a time when the city was filled with abolitionist debates and controversy. He was apprenticed in a lithography shop in the mid-1850's before taking up work as a freelance illustrator and then training as a fine artist in 1859 at the National Academy of Design, where he exhibited his first work the following year. After the outbreak of the Civil War, Homer joined the Union campaign as an artist-reporter for *Harper's Weekly*. He was also commissioned by the publishers Louis Prang and Co. in 1863 and 1864 to design sets of campaign sketches which were reproduced in lithographic form.

164 One of the earliest images Homer produced was *Bivouac Fire on the Potomac*, which appeared as a wood engraving in the December 21, 1861 issue of *Harper's Weekly*. As was the case with most of his war images, this one focuses on camp life rather than the battle front. The image is similar to the scene drawn eight years later by Davis for *Harper's Weekly* that was 149 discussed in Chapter 6. This time, however, an African American, rather than Native Americans, dances around the fire for the pleasure of the white Union soldiers. Homer has utilized all of the stereotypes then in place for the depiction of African Americans—the shabbily clothed high-stepping dancer with corkscrew curls, and the grinning, fat-lipped fiddler sitting at the edge of the fire playing for the dancer. Such antics and physiognomical distortions had become even more entrenched in both popular and fine art imagery with the introduction in the 1840's of a new genre of entertainment, the minstrel show, and its subsequent widespread success. Performed by white men in black face, with tattered clothes and broad, grinning lips painted on their faces, minstrel shows were, according to the art historian Albert Boime, "a white fantasy projected upon black people—no wonder the safe, familiar vision of the grinning black who could 'hoof it off' through thick and thin had a powerful and lasting appeal for American whites."

An even more grotesque caricature of the dancing African

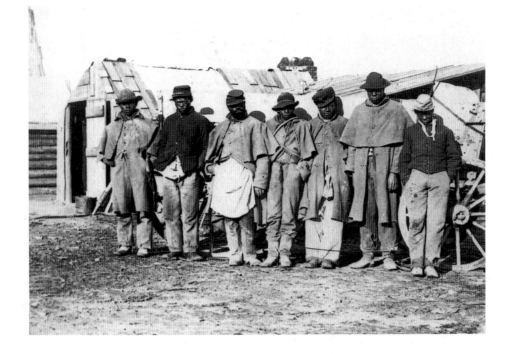

American appears in Homer's lithograph *Our Jolly Cook* (1863), while the grinning musician, this time a banjo player, is found once again in his 1864 painting of Confederate forces entitled *Inviting a Shot before Petersburg, Virginia*. By adopting such stereotypes, Homer reinforced the subservient place of African Americans (and their satisfaction with this place), whether as contraband, enlisted men, or slave laborers, within both the Union and Confederate Armies.

162 War Photograph and Exhibition Company *A Group of "Contrabands"* ca. 1861–5.

163 Taylor and Huntington Publishers *Execution of a Colored Soldier* 1864.

One of Homer's first moves away from such stereotypical depictions of African Americans during the Civil War, a direction he would increasingly follow, can be found in his 166 small painting *The Bright Side* (1865). The painting depicts five mule drivers, four of whom are caught asleep, leaning against the sunny side of a tent. Only the head of the fifth man is visible, appearing out of the opening in the tent. Homer claims to have sketched the scene from life, with the fifth man appearing from inside the tent just as he had finished drawing the first four. When the painting was first exhibited at the Brooklyn Art Association's Spring Exhibition in March 1865 and at the National Academy of Design Annual Exhibition in April of the same year, it received favorable critical and popular reviews. This favorable opinion was at least in part responsible for Homer's acceptance into the Academy in May 1865.

Critics praised *The Bright Side* for both its "truthfulness" and its "humor." One critic wrote: "The lazy sunlight, the lazy, nodding donkeys, the lazy, lolling negroes, make a humorously conceived and truthfully executed picture." For this critic, and for many others, a "truthful" depiction of

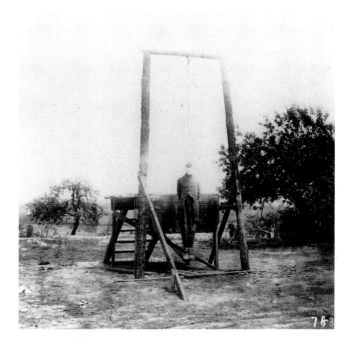

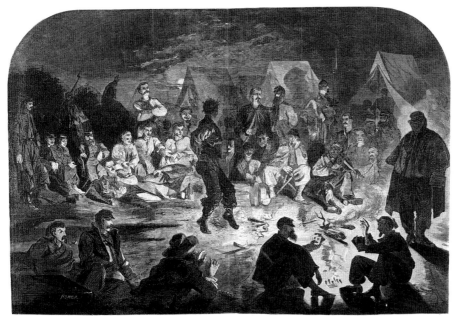

164 WINSLOW HOMER *A Bivouac Fire on the Potomac* 1861. 13¾ × 20 (34.9 × 50.8)

165 WINSLOW HOMER *Our Jolly Cook* 1863. 13⅞ × 11⅛ (35.2 × 28)

African Americans was, inherently, humorous. According to the scholar Robert F. Lucid, "the convention was that a negro, as such, was funny." He was also lazy, despite ample record of the often brutal labor that was involved in the work of a teamster. Teamsters were frequently compared with the mules they drove, animals regularly described as unintelligent, stubborn and lazy, despite, again, evidence to the contrary.

The critical response to *The Bright Side* shows how critics often see what they want to see, rather than necessarily what is there. Many viewing this painting did not want to give up their stereotypes. The man whose head appears through the tent door was repeatedly described as comic and grinning, despite his serious expression and direct gaze, a gaze that recalls those of the teamsters in the photograph *A Group of "Contrabands,"* taken around the same time Homer was composing his scene. Not that humor is totally absent from this piece. Homer was undoubtedly quite aware of the comic tales of teamsters and their mules and knew that painting such a scene would produce a few laughs. There is also an element of philosophical playfulness in the title of the painting. On the surface, *The Bright Side* refers to the sunny side of the tent. But it could also be read as a commentary on the occupation of the five men and their physical location. Driving mules for Union forces behind Union lines was preferable to laboring as a slave in the cotton fields of the South, although Homer must have been well aware of the fact that contraband teamsters were often immediately killed if captured by Confederate forces.

According to the art historian Marc Simpson, "if a seemingly racist humor can be found in Homer's painting of the teamsters, complicating elements are also there that require more than a chuckle in response." The direct gaze of the central teamster is one such complicating element. The depiction of all five men as closely observed individuals rather than stock characters is another. However, while Homer abandons the physiognomical stereotypes of African Ameri-

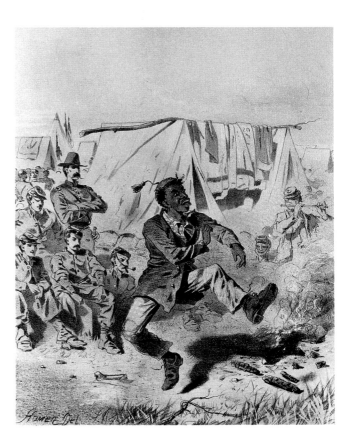

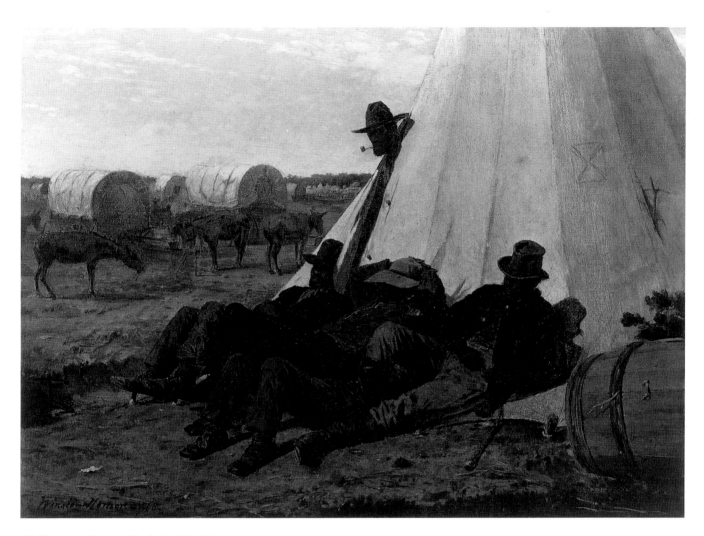

166 WINSLOW HOMER *The Bright Side* 1865. 13¼ × 17½ (33.7 × 44.4)

cans, he still places them in a setting that allowed most viewers to deny the individuality of the figures in favor of the generalizing stereotypes.

Another artist who covered the Civil War for *Harper's Weekly* was Thomas Nast (1840–1902), best known for his scathing political cartoons of the late nineteenth century. Born in Germany, he came to the U.S. in 1846 and studied with Kaufmann, later entering the National Academy of Design. After working for *Frank Leslie's Illustrated Weekly* and the *New York Illustrated News*, Nast was engaged by *Harper's Weekly* in the summer of 1862 to cover the Civil War. In 1865 he produced an image that was strikingly different from the majority of portrayals of African Americans during the war. *Entrance of the Fifty-fifth Massachusetts (Colored) Regiment into Charleston, South Carolina, February 21, 1865* (1865) shows the volunteer all-black Fifty-fifth Regiment from Massachusetts under the leadership of the white Colonel Robert Gould Shaw. Nast's drawing is one of the few images

that acknowledges the presence of African Americans as active Union soldiers who fought in many of the major battles of the Civil War. Once Lincoln's initial resistance to the enlistment of African Americans in the Union Army had been overcome, the numbers joining up increased throughout the war. Official records indicate that approximately 185,000 African Americans joined the Union Army. Over 200,000 African American civilians also worked in Union camps. Historians now agree that the presence of such large numbers of African Americans in the northern forces turned the tide against the Confederate Army in 1864 and 1865. The African American in the center foreground of Nast's drawing, therefore, is dancing not for the pleasure of Shaw, who confronts him on horseback, but in joy at the arrival of the heroic African American regiment into Charleston. The price of their victory is graphically present in the ruins towering over the regiment, ruins that are reminiscent of the many burned-out buildings that filled the photographs taken at the end of the war. Indeed, there is speculation that Nast's drawing is based, at least in part, on a photograph.

During the Civil War over half a million slaves fled the South. Four million remained, yet it was only a matter of time before many of them would also escape to the North. The African American activist and scholar W. E. B. DuBois later wrote in *Black Reconstruction* (1935):

> Either the south must make terms with its slaves, free them, use them to fight the North and thereafter no longer treat them as bondsmen; or they could surrender to the North with the assumption that the North after the war must help them to defend slavery as it had before.

General Robert E. Lee chose the latter route, surrendering to General Ulysses S. Grant at Appomattox on April 9, 1865, five days before the assassination of President Lincoln. While slavery was never officially restored in the South, white politicians in the North did, in fact, collude with their counterparts in the South to reinforce in new ways the subservience of African Americans.

IMAGES OF RECONSTRUCTION: PRISONERS FROM THE FRONT AND VISIT FROM THE OLD MISTRESS

In the decade after the end of the Civil War, known as the Reconstruction Period, education was opened to African Americans in the South, and African American men were given the vote and allowed to run for political office. Many were elected to local, state, and federal positions. Discrimination in the use of public facilities was outlawed by the Civil Rights Act of 1875. Southern whites, however, did not accept these new laws and organized groups such as the Ku Klux Klan (founded in 1866) to terrorize African Americans and prevent them from exercising their new freedoms. As long as the Union Army remained in the South, African Americans were protected to a certain degree from these attacks. But in 1877 troops were withdrawn as part of a larger political deal in which Republicans agreed not to interfere with the reestablishment of white control of the South if southern Democrats would give the Republican presidential candidate Hayes enough electoral college votes for him to become president. In 1883 the Civil Rights Act was nullified by the Supreme Court, which found the Act unconstitutional. It was replaced in 1896 with a Supreme Court decision allowing railroads, and thus, by precedent, all other public services, to segregate black and white if the segregated facilities were "equal." By 1900 all southern states had written into law the disenfranchisement and segregation of blacks.

Homer produced a number of paintings which addressed the tensions and accommodations produced by the end of the war and by the attempt to "reconstruct" the South. One such painting is *Prisoners From the Front*, painted in 1866. This work draws upon the well-established compositional conventions of confrontation scenes, which generally take place between the vanquished and the victor after a battle. In many major European paintings of confrontation scenes connected to specific military enterprises, such as the campaigns of Napoleon, the designation of victor and vanquished is clearly marked. The vanquished kneel or dramatically bow down on the left, guarded by members of the victorious army. The victor stands to the right surveying the vanquished, often surrounded by his military retinue. A good example is Gros's *The Capitulation of Madrid, December 4, 1808* (1810).

The general outlines of this compositional scheme have been maintained by Homer but he has made certain significant alterations. To the left of center stand three Confederate soldiers who have just surrendered. Two Union soldiers stand to the right and just behind this group. Facing the Confederate soldiers is a Union officer. He stands alone, although behind him at a distance are more Union soldiers with their horses and a Division flag. They all stand in a barren landscape, the young trees and bushes having been cleared by the advancing armies for firewood and to facilitate the movement of troops.

The Confederate soldiers have indicated their surrender by placing their rifles on the ground. They do not, however, bow down in submission. The prisoner closest to the Union officer stands defiantly, hand on hip, staring directly at his Union counterpart. Both appear to be in their twenties or thirties. The other two prisoners are of markedly different ages. The old man in the middle sports a full white beard and white hair and is the most submissive of the three, standing with his hands clasped in front of him. To the left of the old man is a very young man, probably in his teens, standing with his hands in his pockets, the slightly worried expression on his face belying his attempt at nonchalance. It is the defiant Confederate soldier who dominates, however. He occupies the center of the painting. Yet none of the figures—the prisoners, their two guards and the Union officer—is positioned above the others. They are all arranged on the same level in a horizontal band across the front of the picture plane, the high horizon line cutting through the head of each figure, locking them in place.

While the painting was well received when it was exhibited at the National Academy of Design Annual Exhibition in 1866 and, along with *The Bright Side*, at the Paris World Exposition of 1867, critics had some difficulty categorizing the work. Was it a figure painting, a genre painting, or a history painting? History paintings usually contained symbolic representations of lofty ideals or permanent truths or, at the very least,

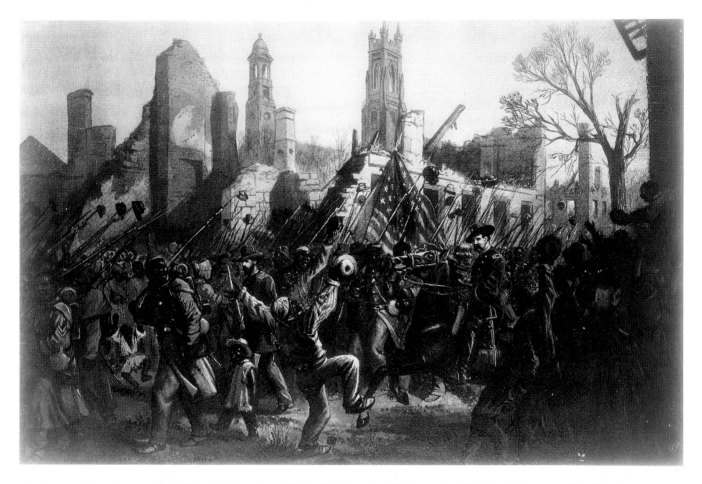

167 THOMAS NAST *Entrance of the Fifty-fifth Massachusetts (Colored) Regiment into Charleston, South Carolina, February 21, 1865* 1865. 14¼ × 21¼ (36.2 × 53.9)

commemorated particular victories or heroes. *Prisoners From the Front* does none of these things. The Union officer is recognizable as General Francis Channing Barlow, a distant cousin of Homer's whom he had visited at the front early in the war, but the identity of the Confederate soldiers is unknown. The taking of prisoners is usually only accorded the privilege of being commemorated in paint if the prisoners are high-ranking and well-known figures, such as in *The Surrender of General Burgoyne at Saratoga, October 16, 1777* (ca. 1822) by the American artist John Trumbull (1756–1843). In certain ways Trumbull's painting more closely follows European confrontation scene conventions, yet like Homer's it downplays the distinction between the victor and the vanquished and the drama of the scene. As with the war between the North and the South, the American Revolution resulted not in a complete break with England, or a subjugation of one country by another, but in a renegotiation of the terms under which the two sides would conduct business.

Many critics, however, did see *Prisoners From the Front* as a symbolic commentary on the Civil War as a whole rather than

simply a factual recording of one event that took place during the war. In this sense it was a history painting rather than an anecdotal genre painting. It was seen as a history painting for other reasons as well. In an 1869 article entitled "Historical Art in the United States," the art critic Eugene Benson argued that history painting should not be about events before the painter's lifetime but should deal with events that are contemporaneous. History painting should "give us art that shall become historical; not art that is intended to be so." He saw *Prisoners From the Front* as a perfect example of such history painting.

What, then, is the nature of Homer's commentary on the Civil War in *Prisoners From the Front?* The critic Sordello (a pseudonym for Benson) wrote the following in April 1866 for the New York *Evening Post* regarding the meaning of the painting:

On the one side the hard, firm-faced New England man, without bluster, and with the dignity of a life animated by principle, confronting the audacious, reckless impudent young Virginian, capable of heroism, because capable of impulse, but incapable of endurance because too ardent to be patient; next to him the poor, bewildered old man, perhaps a spy, with his furtive look . . . ; back of him "the poor white," stupid, stolid, helpless, yielding to the magnetism of superior natures and incapable of resisting authority. Mr. Homer shows us the North and South confronting each other; and looking at *his* facts, it is very easy to know why the South gave way. The basis of its resistance was ignorance, typified in the "poor white," its front was audacity and bluster, represented by the young Virginian—two very poor things to confront the quiet, reserved, intelligent, slow, sure North, represented by the prosaic face and firm figure and unmoved look of the Union officer.

Sordello was not the only critic who remarked on the contrasting class and breeding of the central characters. Another commented that "the Southern officer and the Northern officer are well contrasted, representing very accurately the widely differing classes to which they belong."

The main characters in the painting were thus read more as types than as individuals, and, as types, they were "keys" to the meaning and causes, and ultimately the outcome, of the Civil War. The defiant Confederate soldier in the center of the painting thus represents the defiance of the South in the face of defeat by the North. The Union officer's contemplative gaze, in turn, represents the North's evaluation of how best to deal with this implacable southern defiance. According to one critic, "the men are both young; they both understand each other." In 1888 another wrote that "the influence of this picture was strong on the side of brotherly feeling." It was this "understanding" and "brotherly feeling" that ultimately led to the deal struck between the North and the South discussed above. A new Union would be created that allowed southern whites to maintain political and economic control through concessions to northern industrialists and politicians. Those who lost out in this deal were those in whose name the Civil War was supposedly fought—African Americans. As early as 1865 and 1866, the years in which Homer was creating *Prisoners From the Front,* vagrancy and apprenticeship laws were being passed by southern legislatures (the Black Codes) which restricted the rights of freedmen.

Does Homer represent this aspect of the Civil War—the betrayal of African Americans—in his painting? The one figure who could possibly function as such is the dark-skinned soldier standing behind the three prisoners. He is the only figure in the foreground of the composition whose facial features are not clearly articulated. There is, instead, merely the faintest suggestion of eyes, nose and mouth. Indeed, the facial features of the figures in the distant right background are more clearly discernible. Even the boots of the soldier are

not completely sketched in. So unfinished is his presentation that it is possible, at first glance, to read this figure as a white soldier cast in shadow. Yet there is no source for such a shadow. The bodies of the Confederate prisoners are the only possible source visible in the painting and their positioning makes such a complete blocking out of the sun impossible. Is this soldier, therefore, African American?

Recent x-radiographs of the painting reveal that this soldier was absent from Homer's original composition. He was added after the Confederate prisoners had been laid in and the brown ground filled in around them, but he was not worked up in the same detail as the other figures. Instead, the face remains marked by the color of the brown ground. Perhaps Homer had intended to create an obviously white counterpart of the other Union guard. Yet in the painting he submitted as "finished" to the National Academy of Design in 1866, the soldier behind the prisoners remained dark-skinned and only faintly articulated. Perhaps after applying the general form of the figure, he realized that the ghostly presence of an African American Union soldier behind the Confederate prisoners would heighten the symbolic significance of the work as a commentary on the war and its aftermath. In other words, the figure would provide a subtle reference to the presence of African Americans in the Union forces and to the extent to which they would be sold out by "brotherly" negotiations between the North and the South.

The second painting by Homer that addresses the Civil War and its aftermath is also a confrontation scene. This time, however, the confrontation is located indoors and takes place between a white woman and her former female African American slaves. In *A Visit From the Old Mistress* (1876) the white woman is dressed, like the Union officer in *Prisoners From the Front,* in black. In addition, as in *Prisoners From the Front,* she confronts three adult figures. The former slaves, like at least two of the Confederate prisoners, are dressed in ragged clothing. Homer's manner of execution is even more "unfinished" in this painting than in *Prisoners From the Front,* although the greatest finish appears in the face and upper costume of the white woman. This is particularly evident if we compare her to the African American woman closest to her whom she confronts directly, whose facial features, like those of the Union guard in the earlier painting, are only barely articulated. Indeed, this adult woman in front of her echoes the guard not only in her schematic manner of execution, but also in the shape and positioning of her head. If the African American has emerged from the shadows of the Confederacy, therefore, it is as a woman in the home rather than a man on the battlefield.

What is the nature of the confrontation being depicted here? Who is the victor and who the vanquished? The title of the painting might suggest that the women on the left are the

168

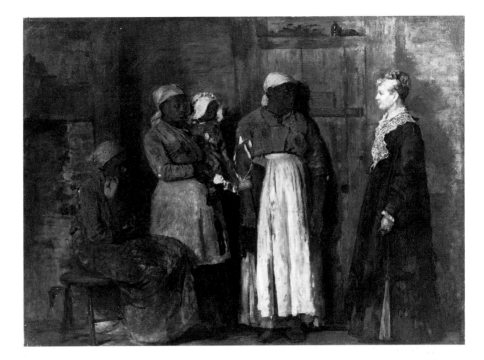

168 **WINSLOW HOMER** *A Visit From the Old Mistress* 1876. 18 × 24⅛ (45.7 × 61.3)

victors. The white woman is, after all, the "old" mistress. Yet "old" could also be read as referring to the age of the woman, for her hair is distinctly gray. In compositional terms, the white woman is located in the position of the victor. She has a slight smile on her face and looks directly at the women in front of her. Yet, as in *Prisoners From the Front,* there is no show of obeisance on the part of the African American women. Rather, there is a distinct sense of suspicion and mistrust, particularly visible in the gesture and facial expression of the seated woman on the far left. In historical terms, the African American women are the victors. This was 1876, over a decade since the end of the Civil War and of the institution of slavery. The fact that the woman on the left remains seated rather than rising at the entrance of the white woman is a sign of the changed relations that now existed between white women and their former slaves. Yet the following year northern and southern politicians struck their deal to put Hayes in the White House, thus effectively ending Reconstruction. It was fitting that this deal was made immediately following the nation's centennial celebrations, for it marked a reaffirmation of the interests of the "founding fathers," many of whom had owned slaves. From this point on, the gains made by African Americans over the previous ten years would be systematically dismantled.

Like *Prisoners From the Front,* therefore, there is no clear-cut victory or defeat in *A Visit From the Old Mistress.* Even the visit of a white woman to her slaves' quarters cannot be read as an act of capitulation. Such visits were common in the earlier slave-holding period, as is indicated in an engraving produced the same year as Homer's painting, *Virginia One Hundred*

Years Ago, by Sol Eytinge, Jr., which appeared in the August 19, 1876 issue of *Harper's Weekly.* Eytinge, Jr.'s engraving was one of a series of similar images that appeared in the 1870's calling up scenes from "the good old days" when slaves knew their place and appreciated the benevolent gestures of their masters and mistresses. The engraving also marks the hierarchy that existed within the slave community, with the personal servant of the master distinguished by dress and attitude.

In creating an enclosed, almost claustrophobic, space for the women in *A Visit From the Old Mistress,* Homer acknowledges the intimate nature of the contact between white women and the African American slaves who worked for them in the plantation mansions. While white men also had personal servants, most of their contact with African American slaves occurred in the fields or potteries or other places of work separate from the home. The world of white women, particularly middle- or upper-class white women in the nineteenth century, was the home. It was in the domestic sphere that white women exerted their control—over their children and over their African American servants. These servants engaged in tasks that directly involved the health and wellbeing of the family—cooking, cleaning, and raising the children. As is suggested in *Uncle Tom's Cabin,* household servants often became the friends of their young white charges, if not of the older members of the household. Such friendships created the basis for an understanding of the inequities of slavery and a willingness to end slavery as a whole. The potential for understanding between the two races appeared to be greater in the female sphere of the home,

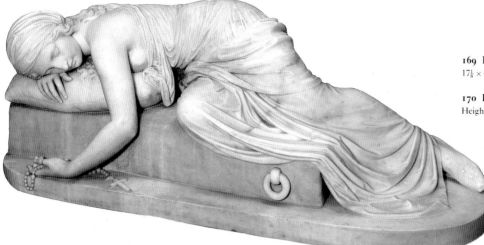

therefore, than in the male spheres of business and politics.

Yet the potential for violence was also great in the home, as indicated by the numerous beatings of household slaves and by the attempts made by these same slaves, often successful, to murder their masters and mistresses. While the work of the household slave was generally lighter than the field slave, it was accompanied by a constant surveillance by whites that forced the continuous wearing of a public mask. Yet, according to Lerone Bennett, Jr., court records of the mid-nineteenth century "yield ample evidence that a large number of slaves refused to play the game of slavery: they would neither smile nor bow. Other slaves bowed but would not smile." Others bowed and smiled but, at the same time, deliberately sabotaged the system from within, breaking utensils or staging slowdowns. The close proximity of the female figures in Homer's painting and their demeanors suggest both the potential for understanding and the potential for harm. The physical and psychological distance between the white and African American women, while filled with tension and mistrust, is also bridgable by a single gesture.

THE AFRICAN AMERICAN ARTIST AT HOME AND ABROAD: EDMONIA LEWIS AND HENRY OSAWA TANNER

As was mentioned earlier, many white abolitionists attempted to bridge this distance by encouraging and supporting the educational and professional pursuits of African Americans. Robert Duncanson was one African American artist who benefited from such patronage. The sculptor Edmonia Lewis (ca. 1845–after 1909) was another. Born in upstate New York in the early 1840's of a Chippewa Indian mother and an African American father, Lewis—originally named Wild-

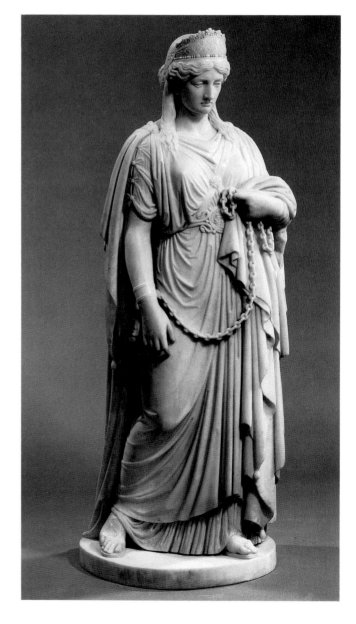

fire—was orphaned at four and raised by her mother's tribe until she was twelve. At thirteen, with the help of her brothers and of various abolitionists, she entered the Young Ladies Preparatory Department of Oberlin College, adopting the Christian name of Mary Edmonia Lewis. While at Oberlin, Lewis was accused of attempting to poison two of her white schoolmates and of stealing. Brought to trial, she was defended by the well-known African American lawyer John Mercer Langston, and acquitted of all charges. Yet she was not allowed to graduate and, with the help of the abolitionist William Lloyd Garrison, settled in Boston where she came into contact with the sculptor Edward Brackett. He lent her sculpture fragments to copy and, along with the sculptor Anne Whitney, helped her develop her skills as an artist.

Lewis's first works were busts and medallions of various abolitionist leaders and heroes, including Garrison, Charles Sumner, Maria Weston Chapman and Colonel Shaw. The portrait of Shaw (1865) impressed his family who organized a group of friends to buy a hundred copies at fifteen dollars each. This money, and the help of her benefactors the Story family, allowed Lewis to finance a trip to Italy in 1865, where she joined the group of women gathered in Rome around the American sculptor Harriet Hosmer. These women went to Europe in search of good marble, historical collections of Classical sculpture, and trained carvers who would teach them. They were encouraged by liberal parents or, as was the case with Lewis, friends who could wholly or partly support them financially. Almost all remained single and devoted their lives to their artistic endeavors.

Harriet Hosmer (1830–1908) provided Lewis not only with a supportive environment within which to work in Rome, but also with examples of images that addressed the issues of slavery and rebellion. In 1857 Hosmer had carved the
169 reclining *Beatrice Cenci*. Cenci was a late-sixteenth-century Roman noblewoman who, with her mother Lucretia, killed her abusive and tyrannical father Francesco. Both women were condemned to death and beheaded, despite numerous pleas for clemency. Hosmer shows Beatrice asleep the night before her execution, having come to terms with her actions and fate through prayer.
170 Two years later Hosmer produced *Zenobia in Chains* (1859). Zenobia was the third-century Queen of Palmyra who was defeated and captured by the Romans. Hosmer presents Zenobia as noble and resolute in her defeat; she gathers up her chains along with her robe, grasping them firmly in her hand as she contemplates her future. When the statue was exhibited in the U.S. in 1863, it was received with great enthusiasm as an example of moral rectitude and resistance to defeat, a fitting symbol for a country in the throes of a civil war. The art historian Whitney Chadwick notes that Hosmer's work stood in striking contrast to another equally well-known and

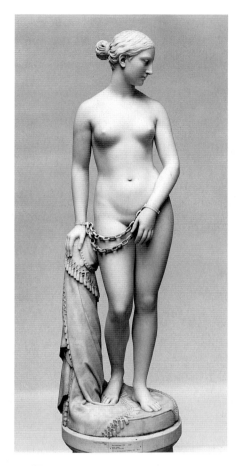

171 HIRAM POWERS *The Greek Slave* 1846 (after 1843 original). Height 65½ (166.4)

popular sculpture of a woman in chains, Hiram Powers' (1805–73) *The Greek Slave* (1843). Both figures are presented as captives, but "*Zenobia*'s resolute dignity stands as a rebuke to *The Greek Slave*'s prurient, if allegorical, nudity. More than one critic lauded Hosmer's figure as an embodiment of the new ideal of womanhood." 171

While Hosmer focused on the political and personal struggles of women against men and male-defined institutions, Lewis turned her attention to the struggles of African Americans against the institution of slavery in the U.S. She created two works on this subject while in Rome, *The Freed Woman and Her Child* (now lost) and *Forever Free* (1867). 172 Originally titled *The Morning of Liberty*, *Forever Free* attempts to capture the emotional impact on African American slaves of Lincoln's proclamation, on the morning of January 1, 1863, that all persons held as slaves (in those areas still fighting the North) "are, and henceforward shall be, free." A woman, the manacle still around her ankle, kneels and clasps her hands in thanksgiving while a man stands above her, one hand on her shoulder, the other raised and holding the manacle and chains that had been previously attached to his ankle. Another manacle remains attached to his wrist,

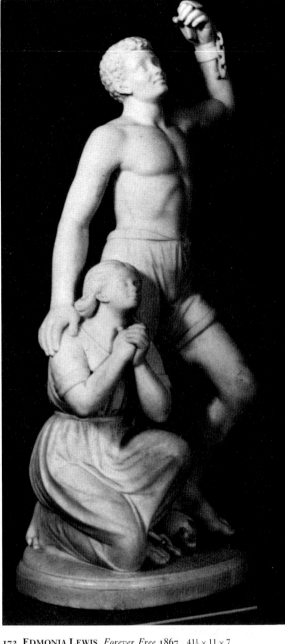

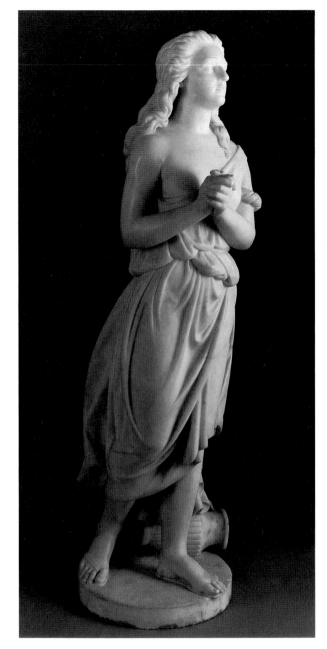

172 EDMONIA LEWIS *Forever Free* 1867. 41¼ × 11 × 7
(104.8 × 27.9 × 17.8)

173 EDMONIA LEWIS *Hagar in the Wilderness* 1868. 52⅝ × 15¼ × 17
(133.6 × 38.8 × 43.4)

however, indicating that freedom has yet to be fully achieved. Both gaze upward, acknowledging the existence and help of a higher power (it was around this time that Lewis converted to Catholicism).

The subservient position of the woman in *Forever Free* may have been a subtle commentary on the struggles that lay ahead for African American women within their own community. Such struggles paled in comparison, however, to the fate of African American women in slavery, who were used not only

as field workers and domestic workers, but also as sexual servants by their white male masters. Lewis chose to focus her artistic attention on at least one subject in which this combination of racism and sexism was present. A year after completing *Forever Free*, she produced *Hagar in the Wilderness* (1868), a tribute to the Egyptian maidservant of Abraham's wife Sarah, who was cast into the desert to escape the rage of Sarah after having borne Abraham a child. The parallel to the situation of African American women in the

173

U.S. is clear. Lewis wrote, in reference to this work, "I have a strong sympathy for all women who have struggled and suffered."

In 1916 the African American writer Freeman Henry Morris Murray wrote of *Forever Free* and of the time in which it had been executed:

Reaction—re-enslavement, I had almost said—had set in.... Miss Lewis and "her people" had felt it. The Sun of Emancipation which had risen in 1863, had seemingly reached its zenith in 1865 with the passage of the 13th Amendment prohibiting slavery. But already it was being obscured by the clouds. Already the sheriff's handcuffs were taking the place of the former master's chains; already the chaingang stockade was supplanting the old slave pen ... The freedwoman was being told that it would be better for her children, even in the North, to go to "separate" schools; and ... accept "separation" on public conveyances and in public places. She was gravely assured that there was no degradation nor detriment in all of this.

It is little wonder, therefore, that despite a growing reputation throughout the late 1860's and early '70's, Lewis remained in Rome and made only brief visits to the U.S. to promote her work. In October 1869 she visited Boston to present *Forever Free* to the Reverend L. A. Grimes at Tremont Temple. In 1873 she traveled to California where five of her works were exhibited at the San Francisco Art Association. She was in Boston in 1876 around the time of the Philadelphia Centennial Exposition, which included her *Death of Cleopatra* (1876). According to Boime, she "often took her show on the road, participating in western fairs to avoid the competition in New York and setting up booths in the form of wigwams, emphasizing the links between the West and her Native American heritage." She also created at least two small works in marble directly addressing her Native American heritage, one of which is *Old Indian Arrowmaker and His Daughter* (1872).

Lewis's financial success attested to her skill at producing the type and quality of work expected by the American art-buying public in the late nineteenth century. Yet, even in Rome, she was continually confronted by the prejudices of an art world accustomed to acknowledging only male members of the white race. She was often viewed as a novelty, as "exotic" because of her gender, her dress (often described as "mannish") and her skin color. Henry James described her as "a negress, whose colour, picturesquely contrasted with that of her plastic material, was the pleading agent of her fame." In other words, her success was the result, not of her artistic talent, but of her novelty, which James sees in terms of a contrast—between her dark skin and the white marble in which she worked. The critic Laura Curtis Bullard wrote in 1871:

Edmonia Lewis is below the medium height, her complexion and features betray her African origin; her hair is more of the Indian type, black, straight and abundant. . . . Her manners are child-like, simple and most winning and pleasing. She has the proud spirit of her Indian ancestor, and if she has more of the African in her personal appearance, she has more of the Indian in her character.

Thus, despite the fact that Lewis was in her late twenties and an accomplished artist at the time this description was written, she was still seen as childlike, winning and pleasing, attributes which made her success and independence as an artist and single woman less threatening to men and to those women who believed in the need to maintain their "femininity" even as they entered professions previously closed to them. Bullard also combines two stereotypes—the "proud" Native American and the "child-like" African American—in

174 **EDMONIA LEWIS** *Old Indian Arrowmaker and His Daughter* 1872. Height 27 (68.6)

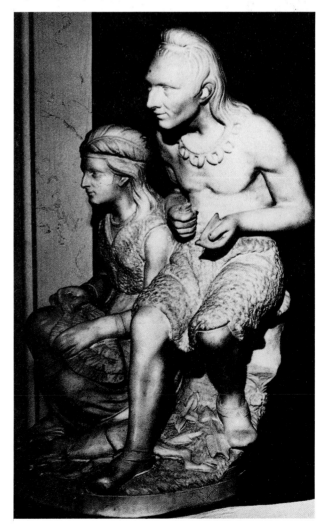

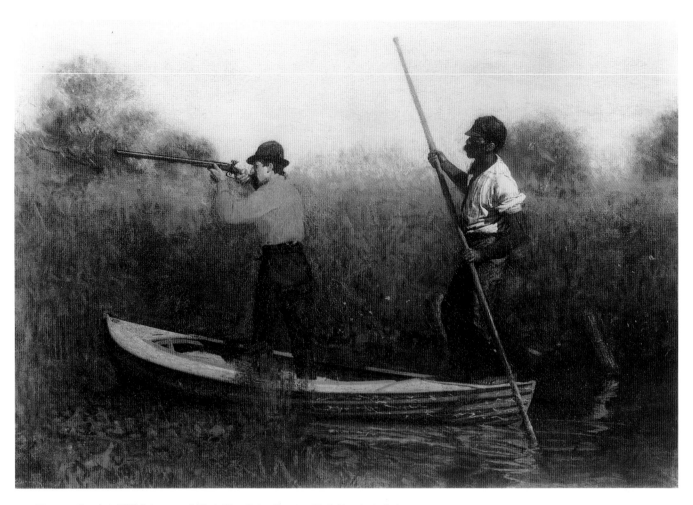

175 THOMAS EAKINS *Will Schuster and Black Man Going Shooting (Rail Shooting)* 1876. 22⅛ × 30¼ (56.2 × 76.8)

her patronizing description of the artist. Little is known of Lewis's career after the mid-1880's. She disappeared from exhibition records and art journals and the last printed reference to her appears to have been in the Catholic *Rosary* magazine, which noted in 1909 that she was aging but "still with us."

Another African American artist who spent most of his adult life in Europe was Henry Osawa Tanner (1859–1937). Tanner was born in Pittsburgh and moved to Philadelphia with his family when he was a child. His father was a minister, and later a bishop, in the African Methodist Episcopal Church (A.M.E.), founded in 1816. The independent African American church movement began in the late 1770's with the founding of the first African Baptist churches in South Carolina and continued to grow throughout the nineteenth century, providing a source of spiritual, political and educational strength and leadership. His father instilled in Tanner a stern belief in the Christian God and in the power of religion as a unifying force in the African American community, one which could help achieve the dignity of *all* human beings,

whatever the color of their skin. Tanner's father was a prolific writer and intellectual, producing *An Apology for African Methodism* (1867), describing the schisms between the African American and white Methodist churches, and *The Negro's Origins and Is the Negro Cursed?* (1869). He was also editor of the A.M.E.'s newspaper the *Christian Recorder* and later founded the *A.M.E. Church Review*. The Tanner household was a gathering place for many of the country's leading African American intellectuals and politicians.

Tanner entered the Pennsylvania Academy of Fine Arts in 1880 in order to study with Thomas Eakins (1844–1916), who had achieved a widespread reputation as a painter of portraits and genre scenes. Yet the latter were not the nostalgic revivals of antebellum or preindustrial America that had become popular after the Civil War, when the social, economic, and political upheavals caused many to wish for a return to "simpler" times. Eakins eschewed the more popular anecdotal rural scenes and chose, instead, to focus on the present and on an emerging socioeconomic group—the professional middle class. He was particularly interested in the work and

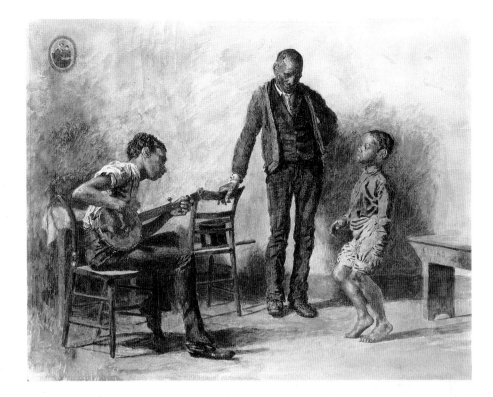

176 THOMAS EAKINS *Negro Boy Dancing*
1878. 18⅛ × 22⅝ (46 × 57.7)

leisuretime pursuits of the men of this class, painting images of surgeons in the midst of operations and men rowing or sculling on the Schuylkill River in Philadelphia (see p. 259). He also collaborated with the photographer Eadweard Muybridge in the 1880's, using sequential still photography to study motion in humans and animals.

Eakins included African Americans in several of his paintings. One such painting is *Will Schuster and Black Man Going Shooting (Rail Shooting)* of 1876. As in his rowing paintings, Eakins presents another leisuretime activity engaged in by many white middle-class men that involved concentration, skill, and discipline. It also involved the employment of a boatman guide who, in this instance, is African American. Each figure is painted with the same meticulous care in terms of clothing and physiognomy. Each figure is also thoroughly engrossed in his task, the hunter in aiming at the bird somewhere outside of the painting, the boatman in watching the bird as well while steadying the boat and preparing for the recoil from the fired gun. While the African American has been named only in terms of his race, the detail with which he is rendered suggests that he, like the many other figures in Eakins' outdoor paintings, is a portrait of a specific individual.

Another painting by Eakins depicting African Americans is *Negro Boy Dancing*, originally titled *Study of Negroes* (1878), executed two years after *Will Schuster and Black Man* and exhibited in that year's American Society of Painters of Water Color Exhibition in New York City. In this work Eakins takes up the theme of the dancing, banjo-playing African American, yet presents it in a way that differs significantly from earlier works like Johnson's *Old Kentucky Home*. Three African American males occupy a room containing two chairs, a small table, a bench, and a small oval portrait on the wall. The objects and figures are arranged in a pyramidal composition, with the old African American man at the apex. To the left sits a younger man, probably in his teens, playing a banjo, while on the right the youngest figure dances. Again, each figure's physical features and clothing are carefully rendered. So, too, are the expressions on each figure's face—the tight-lipped concentration of the youngest boy, the pleased smile on the face of the old man, the silent encouragement on that of the banjo player. The three figures constitute a self-contained, self-supporting unit. As in *Will Schuster and Black Man*, all concentrate intensely on the task at hand. The bareness of the room allows us to focus on the actions and attitudes of its inhabitants. While the top hat and cane on the chair suggest that this private lesson will lead to a public performance, for the moment the concern is learning a skill, passing on knowledge from one generation to the next.

Education, both formal schooling and informal transmission of cultural traditions, was of utmost importance to former slaves, who had been systematically denied access to education in the South. Many artists portrayed scenes of African Americans pouring over books in the home or in roughly constructed schoolrooms. Eakins refers to this formal book-learning in the small oval portrait of Lincoln and his son

"Tad" examining a book together, taken from a Mathew Brady Studio photograph of 1864, in the top lefthand corner of his painting. The focus of the painting, however, is the passing on of a broader cultural knowledge—dancing and playing the banjo—from one generation to the next and the pride and sense of hope and self-fulfillment attached to the acquisition and maintenance of this knowledge.

177   Eakins' *Negro Boy Dancing* may well have inspired Tanner's own tribute to the transmission of knowledge from one generation to the next, *The Banjo Lesson* (1893). This painting speaks to the theme of education on three levels: 1) the education of Tanner as an artist; 2) the education of the child by the grandfather; and 3) the education of the art-viewing public by the painting itself.

While Tanner had benefited artistically from his lessons at the Pennsylvania Academy of Design, he could not escape the racism that forced so many artists of color either to abandon their pursuits or to leave the U.S. In his autobiographical work *Adventures of an Illustrator* (1925), Joseph Pennell, who attended the Academy at the same time as Tanner, described a scene where a young "octoroon, very well dressed . . . quiet and modest," with short cropped "wool" and a moustache, was tied to his easel in the middle of Broad Street one night by a group of white students "when he began to assert himself." "This is my only experience of my colored brothers in a white school," remarked Pennell, "but it was enough." While Pennell does not name Tanner, the physical description matches photographs of Tanner at the time.

In 1891 Tanner traveled to Paris where he entered the Académie Julian to study with artists such as Jean-Joseph Benjamin-Constant and Jean-Paul Laurens, and joined the American Art Students' Club of Paris. He also made trips to the village of Pont-Aven on the Brittany coast and enjoyed the company of fellow artists in an environment that was substantially less racist than the one he had left in Philadelphia. Tanner's early paintings were primarily seascapes, landscapes, and animal paintings. It was not until the mid-1890's that he began to take up the theme that would become the major focus of his work in the early twentieth century—religion. Before that, he took a brief detour and created a small number of genre paintings that addressed the life of African Americans, the best-known of which is *The Banjo Lesson*.

Tanner returned to Philadelphia in the summer of 1893 to recover from a bout with typhoid fever. In August he delivered a paper at the World's Congress on Africa, part of the World's Columbian Exposition in Chicago, on "The American Negro in Art." This paper, plus his return to Philadelphia and the inevitable re-encounter with a racism that he had fled two years earlier, may have prompted him to turn his attention to African Americans as subject matter. He gives a further indication of his reasons for painting African

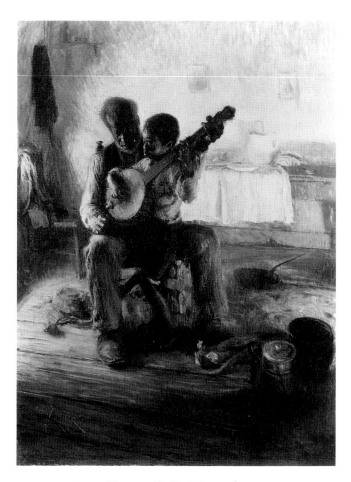

177 HENRY OSAWA TANNER *The Banjo Lesson* 1893. 48 × 35 (121.9 × 88.9)

Americans in a statement the following year, referring to himself in the third person:

> Since his return from Europe he has painted many Negro subjects, he feels drawn to such subjects on account of the newness of the field and because of a desire to represent the serious and pathetic side of life among them, and it is his thought that other things being equal, he who has most sympathy with his subject will obtain the best results. To his mind, many of the artists who have represented Negro life have only seen the comic, the ludicrous side of it and have lacked sympathy with and affection for the warm big heart within such a rough exterior.

Tanner may well have been thinking of paintings by artists such as Krimmel and the early Johnson.

How does Tanner's painting differ from the work of artists who saw only the "comic" or "ludicrous" side of African American life? While Johnson drew on the anecdotal genre scenes of peasant life painted by seventeenth-century Dutch artists, Tanner looked to another seventeenth-century Dutch artist for inspiration—Rembrandt van Rijn. In adopting Rembrandt's looser brushwork and in paring down the objects in the painting, Tanner forces the viewer to focus on the central figures in the scene and on their activity rather than the details of their costume or physiognomy. In addition, his use of a golden light entering from the side, which marks so many of Rembrandt's paintings and which highlights the faces and sharpens the outlines of the figures against the background, adds a sense of solemnity and religiosity to the painting. Tanner would develop this brushwork and use of light even further in his biblical paintings of the subsequent decades. Here, however, the sense of devotion is focused on the daily life of African Americans, on an elevation of the lives of the poor. In this respect Tanner once again reflects on Rembrandt and his own respect for the poor in seventeenth-century Holland.

Following Eakins' example, Tanner portrays the two figures in *The Banjo Lesson* as distinct individuals intensely absorbed in the task at hand. The banjo becomes a conduit, a connection from one generation to the next. It also represents a bridge between Africa and America, for the banjo was developed from a stringed instrument brought over from Africa. In her 1990's work on the banjo in American popular culture, Karen S. Linn has traced the changing and conflicting meanings attached to the banjo as a result of its integration into national commercial culture after the Civil War. Before the Civil War the banjo was seen as primarily an African American instrument. In the late nineteenth century, however, urban entrepreneurs attempted to introduce the banjo into elite white culture and, in the process, to downplay its connections with the lives and culture of African Americans. One way of doing this was to promote a new style of playing. Instead of continuing the downward strokes and chording of minstrel performers whose songs grew out of African American culture, the "new" banjo players plucked the strings separately and upward, like a guitar, in order to play the new parlor music of the day. Many white colleges and youth social clubs took up the banjo in the 1880's and '90's, in part because of the promotion of the instrument as comparable to the guitar and piano, and in part because of its

connection to the "unofficial," off-limits world of African American culture.

The 1884 dime novel by S. S. Steward *The Black Hercules, or the Adventures of a Banjo Player* shows, however, that many African American banjo players soon mastered the new way of playing and, like Horace Weston and the Bohee brothers, performed in concert tours throughout the U.S. and England. Indeed, the boy in Tanner's *The Banjo Lesson* has his right hand positioned so as to facilitate the upward plucking motion involved in the new banjo technique. Tanner's painting could have been read as a reaffirmation, therefore, of the banjo as a distinctly African and African American instrument and of the ability of African Americans in this field, as in many others, to master new techniques and acquire new knowledge. One could add musicians, therefore, to the painters and sculptors referred to in Tanner's talk at the World's Congress on Africa, which was described as follows in a report on the Congress: "Professor Tanner (American) spoke of negro painters and sculptors, and claimed that actual achievement proved negroes to possess ability and talent for successful competition with white artists."

Tanner's *The Banjo Lesson* was exhibited in October 1893 at Earle's Galleries in Philadelphia and the following year in the annual Paris Salon. It was purchased by Robert C. Ogden, a partner in John Wanamaker's dry-goods business and a promoter of African American public education who, in November 1894, donated the painting to the Hampton Institute. It was appropriate that a school committed to the education of Native American and African American children should come to possess a painting that presented in such a compelling and dignified way the role of education in African American life. It undoubtedly helped counteract the display of cowboys and Indians so graphically present in Johnston's photograph *Class in American History*. Rather than an image 152 of cultural assimilation, which relegated Native American and African cultures to the past, Tanner produces a testimony to the changing and vital nature of cultural traditions and to the persistence with which African Americans (and Native Americans) would pursue the knowledge necessary to continue their struggles for equality into the twentieth century.

· 8 ·

THE GENERATION OF 1830 AND THE CRISIS IN THE PUBLIC SPHERE

ROMANTICISM AND THE CRISIS OF MEANING

THE POPULARITY OF EARLY NINETEENTH-century landscape painting would probably have surprised its creators; it is now admired for precisely those qualities that were once most disparaged—abstraction and expression. "The great vice of the present day," wrote Constable himself in 1802, "is *bravura*, an attempt to do something beyond the truth." A generation later, Friedrich wrote: "It is the [unfortunate] taste of our time to relish strong colors. Painters outdo one another in applying make-up to cheeks and lips in their paintings; the landscape painters carry exaggeration even further and put make-up on trees, rocks, water and air. . . . Landscape painting these days no longer aims for a spiritual conception of its subject." In contrast to this nineteenth-century unease, the twentieth century has embraced bravura and exaggeration in landscape; Turner, Constable, and Friedrich have been celebrated as prescient forerunners of the Impressionists and the Expressionists, and their virtuosity is seen as its own justification. Indeed, we are moved, and assured of Constable's integrity, when in 122 *Hadleigh Castle* (1829) he loosens his hold on mimesis and paints his feelings; we receive a shock of recognition, and are convinced he is speaking to posterity when he writes in 1821: "Painting is for me but another word for feeling."

More than any previous generation of artists and writers, the Romantics prized personal autonomy and creative originality. Conceiving themselves independent geniuses above the common mien, they claimed to possess the almost divine gift of Imagination, which offered, as Blake wrote: "A Representation of what Eternally Exists, Really and Unchangeably." As Blake's, Constable's, Ruskin's, and Friedrich's

remarks suggest, the Romantics were not proclaiming unfettered artistic abstraction and license. Art must engage "what Eternally Exists" and it must also be more than sheer mimesis and personal expression. Even landscape painting—in a sense the genre most free of moral implications by virtue of its focus on the natural instead of the human world—was tasked by them with a public moral and ethical imperative beyond both virtuosity and expressivity. Ruskin exemplified this traditional and idealist view of art; he judged the landscape art of Turner "invaluable as the vehicle of thought but by itself nothing." In *Modern Painters* (1843) he wrote that "all those excellencies which are peculiar to the painter as such, are merely what rhythm, melody, precision and force are in the words of the orator and the poet, necessary to their greatness, but not the test of their greatness. It is not by the mode of representing and saying, but by what is represented and said, that the respective greatness either of the painter or the writer is to be finally determined."

Ruskin's view that the artist had a responsibility to imitate the essential truths of society, as he elsewhere wrote—and not just the appearance of nature—was shared even by those with very different politics and tastes. Although Constable was a Tory and Ruskin an early Socialist, the painter shared the critic's belief in the moral and ethical responsibility of landscape painters. It was his ambition, we have seen, scientifically to record, for purposes of instruction and moral suasion, his vision of England as richly productive, a land of social peace and hierarchic stability. Indeed, Constable's "six-footers" were intended to carry the ideological burden of history paintings: they were to enshrine for future generations the conservative social vision of the class of industrious rural gentry to which the artist belonged.

In Germany, the landscapes of Friedrich were also

intended to offer moral lessons; the artist described his works as transcendental exercises with the potential to help overcome the spiritual alienation of individuals within society. "Close your eye," he instructed painters, "so that your picture will first appear before your mind's eye. Then bring to the light of day what you first saw in the inner darkness, and let it be reflected into the minds of others." The task of the painter was thus again, as with Constable, to reconcile self and other, self and society, nature and society through the unique procedures of landscape mimesis and idealization. The artist, the nature-philosopher F. W. Schelling wrote, must "withdraw himself from [nature] . . . but only in order to raise himself to the creative energy and to seize [it] spiritually. Thus he ascends into the realm of pure ideas; he forsakes the creature, to regain it with thousandfold interest, and in this sense to return to nature." Schelling's language is abstract, but his injunction to artists is unmistakable: they must show us that transcendent truths do exist by creating works that are in equal parts ideal and real. Art is a means by which people can be made to understand that their freedom resides precisely in their submission to morality.

In sum then, we have seen that however experimental, virtuosic and original it may have been, English and German and also American landscape painting in the Romantic age was also expected to play an important discursive role in the unfolding of politics, ethics, and morality. Yet the very fact that painters and critics were beginning to notice a widening gap between artistic expressiveness and public meaning reveals that a cultural crisis was already underway. Increasingly estranged from a public they viewed as capricious and "simple minded" (in the English poet Shelley's phrase), artists were uncertain to whom exactly they owed allegiance. Increasingly subjected to the thrall of a market they saw as vulgar and factious, artists grew unsure about precisely how to measure their successes and failures. At once freed from oppressive structures of patronage and cut off from supportive communities, Romantic artists, finally, were unsure about just what values, morals, and precepts should be represented in their works. This crisis of cultural meaning, which ultimately led to the creation of a modern and critical nineteenth-century art, was nothing less than a crisis of the public sphere itself.

The "public sphere," writes the critical philosopher Jürgen Habermas, is "that realm of our social life in which something approaching public opinion can be formed. Access is guaranteed to all citizens. A portion of the public sphere comes into being in every conversation in which private individuals assemble to form a public body." In England, the Royal Academy exhibitions, established in 1768, were important arenas for the formation of a progressive bourgeois public sphere; there (as in the French Salon exhibitions inaugurated

a generation earlier) artists, patrons, and public could informally assemble to discuss, debate, and negotiate—through the medium of works of art—the new Enlightenment principles of liberty and equality, the hierarchies of class and gender, the roles of public and private authority, and the political structures of state and empire, among other issues. Artworks of every genre and description—especially history painting but also landscape—played parts in this drama of discursive exchange, helping to cement bourgeois class solidarity, and ultimately to secure its political hegemony. (A taste for art and literature, and the requisite skills of interpretation, was a measure of one's status within the bourgeoisie, and thus too an instrument of cultural power.) Ideally suited—by virtue of its simultaneously empirical and commodity character—to its role within the bourgeois public sphere, painting played a pivotal cultural part in the unfolding of world historical events in the eighteenth century. That elevated cultural status, however, could not outlive the public sphere itself.

What a bourgeois public sphere cannot tolerate is the intrusion of cultural and class factions whose beliefs and attitudes contradict its own cherished notions of reason and common sense. This was precisely what began to occur in England and France in the second and third decades of the nineteenth century. By around 1820, the temper of public life in England had indeed changed: trade unions, working-class corresponding (debating) societies, utopian socialism, dissenting churches, feminism, and an expanding radical press were signals of the decline of consensual politics and the breakup of the bourgeois public sphere that had prevailed (though not without significant strains) for a hundred years. The task of the bourgeois public sphere—debate, negotiation, and consensus building among like-minded men—had become a paralyzing and debilitating burden in the midst of a social totality fractured by working-class dissent. The later landscape paintings of Constable may be seen as a symptom of the crisis. In the midst of rural revolt and economic hard times in 1823, Constable wrote to his friend Archdeacon Fisher: "Though I am here in the midst of the world, I am out of it, and am happy, and endeavour to keep myself unspotted. I have a kingdom of my own, both fertile and populous—my landscape and my children." Indeed, it was precisely Constable's attempt to keep his art "unspotted" by the plagues of insurrection and Luddism that, as we saw in an earlier chapter, precipitated the dichotomy of representation and abstraction in his last works. That division, prefigured nearly a generation before in the recondite and mystic imagery of William Blake, would soon come to dominate English and especially French nineteenth-century art. The accepted name for the phenomenon—whereby the truth of a representation is doubted and the materiality of its form embraced—is "modernism"; it arose wherever a well-entrenched set of cultural traditions (for example, those associated with the term Classicism) collided with a new complex of social and political hierarchies.

Constable's artistic crisis, therefore, which I see as foreshadowing the exigencies of many subsequent European and American artists, was also a public sphere crisis. His historical situation and painterly response may be summed up as follows: the breakdown of political consensus—long in coming but accelerated by the boom and bust cycle of the 1820's—was marked by the rise of working-class "combinations," the growth of rural radicalism, and demands for economic and political enfranchisement. In the face of these challenges, the Tory Constable retreated more and more into an expressive, confessional, and idiosyncratic "kingdom of [his] own." Yet his quixotism was soon judged by critics to be a cipher of the very alienation Constable sought so desperately to fend off. "Nature [in Constable]," wrote the author of an 1837 obituary, "is one vast factory and every element in it condemned to perpetual toil." Constable's defensive response to political and cultural dissidence, in other words, was itself seen as dissident. How could the painter not retreat still further into the emotional sanctuary of "bravura" if even he was judged by his contemporaries to be radical?

In Constable's personally logical, but culturally ambiguous, response to the breakdown of the bourgeois public sphere, appears a premonition of the subsequent directions of nineteenth-century art. At once defensive and aggressive, conservative and radical, traditional and modern, Constable died at a time when art was undergoing an epochal transition. After the collapse of the bourgeois public sphere, painters and sculptors in England, France, the United States, and elsewhere in the West pursued several different but inevitably risk-filled and contradictory strategies.

1) Accepting without plaint the breakdown of the public sphere, many artists settled for a new, culturally diminished role for themselves. Ideologically plaint, culturally complacent, and stylistically eclectic, the art they made might be sponsored by the church or state, or produced "on spec." Regardless of its origin or destination, however, this work would always flatter and entertain. It might inform audiences of what they already knew, or cynically remind them of what they knew they were supposed to believe. The names given today to this varied art—which arose in France with Louis-Philippe and became anachronistic within two generations—are Academic and Official Painting. (The former is the art supported by the Académie des Beaux-Arts, the latter the art sponsored by the successive state administrations—the two were generally, but not always, in basic agreement.) With hindsight, Academic and Official Painting may be seen as early instances of "mass culture" or "kitsch;" they were part

of the French and European general provisions of bread and circuses intended to secure working-class and petit-bourgeois allegiance to capital. (A more or less straight line runs from the French Academician Paul Delaroche [1797–1856] to the Hollywood director Cecil B. DeMille). The historical origins and stylistic variety of this art will be explored later in this chapter under the subheading "Art of the July Monarchy" and in the next chapter (9), under "Individualism and Naturalism in French Salon Art."

2) Reasserting cultural authority and political engagement, a few artists embraced a newly emergent "counter-public sphere." By representing the interests of audiences, constituencies, and patrons from outside of the bourgeoisie—that is, from among the peasantry, proletariat, and petit bourgeoisie—artists once again created works that become vehicles for public and political debate, contest, and consensus. This ambitious direction in art, especially pronounced in France because of the salience of its revolutionary history, was fraught with personal and professional risk, because it generally fell foul of cultural, political, and military authority, and because it sought to address an audience lacking in political, financial, and critical wherewithal. As a result, this artistic mode—described below as Avant-Garde—was generally pursued only during periods of bourgeois vulnerability or subaltern empowerment. Avant-garde art arose in France during the Second Republic (1848–51); its great apostle was the Realist Gustave Courbet. Its re-emergence there some years later among Manet and the Impressionists and in Italy among the Macchiaioli was coincident with the decline and fall of the Second Empire (1870) and with the Italian movement for unification and independence called the Risorgimento. Moments of avant-garde volition are, however, visible (avant la lettre) earlier in the century—as we have seen with Goya and Géricault—and later, as in the works of Vincent Van Gogh, Georges Seurat, and perhaps Paul Gauguin.

3) Seeking no social or political role at all—neither within a "counter public sphere" nor within the domain of Official and Academic entertainment—a small but gradually expanding number of artists pursued the chimera of autonomy. Carefully cultivating their posture of expressive and ideological disinterest, they were sponsored by few and criticized by all. At once embracing and disdaining modern life, these artists sought sanctuary in remote places or among people without clearly fixed class allegiances or ideological identities—the lumpen-proletariat, the petit bourgeois, and foreign and domestic "primitives." This artistic route—the origins of which, as indicated above, may be traced back at least to Goya, Blake and Constable—is conventionally called "modernism." It flourished in periods of historical transition, political stasis, or cultural pessimism, especially during the Second Empire

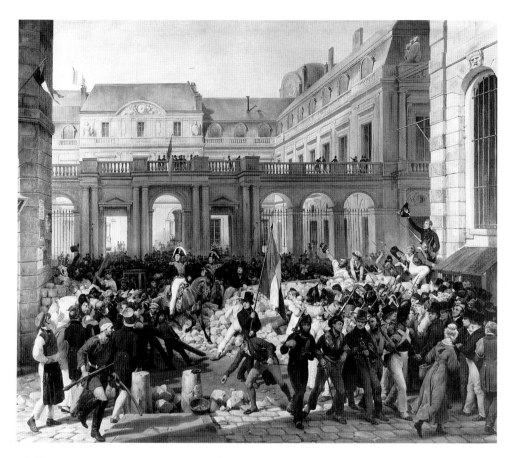

178 HORACE VERNET *The Duc d'Orléans Proceeds to the Hôtel-de-Ville, July 31, 1830* 1833. 89¾ × 8′ 4½
(228 × 258)

with Manet, and during the *fin-de-siècle* with the Symbolists. (The art of Edouard Manet, we shall discover, engaged all three of these strategies.)

Surrender, defiance, and withdrawal—these terms broadly represent the gamut of critical responses to the crisis brought about by the decline of the bourgeois public sphere in the third and fourth decades of the nineteenth century. Academic and Official, Avant-Garde, and Modernist—these labels provide a framework for examining the visual arts of the middle and late years of the century; they also provide a vantage point from which to view the expanding critical consciousness of nineteenth-century art.

THE JULY MONARCHY AND THE ART OF *JUSTE MILIEU*

In France the crisis of the bourgeois public sphere grew acute in the years following the revolution of July 1830. Striving to reinvigorate the genre of history painting, Eugène Delacroix created *The 28th of July: Liberty Leading the People* in time for exhibition at the Salon of 1831. Far from the triumph he had

hoped for and expected, the picture was little short of a public disaster. Boldly painted with the discordant colors of the French *tricoleur*, populated with workers, students, and bourgeois alike, *Liberty* was too literal a depiction of the sustaining myth that the July Revolution was the creation of all the classes of Paris acting in harmony. It was one thing for Delacroix to embrace, as the officially sanctioned Horace Vernet did in *The Duc d'Orléans Proceeds to the Hôtel-de-Ville, July 31, 1830* (1833), comforting homilies about solidarity, but quite another thing to see Liberty herself wearing the disheveled costume of the proletariat: "Was there only this rabble . . . ," asked Dumas, "at those famous days in July?" Although purchased (cheaply) by the French Interior Ministry and exhibited at the Musée Luxembourg in 1832, *Liberty* was thereafter secreted from sight out of fear that it would incite sedition. The concern was not unreasonable.

No longer the social *mélange,* or *sans-culottes* of 1789, the Paris workers who fought on the barricades in July were becoming self-conscious *prolétaires* (the term was first used in its modern sense by Auguste Blanqui in 1832). For them, the Revolution was fought not only for restoration of the constitutional charter usurped by the Bourbon Charles X, but

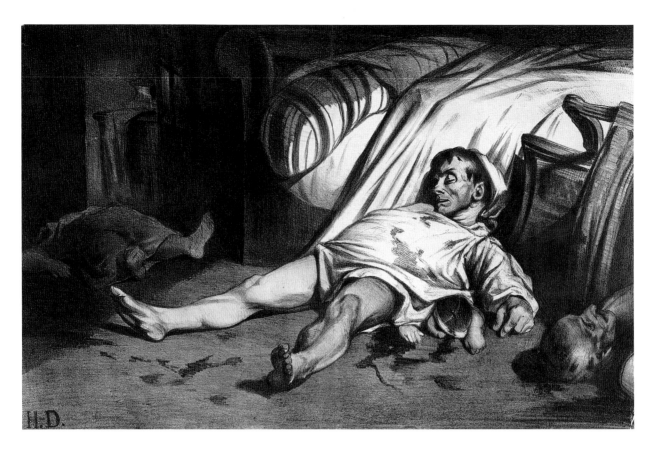

179 HONORÉ DAUMIER *Rue Transnonain April 15, 1834* 1834. 11½ × 17⅝
(29.2 × 44.8)

180 PAUL DELAROCHE *Artists of All Ages* 1836–41. 12′5 × 82′
(388.6 × 2499.4)

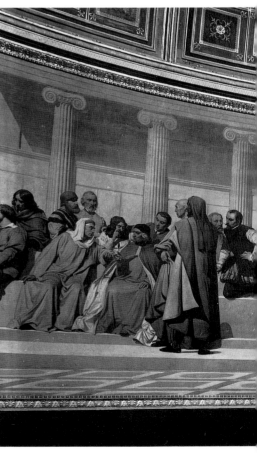

for the right to work, the right to a fair wage, and the right to
organize trade unions. Within a year of the Revolution, a new
round of insurrections had begun: in November 1831, the silk
workers of Lyons were on strike in protest against economic
laissez-faire and a low *tarif* (scale of wages for piece-work); in
1832, workers in Paris rose up in rebellion after the funeral of a
popular Bonapartist general; in 1834, it was once again the
turn of Lyons workers who, backed by a local Republican
party, fought police and national troops in a six-day pitched
battle which left hundreds dead. Within days of the Lyons
uprising in April, workers in the French capital rose in anger
at the closure of a radical newspaper and the arrest of the
leaders of the proletarian Society of the Rights of Man. On
April 14, barricades were erected by the workers to block the
passage of troops through the proletarian *faubourgs* of Paris.
The tactic was unsuccessful, however, and within a short
time, the uprising was defeated and dozens of workers were
dead on the streets or in their homes. The government
massacre was depicted by the young caricaturist Honoré

Daumier (1808–79) in a large lithograph exhibited in a shop-window in October, *Rue Transnonain April 15, 1834* (1834). A few months later, a series of strict press censorship laws were passed, and the facade of constitutionalism dropped. Neither history paintings like Delacroix's, nor even political caricatures such as Daumier's "*You have the floor, explain yourself*" (1835), created during the trial of the rebels of 1834, would be permitted to engage the public sphere.

For nearly two decades following the July Revolution, French painting and sculpture were severely circumscribed by the policies and preferences of the French Académie and the regime of Louis-Philippe. The Classical tradition—once the grand, metaphoric language of enlightenment and revolution—was now compromised by bourgeois historicism, as in Delaroche's semicircular mural painting *Artists of All Ages* (1836–41). Created for the hemicycle auditorium in the Ecole des Beaux-Arts in Paris, the work (more than eighty feet wide at its base) depicts seventy-five figures representing the progress of art from ancient to modern times. Unlike Ingres's *Apotheosis of Homer*, however, which was its ostensible inspiration, Delaroche's hemicycle is anecdotal and conciliatory. Here artists—from Cimabue to Puget—are seen relaxing and kibitzing as if they were gathered during a theatre intermission. The Romantic sculptor David d'Angers called it

a "scholarly genre painting," succinctly exposing its essentially intimate (despite its size) and antiquarian character.

Just as the Classical tradition of art was giving way to antique costume drama during the regime of Louis-Philippe, so too history painting itself (*tableau d'histoire*) was giving way to a hybridized historical genre painting (*genre historique*). Seeking to discourage the creation of large-scaled, politically tendentious subjects taken from Greek and Roman antiquity, the state and the Academy encouraged instead the exhibition and sale of easel-sized pictures representing nationalistic, patriotic, and familial themes drawn from past and present history. This new *genre historique*, as critics called it, consonant with the historical writings of François Guizot, Adolphe Thiers and Jules Michelet, emphasized the achievements of the *grands hommes* of French history, as well as depicting the beliefs, manners, habits, and conditions of the everyday people of the past. The political impetus behind such works, represented by Ary Scheffer's (1795–1858) sentimental *St. Augustine and St. Monica* (1846) and Jean-Léon Gérôme's (1824–1904) lubricious *Cockfight* (1846), is of course profoundly conservative. While the Scheffer, for example, enshrines Catholicism and the Gérôme masculinism, both occlude historical change by implicitly arguing that the difference between the past and the present is only a

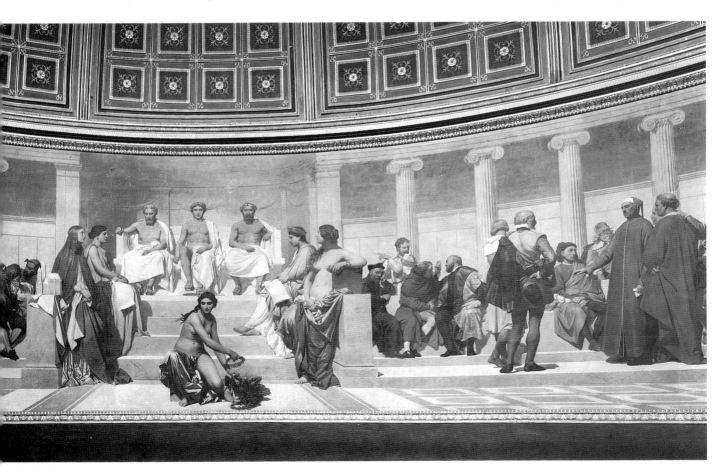

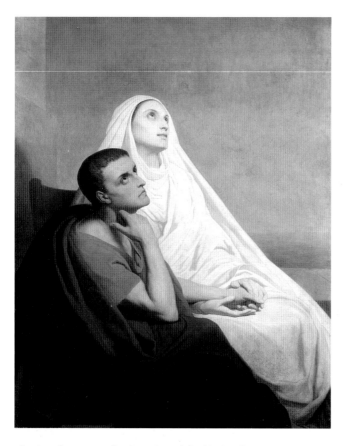

181 ARY SCHEFFER *St. Augustine and St. Monica* 1854. 53¼ × 41¼
(135.2 × 104.7)

matter of costume. Unlike previous history paintings intended to function as *exemplum virtutis*, the *genre historique* was intended to elevate the present by diminishing the splendor and distinctiveness of the past. (Official and Academic painting was completely successful in this latter regard: by the time of Thomas Couture's *Romans of the Decadence* [1847, see pp. 202–05], the Classical vocabulary was suited, for the most part, only to irony, satire, and melodrama.)

The *genre historique* may be observed in the medium of sculpture as well as painting during the July Monarchy. Although exhibited at the pre-revolutionary Salon of 1827, 182 Félicie de Faveau's (1799–1866) plaster *Christina of Sweden Refusing to Give Mercy to Her Squire Monaldeschi* (ca. 1827) exemplifies the tendency in the 1830's for relief sculpture to become portable, anecdotal, historicist, and intimate. Her work is, however, a remarkable example of the genre, because of both its treatment and its theme. The relief is serious and restrained in its dramatic action and setting, consisting of two distinct but proximate figural groupings set against a blank background. The subject is no less compelling, representing an act of militancy and resolve, not unlike the actions of the

sculptor herself, who was briefly imprisoned in 1832 for her participation in a Bourbon Legitimist plot against Louis-Philippe.

More representative of July Monarchy sculpture, however, is the work of Antoine-Louis Barye (1796–1875). Like most sculptors of the period, Barye came from an artisanal background and maintained strong ties to the industrial and decorative arts traditions. He was a pioneer (along with the slightly older David d'Angers) in the revival of bronze sculpture, and was among the first serially to reproduce his designs in order to reach a large middle-class audience. Barye's class background, technical innovativeness, and longstanding association with unionized bronze-foundry workers, however, did not affect his thoroughly Orléanist political allegiances. His *Lion Crushing a Serpent* (1833), 183 which won for him the *Légion d'honneur*, was widely regarded as an allegorical celebration of the July Revolution; it could be interpreted as the French people crushing the Bourbon dynasty, or alternatively as Orléanist law destroying Republican anarchy. (Both of these messages were fully consonant with Louis-Philippe's promotion of himself as the promulgator of moral order and national prosperity.) Although Barye thereafter only rarely ventured into the mode of political allegory, his many bronze sculptures of animals in combat appealed to the regime's taste for melodrama and scientific naturalism. Partly derived from ideal ancient and Renaissance prototypes, and partly from naturalist observation at the Paris Cabinet d'Anatomie Comparée (established in the late eighteenth century by Georges Cuvier), Barye's bronzes are thus the products of typical July Monarchy compromise.

Like Barye, most artists of the July Monarchy sought to achieve in their works the same *juste milieu* (golden mean) that the king was seeking to achieve in matters of state. Louis-Philippe saw his state as the preordained reconciliation of 1789 with the Restoration; his regime would pay homage to the memory of the heroic Bonaparte even as it set store by such men as the stolid bourgeois M. Louis-François Bertin, 184 painted by Ingres in 1832. Freedom and order, democracy and stability, science and faith, progress and business-as-usual—these were the paired pillars of the *juste milieu*, paralleling France's dual revolutionary and monarchical traditions. Thus the king and his *idéologues* (the term had been coined by Napoleon) courted both eclecticism and synthesis in their cultural and economic policies alike. Alongside the new industrialization grew parochial monopolies; among the new national banks arose domestic tarifs and foreign protectionism. Together with the Classicism of Ingres was the Romanticism of Delacroix; beside the official, Romantic idealism of Scheffer was the academic, Neoclassical verisimilitude of Gérôme.

As Boime has shown, the politics and art generally pursued

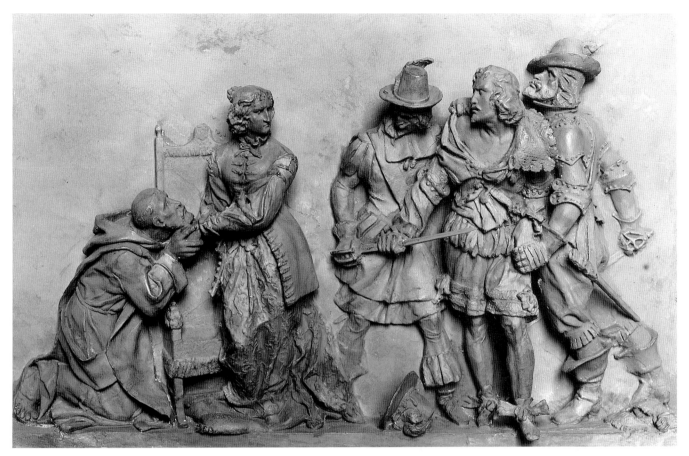

182 FÉLICIE DE FAVEAU *Christina of Sweden Refusing to Give Mercy to Her Squire Monaldeschi* ca. 1827. 15¾ × 22⅞ (40 × 58)

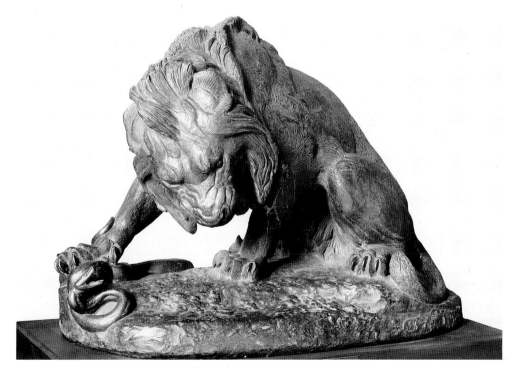

183 ANTOINE-LOUIS BARYE *Lion Crushing a Serpent* 1883. Length 70 (177.8)

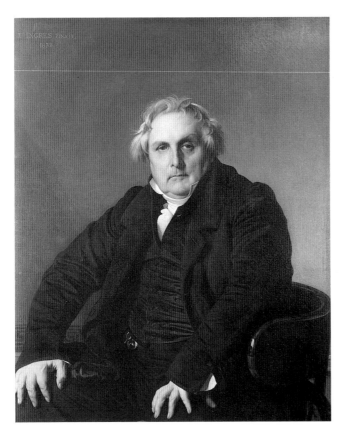

184 JEAN-AUGUSTE-DOMINIQUE INGRES *M. Louis-François Bertin*
1832. 46 × 37½ (116.8 × 95.3)

during the July Monarchy were those which harmoniously blended these irreconcilables. "Take a portion of monarchy, a portion of aristocracy and a portion of democracy," wrote the socialist and cynic Pierre Leroux in 1839, "and you will have the Restoration or the *juste milieu,* and that will be eclecticism." "Genius is a ready and sure perception of the right proportion [of] the ideal and the natural, form and thought," wrote the influential philosopher Victor Cousin in *Du vrai, du beau et du bien* (1853). "This union is the perfection of art: masterpieces are produced by observing it." Like *juste milieu* politics, however, *juste milieu* art was ultimately contradictory and unstable. Two cases in point, dating from the beginning and end of the July Monarchy, are David d'Angers's sculpted pediment for the Pantheon and Couture's painting for the Salon of 1847, *The Romans of the Decadence.*

187
185–6

THE PARADOX OF PATRIOTISM: D'ANGERS'S PANTHEON PEDIMENT

Begun in 1830, the year Delacroix was painting *Liberty Leading the People,* David d'Angers's pediment of the

Pantheon was an effort to engage the imagination and energy of a progressive and patriotic bourgeoisie. Like the painting, the relief combines real and allegorical figures in a stirring but heteroclite ensemble. Like the painting too, the colossal sculpture was received by political moderates and conservatives with anger and incomprehension, revealing a widening schism in the public sphere. Beneath the relief appears an inscription which announces its theme: "AUX GRANDS HOMMES LA PATRIE RECONNAISSANTE" ("In gratitude to the great men of the Fatherland"). At the center of the pediment stands the allegorical figure of La Patrie, distributing laurel wreathes handed to her by Liberty, seated at her right. History sits at La Patrie's left, inscribing on a tablet the names of the *grands hommes* of military and civic affairs who are to be honored.

Military men occupy the right half of the pediment, led by the young Bonaparte, who reaches past History to take his crown. With the exception of the legendary drummer from the battle of Arcole, the remainder of the military figures are anonymous soldiers of the Revolution and Empire, assembled left to right, in decreasing order of rank. The men of civic and cultural affairs fill the left half of the pediment, and represent a liberal Enlightenment canon. They include Rousseau and Voltaire (seated side by side on a bench), J.-L. David (standing, with palette and brushes), the jurist and victim of the Terror Malesherbes (standing, with counselor's robes), and behind him the deputy Manuel, expelled in 1823 from the Chamber of Deputies for his opposition to French intervention on behalf of the monarchy in Spain. Among the others are Cuvier, the Archbishop Fénélon, and the Marquis de Lafayette, who was instrumental in conferring the crown on Louis-Philippe but who soon thereafter became disenchanted with the monarchy.

For the most part, David d'Angers's patriotic pantheon represents the range of his own generally liberal-to-Jacobin political sympathies, as well as reflecting the liberalism of the Orléans regime at its inception. (Even the inclusion of the monarchist Malesherbes does not detract from the overall left politics: he was as renowned for helping to end the issuance of *lettres de cachet* as for advocating the life of Louis XVI.) Yet the unanimity of artist, patron, and audience that underlay the program for the pediment would not survive 1830. As the revolutionary summer passed into a repressive winter and spring, d'Angers's cast of characters—like Delacroix's—was increasingly seen as tendentious, incendiary, or simply incoherent. Attempts were made by successive ministers of the interior in 1832–4 to block completion of the project, and the actual unveiling of the work was postponed in July 1837, probably out of nervousness over its political content. D'Angers was relentless, however, in his determination to finish and display his work, and in September 1837 he finally succeeded in having the obscuring canvas and scaffolding removed.

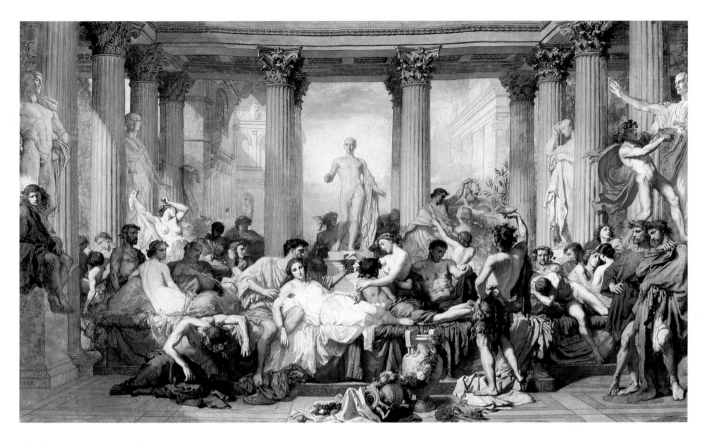

185 THOMAS COUTURE *Romans of the Decadence* 1847. 15′6½ × 25′10 (473.7 × 787.4)

During the succeeding months and years, the Pantheon pediment was vehemently criticized from the Legitimist and Ultramontane right and the Orléanist center of the political spectrum. D'Angers's depiction of the atheists Voltaire and Rousseau among others, on the facade of a building originally consecrated in honor of Sainte-Geneviève (built 1755–80), was anathema to conservative Catholics, who included Queen Amélie. In addition, his embrace of the principles and personages of the Revolutions of 1789 and 1830 was seen in official circles as both anachronistic and provocative: anachronistic because the King had already rejected the very revolutionary principles that brought him to power, and provocative because a series of recent ministerial and economic crises threatened to precipitate a new uprising; reconciliation and quietism were now most wanted in the arts. As might be expected, therefore, the left (its voice, however, muted by press restrictions) was much more favorably disposed toward the pediment than the right, seeing in it a condemnation of Catholic revanchism, Orléanist authoritarianism and bourgeois corruption.

Yet it would probably be incorrect to view d'Angers's pediment as existing wholly outside the *juste milieu* ideological orbit. For one thing, its representation of the concept of *grands*

hommes was consonant with the historicist preoccupations of the Orléans court and its official historian, François Guizot. (We have already considered Delaroche's *Artists of All Ages* as one *juste milieu* result of that interest.) For another, d'Angers's creation of a bourgeois Enlightenment martyrology repudiates emerging radical ideas about the centrality of the proletariat in the revolutionary process, such as those held by Auguste Blanqui, represented by his friend the artist in 1840. Stylistically, too, the pediment is marked by *juste milieu* compromise, combining as it does Baroque Classicism with elements from the *genre historique*. Like his freestanding monument to Cuvier (1845), d'Angers's pediment possesses the majesty and hierarchism found in works by the greatest sculptors of the late *ancien régime*—especially Bouchardon, Pigalle, and Pajou—yet individual figures also display an informality, particularism, and even homeliness suggestive of works by Delaroche, Scheffer, and Gérôme, among others.

In one significant way, however, David d'Angers's version of *juste milieu* stands apart from that of his contemporaries, and anticipates an emerging attitude of avant-gardism: his best sculptures achieve their power and perspicacity by embracing popular artistic traditions outside of the official mainstream. The proportion, physiognomy, and placement of

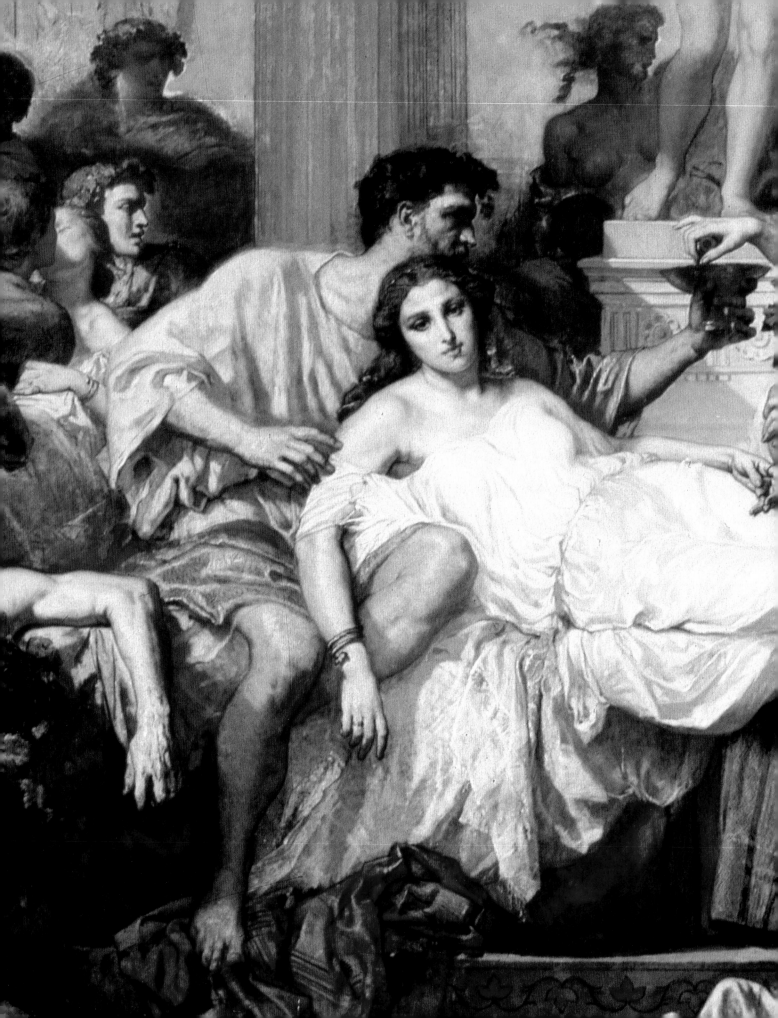

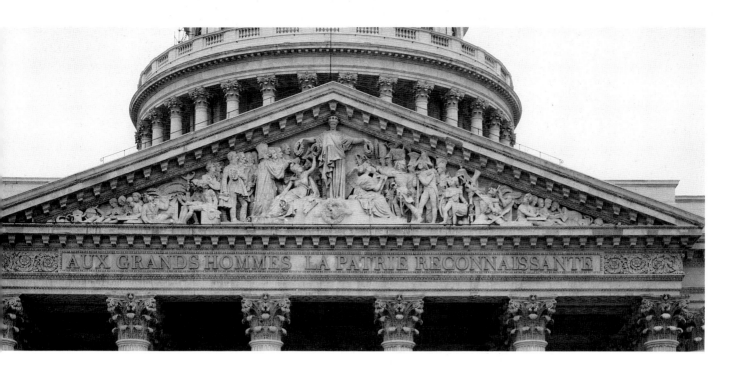

187 PIERRE-JEAN DAVID D'ANGERS, the pediment of the Pantheon, Paris, 1830–37

figures in his pediment were probably influenced by the popular prints then being issued in great numbers from the town of Epinal in northeastern France. In d'Angers's pediment and in F. Georgin and J.-B. Thiébault's woodcut 188 *The Apotheosis of Napoleon* (1834), for example, the Academic canons of graceful human proportion are rejected in favor of more squat or compact formulae. In addition, both works employ perspective only minimally; this flatness is immediately apparent in the serried ranks of soldiers in the woodcut, but it is also visible in the sculpture. Instead of conceiving the pedimental space as coextensive with the actual three dimensions of the lived world, d'Angers had created a telescoped space of shallow planes in which figures are overlapped or superimposed, one above another. To some extent, this approach to composition is dictated by the peculiar triangular format, but d'Angers's stylistic populism 190 is equally apparent in his rectangular relief panels, such as *The Motherland Calling Her Children to the Defense of Liberty* (1835) in the vault of the Arc de Triomphe at the Gate of Aix, in Marseille. Here the heroic plebeians are jumbled together in shallow relief and comic cacophany, at once recalling the paintings of Pieter Breugel the Elder and anticipating the frescos of Diego Rivera.

David d'Angers's skill at synthesizing diverse styles and traditions was shared by two other outstanding sculptors of the July Monarchy—François Rude (1784–1855) and Antoine-Augustin Préault (1809–79). In Rude's famous 191 *Marseillaise* (or *The Departure of the Volunteers of 1792*, 1833–6), on the Arc de Triomphe in Paris, the sculptor depicts war as an ugly siren calling the volunteers of '92 to order and arms. Part of an elaborate sculptural program intended to promote domestic tranquility, Rude's relief is marked at once by violence and humor. The figure of War above emits a blood-curdling alarm while the soldiers below react with confusion; their dishevelment and *déshabille* lends the scene a quotidianism that is at variance with its ostensible heroism. A similar combination of high and low, or ideal and anecdotal, elements may be seen in the work of Préault, who was for a time a student of d'Angers.

In Préault's plaster relief *Slaughter* (1833–4, later cast in 189 bronze), the artist represents the massacre of a family by a helmeted warrior and a black man shown at the upper left. (The precise subject of the work, if there was one, remains unknown.) Though partly inspired by reliefs by the Baroque sculptors Pierre Puget and Alessandro Algardi, the work is remarkably abstract and experimental. The composition has the compactness of an ancient "episodic fragment of a low relief" (in the artist's words), and the flattened space of Epinal prints. Yet there is nothing static about *Slaughter*: indeed, its two-dimensionalism is almost Cubist in its jostling and juxtapositioning of forms and figures. (A century later, the figure of the screaming mother provided a model for Picasso's *Guernica*.) Préault's *Slaughter* did not find a sympathetic audience; after exhibiting it at the Salon of 1834 (the year of the slaughter of Transnonain), he was excluded from Salon exhibitions for the next fifteen years.

Less confrontational and better connected than his pupil, David d'Angers did not suffer a similar exile from patronage.

PARADOX OF PATRIOTISM · 199

◀ 186 Detail of Plate 185

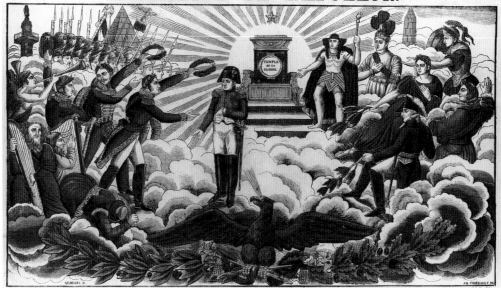

188 **F. Georgin** and **J.-B. Thiébault** *The Apotheosis of Napoleon* 1834. 16 × 23 (40.6 × 58.2)

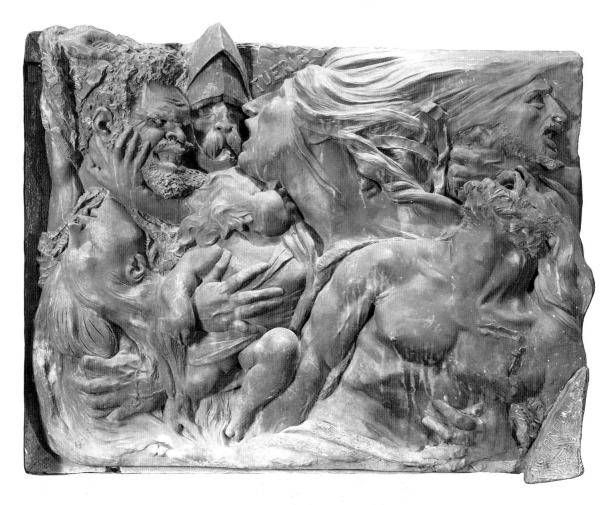

189 **Antoine-Augustin Préault** *Slaughter* 1833–4. 43 × 55 (109.2 × 139.7)

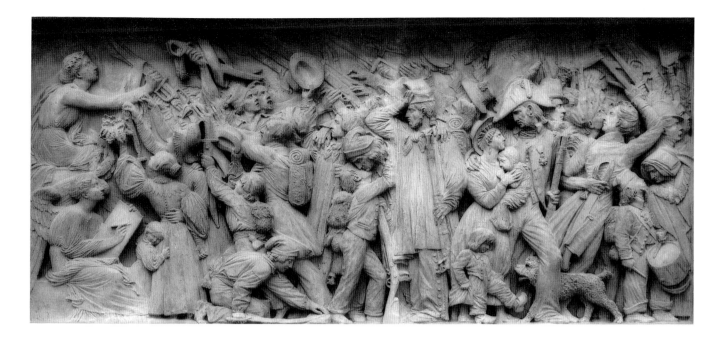

190 **PIERRE-JEAN DAVID D'ANGERS** *The Motherland Calling Her Children to the Defense of Liberty* 1835. $53\frac{1}{4} \times 10'11\frac{1}{8}$ (135×333)

191 **FRANÇOIS RUDE** *The Marseillaise* (*The Departure of the Volunteers of 1792*) 1833–6. Height 42' (504)

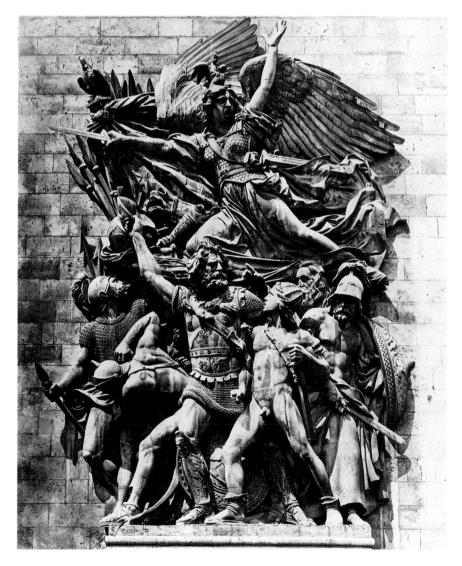

However, for the remainder of his career after the Pantheon pediment he was forced to grapple with the political paradoxes of public sculpture. Indeed, it would seem that his very project had become untenable in the era in which it was conceived. The construction of an Enlightenment canon, the celebration of the principles of 1789, and the embrace of alternative or popular art traditions, were acts that engaged a progressive bourgeois public sphere that for the most part no longer existed. The insurrectionary events in Paris and Lyons had put an end to the myth of solidarity between classes on behalf of *liberté*. From now on, artists would either have to abjure highminded political principle or else embrace it and thereby unleash the very divisive ideological forces that the July Monarchy sought to control. The public sphere and the bourgeois *juste milieu*, in others words, were incompatible.

D'Angers's last years were marked by political engagement (he was elected a departmental deputy during the Second Republic) and artistic hope. His dream of a great *Monument to Emancipation*, however, would remain unfulfilled with the exception of a few drawings and models, while his small bronze medallions in commemoration of *grands hommes* would multiply to more than five hundred. In January 1841 he wrote to the German physician and painter Carl Gustav Carus (1789–1869) concerning a small terracotta statuette of Liberty: "I am very much afraid that the figure of Liberty that I am sending you will be confiscated by the German customs. The rulers of all countries fear it even in painting. They are right because Liberty is the sword of Damocles suspended continually above their heads. It is the powerful voice of humanity that will be heard some day from one end of the earth to the other." Within a decade, that voice would indeed be heard again in France, and a new, avant-garde art would be born in response.

THOMAS COUTURE: CLASSICISM AND THE WOMAN QUESTION

185–6   At the end of the July Monarchy, Thomas Couture (1815–79) painted *Romans of the Decadence* (1847) in an effort to revive monumental history painting for the public sphere. In many ways, as Boime has argued, the picture is a summation of *juste milieu* culture, combining history painting and the *genre historique*, Classicism and Romanticism, eroticism and sexual repression, political criticism and Orléanist ingratiation. At the Salon of 1847 it achieved a success as vast as its size and ambition, and was soon among the most widely admired, discussed, and reproduced paintings of the nineteenth century. Yet for all its celebrity, *Romans* was as much an end as a beginning; like d'Angers's Pantheon pediment, Couture's painting was contradictory and paradoxical, and may actually

have helped to destroy public, monumental, and Classicizing art in the attempt to save it.

Romans of the Decadence represents the debauched morning after an orgiastic night before. Within a columned hall, some forty figures in Roman costume are seen lounging, sleeping, dancing, embracing, or, in the case of the two standing men at the right, casting censorious glances. On the intarsia marble floor in the foreground is a still life of fruit, flowers, and amphoras. On the triclinium (three-sided sofa) in the middleground are the bulk of the figures, organized into large and small groups and appearing as a frieze parallel to the picture plane. Surrounding the revelers and bordering the chamber are alternating Corinthian columns and statues of august Romans, including Germanicus at the center of the picture. In the background is a courtyard or atrium, articulated with Classical columns, arches, pilasters, niches, cornices, and friezes.

Couture's bacchanal has formal and thematic antecedents in the work of the Renaissance artists Bellini, Titian, Raphael, and Veronese and in the painting of Géricault, Ingres, and Delacroix, among many others. Two especially apposite sources for *Romans* are Delacroix's *Women of Algiers* (1834)   192 and Dominique Papety's (1815–49) *The Dream of Happiness*   193 (1843). Together they provided a basis for Couture's attempted unification of Romantic color and Classical draftsmanship, as well as his idiosyncratic combination of sensualism and moral rectitude.

Delacroix's picture, inspired by the artist's visit to a Moroccan harem in 1832 (which in turn was made possible by the recent French occupation of the region) is a dream image of "Oriental" indolence. The three harem women and their servant are the embodiment of the European masculinist image of Middle Eastern and North African people as sensual and irrational. The third woman from the left, who is the source for the nude in profile at the center of *Romans*, holds the tube of a hookah, suggesting the timelessness of intoxication and sexual delight. Unlike Delacroix's *Liberty Leading the People*, which honors the classes and heroic individuals that made the July Revolution, *Women of Algiers* celebrates social and cultural passivity: the Orient is vividly represented by the artist as a land of erotic freedom and languor outside of politics, history, and class. "It must be hard for them to understand," Delacroix wrote in his diary from Tangier, "the easy-going ways of Christians and the restlessness that sends us perpetually seeking after new ideas. We notice a thousand things in which they are lacking, but their ignorance is the foundation of their peace and happiness. Can it be that we have reached the end of what a more advanced civilization can produce?"

For Delacroix and a succession of Orientalists culminating in the Symbolist Paul Gauguin, "the East" functioned as an

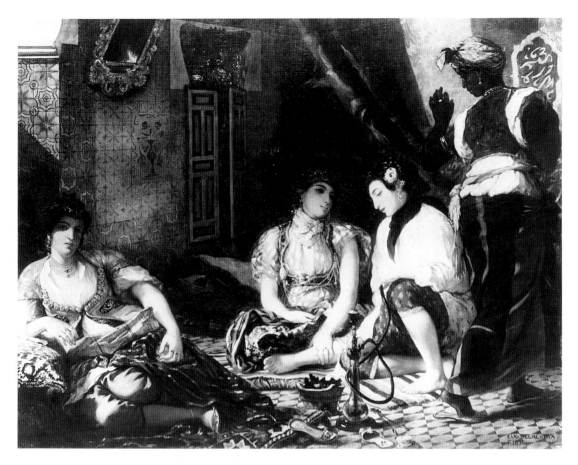

192 EUGÈNE DELACROIX *Women of Algiers* 1834. 70⅞ × 90⅛ (180 × 229)

ideal respite from the dispiriting sexual and ideological conflicts that existed in "the West." Whereas in Paris women had begun articulating demands for the reform of property, child-custody, and divorce laws, in the East women appeared to be chattel slaves; whereas in Paris, the feminist and radical Flora Tristan (1803–44) published several tracts and a novel (*Méphis,* 1838) describing the liberation of women and the *prolétaire* as necessary and interrelated projects, in the Orient gender and class hierarchies appeared stable and timeless. Yet however racist and sexist it might be thought today, *Women of Algiers* is also a utopian tract. Like the Saint-Simonian philosopher Prosper Enfantin who dreamed in 1832 of a "beautiful army" of prostitutes destined to sanctify the flesh by fulfilling natural desire, Delacroix imagined a vividly colored Oriental utopia of feminine sexual pleasure in *Women of Algiers.* "This is a place for painters," Delacroix wrote from Tangier. "Economists and Saint-Simonists would find much to criticize here, from the point of view of the rights of man and equality before the law, but beauty abounds. . . . Here you will see a nature which in our country is always disguised, here you will feel the rare and precious influence of the sun which gives an intense life to everything." Delacroix's *Women* is thus both a testimonial to and a condemnation of the "advanced [European] civilization" of its day. In offered Couture a model of sexual blame and praise.

In Papety's *The Dream of Happiness,* exhibited at the Salon of 1843, some two dozen men, women, and children rest, lounge, read, sing, and cavort in a bower framed by Classical sculpture and architecture. The picture is explicitly indebted to the utopian socialist doctrines of Charles Fourier (1772–1837), whose treatise *Unité universelle* is read by the young men and women at the lower right. Couture, who worked beside Papety in the studio of their teacher Delaroche, borrowed the motif of the young man offering a toast to the statue of a flute player, for his own semi-nude male toasting the statue of Germanicus in *Romans.* Like the *Women of Algiers, The Dream of Happiness* is located outside of European history; Papety represents a future utopia of abundance, peace, and pleasure modeled on an idealized past that combines the "noble simplicity and quiet grandeur" of the Classical age with the sumptuousness and indolence of the French *ancien régime. The Dream of Happiness* is a kind of *juste milieu* nudist colony, at once ascetic and libertine, which gave Couture a model marriage of conformism and liberalism.

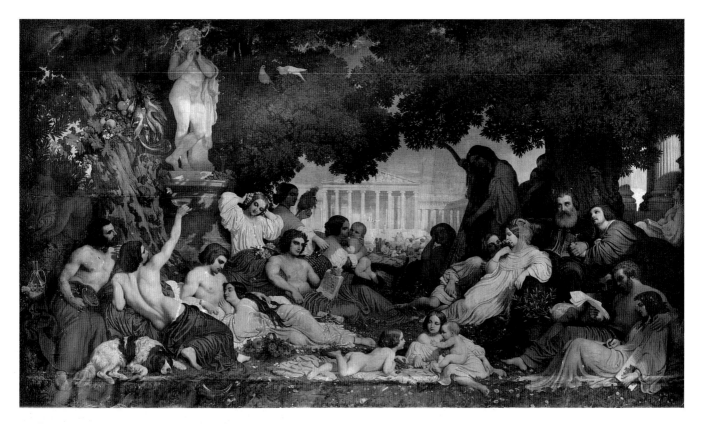

193 DOMINIQUE PAPETY *The Dream of Happiness* 1843. 12′1¾ × 20′8 (370 × 635)

Although inspired by these and many other works, *Romans of the Decadence* has its own specific content and origins. Its subject was taken, according to the 1847 Salon catalog, from two verses of the Roman writer Juvenal's sixth *Satire,* "Against Women," which compares the "plague" of feminine sexuality and betrayal in his age to the "blessings" of feminine chastity and loyalty in an earlier time: "Now we suffer the evils of long peace. Luxury hatches terrors worse than war, avenging a world beaten down." Juvenal's misogynist paean is succinctly represented at the center of Couture's picture by a

186 crucial juxtaposition: the reclining woman (identified by contemporaries as a courtesan) beneath the erect statue of Germanicus. Just as sexually demanding women destroyed the might of Rome—so the modern argument went—the courtesan threatens the nobility and honor of France. If the Classical tradition has been brought low, it is the fault of modern women. In Couture's *Romans,* in short, feminine sexuality is figured as tragic decadence.

Couture's reclining courtesan, along with the other sexually usurpatious women in the picture, is an important instance of the increasingly widespread representation of the erotic female as the embodiment of modern decadence and death. In

194 *Romans,* as in the exactly contemporaneous *Woman Bitten by a*
195 *Snake* by Jean-Baptiste Clésinger (1814–83) and *Two Young*

Girls or The Beautiful Rosine by the Belgian Antoine Wiertz (1806–65), Woman is the repository of bourgeois fear and masculine loathing; by her erotic independence she is both a threat to male political prerogatives and a mockery of masculine sexual desire. At the same time as these artists, the poet Charles Baudelaire was beginning to sketch the theme of the vicious courtesan for his *The Flowers of Evil* (*Les Fleurs du Mal,* 1861) and *Paris Spleen* (*Le Spleen de Paris,* 1869). Unlike Delacroix, who appears to revel in what he takes to be the sexual freedom of the harem, Baudelaire hates the prostitute for her resemblance to himself. Subjected to the vicissitudes of the marketplace, the prostitute's sexuality—like the journalist's independence—is a mere sham of freedom. Irony is thus the rhetoric of Baudelairean sexuality: "Not so many years ago," says one of the old roués in "Portraits of Mistresses" from *Paris Spleen,* "Fate granted me the possession of a woman who was without doubt the sweetest, the most submissive, and the most devoted creature in the world, and who was always ready! And without enthusiasm!" The woman in the center of *Romans of the Decadence,* by contrast, is not lacking enthusiasm: her ennui is only the result of her insatiety. "What impossible sensuality," asked the critic Théophile Gautier, "does she dream of after that night of orgiastic passions?"

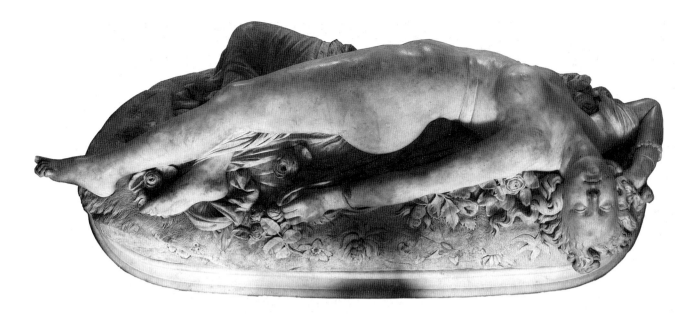

194 JEAN-BAPTISTE CLÉSINGER *Woman Bitten by a Snake* 1847.
Length 31 (78.7)

195 ANTOINE WIERTZ *Two Young Girls or The Beautiful Rosine*
1847. 55⅛ × 39⅜ (140 × 100)

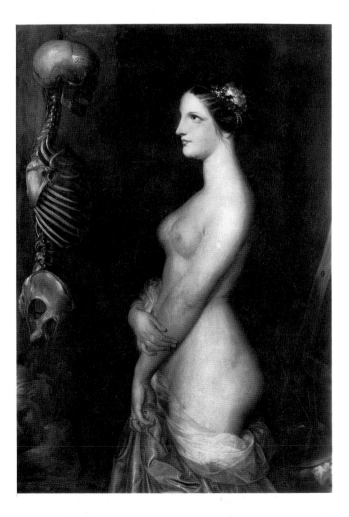

A year after the exhibition of *Romans*, the cliché of the
temptress undermining virtue and ridiculing masculine desire
would be supplemented by a still more virulent allegory: the
modern prostitute would be identified with the radical
proletariat leading society headlong to chaos and perdition.
The origins of the "red whore" motif are to be found much
earlier than 1848; certainly it may be detected in the
conservative response to Delacroix's *Liberty*, described by the
German poet and critic Heinrich Heine as an "alley-Venus."
But amid the generalized panic of the months following the
proletarian rising of June 1848, the image of the prostitute on
the barricades became seared in bourgeois memory. Jean-
François Millet depicted the subject in a lost pastel, as did a
host of reactionary caricaturists. Indeed, for the generation
that followed the 1848 Revolution, the body of the prostitute—in fact and image—would become a battleground upon
which class and gender struggles would be waged. Couture's
Romans of the Decadence stands at the threshold of that new
period of sexual and political antagonisms, just as surely as it
stands at the close of an epoch in which the Classical tradition
was the preferred metaphoric language for contest and debate
within the bourgeois public sphere.

· 9 ·

THE RHETORIC OF REALISM: COURBET AND THE ORIGINS OF THE AVANT-GARDE

RHETORICS OF REALIST ART AND POLITICS

GUSTAVE COURBET (1819–77) BELONGED TO THE Post-Romantic generation of French artists and writers that included Honoré Daumier, J.-F. Millet, Gustave Flaubert, and Charles Baudelaire. They were born at the close of an heroic age. In their youth, they witnessed the breakdown of a common language of Classicism, the dissipation of revolutionary idealism, and the growing division between artists and public. In their maturity, they saw the abandonment of Enlightenment principle and widespread accommodation of authoritarianism. At the end of their lives, they beheld the promise and threat of Communist insurrection and the complete collapse of a bourgeois public sphere. Together, these crises and caesuras combined to convince the artists and writers of the mid-century that they were living through a cultural rupture of unprecedented dimension: the name given for that broad epoch of change was "modernity," and the name for that specific post-Romantic generation was Realist. "I am not only a socialist," Courbet wrote provocatively to a newspaper in 1851, "but a democrat and a Republican as well—in a word, a partisan of all the revolution and above all a Realist . . . for 'Realist' means a sincere lover of the honest truth."

The rhetoric of Realism, however, is not confined to artists' manifestos or to France; it is written across the age and across Europe, in its politics, literature, and painting. The artists and writers mentioned above may not have read Marx's *Manifesto of the Communist Party* (1847), but their works shared with it a depiction of epochal anxiety, transformation, and desacralization:

The bourgeoisie has stripped of its halo every occupation hitherto honored and looked up to with reverent awe. It has converted the physician, the lawyer, the priest, the poet, the man of science into its paid wage-laborers. . . . Constant revolutionising of production, uninterrupted disturbance of all social conditions, everlasting uncertainty and agitation distinguish the bourgeois epoch from all earlier ones. . . . All that is solid melts into air, all that is holy is profaned, and man is at last compelled to face with sober senses, his real conditions of life, and his relations with his kind.

Marx's words are redolent with images from Realist art and literature. Physician, lawyer, priest, poet, and man of science are veritably the cast of characters in Flaubert's bitter satire of country life, *Madame Bovary* (1857); the depressing results for humankind of the "uninterrupted disturbance of all social conditions" are exposed in Daumier's *The Third-Class Carriage* (ca. 1862), Millet's *The Gleaners* (1857), and Courbet's *The Stonebreakers* (1850); the poet stripped of his halo is the subject of Baudelaire's ironic prose-poem "The Loss of a Halo" in *Paris Spleen* (1869).

In the art and literature of Courbet and Flaubert, reverence for the ideal and honor of the Classic have no place: the former depicted gross wrestlers, drunken priests, peasants, prostitutes, and hunters; the latter described common scribes, pharmacists, journalists, students, and adulterers. In the caricatures of Daumier and the poems of Baudelaire, there appear no Romans in togas (except for purposes of satire) or medieval knights in armor: they preferred to honor ragpickers in their shreds and patches, country bumpkins in their ill-fitting city clothes, and bourgeois men in their black suits. "It is true that the great tradition has been lost," wrote Baudelaire

196
197
206

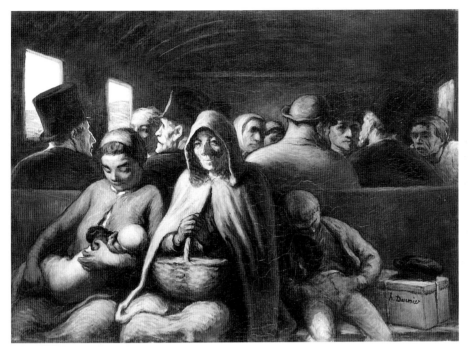

196 HONORÉ DAUMIER *The Third-Class Carriage* ca. 1862. 25¼ × 35½ (65.4 × 90.2)

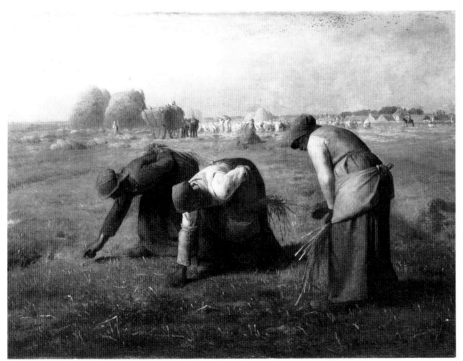

197 JEAN-FRANÇOIS MILLET *The Gleaners* 1857. 33 × 44 (83.8 × 111.8)

at the dawn of this new age, in "On the Heroism of Modern Life" (1846),

> and that the new one is not yet established. . . . But all the same, has not this much abused garb its own beauty and its native charm? Is it not the necessary garb of our suffering age, which wears the symbol of a perpetual mourning even upon its thin black shoulders? Note, too, that the dress-coat and the frock-coat not only possess their political beauty, which is an expression of universal equality, but also their poetic beauty, which is an expression of the public soul—an immense cortège of undertakers' mutes (mutes in love, political mutes, bourgeois mutes . . .). We are each of us celebrating some funeral.

Compared to modern men in "frock-coats," like those from Balzac's novels, the poet then explains, "the heroes of the Iliad are but pygmies."

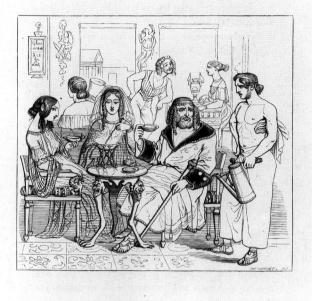

198 GRANDVILLE "Apple of the Hesperides and rum ice," from *Un Autre Monde* 1844.

In contrast to Baudelaire's irony, Daumier and his fellow caricaturist Grandville (J.-I.-I. Gérard, 1803–47) chose anachronism to satirize the "real conditions" of their "suffering age." In the 1840's, they highlighted the dubious heroism of the present by depicting the stylishness of figures 198 from the Classical past, as in Daumier's lithograph "The Abduction of Helen," from *Le Charivari* (1842), and Grandville's engraving of Romans ordering an "apple of the Hesperides and rum ice." In the latter sheet, from the Fourierist *Un Autre Monde* (1844, see pp. 203 and 298), a modish ménage wearing Roman sandals are seated in a bistro, being served drinks by a surly waiter standing in Classical *contra-posto*. Once again the rhetorics of Realist art and politics may be seen to overlap. Anachronism and caricature were the linguistic weapons of choice for Karl Marx a few years later when he sought to describe the hypocrisy and servility of the bourgeoisie who permitted Louis Napoleon (nephew to the first Napoleon) to destroy the Second Republic in a *coup d'état* on December 2, 1851:

Hegel remarks somewhere that all great, world-historical facts and personages occur, as it were, twice. He forgot to add: the first time as tragedy, the second as farce. Caussidière for Danton, Louis Blanc for Robespierre, the Mountain of 1848–51 for the Mountain of 1793–1795, the Nephew for the Uncle. And the same caricature occurs in the circumstances in which the second edition of the Eighteenth Brumaire is taking place. [18 Brumaire is the date in 1799, according to the Revolutionary calendar, when Napoleon I assumed supreme power.]

No longer can Classical antiquity be plausibly invoked, Marx argues, to cloak from the men and women of 1851 the real nature of their unheroic deeds and attitudes. Neither the bourgeoisie nor their proletarian interlocutors can any longer have recourse to such idealist "self-deceptions." Because 1789 served to liberate only the bourgeoisie and not all of humanity from oppression, Marx writes, the revolutionists of that day "required world-historical recollections in order to drug themselves concerning their own content." Since, on the other hand, the present revolution was being waged by the proletariat on behalf of all humanity, it required absolute clarity as to means and ends. "In order to arrive at its content," Marx says, "the revolution of the nineteenth century must let the dead bury their dead. There the phrase went beyond the content; here the content goes beyond the phrase."

In England no less than France, the style and phrase of Classical antiquity—there only recently embraced—quickly gave way to an art and literature that emphasized fidelity to the materiality of things, directness of emotional appeal, and honesty to natural appearances. The artists who formed the Pre-Raphaelite Brotherhood (PRB) in 1848—William Holman Hunt (1827–1910), John Everett Millais (1829–96), and Dante Gabriel Rossetti (1828–82)—were inspired by the revolutionary events on the Continent and by the English working-class movement for a People's Charter, to attempt a reform of British art. Rejecting the mannerism of the later Raphael as much as the formulas of the Royal Academy, the PRB turned for inspiration to fifteenth-century Italian and Flemish painting and to early nineteenth-century German art by Runge, Friedrich, and the Nazarenes. (The Nazarenes, so called for their beards and long hair, were a brotherhood of Catholic-converted German artists active in Rome after 1810. They included Peter Cornelius, Johann Friedrich Overbeck, and Franz Pforr.) From these near and distant sources, the PRB sought the bases for a regeneration (the group's journal was named *The Germ*) of British culture and society.

Millais dispensed with Classical costume and architecture as well as with High Renaissance grace and timelessness in *Christ in the House of His Parents* (1850). The genre scene of 199

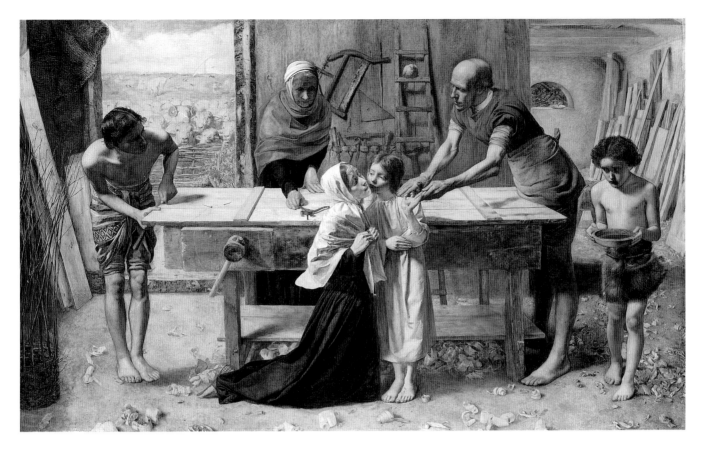

199 JOHN EVERETT MILLAIS *Christ in the House of His Parents*
1850. 33½ × 54 (85 × 137.2)

200 WILLIAM HOLMAN HUNT *The Awakening Conscience* 1853. 29½ × 22
(74.9 × 55.8)

the boy-Christ and his working-class family instead enshrines matter-of-factness, physical labor, and the unidealized body. Derived from his observation of a carpenter's shop on Oxford Street in London, Millais's interior is filled with accurate details of *métier*—tools and wood shavings—connoting the human and spiritual worth of sweat and handcraft.

By contrast with Millais's *Christ*, the interior of Hunt's *The Awakening Conscience* (1853) is filled with all manner of Victorian gewgaws and bric-a-brac. The picture records the moment when a young woman, "with a startled holy resolve," in the painter's words, determines to escape her sinful, fallen life. Like the woman and man themselves, the drawing-room has a physiognomy that tells a story which is, as Ruskin wrote, "common, modern, vulgar . . . tragical." Furniture, rugs, curtains, tapestry, book, clock, and picture all possess a "terrible lustre" and "fatal newness" which bespeak, in Ruskin's words, "the moral evil of the age in which it is painted." As with Couture's *Romans of the Decadence*, Hunt's *Awakening Conscience* argues that the issue of moral and material degeneracy is inseparable from "the woman question," but whereas the one depicts a female as the heedless agent of modern society's corruption, the other sees her as its guileless victim.

200

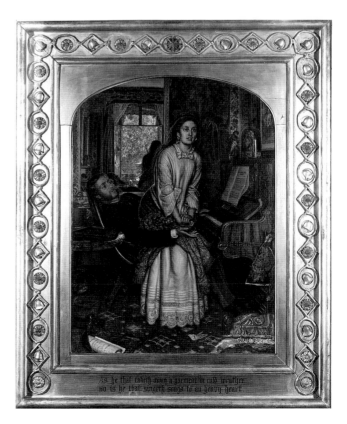

Like Millais's *Christ in the House of His Parents*, Ford Madox Brown's (1821–93) monumental and complex painting *Work* (1852–65) preaches the Christian Socialist gospel of work as the cure for the social unrest and moral iniquity that plagued mid-Victorian England. (Both paintings, in fact, were commissioned by the same evangelizing patron, the Leeds stockbroker and philanthropist Edward Plint.) Unlike the former painting, however, Brown's is based on contemporary London life, not on biblical narrative. The scene is set in mid-afternoon at Heath Street in Hampstead; a group of men known as navvies—"representing the outward and visible type of *Work*," as Brown wrote in his extended explication of the picture—is shown digging a trench into which a new waterworks main will be laid. To the left, carrying a basket of wildflowers for sale, stands a "ragged wretch," a representative of the *lumpen* (ignorant and disenfranchised) proletariat. In contrast to the "fully-developed navvy who does his work and loves his beer," he "has never been *taught to work* . . . [and] doubts and despairs of every one." Above him, on horseback and on foot, are the idle rich who "have no need to work." One of them—with umbrella, bonnet, and downward-cast eyes—has just handed a temperance tract to a navvy who returns a skeptical glance. To the far right of the painting stand "two men who appear to have nothing to do," but who are in fact "brainworkers." Their job is to think and criticize, like the "sages in ancient Greece," thereby helping to assure "well ordained work and happiness in others." These "sages," in fact, are the Christian Socialist Frederick Denison Maurice at right and the great polemicist and "reactionary socialist" (as Marx wrote in 1848) Thomas Carlyle at left.

Indeed, amid the extraordinary welter of persons, anecdotes, and details, "not the smallest [of which] has been considered unworthy of thought and deep study" (as the artist's granddaughter noted), the presence of Carlyle is especially significant. In his *Past and Present* (1843), Carlyle condemned the loss of affective human bonds in contemporary British society, and their replacement by a cold and impersonal "cash-payment nexus." The solution to the present crisis, he believed, lay in leadership by an aristocracy of talent, and in the cleansing power of hard work. Physical labor, he wrote: "[is like] . . . a free-flowing channel, dug and torn by noble force . . . draining off the sour, festering water . . . making instead of a pestilent swamp, a green fruitful meadow." In *Work*, Brown made the Carlyle metaphor concrete and *real*. His navvies are laying pipe, as the art historian Gerard Curtis has discussed, to provide fresh water to replace the fetid streams that turned working-class neighborhoods into filthy and pestilential slums. Hard work, Brown and Carlyle believed, is essential to human health and human nature itself; it ennobles people and cleanses their very

souls in the face of a system that would otherwise degrade them, and enslave them to filthy lucre.

Millais, Hunt, and Brown's pictures, like many others by the PRB and their associates in their first decade and a half, were disdained by critics precisely for their insistent particularity, contemporaneity, and topicality, regardless of the subject depicted. Indeed, at almost the same moment when Courbet's paintings of proletarian labor and ritual were condemned at the Paris Salon for their ugliness and vulgarity, Millais's *Christ* at the Royal Academy Exhibition was being attacked by Charles Dickens for its rejection of "all elevating thoughts . . . or beautiful associations" in the name of "what is mean, odious, repulsive and revolting." Brown's painting was subjected to no such obloquy when it was finally finished and exhibited in 1865; instead it was ignored for the most part, by critics and public alike. At no time in the nineteenth century were the visual cultures of England and France closer than during the European turmoil of 1848 and its aftermath.

In the exact middle of the nineteenth century, "the content went beyond the phrase," to repeat Marx's formulation, in both politics and art. A cataclysmic, European-wide economic decline during the years 1846–8, coinciding with a series of national political crises, led to an outbreak of revolution in France in February 1848. Uprisings quickly followed in Germany, Austria, Hungary, Poland, and Italy, among other states and kingdoms. The February revolution in France, however, was succeeded in June by a second and still more significant insurrection. The closure of the National Workshops—whose recent establishment had been a half-hearted attempt by the Provisional Government to placate the left— led to a massive proletarian rising on June 23. On the following day, barricades rapidly ribboned through the old twisting streets of Paris and a pitched battle was waged between working-class insurgents and the National Guard supported by a bourgeois and peasant "party of order." By the 26th, the workers (and such intellectual fellow-travelers as Baudelaire) were isolated in their *faubourgs*, their defenses were in tatters, and their cause was doomed; 1500 died in the three days of battle, 3000 more were slaughtered in the immediate aftermath, and many thousands in addition were arrested, imprisoned, and transported to distant penal colonies. The June days, the conservative political theorist Alexis de Tocqueville wrote, were "a struggle of class against class"; Marx was in agreement, calling the insurrection "the first great battle . . . between the two classes that split modern society." The revolution was defeated in France and everywhere else in 1848, but the image of the *quarante-huitard*, armed and brimming with revolutionary ardor, informed the rhetoric of the age.

During and after 1848, artists and revolutionaries in France (the names of the latter include P.-J. Proudhon, Louis Blanc

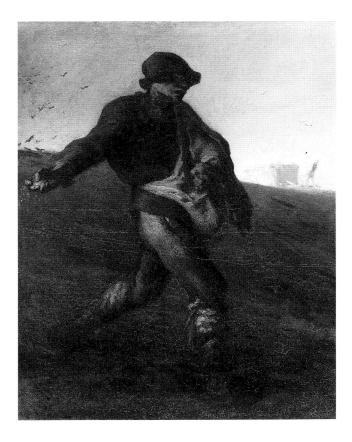

201 JEAN-FRANÇOIS MILLET *The Sower* 1850. 39¾ × 32½ (101 × 82.5)

and Auguste Blanqui) felt compelled as never before "to face with sober senses [the] real conditions of life and [man's] relations with his kind." Many now believed that, regardless of the immediate outcome of the insurrection, a new stage in European evolution had been reached in which working people—pressed by circumstance to forge alliances and form opinions of their own—were on the point of overturning or transforming not just single policies, ministries, or even governments, but society itself. On this point there was a strange unanimity between right and left, and between sober politicians and wisecracking artist journalists: writing in the tense interregnum between February and June 1848, the right-leaning de Tocqueville exclaimed that he saw "society cut into two: those who possessed nothing united in a common greed; those who possessed something in common terror." At the same time, the left-wing Daumier depicted a conversation between a peasant and his local mayor in *Le Charivari* (May 5, 1848): " 'Tell me, what is a communist?' 'They are people who want to keep money in common, work in common and land in common.' 'That's fine, but how can it happen if they have no common sense?' "

Of the existence of a dominant rhetorical timbre to the French art and literature of mid-century, there can be little

doubt. Such diverse writers as Flaubert, Baudelaire, and de Tocqueville, and such varied painters as Courbet, Millet, Octave Tassaert, and Isidore Pils shared a perception of social dislocation, alienation from the Classical past, and concern or joy about a pending revolution. The Realist Daumier, who lived at this time in the midst of the working-class 9th Arrondissement of Paris, described and depicted in his paintings and caricatures, contemporary urban street life and leisure, and the domestic hardships and joys of working people. The Realist Millet, who left Paris in 1849 for the peaceful rural village of Barbizon, represented in *The Gleaners* and *The Sower* (1850) the virtue of agricultural labor and the biblical nobility of rural poverty. Both artists are Realists by virtue of their common focus upon contemporary working-class life and urban and rural conflict. Yet the very commonality of this rhetoric of Realism should serve as a warning that we are in the presence of an ideology whose function was to obscure as much as it was to reveal "the content beyond the phrase" of 1848. Indeed, by 1855 the dictator Louis Napoleon had succeeded in establishing a conservative school of official realism—including Pils, Tassaert, Jules Breton, Rosa Bonheur, Théodule Ribot, and many others—in opposition to the insurgent Realism of Courbet. Thus, what was hidden beneath the Realist consensus was a fierce struggle among artists and art institutions over precisely the measures to be taken in either advancing or retarding the great historical changes then underway in France and the West.

The key question about Courbet and the Realists, therefore, does not primarily concern his and their particular *attitudes* toward modernity: all Realists more or less shared Daumier's credo *il faut être de son temps*; all more or less agreed with the novelist, critic, folklorist, and political chameleon Champfleury (Jules Husson) that art must represent the everyday life of common people. Rather, the issue concerns the actual *position* and *function* of Realist works within the mode and relations of production of their time. "This question," Walter Benjamin writes, "is concerned, in other words, directly with the [artistic] *technique* of works." Thus the argument made below will be that the innovative technique of Gustave Courbet—more than any other artist of the day—propelled political change by challenging the existing institutional relationship between art and the public.

Like Jacques-Louis David before him, Courbet employed a technique alien to the established traditions and audiences for art. For the Enlightenment David, this alienation arose from his rejection of Rococo and aristocratic *bon ton,* and his embrace of Neoclassical and bourgeois *noblesse.* For the Realist Courbet, this alienation entailed a rejection of academic and bourgeois *juste milieu,* and an espousal of the formal principles found in nonclassical and working-class

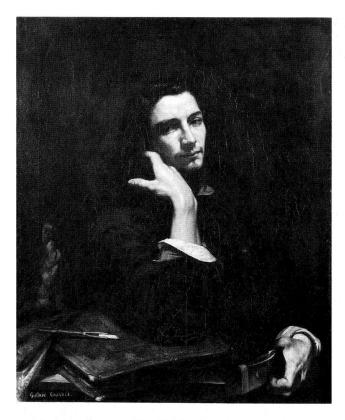

202 GUSTAVE COURBET *Man With Leather Belt* ca. 1845. 39⅜ × 32¼ (100 × 82)

popular art. By this means, Courbet attempted to turn formerly neglected peasant and proletarian Salon spectators into artistic collaborators, thereby potentially ennobling and empowering them at the expense of their putative betters. In the course of the decade following 1848, Courbet enacted an interventionist cultural role that has since been defined as avant-garde. Avant-garde art, I shall argue at the end of this chapter, is exceptional in the nineteenth century, and exceptionally fragile. By the end of Courbet's life, it had mutated into a nearly quietist modernism.

COURBET'S TRILOGY OF 1849–50

Courbet was born in the village of Ornans, near Besançon in the region of central-eastern France called the Franche-Comté. His father Régis was a wealthy farmer who resisted his son's decision to become an artist, but nevertheless paid his way to Paris in 1839. There, Courbet studied in the private studios of a succession of mediocre academic masters, learning at first a somewhat labored Romanticism which recalls the "Troubador Style" practised by Couture and others in the 1840's. Yet even as a young artist, Courbet demonstrated independence and self-assurance: his self-portraits including

Man With Leather Belt (ca. 1845) and *The Wounded Man* (ca. 1844–54) in fact mark a kind of liberation from the reigning *juste milieu*. In place of the Neoclassical linearism of contemporary portraits by, for example, Hippolyte-Jean Flandrin and Théodore Chassériau (*Portrait Drawing of de Tocqueville*, 1844), Courbet's self-portraits reveal a Romantic painterliness combined with a compositional informality or even awkwardness. In place of the sentimentality found in genre paintings by the emerging official Realists, such as Tassaert, Ribot, and Pils (*The Death of a Sister of Charity*, 1850), Courbet's paintings convey a psychological complexity, physical proximity, and eroticism that has its only precedents in Caravaggio and Géricault. (The former's *Ecstasy of Saint Francis* is perhaps a source for *The Wounded Man*; the latter's "portraits of the insane" are likely sources for *Man With Leather Belt*).

202

203

204

61

By 1848 Courbet was dividing his time among the Paris museums, his own atelier on the Left Bank, and the bohemian Brasserie Andler; at the Brasserie he came into contact with some of the most progressive and idiosyncratic figures of the day, including Baudelaire, the anarchist Proudhon, the leftist balladeer Pierre Dupont, and Champfleury. Bohemianism was a relatively new and contradictory subcultural stance in Paris—composed in equal parts of estheticism, asceticism, defiance, and sycophancy—and it functioned as a kind of laboratory for testing the various rhetorics of Realism. In January 1848 Courbet wrote to his family: "I am about to make it any time now, for I am surrounded by people who are very influential in the newspapers and the arts, and who are

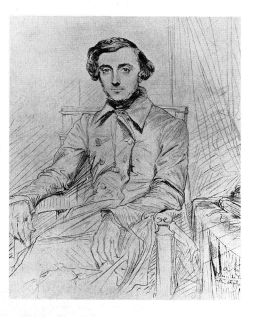

203 THÉODORE CHASSÉRIAU *Portrait Drawing of de Tocqueville* 1844. 11⅞ × 9½ (30 × 24)

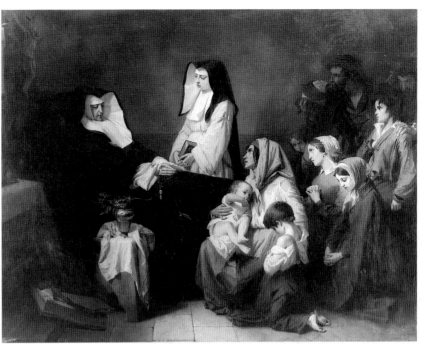

204 ISIDORE PILS *The Death of a Sister of Charity*
1850. 95 × 10′ (241 × 305)

205 GUSTAVE COURBET *After Dinner at Ornans*
1849. 76¾ × 8′5⅛ (195 × 257)

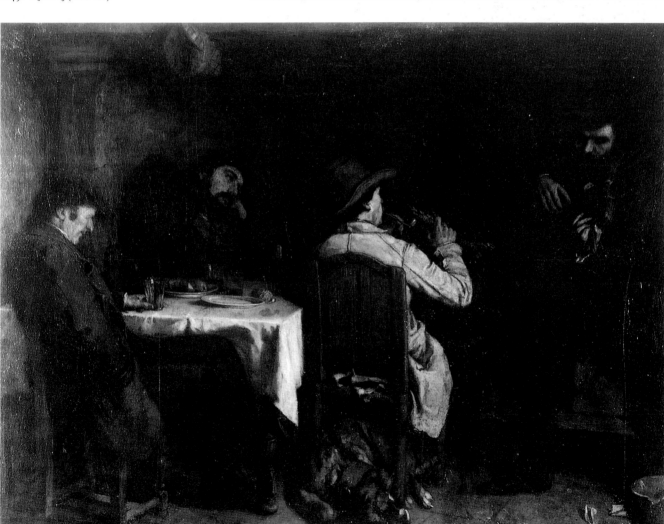

very excited about my painting. Indeed, we are about to form a new school, of which I will be the representative in the field of painting." Courbet was correct in his predictions, though he could not have known that a revolution would be necessary to help him accomplish his goals.

According to his letters, Courbet remained on the sidelines during the fighting in February 1848, though he was immensely pleased at the overthrow of Louis-Philippe and the establishment of a Republic. In June, too, he kept a safe distance from the shooting, stating in a letter to his family: "I do not believe in wars fought with guns and cannon. . . . For ten years now I have been waging a war of the intellect. It would be inconsistent for me to act otherwise." Despite this expression of principled pacifism, Courbet's abstention from battle was probably the result of strategic as much as moral calculation: like many others, he quickly recognized the brutality and implacability of the bourgeois and peasant "party of order," and understood that a war fought for "the democratic and social republic" could not be won on the barricades of June. On the contrary, the struggle for labor cooperatives, fair wages, housing, debt relief, and full political enfranchisement for workers and peasants would require organization, propaganda, and a broadly based mass movement. Disdaining bayonets, therefore, Courbet became resolved to wage his combat with images; the time was ripe for such a battle, and he would not waste his chance.

After February, the exhibition policies of the Salon were liberalized, permitting Courbet free access for the first time. Whereas he had managed to show only 3 paintings in the previous seven years, he exhibited 10 works in 1848 and 11 the following year, including the peculiar *After Dinner at Ornans*. An ambitious and provocative picture, *After Dinner* was oddly oversized for its genre, indefinite in its lighting and compo-

205

sition, and indeterminate in its mood and subject. For all these anomalies, however, it sufficiently resembled Dutch genre paintings—then in renewed vogue—for it to garner praise from a number of Salon critics and the award of being purchased by the state.

The historical significance of *After Dinner* lies in two factors outside of its particular artistic weaknesses or merits: first, the gold medal Courbet received for it in 1849 automatically entitled him to free entry to the 1850 Salon; secondly, *After Dinner* is a precise mirror of Courbet's interest in the concurrent crises of French rural and urban life. In the wake of agrarian recession and urban insurrection, the definitions and political allegiances of both country and city were up for grabs, and any picture that treated ambiguously both realms could have been incendiary. The figures in *After Dinner* might as well be bohemians at the Andler as peasants at the home of the artist's Ornans friend Cuénot, thus potentially calling into question the opposition between worker and peasant that had ensured the failure of the insurrection of June. *After Dinner* was not scandalous in 1849, but its subject was and Courbet knew it. Therefore, in October 1849 Courbet left Paris and returned to Ornans in order to reflect upon and plan his future "intellectual" interventions. "I am a little like a snake . . . in a state of torpor," he wrote to his friends the Weys at the end of October. "In that sort of beatitude one thinks so well! . . . Yet I will come out of it . . ." Indeed, in the course of the next eight months, Courbet painted three colossal pictures that changed the history of art—*The Stonebreakers* (destroyed), *A Burial at Ornans*, and *Peasants of Flagey Returning From the Fair*. As the art historian T. J. Clark has shown, and as will be summarized here, each work constituted an attack upon the technical foundations of bourgeois art and a disquisition upon class and political antagonisms of the day.

206
209
210

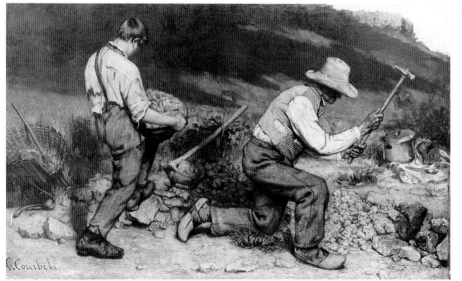

206 GUSTAVE COURBET *The Stonebreakers* 1850. 63 × 8'6 (160 × 259)

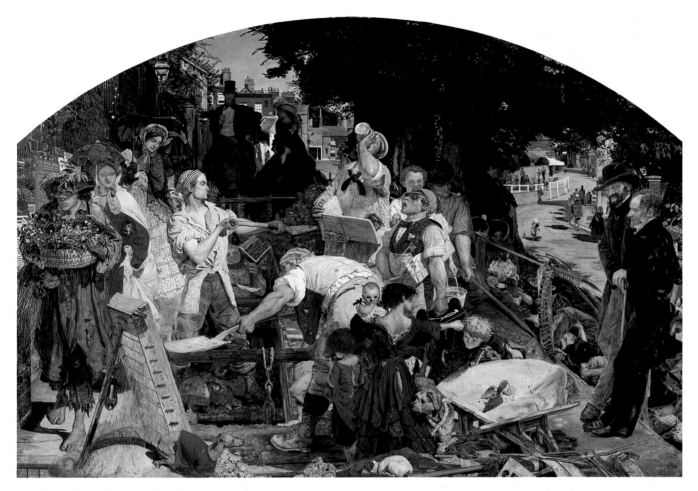

207 FORD MADOX BROWN *Work* 1852–65. 54 × 78 (137 × 197.3)

The Stonebreakers, its author said, "is composed of two very pitiable figures," taken from life. "One is an old man, an old machine grown stiff with service and age. . . . The one behind him is a young man about fifteen years old, suffering from scurvy." Stonebreaking for roads was a rare, though not unprecedented, subject for art, but it had never been treated so unflinchingly and so monumentally (the painting was nearly 5½ by 8 feet). Two nearly lifesize figures are set against a hillside, in approximate profile. Their gazes are averted from view, their limbs are strained by effort, and their clothes are in tatters. The colors and surface of the picture (such as can be surmised from its prewar photograph and the surviving oil study) are earthen and clotted, and the composition is uncomplicated. The predominant impression, as Courbet's words suggest, is of humans acting as machines: hands, elbows, shoulders, backs, thighs, knees, ankles, and feet are all treated as alien appendages that only serve, as Ruskin wrote in *The Stones of Venice* (1853), to "make a tool of the creature."

209   For *A Burial at Ornans,* Courbet gathered together some fifty-one men, women, and children on the grounds of the new

cemetery, and painted their portraits on a canvas almost 22 feet long. The mourners include the artist's father and sisters, the town mayor, Courbet's late grandfather, and a spotted dog. The coffin, draped in white with black teardrops and crossbones, belongs to one C.-E. Teste, a distant relative of Courbet; the ostentatious pair dressed in red with bulbous noses are beadles. No one in the picture is paying much attention to either the coffin or the future resting place of the deceased; indeed, the crowd is composed of at least three discrete groups—women mourners at right, clergy and pall bearers at left, and a *bourgeois* and mongrel dog at center right—that are compositionally and emotionally disconnected from each other and the funeral ritual. (How different from the postures and expressions of rapt piety among the mourners in Pils' exactly contemporaneous and acclaimed *The Death of a Sister of Charity!*) Adding to the impression of 204 artifice and distraction in Courbet's work is the insistent black and white of the canvas (compare the dog's coat to the drapery over the coffin), as well as the odd superimposition of figures above one another.

Tonal simplicity, compositional fracture, and emotional

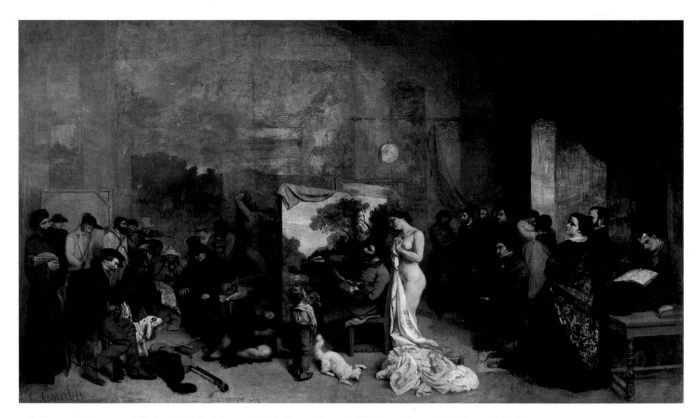

208 GUSTAVE COURBET *The Studio of the Painter: A Real Allegory Summing Up Seven Years of My Artistic Life* 1854-5. 11'10 × 19'8 (360.7 × 599.4)

210 opacity also characterize the *Peasants of Flagey*. Like the *Burial*, its subject was conventional (for example, Thomas Gainsborough's *Road from Market*, ca. 1767) but its treatment certainly was not. The *Peasants* is made up of discrete groupings of figures and animals unified only by a dull repetition of color and tonality: foreground and middle-ground planes awkwardly collide at the edge of a road extending from lower left to middle right; a boy and two peasant women are oddly insinuated among the inconsistently scaled horses and cattle; a man being led by a pig seems to float across the surface of the picture. Unlike Rosa Bonheur (1822-

211 99), whose *Plowing in the Nivernais: The Dressing of the Vines* (1849) records with patriotic specificity the agricultural practises of a particular region, Courbet disregards the cultural and physiognomic particulars of his human and animal subjects in *Peasants*. (Are those Jersey or Charolais cows under yoke?) Unlike Jules Breton (1827–1906), whose *The Gleaners* (1854) depicts the poor peasants of Marlotte as a faceless herd, Courbet provides his protagonists with individual and class identity, albeit ambiguous. (Is the man with peasant smock and stovepipe hat the same Régis Courbet who wears a bourgeois greatcoat in the *Burial*?) In place of the reassuring binary oppositions that will soon dominate official realism—city/country, bourgeois/peasant, proletarian/peasant—Courbet proposes a countryside that is as awkward,

indefinite, and contingent as the immigrant city of Paris.

Like the *Stonebreakers* and the *Burial at Ornans*, therefore, the *Peasants of Flagey Returning From the Fair* is all about the awkward antagonisms and injuries of social class. In the *Stonebreakers*, two peasants, reduced to penury, resort to stonebreaking in order to survive; in the *Burial*, a peasant community, got up in its Sunday bourgeois best, celebrates a funeral; in *Peasants*, a motley group of men, women, and animals, returning from an agricultural fair, meet a rural bourgeois in waistcoat walking his pig. This was the ungraceful form and subject of Courbet's much attacked triology shown in Paris at the Salon of 1850–51.

It would be easy to expound further—as the critics and caricaturists of 1851 did—upon the strange formal and thematic disjunctiveness of the *Peasants*, the *Stonebreakers*, and the *Burial*. Yet to do so would be to risk overlooking a new and provocative coherence in the works. In place of the old academic and political logic based upon Classical mimesis and clear class difference, Courbet has erected an alternative coherence based upon popular culture and social or class ambiguity and opacity. As Meyer Schapiro and T. J. Clark have shown, the formal touchstone for Courbet's trilogy was the "naive" artistic tradition—Epinal woodcuts and popular broadsheets, catchpenny prints and almanacs, chapbooks and songsheets—then being revived and contested across France as a component of the political and class war of 1848. Especially in the months before the Napoleonic *coup d'état* of December 2, 1851, popular culture—best defined negatively as the unofficial culture of the non-elite—was a weapon used by peasants, workers, and their urban, bourgeois allies to help secure the *égalité* promised but not delivered by the first French Revolution. Courbet was a soldier in this war and the trilogy was his weapon.

In its lack of depth, its shadowlessness, stark color contrasts, superimposition of figures, and emotional neutrality, the *Burial* especially recalls the style and aspect of popular woodcuts, engravings, and lithographs, such as those used to decorate the many generic *souvenirs mortuaire* printed to help rural communities broadcast and commemorate local deaths, or the woodcuts that illustrated the traditional *Funeral of Marlborough* or other tales and ballads. (Indeed, in a letter to the Weys from 1850, Courbet cites the nonsense refrain "*mironton, mirontaine*" from the popular ballad of Marlborough.) Courbet was fascinated by popular culture during this period; in addition to composing several folk ballads and pantomimes, he illustrated a broadsheet of songs dedicated to the Fourierist apostle Jean Journet in 1850, and a decade later executed two drawings for Champfleury's *Les Chansons populaires de France*. Further examples of the artist's interests in popular culture are his 1853 depiction of a wrestling match, and his employment, a year later, of an Epinal print of the Wandering Jew as the basis for his autobiographical painting *The Meeting* (1854).

In embracing popular art and culture—its audience, its subjects, and even its ingenuous and anonymous style—Courbet was explicitly rejecting the hierarchism and personality cult fostered by the regime of President and then Emperor Louis Napoleon, and represented in Flandrin's *Napoleon III* (1860–61). Indeed, even as Courbet was exhibiting his works in Paris during the winter of 1850–51, Bonapartists in the rural provinces were clamping down the activities of a legion of *colporteurs,* balladeers and pamphleteers who they judged were active in the revival of popular culture and the establishment of a radical, peasant solidarity. In Paris, too, the popular entertainers—clowns, street musicians, mountebanks and *saltimbanques*—were viewed by the police and the Prefects as the natural allies of subversives and Socialists; their activities were curtailed after 1849 for being inconsistent with order and social peace. In this feverish political context, when a celebration of the popular was understood as an expression of support for the "democratic and social republic," it is not surprising that Courbet's works were received with fear and hostility. "Socialist painting," one critic said of Courbet's Salon entries in 1851; "democratic and popular," said another; "an engine of revolution," exclaimed a third.

What appears to have most disturbed conservative critics about Courbet's art, and what prompted these and other charges, was its "deliberate ugliness," which meant its embrace of both a popular ("ugly") content and a popular (working-class) Salon audience. Artwork and audience waltzed in a strange and morbid syncopation, critics of the Salon suggested, and vainglorious Courbet was dancing-

209 GUSTAVE COURBET *A Burial at Ornans* 1849. 10′4 × 21′9 (315 × 663)

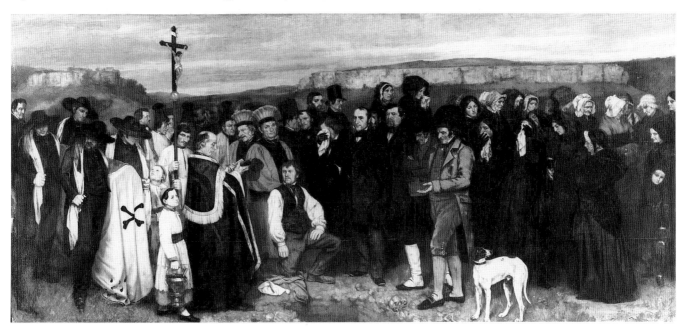

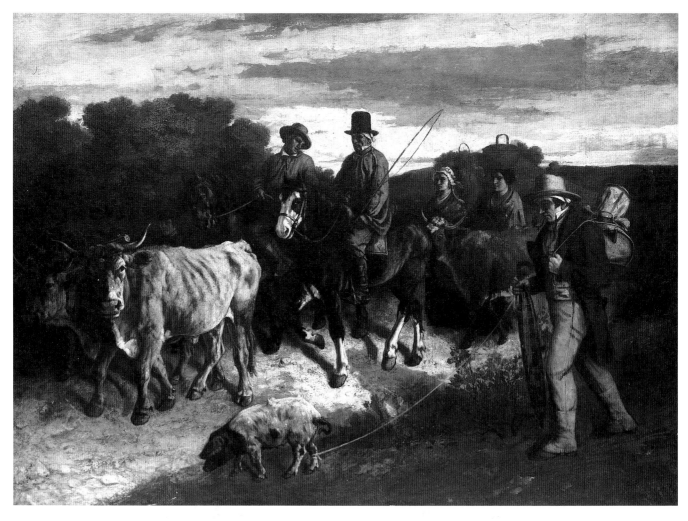

210 GUSTAVE COURBET *Peasants of Flagey Returning From the Fair* 1849. 81½ × 9′1½ (206 × 275)

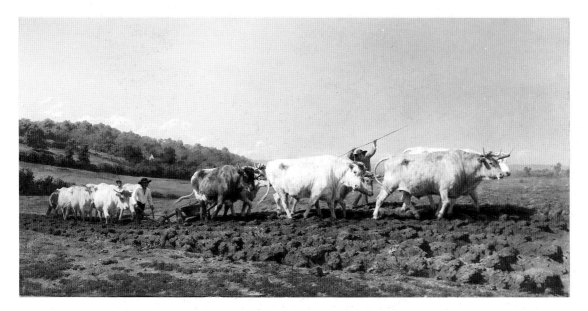

211 ROSA BONHEUR *Plowing in the Nivernais: The Dressing of the Vines* 1849. 69 × 8′8 (175.3 × 264.2)

master. After surveying the critical response to the artist's trilogy, T. J. Clark summarized Courbet's historic achievement: "He exploited high art—its techniques, its size and something of its sophistication—in order to revive popular art. . . . He made an art which claimed, by its scale and its proud title of 'History Painting', a kind of hegemony over the culture of the dominant classes." It should be mentioned that the claim was fragile, and turned out to be short-lived, but that to many at the time it appeared powerful enough to threaten the stability of the public sphere. Courbet's grand and sophisticated popular art could not survive intact the *coup d'état* and the inevitable dissipation of revolutionary consciousness that followed. Nevertheless, his trilogy has survived until the present as a model of artistic activism.

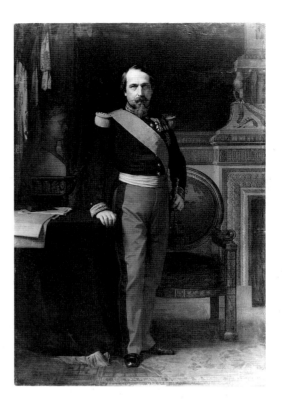

212 HIPPOLYTE-JEAN FLANDRIN *Napoleon III* 1860–61. 83½ × 58 (212 × 147)

213 GUSTAVE COURBET *The Meeting* 1854. 50¾ × 58⅝ (129 × 149)

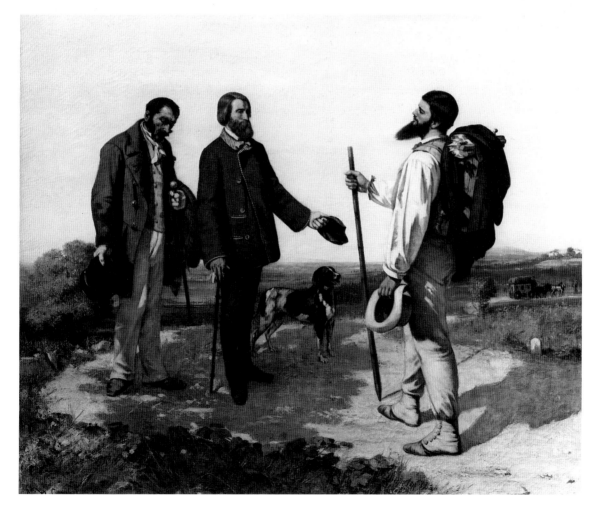

Indeed, it may be argued that Courbet's three pantings and the scandal they precipitated proved to be the historical point of origin of avant-gardism as a cultural stance of ideological opposition and political contestation. The goal of the artistic avant-garde, from Courbet to the Surrealists, has been to intervene in the domain of real life by changing the language of art so as to turn passive spectators into active interlocutors. Like the many artists who followed—Manet, the Impressionists, Van Gogh, Seurat, and the Russian avant-garde—Courbet sought to effect this intervention by recourse to the "popular," that is to a cultural form or tradition from without the fixed canon of cultural legitimacy and ruling-class authority. Yet like those artists too, Courbet was ultimately unable to pursue his ambition to its promised end—events overtook him and the overwhelming assimilative powers of the dominant culture won out. Thus his trilogy also marks the onset of modernism as a formal procedure of esthetic self-reference and political abstention. The loss of an active and engaged oppositional public following the consolidation of the Second Empire (especially after 1857) led to the abstraction and generalization, as Thomas Crow has described it, of the antagonistic pictorial strategies adopted by Courbet in 1850. From this point forward, the interventionist goals of the avant-garde faded before the ultimate aim of modernism which—from Courbet to Frank Stella—was the achievement of artistic autonomy. Indeed, for Courbet, political insignificance always lurked just the other side of popular engagement. In July 1850, while crating his pictures for shipment to Paris, he wrote to the Weys:

> The people have my sympathy. I must turn to them directly, I must get my knowledge from them, and they must provide me with a living. Therefore I have just embarked on the great wandering and independent life of the bohemian.
>
> Don't be mistaken, I am not what you call a flimflammer. A flimflammer is an idler, he has only the appearance of what he professes to be, like the members of the Academy and like toothdrawers who have their own carriages and handle gold.

For Courbet as for later ambitious French and European artists, avant-garde and modern are the two sides of a coin that doesn't add up to a whole; the one connotes community, the other individuality; the one implies engagement, the other an ivory tower; the one invites bohemianism, the other flimflammery. In fact, however, avant-garde and modern possess the same specific gravity since the technical procedures that make possible the first are the very ones that inevitably conjure up the second. My argument in sum is this: the interventionist stance of the avant-garde entailed a rejection of established academic procedures and an embrace of the formal simplicity,

clarity, and flatness of popular art as found in nineteenth-century broadsheets, chapbooks, Epinal prints, and tradesmen's signs, as well as in the performances of *saltimbanques*, balladeers, and café singers. To employ such forms—such a new technique—was to carve out a new position for art within the means and relations of production of the day and thereby potentially to turn formerly alienated or passive working-class spectators into active participants. The cool self-regard of modernism entailed many of the same formal strategies, but in the absence of an oppositional public of like mind, the techniques were no more than vestiges of the dreamed interventionism. After 1852, avant-garde and modern marched in virtual lockstep. Courbet noticed this and made an allegory on the subject in 1855.

COURBET'S *THE STUDIO OF THE PAINTER*

On May 8, 1853 a decree was published announcing that the Salon of 1854 was canceled, but that a colossal art exhibition would be included among the exhibits of a great Universal Exposition to be held in 1855. The idea of the fair was to display to the world the marvelous industrial, cultural, and social progress achieved in France since Napoleon III's assumption of dictatorial powers in 1851. As a demonstration of his liberalism and magnanimity, the Emperor had his Intendant des beaux-arts, the Comte de Nieuwerkerke, invite Gustave Courbet to luncheon in order to propose that the artist cooperate with his government's plans, and submit to the Exposition jury a work of which the Comte and the Emperor would approve. In a letter to his friend and patron Bruyas, Courbet described his indignant response to this naked effort at cooptation:

> You can imagine into what rage I flew after such an overture . . . first, because he was stating to me that he was a government and because I did not feel that I was in any way a part of that government; and that I too was a government and that I defied his to do anything for mine that I could accept. . . . I went on to tell him that I was the sole judge of my painting; that I was not only a painter but a human being; that I had practiced painting not in order to make art for art's sake, but rather to win my intellectual freedom, and that by studying tradition I had managed to free myself of it; that I alone, of all the French artists of my time, had the power to represent and translate in an original way both my personality and my society.

Courbet's letter went on to describe the rest of his tense and abortive luncheon with Nieuwerkerke—additional sparring, dressings-down, and protestations of sincerity and pride—and the artist's intention to press ahead in his artistic project "with full knowledge of the facts." What is perhaps most salient about the letter, however, is that it announces a kind of program for future work, in particular for the very painting that Courbet would make and then insinuate into the heart of the Exposition grounds, *The Studio of the Painter: A Real Allegory Summing Up Seven Years of My Artistic Life*. According to his remarks above, Courbet was seeking in his painting to explore the social and cultural position of the artist; to cast off "art for art's sake" while nevertheless maintaining independence; and to explore the complexities of reality in order to "represent and translate . . . my personality and my society." Courbet's manifesto in paint was underway by November 1854 and finished six months later, just in time for it to be rejected by the Exposition jury.

The Studio is a vast (almost 11 by 20 feet) and somewhat lugubrious depiction of the artist's atelier and its thirty-odd occupants. The composition is divided into two parts with the painter himself in the middle. He is seen painting a landscape and is accompanied (in perfect Oedipal fashion, as Linda Nochlin has said) by a small boy and nude woman who cast admiring glances. To the right are the painter's "shareholders," as he called them in a letter to Champfleury, that is, his various artistic and bohemian friends. These include Baudelaire (at the far right, reading), Champfleury (seated), and Bruyas (with the beard, in profile). To the left are "the people, misery, poverty, wealth, the exploited and the exploiters, the people who live off death." The identification of this group is less clear, but it appears to include Louis Napoleon (seated, accompanied by spaniels), the Minister of State Achille Fould (standing with cask, at far left, and described by the artist as "a Jew whom I saw in England"), the late regicide Lazare Carnot (in white coat and peaked hat), and perhaps the European revolutionaries Garibaldi, Kossuth, and Kosciuszko. The upper half of *The Studio*, above the heads of all of the figures, consists of an expanse of brown paint ("a great blank wall") that inadequately covers the ghost of *The Peasants of Flagey*.

Denied the chance to display the puzzling *Studio* alongside his other accepted works, Courbet decided to erect a "Pavilion of Realism," in the form of a circus tent, on land just opposite the entrance to the Exposition. There he would display his new paintings as well as his most controversial older works, and steal the thunder from the officially sanctioned Ingres, Delacroix, Vernet, and Descamps, among others.

With the financial assistance of Bruyas, the "Pavilion of Realism" was indeed quickly built, but the public response was not what Courbet hoped for and planned: attendance was poor and the critics were largely indifferent. The most considered response to Courbet's *Studio*, in fact, is found in the private diaries of Delacroix:

Paris, 3 August
Went to the Exposition, where I noticed the fountain that spouts artificial flowers.

I think all these machines are very depressing. I hate these contrivances that look as though they were producing remarkable effects entirely on their own volition.

Afterwards I went to the Courbet exhibition. He has reduced the price of admission to ten sous. I stayed there alone for nearly an hour and discovered a masterpiece in the picture they rejected . . . In [*The Studio*] the planes are well understood, there is atmosphere, and in some passages the execution is really remarkable, especially the thighs and hips of the nude model and the breasts. . . . The only fault is that the picture, as he has painted it, seems to contain an ambiguity. It looks as though there were a real sky in the middle of the painting. They have rejected one of the most remarkable works of our time, but Courbet is not the man to be discouraged by a little thing like that.

Delacroix's chief insights occur at the beginning and near the end of this passage. His remark about the "machines . . . acting entirely on their own volition" constitutes a succinct account of "commodity fetishism," a term coined and defined a few years later by Marx in *Capital* (1867) as the disguising of the "social relation between men . . . [in] the fantastic form of a relation between things." The 1855 Exposition, which consisted primarily of the mass display of consumer goods and the machines that produced them, was indeed an early important landmark in the fetishization of commodities. It heralded the beginnings of a world that would increasingly identify progress with the rationalization of production, liberty with the freedom to consume standardized goods, and human intimacy with the market exchange of sex. Delacroix appears to have understood something of this historic aspect of the Exposition, and found it (with unusual understatement) depressing. Courbet's picture was thus judged a triumph in opposition to this sobering exhibition of modernity.

Delacroix's other insights into Courbet's *The Studio of the Painter: A Real Allegory Summing Up Seven Years of My Artistic Life* are contained in his comments about the "remarkable" execution of the thighs, hips, and breasts of the nude and the "ambiguity [of] a real sky in the middle of the picture." In these few lines, the Romantic painter has encapsulated the woman/nature dyad that constituted Courbet's personal response to the dispiriting forces of modernization on display at the Exposition. For Courbet, woman and nature are the "real" touchstones for the personal and political "allegory" that began in 1848 and ended with the exhibition of 1855.

The nude woman in *The Studio* (as Delacroix and Courbet both wrote) is a model and nothing more: she is not Venus.

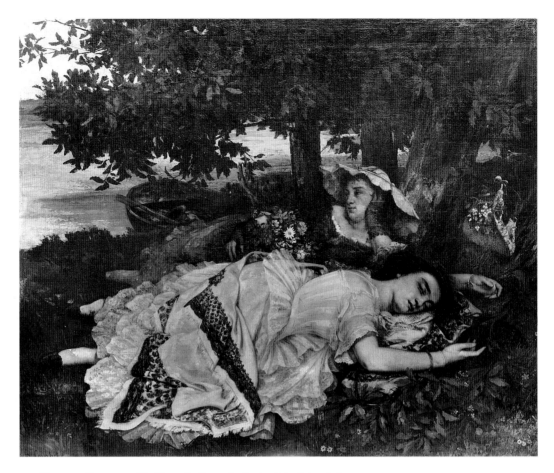

214 **GUSTAVE COURBET** *The Young Ladies on the Banks of the Seine* 1856–7. 68⅛ × 81⅛ (173 × 206)

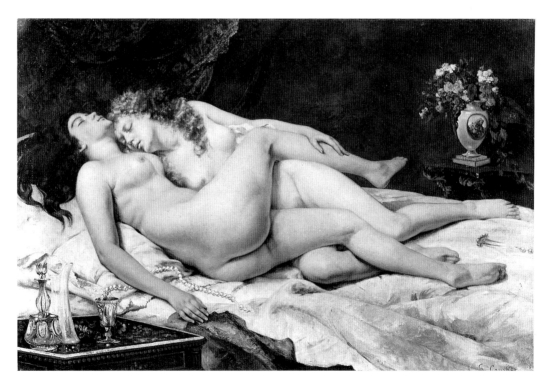

215 **GUSTAVE COURBET** *Sleepers* 1866. 53⅛ × 78¾ (135 × 200)

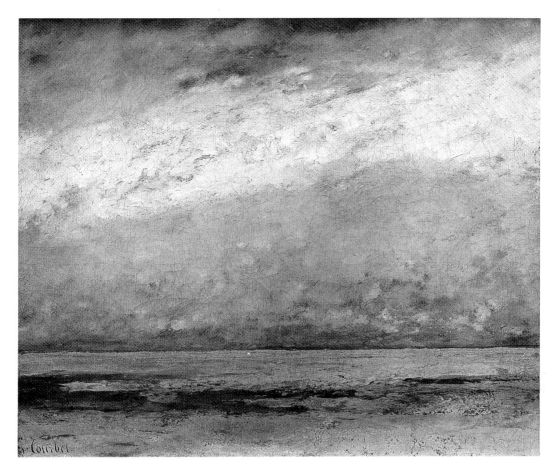

216 **GUSTAVE COURBET** *Seaside* 1866. 21⅛ × 25¼ (53.5 × 64)

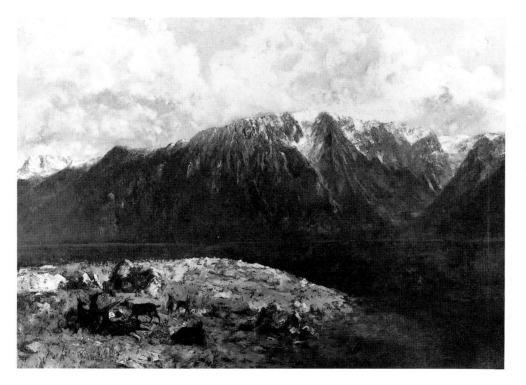

217 **GUSTAVE COURBET** *Grand Panorama of the Alps With the Dents du Midi* 1877. 59½ × 82¾ (151 × 210)

She is not muse or *Source*, as in Ingres's painting of 1856; she is not the allegory of Liberty, the Republic, Spring, Misery, Tragedy, or *War* and *Peace*, as in Pierre Puvis de Chavannes's paintings of 1867. At once freed of the allegorical burdens placed upon her by innumerable academic artists of the Second Empire, and stripped of her only sources of cultural power, she is instead a blank canvas, like the cloth she holds, upon which the modern male painter will figure his authority and independence. In painting after painting until the end of his life, including *The Young Ladies on the Banks of the Seine* (1856–7) and *The Sleepers* (1866), Courbet reenacted this dialectic of the feminine. Divested of any but sexual power, Courbet's women are reduced to mere passive vehicles of painterly dexterity and authority; relieved of the burden of allegorization, women are for perhaps the first time in the history of Western art shown actually to possess a sexuality. (The politically incendiary aspect of this latter emancipation would be strikingly exposed in the critical response, a decade after *The Studio*, to Edouard Manet's *Olympia*.)

Just as Courbet's nude model functions as a cipher of artistic volition, so too does the landscape and "real sky," in Delacroix's words, function as an anchor for painterly autonomy. For the Realist, landscape—especially the type of rugged and inaccessible woodlands represented on the artist's easel—constituted the dream space of personal freedom, and the idealized locus, as the art historian Klaus Herding has described it, of social reconciliation. In landscape painting after landscape painting, from the *Chateau d'Ornans* (1850) to *Seaside* (1866) to the *Grand Panorama of the Alps With the Dents du Midi* (1877), Courbet represented his dreamed

personal autonomy and social equality ("I too was a government") by his rejection of the traditional formulas of the genre. His landscapes, like those of the Impressionists who followed, lacked compositional focus, internal framing devices, *repoussoir* elements, atmospheric perspective, and coloristic sobriety and balance. They were instead painterly, sketchy, vibrant in color, bright in tonality, spatially flat (though texturally three-dimensional), and democratic, meaning that the painter paid nearly equal attention to all parts of the picture—the sides, bottom, top, and corners, as well as the center of the picture.

Courbet's *The Studio of the Painter* is thus as much a foretelling of the painter's future as it is a summary of his past. In addition, it is an early instance of the modernism—represented by the nude, the landscape, and the great swathe of brown paint that constitutes the upper half of the painting—that would flourish in succeeding generations. Modernism is the name for the visual art that would increasingly de-emphasize representation in favor of the integrated material surface; it is the art that would avoid direct engagement in the ongoing battle of classes and interests in the name of individual and pictorial autonomy. Another way to describe the development of modernism is simply to say that it involved the rejection of *allegory* and the embrace of the *real* in all its contradictoriness. "The people who want to judge [*The Studio of the Painter: A Real Allegory*]," Courbet wrote to Champfleury, "will have their work cut out for them." The numerous, conflicting, and often convoluted interpretations of the painting (not excepting this one) bear out the artist's words, but it may be that Courbet himself supplied the painting's best gloss in its title.

· 10 ·

THE DECLINE OF HISTORY PAINTING: GERMANY, ITALY, AND FRANCE

THE RISE OF NATURALISM IN GERMANY

DURING THE TWO DECADES FOLLOWING THE Universal Exposition (1855), the status of history painting declined precipitously in Europe. Indeed, by the time of the first Impressionist exhibition in Paris in 1874, the creation and display of complex narrative paintings of Classical or religious subjects had nearly ended in France and other European countries, replaced by the depiction of contemporary history, daily life, landscape, and still life. The decline and fall of history painting had been long in coming (and the end came as something of a relief to all concerned) but was nonetheless momentous. Now for the first time, painting was fully liberated from its parasitical dependence upon an anachronistic complex of cultural hierarchies, academic regulations, and codified *ancien-régime* tastes. Now for the first time, too, painting was freed from the responsibility—implicit since David and the Revolution—of representing the bourgeois Enlightenment dream of an infinite advance toward intellectual, social, and moral betterment. Hereafter, painters were free to focus their attentions upon the transience and ephemera of modernity, which is just another way of saying that, like other petty manufacturers, artists were now independent commodity producers, and every bit as liberated and as subservient as that position implies: on the one hand, they were individuals who sought (and to a degree achieved) autonomy from a dominant bourgeois society that tailored all cultural production to the narrow ends of profit, and on the other, they were the very mirror of that society by virtue of their masculinist and entrepreneurial stance of heroic individualism. Modern art—in all its complexity and contradictoriness—arose in France and elsewhere from the ashes of history painting and the seeds of modern capital.

In Germany, history painting may be said to have died with

the painter Peter Cornelius in 1867, though morbid symptoms had been apparent for nearly a generation. By mid-century, in fact, the Classical revivalism that had dominated German painting since the rise to power of Ludwig I of Bavaria (1825) and Friedrich Wilhelm III of Prussia (1797), was succumbing to both naturalism and a *juste-milieu* historicism similar to that which arose in France. In Munich and Berlin, private and parochial values and sentiments were replacing public and enlightened ones, as the generation of Winckelmann, Mengs, Carstens, and the subsequent Nazarenes was fading from memory and view. No longer would there be heroic Neoclassicists, like the Danish-born Carstens, living in Rome, who protested against an official summons to Berlin: "I belong to Humanity, not to the Academy of Berlin." In their place would arise naturalists such as Adolph von Menzel (1851–1905) who employed what one contemporary called "daguerreotypical reality" in his depictions of the life of Frederick the Great, such as *The Roundtable of Frederick II at Sanssouci* (ca. 1857).

No longer, either, would there be committed Romanticists, such as the Nazarene Cornelius or his student Wilhelm von Kaulbach, whose many grandiose murals for religious and state buildings in Munich were replete with the trappings of religious and historical allegory and symbol. In their place would emerge Munich artists like the celebrated Karl von Piloty (1826–86), whose at once idealizing and anecdotal scenes from German history, such as *Seni Before Wallenstein's Corpse* (1855), were derived from Delaroche's bathetic *genre historique*. Piloty's many pupils, including Gabriel von Max (1840–1915), Franz von Defregger (1835–1921) and Wilhelm Leibl (1844–1900) continued their teacher's tendency to sentimentality, but gradually abandoned the depiction of history subjects altogether. Indeed, Leibl—an admirer of Courbet and painter of such ingenuous works as the 1877

218

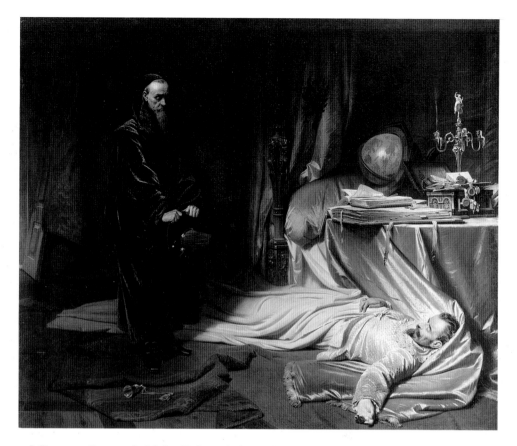

218 KARL VON PILOTY *Seni Before Wallenstein's Corpse* 1855. 10'2¾ × 11'11¾ (312 × 365)

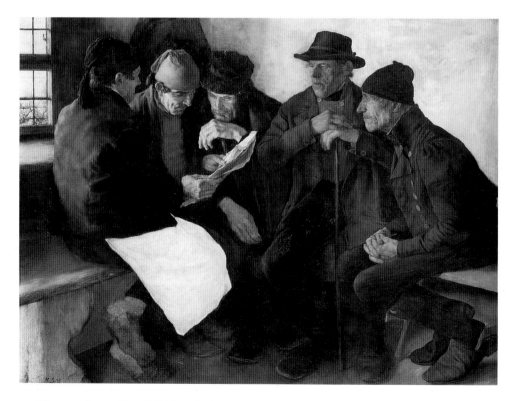

219 WILHELM LEIBL *Town Politicians* 1877. 30 × 38⅛ (76 × 97)

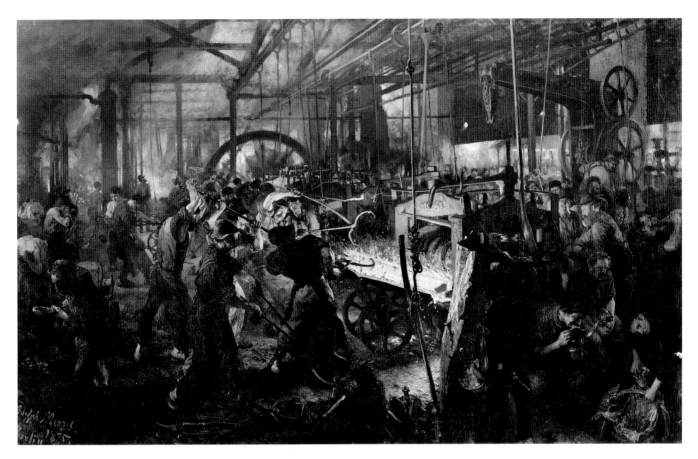

220 ADOLPH VON MENZEL *Iron Rolling Mill* 1872–5. 60¼ × 99⅝ (153 × 253)

219 *Town Politicians*—expressed the now widespread rejection of history painting when he cheerfully confessed in a letter written the same year as the above work: "You know that I am used to painting according to nature, and that it is a matter of indifference to me whether I paint a landscape, people or animals."

By the time of Leibl, a critical discourse in support of naturalist landscape and genre painting was well established. To the Munich critic Anton Springer, Classicism and antiquarianism were no more than feeble ruses through which to escape the present. "If our history painters only possessed half the courage of our landscape painters," wrote Springer in his 1858 review of the All-German Historical Exhibition in Munich, "if they had the courage to look without prejudice and to forget about worn out aesthetic concepts, the artistic value of contemporary life would soon be looked upon differently." The Berlin painter von Menzel, in addition to the young artists in the Munich Piloty school, apparently took the critic's words to heart; between his *The Flute Recital* 220 (1852) and the monumental *Iron Rolling Mill* (1872–5), Menzel gradually rid his work of the anecdotal "stylistic embellishments" that, Springer believed, stood in the way of the historical self-realization of the German people.

In the latter painting, Menzel memorialized and mythologized Germany's refulgent industrial capitalism (its share of world industrial production was growing at the expense of its rival Great Britain's) by depicting the Königshütte iron rolling mill in Upper Silesia as a kind of rationalized Vulcan's forge. If anecdotalism is diminished in Menzel's naturalist art, however, Classicism is not: his workers are disposed in space like the disciples in Tintoretto's *Last Supper*, and their heroic poses are derived from, among other works, Pollaiuolo's *Battle of Nudes* and Velázquez's *Triumph of Bacchus*. Thus despite its thematic modernity, Menzel's *Iron Rolling Mill*, like Leibl's nearly contemporaneous *Town Politicians*, exposes the limits of artistic modernization in Germany during the second half of the nineteenth century. History painting in Germany may have ended with the death of Cornelius, but the naturalism that arose and flourished in its place drew upon many of the same academic conventions and Classical sources. Naturalism was thus in Germany—as elsewhere, we shall discover—an art of compromise between an insurgent, modernizing Realism and a persistent, academic Classicism.

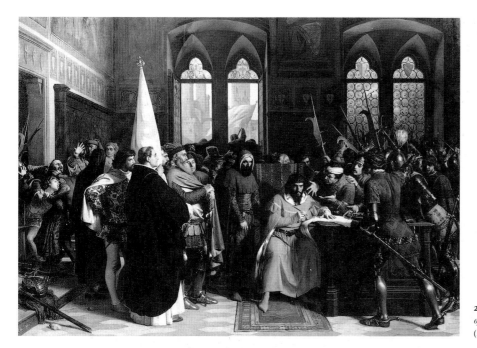

221 STEFANO USSI *The Expulsion of the Duke of Athens From Florence* 1861. 10'6 × 14'10 (320 × 452)

THE ITALIAN MACCHIAIOLI

In Italy, history painting was faring only a little better; its last hurrah was probably sounded in 1861 at the Fine Arts section of the Esposizione Nazionale held in Florence. There, amid nationalist and entrepreneurial celebration, were exhibited the works of three generations of Florentine history painters, including Pietro Benvenuti (1769–1844), his pupil Giuseppe Bezzuoli (1784–1855), and his pupil's pupil, Stefano Ussi
221 (1822–1901). The latter's *The Expulsion of the Duke of Athens From Florence* (1861), along with the young Odoardo
222 Borrani's (1833–1905) *The 26th of April 1859* (1861), were the sensations of the show, and represented the past and future of Italian art. Ussi's painting, which depicts the final dispatch of the French usurper Walter de Brienne from the Palazzo Vecchio in 1343, was rendered with the dramatic focus found in works by Bezzuoli, and the coloristic radiance of those by the Italian "purists" Luigi Mussini and Enrico Pollastrini (who, in turn, were influenced by the German Nazarenes). Borrani's painting, on the other hand, while similarly depicting an act of patriotism—the sewing of the Italian tricolor flag on the day before the expulsion from Florence of Grand Duke Leopold II—was small, domestic, intimist, and composed out of sharp tonal contrasts and luminous patches (*macchia*) of color. By virtue of its technique and scale, therefore, the work represented a stern rebuke to the established academic tradition of history painting. "Never was there such an empty, slovenly style of work," complained one critic, upon viewing the history paintings and landscapes of Borrani and the other painters who the following year

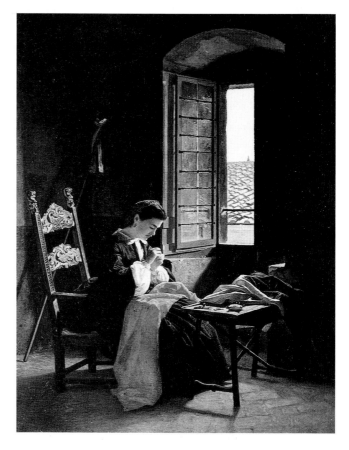

222 ODOARDO BORRANI *The 26th of April 1859* 1861. 29½ × 22⅞ (75 × 58)

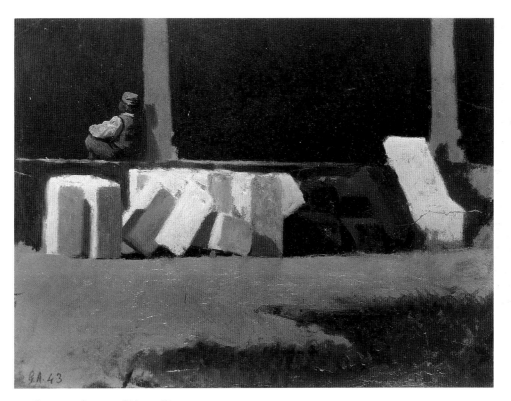

223 GIUSEPPE ABBATI *Cloister* 1861–2. 7⅝ × 10 (19.3 × 25.2)

would be dubbed the "Macchiaioli." Yet it was the persistent hammer-blows of these same artists that would doom history painting in Italy to collapse and fall, as the critic Pietro Selvatico wrote in 1861, "as a dead body falls under the blows of prosaic realism."

To Selvatico and many others at the time, the only hope for the future of a unified Italian art lay in "another kind of painting which is historical with respect to the daily life of society, but does not depict particular events except as revelations of the feelings, affections, and special tendencies of our time." The artists who would principally answer this naturalist and modernist call were the Macchiaioli, though the academic stickler Selvatico in fact questioned their tendency to elevate painted, chiaroscuro sketches employing *mezza-macchia* ("half-effects") to the status of finished works of art. These young painters (most were born around 1830) were veterans of the Italian movement for independence and unification (the Risorgimento) and habitués of the Caffè Michelangiolo, a hotbed of Florentine bohemianism and political radicalism. Beginning about 1855, the painters Telemaco Signorini, Vito D'Ancona, Giovanni Fattori, Raffaello Sernesi, and Silvestro Lega, among others, began to meet at the café to discuss Risorgimento politics and an art characterized by what Signorini called a "violent chiaroscuro." By the end of the decade, they had created a body of paintings remarkable for their depiction of the informal activities and ceremonies of bourgeois and working-class daily life, through an equally informal vocabulary of tonal and color contrast, and compositional and mimetic relaxation.

Sernesi's (1838–66) *Roofs in Sunlight* (1860–61) and Giuseppe Abbati's (1836–68) *Cloister* (1861–2) are typical of the best Macchiaioli paintings: they are very small and quickly brushed, but monumental in scale and fully completed. The former work, just 4⅞ by 7½ inches, depicts a compact cluster of Florentine walls, roofs, eaves, and chimneys beneath a brilliant blue sky. A white, dolphin-shaped cloud or puff of smoke at the upper left rests on top of a chimney-pipe or smoke-stack ambiguously located in the middle or background. The latter painting, only 7⅝ by 10 inches, represents a row of cream and gray-colored marble blocks in the middle-ground, set against a low cloister wall upon which is perched a boy with a brown vest and pants and a cool-blue cap. The lower and upper thirds of the painting are dominated by broad and loosely brushed areas of cool tan and warm sienna, representing a vacant foreground and a sheltered background. Both paintings articulate a dialectic of flatness and depth. The insistent geometries of walls, blocks, and midday shadows echo the very shape and materiality of the cardboard panels upon which the scenes are painted; the dominance of chiaroscuro in each—indeed, the reduction of tonal contrast to the simple on/off of *mezza-macchia*—similarly reiterates the two-dimensionality of the medium and the basic terms of pictorial facture. At the same time, however, the deep shadows in the two paintings, combined with the slightly oblique viewpoint—a characteristic Macchiaioli device found in Cristiano Banti's uncompromising painting *The Brush Gatherers (Le Macchiaole)* (ca. 1861)—create a compelling spatial depth and physical breadth.

In paintings by the Macchiaioli, Boime has persuasively argued, the formal structures that underlay the grand fictions of mimesis are unambiguously revealed. In the works discussed here, and many others, light and dark, line and color, surface and depth, impression and composition, discovery and understanding are unguardedly exposed in utter disregard for the formal injunctions of the Florentine Academy on the need for finish. Yet in estranging themselves from their academic predecessors and contemporaries, the Macchiaioli were in fact seeking the revival of an Italian art that had once been marked by a dialectic of individual genius and national consensus. By honestly exposing the techniques and preconceptions that underlay pictorial representation, these Risorgimento artists were celebrating their unique individuality within a national culture that they themselves were forging, both by their political activity and by their depictions of workers, bourgeoisie, soldiers, fields, farmhouses, cloisters, and city streets. The Macchiaioli movement was short-lived—by the late 1860's its dialectics were compromised by an excessive embrace of the Quattrocento—but it had already succeeded in ending history painting in Italy, and inaugurating, as Selvatico wrote, "another kind of painting which is [only] historical with respect to the daily life of society."

INDIVIDUALISM AND NATURALISM IN FRENCH SALON ART

In France, history painting had been distressed since at least the Romantic generation of 1830, but it was probably the combined attacks of Courbet and Louis Napoleon during the early years of the Second Empire that accelerated the art's demise. The Realist painter's role in the tragic drama was to undermine the elite class status of the genre by employing its scale, sophistication, and ambitiousness for the purpose of creating a new and politically contentious popular art intended for an audience of workers and peasants. The dictator's part was to forbid the free expression upon which a progressive and enlightened bourgeois public art depended and, further, to criminalize even the marginal avant-garde culture that arose in its wake. Indeed in 1857, the same year that Courbet exhibited his ironically titled (and scandalous) *The Young Ladies on the Banks of the Seine*, Flaubert and Baudelaire were brought separately to trial on charges of

"immorality" and "irreligion" for their *Madame Bovary* and *Flowers of Evil*. (The former was acquitted while the latter was convicted.)

The censorious cultural policies of Louis Napoleon and his ministers were accepted by working class and bourgeoisie alike with more or less complaisance—the one was exhausted from revolution and the other was hushed by money gained from bribes, industrialization, and speculation. Indeed, the French bourgeoisie of the Second Empire—effectively caricatured by Daumier in his sculpture of the jaunty and duplicitous *Ratapoil* (ca. 1851)—willingly swapped its Revolutionary artistic and political inheritance for "the protection," as Marx venomously wrote, "of a strong and unrestricted government. It declared unequivocally that it longed to get rid of its own political role in order to get rid of the troubles and dangers of ruling." (The two decades following the Napoleonic *coup d'état* were in fact a period of tremendous economic expansion and modernization in France; during that time, overall industrial production more than doubled, the percentage of people who gained their livelihood by agriculture, forestry, or fishing dropped below fifty percent, and the number who worked in industry, transport, trade, and banking reached nearly forty percent.)

Thus, with political and cultural authority vested as never before in the person of a vain and parochial Caesar, French artists and authors were discouraged from engaging the public culture and moral life of their nation. Daumier kept his sculpture of Ratapoil hidden during the Emperor's reign (the former shared the latter's extravagant moustache) and generally pulled punches in the lithographs based on the figure. In addition, the legion of history painters trained at the Ecole lowered their sights, often enough, from Grand Manner to Grand Guignol, as in Auguste-Barthélemy Glaize's (1807–93) allegory of women's descent into debauchery, *Misery the Procuress*, shown and acclaimed at the Salon of 1861. By the time of Louis Napoleon's political liberalizations of the 1860's, it was too late; ambitious history painting was moribund, and in its place had arisen, we shall soon discover, a bewildering variety of uniformly depressing substitutes.

Attempting to put a positive gloss on this unprecedented situation of political evacuation and cultural impoverishment, the young critic Jules Castagnary described the current sad fate of history painting as the natural result of the aging of certain outmoded social institutions. In his "Salon" of 1857 he wrote: "Religious painting and history or heroic painting have gradually lost strength as the social organisms—theocracy and monarchy—to which they refer become weakened. Their elimination, which is almost complete today, leads to the absolute domination of genre, landscape, and portraiture, which are the result of individualism: in art, as in contemporary society, man becomes more and more himself."

214

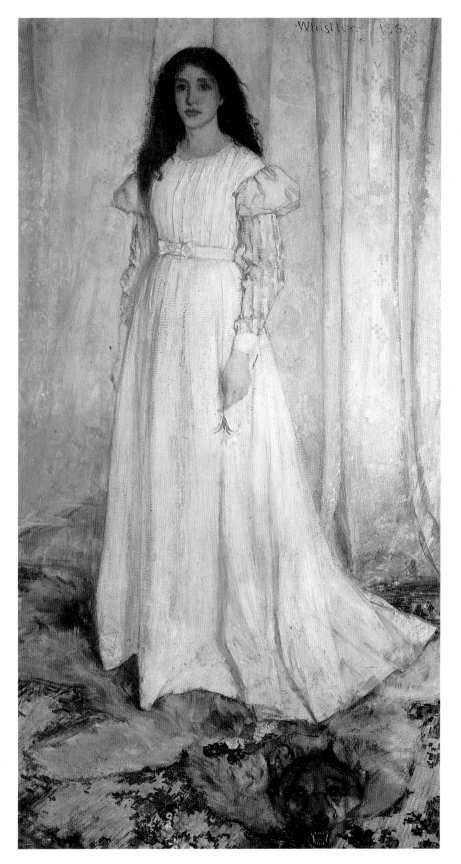

224 JAMES ABBOT MCNEILL WHISTLER *The White Girl* 1862. 84½ × 42½ (214.6 × 107.9)

Castagnary's final confident phrases, which he developed in a series of incisive published "Salons" extending into the early years of the Third Republic, may be taken as a summary of the ambitions and self-perceptions of a subsequent generation of French artists. Individualism—whether in the form of genre, landscape, or portraiture—was what replaced the grand public art of history painting; it was pursued with a vengeance at official Salon and unofficial avant-garde venues alike, and soon became the dialectical basis of modernism.

Although the word individualism was a neologism that came into parlance in the 1820's as a term of disparagement used against Jacobins, Romantics, and Liberals, it had largely shed its negative cast by the time of Castagnary's usage in 1857. Indeed, in many respects, individualism was developing into one of the most important ideological paradigms of the Second Empire and the subsequent Third Republic. Seeking to enfold or outflank all dissident or insurgent cultural tendencies in a vast authoritarian structure called "eclecticism," as the art historian Patricia Mainardi has shown, Louis Napoleon and his diverse apologists—ranging from the religious historian Ernest Renan to the anarchist P.-J. Proudhon—began to celebrate an emerging spirit of individualism in politics, philosophy, and art. By the 1860's and '70's, the word—but more importantly the concept of subordinating the interests of the social whole to the particular commercial and affective interests of the individual—may be said to have become hegemonic; it was basic to the emergent ideologies of entrepreneurial capitalism, political liberalism, and even revolutionary anarchism. In addition, it provided a basis for the new, naturalist art theory and criticism practised by, among others, Castagnary, Edmond Duranty, and Emile Zola, and it offered a common vocabulary and studio jargon for practising artists. "Individualism is the idea of the century," wrote the historian Hippolyte Castille in 1853, and its artistic correlatives were first visible at the Salons.

The demise of history painting did not diminish the popularity of the Salons or the other state-sponsored exhibitions of fine art. On the contrary, exhibitions of contemporary painting and sculpture were mass cultural attractions during the Second Empire and early Third Republic as they never had been before and never would be again. At the 1855 Exposition Universelle des Beaux-Arts, nearly 2000 works by 700 painters were seen by almost a million visitors during a six-month run. In 1857, the biennial Salon des Beaux-Art exhibition held at the same Palais de l'Industrie, included almost 3500 works by 500 artists and was seen by more than 100,000 people during two months. In 1868, 4200 works were exhibited at the Salon. In 1870, a more conservative jury accepted just 2000 works for display, but by 1880 the number had climbed back to over 7000 works, seen by perhaps a half-million people. On any given Sunday, when admission was free, more than 50,000 visitors might pass through the Salon turnstiles.

The generally massive scale of these Salons and other exhibitions, however, was not always greeted with equanimity by their sponsors. By 1863, the number of submissions for the Salon was judged by authorities to be excessive and their quality inferior; thus an effort was undertaken by the state to persuade the Academic jurors to be more selective. This "reform" turned out to be more successful than was perhaps intended: of the approximately 5000 works submitted in that year by 3000 artists, more than seventy percent were rejected, occasioning the need for a special Salon des Refusés at the nearby Palais de l'Expositions. This officially sanctioned anti-Salon, consisting of more than 600 paintings by dozens of artists—including Edouard Manet, Théodore Fantin-Latour, J. A. M. Whistler, and Camille Pissarro—was an unexpected, if modest, success, attracting 3–4000 rictus visitors on Sundays, and much shrill publicity.

The most discussed and abused painters at the Salon des Refusés were undoubtedly Whistler (1834–1903), whose *The White Girl* (1862) was conspicuously hung near the entrance to the exhibition, and Manet, whose *The Bath* (better known as *Le Déjeuner sur l'herbe* [*Luncheon on the Grass*]) was judged "shameless" and "slipshod" by the reviewer Louis Etienne, among others. The socialist critic Théophile Thoré, on the other hand, applauded these artists for their very "barbarity," comparing them to the painter of Native Americans, George Catlin. In remarks that anticipate the writings of the Impressionists and especially Paul Gauguin, Thoré continued: "It seems that these artists are taking art back to its origin, without having to worry about what civilized men have been able to do before them." Thus the Salon des Refusés, according to the critic, marked a kind of return of Realist populism: "It is even good to descend, or, if you will, to rise once more to the classes that scarcely ever had the privilege of being studied and put into the light of painting. . . . The portrait of a worker in his smock is certainly worth as much as the portrait of a prince in his golden costume." Public discussion and implicit political debate, such as between Etienne and Thoré over the relative merits of pauper and prince, were certainly never sanctioned by Napoleon III when he decreed the establishment of an exhibition of rejected artists. In fact, the Salon des Refusés turned out to be a one-shot deal (though there was a half-hearted reprise in 1864): despite repeated pleadings, cajolings and even harrassing petitions by rejected artists (such as the young Paul Cézanne) for the rest of the decade, the Emperor and his ministers never again repeated this experiment in cultural democracy.

As the controversy over the Salon des Refusés indicates, Second Empire arts policy was often a matter of experiment,

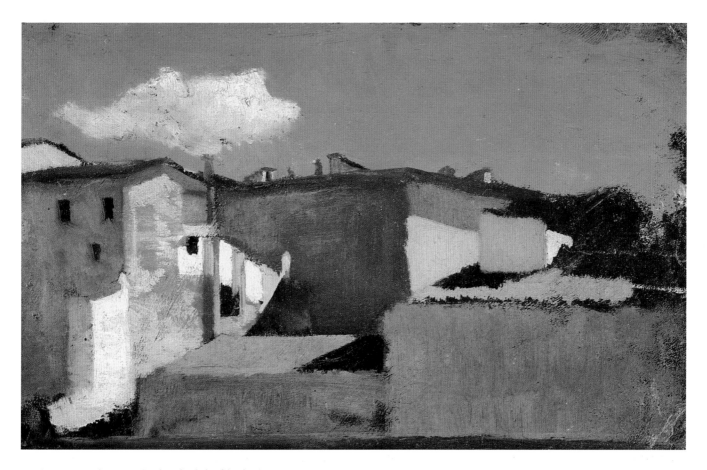

225 RAFFAELLO SERNESI *Roofs in Sunlight* 1860–61. 4⅞ × 7½ (12.3 × 19)

improvisation, misstep and correction. From 1855 until the end of Louis Napoleon's regime, there were frequent changes of rules governing the selection of judges, the number and type of acceptable submissions, exhibition frequency and duration, and even admission price. Yet none of these variations—excepting perhaps the unique experiment of the Salon des Refusés—appears to have had any significant effect upon the actual type or quality of the art on display; a superficial diversity, in short, masked an underlying uniformity. With history painting approaching obsolescence, as Castagnary observed, Salon painting was dominated by genre, landscape, and portraiture; with the authority of the Académie des Beaux-Arts in decline, artists could be roughly divided, he said, "into three principle groups: the classicists, the romanticists, and the naturalists."

The Classicists, descended largely from David and Ingres, included H. J. Flandrin (1809–64), J.-J. Henner (1829–1905), Jean-Léon Gérôme, Alexandre Cabanal (1823–89) and William-Adolphe Bouguereau (1825–1905) (the latter two artists were in fact pupils of F. E. Picot but Castagnary understandably grouped them with artists of like temperament). As might

be expected, they emphasized precise drawing, contour, and finish in their paintings, and strict adherence to the rules of anatomy, perspective, academic modeling and physiognomic expression. Their works often represent Classical, mythological, allegorical, or Orientalist themes in addition to contemporary history. The latter three subjects, for example, are represented in Gérôme's *Reception of the Siamese Ambassadors by Napoleon III and the Empress Eugénie at Fountainebleau, June 27, 1861* (1861–4). This grandiose work was commissioned by Nieuwerkerke in 1861 in commemoration of an historically insignificant meeting between Louis Napoleon and a group of Siamese ambassadors in the Salon d'Hercule following the conclusion of several minor trade agreements.

Deriving the composition of the *Reception* primarily from David's *Coronation of Napoleon*, Gérôme strives to imbue the Imperial nephew with the same grandeur as the uncle: seated at the far right beside the Empress, Napoleon receives tribute from the first in a double line of Siamese ambassadors seen crawling in obscene supplication before their French master and mistress. The ambassadors' gifts, rendered with the same painstaking exactitude as the costumes, the carpets, the

226

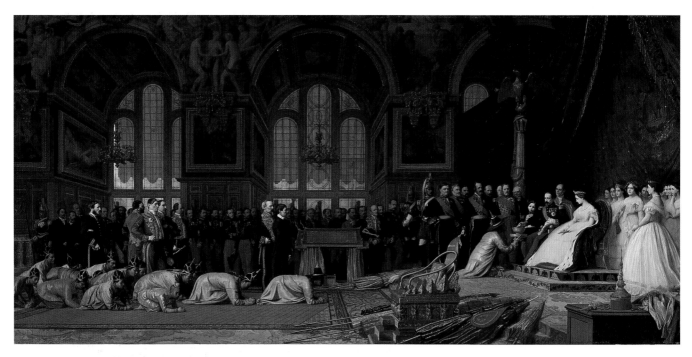

226 JEAN-LÉON GÉRÔME *Reception of the Siamese Ambassadors by Napoleon III and the Empress Eugénie at Fontainebleau, June 27, 1861* 1861–4. 50⅜ × 8′6⅜ (128 × 260)

chandeliers, and the Primaticcio-frescoed ambience, are piled up in the right foreground as if in allegorical expression of the benefits of France's imperialism. (In fact, the painting is an exercise in colonialist wishful thinking since Britain remained dominant in Siam until 1893, when France seized control of trade in the eastern part of the country, a region adjacent to its other Indochinese holdings.) Gérôme's depiction of Thais in the *Reception*, like his representation of Arabs and Black Africans in *Slave Market* (1867) and other pictures, is racist; it may have been influenced by the Bonapartist ideologue Arthur de Gobineau's tripartite division of humanity in his *Essay on the Inequality of the Human Races* (1853–5). In that work, a veritable primer in European racial theory, Gobineau described people of the "yellow race" as apathetic, material-istic, and respectful of order, just as Gérôme represented them in the *Reception,* and people of the "black race" ("Hami-tic")—including Arabs—as violent, capricious, and pos-sessed of "an intensity of desire . . . which may be called terrible." This "strength of sensation" resulted in an indifference to human life among the Hamites, and an embrace of slavery and prostitution, such as depicted in Gérôme's *Slave Market.*

Not all Classicist painting was so nakedly subservient to Imperialist ideology as Gérôme's, but most acceded to governing class, gender, and racial hierarchies, employed a highflown (and anachronistic) rhetoric of facial expression and physical gesture, and strove to impart religious, historical,

scientific, political, or moral lessons through narrative anec-dote. Classicist Salon painting of the Second Empire, in sum—like the *genre historique* of the July Monarchy before it—by its combined highmindedness and vulgar anecdotalism tended to bathos; indeed, it is the very glut of Imperial pomp and Orientalist circumstance in Gérôme's *Reception* and *Slave Market* that ultimately undermines our confidence in the seriousness and authority of these pictures. A similar ideological instability, resulting from the awkward combi-nation of grand style and vulgar subject, is apparent in works by Cabanal and Bouguereau, as well as in the paintings of the Romanticists discussed next.

The second group of artists described by Castagnary in his 1863 Salon review was the Romanticists, descended in spirit, if not in actual training, from Géricault, Gros, and Delacroix, but now much reduced in number and influence. Chassériau, Scheffer, Descamps, Vernet, and Delacroix would all be dead by the year's end, and their places taken by a small number of artists that included, for lesser and greater periods of time, Léon Bonnat (1833–1922), Fantin-Latour (1836–1904), and especially Gustave Moreau (1826–98). Moreau's *Oedipus and* 227 *the Sphinx* (1864), shown at the Salon of 1864, well represents the tendency toward the exotic, the violent, and the grotesque (Castagnary's "rain of sulphur") that characterized the earlier Romantic generation of Hugo, Goethe, Delacroix, and Ingres. Notwithstanding these basic, common themes, however, Moreau differs profoundly from the earlier authors and artists in his sacrifice of dramatic breadth and panoramic viewpoint in favor of the evocation of psychic and spatial claustrophobia.

228 Compared with Ingres's prototypical *Oedipus and the Sphinx* (1808), which celebrates the Classical Greek ideal of a combined physical and intellectual self-prepossession, Moreau's painting is all about sexual terror and emotional impenetrability. His archaic Oedipus, pressed against a cliff and threatened by the Sphinx (like Prometheus tortured by the eagle), shrinks at once from woman and knowledge—each threatens the frigid integrity of his body and mind. "[The Sphinx] is a terrestrial chimera," Moreau wrote in one of his notebooks, "as vile as earthly matter and equally bewitching, represented by that charming head of a woman, with a winged body . . . [it offers] promises of the ideal, but with the body of a monster, of the carnivore who tears prey to shreds." Moreau's subsequent Salon successes—culminating in his *Salome* and *Hercules and the Hydra of Lerna* (both 1876)—were increasingly dominated by his misogyny and bloodlust as well as by his obsessive concern for Orientalist detail. The later praise and blame of Moreau from the likes of Odilon Redon and Edgar Degas are indicative of the general fate of the Second Empire Salon Romantics: "What admirable virtuosity," wrote Redon, "in the accessory effects!" "He would have us believe," quipped Degas, "that the gods wear watch chains." By surrendering to the lure of "accessory effect" and surface accoutrement, Romanticism succumbed to the thrall of a superficial Naturalism.

More than Classicism and Romanticism, it was Naturalism, according to many critics, that represented the future of art at the Salon. Inaugurated, the Republican Castagnary wrote, a generation earlier by the Barbizon landscapists—who included Jules Dupré (1811–89), Millet, Théodore Rousseau (1812–67), Constant Troyon (1810–65) and Narcisse Diaz (1808–76)—Naturalism was claimed by him to represent a new principle of equality and individualism in society and culture: Naturalism "springs from our politics," he wrote, "which, by taking for a principle the equality of individuals and the equality of conditions as a *desideratum,* has banished from the mind false hierarchies and lying distinctions." The basis for Castagnary's linkage of Naturalist art and democratic politics was his belief, especially widespread during the first decade of the Second Empire, that nature, particularly the unspoiled Barbizon of the eponymous painters, or the untrammeled Franche-Comté of Courbet, represented the only remaining loci for personal fulfillment and independence during a time of mass urbanization and Bonapartist absolutism. As such, it was the fundamental principle upon which all artistic creations, regardless of genre, must be constructed.

Indeed, Castagnary and other critics increasingly applied the label Naturalism to more artists than just the insurgent Courbet and the Barbizon group, citing, for example, the

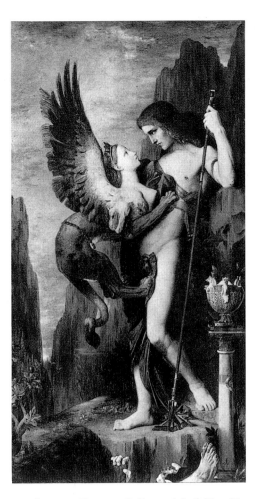

227 GUSTAVE MOREAU *Oedipus and the Sphinx* 1864. 80⅝ × 41 (204.7 × 104.1)

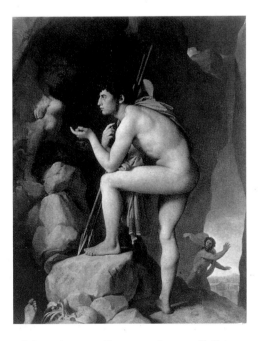

228 JEAN-AUGUSTE-DOMINQUE INGRES *Oedipus and the Sphinx* 1808. 74⅜ × 56⅝ (188.9 × 143.8)

Bonapartist animal painter Rosa Bonheur and the Catholic peasant artist Louis Cabat (1812–93). Thus the rubric, despite its defining "principle of equality," was in fact increasingly an expression of that official eclecticism which masked a profound hierarchism at the Salons of the Second Empire. The Naturalists who were most favored by patrons and jurors during these years were not the radicals—Courbet, Rousseau, and Millet—but the idealists, like Alexandre Antigna (1817–78) and Jules Breton, who upheld the superiority of the ruling notables, the value of simple peasant virtues, and the need for proletarian subservience. In Breton's award-winning *Blessing the Wheat in the Artois,* for example, shown at the 1857 Salon, the rural laborers literally bow before higher authorities. Employing a composition that echoes Courbet's *A Burial at Ornans* and anticipates Gérôme's *Reception of the Siamese Ambassadors,* Breton depicts a ragged group of peasants in the foreground kneeling in supplication before a procession representing Church (priests), Commerce (the bourgeoisie in suits), and State (the uniformed gendarme). Few works of the period represent more clearly the tripartite foundation of Second Empire authority, or the tendency of Salon Naturalists to adhere to class and ethnic *idées reçues.*

The extreme of Naturalist reticence about depicting social complexity and contradiction was probably achieved by the animal painter Rosa Bonheur. Undoubtedly the most celebrated woman artist of the nineteenth century (she was awarded a *Légion d'honneur* in 1865), Bonheur maintained a menagerie at her By estate precisely in order to avoid unpleasant interactions with society. Despite her misanthropy, however, celebrity and wealth came early to Bonheur. Encouraged by her Saint-Simonian father Raimond to become an independent woman and an artist, she copied both

from earlier animal painters and life, and by 1849 had achieved a considerable success at the Salon for her *Plowing in the Nivernais: The Dressing of the Vines.* In that work, as in *The Horse Fair* (1853), shown at the 1853 Salon and the 1855 Exposition Universelle, humans are reduced to mere appendages beside the yokes of cattle or the magnificent Percheron horses. Observing Bonheur's transformation of people into mere operatives, John Ruskin objected in 1855: "This lady gains in power every year, but here is one stern fact concerning art which she would do well to consider. . . . No painter of animals ever yet was entirely great who shrank from painting the human face; and Mlle. Bonheur clearly *does* shrink from it. . . . In the *Horse Fair* the human faces were nearly all dextrously, but disagreeably, hidden, and the one chiefly shown had not the slightest character." By now, however, Bonheur was largely exempt from criticism: granted a special police dispensation to dress as a man, she contentedly retreated to her estate and sold her works privately, independent of critical or Salon sanction.

French Salon art of the Second Empire, in conclusion, came in countless shapes and sizes, and critics past and present have sweated over the best labels. History painting, historical genre, Orientalist, eclecticist, academicist, Classicist, Romanticist, Naturalist, and Realist are all terms that have been used to describe this art in whole or in parts. Perhaps the only safe conclusion that can be drawn is that Salon art was a mixed and variable body of work that nevertheless shared a single fundamental aspect and purpose—reducing the act of vision to seeing only what has been seen before.

Indeed, more than anything else, Salon painting positively reveled in stereotypes and clichés; it consistently displayed

229 JULES BRETON *Blessing the Wheat in the Artois* 1857. 51 × 10′6 (129.5 × 320)

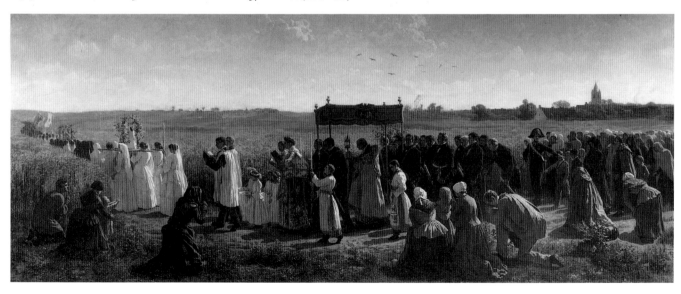

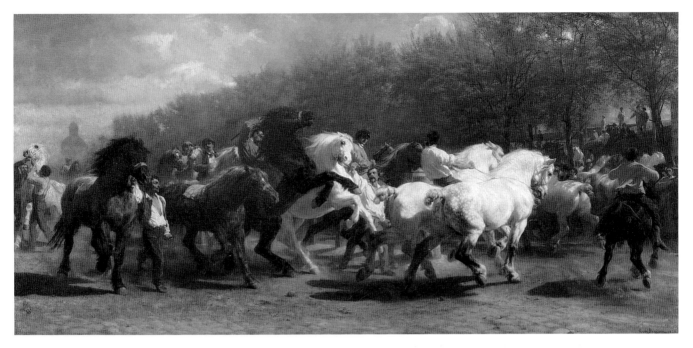

230 ROSA BONHEUR *The Horse Fair* 1853. 94¼ × 16'7½ (239.3 × 506.7)

an attitude of tongue-in-cheek and wink-and-a-nod, inviting spectators to believe that they were being let in on a joke at someone else's expense. (As we shall soon see, that someone else was usually a woman.) Salon art therefore performed its ideological work not by facilitating audience absorption in the object—whether through illusionistic tricks or narrative power—but on the contrary by encouraging a stance of diffidence and self-consciousness before the work. In this way, Salon spectators were encouraged to exercise and gratify their individual powers of esthetic delectation and connoisseurship—to become experts—the better to identify with the particular received idea on view. What was positively discouraged at the Salon was the exercise of any insurgent, collective, or class consciousness: that is, any identification with the outmoded "social organisms," as Castagnary wrote, that might interfere with the development of a society in which "man becomes more and more himself." Individual consumption, not class solidarity—individual retreat into nature, not collective resistance to the alienation of society—was promoted at the Salons of the Second Empire.

Individualism and commodified consciousness—masked and justified by a crude ideology of Naturalism—was what replaced history painting in Germany, Italy, and France around the middle of the nineteenth century. In Risorgimento Italy, the Macchiaioli briefly intruded upon this bleak horizon by depicting non-elite classes, occupations, and locations in a style that was honest about its own facture and fictitiousness. In France, where a critical consciousness of society was profoundly rooted in three quarters of a century of insurgency and revolution, Courbet, Manet, and the Impressionists offered a still more compelling challenge to the new Salon paradigm. Among these artists, individualism was dialectically redefined to include both personal autonomy and the popular collectivity: thus was modernism born, in Paris, at the close of the Second Empire.

MODERN ART AND LIFE

· 11 ·

MANET AND THE IMPRESSIONISTS

EDOUARD MANET AND HAUSSMANNIZATION

Edouard Manet was born in Paris in 1832 and died there in 1883, a lifespan largely coincident with the modernization of the French capital. Until 1850, Paris was still in many respects medieval: its streets were narrow and twisting, many houses were made of wood, and water and sewage facilities were inadequate at best. As the population of the city grew—it reached one million by 1836 and one and a half million by 1856—city squares, parks, and cemeteries were built over, seriously restricting the healthy passage of light and air and the movement of people and goods. The progress of commerce and industry and the battle against tuberculosis and cholera were thus seriously compromised at mid-century, by the occluded urban pattern and decrepit infrastructure of Paris.

All this began to change in 1852. Within days of the Napoleonic *coup d'état*, the Emperor announced a massive public works project to redesign and rebuild the city of Paris. Implemented under the supervision of a city superintendent, Baron Georges Haussmann, the campaign—which lasted for the entire Second Empire—resulted in the construction of new water and sewer systems, the cutting of new boulevards and the straightening and widening of old ones, the installation of street lighting, the creation of parks and transportation hubs and the building of new, speculative residential and commercial structures.

In addition to improving health and transportation, the intention of the Emperor and his superintendent was to secure popular consent or obedience to undemocratic rule: the public works program provided employment for thousands at a time of massive unemployment, and the urban renewal broke up the radical communities that existed in the Cité and the

Faubourg Saint-Antoine, among other places. The rebuilding of Paris was thus a strategic as much as it was an economic endeavor, and while it may not be strictly true, as many at the time believed, that the boulevards were straightened to facilitate the flight of canonballs, the idea cannot have been wholly absent from the minds of the governors of a city that had already witnessed three revolutions in as many generations. Indeed, those fine, straight avenues were put to efficient use during the mass executions that followed the defeat of the Paris Commune in the late Spring of 1871, as shown by Manet in his drawing called *The Barricade* (ca. 231 1871).

The social and cultural, as much as the economic and strategic, effects of Haussmannization (as the rebuilding came to be called) were tremendous. Within a generation, Paris became the place we know today, a city of fashion, elegance, effrontery, and detachment. Architectural homogeneity replaced urban syncretism; class segregation replaced social integration; a *blasé* public attitude replaced a changeable and energetic mien. Where rich and poor had once lived in relative proximity, they were now increasingly separated from each other, the former in the smart new apartment blocks lining the *grands boulevards* on the right bank of the Seine, and the latter in the houses and tenements of the *communes annexées*, such as Ménilmontant, Belleville and La Villette, outlying the city. Whereas in former times the center of the city was marked by the confused crush and din of carriage traffic, travelers, beggars, entertainers, and street hawkers of every kind—old-clothes men, crockery menders, dog barbers, and others—it was now, as Baedeker's wrote, "a far less noisy place than many other large cities . . . [a place of] comparative tranquility." Whereas in a previous age, the signs of social class, occupation, and sexual availability were instantly readable in costume and deportment, the mass-produced clothes sold in the new department stores, combined with the growth of a lower middle class between bourgeois and proletarian, made such identifications more difficult. The city became a place inhabited by strangers, orphans, and refugees.

The extent of the erosion of the rich and complex symbolic life in Paris during the Second Empire can easily be exaggerated. The fear and disparagment of modernity, after all, are integral parts of modern culture itself, and can be traced, as Raymond Williams has shown, to the time of Piers Plowman if not before. Alarms concerning urban desecration and alienation in Paris were being issued by Victor Hugo in the preface to *Nôtre-Dame de Paris* from 1830 and by Balzac in *Les Petits Bourgeois* a decade later. Nevertheless, the appearance in Paris of a number of strange and neurotic symptoms at approximately mid-century would seem to point to the uniqueness of the changes that overtook the capital at this time. *Flaneurie* and modernist painting are two related examples of this symptomatology.

Seeking to cushion themselves against the shocks of capital, or to carve out an identity in an environment increasingly bereft of social markers, a number of individuals, including the poet Baudelaire and the painter Manet, adopted the subcultural stance of the *flaneur*. The very embodiment of the modern male individualist "become more and more himself," the *flaneur* was a perpetual idler, browser, or window-shopper who saw the city of Paris as a spectacle created for his entertainment, and judged commodities to be icons made for his veneration. "The street becomes a dwelling place for the *flaneur*," Walter Benjamin has written:

> he is as much at home among the facades of houses as a citizen is in his four walls. To him the shiny, enamelled signs of businesses are at least as good a wall ornament as an oil painting is to a bourgeois in his salon. The walls are the desk against which he presses his notebooks; news-stands are his libraries and the terraces of cafés are the balconies from which he looks down on his household after his work is done. That life, in all its variety and inexhaustible wealth of variations . . . [thrived] among the grey cobble streets and against the grey background of despotism.

The *flaneur* slowly strolled the streets of Paris, scrutinizing everything he saw, like a detective searching for clues to help him solve a mysterious crime. In such difficult cases, every piece of evidence counts: the cut of a sleeve or trouser, the sheen on a piece of satin, the trim of whiskers, and the depth of a plunging neckline are all prerequisite for the discovery of identity in a city of strangers. And the work of detection in Paris was all the more subtle and rewarding given the meagerness of the signs of social and psychological difference on display, as, for example, in the Tuileries park, in Manet's

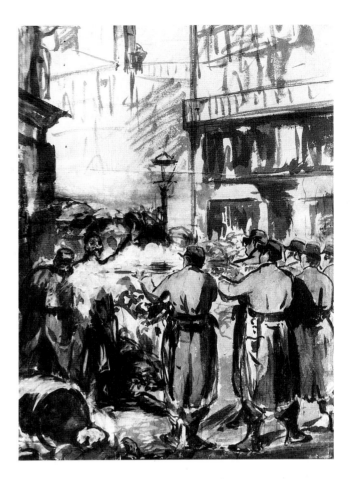

231 EDOUARD MANET *The Barricade* ca. 1871. 18⅜ × 13⅛ (46.5 × 33.4)

Music in the Tuileries (1862), or on a balcony, as in his *A Balcony* (1868–9). 232–3

In *Music in the Tuileries*, perhaps the "earliest true example of modern painting in both subject matter and technique," as the art historian and curator Françoise Cachin wrote, Manet has interspersed his many fashionable friends and acquaintances among a larger cross section of elegant society. Manet himself stands at the far left, brush in hand; Baudelaire stands in lost profile, coincident with the largest tree at middle left; beneath him sit the Mmes. Lejosne and Loubens, distinguished wives of notable men in government and education; Eugène Manet—the painter's brother—also stands in profile, bowing and facing left in the middle right foreground; seated just to the right is the composer Jacques Offenbach, with moustache, no beard, and neatly circumscribed by the largest tree at middle right. The painting constitutes, in brief, a kind of Parisian, elite *roman à clef*, in which the table is turned upon the *flaneur*; now he is subject to perusal; now his costume and features—hidden beneath a blur of white, black, and tan and a confused tangle of phallic trees (or exclamation points!)—will be spied for signs of class and temperament.

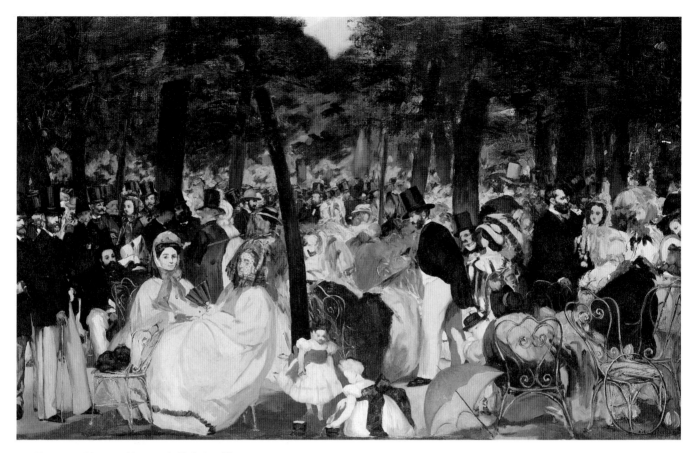

232 EDOUARD MANET *Music in the Tuileries* 1862. 30 × 46¼ (76 × 118)

A similar reversal of the position of seer and seen is effected
in *A Balcony* (and in Cassatt's *Woman in Black at the Opera:*
see pp. 263–4). There, two women dressed in white with green
accessories, a man in black with blue cravat, a servant in the
upper left shadows, and an uncertain breed of dog at the lower
left, all pose behind a green iron balcony and between green
shutters. The seated woman is the painter Berthe Morisot
(1841–95), whose particular keenness of vision and insight
would be revealed in her paintings of the next decade (see also
pp. 253–4). They cast their eyes left, right, and center in
imitation of the shifting gaze of the bewildered spectators who
saw the work at the Salon of 1869. "This contradictory
attitude [of the two women in *The Balcony*]," Castagnary
wrote, "bewilders me. . . . Like characters in a comedy, so in a
painting each figure must be in place, play its part and so
contribute to the expression of the general idea." Manet
would accept no such circumscribed role for his women
characters or for himself. He pursued the much vaunted
principle of individualism even at the cost of public incomprehension, comforted that he lived and worked among like-
minded artists and writers on the borderland between
bohemia and high society.

Artists like Manet and the painter and graphic artist
Constantin Guys (1802–92)—who worked outside of the
institutional framework of the Academy—were natural
flaneurs; they had no fixed occupation and hardly even a
settled abode, traveling between home and studio and
vagrantly searching the city for models and motifs. "The
crowd is his domaine," wrote Baudelaire about Guys, author
of the vacuous drawing *The Champs-Elysées* (1855), "as the air
is for birds and water is for fish. His passion and his profession
is to marry [épouser] the crowd." Like Baudelaire, the male
artist-*flaneur* was a politically contradictory figure. By virtue
of his furtive insinuation into the middle of the crowd, and his
deadpan style and humor, the *flaneur* was a minor thorn in the
side of a despotic regime that survived on the pageant of
manipulated consent. He was, for the most part, no patriot
and no cheerleader, and was totally lacking in ingenuousness.
Yet he was at the same time an eager propagandist for
modernity and thus of some use: by believing with his entire
heart and soul that the mass-produced clothes slung across the
mannequins in the Au Bon Marché department store or
draping the sloped shoulders of the good bourgeois on the
Boulevard des Capucines contained the clues to a unique

identity, he was accepting and propagandizing the commodity fetishism that buttressed both the dazzling facade of the Second Empire and its "grey background of despotism." Paris was both phantasmagorical and dictatorial; it was a perpetual-motion machine that seemingly worked its magic—as Delacroix had noted at the 1855 Exposition—entirely of its own volition and independent of the labor of workers or the struggle of classes and genders. Paris, with its gaslighted boulevards and omnibuses, glass-fronted stores that functioned like reliquaries, glass-roofed arcades that resembled Gothic cathedrals, and mock festive *café-concerts* with names like Alcazar, El Dorado, and Ambassadeurs, was a modern city born of the commodity and dedicated to keeping that fact a secret. *Flaneurie* was complicit in commodity fetishization and intrigue, as was the artist Manet in these pictures.

OLYMPIA

At times, however, Manet appeared to resist the given structures of class and gender ideology, thereby achieving something of the individualism or autonomy which he and his contemporaries claimed to seek. *Olympia* (1863, exhibited 1865), which immediately eclipsed his own *Déjeuner sur l'herbe* (1863) as the most notorious painting in the history of art, is the case in point. It depicts a naked white woman reclining on a bed gazing at the viewer, and a clothed black woman holding a bouquet of flowers and gazing at Olympia. A black cat arches its back at the lower right, a green drape is drawn back at the upper left, and a partition and curtain fail to meet in the middle—behind Olympia—permitting a glimpse into an alcove or waiting area beyond. The plane of the bed upon which the protagonist lies is almost exactly parallel to the

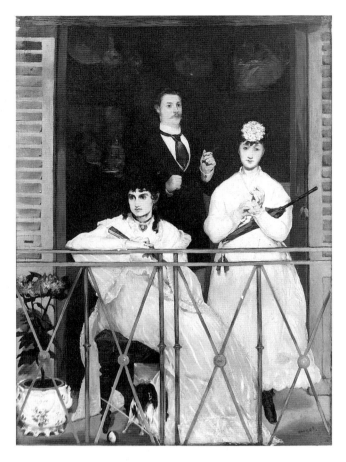

spectator's line of sight, and the bedclothes at lower left and dressing-gown at lower right cascade into the viewer's space. The painting's composition is thus rather mechanically balanced between left and right, and top and bottom, further highlighting by contrast its immodest or imbalanced subject.

The handling of paint in *Olympia* is as discordant as its contents and composition. Whereas academically approved

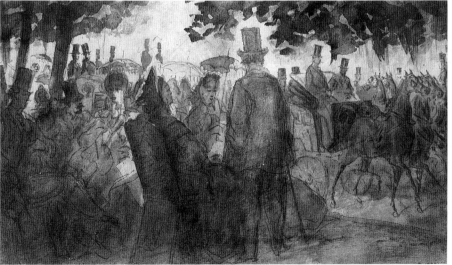

233 EDOUARD MANET *A Balcony* 1868–9. 66½ × 49¼ (169 × 125)

234 CONSTANTIN GUYS *The Champs-Elysées* 1855. 9½ × 16⅜ (24.1 × 41.6)

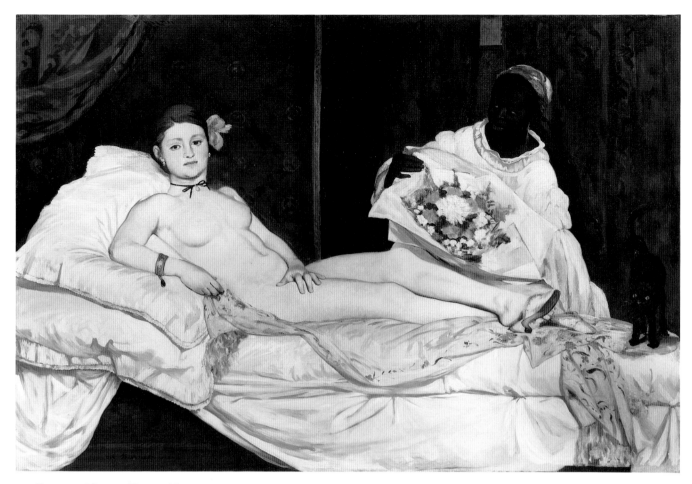

235 EDOUARD MANET *Olympia* 1863. 51⅜ × 74⅞ (130.5 × 190)

Salon painting was generally highly polished, with its brushstrokes invisible and its forms smoothly modeled, *Olympia* presents something of the appearance of an *ébauche* (preliminary, rough underpainting), with its clearly distinct touches of color and abrupt contrasts of tonality, as for example on the nude's shoulders, breasts, belly, and hips. In addition, the bedclothes, dressing-gown, nude body, and paper are all hard and angular, like the drapery in works by the early Flemish painters. The overall pictorial effect of this refusal of modeling and subtle chiaroscuro, as well as of the mechanically poised compositional elements and angularity, is a flatness and ungainliness such as found in "primitive" and children's art or in Epinal prints. Like Courbet, then, Manet has sought refuge and resource in the naive and the popular: therein lies his avant-garde suit to the Salon public, one very different from the disingenuous entreaties of Academic and Official art.

The times were inauspicious for popular art, however, and Manet's *Olympia*—exhibited alongside his *Christ Mocked* at the 1865 Salon—was lambasted by the critics: "We find him again this year," wrote the usually sensible Jules Claretie, "with two dreadful canvases, challenges hurled at the public, mockeries or parodies, how can one tell? Yes mockeries. What is this Odalisque with a yellow stomach, a base model picked up I know not where who represents Olympia? . . . A courtesan no doubt." Another critic, cited by T. J. Clark in his indispensable study of the picture, spoke of Olympia as "a courtesan with dirty hands and wrinkled feet . . . her body has the livid tint of a cadaver displayed in the morgue; her outlines are drawn in charcoal and her greenish, bloodshot eyes appear to be provoking the public, protected all the while by a hideous Negress."

Manet indeed provoked critics and bourgeois public alike by his subversion of the genre of the nude and his rejection of the received ideas of sex and race. To depict nudes, "fallen" and alluring women, was, we have seen, common enough in nineteenth-century France. Couture, who was Manet's teacher between 1850 and 1856, had made a courtesan the focus of his 1847 *Romans of the Decadence*, and by 1865 the Salon walls would have seemed half-bare without their full complement of dissolute Venuses, Bacchantes, Nymphs, Sapphos, Salomes, Dianas, and Odalisques, by the likes of Bouguereau, Cabanal, and Paul Baudry. In addition, before the decade ended, the sculptor Jean-Baptiste Carpeaux (1827–75) and the painter Claude Monet (1840–1926) ventured to create what they believed to be more naturalistic representations of female figures—naked, clothed, and in ensemble. In both Carpeaux's *The Dance* (1867–9) and Monet's *Women in the Garden* (1866–7) women are represented in counter-clockwise orbit around a central axis; in the Monet, the fashionable women encircle a slender and animate tree, and in the Carpeaux around an adolescent male personifying "the Genius of Dance." When Carpeaux's sculptural group on the facade of the new Paris Opera was unveiled in 1869 it caused a scandal by what was seen as its "immodesty," "realism," and modernity; in fact, it was profoundly influenced by Raphael, Michelangelo, and Bernini, and formed part of the decorative ensemble of the very building that symbolized the regime of Napoleon III with all its imperial and Classical pretensions. Monet's early Impressionist *Women in the Garden* was also rejected, by the jury of the Salon, reportedly because of its potential to corrupt youthful artists, despite its Classical and hierarchically structured composition. Images of women—painted, sculpted, academic, and modern—positively dominated the visual culture of the Second Empire, but none was so controversial as Manet's.

245
246

236 FRÉDÉRIC BAZILLE *La Toilette* 1870. 83 × 79 (211 × 201)

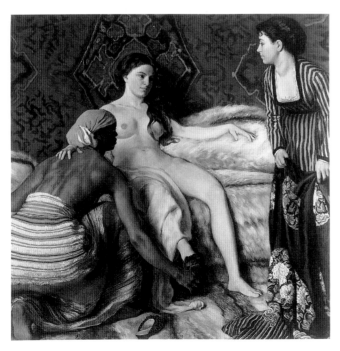

The practise of depicting "negresses" in art, though less common, was nearly as longstanding and revered as the representation of "fallen" women: black women began to appear in painting, sculpture, and the decorative arts in the middle of the eighteenth century as allegories of Africa or in order to signal the presence of illicit or animal-like sexuality. By the early nineteenth century, when racist theories of polygenesis (the notion of the separate biological origins of humans) prevailed, they represented lasciviousness and evolutionary retardation. Delacroix, for example, whose colorism and expressive drawing style profoundly influenced Manet, had depicted a turbaned black African serving woman in his hothouse *Women of Algiers*. By the early Second Empire, black women became almost ubiquitous in the Orientalist pictures of Ingres, Gérôme, Chassériau, and Eugène Fromentin, among others. In 1870, the young Impressionist Frédéric Bazille (1841–70) painted *La Toilette* in which a black woman at the lower left—perhaps the same Laura (last name unknown) who posed for Manet—is shown dressing a naked and voluptuous white woman in the center. (The composition, as well perhaps as the subject, is derived from the central figural group of Courbet's *Toilette of the Bride*, 1865, which depicts the preparation of a body for burial.) Unlike these artists, however, Manet offered his male spectators neither secure art historical moorings nor any patriarchal consolation in *Olympia*.

192

236

The body of Olympia lacked pliancy and suppleness, suggesting instead an independent sexuality which emerged, as a critic wrote, "[from beneath her] hand flexed in a sort of shameless contraction." She was not a grand courtesan paid to confirm the myths of masculine desire, but a proletarian who owned only her labor power and her sex. And as such, critics argued, she was subhuman: "A sort of female gorilla . . . ape[s] on a bed," wrote one, "a monkey," wrote a second, and "a corpse . . . from the [working-class] Rue Mouffetard," stated a third. The repeated references to Olympia's blackness and simian aspect suggest that a critical elision between the nude and the West Indian maid has occurred. The body of the lower-class prostitute and the body of the Afro-Caribbean woman, according to Manet's interlocutors, were linked by their common *dégénérescence*, that is, by their combined intellectual, physical, and moral depravity, morbidity, and inferiority. (Black women and prostitutes were widely understood, according to the science of the day, to possess congenitally deformed genitals that preconditioned them to hypersexuality.) Each was judged more grotesque than the other and harbingers of the feared degeneracy which, according to the respected doctor Bénédict Augustin Morel—author of the *Treatise on Degeneracy* (1857)—was infecting French society as a whole. Manet's picture represented something of that decay, and for that reason—as well as for its overall pictorial strangeness—precipitated the very compli-cated, fantastic, and idiotic chain of criticisms that constituted its scandal.

In the end, it must be observed that Manet's *Olympia* was probably more modern than it was avant-garde, in the senses those terms have been used here. Although it represented two proletarian women, they were of the politically ambiguous *lumpen* variety; though it employed the two-dimensionality of popular art, it did so within the confines of a genre—the nude—that was, for all its rebarbativeness in Manet's case, still constitutive of the old class and gender hierarchies; and finally, though *Olympia* incited a frenzy of shrill critical antagonism, it did so in the name of no other clearly particular social class, political principle, or oppositional ideology. Manet did not succeed in fashioning a new, artistic public sphere in 1865; still less did he create a new sort of history painting to replace the once exalted and now moribund genre. "You are only the first in the decrepitude of your art," wrote Baudelaire to him in 1865 and, indeed, *Olympia* was a suitable end and beginning of painting. It marked the conclusion of a heroic tradition of art for an enlightened bourgeois public, and the origins of a modern art that instead denies or negates the verities of that class's rule. In addition, it signaled the (temporary) end of the Courbetist dream of a Realist art for the masses, and the beginning of an equally idealist dream of an autonomous art intended for a society of free individuals.

IMPRESSIONISM AND THE COMMODITY

Like the *flaneur* Manet, the Impressionists were determined to discover for themselves a semblance of the individual freedom, self-determinacy, and sensual pleasure that consti-tuted the utopian legacy of enlightenment and revolution. Unlike him, they generally lacked irony and guile, seeing in the existing urban, and especially the suburban, spaces of modernity the dream-terrain of that quest. "Early Impressionism," as Meyer Schapiro wrote:

had a moral aspect. In its discovery of a constantly changing phenomenal outdoor world of which the shapes depended upon the momentary position of the casual or mobile spectator, there was an implicit criticism of symbolic social and domestic formalities, or at least a norm opposed to these. It is remarkable how many pictures we have in early Impressionism of informal and spontaneous sociability, of breakfasts, picnics, promenades, boating trips, holidays and vacation travel. These urban idylls not only present the objective forms of bourgeois recreation in the 1860s and 1870s; they also reflect in the very choice of subjects and in the new aesthetic devices the conception of

art as solely a field of individual enjoyment . . . for an enlightened bourgeois detached from the official beliefs of his class.

The Impressionists were indeed individualists who lacked the world-historical ambition, Romantic fervor, and avant-garde convictions of the two previous generations of French and European artists. Born around 1840, they were too young to be firebrand *quarant-huitards,* but were old enough to watch in shock and horror (mostly from a safe distance) the Prussian dismemberment of France in 1870–71, and the French massacre of its own citizens during the suppression of the Commune that followed. They beheld the industrialization of agriculture in the provinces and the Haussmannization of urban space in Paris, and understood that the old France of agrarian autarchy and distinct urban *quartiers* was no more. To all of these events and transformations, they responded for the most part with the officially approved mix of nostalgia for the old and complacency at the new. The Impressionists were thus in the main passive witnesses of, or willing propagandists for, the emerging and modern "forms of bourgeois re-creation" of their day, but the acuity of their observation and the depth of their enthusiasm was such that they nevertheless managed to precipitate a crisis of representation that ended only with the severance of the formerly existing relationship between art and its public.

The term Impressionism, used after 1874 to define the group of eponymous artists, derives from the word *impression,* which Emile Littré defined in his *Dictionnaire* (1866) as "the more or less pronounced effect which exterior objects make upon the sense organs." In 1870, the word was applied by the critic Théodore Duret to Manet: "He brings back from the vision he casts on things an impression truly his own. . . . Everything is summed up, in his eyes, in a variant of coloration; each nuance or distinct color becomes a definite tone, a particular note of the palette." Duret thus described two aspects of Manet's art that have already been considered: first, its utter individuality, and secondly, its structure of discrete color "notes" juxtaposed against, but not blended with, their adjacent tone. The dual nature of Impressionism also underlay Castagnary's celebrated description of the thirty artists who exhibited together for the first time under the name Société Anonyme at the Paris studios of the photogra-pher Nadar in 1874: "They are *Impressionists* in the sense that they render not the landscape but the sensation produced by the landscape. . . . [The Impressionists] leave reality and enter into full idealism." By "idealism," as the art historian Richard Shiff has shown, Castagnary meant the individualism of the artists, that corresponded to their technique of laying down a mosaic of colors and forms determined by the peculiar impression of the exterior world upon their sense organs.

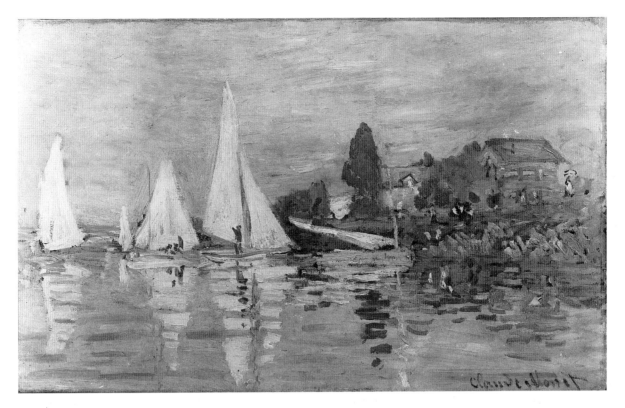

237 **CLAUDE MONET** *Regatta at Argenteuil* 1872. 19 × 29½ (48 × 75)

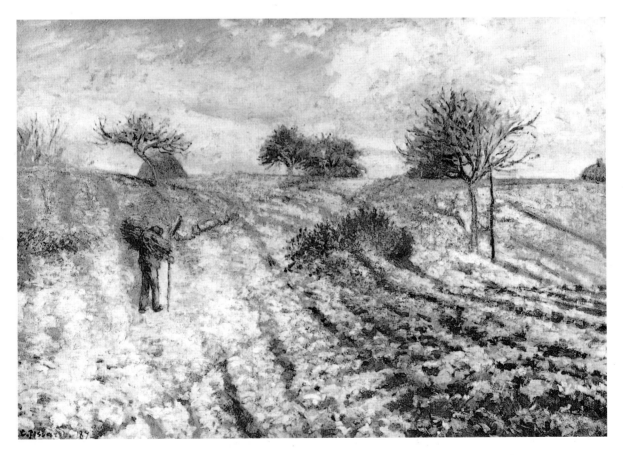

238 **CAMILLE PISSARRO** *Hoarfrost* 1873. 25⅝ × 36⅝ (65 × 93)

In 1874, therefore, the term Impressionism connoted a vaguely defined technique of painting and an attitude of individualism shared by a group of allied artists unofficially led by Manet (who, however, never exhibited with them). Indeed, the two definitions are aptly conjoined, since the formal and technical innovations of the movement effectively served to represent an ideal of personal pleasure and individualist freedom. These innovations may be summed up under three rubrics: 1) the rejection of chiaroscuro; 2) the depiction of the interaction of light and color *en plein air*; and 3) the equalizing of brushstrokes across the surface of the canvas.

1) Academic painting depended upon chiaroscuro (the modeling of form and space through light and dark gradation and contrast) for its drama and putative three-dimensionality. In the early stages of their paintings, academically trained artists employed a dark, often reddish brown underpainting in order to establish a deep pictorial space even before they painted anything else. By proceeding to leave areas of shadow thinly painted and areas of mass thickly painted with bright colors and highlights, they were able to establish strong contrasts between dark and light, shadow and mass, and far and near. In Monet's *Regatta at Argenteuil* (1872) and Camille Pissarro's (1830–1903) *Hoarfrost* (1873), by contrast, a light-toned underpainting—creamy yellow in the first case and grey in the second—is employed instead of the conventional reddish brown. In addition, dark tones are largely eliminated from the mixtures of hue, and paint is applied in a fairly uniform thickness all across the surface of the picture. The effect of these changes from academic practise, in conjunction with others noted below, is greatly to reduce tonal contrast in the pictures and thereby to flatten them. Although Monet and Pissarro include fore-, middle-, and backgrounds in their *Regatta* and *Hoarfrost*, their elimination of chiaroscuro causes us to see all three zones as lying on approximately the same shallow, foreground plane.

2) Before the nineteenth century, artists drew but rarely painted out of doors. By the middle of the century, the painting of small outdoor *études* was common to Corot and the Barbizon school, and to the "Pre-Impressionist" painters Eugène Boudin and J.-B. Jongkind, who were active in Normandy. Yet these artists seldom painted fully finished compositions out of doors, and equally rarely exhibited their *études* at the Salons. The Impressionists, on the other hand—especially Monet, Pissarro, Pierre-Auguste Renoir (1841–1919), Morisot, and Alfred Sisley (1839–99)—painted many of their most ambitious works *en plein air*, and discovered a technique for evoking the interaction of light and air in nature. Monet's *Women in the Garden*, considered earlier for the conservatism of its subject and composition, was nevertheless almost unprecedented in its depiction of colored shadows and

light. Painted almost entirely *en plein air* (the artist actually dug a trench into which he could lower the work so as to paint its upper reaches without changing his point of view), *Women in the Garden* features colored shadows and the juxtaposition of warm and cool hues to achieve modeling of faces and hands. The dress of the woman at left is tinted green from the filtration of light through the canopy of trees, and the shadows on the dress of the seated woman in the foreground are tinted violet, the complement of the yellow light of the sun. The women's faces and hands, as well as their bouquets of flowers, are made vivid by the juxtaposition of similar, and especially complementary, colors—red/green, blue/orange, and yellow/violet—and by the use of thick, broad patches of paint. The optical effect of complements, which are pronounced in *Regatta at Argenteuil* (red/green) and Pissarro's *Hoarfrost* (yellow/violet), was described by Monet in 1888: "Color owes its brightness to force of contrast rather than to inherent qualities; . . . primary colors look brightest when they are brought into contrast with complementarities."

3) Most paintings submitted for exhibition at the Salons had a surface that was smooth, clean, and impersonal, whereas most paintings shown at the eight Impressionist exhibitions held between 1874 and 1886 had coarse, irregular, and idiosyncratic surfaces. Indeed, as much as for its rejection of chiaroscuro and its embrace of *plein air*, Impressionism was notable in its day for the use of discrete patches (*taches*) of color. To be sure, a loaded brush and impasto technique were deployed by Rubens and Rembrandt among many other artists from the past, but rarely had they covered their works with such a density of paint regardless of the subject depicted. In Pissarro's *Corner of a Village in Winter* (1877) and Renoir's *Bal du Moulin de la Galette* (1876) the entire canvas surface is densely clotted with paint. Individual brushstrokes are varied in width, breadth, and direction, and the pictorial field is uniformly animate, agitated, and immediate. The complex and dynamic Impressionist *tache* was largely responsible for the incomprehension and anger of the critics: "Seen up close [Pissarro's landscapes] are incomprehensible and hideous;" wrote Léon de Lora in 1877, "seen from a distance they are hideous and incomprehensible." "I recommend Renoir's *The Swing* [1876]," wrote Bertall (Charles Albert d'Arnoux) in 1876, "sublime in its grotesqueness . . . and *Bal du Moulin de la Galette*, which is in no way inferior to his other work in its incoherence of draftsmanship, composition, and color."

In the face of the reigning formal and technical paradigms of Salon art, Impressionism offered nothing less than a redefinition of the pictorial. If the Classical and academic tradition insisted that a picture should be a recreation in two dimensions of the three-dimensional world, that is, if painting was previously conceived as first and foremost mimetic, Impressionist art was first of all optical. In 1876, the poet

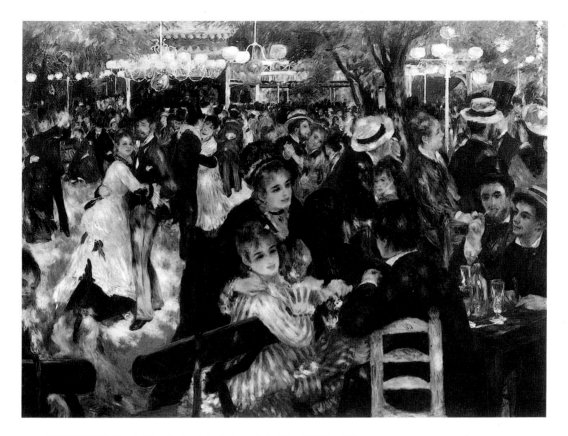

239 AUGUSTE RENOIR *Bal du Moulin de la Galette* 1876. 51½ × 68⅞ (131 × 175)

Stéphane Mallarmé wrote an essay entitled "The Impressionists and Edouard Manet," in which he precisely described Impressionism as the return of art to its "simplest perfection:"

> The scope and aim . . . of Manet and his followers is that painting shall be steeped again in its cause, and its relation to nature. But what, except to decorate the ceilings of saloons and palaces with a crowd of idealized types in magnificent foreshortening, what can be the aim of a painter before everyday nature? To imitate her? Then his best efforts can never equal the original with the inestimable advantage of life and space. . . . [That] which I [the artist] preserve through the power of Impressionism is not the material portion which already exists, superior to any mere representation of it, but the delight of having recreated nature touch by touch. I leave the massive and tangible solidity to its fitter exponent, sculpture. I content myself with reflecting on the clear and durable mirror of painting, that which perpetually lives yet dies every moment, which only exists by the will of Idea, yet constitutes in my domain the only authentic and certain merit of nature—the Aspect.

Although sculpture may be fit to reproduce the tactile qualities of nature, Mallarmé's ideal Impressionist argues, painting is not. It can only focus upon "the clear and durable mirror of painting," that is, upon the flattened, optical screen which constitutes the artist's field of vision; the Impressionist painter's responsibility and delight is to reproduce nature's "aspect" touch by touch.

The Impressionist world, according to this view, is one which cannot be manipulated, grasped, or even touched, except with the eyes. It is a world where use-value has been banished, and exchange-value—which posits the universal equality of things—enshrined instead. For the Impressionist painter, nature and the built environment appear as commodity-forms, or fetishes (as defined by Marx), alienated from the biological processes or human labor that brought them into being. Indeed, Impressionist optics and style—defined by their negotiation and compromise between hues across the flat expanse of the picture surface—may be said to repeat the mistaking of illusion for reality that constitutes the basis of commodity fetishism. In the first volume of *Capital* (1867) Marx described the "mysterious character" of the commodity-form as consisting in the fact that it (mis)represents the social and class relations of the human labor that produced it as an autonomous relationship between things:

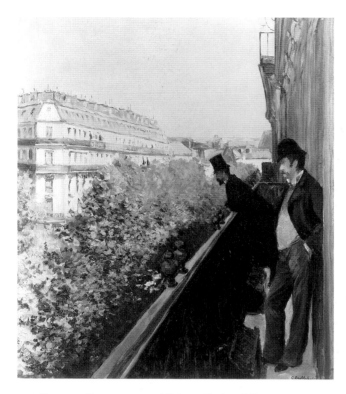

Through this substitution [by the social relations between objects for the social relation between producers], the products of labor become commodities, sensuous things which are at the same time suprasensible or social. In the same way, the impression [*Lichteindruck*] made by a thing on the optic nerve is perceived not as a subjective excitation of that nerve but as the objective form of a thing outside the eye.

Impressionist art is precisely concerned with the bestowal of a phantasmagorical reality upon "the objective form of thing[s] outside the eye." In 1883, the poet Jules Laforgue described the magic of Impressionist color:

> In a landscape flooded with light . . . where the academic painter sees nothing but a broad expanse of whiteness, the Impressionist sees light as bathing everything not with a dead whiteness, but rather with a thousand vibrant struggling colours of rich prismatic decomposition. Where the one sees only the external outline of objects, the other sees the real living lines built not in geometric forms but in a thousand irregular strokes, which at a distance, establish life. . . .
> The Impressionist sees and renders nature as it is—that is, wholly in the vibration of color. No drawing, light,

240 GUSTAVE CAILLEBOTTE *A Balcony, Boulevard Haussmann* ca. 1880. 26¾ × 24 (67.9 × 61)

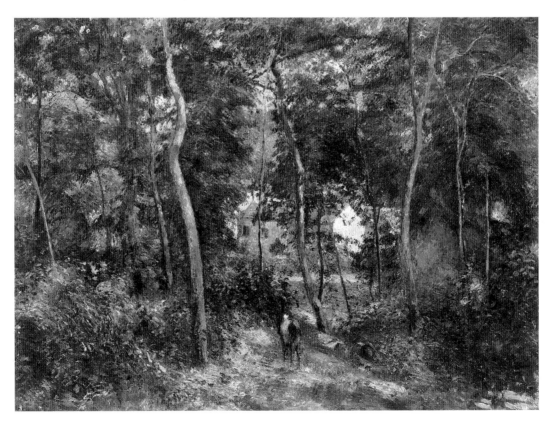

241 CAMILLE PISSARRO *Edge of the Woods, or Undergrowth in Summer* 1879. 49⅝ × 63¾ (126 × 162)

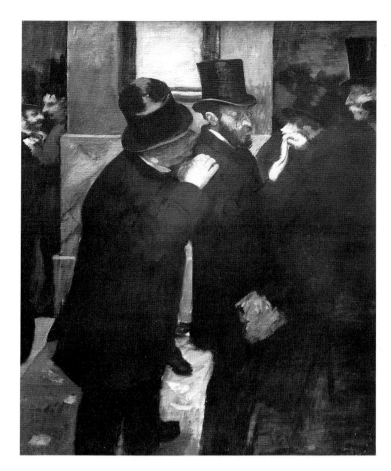

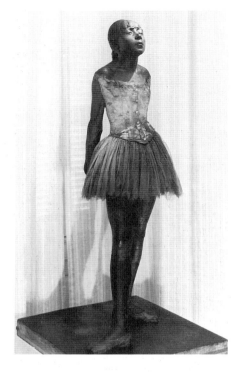

242 (*left*) **EDGAR DEGAS** *Portraits at the Stock Exchange* ca. 1879.
$39\frac{3}{8} \times 32\frac{3}{8}$ (100 × 82)

243 (*above*) **EDGAR DEGAS** *Little Dancer Aged Fourteen* ca.
1881. Height 39 (99.1)

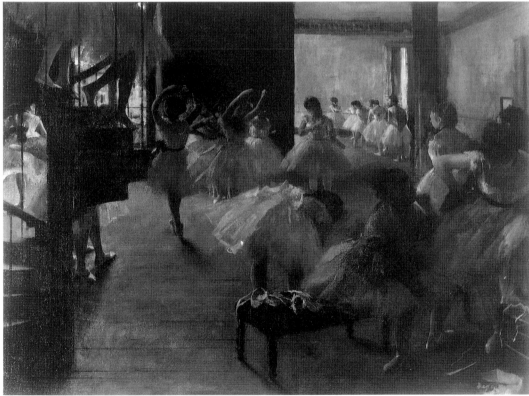

244 **EDGAR DEGAS** *The Dance School* 1873. $19 \times 24\frac{5}{8}$ (48.3 × 62.5)

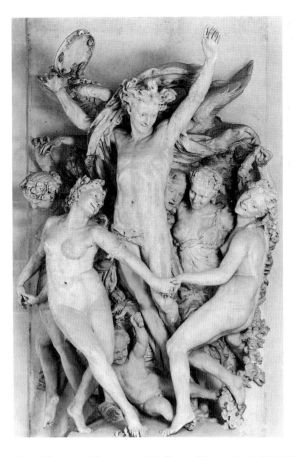

245 JEAN-BAPTISTE CARPEAUX *The Dance* 1867–9. Height 13'9⅜ (420)

modelling, perspective or chiaroscuro, none of those childish classifications: all these are in reality converted into the vibration of color and must be obtained on the canvas solely by the vibration of color. . . . [In the work of] Monet and Pissarro, everything is obtained by a thousand little dancing strokes in every direction like straws of color—all in vital competition for the whole impression.

The fetishistic character of Impressionist art, with its "real living lines" which "establish life," has of course been revealed by its subsequent commercial and institutional history. As early as the mid-1880's, the French dealer Paul Durand-Ruel, backed by the financier Charles Edwards, succeeded in establishing an international market for Impressionist works, with exhibitions and sales in Berlin, Boston, New York, Rotterdam, and London, as well as Paris. Indeed, the key years for the transformation of French art dealers from petty tradesmen to international entrepreneurial capitalists coincided with the rise and success of Impressionism. (To this day, works by Monet, Renoir, Degas, and the others are common tender in the international art market.) Moreover, the exchange-value represented by Impressionist art did not

remain circumscribed by the narrow confines of the trade. Since the beginning of the twentieth century, the forms and imagery of Impressionism have informed and invigorated the publicity apparatus of many of the key culture and leisure industries of Europe, North America, and (more lately) Japan, including suburban, vacation, and retirement homes, travel and tourism, automobiles, home gardening, sportswear, and health and exercise products. The modern bourgeois world, it may be claimed with only slight exaggeration, has modeled itself upon the "aspect" of Impressionism.

But the gift of ideology has not been all in one direction. The triumph of modern tourism and leisure has also tended to inform prevailing interpretations of Impressionism, masking the genuinely counter-cultural and even subversive aspects of the movement. Indeed, in the years between its first (1874) and third (1877) exhibitions, the self-proclaimed Société Anonyme was often dubbed in the press "the Intransigents," a term from the contemporary political lexicon, as I have shown elsewhere, meaning radical, anarchist or communist. "At first they were called 'the painters of the open air'," wrote the critic Marius Chaumelin in 1876: "They were then given a generous name, 'Impressionists,' which no doubt brought pleasure to Mlle Berthe Morisot and to the other young lady painters who have embraced these doctrines. But there is a title which described them much better, that is the *Intransigents*. . . . They have a hatred for classical traditions and an ambition to reform the laws of drawing and color. They preach the separation of Academy and State. They demand an amnesty for the 'school of the *taches*,' of whom M. Manet was the founder and to whom they are all indebted." With less irony, the critic for the official *Moniteur Universel* flatly stated: "The Intransigents in art holding hands with the Intransigents in politics, nothing could be more natural."

At the same time that these critics were condemning the Impressionists as political Intransigents, Mallarmé was applauding them for the same reason. In the essay cited above, he forthrightly argued that Impressionist art was an expression of working-class—not bourgeois—vision, and a celebration of the newly emergent ideology of collectivism:

At a time when the romantic tradition of the first half of the century only lingers among a few surviving masters of that time, the transition from the old imaginative artist and dreamer to the energetic modern worker is found in Impressionism. The participation of a hitherto ignored people in the political life of France is a social fact that will honour the whole of the close of the nineteenth century. A parallel is found in artistic matters, the way being prepared by an evolution which the public with rare prescience dubbed, from its first appearance, *Intransigent*, which in political language means radical and democratic.

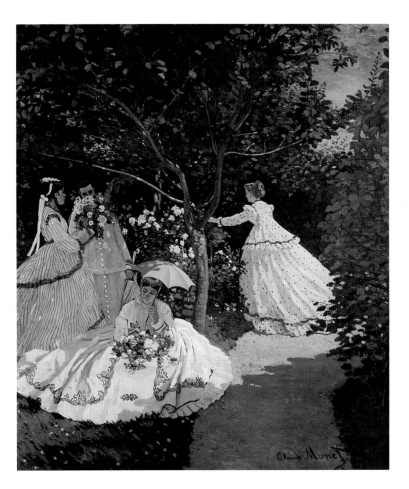

246 CLAUDE MONET *Women in the Garden* 1866–7. 8′4 × 81
(255 × 205)

247 BERTHE MORISOT *Laundresses Hanging Out the Wash*
1875. 13 × 16 (33 × 40.6)

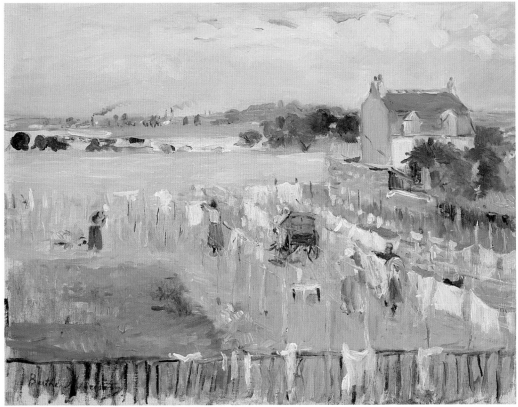

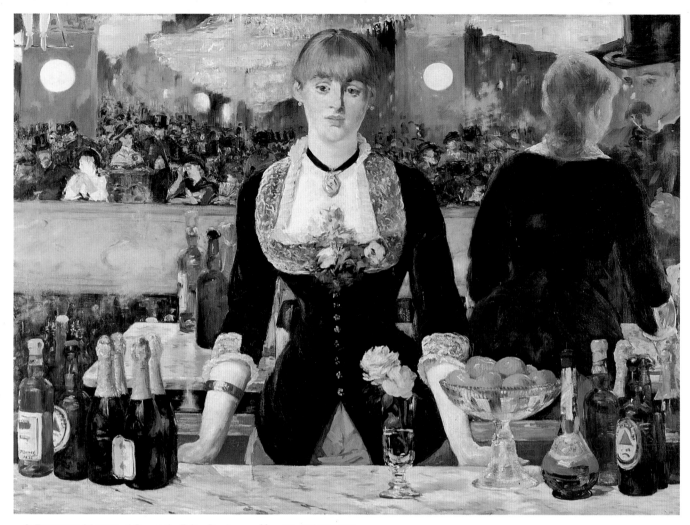

248 EDOUARD MANET *A Bar at the Folies-Bergère* ca. 1882. 37¾ × 51⅛ (96 × 130)

To Mallarmé, therefore, Impressionism marked a new stage in the social and cultural evolution of France; it was an art of "truth, simplicity and child-like charm," he wrote, which affirmed and paid homage to the mode of vision of a new and surging working-class "multitude [which] demands to see with its own eyes."

Two conflicting interpretations of Impressionism thus appear to be on offer: one situates the movement beside the other early manifestations—vaudeville shows, spectator sports, World's Fairs, and Sundays in the country—of the emergent culture of commodity capitalism; the other locates the movement within the radical confines of the avant-garde, accepting Mallarmé's contention that Impressionism—by rejecting Classical mimesis and Romantic fantasy—was the vision and voice of an increasingly self-conscious and confident proletariat. In fact, both interpretations have validity, because modern capital has consistently fed from the plate of the avant-garde. From its shaky origins in Haussman-

nized Paris, to its swaggering maturity today, mass (commodity) culture has learned about what desires it can exploit from observation of the ways in which avant-gardes and other subcultures devise strategies for self-fulfillment and individual expression. Impressionist leisure and vision—with its easefulness, unproductiveness, ephemerality, intangibility, luminosity, colorism, and overall opticality—was one such strategy for sensual emancipation and personal pleasure that could not be ignored. It was not, and a certain part of the world was eventually made over into its image.

As for the artists themselves, they resisted labels of all kinds; by the mid-1880's, the shifting alliance of men and women that first coalesced in 1874 had rejected the names Société Anonyme, Impressionist, Intransigent, and even Independent, preferring to designate the various group and solo exhibitions simply by the word "Exhibition." Indeed, the group's struggles over nomenclature signal the presence of a specifically modernist, formal strategy of evasiveness, displacement, effacement, and abstraction. In their art as well as their ideology, the Impressionists sought refuge on the margins or in the shadows: they cultivated the borderlands of city and country at Montmartre or Gennevilliers (where the solid waste of Paris was spread as manure), as in Morisot's 247 sketchy *Laundresses Hanging Out the Wash* (1875); they spied from balconies or crouched in woodland glades, as in Gustave 240 Caillebotte's (1848–94) *A Balcony, Boulevard Haussmann* (ca. 241 1880) and Pissarro's *Edge of the Woods or, Undergrowth in Summer* (1879); and they secreted themselves backstage at the ballet, or amid the crowd outside the Bourse, as in Degas's 244 (1834–1917) *The Dance School* (1873) and *Portraits at the* 242 *Stock Exchange* (ca. 1879).

In the latter two works, exhibited respectively at the third and fourth Impressionist Exhibitions in 1877 and 1879, Degas displayed his peculiar naturalist and conspiratorial penchants. The dancers are so many diverse examples of a single common species; they bend, stretch, gaze vacantly, scratch, bite thumbs, practise at the bar, and stand on toes. The alien character of Degas's dancers is perhaps even more apparent in the dozens of mostly small wax figures he made between 243 approximately 1870 and his death. His *Little Dancer Aged Fourteen* (ca. 1881), the only sculpture by him exhibited in his lifetime, was described by critics as a "monkey," and "a monster . . . [from] a museum of zoology." In *Portraits*, Degas has chosen to examine another modern institution—no less exotic and marked with *dégénérescence* than the world of the ballet—the Stock Exchange. "A few minutes before noon," writes Baedeker's (1882), "the Place de la Bourse begins to present a busy scene . . . [as] the money-seeking throng hurries into the building. . . . [Inside], amidst the Babel of tongues, are heard the constantly recurring words '*J'ai . . .* ; *qui-est qui a . . . ? je prends*; *je vends!*'" Standing on the threshold of the Bourse, the Jewish banker and art collector Ernest May is shown receiving a note from a man in front of him (actually only a detached hand and profile head), and a conspiratorial tap on the shoulder from a man behind (Nochlin has defined the gesture as "confidential touching"). In the wings at left are two more figures whose prominent noses and abbreviated brows connote—according to the physiognomic and psychological theories of the day—both degeneracy and Jewishness. (Indeed, in 1881 Degas depicted a similar pair of heads in pastel and called them *Criminal Physiognomies*.) In *Portraits at the Stock Exchange*, therefore, Degas has indulged that most pernicious and consequential of modern myths—announced by the "Young Hegelian" philosopher Bruno Bauer in 1843, reiterated by Marx, and espoused as gospel by a subsequent generation of anti-Semites that included the notorious Frenchman Edouard Drumont and Degas: "The Jew, who may be entirely without rights in the smallest . . . state, decides the destiny of Europe." "Anti-Semite" was in fact the only

label that Degas ever wholeheartedly embraced, but for him as for others it too functioned as a disguise, hiding class and gender antagonisms behind a false brotherhood built upon a common hatred.

Fortunately, Impressionist evasiveness and disguise were rarely so paranoid and humorless as they were with Degas. More often they involved mysterious masks at fancy-dress balls and preposterous boating clothes at the dockside as in Manet's *Masked Ball at the Opéra* and *Argenteuil* (1874); at other times, they took the form of bathing costumes worn by the petit bourgeois at La Grenouillère, a popular bathing spot on the Seine, near Bougival, painted in 1869 by Monet and Renoir, or else of garishly illumined evening clothes at *café-concerts* such as the Folies-Bergère, painted by Manet in his last major work, *A Bar at the Folies-Bergère*, shown at the 248 Salon of 1882. Indeed, *café-concerts*, which were popular hang-outs for Degas, Manet, and the young Georges Seurat, were devised precisely in order to accommodate disguise: "Here [at the café Eldorado] amid volumes of smoke," the guide-book author Galignani informed the tourist in 1862, "the blouse and the frock-coat are conspicuous, interspersed here and there with a muslin cap and merino gown, listening to the comic scenes, or snatches from favorite operas, retailed to the audience by the performers."

The *Bar* by Manet, with its recalcitrant mirror and equally refractory barmaid, reveals a complex understanding of class and gender that is also apparent in works by Berthe Morisot. In the *Bar*, as in Morisot's *The Psyché* (1876), a woman stands 249 before a mirror that fails accurately to reflect her. The barmaid who confronts the spectator is upright and poised whereas her mirror image is bent forward in unsavory conversation with the top-hatted customer at right. Moreover, the location of the barmaid and reflected dandy implies that the mirror is curved, whereas the reflections of the bottles and the marble-top bar suggest that it is flat or parallel to the picture surface. The result of this purposeful ambiguity (the painted study in Amsterdam has the reflection approximately right), and of Manet's studied indifference to face painting, is the creation of a peculiar tension—a sense of "detachment," as T. J. Clark writes—between the barmaid and her glittering modern ambience. Unlike Galignani's securely classed café patrons, she wears her costume and expression uneasily, and the (male) spectator responds with doubts about the stability of the game of class and gender which he plays.

In Morisot's painting, too, the empirical validity of "the mirror of painting," in Mallarmé's phrase, is challenged. The woman who stands bunching her loose peignoir before the psyché mirror, exposes a seductively supple shoulder, downcast eye, and pouty mouth, whereas the image in the mirror reveals no such conventional signs of *coquetterie* (save the Olympia-like neck ribbon). Instead of celebrating the mascu-

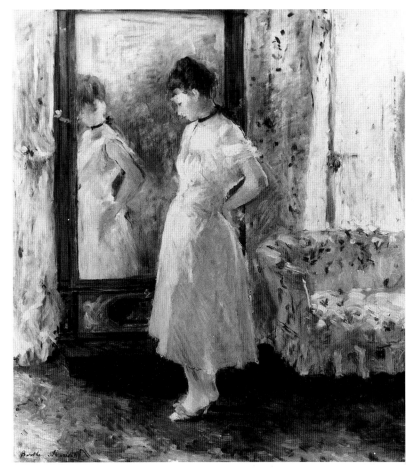

249 **BERTHE MORISOT** *The Psyché* 1876. 25¼ × 21¼ (64 × 54)

line prerogative to see and the feminine responsibility to be seen, therefore, Morisot's toilette paintings such as this one expose the artifice and irony of modern painting made by a woman. To paint a picture, Morisot seems to claim, is no more, but also no less, than artistically to adorn one's own body. In both *The Bar at the Folies-Bergère* and *The Psyché* the established circuits of sexual seeing and knowing—of temptation and desire—are crossed and produce a spark of insight. *Café-concert* and boudoir are thus alike in modern Paris; they are the places where class and gender—at once hidden and revealed by the fashionable dazzle of electric lights, trapeze, make-up, and lace—are made over into commodities to be bought and sold like so many bottles of beer or bolts of chiffon.

Impressionisme is a masculine noun, Larousse tells us, but in its intimacy with fashion and the commodity it was gendered feminine. Indeed, among the greatest practitioners of Impressionism, only Berthe Morisot and to a lesser extent Mary Cassatt managed to escape the withering criticisms flung at the movement. Praised for possessing charm, sensibility, grace, and delicacy, paintings by the two women were exempted from the usual charge against Impressionist works, that they were merely unfinished sketches. Impulsiveness, sensuousness, and lightness of touch were deemed essential to women's nature and therefore wholly appropriate in Impressionist works by women. Thus in addition to the marginality and elusiveness described above, a final transgressive feature of Impressionism must be noted: unlike contemporary Salon painting, it did not wholly reiterate the prevailing gender stereotypes about artmaking. Impressionisms's chief practitioners were either males who painted in a style judged appropriate only for women, or women who painted with the ambition and conviction which it was then thought could be found only among men. Cassatt, however, went still further: she actually painted the liberation of women, and in so doing helped turn American painting from a local into an international achievement.

· 12 ·

ISSUES OF GENDER IN CASSATT AND EAKINS

LINDA NOCHLIN

GENDER AND DIFFERENCE

THE TENSIONS, OPPOSITIONS, AND ACHIEVEMENTS of American painting of the late nineteenth century can best be approached through an examination of two of its major practitioners—Mary Cassatt and Thomas Eakins. A careful analysis of their work also reveals the difficulty of making clear-cut stylistic distinctions in high art based on either national origin or gender. Of course, until recently, the question of national origin—what is American about American art?—might have loomed much larger than that of gender. In recent years, on the contrary, the fact that Cassatt was a *woman* artist has been central to the more complex and problematic readings of her work by such revisionist art historians as Nancy Mowll Mathews and Griselda Pollock. Yet it seems to me that there is no better way of exploring the vexed issues of American-ness versus the cosmopolitanism represented by the French vanguard of the period or male versus female production than in exploring, in detail, the lives and works of these two artist-contemporaries, so alike in their ambitions and stature, so unlike in their choice of milieu and their pictorial language.

Mary Cassatt and Thomas Eakins had a good deal in common as far as biography goes. Both were born almost mid-century, in the year 1844; both were born in Pennsylvania; neither had to depend on painting to make a living; both studied at the Pennsylvania Academy of the Fine Arts and later in Europe, Eakins in France with Gérôme from 1866 to 1870, Cassatt traveling to Spain, like Eakins, and to Italy as well, yet basically French in her orientation, settling in Paris in 1866. Both were painters dedicated to the representation of the human figure, primarily the portrait. Yet there are extraordinary differences between them, too, differences inscribed in their work itself, as their self-portraits clearly

reveal (Cassatt's of 1878, Eakins' of 1902). Cassatt came from a much wealthier and more socially prominent family than Eakins; she learned in Paris not from the relatively conservative Gérôme but from the pictorial radicals Manet and Degas; she did not return to conservative Philadelphia to pass the rest of her life, as a loner, like Eakins, but stayed on in Paris where she actively participated in the most advanced painting movement of her time, Impressionism. Indeed, she was one of the most faithful participants in the Impressionist exhibitions, showing with the group in 1879, 1880, 1881, and 1886.

Equally important in establishing the difference between the two is the fact that Eakins was a man and Cassatt a woman. This gender difference seems to me of prime importance in the interpretation of the salient characteristics of their work. Gender difference, however, must not be interpreted as directly expressed in the work in terms of some formal structure or inevitable iconographic choice; nor should gender be understood in terms of essential, fixed, timeless, inborn qualities of masculinity or femininity. Rather, gender must be envisioned as a social construct, mediated by historical conditions and the specific practice of painting. It can only signify through the concrete qualities of pictorial language in specific situations. In other words, the readings must be at once incisive and subtle; forceful yet complex. Nor must the sex of the artist be seen as always and in every circumstance the determining factor. Both Eakins and Cassatt, for example, strikingly reject (whether completely consciously or not) the notion, taken for granted at the time, that the portrait of a woman, especially a commissioned portrait, must be flattering in order to be successful. Both artists seem resolutely to refuse to idealize or prettify their female sitters. In Cassatt's pastel portrait of her friend, the important art collector and suffragist, Louisine Elder Havemeyer (ca. 1896), the sitter is represented as uncompromisingly unglamorous and serious.

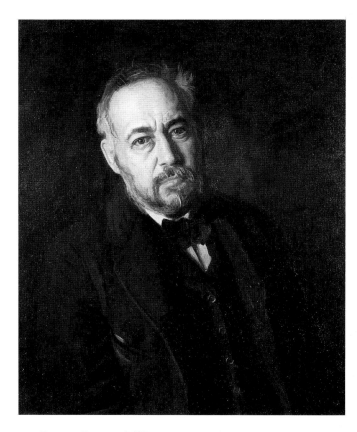

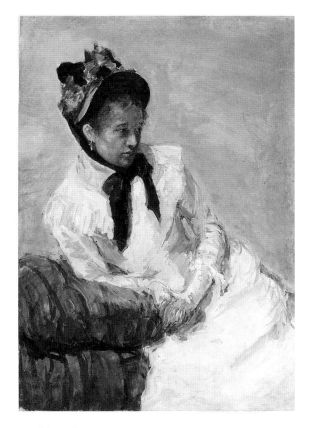

250 THOMAS EAKINS *Self-Portrait* 1902. 30 × 25 (76.2 × 63.5)

251 MARY CASSATT *Self-Portrait* 1878. 23½ × 17½ (59.6 × 44.4)

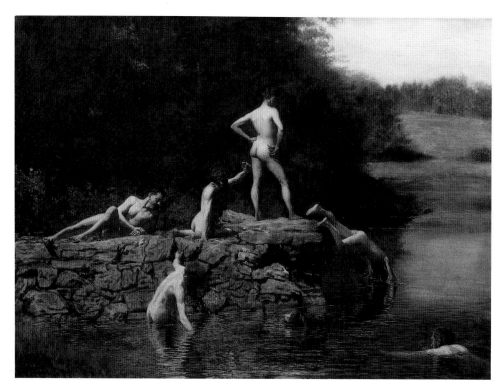

252 THOMAS EAKINS *The Swimming Hole* ca. 1883–5. 27 × 36 (68.5 × 91.4)

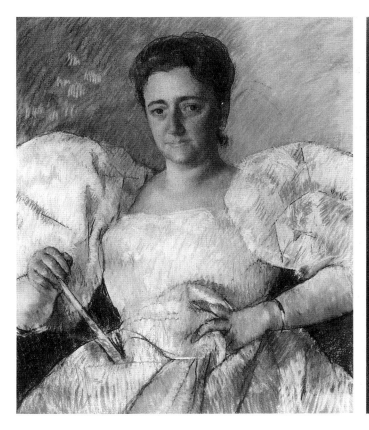

253 **MARY CASSATT** *Portrait of Louisine Elder Havemeyer* ca. 1896. 29 × 24 (73.6 × 61)

254 **THOMAS EAKINS** *Portrait of Mrs. Edith Mahon* 1904. 20 × 16 (50.8 × 40.6)

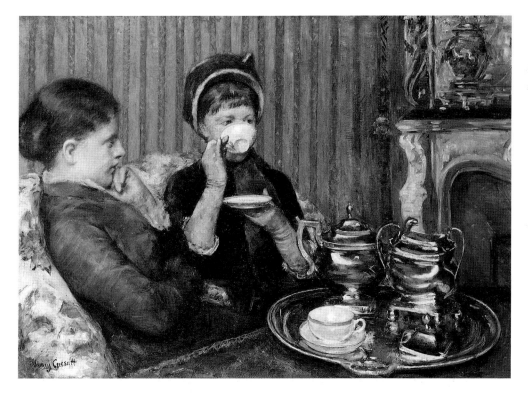

255 **MARY CASSATT** *Five O'Clock Tea* ca. 1880. 25½ × 36½ (64.7 × 92.7)

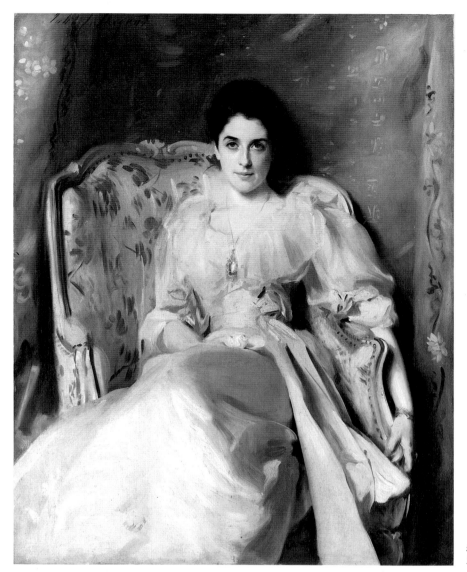

256 JOHN SINGER SARGENT *Lady Agnew of Lochnaw* ca. 1892–3. 49½ × 39½ (125.7 × 100.3)

Mrs. Havemeyer is middle-aged, dark, powerful. Despite the diaphanous white butterfly wings of her puffed-sleeved, low-necked dress, or perhaps in purposeful contrast with them, the somber, square-cut head with its deep-set eyes and irregular yet sensitive mouth conveys a sense of that forceful individual character usually reserved for the male sitter, rather than the conventional beauty and elegance considered appropriate to the upper-class female one; the same might be said, to a lesser degree, of the unbeautiful head, rather like that of a sympathetically introverted bull-dog, and lack of coquettish self-consciousness of the sitter in Eakins' *Portrait of Mrs. Edith Mahon* of 1904.

Yet the two artists seem to me more strikingly different than similar. Often, it is a difference created by the subjects male and female artists were encouraged, or permitted, to paint. Gender difference is easiest to discern when a simple opposition in iconography is involved: young men and boys swimming naked out of doors in Eakins' *Swimming Hole* (ca. 1883–5) versus ladies taking tea in an elegant parlor in Cassatt's *Five O'Clock Tea* (ca. 1880). But even where it is simply a question of quintessentially "male" versus "female" subject matter, the issue is complicated. Are Eakins' naked men versus Cassatt's tea-drinking ladies reducible to a mere question of gender, to what is permitted to or socially acceptable for the male artist versus the female one? Isn't the issue of class also implicated, or even the artist's relationship to the social order as a totality?

Eakins' *Swimming Hole* projects a heady sense of escape from social constraint through sheer bodily freedom. The youthful male nudes, including Eakins himself in the foreground, are represented modestly, from the back or with strategically bent leg, in the classical *Dying Gaul* posture, and evoke moral qualities of honesty and purity in the out-of-doors context. In other words, in the Eakins painting,

254

252

255

democratic freedom is signified by the youthful male American body in the American landscape: to be American is at once to be natural and to have a privileged relation to Nature. In Cassatt's *Five O'Clock Tea*, a more cosmopolitan sense of the operations of social convention is conveyed through the refinement and elegance of pose, setting, and accoutrements. Rejecting the timelessness of the nude, or more accurately, deprived of access to the representation of unclothed bodies, Cassatt deploys fashion to define a specific historical moment, a concrete social milieu within the supposed a-historicity of the female domestic realm. Fashion and objects also specify the social milieu: these are not "just folks", not "natural" country women but refined members of the upper class. The painting, featuring the artist's sister Lydia and a visitor, is set in Cassatt's tastefully decorated Parisian drawing-room, with a silver tea-set, an heirloom which had been made in 1813 for the artist's grandmother, Mary Stevenson, prominent in the foreground. Not freedom, but what the poet William Butler Yeats described as "the ceremony of innocence" is recorded here in all its significant detail. One might say that gender difference is always overlaid with and intersected by other kinds of difference as well in the paintings of these two American artists.

The complex nature of the differences between the work of Eakins and that of Cassatt becomes even more obvious when the subjects in question are extremely close or indeed almost identical, as they are in Eakins' *Max Schmitt in a Single Scull* of 1871 and Cassatt's *The Boating Party* of 1893–4—an oarsman in a boat on the water. Eakins, in this early painting, was constructing an image to represent the democratic hero, not just a hero of modern life but of *American* modern life, a theme he was to pursue throughout much of his career. Schmitt was a friend of Eakins and a prominent oarsman, at a time when rowing was becoming increasingly popular in both the United States and France. The painting, one of nineteen by the artist representing the sport of rowing, celebrates a champion. Yet at the same time that it is a portrait of an amateur hero of sport, it may also be said metaphorically to celebrate Eakins' recent return from France to his native turf, specifically the Schuylkill River and the banks of Fairmont Park. Schmitt had just won an important and well-attended race of single sculls, so the portrait commemorates a specific victory, but in the larger sense it also celebrates the moral and physical virtues of rowing—above all, single-scull rowing— as a demanding sport which provided a much-needed respite from the crowds and urban confusion then seen to threaten the American citizen. The social historian Jackson Lears has pointed out the prominent position occupied by sport in the putative redemption of the decadent American male psyche in late nineteenth-century medical and social discourse: "To a bourgeoisie feeling enervated and fearful of lower-class

unrest, the worship of force presented paths to class revitalization . . . the mania for sport reinforced bourgeois values of discipline and productivity . . . Outdoor exercise seemed the perfect antidote to 'morbid self-consciousness' and excessive mental work."

Cassatt, on the other hand, cannot be said to celebrate the heroic virtues of sport, much less its prophylactic qualities, in her painting: on the contrary, her oarsman is hired help, distinguished as a member of the working classes by his sash and beret. Although the oarsman is prominent in the foreground of the painting, the figure is certainly not meant as a portrait: one can only glimpse his face in *profil perdu*. Rather, this rower's effort is constructed as part of a scene of leisure, of which the "real" subjects are the charming and fashionably dressed mother and child in the front of the boat. Yet even these differences in intention and iconography cannot account for the striking dissimilarity in total effect created by these works, a dissimilarity in which the construction of gender may play only a partial role.

For Eakins, a more traditional painter, the canvas functions

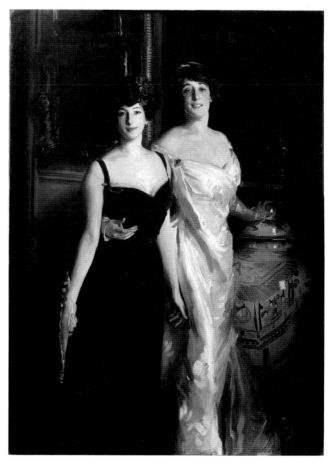

257 JOHN SINGER SARGENT *Ena and Betty, Daughters of Mrs. and Mrs. Asher Wertheimer* 1901. 73 × 51½ (185.4 × 130.8)

as a transparent window through which we see a vividly reconstituted three-dimensional space, with a vanishing point drawing our eye to the horizon. Near, middle, and distant space are constructed within this illusory world: brushstrokes are rendered modestly invisible in their task of conveying the glassy surface of the water, the fuzzy texture of autumnal trees, the fluffiness of clouds, the diaphanousness of air, the solid flesh and blood of the portrait subject himself, isolated in the fictive solitude at the center of the painting. We, the viewers, are positioned at a seemly distance from the subject; we move into the pictorial world over a period of time.

Cassatt's work, on the contrary, taking its cue from Manet's *Boating* of 1874, erases space and eradicates the temporal factor suggested by Eakins'. Cassatt erases as well the meaningful, narrative implications of spatial depth and temporal endurance produced by shadow, modeling, and linear and aerial perspective, in favor of surface, immediacy, and focus on the formal means of construction. Boat and figures are tilted up onto the surface of the canvas: Manet and Japanese prints rather than nature rendered through traditional perspective lie behind this construction; the horizon is almost, but not quite, obliterated in the interest of destroying depth. Shapes, forms, and color-areas are boldly reiterated as focal factors: the cut-off sail is related both to the triangular shape of the boat's bow and the woman's hat; the lines of the thwarts reiterate horizontally the diagonal of the oar; the varying blue shapes of the oarsman's suit, his sash, the bottom of the boat and the flat, textured surface of the water create interrelated flat patterns. Cassatt, as opposed to Eakins, is resolutely antidepth, whether we take this word literally or metaphorically, and thus her project must be related to that of the French avant-garde of her time in a way that Eakins' most definitely cannot.

THE PORTRAIT

Before turning to a detailed analysis of Eakins and Cassatt as portrait painters, a few words are in order about the portrait in general and the portrait in the nineteenth century specifically. The Western tradition of the portrait, which reached its full development with the stress on individualism initiated by the Renaissance, obviously tells us as much about the artist—the period when, the place where he or she is working, the patron who commissioned the image or the free choice of subject—as it does about the sitter represented.

By the late nineteenth century, the portrait genre could also establish the social class of the sitter, as it does most preeminently in two works by Sargent and Van Gogh 256 respectively, *Lady Agnew of Lochnaw* (ca. 1892–3) and *La* 295 *Berceuse (La Mère Roulin)* (1889). Aside from fulfilling the

obligation to body forth their respective artists' stylistic identities, these portraits also constitute iconic models for identifying "the aristocrat" versus the "working-class" woman.

Did the American-born cosmopolite John Singer Sargent (1865–1925) accept commissions to paint only lovely women? Or was the veil of glamor he cast over his female subjects merely an essential element of the *imaginaire* of upper-class appearance of his time, an element contravened, it must be added, by the portraiture of both Eakins and Cassatt? In portraits of American aristocrats, like *Mr. and Mrs. I. N. Phelps Stokes* (1897), Sargent skillfully established a new iconography of elongated, fine-limbed, casually superior beauties, ancestors of those young women whose sheer physical confidence, not to speak of social self-assurance, were to give girls from Brooklyn like me an inferiority complex at Vassar half a century later. That there are no ugly members of the upper classes is the lesson these suavely painted portraits teach, although admittedly, the artist seems to have had to work harder deploying what Henry James referred to as his "pure tact of vision" when the subjects were even slightly marginal—Jewish, for example—like *Ena and Betty,* 257 *Daughters of Mr. and Mrs. Asher Wertheimer* (1901). Here, the smallest hint of a thick waist, a short neck is raised but quickly obliterated by dazzling brushwork and overpowering elegance of setting and costume. But of course, these people are merely rich, not born aristocrats.

Sargent stirred up a rich pictorial brew, concocted from ingredients drawn from the European tradition of aristocratic and high bourgeois portraiture of the seventeenth and eighteenth centuries—Velázquez, Van Dyck, and Hals—and spiced with more up-to-date precedents, like those offered by his teacher, the fashionable French portraitist Carolus-Duran, as well as, more discreetly deployed, those of Manet and Monet. Clearly, he was offering the wealthy clients who commissioned his portraits up-to-date esthetic value for their money as well as a mere likeness. In the exemplary case of *Lady Agnew*, the physicality of the body of the sitter is almost denied, dissolved by pale, diaphanous or silky fabrics. The delicate amethyst of the huge but simple jewel about Lady Agnew's throat is repeated in the mauve-violet sash about her waist and the bows on her sleeves; this pale simplicity is enlivened by the printed silk fabric of the chair she sits in as well as the exotic pale blue Chinese hanging which marks the back plane of the portrait, adding a touch of esthetic refinement to the scene.

The sitter's class position is signified through the sheer physical grace of her being as well as by dress and decor: her impossibly slender waist, her lovely dark eyes set beneath perfectly modeled dark brows, her delicate features haloed by a cloud of tastefully coiffed dark hair. The frankness of her

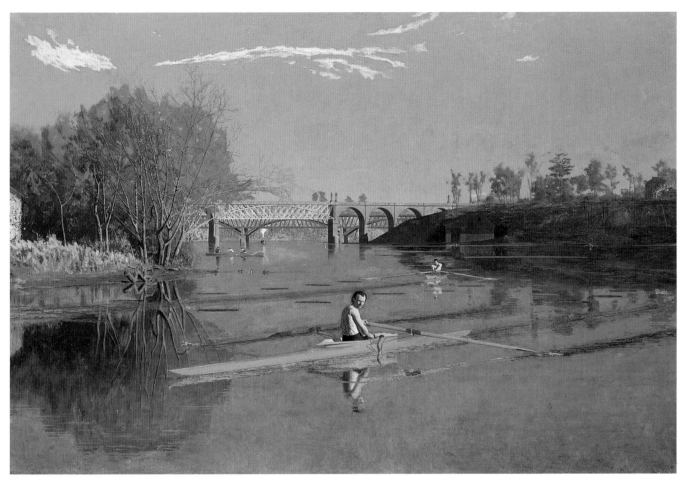

258 THOMAS EAKINS *Max Schmitt in a Single Scull* 1871. $32\frac{1}{4} \times 46\frac{1}{4}$ (81.9 × 117.5)

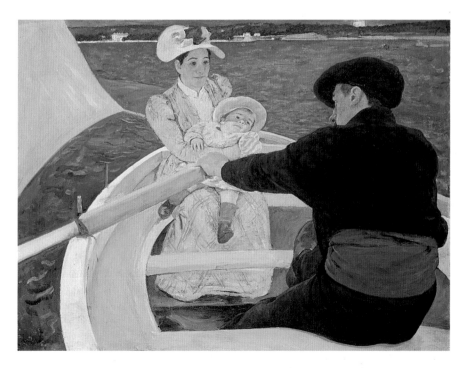

259 MARY CASSATT *The Boating Party* 1893–4. $35\frac{1}{2} \times 46\frac{1}{8}$ (90.1 × 117.1)

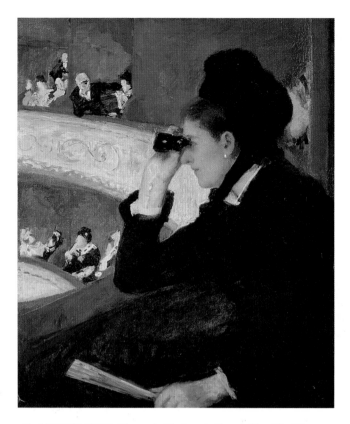

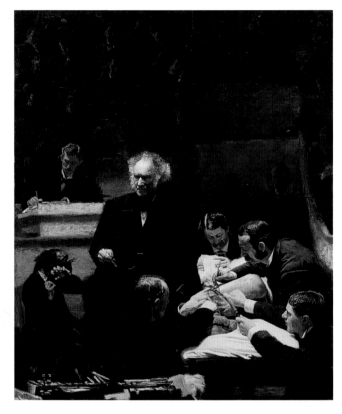

260 MARY CASSATT *Woman in Black at the Opera* 1880. 31½ × 25¼ (80 × 64.8)

261 THOMAS EAKINS *The Gross Clinic* 1875. 96 × 78 (243.8 × 198.1)

glance reveals—nothing. The well-brought up woman gives nothing away. Her pose is at once dignified yet relaxed, the *désinvolture* of her posture emphasized by her asymmetric placing on the chair, an asymmetry which nevertheless does nothing to lessen her casual dominance of the pictorial space. All of this bespeaks wealth and breeding, a classy portrait of a high-class woman: the portrait of a lady, in short.

Van Gogh, on the contrary, establishes the working-class credentials of La Mère Roulin by emphasizing the proletarian maternal stockiness of her body, the angularity and awkwardness of both her pose and his draftsmanship, the crude, burning oppositions of the color relationships and the honest expressive directness of the material application of the paint itself. *La Berceuse* is indeed one of the artist's group of works in which he explores the relatively novel notion that the lower classes were as much entitled to the commemorative homage of portraiture as their "betters." Following the precedent established by English graphic artists of the time, he announced his intention to create "portraits of the People," uncommissioned images which, in his view, engaged that specificity of individual appearance and character, as well as that aura of spiritual dignity, up to this time deemed a specifically middle- and upper-class privilege.

As early as the first decade of the nineteenth century, the inspired and inventive French portraitist Ingres had constructed pictorial configurations to establish gender difference as an easily readable variable: in the case of the portraits of a husband and wife like the Rivière couple (*M. Rivière* and *Mme. Rivière*, both 1807), by means of relatively subtle but telling differences in pose, relation to space, drawing style, and elaboration of decorative texture.

Eakins too, in his portraits, established subtle yet powerful signifiers of difference for the representation of male and female sitters (*Miss Van Buren*, 1891, and *Portrait of Professor Rand*, 1874). Miss Van Buren is a being wrapped in her own thoughts, a representative of the inner world rather than the outer one of practical intellect represented by the professor. She muses or meditates, without specific focus, diffusely, resting her head on her hands, her posture slightly off balance; he, on the contrary, thinks, his attention studiously concentrated. Professor Rand, a physician, had been Eakins' chemistry and physics teacher in high school and later joined Dr. Gross at Jefferson Medical College in Philadelphia. His character is defined by his intellectual and worldly achievement. The painting crackles with energy, as though charged with the intellectual concentration of its subject. Details like

264→

the microscope and the test-tubes establish Dr. Rand's professional credentials: this is a *portrait à l'apparat*. His studiousness and concentration are attested by his glasses, slightly wrinkled forehead, and his forefinger pressing down the pages of the book he reads with such relentless single-mindedness, and by the firmness of his grasp on the cat (pet or object of scientific observation? we are unsure just which) on the table before him.

If, to paraphrase the title of the art historian Elizabeth Johns' study of Eakins, the artist's male sitters are indeed in some sense "heroes of modern life," conceived of as active contributors—professionals, artists, religious dignitaries—to the welfare of democracy and humanity, then his women subjects, like those represented in *The Coral Necklace, The Old Fashioned Dress (Portrait of Helen Parker)* (ca. 1908) or

254   *Mrs. Edith Mahon* (1904), act as a kind of counterweight, a contrary and supplementary force. On them is laid the burden of inwardness, of diffuse if subtle emotionality, of passive acceptance of or resistance to life and its depredations. A common inner anxiety, an air of longsuffering-ness—of martyrdom, even—a veiled appeal tinged with self-withdrawal seems to characterize all of Eakins' female sitters. The same half-conscious awareness of time and its depredations—the past for the mature, the future for the women sitters—scars them all, holds them in wistful yet uneasy bondage.

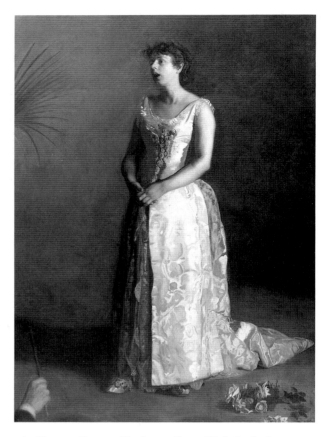

262   THOMAS EAKINS   *The Concert Singer (Weda Cook)* 1892. $75\frac{3}{8} \times 54\frac{3}{8}$ (191.4 × 138.1)

CASSATT AND THE GAZE

263   AUGUSTE RENOIR   *The Loge* 1874. $31\frac{1}{2} \times 25\frac{1}{8}$ (80 × 64)

Nothing would seem more different in pose, glance, and the
264   spatial setting associated with refined femininity in Eakins'
Miss Van Buren than the image created by Cassatt in her 1880
260   portrait of a young woman at the opera (*Woman in Black at the Opera*). Cassatt's woman is all active, aggressive looking. At a time when women were rarely understood to possess what recent psychoanalytic theory has denominated as "the power of the gaze," Cassatt has given it forcefully and completely to her opera-goer. She holds the opera-glasses, that prototypical instrument of male specular power, firmly to her eyes; even her fan is somewhat raised in the tense excitement of her active looking (as opposed to the relaxed horizontal position of the fan locking Eakins' *Miss Van Buren* into the enclosure created by the arms of her overpowering chair). Energy, control, the vividness of active looking, even the suggestion of veins standing out beneath the glove on the wrist of the hand which grasps the opera-glasses; all this and the forcefulness of the dark silhouette against the light of the house behind: one can see this portrait in some way functioning as a self-image of the modern woman artist herself.

This is not to say that Eakins never represented what one

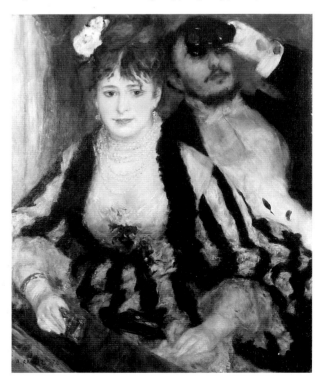

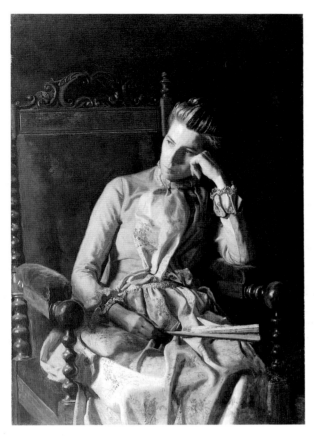

264 THOMAS EAKINS *Miss Van Buren* 1891. 45 × 32 (114.3 × 81.2)

265 THOMAS EAKINS *Portrait of Benjamin Howard Professor Rand* 1874. 60 × 48 (152.4 × 121.9)

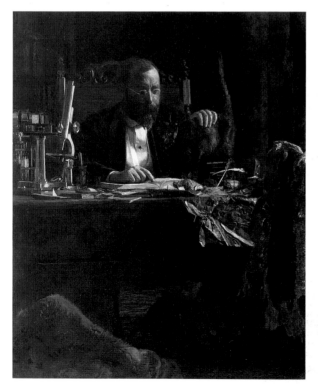

might call "heroines of modern life." He did paint portraits of women singers, most notably in *The Concert Singer (Weda Cook)* (1892). But although Cook is shown actively perform- 262 ing, on the stage, she is in some sense figured as less active, less self-propelled than Cassatt's *spectator* of the performance in *Woman in Black at the Opera*. As Johns has pointed out, the pose of the singer is a relatively pliant, wavering one rather than a posture of easy command. She seems to have surrendered her separateness to the spell of what she is doing. To put it another way, Eakins interprets the female singer as the instrument of the music that flows forth from her rather than as a creator in her own right. Indeed, this notion of instrumentality is carried further by the presence of the male hand to the lower left, meant as a synecdochal reference to the otherwise invisible orchestra leader. Yet the hand can also be read as a sign of masculine control and dominance; it is, in fact, the hand of Weda Cook's teacher, Dr. Schmitz: his almost unseen masculine presence figures as the active, generating force of the artistic creativity bodied forth in the painting.

Cassatt's painting stands out as something of an anomaly even within the context of (male) Impressionist painting itself. Renoir's vision of a lovely young woman at the opera in *The* 263 *Loge* (1874) positions her clearly as the object of the masculine viewer's gaze, both within the paintings and outside it; it is the male companion who has the privilege of wielding the opera- glasses. In the same artist's *First Evening* (1876), similar to Cassatt's painting in its profile representation of a young woman at the opera, the subject is depicted as though relegated by youthful shyness to a sheltered position in relation to the viewing audience, rather than pressing tensely forward to satisfy her own visual concerns. Cassatt, in fact, emphasizes the novelty of her construction of the feminine subject here by including in her painting the conventional male viewer watching the young woman; but he has no effect on her independence or self-motivation.

EAKINS AND THE AMERICAN HERO

Eakins, on the contrary, in his major portrait of a hero of modern life, *The Gross Clinic* (1875), positions the one woman 261 in the composition as the one—the only one—who *cannot* look, who *will* not look. As the mother of the young victim undergoing the operation, she functions both as the repository of feeling and as the signifier of a momentary, irrational reaction to the event: the figure whose loss of control, as she is hysterically swept away by emotion, is opposed to the reasoned, longterm attention to ends and means embodied in the sober and restrained male medical personnel and audience, all of whom have their eyes fixed dispassionately on the business at hand.

In this, possibly his greatest portrait, specifically a group portrait, and certainly his most ambitious attempt to depict the heroic quality of American professional achievement, Eakins obviously turned to the precedent established by Rembrandt in his famous portrait of a professional group, the *Anatomy Lesson of Dr. Tulp* (1632). But aside from the fact that Eakins is representing a more philanthropic and practical activity in line with nineteenth-century American standards of heroism—a life-saving operation on a living person rather than an anatomical demonstration carried out on a corpse—he has changed the format of his illustrious prototype from horizontal to vertical, thereby changing the focus from concentration on the group of observers and the corpse to the isolated, light-revealed hero, Dr. Samuel D. Gross, who is represented performing an operation—the removal of a piece of dead bone from the thigh of a child—in the cavernous amphitheater of Jefferson Medical College in Philadelphia. The scene is an extremely dramatic one, perhaps even melodramatic, and its intensity is highlighted by Eakins' skillful manipulation of his pictorial means—light, space, color, brushwork—to focus on the meaning of the action and its moral overtones. The dominating figure is of course the good doctor who turns from his work to explain some detail of his procedure to an audience of future physicians and surgeons: heroes of modern life in the making, as it were, and the frightening, even the morbid aspects of this challenging feat are directly conveyed not so much by narrative description as by color—the all-over presence of the color red, suggesting blood, token of mortality as well as the life-force at stake. Johns has pointed out that the underpainting is red, there is red in the doorway and in the depth of the

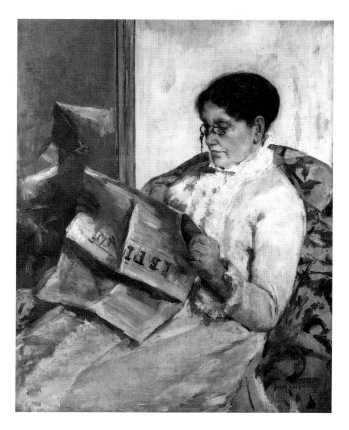

amphitheater as well as the blood-stained dressings on the left of the tables; more red in the sawdust box and red in the pen of Franklin West on the left, in Eakins' own pen on the right, and again on the shirt cuffs of the assisting surgeons and on Gross's coat, in the patient's incision, and, as a kind of climax, on Gross's hand and scalpel. As in portraits and self-portraits of artists (to which this may in some sense refer), the paint, as

266 MARY CASSATT *Reading Le Figaro* 1883. 41 × 33 (104 × 83.7)

267 MARY CASSATT *Lydia Working at a Tapestry Frame* ca. 1881. 25⅞ × 36¼ (65.5 × 92)

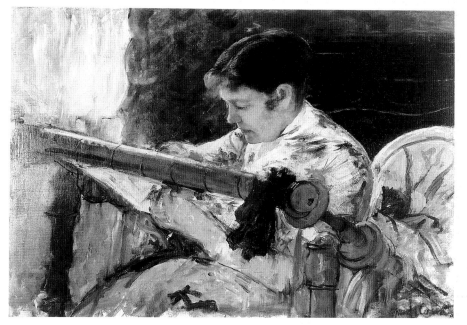

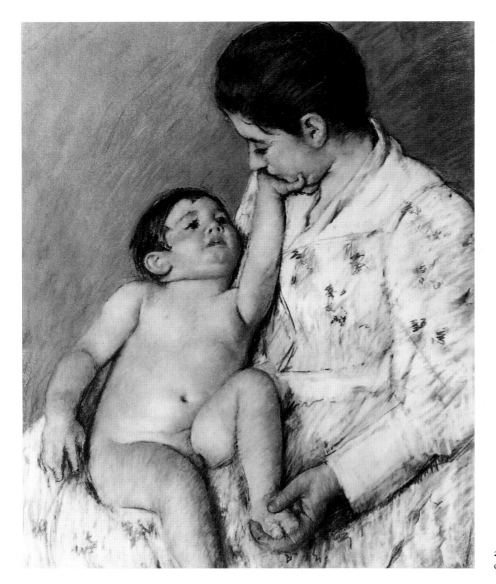

268 MARY CASSATT *The First Caress*
ca. 1890. 30 × 24 (76.2 × 61)

the art historian Michael Fried has shown, is densest and most vivid here, at the site of the working hands of the protagonist.

WOMEN AND CHILDREN

For Cassatt, this world of public performance and professional achievement—the male-coded "heroism" of modern life—did not exist as a subject for painting. Her world was the world of women and their children, a world of cultivated, well-bred, upper-class family members, friends, and acquaintances—a world private and intimate in its relationships rather than public and heroic. Yet bound by convention and restriction though this world may have been, there is nothing conventional or restricted about her conception of it, or the formal means she uses to embody it. Cassatt's formal language is at once forceful and sophisticated, whether she is portraying her sister or her mother absorbed in reading or a family friend presiding over one of the rituals of genteel sociability.

Her mother in the dignified, concentrated pose of the thinker (*Reading Le Figaro*, 1883) or Mrs. Riddle at her tea 266 table (*Lady at her Tea Table (Mrs. Robert Riddle)*, 1883–5)— both of these older women of considerable presence and dignity—are neither overwhelmed nor oppressed by the passage of time or the ominous shadows of interior space, but are constructed as firmly in control and at ease in their social and pictorial settings. Her sister Lydia is shown calmly absorbed in her tapestry work, or crocheting in the garden (*Lydia Working at a Tapestry Frame*, ca. 1881, and *Lydia* 267 *Crocheting in the Garden at Marly*, 1880).

Yet from the 1880's on, Cassatt did focus on a theme which might be considered the female equivalent of the notion of modern heroism—modern motherhood. In a series of works in oil, pastel, and print, she invented and constructed a gendered alternative for the masculine hero—the female nurturer and her offspring. Two relatively early representations of the motherhood theme, *Emmie and her Child* (1889) and *The First Caress* (ca. 1890), reveal Cassatt's Impressionist ability to capture the momentary, the intimate, and the playful; her gift of observation and for creating fresh pictorial equivalents for what she has observed are striking. Later examples from the beginning of the twentieth century (like *The Caress*, 1902, and *Mother and Child*, 1908) are more formal, more highly finished, with perhaps certain Symbolist overtones and muted references to the art of the Italian Renaissance which she had admired earlier in her career. In Cassatt's passionate devotion to the nude, childish body, one senses the presence of desire, but a different desire. One might almost speak of Cassatt's lust for baby flesh, for the touch, smell, and feel of plump, naked smooth-skinned bodies, kept carefully in control by both formal strategies and a certain emotional diffidence, in rare cases—the less successful ones— displaced and oversweetened as sentimentality. The psychoanalytic terms "displacement," "repression," and "sublimation" inevitably creep into the discourse when the subject of sexuality is broached in relation to the works of both Cassatt and Eakins. Yet we must be wary of anachronistic readings of the mobility of desire and its objects. For the nineteenth century, the naked bodies of children were often envisioned as simultaneously pure and desirable, as exemplified in the seductively nude or nearly nude photographs of little girls by the English Reverend Dodgson, otherwise known as Lewis Carroll. Although it is tempting to see Cassatt's lusciously nude babies as examples of Freudian "displacement"—to assert that in the absence, in the representational codes of the time, of socially acceptable mature objects of female desire she simply displaced that desire onto immature ones—this may not be the case at all. Desire takes many different forms at different historical moments and in different situations and we decide what is "normal," what "displaced" or "repressed" at our peril. What Eakins and his contemporaries might have envisioned simply as healthy male bonding in the out-of-doors, in his various representations of naked men, boys, and adolescents, may well be read as homosocial or even repressed homosexual desire today. A troubling female sexuality seems closer to the surface in some of Eakins' proto-Balthusian representations of pubescent or pre-pubescent girls like *Home Scene* of 1871 (surely based on Courbet's renditions of the daughters of P.-J. Proudhon in his portrait of the anarchist philosopher of 1865) or his *Girl With Cat* (1872), where the young woman, drenched in shadow, is teasing the animal crouched in her outspread lap, her burgeoning sexuality reiterated by the suggestive shape of the open fan in her hand.

Perhaps nowhere is the theme of mother and child treated

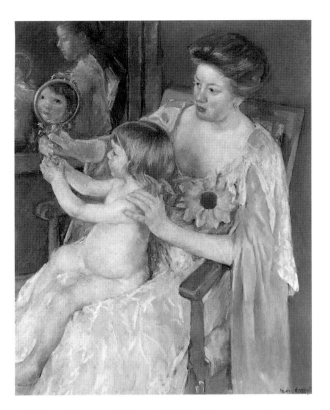

269 MARY CASSATT *Mother and Child* 1908. 36¼ × 29 (92.1 × 73.7)

270 THOMAS EAKINS *Girl With Cat* 1872. 62¾ × 48¼ (159.4 × 122.6)

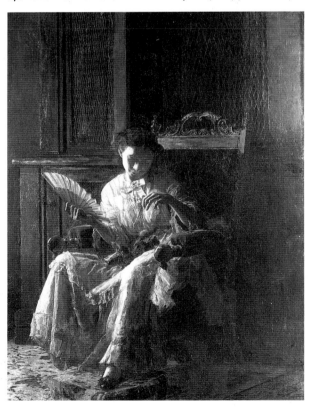

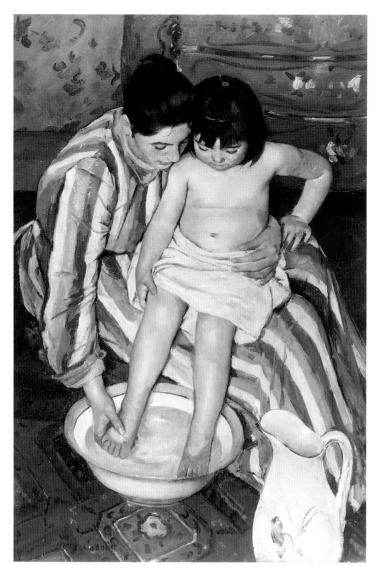

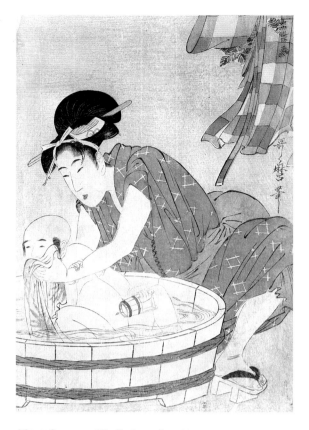

271 MARY CASSATT *The Bath* ca. 1892. 39 × 26 (99 × 66)

272 KITAGAWA UTAMARO *A Mother Bathing Her Son*
Edo period, eighteenth century. 14¾ × 9⅞ (37.5 × 25)

with more formal boldness, more emotional restraint than in Cassatt's representations of mothers bathing their children, like two works titled *The Bath* (a print of 1891 and an oil of ca. 1892). One has only to think of all the adult female *Bathers* of the period, from Courbet through Degas and Cézanne, to see how Cassatt makes this theme particularly her own. Any of the sentimental clichés natural to this theme, and not always completely expunged from it by Cassatt herself, are canceled in these cases by the lessons of the Japanese Ukiyoe, like Utamaro's *A Mother Bathing Her Son* (eighteenth century), and Cassatt's respect for the formal demands of the surface— carefully deployed in pattern, texture, and color—which moves our eye up and across the canvas rather than into it, or, in the case of the print, the demands of the technically difficult drypoint and aquatint medium.

Indeed, one might say that Cassatt's masterpiece was the series of color prints she executed in etching, drypoint, and aquatint in the beginning of the '90's, at the height of her career (*Maternal Caress,* ca. 1891, and *The Mother's Kiss,* 1891). These prints encapsulate the undramatic events constituting the daily life of the upper-class woman, the woman of refinement and leisure. They include: playing with the baby; the private preparations of the body or clothing; letter-writing; visiting; and riding on the omnibus. In the latter cases, despite the fact that the subject demands venturing into the outside world of a great city, the female subject is always represented existing within a protected and enclosed—even encapsulated—world. The closed, protected world of genteel womanhood is daringly filtered through the stylized and elliptical rendering of reality characteristic of the Japanese print, whose lessons her friends and fellow Impressionists Degas and Pissarro were also taking seriously at the same time; the artists often shared ideas, technical data, and criticism (*The Coiffure,* 1891, and *The Fitting,* 1891). Cassatt transposes the Ukiyoe idiom into her own modern and Western terms, terms in which feminine experience functions as a complete language system, with its own tropes and inventions. Here Cassatt completely erases the meaningful narrative implications of temporality, traditionally produced by shadow, modeling or deep space, signifiers of the unfolding of time in painting, in favor of surface, presentness, and antinarrative surface in a series of subjects, which, because of their very unimportance, their antiheroic qualities, lend themselves perfectly to the idiom of modernism (*The Letter,* 1891, and *The Lamp,* 1891). The transformation of intimate spaces into formal elegance by means of bold reduction and sophisticated patterning is one of Cassatt's many achievements in these works, like *Afternoon Tea Party* (1891) or *The Omnibus* (1891). Worldly sociability, the tête-à-tête of two fashionably dressed ladies, can serve as the basis of a print of great coloristic and compositional subtlety, playing the black of the visitor's jacket against the white of the hostess's gown, which is, of course, created by the white of the paper itself. In *The Omnibus,* a trip into the world is represented as so protected that the public vehicle, whose open windows

provide an admirable formal scaffolding for the composition, is figured like a traveling parlor for elegant mother, baby, and nursemaid, and the city of Paris itself, locus of so much Impressionist attention, functions as a mere backdrop for the domesticated interior.

CASSATT, EAKINS, AND THE MODERN ALLEGORY

Like Eakins, Cassatt also created an allegorical painting, and, like his, it is an allegory referring to their trade, or craft, or calling—the creation of art. Eakins' *William Rush Carving His Allegorical Figure of the Schuylkill River* (1877) is an allegory of the past, commemorating a sculptural commission completed in 1809 for the city of Philadelphia. The painting evokes the history and the deeper meaning of artistic creation by means of its shadowy spatial setting with a glinting light which sets the artist himself in vague and enveloping darkness, transforming him into a mere metaphor of the artist in general, and setting his source of inspiration in relative

273 MARY CASSATT *The Mother's Kiss* (5th state) 1891. 17⅛ × 11⅞ (43.5 × 30)

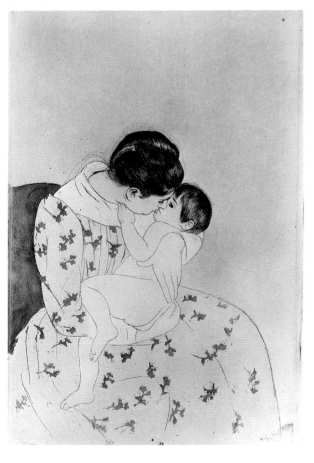

274 MARY CASSATT *The Coiffure* (5th state) 1891. 19 × 12⅛ (48 × 30.9)

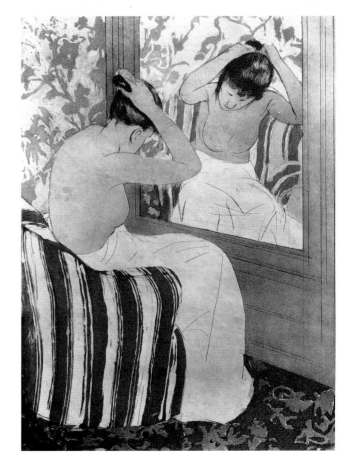

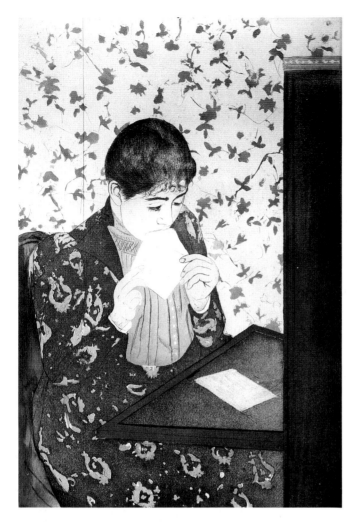

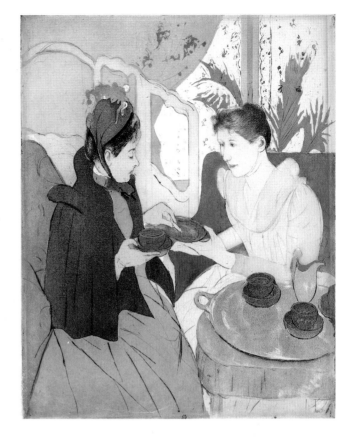

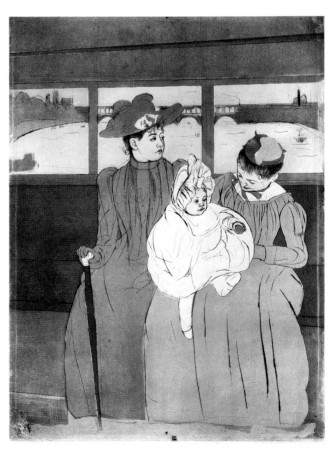

275 MARY CASSATT *The Letter* (3rd state) 1891. 13¾ × 9 (34.7 × 22.8)

276 MARY CASSATT *Afternoon Tea Party* (4th state) 1891. 16¼ × 12¼ (42.5 × 31.1)

277 MARY CASSATT *The Omnibus* (4th state) 1891. 18 × 12⅜ (45.7 × 31.4)

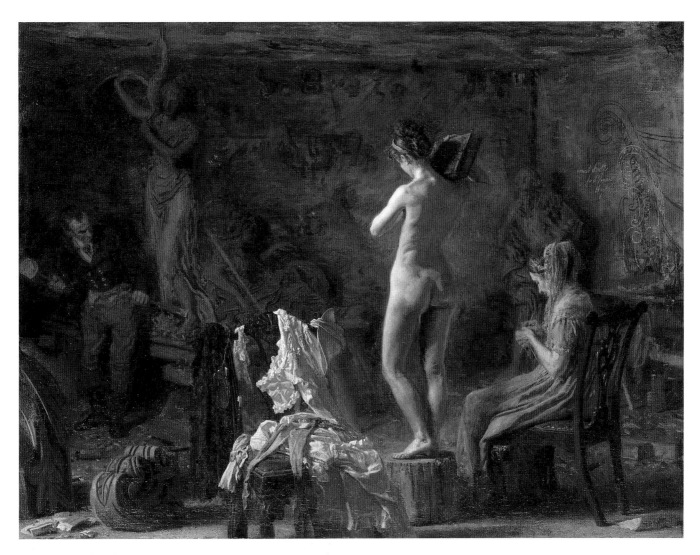

278 **THOMAS EAKINS** *William Rush Carving His Allegorical Figure of the Schuylkill River* 1877. 20⅛ × 26⅛ (51.1 × 66.3)

brightness. Color is muted, surface dissolved into suggestive adumbration. Cassatt's, on the contrary, is an allegory of the present and future. Prepared for the North tympanum of the Woman's Building at the World's Columbian Exposition of 1893 in Chicago, Cassatt's mural (later lost or destroyed) was entitled *Modern Woman*. Cassatt became involved in this monumental project through the intermediary of Bertha Potter Palmer, a prominent suffragist and member of high society in Chicago who was President of the Board of Lady Managers for the Woman's Building. Mrs. Palmer met Cassatt in Paris in 1892, admired her work, and commissioned her to do one of the two murals for the Hall of Honor (the other, more traditional, theme of "Primitive Woman" being allotted to the more academic Mary Fairchild MacMonies). For the large-scale canvas, which measured about 12 feet by 58 feet, Cassatt had a glass-roofed studio constructed at her summer house in Bachivilliers; as Monet had done for his

earlier *Women in the Garden*, she had a trench dug in the studio so that she could raise and lower the canvas as she needed to. By so doing, she secured the advantages of *plein-air* painting and those of monumentality at the same time.

The central panel represented a scene of young women 279 picking fruit, allegorizing the notion of "Young Women Plucking the Fruits of Knowledge and Science" in an Eden-like garden; to the left, in *Young Women Pursuing Fame*, young women were represented allegorically—and rather humor-ously—running after what looks like a kite but is actually a little winged figure, with geese at their heels. To the right, *Arts, Music, Dancing* are represented by young women engaged in these activities. Although the originals have been lost, a sketch provides some notion of the brilliance of the color in the final version. It is clear from examining related works of the period (*Baby Reaching for an Apple*, 1893) that Cassatt conceived *Modern Woman* boldly, as a large-scale decorative project. It is equally clear from textual evidence of approximately the same time that she intended to demonstrate that in *her* garden the picking of the fruit of knowledge by women was *not* a condemned activity: on the contrary, it was to be strongly encouraged. The promoters of the Woman's Building had stated their purpose as follows: "We [women] have eaten of the Tree of Knowledge and the Eden of Idleness is hateful to us. We claim our inheritance, and are become workers not cumberers of the earth." Nevertheless, Cassatt refuses to make her allegory grim, moralistic or formally old-fashioned: on the contrary, her style is that of the vanguard of the day, Postimpressionist or Symbolist. She was fully aware of the modernity and innovativeness of her project and emphasized the seriousness of her commitment to its formal aspects. At the same time, she wrote to Mrs. Palmer of her work-in-progress as follows, using words and phrases that stress her belief in a new, strong role for women:

> I have tried to express the modern woman in the fashions of the day, and I have tried to represent those fashions as accurately and in as much detail as possible. I took for the subject of the centre and largest composition Young Women Plucking the Fruits of Knowledge and Science ... An American friend asked me in rather a huffy tone the other day "Then this is woman apart from her relations to man?" I told him it was. Men I have no doubt are painted in all their vigour on the wall of the other buildings; to us the sweetness of childhood, the charm of womanhood, if I have not conveyed some sense of that charm, in a word if I have not been absolutely feminine then I have failed . . . I will still have place on the side panels for two compositions, one which I shall begin immediately is Young Girls pursuing Fame. This seems to me very modern ... The other panel will represent the Arts and Music (nothing of St. Cecilia).

Cassatt had become more and more radical in her politics with the passage of time. She was a supporter of Dreyfus at the time of the Affair and, increasingly, she felt herself allied with the cause of feminism. Writing to Mrs. Palmer, she declared: "After all give me France. Women do not have to fight for recognition here if they do serious work," and she refers positively to women's determination to be *someone* rather than *something*. She participated enthusiastically in a benefit exhibition for the suffragettes in New York in 1915, and wrote to her activist friend Mrs. Havemeyer, "You know how I feel about *the*, to me, question of the day, and if such an exhibition is to take place, I wish it to be for the cause of Woman Suffrage."

Eakins never engaged in politics so overtly: his late work is, in fact, rather conservative. It is difficult to imagine him supporting feminism in such outspoken terms, although he seems to have encouraged some of his female students and to have demanded greater availibility of the nude model in his classes. Yet together, these two artists, so different in their formal conceptions and their notions of human existence and the social order inscribed by painting, transformed American art from a provincial, rather limited pursuit into a world-class enterprise.

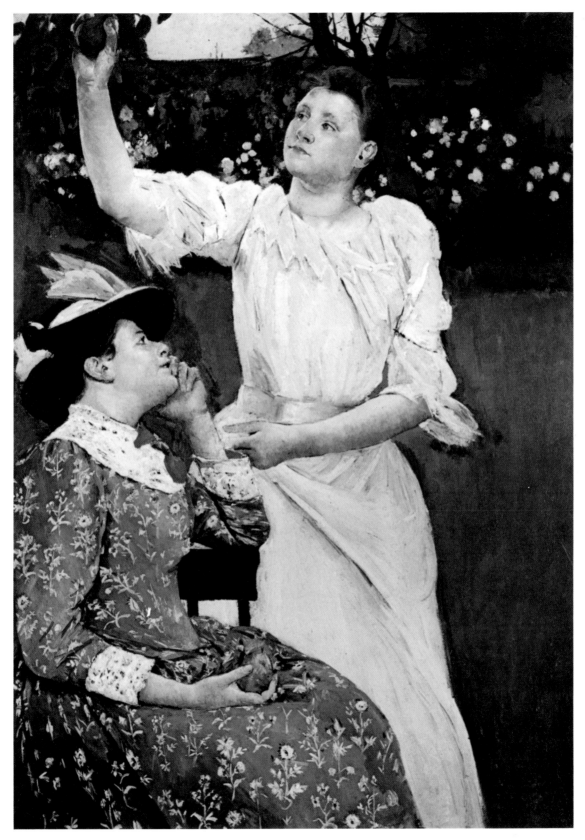

279 **MARY CASSATT** *Young Women Picking Fruit* 1892. 52 × 36 (132 × 91.5)

· 13 ·
MASS CULTURE AND UTOPIA: SEURAT AND NEOIMPRESSIONISM

THE ANTINOMIES OF GEORGES SEURAT

IN 1929, THE BRITISH CRITIC ROGER FRY WROTE THAT the art of Georges Seurat (1859–91) was stretched between the poles of "photographic literalness" and a condition "as abstract . . . as pictorial art ever attained." This basic antinomy, I believe, accurately describes the efforts and achievements of Seurat and his Neoimpressionist followers. Born nearly a generation after the Impressionists, these artists sought to return Impressionism to its collective and democratic roots, while at the same time maintaining their personal and expressive autonomy. The goal was largely impracticable given the social and cultural constraints of the age, and resulted in an art of paradox: Neoimpressionism was guided at once by the lessons of science and by an often abstruse idealism; it was influenced both by popular culture and the elite art of the Classical and Academic tradition; it aimed to be at the same time politically tendentious and formally pure; it represented together the alienation of modern life and the utopian dream of a life of leisure and unending pleasure; and it was, in sum, intellectually rigorous and an "armchair for the tired businessman," in Matisse's words. By these antinomies, therefore, the art of Seurat and his followers laid the foundation for twentieth-century modernism, whose antinomies are named Picasso and Matisse, Mondrian and Miró, Albers and Rivera.

SEURAT'S DRAWINGS AND THEIR DISPERSION OF MEANING

The founder and leader of Neoimpressionism (and its only genius) was undoubtedly Georges Seurat. Apart from a few summers spent on the Normandy or Brittany coasts, he lived his entire brief life in Paris, either in the company of his family in their apartment at 136 boulevard Magenta (halfway between the new Gare du Nord and the old Saint-Lazare Prison) or in his own apartment-studio. His mother was the daughter of a coachman turned jeweler, and his father was a minor civil servant and real estate speculator who retired early and spent his free time at a suburban villa at Le Raincy. The success of Antoine Seurat permitted Georges to take up an artist's career without financial worry, but the young man was clearly affected by more than just the fortunate financial circumstances of his upbringing: he must have been impressed as well by the modernity of the section of Paris in which he lived, by the cultural novelty of suburban life at Le Raincy, and by the power of his father's capital; these are all subjects represented in his mature art.

Initially trained in the industrial and decorative arts, Seurat applied for, and was granted, admission to the Ecole des Beaux-Arts in 1878. He studied in the atelier of Henri Lehmann (1814–82) for a little more than a year before leaving on account of boredom, poor grades, and political ostracism (his fellows called him a *communard*). After a year of compulsory military service, Seurat returned to Paris, rented a studio with his friend Edmond-François Aman-Jean (1860–1935), and immediately proceeded to develop and refine a style of drawing that was utterly without precedent. In *Aman-jean* (1882–3) and *Echo* (1883), among many other works, Seurat largely dispensed with line, the one indispensable element of all previous drawings. In so doing, he also dispensed with meaning in the work of art, as formerly understood.

Aman-Jean is a large ($24\frac{1}{2}$ by $18\frac{1}{4}$ inches) independent portrait drawing in conté crayon on rough Michallet paper. The male subject is depicted in half-length profile with gaze directed to the lower right. His right hand is extended and

280
281

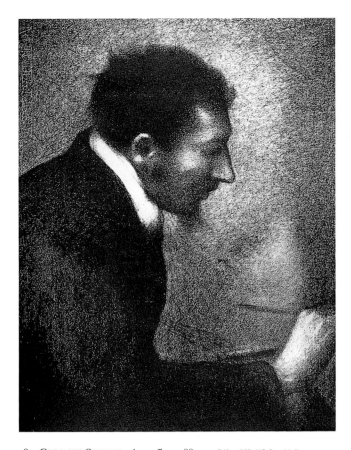

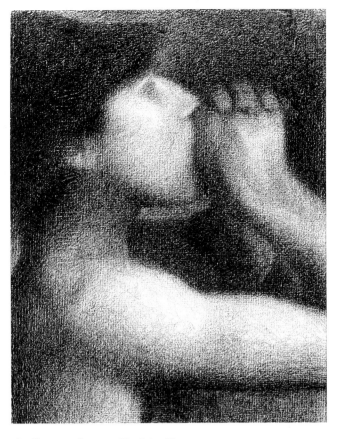

280 GEORGES SEURAT *Aman-Jean* 1882–3. 24½ × 18¼ (62.2 × 46.4)

281 GEORGES SEURAT *The Echo* 1883. 12¼ × 9¼ (31.1 × 23.4)

holds a small brush with which he makes a mark on a surface nearly coincident with the right margin. *Echo* is exactly half the size of *Aman-Jean,* and is a highly finished study for Seurat's first major painting, *A Bathing Place, Asnières* (1883– 4). The boy in the drawing is shown close up and in profile. His back and extended arms form an "L" which echoes the left and bottom margins of the paper; his cap is shaped into an isosceles triangle, and his nose and right forearm create a diagonal extending from upper left to lower right. His hands are cupped around his mouth in order to amplify a shout.

In both of these drawings, Seurat rubbed the greasy black crayon all over the surface of the paper in order to create a subtle continuum of dark and light uninterrupted by the hard contour of a line. (The only exception to this exclusion of line is the reinforcement of the profile of Aman-Jean.) Relief is created by the absense of crayon, as in the bare shoulders of the boy in *Echo,* and by contrasts of light and dark, as in the shirt collar and jacket lapels of *Aman-Jean.* Yet to speak of relief, modeling, and volume in these drawings is misleading; a simultaneous evanescence and tangibility is present here in areas of mass as much as in areas of shadow. Physical presence and absence commingle in a single, haunting rhetoric. *Aman-*

Jean and *Echo* are thus, in a sense, not representations at all. They are useless as interrogations of human character, they reveal nothing of the physical nature of the subjects they depict, they refuse any clear distinction between figure and ground, and they are valueless as renderings of the artist's personality or psyche. By abjuring line in his drawings, Seurat thus more closely approached pure abstraction than any artist we have considered so far. Because these drawings are so central to an understanding of Seurat's break with the Classical tradition, they must be considered a little further before we turn to his equally epochal paintings.

Since before the Renaissance, the art of drawing was based upon the control and manipulation of line: contour, move-ment, direction, volume, light, and expression were all judged dependent upon it. To Federico Zuccaro at the end of the sixteenth century, linear drawing had attained a nearly divine status: as the material expression of the Platonic *Idea,* drawing was the essential instrument for the representation of the divine within the human. Lines for him were both the means by which bodies were physically manifested in works of art (*disegno esterno*), and the material traces of the imagination and genius of the artist (*disegno interno*). Thus, the art of

282

drawing with lines had a moral, as well as a representational, value that allowed it to become the foundation for seventeenth-century history paintings concerned with the great men and deeds of history, mythology, and religion. By the early nineteenth century, this Classical and idealist tradition of linear drawing was principally upheld by Ingres, who instructed his pupils (including Seurat's teacher Lehmann): "To draw does not simply mean to reproduce contours; drawing does not simply consist of line: drawing is also expression, the inner form, the surface modeling. . . . That is why the painters of expression among the moderns happen to have been the greatest draftsmen—witness Raphael!"

In addition to Ingres and his pupils, support for the tenets of Neoclassical art theory with its championing of the role of line in drawing came from Charles Blanc. An influential critic, esthetician, and pedagogue, Blanc wrote in his *Grammaire des arts du dessin* (1867), "that lines—straight, curved, horizontal and oblique—are directly related to our sentiments, and can themselves be expressive and eloquent." Even Delacroix and Manet, both of whom sought to dethrone line from its exalted rank, nevertheless found it indispensable for the creation of movement and plasticity in drawings. Yet in the hands of Seurat the tradition of linear drawing is ended and in its place is substituted the abstraction of what the art historian Bernd Growe has called a "light-dark continuum." Solid bodies are dissolved by the light emitted from beneath a carpet of conté crayon; light is given material substance by the ebb and flow of tonality. In *Aman-Jean* and *Echo*, the unseen canvas upon which the artist labors and the unheard shout of a working-class boy are perhaps Seurat's real subjects. "Meaning" in these drawings of Seurat, as in others, is thereby dispersed beyond the ragged and indefinite edges of the Michallet paper into a spectatorial space that is dynamic and contested. In this way, Seurat's drawings are very like his paintings: they are unusually, and radically, *critical* in their effort to spark an exchange between the artwork and the diverse classes and cultures the artist saw and depicted. By their rejection of meaning as it was formerly conceived—*within the circumscribed frame of the artwork*—Seurat's drawings and paintings therefore mark an attempt to restore social and political meaning to the work of art. Now their significance is to be determined, almost as never before, by a broad and diverse community of spectators responsive to the formal imperatives of art. Even as the works reject important aspects of Neoclassical art theory, they mark a return to the values of Revolutionary, Neoclassical history painting as practised by David exactly one hundred years earlier.

Seurat studied and understood the contested spaces and cultural diversity of the city that lay beyond the frame of his canvas and studio door. In his youth he frequented the newly built working-class park of the Buttes-Chaumont just a few blocks east of his family's apartment. Further east was his father's retreat at Le Raincy, a suburban area only recently subdivided into lots for middle-class "villas." Thus Seurat was already familiar with the complex signs of social class on display in the Haussmannized urban and suburban leisure spaces of Paris, when he and some of his friends began to spend time at Clichy, Asnières, and the Island of the Grande Jatte. *Bathing Place, Asnières* is a heroically scaled (79 by 118 inches) depiction of working-class men and boys relaxing and bathing at a well-known if somewhat down-at-heels resort on the left bank of the Seine. The picture, composed out of a regularized and systematized Impressionist palette and facture, was refused by the Salon judges, and was instead shown twice in 1884 at jury-free exhibitions of the Artistes Indépendants, a large group which included Odilon Redon and Paul Signac (1863–1935). There it was acclaimed by a handful of Naturalist writers, critics, and artists, including Signac, who would form the nucleus of a movement dubbed by the writer, art critic, and anarchist Félix Fénéon "Neo-impressionism." The "manifesto" of the new movement, however, as the critic Maurice Hermel called it, appeared two years later at the eighth and last Impressionist Exhibition, in the form of Seurat's *A Sunday Afternoon on the Island of the Grande Jatte* (1884–6).

A "MANIFESTO PAINTING": *A SUNDAY AFTERNOON ON THE ISLAND OF THE GRANDE JATTE*

Seurat's *Grande Jatte* is a life-sized depiction of a Sunday idyll 284–5 at a suburban park located on a small, narrow island opposite the banks of Asnières. Women, men, and children of all classes are got up in their good clothes to picnic, promenade, boat, fish, and gaze upon one another on this particular sunny, Sabbath noon. A black labrador grazes, a pug gambols, and a monkey poses in the foreground. Above, trees form an intermittent canopy while a cotton swab floats across the sky at upper left. The island and its habitués constitute a modern Cythera, but with this difference: the pleasure appears extremely vitiated. The critic Henri Fèvre wrote in May 1886:

Little by little, one understands the intention of the painter; the dazzle and blindness lift and one becomes familiar with, divines, sees and admires the great yellow patch of grass eaten away by the sun, the clouds of golden dust in the treetops, the details that the retina, dazzled by light, cannot make out; then one understands the stiltedness of the Parisian promenade, stiff and distorted; even its recreation is affected. . . . It is materialist Puvis de Chavannes, a coarse summary of nature, savagely colored.

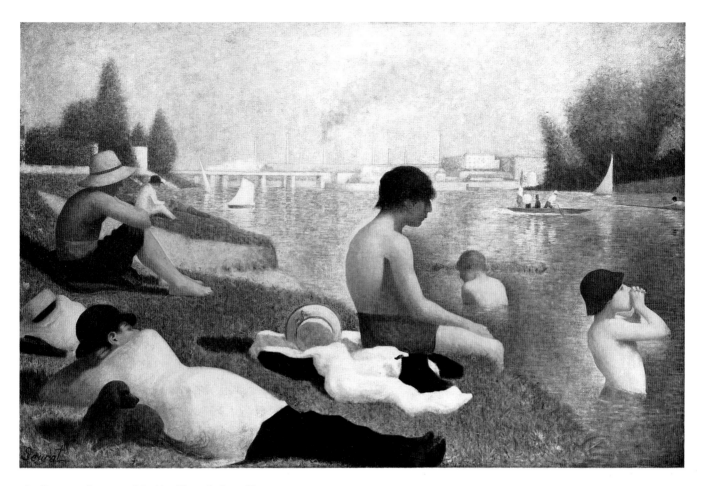

282 GEORGES SEURAT *A Bathing Place, Asnières* 1883–4. 79⅛ × 9′10 (200.9 × 299.7)

Another critic, Alfred Paulet, wrote: "The painter has given his figures the automatic gestures of lead soldiers, moving about on regimented squares. Maids, clerks, and soldiers all move around with a similar slow, banal, identical step." Seurat's *Grande Jatte* is thus at once an ingenuously Impressionist image of suburban recreation and leisure, and a critical Realist picture of the artifice and alienation of modern class society. His mentors are at once Monet, the author of *La Grenouillère* (*The Frog Pond*), and Manet, the painter of *Le Déjeuner* (*Luncheon*).

Even a cursory glance at the picture, however, reveals that its style differs markedly from works by either of these two painters. Unlike them, but in common with some academicians, Seurat is rigid and systematic in his method. "The Pan-Athenaic Frieze of Phidias [on the Parthenon] was a procession," Seurat told his friend the poet and critic Gustave Kahn in 1888, "I want to make the moderns file past like figures on that frieze, in their essential form, to place them in compositions arranged harmoniously by virtue of the directions of the colors and lines, line and color arranged in accordance with one another." Like the Academic muralist Pierre Puvis de Chavannes (1824–98), whose *The Sacred Grove* (1884) was exhibited at the Salon in the very year the *Grande Jatte* was begun, Seurat has subjected his landscape and especially his figures to a strict proportional and Classical schema based upon Vitruvius: heads are $\frac{1}{7}$ the height of bodies, and faces are turned precisely full frontal, $\frac{3}{4}$ view, full profile, $\frac{3}{4}$ from the back, or full back. Seurat is equally rule-bound in his application of color, though in this case the source is contemporary color theory written by Michel-Eugène Chevreul, Charles Henry, and especially Ogden Rood. Atop a thin underpainting consisting of broad, rectangular strokes of a few closely related hues of local color, Seurat carefully placed curved, horizontal, vertical, or crisscrossed strokes of unmixed or partially blended paint. Above this he applied myriad, nearly identically sized dabs or points of mostly unblended complementary and adjacent colors, animating the surface and causing it to take on the quality of a mosaic.

Rejecting the relative tonal sobriety of Puvis, Seurat employed this technique of "Chromo-luminarism," as he

283

called it, in order to achieve a luminosity that would exceed even that in Impressionist paintings. Fénéon was informed by Seurat of his methods in 1886 and published them that year:

> These colors, isolated on the canvas, recombine on the retina: we have, therefore, not a mixture of material colors (pigments), but a mixture of differently colored rays of light. Need we recall that even when the colors are the same, mixed pigments and mixed rays of light do not necessarily produce the same results? It is also generally understood that the luminosity of optical mixtures is always superior to that of material mixture, as the many equations worked out by M. Rood demonstrate.

The following year, Fénéon again expounded the technique of Seurat and his colleagues Signac, Lucien Pissarro (1863–1944, Camille's son), Maximilien Luce (1858–1941), Charles Angrand (1854–1926), and Albert Dubois-Pillet (1845–90), whose works were on display at the third annual exhibition of the Société des Artistes Indépendants. Calling them "Neoimpressionists" for their rejection of Impressionism's "fugitive appearances," he described their attempts, in such works as 286 Signac's *The Gasometer at Clichy* (1886) and *The Dining Room, Breakfast* (1886–7), to "synthesize the landscape in a definitive aspect which perpetuates the sensation [it produces]. . . . Step back a bit [from their pictures] and all these variocolored spots melt into undulating, luminous masses; the brushwork vanishes, so to speak; the eye is no longer solicited by anything but the essence of painting." Even the mature Camille Pissarro was intoxicated by Chromo-luminarism, practising it for approximately five

years between 1885 and 1890. His *L'Ile Lacroix, Rouen, Mist* 287 (1888) employs a subtle palette of white, pink, and green in the brightly lit areas, and complementary orange and blue in the shadows. Its carefully divided brushstrokes were an attempt to master the "laws" of colored light, and to produce, as he wrote, "a robust art, based on sensation."

In fact, however, Fénéon, Seurat, and his followers misunderstood the color theories of the American physicist Ogden Road, believing he had claimed that *every* material mixture was deficient in luminosity when compared to color achieved by optical mix. This misunderstanding resulted in colors in the *Grande Jatte* that Emile Hennequin, as early as 1886, correctly perceived to be "dusty or lusterless" and "almost entirely lacking in luminosity," especially in those areas, such as the trousers of the reclining man in the left foreground or the dress of the woman with the fishing pole, where complementary dots or strokes of paint have been intermingled. Nevertheless, Seurat continued in his pursuit of a scientific esthetic, and was soon convinced that he had indeed discovered, as Kahn wrote, "scientifically, with the experience of art . . . the law of pictorial color."

In a short letter of 1890, Seurat described his method. Under the rubric "Esthetic," he wrote:

> Art is Harmony.
> Harmony is the analogy of opposites, the analogy of similarities of *tone, of tint, of line*, taking account of a dominant, and under the influence of the lighting, in combinations that are gay, calm or sad.

Further on, beneath the word "Technique," he wrote:

283 PIERRE PUVIS DE CHAVANNES *The Sacred Grove* 1884. $36\frac{1}{2} \times 91$ (92.6 × 231)

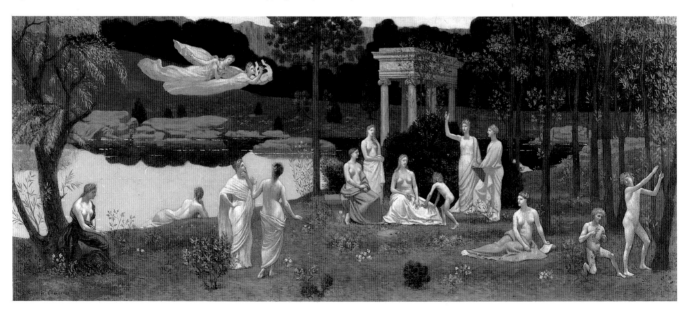

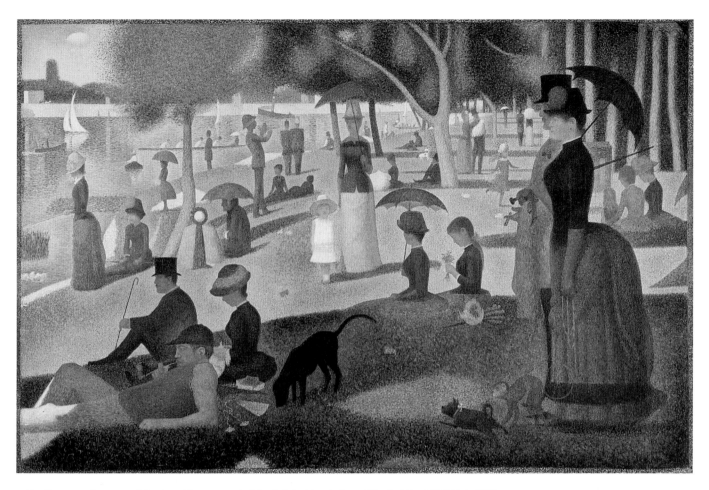

284 GEORGES SEURAT *A Sunday Afternoon on the Island of the Grande Jatte* 1884–6. 81¾ × 10′1¼ (207.6 × 307.9)

Given the phenomenon [. . .] of the duration of the luminous impression on the retina, [. . .]

Synthesis is logically the result.

The means of expression is the optical mixture of tones, of tints (of local color and the illuminating color: sun, oil lamp, gas, etc.), that is, of the lights and their reactions (shadows) following the laws of *contrast*, of gradation, of irradiation.

The frame [. . .] is in a harmony opposed to those of the tones, tints and lines of the [. . .] picture.

The basis of Seurat's method, as he wrote, was color "contrast" and "synthesis;" his motto "Art is Harmony" was thus a proclamation that beauty arises from a continuous process of opposition and resolution among contrasting colors, values, and lines. (Line must here be understood primarily to mean direction.) This dynamic relationship, moreover, was extended by Seurat beyond the limits of the canvas to the frame, and then beyond the frame to the world of the spectator. According to the testimony of the poet and critic

Emile Verhaeren, Seurat compared his painted frames, spectacularly represented by his landscape *Le Crotoy,* **288** *Upstream* (1889), to the stagecraft of Wagner's opera house at Bayreuth, in which the contrast between the illuminated stage and the darkened theater "is continued and extends itself to meet the eye of the spectator."

By means of Seurat's scientific and dialectic approach to painting, in which the barriers between artwork and world are broken down, he sought to restore to painting the cultural significance it had lost with the demise of Classicism and Academic history painting. The artist's only known comment about the *Grande Jatte*, set down much later by Signac, should be taken as an indicator of his respect for the Davidian paradigm: "In another vein I would just as willingly have painted the struggle between the Horatii and the Curatii." By means of his relentless focus upon the laws of harmony, Seurat sought as well to return to the enterprise of painting the social and collective meaning it had lost with the destruction, as we have seen, of Courbet's project of Realism. Indeed, Courbet's *Burial at Ornans,* despite the differences in color and tonality, **209**

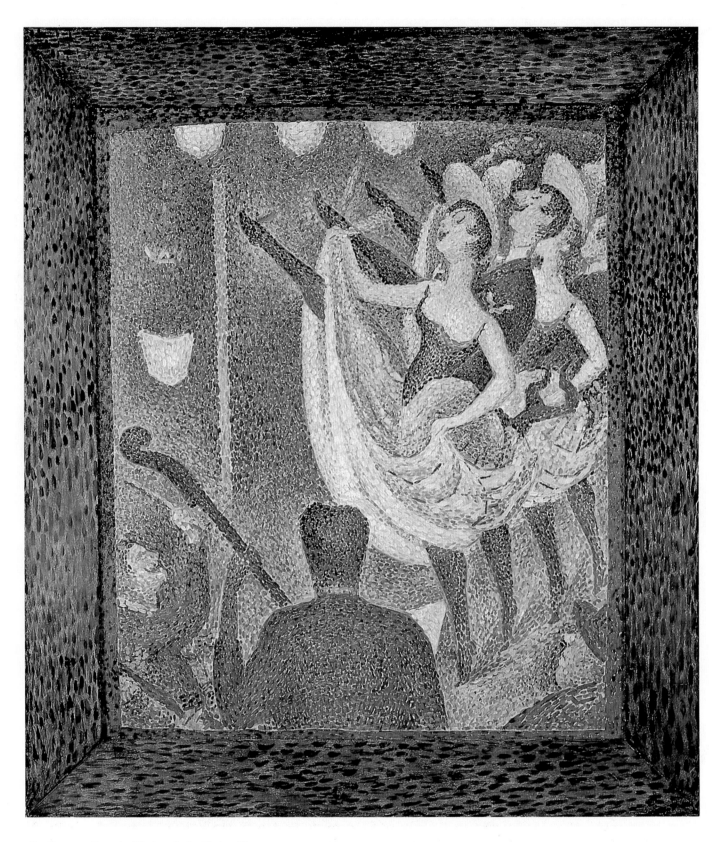

285 **GEORGES SEURAT** Final study for *Chahut* 1889. $21\frac{7}{8} \times 18\frac{3}{8}$ (55.6 × 46.7)

is recalled by the *Grande Jatte:* both are large, indeed heroically, scaled pictures depicting occasions of awkward, and ambiguously classed, rituals.

Idealist and Realist, Classical and modernist, the *Grande Jatte* may thus be said to possess, like its author, in Meyer Schapiro's words, "an earnest democratic spirit;" it affirms the right and opportunity of a diverse audience, like the Sunday crowd in the picture itself, to become legitimate and critical spectators of painting. Like many modernists to follow, Seurat sought to break down the distinction between artist and worker, fine and industrial art. It is significant that when asked by his friend the critic Octave Maus the selling price of *The Models* (1886–8), a depiction of working-class models relaxedly posed against the starched bourgeoisie in the *Grande Jatte,* Seurat computed its value like a day laborer would figure his wages: "one year at 7 francs a day." When asked by Angrand about the significance of his works, Seurat replied: "They [writers and critics] see poetry in what I do. No. I apply my method and that is all." Indeed, for Seurat and the Neoimpressionists, as for few other artists of the time, the division between the physical creation and intellectual cognition of the artwork was nearly absolute. Painted in discrete dots of color, applied according to a preconceived system, Neoimpressionist pictures are a kind of exaggeration or parody of the very type of industrial and alienated labor then expanding in France, in which workers see no relationship between their individual work-gesture and the final product. To what, then, can be attributed the sense of alienation and isolation perceived by contemporary and subsequent critics of the *Grande Jatte?* Precisely this: that it was a picture which sought to discover and employ a rationalized, esthetic formula for the representation of idleness, quietness, and pleasure. Short of a revolution in daily life and labor, these two halves could not make a whole; the result was parody.

MASS CULTURE AND THE PARADOX OF PLEASURE: *CHAHUT*

The paradoxical nature of Seurat's quest for harmony is unmistakably manifest in his pictures of popular entertainments—*Sideshow* (1887–8), *Chahut* (1889–90), and *Circus* (1890–91)—all shown at exhibitions of the Salon des Indépendants. In *Chahut* Seurat depicts two men and two women performing the vulgar quadrille known as the Chahut on a stage in a dance hall like those he knew in Montmartre (it is almost certainly the *café-concert* known as Le Divan Japonais at 75 rue des Martyrs). In fact, we are seeing the climax of the performance, or the curtain call, when the dancers break out of their square, form a line, and perform a

few last high kicks for the crowd. The members of the orchestra are embraced by the extended legs of the foreground female dancer, like a great erotic parenthesis; the bass player is seen in the extreme foreground with his back to us and his instrument pointed upward and to the left; the flute player is recognizable by his hands and instrument in the lower left corner; the conductor is shown in profile with raised head, arm, baton, and moustache; and two fiddlers are indicated by the presence of their raised bows.

The audience in *Chahut*, seated in the *parterre* or pit beside the musicians, consists of a gentleman in the lower right, described by Kahn as "pig-snouted," but otherwise nattily dressed in hat, cane, and overcoat with flowered lapel, and three other figures on the opposite side of the runway—from right to left, a woman wearing a crown like the Statue of Liberty's, a woman wearing a feathered toque, and a man with a bald head and beard. Everything else about the picture is obscure—the gas lamps at the top and those suspended in mid-air at the left, the vertical bar or pole approximately one quarter the distance from the left margin, the location of the rear wall, the precise arrangement of seating for audience and orchestra, and the curious vignette-shape of the picture itself within its painted frame. Equally mysterious is the mood of the picture. In *Chahut*, it would seem, Seurat paradoxically depicts both a dream of unrestrained pleasure and a nightmare vision of vulgarity.

The opposition was observed and ascribed political significance at the time by Kahn when he wrote: "If you are looking at all costs for a 'symbol,' you will find it in the contrast between the beauty of the dancer, an elegant and modest sprite, and the ugliness of her admirer; in the hieratic structure of the canvas and its subject, a contemporary ignominy." Signac had a similar view of the picture, which he expressed in 1891, just a few months after Seurat's death. He wrote that by painting images of working-class life, "or better still, the pleasures of decadence like dance halls, *chahuts* and circuses—as the painter Seurat did, who had such a vivid perception of the degeneration of our transitional era—[the Neoimpressionists] bring their evidence to the great social trial that is taking place between workers and Capital." One way to understand the opposition of dream and nightmare in *Chahut* is simply to say, following Kahn, that in the Montmartre cabarets where Chahuts are performed, the dancers experience the utopian delight of free and expressive movement while the audience is subjected to the dystopia of bad food and spirits, seedy surroundings, and lewd display. In fact, however, the opposite can just as easily be claimed. We may say, following Signac, that in the Parisian dance called Chahut, the performers are no "sprites," but are reduced to mere automata; their limbs, buttocks, breasts, crotches, and smiles are visibly alienated from their bodies and their minds

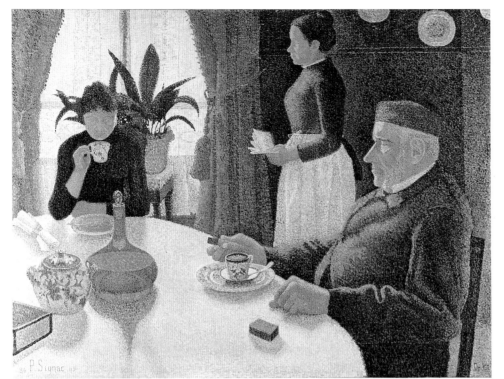

286 PAUL SIGNAC *The Dining Room,
Breakfast* 1886–7. 35 × 45½ (89 × 115)

287 CAMILLE PISSARRO *L'Isle
Lacroix, Rouen, Mist* 1888. 18¼ × 21⅞
(44 × 55)

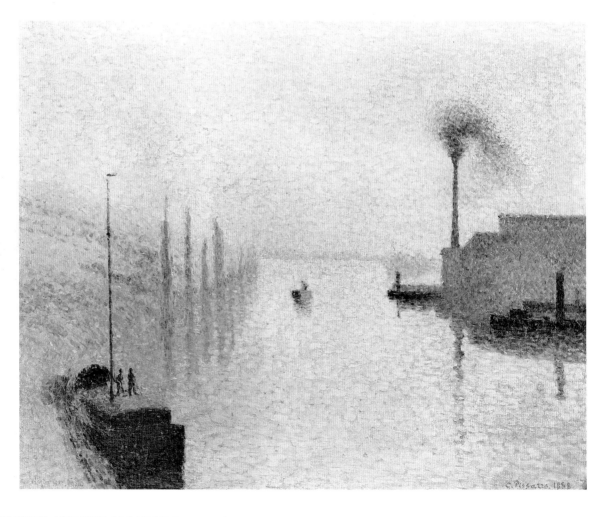

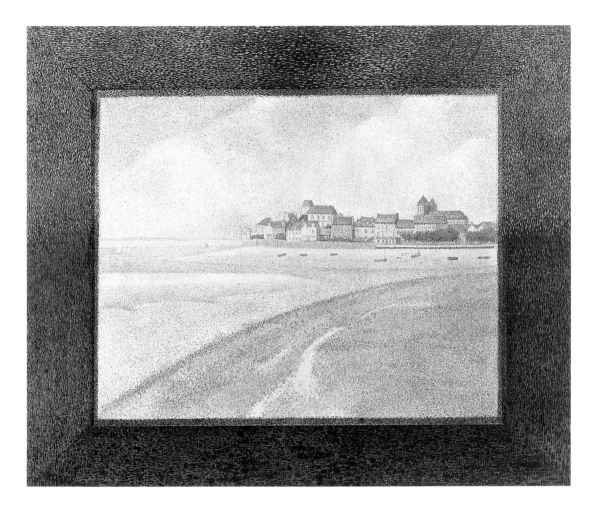

288 GEORGES SEURAT *Le Crotoy, Upstream* 1889. 28¾ × 36¼ (73 × 93.3)

289 GEORGES SEURAT *The Models* 1886–8. 79 × 98¾ (200.6 × 250.8)

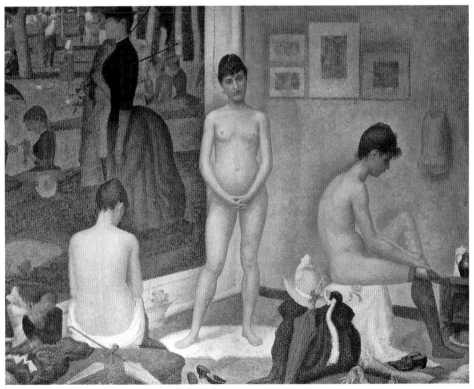

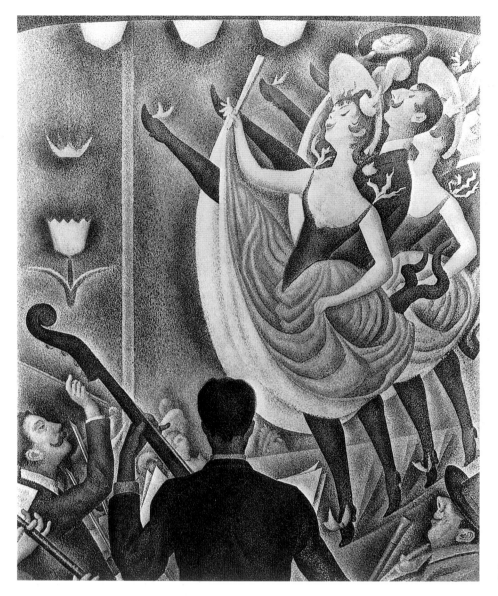

290 GEORGES SEURAT *Chahut* 1889–90.
66⅛ × 55½ (168.9 × 140.9)

in a dystopia of fetishism and objectification. At the same time, the spectators are treated to the utopian pleasures of music, light, frenetic dance, and sexual stimulation.

Each of these antinomies is equally plausible and implausible: how can the performers actually have experienced the delight of free and expressive movement when we know that their dance was designed precisely to subordinate expressivity in favor of crude sexual display? On the other hand, how can the performers have felt alienated and degraded when their kicks are so clearly exuberant and they wear such broad smiles? Regarding the spectators, how can they have suffered the dystopia of degradation and exploitation, when they are so clearly enraptured and so splendidly attired? On the other hand, how can we assert that the audience has experienced the joyous utopia of sensual stimulation and erotic delight, when they themselves are barred from the dance and, apparently,

from human companionship? Everyone came alone to the Chahut. (The bald man with the beard and the woman with the toque might just belong together, but they are separated by the neck of the bass viol and anyway make an unlikely couple.)

The question which arose in considering the *Grande Jatte* must be considered again: is *Chahut* a satire? If so, why did Seurat go to such lengths to include tonal, linear, and coloristic devices that, he believed, would guarantee that his picture would stimulate feelings of joyousness in his audience? The predominating high luminosity, warm hues, and upward pointed angles and accents (lines) were believed by him to be conducive to happiness. In the letter cited earlier, Seurat wrote: "*Gaiety of tone* is the luminous dominant, *of tint*, the warm dominant, *of line*, lines above the horizontal." *Chahut* contains just this vocabulary of gaiety. In *Chahut*, it would

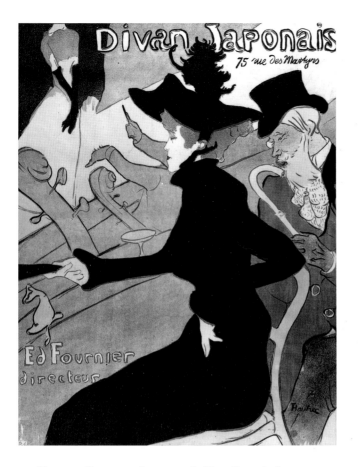

291 HENRI DE TOULOUSE-LAUTREC *Le Divan Japonais* 1892–3.
31⅞ × 24 (80.8 × 60.8)

contradictory. Upon entering Seurat's Divan Japonais, Degas's Cirque Fernando (in his *Miss Lola at the Cirque Fernando*, 1879), Manet's Folies-Bergère, or the hundreds of other theaters and places of entertainment depicted by French and European artists of the late nineteenth century, things were not what they seemed. Take the question of the theater audience, for example. Occupying "the center seats in the pit, under the chandelier or *lustre*," writes Baedeker's in 1888, "the *claque*, or paid applauders, form an annoying, although characteristic feature in most of the theatres . . . and are easily recognized by the obtrusive and simultaneous vigor of their exertions. There are even *entrepreneurs de succès dramatique*, a class of mercantile adventurers who furnish theaters with *claques* at stated terms."

At the many Paris *cafés chantants*, or nightclubs, the guide continues, "the music and singing is never of a high class, while the audience is of a very mixed character. . . . The alluring display of the words *entrée libre* outside the *cafés chantants* is a ruse to attract the public, as each visitor is obliged to order refreshments (*consommation*), which are generally of inferior quality." If the innocent visitor chooses

292 JULES CHÉRET *Le Bal du Moulin Rouge* 1889. 23½ × 16½ (59.7 × 41.9)

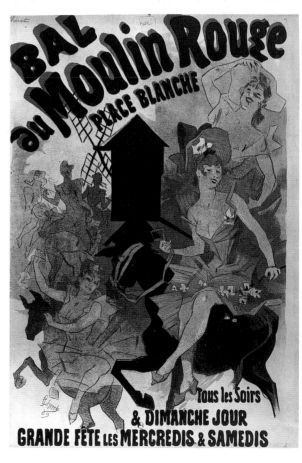

seem, Seurat set out to make a democratic and happy picture.

And yet, no matter what we know of Seurat's esthetic theories and practise, the imputation of satire remains inescapable when actually viewing *Chahut*. The conviction is even further strengthened if we compare the painting to Henri de Toulouse-Lautrec's (1864–1901) lithographed poster of the same cabaret, *Le Divan Japonais* (1892–3). Toulouse-Lautrec depicts uncritically the Parisian world of fashion and celebrity; the popular *chanteuse* Yvette Guilbert is shown on stage (her head audaciously cut off by the top edge of the poster), above the dancer Jane Avril (in one of her famous and outlandish hats) and her companion Edouard Dujardin, the dandified founder of the avant-garde *Revue Wagnérienne*. No such celebrity and playful in-joking is in evidence in Seurat's picture. At some level, then, Kahn and Signac must be right in their perception of social and political criticism in *Chahut*. As with the *Grande Jatte*, Seurat has created a painting which records the paradox—both the alienation and the delight—of modern leisure and mass culture.

Indeed, mass culture in Seurat's day was, as we have already begun to understand (see Chapter 11), new and instead to attend one of the innumerable balls or dance halls of Paris, things are no better:

> The balls, which take place all the year round at public dancing rooms, may be regarded as one of the specialities of Paris. Many of these entertainments, however, have for some years past been to a great extent "got up" for the benefit of strangers, numbers of the supposed visitors being hired as decoys by the lessee of the saloon. . . . At the Bal Bullier . . . a famous establishment in its way, the dancing of the students and artisans with their *étudiantes* and *ouvrières* is generally of a wild and Bacchanalian character. Here the famous Can-Can may be seen.

In *Chahut*, Seurat appears to have depicted a fully professionalized performance, and not a mock amateur can-can danced by ersatz students and workers. The audience seems genuine enough (they are not applauding), and no particular inducements are in evidence. But if Seurat omits from his painting any obvious clues as to the put-on nature of the audience, the location, and the performance, it is only because he understood that these entertainments were sufficiently effective and insidious even without ostentatious guile. His knowledge and respect for the power of mass culture is revealed, for example, by his admiration and even occasional emulation, as the art historian Robert Herbert has shown, of the cabaret posters of Jules Chéret (*Le Bal du Moulin Rouge*, 1889, for example). In 1891, Verhaeren described Seurat's affinity for Chéret: "The poster artist Chéret, whose genius he greatly admired, had charmed him with the joy and the gaiety of his designs. He had studied them, wanting to analyze their means of expression and uncover their aesthetic secrets." Chéret had apparently understood the secret allure of mass culture and found a recipe for representing it in his posters. Perhaps Seurat could take a lesson from him and also discover what underlay the hypnotic power of the nascent culture industry.

A highly cultured and circumspect man (Degas called him "the notary"), Seurat must have felt a profound ambivalence about the world of artifice and contrived pleasures in *Chahut* and *Circus*, his last painting. On the one hand, he surely deplored its vulgarity and reduction of the spectator to the condition of passive spectator, but on the other, he probably saw it as offering working people a place of refuge—even perhaps a sense of honor; notice the serried ranks of smiling spectators in *Circus*. Like the modern factory, the sideshows, dance halls and circuses were alienating, yet the alienation was collective. Perhaps some sense of camaraderie, some collective desire for freedom and autonomy could be salvaged from even this world; perhaps the artist could be instrumental in providing a new (harmonic) vocabulary through which this freedom could be felt and even acted upon by everyone?

At Asnières, the Grande Jatte, and the other new haunts provided by a growing culture industry, Seurat understood that he was witnessing the very utopia of which he dreamed, as well as its opposite. This dialectic was succinctly described by the social critic and philosopher Herbert Marcuse in 1937, in terms that might have been inspired by the pictures of Seurat:

> In suffering the most extreme reification, humans triumph over reification. The artistry of the beautiful body, its effortless agility and relaxation, which can be displayed today only in the circus, vaudeville and burlesque, herald the joy to which humans will attain in being liberated from the ideal. Once humankind, having become a true [independent] subject, succeeds in the mastery of matter . . . when sensuality, in other words, is entirely released by the soul, then the first glimmer of a new culture emerges.

In the very degradation of the performers at these venues, in the very objectification of the body, in the very focus upon the erotic at the expense of the ideal, Seurat must have seen anticipations of the world of harmony and pleasure of which he dreamed. Indeed, modern mass culture, of which the parks, cabarets, and circuses of Paris are early examples, is construed from just this dialectic of alienation and freedom: the pleasures it offers are at once the result of the extremely circumscribed act of commodity consumption and of the anticipatory utopian joy of "effortless agility" and the "mastery of matter." Seurat's achievement was to explore this paradox through an art that was itself dialectical. The drawings and paintings of Seurat are at once relentlessly scientist and ingratiatingly popular; they are by turns abstract and literal, formalist and naturalist. Along with the works of Van Gogh, to which we shall now turn, they were among the last such synthesizing efforts of the nineteenth century.

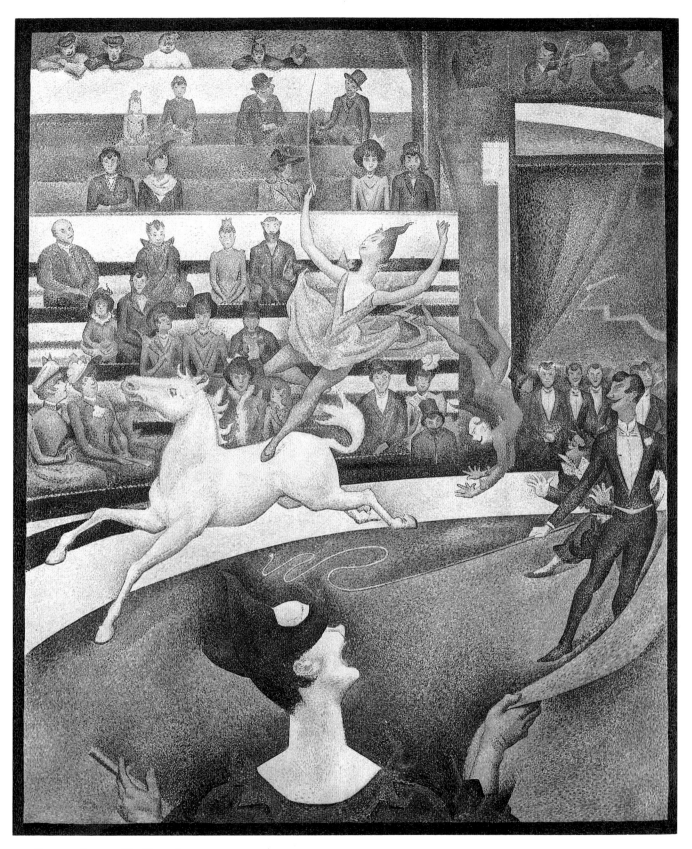

293 GEORGES SEURAT *The Circus* 1890–91. 73 × 60 (185.4 × 152.4)

· 14 ·

ABSTRACTION AND POPULISM: VAN GOGH

SEURAT AND VAN GOGH COMPARED

Close contemporaries whose paths several times crossed, Vincent Van Gogh (1853–90) and Georges Seurat are nonetheless often seen as opposites. Whereas the Dutch-born artist, it is said, was essentially a man of nature and the countryside, the Frenchman was archetypically urban and cosmopolitan. Whereas the one was unsettled and passionate in his temperament and his art, the other was generally calm and dispassionate in both. And whereas Van Gogh's painting was romantic and self-expressive, Seurat's was classical and disciplined. The list of such oppositions could easily be lengthened to include those other binaries—Baroque/Classical, Modern/Ancient, *Rubéniste/Poussiniste*—that have provided a comforting structure to nineteenth-century and subsequent art historical thought. Yet the dichotomy is mostly false, as can immediately be seen by a comparison of Van Gogh's portrait of Madame Augustine Roulin, called by him *La Berceuse* (1889), and Seurat's portrait of his mistress, Madeleine Knoblock, called *Young Woman Powdering Herself* (1889–90).

Both paintings are three-quarter-length seated portraits of women. Each woman's body and gaze is oriented to the left, while her preponderant bulk is anchored at the lower right. Each is accompanied by an attribute—a make-up kit, and a rope attached to an unseen cradle—which determine the picture's title. Flowers are a prominent part of the decorative ensemble of each painting, serving at once to disperse the viewer's attention across the surface of the picture and to reinforce an overall flatness; in the Seurat, flowers are seen on the background wallpaper and reflected in the bamboo-framed mirror at the upper left, while in the Van Gogh they are found only—but spectacularly—in the background wallpaper. Each painting, moreover, is structured according

to Neoimpressionist principles of divided color. Seurat's portrait contains a complex mixture of tints of blue, red, green, orange, yellow, and purple, with a predominant blue/orange complementary pairing. Van Gogh employs divided color everywhere in the painting: in the red/green complements of the floor and Madame Roulin's ample skirt and sweater, in the orange/blue complements of her eyes, collar, and sleeves and especially in the hallucinatory wallpaper, composed of flowers of pink, white, red, green, and yellow, floating above a pattern of green and yellow paisley above a field of black ovals surrounding orange dots above a sea of dark green. (The peculiar wallpaper may have been derived from the wallpaper pattern in Dubois-Pillet's *Portrait of Mlle. M. D.*, 1886).

Van Gogh's portrait of his friend Madame Roulin, who had offered him succor during a period of convalescence, was clearly intended as a composition in restfulness and harmony, orchestrated with the instruments of Chromo-luminarism, or what Seurat called "the harmony of opposites." In January 1889, Van Gogh described *La Berceuse* in a letter written to his friend the Dutch painter Koning in Paris:

> At present I have in mind, or rather on my easel, the portrait of a woman. I call it "La Berceuse," or as we say in Dutch . . . "our lullaby or the woman rocking the cradle." It is a woman in a green dress (the bust olive green and the skirt pale malachite green). The hair is quite orange and in plaits. The complexion is chrome yellow, worked up with some naturally broken tones for the purpose of modeling. The hands holding the rope of the cradle, the same. At the bottom the background is vermilion (simply representing a tiled floor or else a stone floor). The wall is covered with wallpaper, which of course I have calculated in conformity with the rest of the colors. This wallpaper is bluish-green

with pink dahlias spotted with orange and ultramarine. . . .
Whether I really sang a lullaby in colors is something I
leave to the critics (Letter 571a).

A few weeks later, Van Gogh wrote to his brother Theo about
his intention to make *La Berceuse* into a work of truly popular
296 art, crafted (as he would later say of his *Bedroom in Arles*) with
a "Seurat-like simplicity." Such a picture, he wrote, could
soothe the hearts and souls of even coarse fishermen:

> I have just said to Gauguin that following those intimate
> talks of ours the idea came to me to paint the picture in such
> a way that sailors, who are at once children and martyrs,
> seeing it in the cabin of their Icelandic fishing boat, would
> feel the old sense of being rocked come over them and
> remember their own lullabys. Now it may be said that it is
> like a chromolithograph from a cheap shop. A woman in
> green with orange hair standing out against a background
> of green with pink flowers. Now these discordant sharps of
> crude pink, crude orange, and crude green are softened by
> flats of red and green. I picture to myself these same
> canvases between those of the sunflowers, which would
> thus form torches or candelabra beside them, the same size,

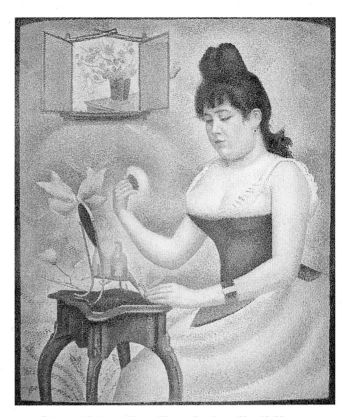

294 GEORGES SEURAT *Young Woman Powdering Herself* 1889–90.
27¾ × 34⅛ (70.4 × 86.6)

295 VINCENT VAN GOGH *La Berceuse* 1889. 36¼ × 28¾ (92 × 73)

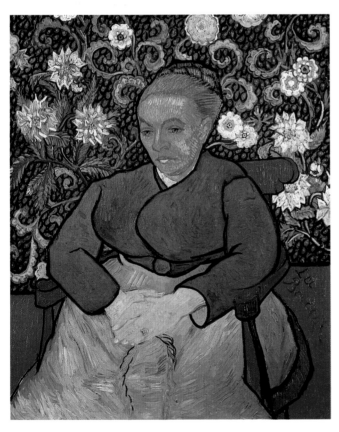

and so the whole would be composed of seven or nine
canvases (Letter 574).

"Perhaps there's an attempt," he later added to Theo, "to get
all the *music* of the color here into *La Berceuse*" (Letter 576).
In his stated emulation of musical effect and quest for
Wagnerian scope, Van Gogh must again be compared with
Seurat, who painted mural-sized works and constructed
chromatic *gesamtkunstwerke* (total works of art) with his
elaborate painted frames.

Comparison of *La Berceuse* with *Young Woman Powdering
Herself*, in short, reveals a quite profound agreement between
their authors as to what constitutes a successful modern
painting. Both artists accepted the validity of the traditional
genre of portraiture (they were among the last modern
painters to do so) but expanded its parameters and range of
affect through a "science" of Chromo-luminarism. Each
sought to stimulate in their audience feelings of harmony, by
which was meant not just a feeling of peace but an ideal and
musical consonance that was both conducive to present social
amity and predictive of a utopian concord that could be
achieved in the future. In addition, each artist desired to
democratize art through the "high" cultural adaptation of
"low" cultural forms, such as cheap chromolithographs
and popular prints. Yet here a distinction must be

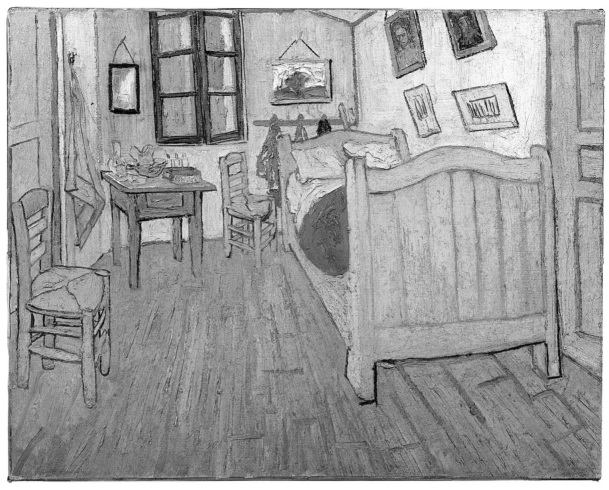

296 VINCENT VAN GOGH *The Artist's Bedroom in Arles* 1888. 28¼ × 35½ (79 × 90)

announced, which will be elaborated in the following pages. The *Young Woman* of Seurat is a modern, fashionable woman of the sort we have met before in paintings by Manet, Degas, Morisot, and Cassatt; *La Berceuse* of Van Gogh is the no-nonsense wife of a proletarian, akin to the heroic working men and women in the Realist art of Daumier, Courbet, and Millet. Whereas Seurat admired as well as sought to capture in his art the promised pleasures of the new *mass* culture of Paris—the cabarets, circuses, and suburban parks—Van Gogh remained wedded to the ideal of an indigenous or autochthonous *popular* culture, more or less traditional and uncontaminated by a modern culture industry. "Yesterday I was at the *Café-concert* Scala," Van Gogh wrote from Antwerp in 1885 to Theo, "something like the Folies Bergères; I found it very dull, and of course insipid" (Letter 438). Later in the same letter, he wrote: "I also have the idea for a kind of signboard, which I hope to carry out. I mean for instance, for a fishmonger, still life of fishes, for flowers, for vegetables, for restaurants. . . . One thing is certain, that I want my things to be seen."

TWO MYTHS ABOUT VAN GOGH

Two myths about Van Gogh must at once be dispelled. First, he was not insane. His progressively worsening mental condition (culminating in suicide), and intermittent institutionalization at the end of his life, were almost certainly the result of an organic dysfunction, probably psycho-motor or symptomatic epilepsy or perhaps some other inner-ear or metabolic disorder exacerbated by liquor, medicines, or poor diet. His doctor at the Hospital of St.-Rémy near Arles wrote to Theo in May 1889: "You ask for my opinion regarding the probable cause of his illness. I must tell you that for the time being I will not make any prognosis, but I fear that it may be serious as I have every reason to believe that the attack which he has had is the result of a state of epilepsy and if this should be confirmed one should be concerned about the future." Vincent Van Gogh apparently agreed with his physician's general assessment, writing at the time to his brother: "I think Dr. Peyron is right when he says I am not, strictly speaking mad, for my mind is absolutely normal in the intervals . . . but during the attacks it is terrible, then I lose consciousness of everything" (Letter 610). Van Gogh obviously could not paint during his seizures or their aftermath, and his art was mature (or well on its way to maturity) long before his first attacks. Thus, though his desperation in the face of what was to him a mysterious and sometimes disabling illness was undoubtedly great, we are probably safe in assuming that his sickness had little or nothing to do with his art.

Secondly, and consequently, Van Gogh's art was not conceived by him as a form of therapy—as a balm for his tormented soul. As we have already begun to see, he became an artist for all the same sorts of reasons, and in pursuit of many of the same goals, as other great nineteenth-century painters. Indeed, he went about his work with as much or more conscious diligence and intellectual resource as any other artist of the century. Van Gogh read voraciously in four languages—Dutch, French, English, and German—and had a modest competence in Latin and Greek. He kept well abreast of local, national, and international news and events and was completely current about contemporary art and literature. Far from being purely instinctual and reclusive, Van Gogh was unusually learned and communicative, and his art was dedicated to dialogue, expression, decisiveness, and action in the world. His more than five hundred published letters to Theo are not primarily a personal diary; they are progress reports to a beloved brother and main financial backer, as well as a selfconscious gloss upon a vast, ambitious, and complex body of art.

VAN GOGH'S FIRST STATEMENTS OF PURPOSE

In 1882, at the dawn of his career as an artist (after a decade as an art dealer, school teacher, and evangelist, among other jobs), Van Gogh wrote to Theo concerning his desire to form a community of artists, and his simultaneous realization that the times were probably not ripe:

One would like to speak [with the authority of] the people of '93 [the year of the French Revolution's Reign of Terror]: this and that must be done, first these have to die, then those, then the last ones, it is duty, so it is unarguable, and nothing more need be said.

But is this the time to combine and speak out?

Or is it better, as so many have fallen asleep, and do not like to be aroused, to try to stick to things one can do alone, for which one is alone liable and responsible, so that those who sleep may go on sleeping and resting? (Letter 248)

Six months later, Van Gogh spoke again about the need for artistic collectives: "I am privileged above many others, but I cannot do everything which I might have the courage, the energy to undertake. . . . Why shouldn't more painters join hands to work together, like soldiers of the rank and file?" Two years later, Van Gogh was confirmed in his determination to act as a kind of cultural insurgent. He wrote again to his brother:

I wish you could just imagine that you and I had lived in the year 1848. . . . [During the revolution of 1848] we might have confronted each other as direct enemies, you before the barricades as a soldier of the government, I behind it as a revolutionary or rebel. . . . Neither you nor I meddle with politics, but we live in the world, in society, and involuntarily, ranks of people group themselves. . . . As an individual one is part of all humanity. That humanity is divided into parties. How much is it one's own free will, how much is it the fatality of circumstances which makes one belong to one party or to its opposite. Well, then it was '48, now it is '84, "le moulin n'y est plus, mais le vent y est encore." [The mill is no longer there, but the wind still blows.] But try to know for yourself where you really belong, as I try to know that for myself. (Letter 379)

To explore social "ranks" or classes, to depict the life and culture of peasants and proletarians, to construct an art that is at once an expression of the individual and of his or her community, and to represent a beautiful dream of utopia— these are among the subjects of Van Gogh's mature art, first announced in the years 1882–4.

EARLY ART IN THE HAGUE AND NEUNEN: *THE POTATO EATERS*

In March 1882, Van Gogh's professional career was launched by a commission from his uncle, C. M. Van Gogh, for two sets of drawings of The Hague, where the artist had that year taken up residence. The works were undoubtedly expected to draw upon the great tradition of Dutch cityscape painting of the seventeenth century (especially by Jan Vermeer and Pieter de Hooch) and upon contemporary Hague School Realism as practised by George Breitner (1857–1923), Jacob Maris (1837–99), Isaac Israels (1865–1934), and Anton Mauve (1838–88), among others. Yet in a drawing from the second set, such as *Carpenter's Workshop and Laundry* (1882), Van 297 Gogh has rejected the comforting balance of land, religion, and working-class industriousness found, for example, in Maris's *The Bleaching Yard* (1870). Whereas the latter 298 combines panoramic landscape, church, and laundress in order to embrace Dutch bourgeois pieties, Van Gogh's work offers an unsentimental cross-section of wage labor and small-scale factories. Van Gogh's patron was apparently

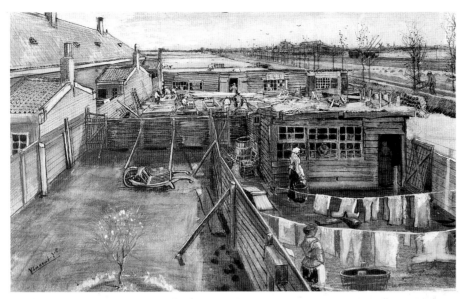

297 VINCENT VAN GOGH *Carpenter's Workshop and Laundry* 1882. 11¼ × 18⅝ (28.5 × 47)

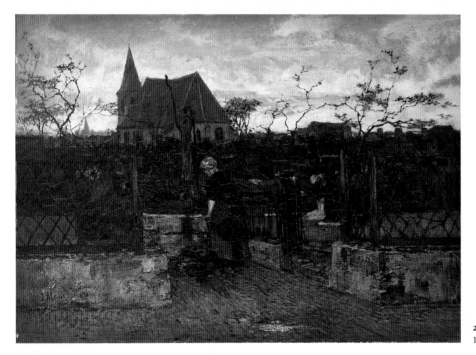

298 JACOB MARIS *The Bleaching Yard* 1870. 16⅛ × 22½ (41 × 57)

disappointed with this and the other drawings in the set, for he paid Van Gogh far less than he promised.

Although drawn with the aid of a perspective window, such as devised by Albrecht Dürer, *Carpenter's Workshop and Laundry* is nevertheless marked with willful violations of perspective and proportion. The diagonal lines at the upper right and left which recede so rapidly toward the horizon belong to a different pictorial order from the lazy dipping and swelling of the foreground zones, as if the space of human labor had to be distinguished from that of nature and its laws. "I have tried to draw the things as naïvely as possible," Van Gogh wrote Theo, "exactly as I saw them before me. . . . As

you can see, there are already several planes in this drawing, and one can look around it and through it, in every nook and cranny. It still lacks vigor . . . but it will come by and by" (Letter 205). The purposeful exaggerations and distortions of light, atmosphere, and anatomy (notice, for example, the angular contours of the idle washerwoman in the right foreground), as well as perspective, which would become so significant a feature of the later oil paintings, are thus already announced in this drawing with pencil, pen, and brush.

Prompted by his acquisition of a collection of popular wood engravings by the English illustrators Luke Fildes, Hubert van Herkomer, Frank Holl, and others, Van Gogh proceeded

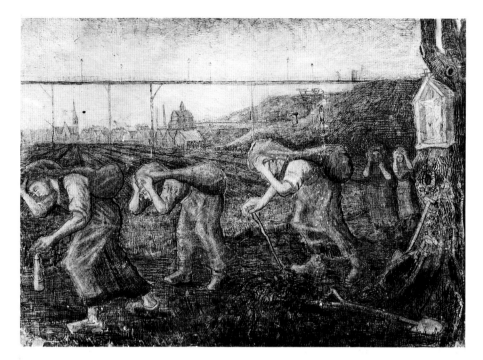

299 VINCENT VAN GOGH *The Bearers of the Burden* 1881. 17 × 23⅝ (43 × 60)

at this time to explore working-class life and labor in a group of over fifty single-figure drawings of men and women from a local almshouse, as well as in dozens of more complex compositions depicting miners, navvies, agricultural workers, and weavers. The artist's perception of these workers is revealed in a letter from 1880, in which he described an excursion from his home in the Borinage (a coal-mining region of Belgium) to a small village of weavers:

> The miners and the weaver still constitute a race apart from other laborers and artisans, and I feel a great sympathy for them. I should be happy if someday I could draw them, so that those unknown or little known types would be brought before the eyes of the people. The man from the depths of the abyss, *de profundis*—that is the miner; the other, with his dreamy air, somewhat absent minded, almost a somnambulist—that is the weaver. . . . And increasingly I find something touching and almost sad in these poor, obscure laborers—of the lowest order, so to speak, and the most despised—who are generally represented as a race of criminals and thieves by a perhaps vivid but very false and unjust imagination (Letter 136).

Van Gogh's words of sympathy reveal the stance of Christian paternalism that dominated his art and thought at the beginning of his career. In *The Bearers of the Burden* (1881), Van Gogh mimics Breugel's parable painting of *The Blind Leading the Blind* (1568), in depicting women in rags weighed down with sacks of coal trudging in a blind and dejected procession. A narrow band of sky above presses down upon these lost and despised souls, while sooty clogs below trace a staggered arc across the foreground. Two years later at Neunen, Van Gogh continued his representation of proletarians in several dozen drawings and small paintings of weavers trapped amid their hand-powered looms. In 1885, he represented peasants in a major work, *The Potato Eaters.*

Composed out of a somber and restricted palette of earth tones—grays, browns, and black—*The Potato Eaters* represents Van Gogh's most accomplished work prior to his move to Paris in 1886. It was completed just three weeks after it was begun and depicts a poor family from the Brabant consuming a humble meal of potatoes and coffee within a meagerly furnished home or *bakhuis* (a small cottage separate from a peasant family's main house, kept exclusively for cooking and eating). An oil lamp casts highlights on men's and women's knuckles, cheekbones, and noses, and upon the various tokens of family wealth: at the upper left are a clock with pendulum and a framed crucifixion scene, and at the upper right a tool rack and a clog filled with spoons. Van Gogh's many visits to his subject-family (the De Groots), dozens of large and small studies in several media (including lithography), and written description of the project, reveal an almost anthropological perspective; his analysis below, for example, exposes a critical self-consciousness at odds with his earlier Christian allegorizing:

> I have tried to emphasize that these people, eating their potatoes in the lamplight, have dug the earth with those very hands they put in the dish, and so it speaks of *manual labor,* and how they have honestly earned their food. I have wanted to give an impression of a way of life quite different

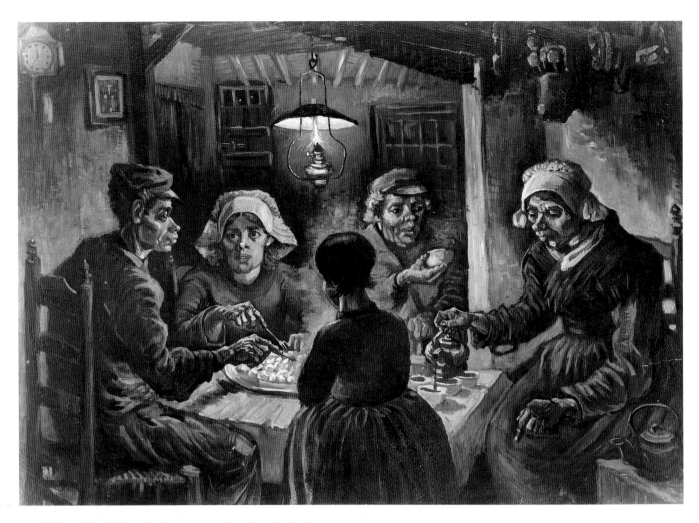

300 VINCENT VAN GOGH *The Potato Eaters* 1885. 32¼ × 44⅞ (82 × 114)

from us civilized human beings. . . . Painting peasants is a serious thing, and I should reproach myself if I did not try to make pictures which will arouse serious thoughts in those who think seriously about art and about life. Millet, De Groux and so many others have given an example of character, and of not minding criticisms such as nasty, coarse, dirty, stinking, etc., etc., so it would be a shame to waver. No, one must paint the peasants as being one of them, as feeling, thinking as they do (Letter 404).

There is no doubt that *Potato Eaters* is profoundly different from other peasant paintings Van Gogh would have known. Whereas Jules Breton emphasized the timelessness of peasant ritual piety, in such works as *Blessing of the Wheat in the Artois* (1857), Van Gogh has relegated Christianity to the crude image of a framed crucifixion; whereas Jozef Israëls (1824–1911) depicted a wholesome and well-washed nuclear family in *The Frugal Meal* (1876), Van Gogh represented the awkward and unclean men and women of an extended and

fatherless family; and whereas William-Adolphe Bouguereau depicted feminine leisure and coquettishness in *The Nut Gatherers* (1880), Van Gogh shows cheap food to be the meager reward for peasant hard labor.

Yet despite Van Gogh's relative distance from bourgeois peasant painting, he was unable completely to rid his art of convention. For one thing, his vision was filtered through innumerable art historical sources, from Rembrandt to Millet to Breton, and *Potato Eaters* shows it. More importantly, as the art historian Griselda Pollock has demonstrated, the intended interlocutors of the painting are not peasants but urban bourgeois—"us civilized human beings," as Van Gogh wrote. In *Potato Eaters*, Van Gogh tried to address a vanguard bourgeois public in an artistic language born, so he thought, in the soot and soil of peasant life itself. Not surprisingly, his efforts were received with indifference or disdain, and he thereupon undertook still another self-refashioning. This entailed a move to Antwerp and then Paris, and the pursuit of an emerging dream of utopia.

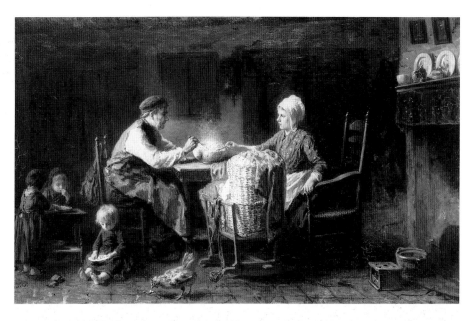

301 JOZEF ISRAËLS *The Frugal Meal* 1876.
35 × 54⅝ (88.9 × 138.7)

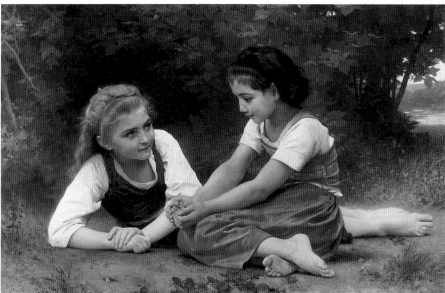

302 WILLIAM-ADOLPHE BOUGUEREAU
The Nut Gatherers 1880. 34⅝ × 52¾ (88 × 134)

ACADEMIC TRAINING AND AVANT-GARDE EDUCATION IN ANTWERP AND PARIS

Van Gogh spent just three months in Antwerp, during which time he attended art classes at the Academy of Fine Arts, studied the paintings of Rubens, and began to collect Japanese woodblock prints. His experience at the Academy was frustrating, as it was for so many others at the Paris Ecole des Beaux-Arts. "First make a contour," Van Gogh was instructed by his teacher, "your contour isn't right; I won't correct it if you do your modeling before having seriously fixed your contour.... Color and modeling aren't much, one can learn that very quickly, it's the contour that is essential

and the most difficult." Van Gogh then exclaimed to Theo: "And now you ought to see how flat, how lifeless and how insipid the results of that system are . . . Like David, or even worse, like [Jan Willem] Pieneman [1779–1853] in full bloom." (Letter 452). A few years earlier, another artist of independent and romantic temperament, Odilon Redon (see Chapter 15), had a similar experience at the Paris atelier of Gérôme: "I was tortured by the teacher. . . . His corrections were vehement to the point that his very approach to my easel upset my comrades. All was in vain. He recommended that I enclose in an outline a form that I saw palpitating. . . . [He] drew with authority a stone, a shaft or a column, a table, a chair, an inanimate accessory, a rock and all of inorganic nature. The pupil saw only the expression, only the expansion

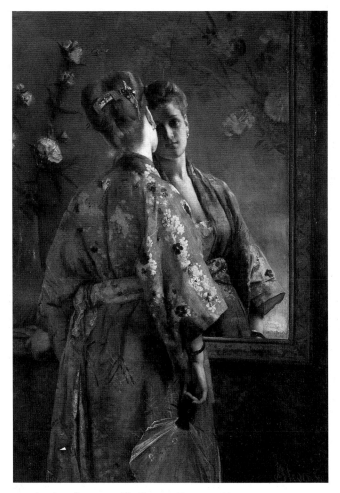

303 ALFRED STEVENS *The Japanese Dress* ca. 1880. 59 × 41½ (150 × 105)

deeply, was he not as simple as a workingman all his life, and so sensitive to all the miseries of others? (Letter 453).

The letter exposes at once Van Gogh's solidarity with the working-class movement and his bourgeois fear and guilt—his political progressivism and his paternalistic conservatism. His solution to the dilemma of class conflict was akin to the utopian one proposed more than two generations before by Henri de Saint-Simon, who wrote in his *Nouveau Christianisme* (1825) that "all men should treat one another as brothers," adding that his new religion would, by "improving the moral and physical well being of the poorest class . . . bring prosperity to all classes of society and all nations with the greatest possible speed." More broadly still, Van Gogh must be understood as one of the many artists, writers, and philosophers of the nineteenth century who shared an attitude of romantic anticapitalism. This perspective, which is especially marked in Van Gogh's favorite romantic authors—including Carlyle, Dickens, and Michelet—may be recognized by its critique of the nineteenth-century economic and social order from the perspective of precapitalist cultural values. For the romantic anticapitalist, the longed for vision of the future is always the reflection of an imagined past. Van Gogh's two years in Paris, from February 1886 to February 1888, would accelerate this already established critical trajectory of his art and thought.

Van Gogh's Paris period taught him the decisive lessons of Impressionism. He grew confident in his treatment of sunlight and prismatic color (lessons gleaned from works by Seurat as well as by Renoir and Monet) and used his new skills to portray modern life, urban and suburban entertainments, and bourgeois and petit bourgeois sociability. In addition, he undertook a thorough study of Japanese Edo Period woodblock prints, exhibiting his personal collection of them at the Café Tambourin in March 1887. In his collecting, Van Gogh was manifesting the Japonisme that had become widespread in the two decades since the display of Japanese arts and crafts at the Paris Universal Exposition of 1867. Yet for him, unlike for the dealer Samuel Bing or the Belgian-born painter Alfred Stevens (1823–1906; see, for example, his *The Japanese Dress,* 303 ca. 1880), Japan was not simply a sign of chicness and exoticism: it was also a dream-image of utopia. Japanese prints appear as the backdrop for his most extraordinary painting of the Paris period, the *Portrait of Père Tanguy* (1887–88). 304 Tanguy was an art dealer, color merchant, and ardent socialist who was especially kind to the often scorned artist, extending him friendship and hospitality as well as considerable credit. They shared, according to their friend the painter Emile Bernard, both poverty and a sustaining faith in the coming dawn of a utopian "era of happiness . . . [and] social harmony." Van Gogh depicts Tanguy seated with eyes

of the triumphant feeling of forms." For both artists, Academic Classicism was at once moribund pedagogy and the token of an elite and discredited social and class hierarchy; for both, Classicism was opposed by what they considered the naive and naturally expressive art of Delacroix, Millet, and Corot. Shortly after describing his academic instruction in Antwerp, Van Gogh wrote again to Theo, but this time about art and politics and the economic depression:

> I do not think it exaggerated to be pessimistic about the various strikes, etc., everywhere. They will certainly prove not to have been useless for the following generations, for *then* they will have proved a success. . . . The laborer against the bourgeois is as justifiable as was the third estate against the other two, a hundred years ago. And the best thing to do is to keep silent, for fate is not on the bourgeois side, and we shall live to see more of it; we are still far from the end. So although it's spring, how many thousands are wandering about, desolate. . . . Corot, who after all had more serenity than anybody else, who felt the spring so

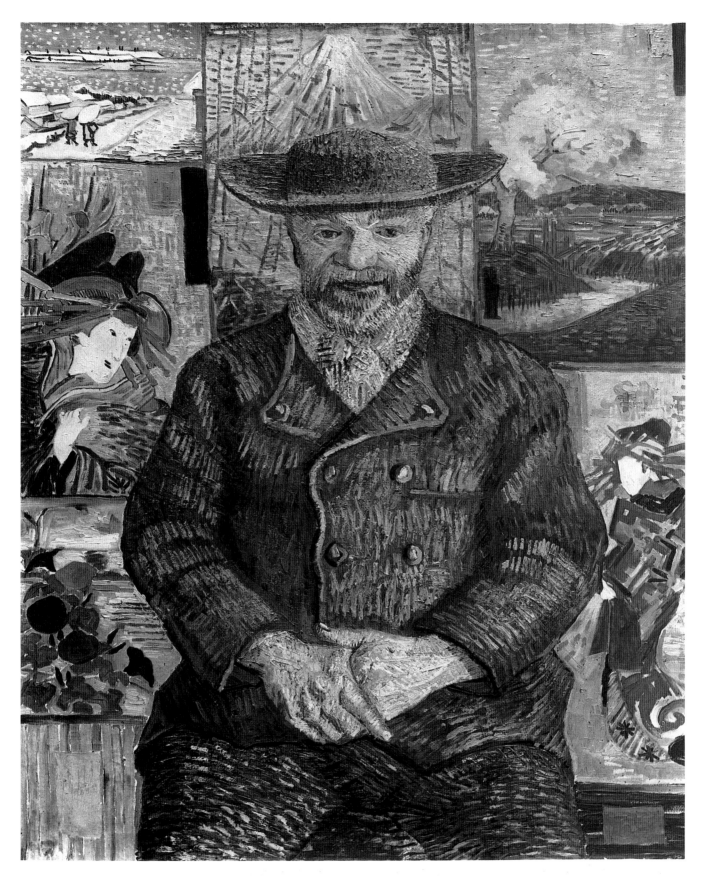

304 **VINCENT VAN GOGH** *Portrait of Père Tanguy* 1887–8. 36¼ × 29½ (92 × 75)

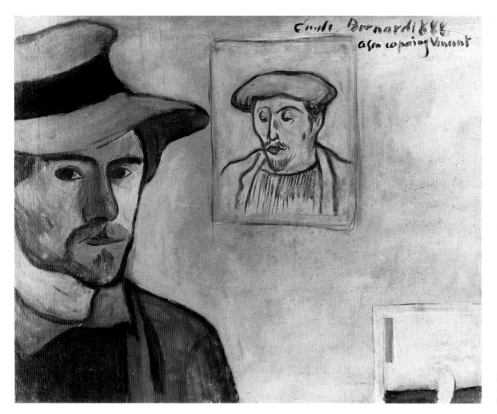

305 EMILE BERNARD *Self-Portrait With Portrait of Gauguin* 1888. 18⅛ × 21⅝ (46 × 54.9)

downcast and hands somewhat stiffly interlocked, in the posture of a Japanese bonze (Buddhist monk). Behind him are at least five freely rendered Japanese prints depicting geishas and landscapes (by Yoshitara, Toyokuni, and Hiroshige), including Mount Fuji, which seems to rise like a crown from Tanguy's hat. By its Chromo-luminarist color and its fashionable "japonaiserie" (a term Van Gogh discovered in Edmond de Goncourt's novel *Chérie,* 1884), the painting is a kind of summary of the artist's assimilation of Parisian avant-garde fashion. Yet in many ways, it is also an announcement, as Fred Orton and Griselda Pollock have written, of the artistic life—the dream of utopia—that was beckoning from Arles in the South of France.

Feeling that his art and life were too narrowly circumscribed by the reigning art institutions and constricting sociability of Paris, Van Gogh had begun to contemplate a move to Arles. There, warmed by a brilliant Provençal sun and solaced by a community of generous and like-minded artist-friends, he would pursue his twin generic ambitions of portrait and landscape painting. All in all, Arles "would be the painter's paradise," Van Gogh wrote in a joyful moment, "it would be absolute Japan" (Letter 543). By the "japonaiserie" of the *Portrait of Père Tanguy,* Van Gogh expressed his utopian hope of creating in France the Orientalist ideal world of Japan—a land of sun-filled peace and pleasure whose artists were all as wise as Buddhist monks.

VAN GOGH IN ARLES

Thus, in February 1888, Van Gogh moved to Arles, eager to renew his health and imagination, and to realize his dream of establishing an artist's commune, called the Studio of the South. This esthetic settlement, part monastery and part Fourierist *phalanstère* (socialist colonies described in the writings of Charles Fourier), would be sustained by the warm dry breezes and timeless popular culture of Provence, as well as by the modest financial support of Theo, who had become an important Impressionist impresario for Goupil and Co. of Paris. Inspired by the example of other avant-garde subcultures, such as the Barbizon school, the Impressionists, and the Pre-Raphaelite Brotherhood, and by fantasies of a primitivistic Oriental paradise in the Occident, Van Gogh set about enlisting the participation of several of his artist friends, particularly the young Emile Bernard (1868–1941), who was then engaged, with Gauguin, in his own utopian fantasizing at Pont-Aven in Brittany. Van Gogh wrote to encourage an exchange of artworks (Bernard's *Self-Portrait With Portrait of Gauguin* [1888], which he inscribed to Van Gogh, was sent in reply), and to persuade Bernard to come to Arles: 305

For a long time now I have thought it touching that the Japanese artists used to exchange works among themselves very often. It certainly proves that they liked and upheld

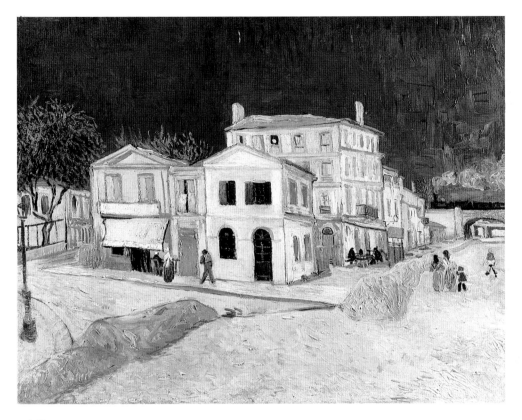

306 VINCENT VAN GOGH *Yellow House at Arles* 1888. 28⅜ × 36 (72 × 91.5)

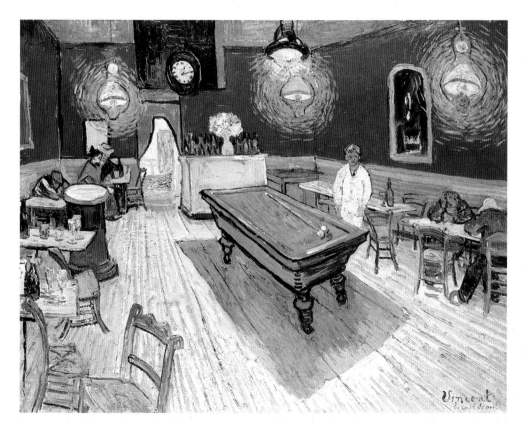

307 VINCENT VAN GOGH *The Night Café* 1888. 28½ × 36¼ (72.4 × 92)

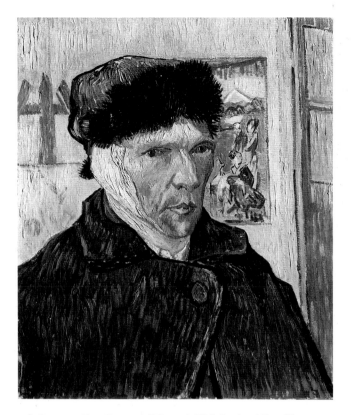

308 VINCENT VAN GOGH *Self-Portrait With Bandaged Ear* 1889. 23⅝ × 19¼ (60 × 49)

tomy, and subtle in their use of color modulation (see Chapter 16) to designate both spatial planes and emotional tenor. Van Gogh described *The Artist's Bedroom in Arles* in a letter to Theo:

> This time it's just simply my bedroom, only here color is to do everything, and, giving by its simplification a grander style to things, is to be suggestive here of *rest* or of sleep in general. In a word, looking at the picture ought to rest the brain, or rather the imagination. The walls are pale violet. The floor is red tiles. The wood of the bed and chairs is the yellow of fresh butter, the sheets and pillows very light greenish citron. The coverlet scarlet. The window green. The toilet table orange, the basin blue. The doors lilac. And that is all—there is nothing else in this room with its closed shutters. The broad lines of the furniture again must express inviolable rest. Portraits on the walls, and a mirror and a towel and some clothes. The frame—as there is no white in the picture—will be white. . . . The shadows and the cast shadows are suppressed; it is painted in free flat tints like the Japanese prints (Letter 554).

Indeed, in spite of the uniformly high-key colors, the painting does achieve balance and restfulness. The buttery yellow bed is kept flat by exaggerated foreshortening, reminiscent of the

each other and that there reigned a certain harmony among them; and that they were living in some sort of fraternal community, quite naturally and not in intrigues. The more we are like them in this respect, the better it will be for us. It also appears that the Japanese earned very little money, and lived like simple workmen (Letter B 18).

At about the same time he wrote to Theo: "Come now, isn't it almost a true religion which these simple Japanese teach us, who live in nature as though they themselves were flowers? And you cannot study Japanese art, it seems to me, without becoming much gayer and happier, and we must return to nature in spite of our education and our work in a world of convention" (Letter 542).

306　　By September 1888, Van Gogh was settled in his *Yellow House at Arles* (1888), the planned center of what the art historian Tsukasa Kodera has called the artist's "primitivistic utopia." At this time, he was painting with an unprecedented rapidity and virtuosity, perhaps in anticipation of the imminent arrival of Gauguin, the only artist who finally came

307　　to live and work with him. Van Gogh's *The Night Café* (1888)
296　　and *The Artist's Bedroom in Arles* (1888) are two of the more than three dozen paintings created during the late summer and fall of 1888. They are simultaneously crude in their disregard of conventional perspective, modeling, and ana-

309 VINCENT VAN GOGH *Joseph Roulin* 1888. 32 × 25¾ (81.2 × 65.3)

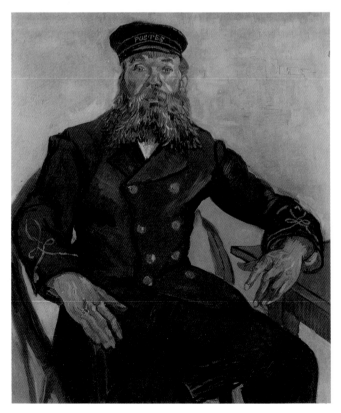

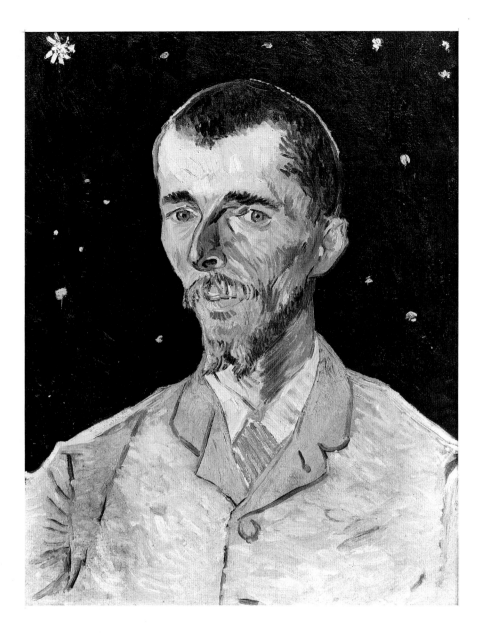

310 VINCENT VAN GOGH *Eugène Boch* 1888.
23⅝ × 17¾ (60 × 45)

vertiginous distortions in works by the Flemish "primitives" (see, for instance, the central panel of the Mérode Altarpiece, ca. 1425–8, by Robert Campin). The warm red-tiled floor is similarly held in spatial equilibrium by the cool blue recessional lines, while the remainder of the picture is constructed out of balanced complements: "The coverlet scarlet. The window green. The toilet table orange, the basin blue." A few large elements on one side of the picture (the door and bed on the right), are balanced against several smaller ones on the other side (window, dressing-table, mirror, rush chairs), anticipating the abstract compositions of the Dutch artist Piet Mondrian (1872–1944), who shared Van Gogh's understanding that the affective quality of color is determined in part by its proximity to other colors and in part by its quantity. Yet for all its subtleties, *The Artist's Bedroom*

in Arles has the aspect of a humbly crafted object; the placement of furniture and accessories in the composition and the thick impasto suggest the ingenuousness of needlework samplers or other pieces of homespun. The whole was conceived, Van Gogh writes, "in harmony . . . of a Seurat-like simplicity."

Precisely such a workmanlike simplicity was sought as well, we have seen, in Van Gogh's portrait *La Berceuse*. Begun in December 1888 during his period of collaboration with Gauguin, the work was only completed in late January after his recovery from the famous and terrible seizure that left him mutilated and hospitalized—as can be seen in his *Self-Portrait With Bandaged Ear* (1889). (Gauguin's stay with Van Gogh at Arles—about which relatively little is known—lasted from October 23 until December 26 1888. Van Gogh's letters

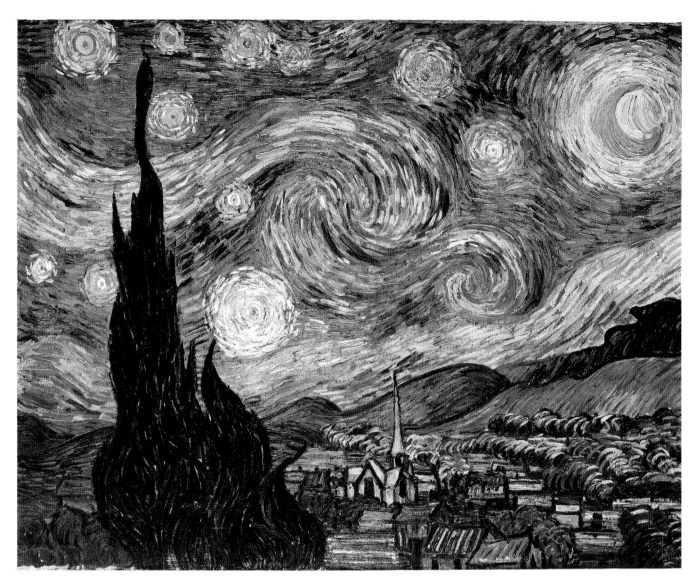

311 VINCENT VAN GOGH *Starry Night* 1889. 29 × 36⅛ (73.7 × 92.1)

to Theo during this period indicate, however, that the two artists got along very poorly; their relationship was marred by mutual suspicion, jealousy, and misunderstanding.) Besides landscapes, portraits and self-portraits now dominated Van Gogh's art; they were, he wrote to Bernard, "*the* thing of the future," part of his effort to record for posterity the physiognomy of a person, a class, a culture, and an epoch. As with the group portrait of the De Groot family in *Potato* 309–10 *Eaters,* the single portraits of *Joseph Roulin* (1888) and *Eugène Boch* (1888) are nearly anthropological in their attentiveness to signs of class and occupation. The postman is posed proud and stiff in his uniform, like the policeman in August Sander's 1925 photograph. Yet unlike the *neue sachlichkeit* (new objectivity) photographer, Van Gogh employed abstraction as well as objectivity to achieve "the great simple thing:

the painting of humanity . . . by means of portraiture" (Letter B 13). He described his portrait of Boch in a letter to Theo:

What a mistake Parisians make in not having a palate for crude things, for [paintings by] Monticelli, for common earthenware. But there, one must not lose heart because Utopia is not coming true. It is only that what I learned in Paris is leaving me, and I am returning to the ideas I had in the country before knowing the Impressionists. . . . Because instead of trying to reproduce exactly what I have before my eyes, I use color more arbitrarily, in order to express myself forcibly. . . .

I should like to paint the portrait of an artist friend, a man who dreams great dreams, who works as the nightingale sings, because it is his nature. . . . So I paint him as he is, as faithfully as I can, to begin with.

But the picture is not yet finished. To finish it I am now going to be the arbitrary colorist. I exaggerate the fairness of the hair, I even get to orange tones, chromes and pale citron-yellow.

Behind the head, instead of painting the ordinary wall of the mean room, I paint infinity, a plain background of the richest, intensest blue that I can contrive, and by this simple combination of the bright head against the rich blue background, I get a mysterious effect, like a star in the depths of an azure sky (Letter 520).

Having always insisted in his letters upon the necessity of drawing and painting from models, Van Gogh now was finding mimesis inadequate to his expressive ends. Dissonance and abstraction are loosed in the clash of complements and the collapsing of foreground and background in portraits and landscapes from the last year of his life.

STARRY NIGHT AND CRITICAL MODERNISM

311 *Starry Night* (1889) is a depiction of the eastern night sky seen from the window of Van Gogh's barred cell on the upper floor of the St.-Rémy mental hospital in the monastery of St.-Paul-de-Mausole, some fifteen miles northeast of Arles. Van Gogh was confined there for one year between May 1889 and May 1890, during which time he painted numerous views of the asylum grounds and the surrounding countryside. *Starry Night* is in many ways a compendium of the artist's interests and preoccupations. Thickly painted in a kind of whorling chain-stitch, the picture has the crafted surface of the "crude things" Van Gogh admired most: "common earthenware," rush-seated chairs, and old pairs of workmen's shoes. Symbols are drawn from a well-thumbed dictionary of romantic anticipitalism: mournful cypress trees, church steeples, peasant cottages with glowing hearths, hills and stars and planets. Indeed, the work is in part a reverie upon a utopian future based on the imagined social integrity of a simpler past. Yet at the same time it is a modernist rejection of the pictorial conventions of Realism and Naturalism. The dichotomy was remarked on by Van Gogh: "[*Starry Night*] is

not a return to romantic or religious ideas, no. Nevertheless, by going the way of Delacroix, more than is apparent, by color and a more spontaneous drawing than delusive precision, one could express the purer nature of a countryside compared with the suburbs and cabarets of Paris" (Letter 595).

In his painting of *Starry Night* and in his brief explication of it to Theo, Van Gogh is revealed as a critical modernist as much as a romantic anticapitalist. "Precision" of representation is "delusive" to Van Gogh exactly because it obscures behind an empirical veil the historically contingent conflicts of class, politics, and ideology that were so keenly felt and understood by the artist throughout his life. Yet the assumption of a critical stance—as we have seen repeatedly in the lives and works of nineteenth-century artists from Goya to Turner to Courbet—entailed considerable risks. Without the old rules of representation (and they have been almost entirely disregarded in such final works as *Roots and Trunks of Trees*, 1890), how can coherence and comprehensibility be upheld? "At one time," Vincent wrote to Theo in 1889, "abstraction seemed to me a charmed path. But it is bewitched ground, old man, and one soon finds oneself up against a wall." For Van Gogh as for so many of his fellow avant-gardists, the old Classical order was dead, but the new modern one could not be born; the goal of creating an art at once radically democratic and completely modern would remain a dream for at least another two generations. Van Gogh, however, would not be part of that continuing quest: for reasons that remain obscure, but which may have been related to despair over his illness, Van Gogh shot himself on July 27, 1890 outside the village of Auvers-sur-Oise, where he had not long before moved. He died in his bed two days later.

As much as Seurat, Van Gogh created an art of antinomy. Traditionalist and revolutionary, he has achieved greater reknown than any other artist of his century, yet at the same time been construed as inscrutable and reclusive. Realist and Symbolist, Van Gogh succeeded in breaking down the barriers between popular and elite art, yet at the same time was taken to exemplify the unbridgeable chasm between the common person and the artistic genius. A summary of the life and art of Van Gogh is thus also a summary of the contradictions of modernism, and especially of the simultaneous "charmed path," and "bewitched ground," of abstraction.

SYMBOLISM AND THE DIALECTICS OF RETREAT

MODERNISM VERSUS SYMBOLISM

Throughout the nineteenth century, modern artists sought to assert their connection to the Classical past by continually strengthening their links to the present: "The true painter we're looking for," we have heard Baudelaire proclaim, "will be the one who can snatch from the life of today its epic quality, and make us feel how great and poetic we are in our cravats and our patent-leather boots." Modernism, it is now possible to state in summary, as it evolved in Europe and North America over the course of the nineteenth century, was not so much a rejection of older European forms as a radical (and more or less last-ditch) effort to keep the Classical tradition alive in all its epic and imperial authority. "All we were really after," the Impressionist Renoir declared, "was to try to induce painters in general to get in line and follow the Masters, if they did not wish to see painting definitely go by the board." The work of Van Gogh revealed as clearly as any other the simultaneous conservatism and revolutionism of this modern cultural strategy.

Van Gogh's primary genre interests—portraiture and landscape—were traditional forms that harked back to the Flemish and Dutch Golden Ages of Breugel, Rembrandt, and Van Ruisdael. Indeed, for all his Chromo-luminarism and use of "arbitrary" color, Van Gogh in such final paintings as *Crows In the Wheatfields* (1890) paid homage not so much to the landscapes of Seurat as to the rural allegories of Breugel: "They are vast fields of wheat under troubled skies," Van Gogh wrote to Theo in July 1890 concerning these works, "and I did not need to go out of my way to express sadness and extreme loneliness. I hope you will see them soon—for I hope to bring them to you in Paris as soon as possible, since I almost think that these canvases will tell you what I cannot say in words, the health and restorative forces that I see in the country" (Letter 649).

Despite his traditionalism, however, Van Gogh expressed in his work the revolutionary stamp and tenor of his times. His landscape subject and facture implicitly criticized the Classical rules and hierarchies of late Renaissance and Baroque painting and its Academic descendants. In addition, his portraits of workers and peasants were efforts to reveal the physiognomy of a dawning twentieth century; by their employment of dissonance or chromaticism, moreover, they suggested the recent music of Wagner. Since the early 1880's, Wagnerism had gained numerous adherents in Paris, especially among the artists and writers who clustered around the poets Jules Laforgue and Stéphane Mallarmé, and the journalists Edouard Dujardin and Théodore de Wyzewa, founders in 1885 of the *Revue Wagnérienne*. For this coterie—which also included the painters Gustave Moreau, Odilon Redon, and Henri Fantin-Latour—Wagner's music represented the long sought esthetic and philosophical unity of sensation, emotion, and intellection, what Wyzewa called "*la vie totale de l'univers*." Van Gogh too was infatuated by Wagnerism, apparently believing that it offered him a means to revitalize an otherwise stultified artistic tradition. "I made a vain attempt to learn music," he wrote to Theo in the summer of 1888, "so much did I already feel the relation between our colour and Wagner's music." Indeed, in *La Berceuse* we saw Van Gogh's modification of the normal harmonic scale progression through the introduction of color accidentals almost to the point of abstraction. But this was an abstraction that was intended not to destroy the art of portraiture but to save it, that is, to make it once more a vehicle for the revelation of human character, the recording of social station, and the expression of feeling. Van Gogh's project of reconciling

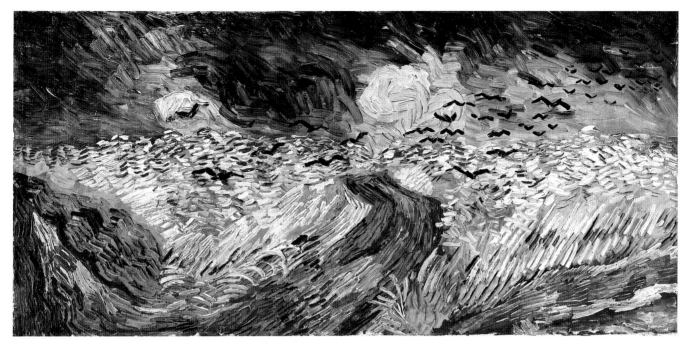

312 VINCENT VAN GOGH *Crows in the Wheatfields* 1890. $19\frac{7}{8} \times 39\frac{1}{2}$ (50.5 × 100.3)

expression and representation, therefore, like the modernist project as a whole, was complex and fraught with difficulty, and engendered an anxiety: how could he keep his work in touch both with modern life and with the masters, without falling victim to either complete abstraction or historicism, both of which signaled to him meaninglessness and the death of art.

At least some of Van Gogh's contemporaries, including the French Gauguin, Auguste Rodin, and Redon, the Belgian James Ensor, the Russian Mikhail Vrubel, the Norwegian Edvard Munch, and the Swiss Ferdinand Hodler had much less anxiety about abstraction. To them, the subtle critical prerogatives of modernism were useless ingenuities in a society tumbling headlong into decay and perdition. To them, painting and sculpture might as well become as abstract or "Symbolist" as imagination demanded, since reality itself was hopelessly degraded and no significant public sphere for art any longer existed. Besides, they reasoned, had not an earlier generation of Romantics shown that form alone—line, color, or pattern—was adequate to convey spiritual meaning and personal expression? "Art is an abstraction;" Gauguin wrote to his friend the painter Emile Schuffenecker in August 1888, "take from nature as you dream, and think more of the creation that will come of it. The only way to rise up to God is by doing like our divine master, by creating." Gauguin's emphasis upon dreams and the spiritual as bases for art was repeated by many others of this generation.

Conceived during a period of widespread European pessimism and disenchantment stemming from a capitalist depression lasting nearly a generation, Symbolism was the artistic symptom of a structural crisis. It was an inward-directed art, antihistorical, intensely personal, and sometimes even confessional. Not daily life but the arcadias of Puvis de Chavannes (see p. 277) and the funereal dreams of the Swiss painter Arnold Böcklin (1827–1901) inspired it. Symbolism marked, therefore, the conclusion of a four-centuries-old tradition of representation founded on Classical concepts of mimesis, and the end of a fifty-year period described by the American art historian Elizabeth Gilmore Holt as "the triumph of art for the public." Yet Symbolism was not only a retreat from representation and public meaning; by rejecting a European mimetic tradition, it also pioneered a new art of sensual liberation and personal expression founded in part on non-Western "primitivism." As much as it was an art of retreat, decadence, and recondite meaning, it was also an engine of cultural criticism, political reinvigoration, and international perspective. Symbolism accelerated the predominant nineteenth-century conflict between Classical representation and critical modernity to a point of crisis; on the horizon lay the irregular terrain of Cubism, the abyss of nonrepresentation, and the revolutionary dreamscape of Surrealism. Symbolism was not an avant-garde subculture—like the Pre-Raphaelite Brotherhood, the Impressionist Société Anonyme or the Neoimpressionist Société des Indépendants—structured societies with membership lists, dues, proscribed exhibition venues, and sectarian rules of

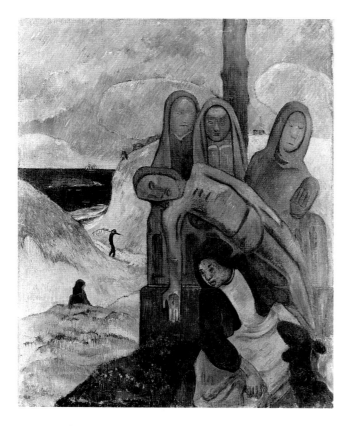

313 PAUL GAUGUIN *Green Christ* 1889. 36¼ × 28¾ (92 × 73)

inclusion and exclusion; it was an international cultural and esthetic direction that, however, spawned numerous local avant-gardes. During the final two decades of the nineteenth century, Symbolism became an irresistible cultural tide that swept across Europe and North America.

THE RHETORIC OF SYMBOLISM

Symbolism may first of all be recognized by its rhetoric. In what many regarded as a Symbolist manifesto, published in the Paris *Figaro Littéraire* on September 18, 1886, the poet Jean Moréas proclaimed the value of pure subjectivity and representation of the "Idea." He wrote: "Symbolic poetry endeavors to clothe the Idea in a sensitive form which, nevertheless, would not be an end in itself, but would be subordinate to the idea while serving to express it . . . art can derive from objectivity only a simple and extremely succinct point of departure." A week later, the poet and critic Gustave Kahn penned a response to Moréas in which he too insisted upon the right of poets and artists to disdain history and contemporaneity and indulge in a world of dream:

> As to subject matter we are tired of the quotidian, the near at hand, and the compulsorily contemporaneous; we wish

to be able to place the development of the symbol in any period whatsoever, and even in outright dreams (the dream being indistinguishable from life). . . . The essential aim of our art is to objectify the subjective (the externalization of the Idea) instead of subjectifying the objective (nature seen through the eyes of a temperament).

Kahn's final pithy formulation, that the artist should "objectify the subjective . . . instead of subjectifying the objective," which Naturalist writers and painters such as Zola and Monet had done, was rapidly seized upon by a diverse array of painters as well as poets as the essential maxim of Symbolist esthetics. Thus, by 1891, the young critic Albert Aurier, in an article called "Symbolism in Painting: Paul Gauguin," was able formally to codify a definition of Symbolist painting under five terms:

1. *Ideist*, for its unique ideal will be the expression of the Idea.
2. *Symbolist*, for it will express this idea by means of forms.
3. *Synthetist*, for it will present these forms, these signs, according to a method which is generally understandable.
4. *Subjective*, for the object will never be considered as an object but as the sign of an idea perceived by the subject.
5. (It is consequentially) *Decorative*—for decorative painting in its proper sense, as the Egyptians and, very probably the Greeks and the Primitives understood it, is nothing other than a manifestation of art at once subjective, synthetic, symbolic and ideist.

In practise, these recipes for Symbolist art were distilled by French, and later other European and American, artists, critics, and a small public down to this simple formula: Symbolism was that theory of art which ascribed the greatest value to the representation of dreams, visions, or other subjective states by means of a restrictive and non-naturalistic vocabulary of line, tone, and color.

Yet if Symbolism had a generally accepted rhetoric, its historical and ideological significance was much less widely agreed upon. To some, such as the painter Maurice Denis (1870–1943) who, along with Paul Sérusier, Edouard Vuillard (1868–1940), and Pierre Bonnard (1867–1947), was a member of the avant-garde group called the Nabis (the word is Hebrew for prophets), Symbolism was a form of "Neotraditionism" that stressed Christian values of quietism, piety, asceticism, and hierarchical stability. In 1890, Denis described how the Symbolist rejection of Naturalism and embrace of formal abstraction was paving the way toward a new and earnestly felt spirituality: "All the sentiment of the work of art comes unconsciously, or almost so, from the state of the artist's soul: 'He who wants to paint the story of Christ must live with

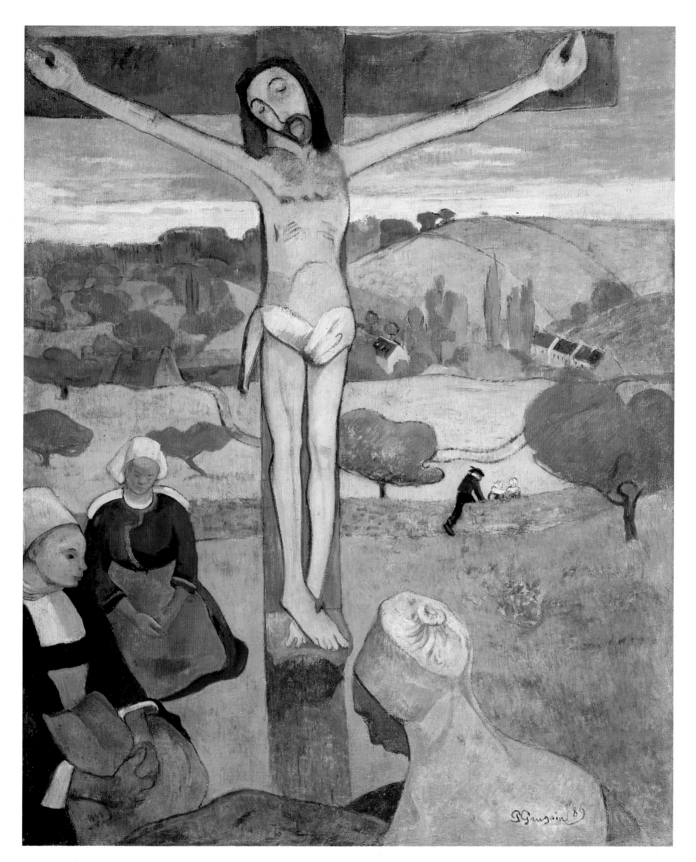

314 Paul Gauguin *Yellow Christ* 1889. 36½ × 28¾ (92 × 73)

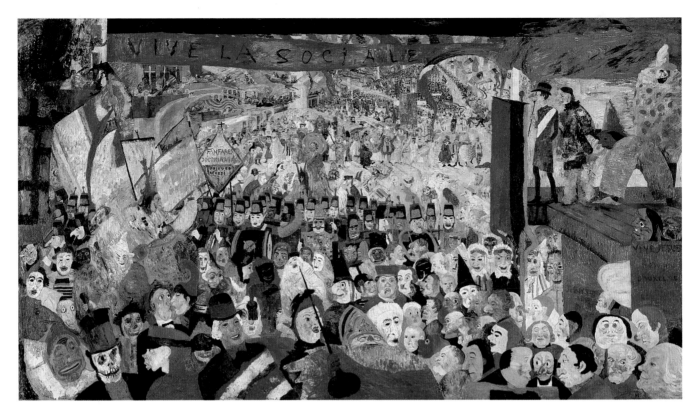

315 **JAMES ENSOR** *The Entry of Christ into Brussels in 1889* 1888. 8'6½ × 14'6 (260 × 430.5)

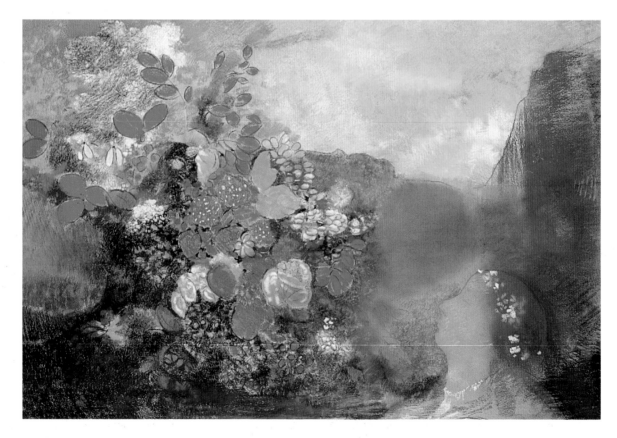

316 **ODILON REDON** *Ophelia Among the Flowers* 1905. 25⅛ × 35⅝ (64 × 91)

313 Christ,' said Fra Angelico. This is a truism. . . . Our . . . impression of moral order opposite [Gauguin's] *Green Christ* [1889] and the bas-relief *Be in Love and You Will Be Happy* cannot spring from the motif or motifs of nature represented, but from the representation itself, forms and coloring."

To other critics, such as the Neoimpressionist apologist Fénéon, Symbolism was an art of creative freedom and sensual liberation that furthered the growing impetus toward revolutionary anarchism. Describing the work of Paul Gauguin (1848–1903) in 1889, he invoked the anarchist dream of free and autonomous nations or communities living side by side in cooperation and harmony:

> Reality for [Gauguin] was only the pretext for a creation quite removed from it: he puts into a new order the material furnished for him by reality; he disdains all illusion, even the illusion of atmosphere; he accentuates lines, limits their number, makes them hierarchic; and within each of the spacious cantons formed by their interlacing, an opulent and sultry color bleakly extends its own pride without in any way threatening the independence of its neighbors, and at the same time without compromising itself.

Fénéon's description of Gauguin's Symbolist painting as political allegory could hardly be more different from Denis's description of it as an "unconscious" rendering of a traditional "moral order." Thus, any adequate definition of Symbolism must take account of the complex ideological distinctions marked by these opposing interpretations. The art of Gauguin was at the time, and remains today, the chief field on which the Symbolist battle was waged; our survey of the movement will therefore begin and end with him. In between, we will briefly examine the results of the improbable collision of an antinaturalist Symbolism and the naturalist genre of landscape painting.

PAUL GAUGUIN AND SYMBOLISM IN BRITTANY

314 While no single artwork succinctly exemplifies all of Aurier's Symbolist preconditions, Gauguin's *Yellow Christ*, contemporary critics generally agreed, came close. Painted in Pont-Aven in Brittany in September 1889, the work depicts a group of three Breton women gathered around a crucified Christ (or sculpture of Christ) planted in the gray rock of Golgotha. The shrill yellow color of the divided fields of grain and of Christ's body, the latter thickly outlined in Prussian blue like the leading around the painted glass in medieval church windows, creates an abstract and therefore *decorative* pattern upon the picture surface. Inspired by an eighteenth-century poly-

chromed wooden Christ which the artist had seen in the rustic chapel of Trémalo near Pont-Aven in Brittany, the painting is purposely crude, populist or *synthetist* in aspect. (*Synthétisme* was the term used by artists who were close to Gauguin at Pont-Aven during 1886–90: a painting was meant to synthesize the artist's impressions and memories. During the Universal Exposition of 1889, an exhibition of *Synthétisme* was held and a Groupe Synthétiste was formed in 1891.) Indeed, examination of *Yellow Christ* reveals the impression of newsprint on its upper third, perhaps the result of being blotted with, or rolled up in newspaper, but in any case anticipating the "low-culture"-inspired pasted paper collages of Picasso and Braque from nearly a generation later. Gauguin's landscape receives a somewhat more complex compositional articulation than his figures, but here too the *ideist* intent—the antinaturalist and decorative aspect—is clearly manifest. The trees are flat red clouds that zig-zag from middle right to background left, the stone wall and serpentine path in the middle-ground are painted without tonal modeling, and the crisp edge of the horizon at upper right is unrelieved by atmospheric perspective. Finally, and in sum, the event Gauguin represented is neither historical nor clearly contemporary, the scene neither quotidian nor clearly visionary, and the technique neither mimetic nor clearly abstract. By these ambiguities the painting is *subjective* and *symbolist* in its suggestion of an alternative reality that lay beyond objective knowledge or sight. The critic Octave Mirbeau assented to the evocativeness of the painting when he described it in 1891 as "a rich, disturbing blend of barbaric splendor, Catholic liturgy, Hindu reverie, Gothic imagery, and obscure and subtle symbolism."

Yet however esoteric its sources or syncretism, what is perhaps most noteworthy about *Yellow Christ* and other Brittany pictures by him, such as *The Vision After the Sermon (Jacob Wrestling With the Angel)* (1888) and *The Green Christ*—and what reveals them to be Symbolist—is what is left largely unpainted and unsaid. Gauguin's decorative, pietistic, and populist representations of Breton spirituality pointedly overlooked the modernizing transformations which the people and their region were then undergoing. During the 1870's and '80's, Brittany experienced an economic boom and cultural redevelopment. Despite a nationwide reduction in wholesale prices and extremely sluggish growth rates in the generation following the (nearly worldwide) "crash" of 1873, Brittany, like some other formerly underdeveloped regions of France, thrived. Agriculture was becoming rationalized (small landholders were dispossessed and the landless made into wage-laborers), fishing and other industries expanded, and tourism rapidly grew. The latter development is especially significant for our account since, ironically, it was the touristic marketing of Breton "primitiveness" that

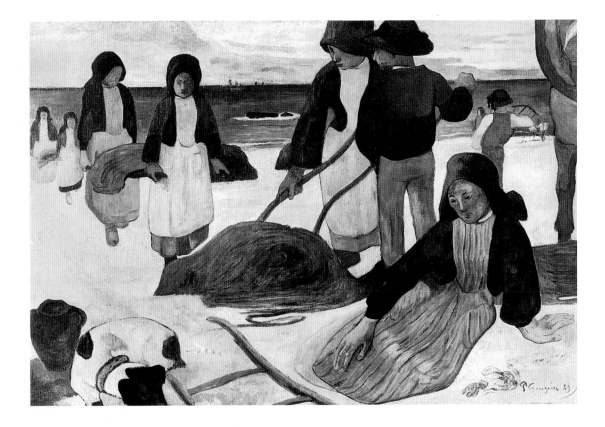

317 PAUL GAUGUIN *The Seaweed Gatherers* 1889. 34¼ × 48½ (87 × 123)

318 PAUL GAUGUIN *Bonjour Monsieur Gauguin* 1889. 44½ × 36¼ (113 × 92)

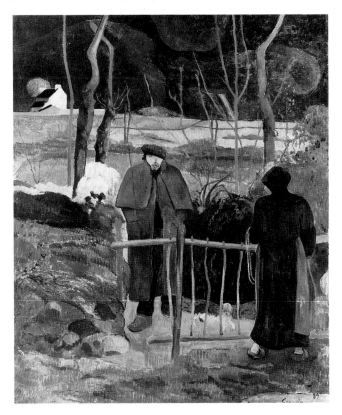

brought Gauguin and many other artists to the region in the first place. The unique and picturesque Breton costumes, for example, which we see represented in works by artists such as Gauguin, Bernard, and Pascal Dagnan-Bouveret, were not a residue of ancient Celtic culture, but rather a complex and modern expression of social hierarchy, class mobility, and cultural aspiration. They permitted people proudly to express their indigenous identities, while at the same time encouraging touristic consumption. Yet Gauguin's representations of what he called in a letter to Theo Van Gogh "savage" and "primitive" Brittany, in pictures created between 1886 and 1890 and again in 1894, largely avoid any reckoning with tourism or with the larger conflict there (and in much of rural agrarian France) between traditional culture and what the philosopher Paul Ricoeur has described as the forces of "universalizing civilization," that is, modern industrial capitalism and its colonizing mass culture.

Gauguin's strategy of evasion thus provides a further preliminary gloss upon Symbolism. The painters who will be considered below—Gauguin, Ensor, Redon, Munch, Vrubel, and Hodler—are Symbolist because their works share certain formal features: flatness, decorativeness, reductiveness, and abstraction; certain iconographic features: a concern with dreams, visions, and the spiritual; and certain ideological features: avoidance of contradiction, disdain for history, and a flight from modernity. Symbolist painting, unlike previous

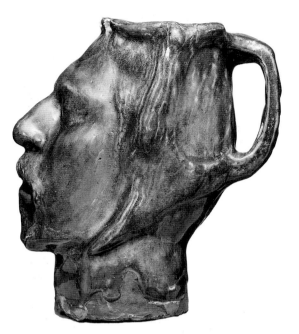

319 PAUL GAUGUIN *Jug in the Form of a Head, Self-Portrait* 1889. Height 7½ (19.3)

320 PAUL GAUGUIN *Christ in the Garden of Olives* 1889. 28¾ × 36¼ (73 × 92)

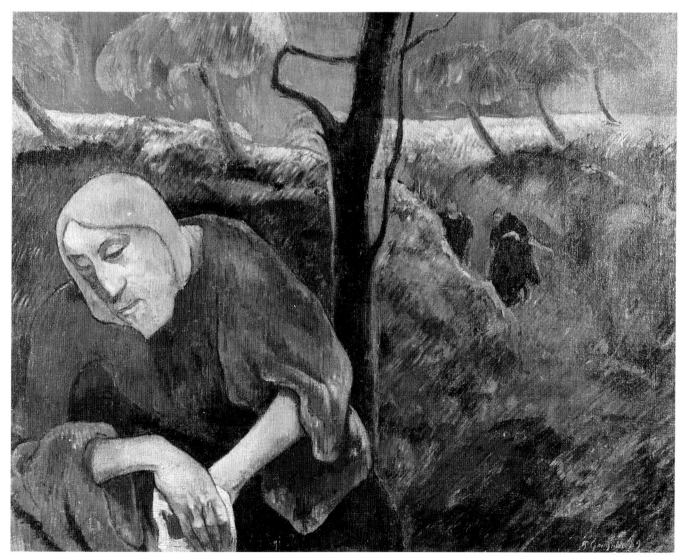

modernisms considered in this book, was as Denis wrote, a form of "Neotraditionism" that upheld a conservative and hierarchical "moral order" in the midst of a society in profound transition. Symbolism was thus "mythical," functioning, as modern European myth does, to "de-politicize speech." "Myth today," wrote the mid-twentieth-century critic Roland Barthes, "turns reality inside out, empties it of history and fills it with nature. . . . [Its function is] to empty reality: it is, literally, a ceaseless flowing out, a hemorrhage, or perhaps an evaporation, in short, a perceptible absence." Barthes argues that at the core of modern myth—embodied today in advertising, mass media, fashion, and tourism—lies an historical amnesia. A similar forgetfulness lurks amid the decorative fanfare of much Symbolist art.

Yet the complexity of Symbolism, and especially the art of Gauguin, does not permit Denis and Barthes to have the final say; Fénéon's words too must be remembered. To him, Gauguin's "synthetist" art from Brittany represented not "Neotraditionism" but a beckoning "new order;" its at once harmonic and independent colors and forms anticipated, he believed, a political future based upon the anarchist principles of mutual respect alongside individual autonomy. Indeed, according to him the art of Gauguin was anything but "de-politicized," despite the fact that it was "removed from reality." Perhaps instead of Barthes, it should be to Claude Lévi-Strauss that we turn for a definition of myth that is germane to Symbolism. The function of myth in "primitive" societies (those without writing), Lévi-Strauss writes, "is to provide a logical model capable of overcoming a contradiction (an impossible achievement if, as happens, the contradiction is real)." Primitive myths are valuable to their cultures not because they mask or occlude contradictions, but because they manage or organize them. In so doing, they underline the prevailing communitarian principle in primitive societies, that, as the anthropologist writes, "self-interest is the source of all evil." Much of the best Symbolist art (especially Gauguin's), I shall argue below, shares this "primitivist" perspective, providing audiences with a new and compelling critique of European culture.

In fact, a closer look at Gauguin's paintings, sculptures, and ceramics from Brittany reveals that he did not entirely abjure modernity and politics. The best works are subtly but forcibly marked by modern signs of artistic alienation, class division, and degrading labor. After organizing in Paris an exhibition of Impressionist and Synthetist art at the Café des Arts (also known as the Café Volpini, after the proprietor), adjacent to the great 1889 Universal Exposition, Gauguin returned to Pont-Aven in June of that year and soon after moved to the nearby hamlet of Le Pouldu. During the next six months, he depicted such modern subjects as proletarian labor in *The Seaweed Gatherers* (1889), subdivided and enclosed grain

317

fields in *Yellow Christ* and other landscapes, and himself as a kind of refugee in *Bonjour Monsieur Gauguin* (1889), a picture inspired by Courbet's *The Meeting* (1854), in which the Realist painter represented himself as the Wandering Jew, forever condemned to walk the earth. In *Christ in the Garden of Olives* (1889) and the extraordinary and disturbing *Jug in the Form of a Head, Self-Portrait* (1889), Gauguin portrayed himself as a savior and a martyr. "This painting is fated to be misunderstood," he said of the *Christ* in a letter to Vincent Van Gogh, "so I shall keep it for a long time." Later he wrote to a journalist: "[*Christ in the Garden of Olives*] represents the crushing of an ideal, and a pain that is both divine and human." What was crushed was the ideal of establishing a harmonious artistic community in "savage and primitive" Brittany in concert with his friends and followers Bernard, Schuffenecker (1851–1934), Louis Anquetin (1861–1932), Jacob Meyer de Haan (1852–95), and Paul Sérusier (1865–1927). Crushed too was the ideal of mutual support and selflessness with Van Gogh at Arles. In Brittany as in the South Seas, Gauguin's response to pain and alienation was the creation of myths, both of the modern and of the primitive sort described above; his Symbolism consisted precisely of a dialectic of avoidance and earnest expression of social contradiction. Many other Symbolist painters, such as Ensor, simply denied modernity outright, finding solace in fantastic imaginings of an ideal past and utopian future.

318

320

319

ENSOR AND POPULISM

James Ensor was born in 1860 at the seaside resort of Ostend, in northwestern Belgium, and died there at the age of 89 in 1949. For most of his life he remained aloof from urban, avant-garde culture as he indulged his carnivalesque imagination in partial emulation of past Dutch and Flemish artists—Van Eyck, Bosch, Breugel, Rembrandt, and Rubens. Thus, like his Symbolist contemporaries in France, Switzerland, and Norway, Ensor was a self-imposed exile from modernization and contemporaneity. "Long live naive and ignorant painting!" Ensor exclaimed in 1900: "Long live the peasant in art . . . Flemish art since Breugel, Bosch, Rubens and Jordaens is dead, truly dead. . . . Long live free, free, free art!" If Ensor was disdainful of modern artistic sophistication and feeling, he was equally scornful of academicism: "All the rules," Ensor wrote, "all the canons of art vomit death like their bronze brethren."

For all his extravagance and vitriol, however, Ensor began his artistic training conventionally enough with private lessons in Ostend, and enrollment in 1877 at the Brussels Academy of Fine Arts. Although he later disparaged the Academy as "that establishment for the near blind," he remained there nearly three years and even earned an award

which artists created art as naturally as trees produced fruit. Ensor was preoccupied with his own failure to achieve such transcendence, and depicted his impotence, marginality, and literal decay in the macabre etching *My Portrait in 1960* (1888).

SYMBOLIST LANDSCAPE PAINTING: MUNCH, REDON, MONET, AND HODLER

The issue of Symbolism's renunciation of modern society (or of what Kahn called "the compulsorily contemporaneous") may be illustrated by examining the movement's position within the history of landscape painting. Since its origins in the late Renaissance, landscape painting has represented not just the physical appearance of land but the social relations between humans in nature. During the seventeenth century, such painters as Claude Lorrain and Nicolas Poussin represented the Italian countryside as a pastoral realm of peace and plenty, recalling a Classical Golden Age described by the Roman poets Virgil and Ovid. In The Netherlands, landscape painting was similarly idealizing and inspiring, although its greater verisimilitude and contemporaneity permitted it to function as an ideological support to an economic order that depended upon rationality, productivity, and expansionism. By the beginning of the nineteenth century, we have seen, during the Romantic period, landscape art (and nature generally) often served as a protest against supposed unnatural intrusions into social life—industrial capitalism, urban living, and the money economy. Yet in all these cases, including of course such art movements as Realism and Impressionism, the relations between nature and society or country and city were intensely dialectical—that is, the mythic stability of the one depended upon the stability of

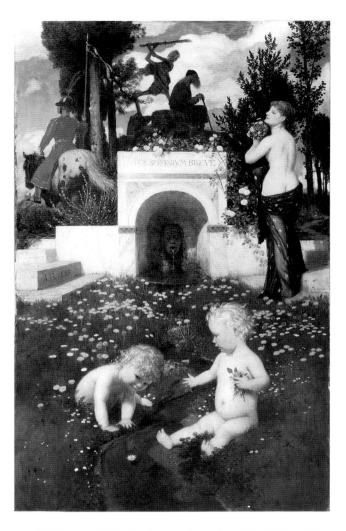

325 **ARNOLD BÖCKLIN** *Vita Somnium Breve* 1888. 70⅞ × 45 (180 × 114.5)

326 **ARNOLD BÖCKLIN** *Island of the Dead* 1880. 29 × 48 (73.6 × 121.9)

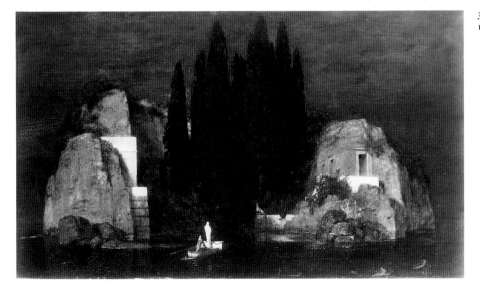

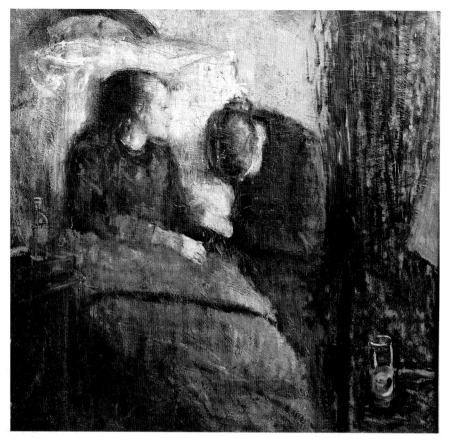

327 EDVARD MUNCH *Sick Child* 1885–6.
47 × 46½ (119.4 × 119)

328 CHRISTIAN KROHG *Sick Girl* 1880–81.
40¾ × 23¼ (103.5 × 51.4)

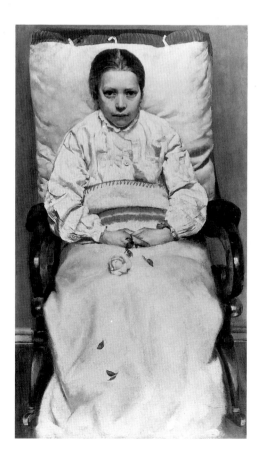

the other, the measure of the one revealed the hidden
dimensions of the other. In this way, nature continued to serve
a progressive function for society, offering itself up as a
measure against which both human accomplishments and
failures could be gauged.

At the end of the nineteenth century, however, the
dialectical relation between nature and society was severed in
the literature and art of Symbolism. During a period of
wrenching economic expansion and contraction, colossal
urban and industrial growth, and the final eradication in
Europe of the remaining pockets of premodern community,
nature came to be considered by some writers and artists as an
inviolable sanctuary and not simply a standard of judgment.
Unlike Caspar David Friedrich, who in the first quarter of the
century depicted nature as a locus for spiritual fulfillment and
social reconciliation, Arnold Böcklin represented it in the last
325 three decades as a place of escape or eternal rest. *Vita
Somnium Breve* [*Life is Short*], an allegorical landscape of
326 1888, and *Island of the Dead* (1880), for example, are siren
songs in praise of blissful solitude and easeful death. In 1937,
the Frankfurt School critic Leo Lowenthal described this
generational sea-change in the representation of nature in his
essay about the popular *fin-de-siècle* Norwegian novelist Knut
Hamsun:

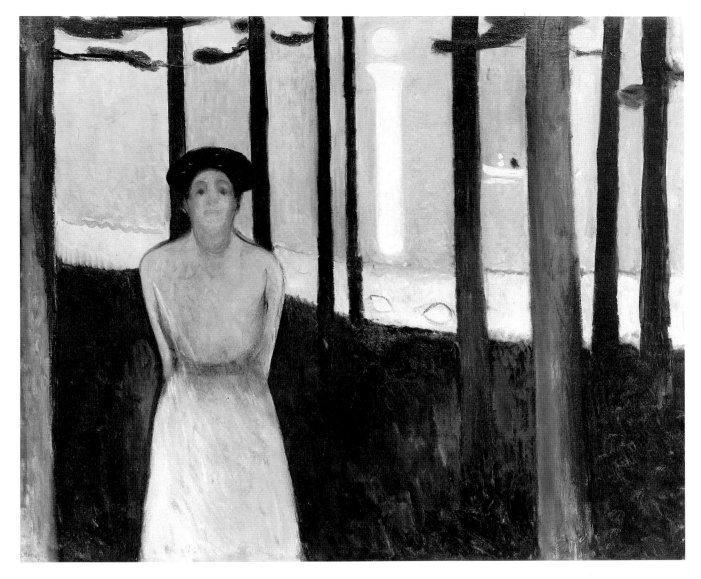

329 EDVARD MUNCH *The Voice* 1893. 34½ × 42½ (87.6 × 108)

However, with the coming of doubt and even despair about personal fulfillment within society, the image of nature was no longer a basis for a new perspective, but became an alternative. Nature was increasingly envisaged as the ultimate surcease of social pressure. In this context, man could submit to nature and feel at peace—at least in fantasy. His soul, inviolable in ideology but outraged in reality, could find solace in such a submission; frustrated in his attempt to participate autonomously in the societal world, he could join the world of nature. He could become a "thing," like the tree or the brook, and find more pleasure in this surrender than in a hopeless struggle against manmade forces. This is the most significant change in man's imagery of his environment to take place in the closing decades of the nineteenth century in Europe. The

novels of Knut Hamsun portray this antinomy of society and nature in an extreme form.

As Lowenthal's remarks indicate, the *fin-de-siècle* was a watershed period in the literary representation of the antinomy between society and nature, but examples from the visual arts are in fact more vivid since only there had the Classical rhetorics which defined the landscape genre—such as the Virgilian pastoral and georgic—continued to exert their thrall. The Symbolist painters of landscape, in short, knew and understood the former paradigms of landscape art, and set out to destroy them. In so doing, they destroyed as well any critical engagement with modernity and created instead a mythic landscape of dreams.

The Norwegian Edvard Munch (1863–1944) began his

career in the circle of Christiania (Oslo) anarchists that included the journalist and activist Hans Jaeger and the naturalist painter Christian Krohg (1852–1925). Munch's *Sick Child* (1885–6), inspired in part by memories of his sister's death from consumption and in part by Krohg's *Sick Girl* (1880–81), is an angry and vivid study of the ravages of a degenerative disease. By its content, large size, and scraped and battle-scarred surface, Munch's *Sick Child* was clearly an indictment of a perceived social and cultural sickness as well as of a tubercular epidemic. The work was bitterly condemned by contemporary critics upon its initial exhibition; Munch soon thereafter retreated to Paris to study drawing at Léon Bonnat's conservative academy, and returned in 1891, a confirmed Symbolist.

In *The Voice* (1893), a painting included among a group of six called by the artist "The Frieze of Life," Munch depicted a lone young woman standing amid trees near the shore of the resort at Asgårdstrand. Starkly dressed in white, she thrusts her chin forward and keeps her hands behind her back; she is as rigid as the trees and as ghostly as the shaft of moonlight at right. This is how Munch described the significance of the six paintings: "The frieze is intended as a series of decorative pictures, which, gathered together, would give a picture of life. Through them all there winds the curving shoreline, and beyond it the sea, while under the trees, life, with all its complexity of grief and joy, carries on." Like his compatriot Hamsun with whom he was often compared, Munch found in nature alone a world of sentiment and pathos. "Have you ever walked along the shoreline and listened to the sea?" Munch asked a friend about Asgårdstrand: "Have you ever noticed how the evening light dissolves into night? I know of no place

on earth that has such beautiful, lingering twilight." In *Pan* (1894), Hamsun wrote: "The sky was all open and clean. I stared into that clear sea, and it seemed as if I were lying face to face with the uttermost depth of the world; my heart beating tensely against it, and at home there." In *The Voice*, as in *Jealousy* (1890), Munch depicted his simultaneous fear and longing to submit to what he saw as the magical, womanly thrall of superior and omniscient natural forces. History is forgotten and human society is powerless before the onslaught of nature, destiny, and the eternal feminine.

The French painter and graphic artist Odilon Redon (1840–1916) similarly articulated the *fin-de-siècle* antagonism between nature and society by portraying humans as passive and powerless objects acted upon by uncontrollable natural forces. In *Ophelia Among the Flowers* (1905), Redon created a meditation upon Shakespeare's irrational Ophelia, seduced by the physical charms of nature. The uniqueness of Redon's image may be judged by a comparison with the Pre-Raphaelite Millais's widely reproduced and much exhibited *Ophelia* of 1851 (Redon may have seen it during his visit to London in 1895). Unlike Millais, Redon chose not to represent the fully stretched out figure of Ophelia, but only her head and shoulders. "Native and indued unto" nature, as Shakespeare wrote, Redon's Ophelia is barely visible; attention is primarily drawn to the clouds of abundant flowers which surround her. Indeed, the heroine is endowed by the artist with no greater personality than the ambient flora; like the ghostly woman in Munch's *The Voice*, she is identified with the irrational and irresistible forces of nature. Similarly, in *Roger and Angelica* (ca. 1908), Redon created a field of glowing hue by means of a technique he called "mutual

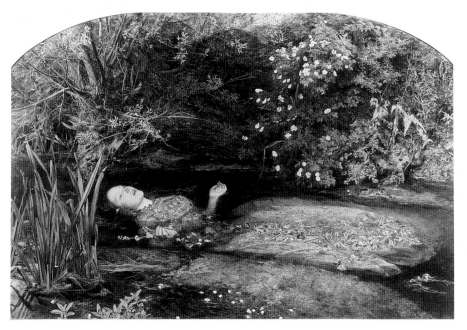

330 JOHN EVERETT MILLAIS *Ophelia* 1851.
30 × 40 (76.2 × 101.6)

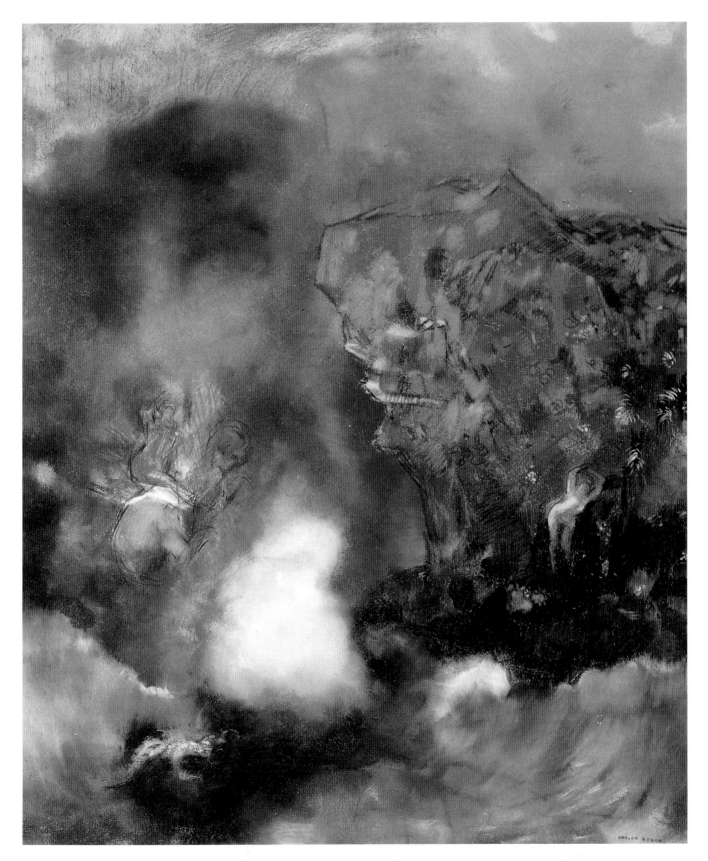

331 **ODILON REDON** *Roger and Angelica* ca. 1908. 36½ × 28¾ (92.7 × 73)

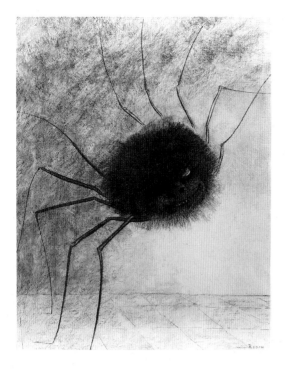

exaltation of colors." The dazzling luminosity of the ultra-marine water and sky is intensified by orange complements, purple and gray-blue adjacents, and the judicious introduction of white or black accents and highlights. The result induces a feeling of disorientation and phantasmagoria.

Created during the twilight of a career marked by isolation and public incomprehension, *Ophelia Among the Flowers* and *Roger and Angelica* eschew the unnatural and assaultive grotesques found in Redon's early *noirs* ("blacks"), such as the nightmarish charcoal *The Eye* (1882) and the lithograph *The Smiling Spider* (1885). In these late works in color, Redon instead focused a pantheistic vision on the minutiae of the natural world: "I cannot say what have been my sources," he wrote in 1903, "I love nature in all its forms; I love it in the smallest blade of grass, the humblest flower, the tree, the ground and the rocks—all things for their character in themselves, more than in the ensemble." In 1904, Redon instructed the novelist André Gide: "Enclose yourself in nature," expressing that desire to "become a thing," as Lowenthal writes: "like the tree or the brook, and find more pleasure in this surrender than in a hopeless struggle against manmade forces."

A parallel surrender before nature is represented in works by the sophisticated and idiosyncratic Russian painter Mikhail Aleksandrovich Vrubel (1856–1910). Rejecting the populism and sentimentality that characterized paintings by the earlier *peredvizhniki* (Wanderers) group—who included

332

332 ODILON REDON *The Smiling Spider* 1885. 10¼ × 8⅜ (26 × 21.5)

333 MIKHAIL VRUBEL *Pan* 1899. 48⅞ × 41⅞ (124 × 106.3)

334 ODILON REDON *The Cyclops* 1905. 25¼ × 20 (64.1 × 50.8)

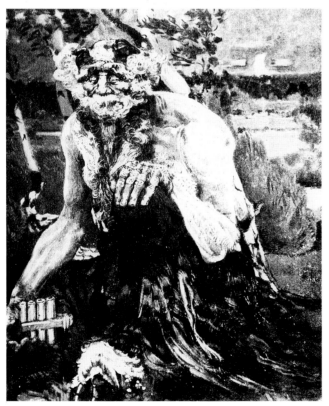

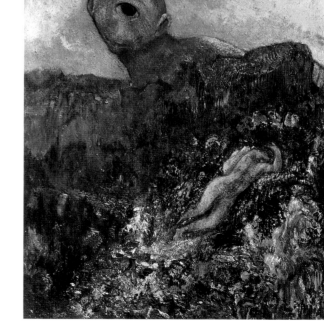

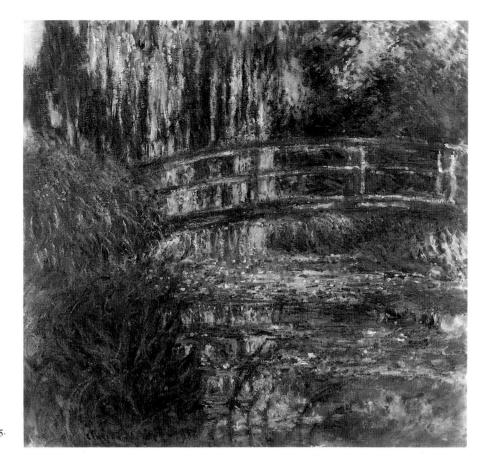

335 CLAUDE MONET *Waterlilies* 1905.
35⅛ × 36½ (89.2 × 92.7)

Ivan Nikolaevich Kramskoy (1837–87) and his student Ilya Efimovich Repin (1844–1930)—Vrubel embraced the stance of the European Symbolist esthete. Possessed, as he wrote, by a "mania" for technique, his paintings are densely packed with broad impastoed planes of color, anticipating the nonobjective works of the early twentieth-century Russian avant-garde. Indeed, Vrubel was conversant with many of the same artists, musicians, and authors who influenced the later generation. He read the works of Tolstoy and Nietzsche, designed stage sets for Rimsky-Korsakov and knew the paintings of Böcklin, Degas, Monet, Moreau, Whistler, and many others through their reproduction in the pages of the Russian journal *Mir Iskusstva* (*The World of Art*). Vrubel's *Pan* (1899), which uncannily anticipates Redon's painting *The Cyclops* (1905), was inspired by Anatole France's story *Le Saint Satyre*. It depicts a kindly satyr—with cloven hoof and pan pipes in hand—who appears to have emerged from the earth. The crescent moon rising on the horizon echoes the shape of the creature's horns and wisps of hair and beard; the cool aqua color of the water at middle right and left is reflected in the blue pools of Pan's gentle eyes. Like the Cyclops in Redon's painting, the Pan in Vrubel's is an autochthonous product of nature who must soon return to its native bourn.

Whereas for Romantic artists, like Friedrich and Turner,

333

334

the confrontation between the autonomous individual and nature signified the limitless potential for human growth or social development, for Redon, Vrubel, and other Symbolist landscape painters, nature is wholly "other," an entity independent of human society or volition, a space designed for passive and private pleasure. A similar vitalism is apparent in the late paintings of Monet, especially the works made at Giverny, such as *Waterlilies* (1905), in which the artist and spectator are immersed in a fantastical world of water, color, and light. The only changes that occur in Monet's garden are seasonal, the result of natural forces. Once again, Lowenthal's remarks are illuminating:

335

> Nature's timetable replaces the timetable of history. . . . Whoever senses and accepts these rhythmic patterns as fundamental has full knowledge immediately and without rational effort. At the same time, the endless reproduction of natural phenomena, the cyclic order of nature, as opposed to the apparent disorder and happenstance of all individual and historical facts, testifies to the powerlessness of humans. It is the extreme opposite of human self-assurance before nature.

Such a conception of nature in the work of these artists arose from the desire to evade social contradiction, history, and contemporaneity, to evade, that is, the dispiriting forces of "universalizing civilization." The antagonism of nature and society that is described here occurred specifically at the moment in history when the colonization and commodification of nature and society had progressed so far that the earlier dialectic conception was ideologically unsustainable. Not a trace of the modern, the quotidian, or the insouciant could be permitted to invade painted landscapes for fear of shattering the Romantic dream of plenitude and thereby admitting the threatening nightmare of alienation and powerlessness. The Symbolist opposition of nature and society is nowhere more compellingly revealed than in the landscapes of Hodler.

The disappearance of an independent peasantry, the erosion of cantonal autarchy, the loss of a rich and vivid "folk" culture, and the concommitant rise of a tourist industry were the factors that led to the artistic segregation of humans and nature in the Symbolist landscapes of Ferdinand Hodler (1853–1918). Indeed, the duration of Hodler's life coincided with a crucially important period of modernization and industrialization, not to say commodification of Switzerland. Apprenticed in 1867 to Ferdinand Sommer, a painter of tourist pictures in the village of Thun in the Bernese Oberland, Hodler was witness to and participant in the explosive growth of the Swiss tourist industry. Yet what marks Hodler's mature landscape art from the 1880's and after is the elimination of nearly all traces of the touristic. The rhetorical justification for this erasure is found in Hodler's Symbolist theory of "parallelism."

After achieving considerable success and celebrity in the 1890's with the exhibition in Paris of such disturbing and dreamlike figure paintings as *The Night* (1891) and *The Chosen One* (1893–4), Hodler increasingly devoted his talents to landscape painting. In 1897, he discussed the essential precepts of that art in a lecture called "The Mission of the Artist," delivered to the Society of the Friends of the Fine Arts in Freiburg. His address repeated many of the prevailing Symbolist tenets of the day, but added a new one:

> *Parallelism,* whether it is the main feature of the picture or whether it is used to set off an element of variety, always produces a feeling of unity. If I go for a walk in a forest of very high fir trees, I can see ahead of me, to the right and to the left, the innumerable columns formed by the tree trunks. . . . Whether those tree trunks stand out clear against a darker background or whether they are silhouetted against a deep blue sky, the main note, causing that impression of unity, is the parallelism of the trunks.

Hodler's first parallel landscape was probably *The Beech Forest* (1885), painted more than a decade before the exposition of the theory, but it was only after 1900, with the series of paintings depicting Lake Leman, Lake Silvaplana, Lake Thun, Lake Geneva, and the summits of the Alps that parallelism came to dominate his art. *Lake Geneva Seen From Chexbres* (1904) consists of an arc of land in the foreground embracing parallel bands of blue, violet, and pink water. The clouds at the horizon resemble identical puffs of smoke from a locomotive passing from right to left; the clouds at the top are a series of parallel and interlocked chevrons. In 1908, Hodler traveled to the Schynige Platte in the Bernese Oberland, a region he had known and loved in his youth, and painted a number of mountain landscapes, including *Eiger, Mönch and Jungfrau Above the Fog* in a still more radically simplified style; the mass of the mountains is rendered with thin oil

342

343

336

336 FERDINAND HODLER *The Night* 1891. 45⅝ × 9'9¾ (116 × 299)

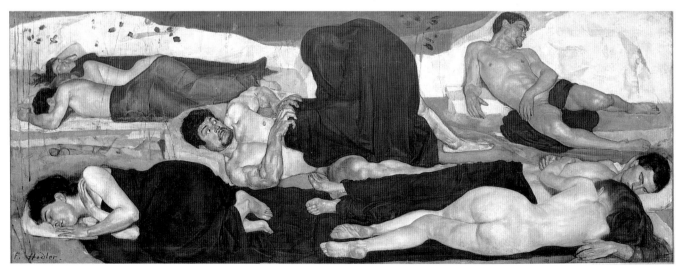

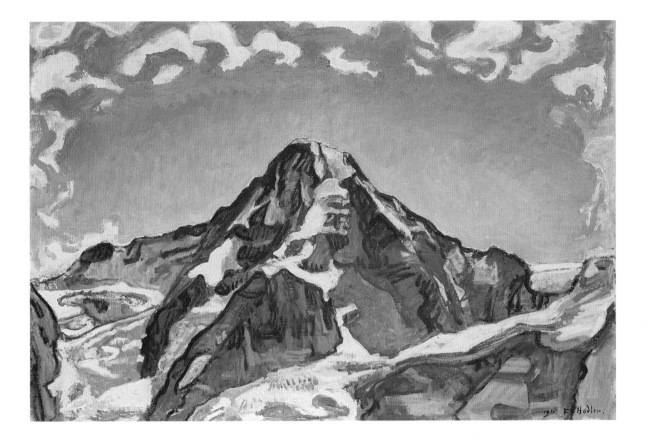

337 **FERDINAND HODLER** *The Mönch With Clouds* 1911. 25⅛ × 36
(64.5 × 91.5)

338 **EDVARD MUNCH** *Madonna* 1895–7. 23⅞ × 17½ (60.6 × 44.5)

washes of gray and blue, while the three summits are precisely
337 outlined in blue, green, and red. Finally, in *The Mönch With
Clouds* (1911), Hodler was at his furthest remove from the
busy tourist pictures of his early career. Here he has depicted
the massif and summit of the second of the three great peaks of
the Bernese Oberland near Grindelwald. The mountain
appears as a steel-blue pyramid with pasty white excrescences;
serpentine clouds, recalling the spermatazoa that enframe
338 Munch's lithograph *Madonna* (1895–7), parallel the picture
surface and rectangular borders, lending by contrast a still
greater mass and stability to the rock.

The late parallel landscapes of Hodler are visions of a world
frozen in time and space. Evacuated and dreamlike, they
conform to no conventional rules of landscape painting and,
unlike the paintings of his exact contemporary Van Gogh, lack
bravura facture and expressionistic color contrasts. Most
striking of all, however, Hodler renounces the integration of
figures or even buildings in his landscapes, a practise essential
for Van Gogh in his representation of agrarian utopias in Arles
and Auvers. Neither are Hodler's landscapes much like the

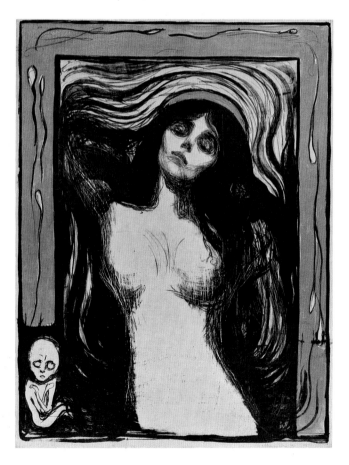

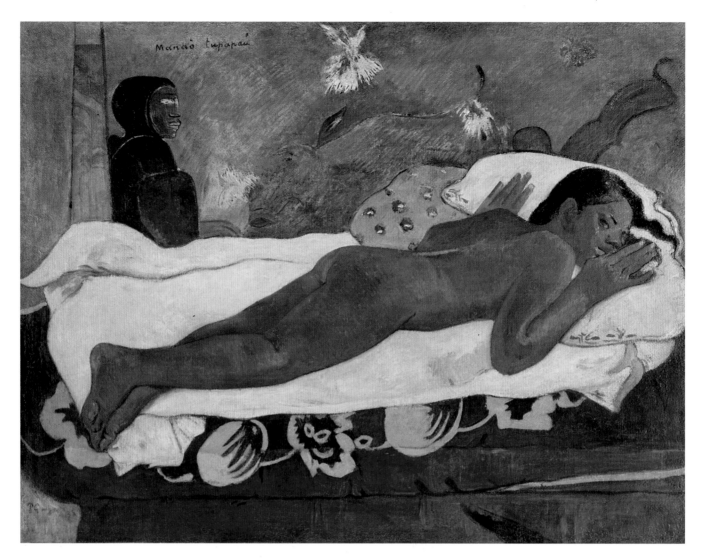

339 PAUL GAUGUIN *Manao tupapau* (*The Specter Watches Her*) 1892. 28¾ × 36½ (73 × 92)

paintings of Cézanne, whose *Mont Sainte-Victoire* (1904–06) would seem to offer the closest analogy to *The Mönch With Clouds*. Both artists sought completeness and stability in their art, but where the latter included in his paintings the unavoidable elisions or lacunas of vision, the former carefully excised all that was fragmentary, untidy, or uncontrollable; where Cézanne captured temporal flux through energetic brushwork, a juxtaposition of warm and cool colors, and a multiplicity of outlines, Hodler's images are largely static, often built of adjacent hues of a single temperature, and of repeated shapes or outlines in accordance with his theory of parallelism.

In "The Mission of the Artist," Hodler stated:

> If we compare these decorative instances [of parallelism in nature] with occurrences from our daily life, we again find

the principle of parallelism. . . . If there is a public festival, you see everybody walking in the same direction. On other occasions, they are grouped around a speaker who represents an idea. Walk into a church during a religious service: the feeling of unity will impress you. When we are gathered for a happy occasion, we do not like to be disturbed by a dissenting voice. In all the examples given, it is easy to see that the parallelism of the events is at the same time a decorative parallelism. . . . The work of art reveals a newly apprehended order of things and is beautiful because it expresses a general harmony.

Hodler's theory of parallelism and the landscape art that arose from it articulated a social or political as much as a compositional imperative. To represent nature and society by means of a system of decorative parallels was to make the unity

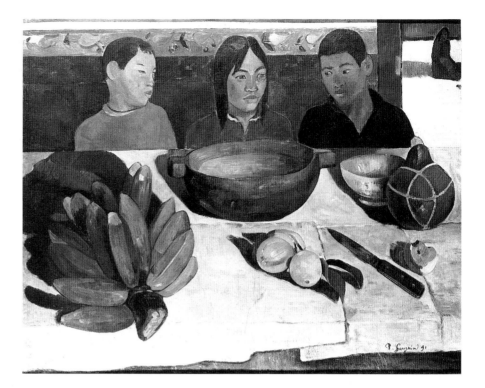

340 PAUL GAUGUIN *The Meal, or The Bananas* 1891. 28¾ × 36¼ (73 × 92)

341 PAUL GAUGUIN *Vahine no te vi (Woman of the Mango)* 1892. 28⅝ × 17½ (72.7 × 44.5)

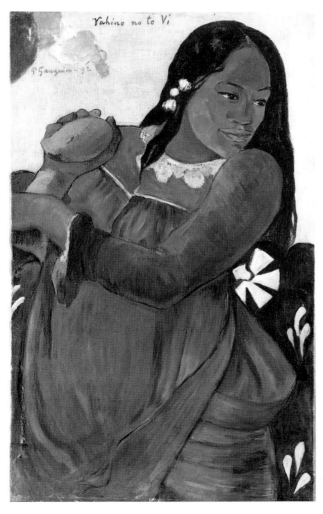

and wholeness of the work of art a substitute for the completeness and social integration lacking in real life; it was, in addition, to endow the artist with heroic powers to re-create at will the harmony and order presumed to characterize an earlier age dominated by festivals, popular democracy, and religious faith. Like Maurice Denis's arcadian *April* (1892), 344 Munch's haunting *The Voice,* and Monet's lyrical *Poplars* (1891), Hodler's *The Mönch With Clouds* displays a decorative balance and hierarchism quite unlike earlier Impressionist or Realist works. Yet the "general harmony" of which Hodler spoke was only the mirror image of a terror that was equally omnipresent in his art; it is seen in *The Night* in the face of the artist shrinking beneath the black-shrouded figure that squats over his loins, and in *Valentine in Agony* (1915) in the face of 345 his lover in the hours before her death. It is visible as well, I would argue, in the jagged profiles of frigid rock that Hodler painted in the Oberland. Symbolist art reveals those feelings of powerlessness and fear that preoccupied a generation. Gauguin too experienced this alienation and fright, and he fled Europe because of it.

GAUGUIN AND SYMBOLISM IN TAHITI

In an effort to restore his fading ideals, health, and finances, Gauguin resolved in 1890 to abandon both Brittany and Paris and move to the French island colony of Tahiti in the Polynesian archipelago. In September, he wrote to Redon:

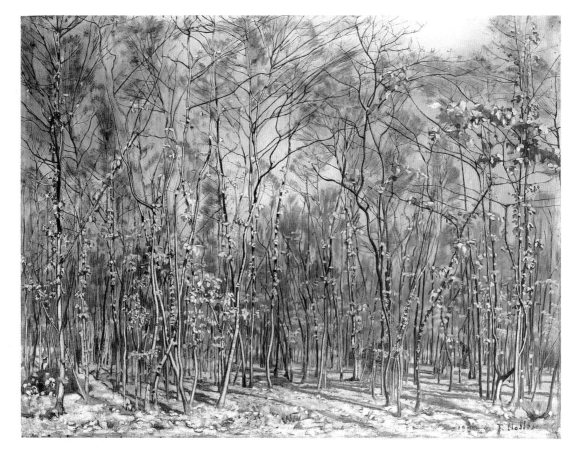

342 FERDINAND HODLER *The Beech Forest* 1885. 39¾ × 51½ (101 × 131)

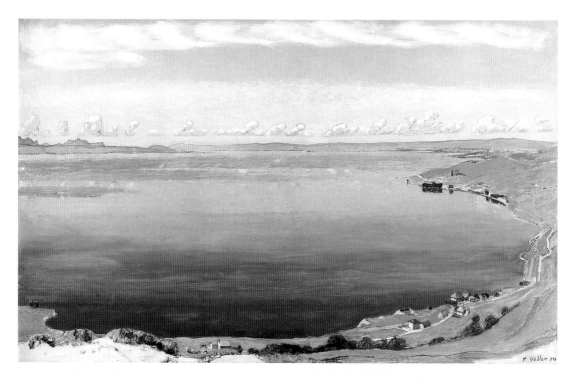

343 FERDINAND HODLER *Lake Geneva Seen From Chexbres* 1904. 27⅝ × 42½ (70.2 × 108)

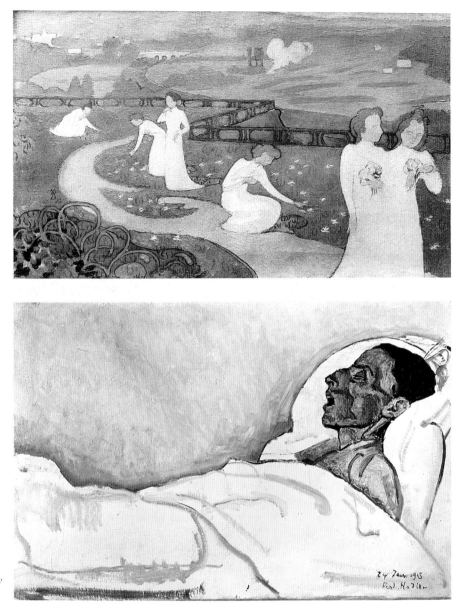

344 MAURICE DENIS *April* 1892. 14¾ × 24 (37.5 × 61)

345 FERDINAND HODLER *Valentine in Agony* 1915. 23⅞ × 35⅝ (60.5 × 90.5)

The reasons you give me for remaining in Europe are more flattering than they are convincing. My mind is made up, although since I returned to Brittany I have modified my plans. Madagascar is still too close to the civilized world; I want to go to Tahiti and finish my existence there. I believe that the art which you like so much today is only the germ of what will be created down there, as I cultivate in myself a state of primitiveness and savagery.

In Tahiti, Gauguin sought to indulge fully his primitivist longing to "go back, far back . . . as far back as the dada from my childhood, the good old wooden horse." As his words suggest, Tahiti for Gauguin represented both a personal and artistic regression. To go and live among indigenes meant to return to his own childhood and, in the familiar Rousseauist

metaphor, to the originary innocence of humanity. Three weeks after his arrival at the colonial capital Papeete, Gauguin described the Tahitian night in a letter to his wife Mette:

Such a beautiful night it is. Thousands of persons are doing the same as I do this night; abandoning themselves to sheer living, leaving their children to grow up quite alone. All these people roam about everywhere, no matter into what village, no matter by what road, sleeping in any house, eating etc., without even returning thanks, being equally ready to reciprocate. And these people are called savages! . . . They sing; they never steal; my door is never closed; they do not kill. Two Tahitian words describe them: *Iorama* (good morning, good bye, thanks, etc.) . . . and *Onatu* (I don't care, what does it matter, etc.) and they are called savages! I heard of the death of King Pomare with keen regret. The Tahitian soil is becoming quite French, and the old order is gradually disappearing.

Our missionaries have already introduced a good deal of Protestant hypocrisy and are destroying a part of the country, not to mention the pox which has attacked the whole race. . . . I should like to have your memory to learn the language quickly, for very few here speak French.

As his letter indicates, Tahiti was at once a dream-become-reality and a profound disappointment to Gauguin; he observed native selflessness giving ground to European greed and traditional sexual freedom surrendering to a cash economy, and responded with nostalgia and bittersweet imaginings. Childhood and native innocence were frequent subjects in Gauguin's Tahitian art at this time, appearing, for example, in *Te tiare farani* (*The Flowers of France*, 1891) and 340 *The Meal, or The Bananas* (1891). In the latter work, three children are shown behind an overlarge table covered with white paper or canvas and an assortment of still-life objects—bananas, lemons, a knife, a half-eaten guava, a gourd and ceramic bowl, and a wooden bowl filled with water. The odd disjunction of scale between the table and children (who appear to be at least on the verge of adolescence) and the simple tripartite division of the composition may be an attempt to represent the meal from a child's point of view, or else to reconstruct childish and native seeing.

Gauguin's depiction of young native women, which dominated his art from his arrival in Tahiti in 1891 until his death in 1903, seems to arise from some of the same personal and cultural impulses as in his paintings of children. Just as children represented a lost and earnestly sought natural innocence, so indigenous women were associated in Gauguin's mind, as in the collective colonialist imagination, with natural fecundity and beneficence, as well as with the restoration of male political authority and sexual prerogative. For the French nation as a whole, the acquisition of colonial possessions (Tahiti was only annexed in 1881) was a means of compensating for a vanished military and demographic vigor: France had suffered an ignominious defeat by Prussia in 1871 and a significant drop in its birth rate since the epoch of Napoleon. For Gauguin as well, the acquisition and depiction of successive colonial *vahines* (wives, women), such as 341 Teha'amana in *Vahine no te vi* (*Woman of the Mango*, 1892), was a means of compensating for a powerlessness before modernity. Once a successful stockbroker, Gauguin was left vulnerable by the spectacular collapse of the Union Générale bank in 1882 to the legitimate demands of his wife, Mette Gadd, and to the caprice of patrons and critics. Now, in his "House of Pleasure" (as he called his last house in the Marquesas Islands), in this land of "amorous harmony"

(Tahiti had indeed once been named La Nouvelle Cythère), he would regain his mastery.

In *Manao tupapau* (*The Specter Watches Her*, 1892), 339 Gauguin depicted a young Tahitian woman whom he identified as Tehura, lying on her stomach on a bed, facing the spectator. She lies on yellow-white sheets, shaded with blue and violet, above a bedspread printed in blue with yellow fruit and flowers. The background is violet, pink, orange, and blue, illuminated with white and green sparks or light-bursts. Above and to the left stands a figure in profile dressed in a black robe and cowl. Gauguin described the genesis of *Manao tupapau* in *Noa Noa*, his Tahitian diary and novel, first published in 1897:

One day I was obliged to go to Papeete. I had promised to return that evening, but . . . I didn't get home till one o'clock in the morning. . . . When I opened the door . . . I saw [her]. . . .

Tehura lay motionless, naked, belly down on the bed; she stared up at me, her eyes wide with fear, and she seemed not to know who I was. For a moment, I too felt a strange uncertainty. Tehura's dread was contagious: it seemed to me that a phosphorescent light poured from her staring eyes. I had never seen her so lovely; above all, I had never seen her beauty so moving. And, in the half-shadow, which no doubt seethed with dangerous apparitions and ambiguous shapes, I feared to make the slightest movement, in case the child should be terrified out of her mind. . . . Perhaps she took me, with my anguished face, for one of those legendary demons or specters, the *Tupapaus* that filled the sleepless nights of her people.

The picture, and the artist's description of it, appears to be a veritable encyclopedia of primitivism and misogyny. That the young native woman is portrayed as "terrified out of her mind" by "specters," suggests that she is ruled by emotion and mysticism and incapable of disinterestedness and rational thought, a characterization consistent with widespread racist stereotypes of native peoples as mentally inferior to Westerners. "The Tahitians are veritable children," Henri le Chartier wrote in his 1887 book on the French colonies of Polynesia, "[and of a marked] fickleness. . . . But the principle trait of their character is superstition: the solitude of the forest, the darkness of the night and especially spirits—tupapaus—frighten them." Moreover, Gauguin's association of the young woman's dread with his own rekindled desire affirms the misogynist canard that women "long to be taken, violently," as Gauguin wrote in *Noa Noa*. At the same time, Gauguin's own Oedipal fear of losing mastery, control, or even bodily integrity before the body of his young lover is suggested by his discussion and representation in *Manao tupapau* of "half-shadows," "dangerous apparitions," "am-

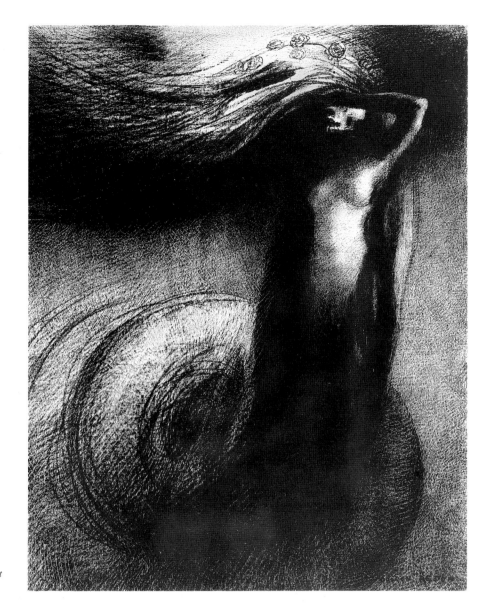

346 ODILON REDON "Death: My Irony Exceeds All Others," from *To Gustave Flaubert* 1889. 10¼ × 7¾ (26.2 × 19.7)

biguous shapes," "demons," and "specters." For Gauguin, as for other Symbolists such as Redon and Munch, women were alternatively blessed virgins and *femmes fatales* whose insistent sexuality portended castration and death. Like *Manao tupapau,* Redon's lithograph "Death: My Irony Exceeds all Others," from his album entitled *To Gustave Flaubert* (1889), and Munch's etching *The Kiss* (1895) represent those unholy unions of lust and death that threaten masculine authority.

Auguste Rodin (1840–1917) also depicted themes of male dominance in his colossal and uncompleted *Gates of Hell* (1880–1917), and his twenty-two illustrations for Baudelaire's *Flowers of Evil* (1887–8), among other works. In the former sculpture, women veritably cascade from the Dantesque portal, twisting and writhing in simultaneous death shudder and orgasm. In the latter ink drawings, women are shown dead and dying, luring and repelling male embraces, entwined

in lesbian love and seized by demons or a skeleton. *Fugit Amor* (ca. 1887), a small independent bronze derived from two similar figural groups on the right-hand panel of the *Gates,* depicts the pair of adulterers described by Dante as inhabiting the Second Circle of Hell. As in the drawing entitled *De Profundis Clamavi* (*Out of the Depths Have I Cried*) from *The Flowers of Evil,* the sculpture represents, as a critic in 1898 wrote, the "dangerous enigma" of the feminine: "She flies along, listless and disdainful, her lips curling with a smile of victorious witchery."

Like the paintings and prints of his contemporaries mentioned above, though unlike the anodyne sculpture *The Waltz* (1891) by his lover Camille Claudel (1864–1943), Rodin based many of his works on clichéd themes of sexual violence and the *femme fatale.* Yet there is at the same time an erotic extremism in some of Rodin's works, such as in the

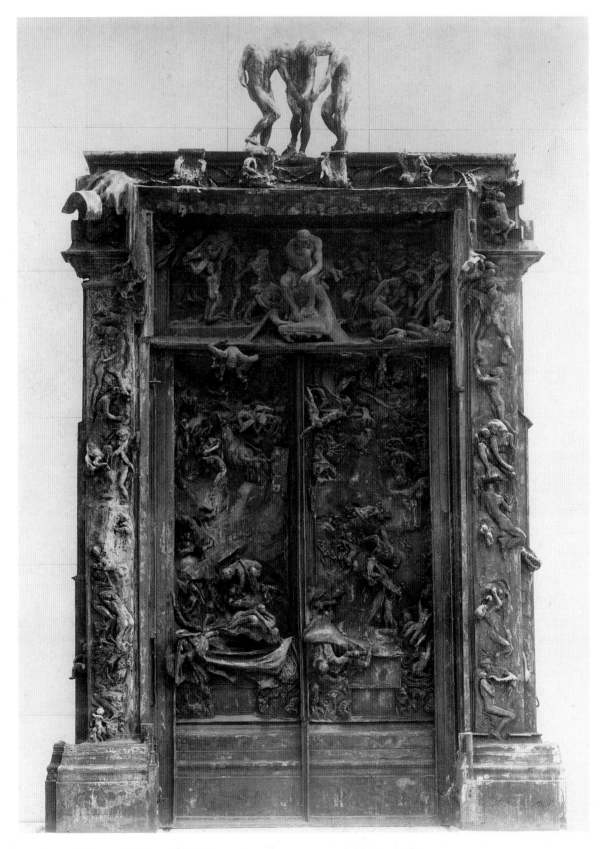

347 AUGUSTE RODIN *The Gates of Hell* 1880–1917. 22'3¾ × 13'1½ × 33½ (680 × 400 × 85)

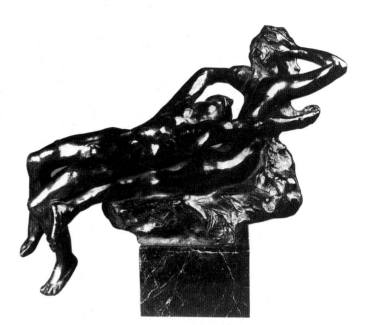

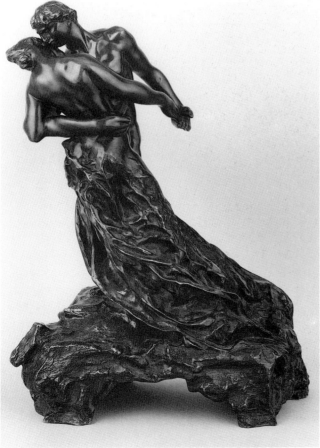

348 **AUGUSTE RODIN** *Iris, Messenger of the Gods*
ca. 1890. Height 37½ (95.3)

349 **CAMILLE CLAUDEL** *The Waltz* 1905.
18¼ × 13 × 7¾ (46.4 × 33 × 19.7)

350 **AUGUSTE RODIN** *Fugit Amor* ca. 1887.
15 × 18⅞ × 7⅞ (38 × 48 × 20)

sculpturally raw and genitally frank *Iris, Messenger of the Gods*   348
(ca. 1890), or in the several masturbation drawings, that would
appear to permit a very different interpretation of sexuality,
one which, as the art historian Anne Wagner has written,
"allows women to possess their bodies." Something of the
same dichotomy between masculine control and dispossession, I believe, is at work in Gauguin's treatment of Tahitian
women and of the cultural construct called "the primitive."
Indeed, the question of Gauguin's primitivism and attitude
toward women is much more complex than initially suggested
by *Manao tupapau*. In depicting *tupapaus* and in employing   339
the Tahitian language in his title, Gauguin was in fact
celebrating aspects of the native culture that the French
colonial authorities were attempting to suppress in the name
of "assimilation," the stated policy of subjecting the islands
and their inhabitants to French legal and economic obligations and cultural controls. Instrumental to this policy was
the effort of Catholic and Protestant missionaries to eradicate
local religious beliefs and instruct the natives in Christian
religion and the French language. Gauguin's depiction of

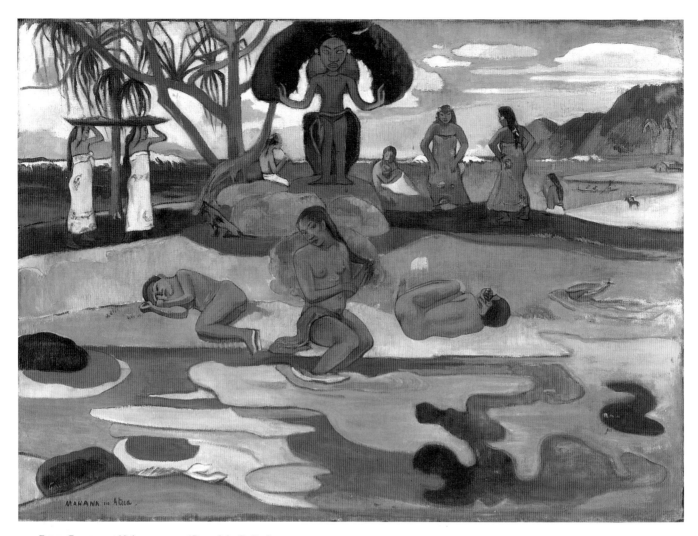

351 PAUL GAUGUIN *Mahana no atua (Day of the God)* 1894. 26⅞ × 36 (68.3 × 91.5)

native "superstition" in *Manao tupapau* and use of a Tahitian title must therefore be seen in the context of native resistance to assimilation and what the artist later called the colonial "reign of terror." Absent from Gauguin's picture is any of the hypocritical smugness or ignorant condescension found in Le Chartier, quoted above, or in the travel writer Mativet, who argued in his 1888 guide to *La Nouvelle Cythère* that tupapaus were simply the result of indigenous confusion between sleep, dreams, nightmares, and reality. Gauguin, by contrast, appears to have recognized that spirits (*Mo'a*) played a crucial role in Tahitian culture and religion. Indeed, spirits such as the tupapaus form one half of the basic "conceptual antithesis" (as the anthropologist Douglas Oliver writes) of Polynesian culture, the other half of which is *Noa*, meaning secular, wordly, or human. To be a Tahitian is to be in almost constant interaction with spirits, which can take the form of sharks, pigs, horses, dogs, cats, and birds. Indeed, that

Gauguin's Tahitian diary novel is called *Noa Noa* is one indication, among others, of his frank recognition of the inevitability of his own separation as a European from Polynesian spirituality.

Thus Gauguin's primitivism, like the phenomenon generally, is not reducible to simple masculinism and Eurocentrism. While nineteenth-century primitivism (or exoticism) was mostly notable for its naked assertion that non-European peoples were fit only for conquest, conversion, or extirpation, it also at times fostered critical reflection upon the differences between Western and non-Western cultures, and upon the failures of the former. In the letter to Redon already cited, Gauguin clearly engaged in this primitivist dialectic:

Gauguin is finished here, and no one will see him anymore. Yet you know that I am an egoist. I carry with me in photographs and drawings, a whole little world of comrades that bring me pleasure; of you, I have memories of all you have done. I also have in my mind the image of a *star*; in following this, in my case to Tahiti, I do not dream of death, I promise you, but on the contrary of eternal life—not death in life but life in death. In Europe, that death with its serpent's tail [Redon's "Death: My Irony . . ."] is inescapable, but in Tahiti, it must be seen with its roots pushing upward among the flowers. . . . I recall a phrase of Wagner that explains my thought: "I believe that the practitioners of great art are glorified, and that, enveloped in a celestial tissue of rays, perfumes and melodious concord, they will be restored for all eternity to the breast of the divine sources of harmony."

On the one hand, Gauguin's vulgar association of the primitive, the non-European, the natural, and the feminine in his letter to Redon conforms to the reigning Eurocentrism that sanctioned violence upon the bodies of real Tahitian women and men during the 125 years since their "discovery" by Captain Samuel Wallis. On the other hand, however, Gauguin's utopian embrace of the natural "harmony" of non-Western cultures was an explicit criticism of the very instrumentalism and hierarchism that sanctioned European exploitation. By jettisoning the "death in life" of Europe and embracing the culture of Polynesia, Gauguin was expressing an internationalism that was as rare as it was potentially subversive in an age of empire. Indeed, Gauguin was a consistent supporter of indigenous rights, jeopardizing his own life in the Marquesas by protesting in support of Polynesian rights in February 1903 (two months before his death) in a letter to the French colonial governor: "This hypocritical proclamation of Liberty, Equality, and Fraternity under the French flag takes on a singular irony with respect to [native] people who are no more than tax fodder in the hands of despotic gendarmes."

351 In Gauguin's *Mahana no atua* (*Day of the God*, 1894), he has juxtaposed, without hierarchy or favor, several religious and pictorial traditions. In the upper third of the painting, women, men, and children are naturalistically depicted beneath an azure sky streaked with white clouds. Behind them are a line of breaking waves, yellow sand, and a distant village with houses, a horseman, and boaters. In the middle of this zone stands the monumental statue of a god inspired at once by Easter Island megaliths, Buddhist figures from the temple of Borobudur in Java, and the feminine Tahitian deity Hina. In the middle third of the painting are three figures, sitting or reclining on pink sand. To the left, a child lies facing us with head resting on hands, legs bent, and toes touching the water; to the right, another child facing away from us, is folded into a fetal posture; in the center a woman is facing us, posed in a graceful *contraposto:* her upper torso is framed by a kind of

green mandorla, her loins are accented by a red *pareu* and her calves are immersed in the phantasmagorically colored water below. The water constitutes the lower third of the painting. Here is seen a jigsaw-puzzle pattern of colors that bears only the merest resemblance to the upper world it would mirror. Here, the sensuality of color has its own way; the lower third of *Mahana no atua* thus represents the abstract, Polynesian antipode to the illusionistic, European manner seen in the two upper registers. Besides Cézanne, no other nineteenth-century painter progressed further than Gauguin in the direction of liberating color from the slavish labor of illusionism, thereby paving a road that leads to the nonrepresentational achievements of Kandinsky and Mondrian, as well as to the new twentieth-century appreciation of the esthetic achievements of non-Western and especially indigenous peoples.

In *Mahana no atua*, as in many of his other Tahitian works such as *Faaturuma* (*Reverie*, 1891), *Te Faaturuma* (*Silence, or To Be Dejected*, 1891), *Fatata te miti* (*Near the Sea*, 1892) and the monumental *Where Do We Come From? What Are We? Where Are We Going?* (1897), Gauguin admits profound uncertainties about his own cultural heritage and posits the

352
353

352 PAUL GAUGUIN *Te faaturuma* (*Silence, or To Be Dejected*) 1891. 36 × 27 (91.2 × 68.7)

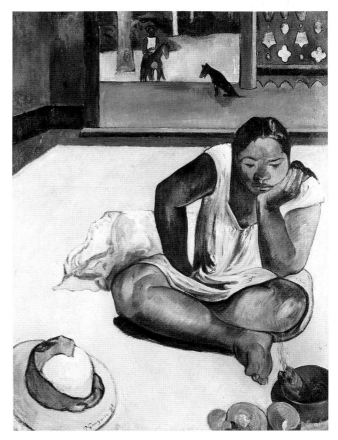

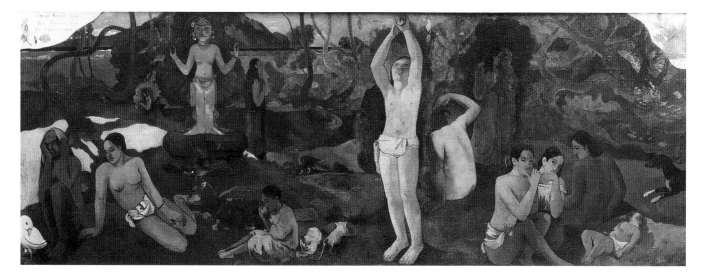

353 PAUL GAUGUIN *Where Do We Come From? What Are We? Where Are We Going?* 1897. 54¾ × 12'3½ (139 × 374.5)

value of a new syncretic and international culture. In these works, Western illusionism is juxtaposed to non-European abstraction and patterning, Christian deities are paired with Hindu, Buddhist, or Tahitian gods, and European narratives of fall and redemption are transformed into parables of healthful eroticism and natural abundance. Moreover, native women are depicted in the works cited above as intellectual and contemplative people (a relative novelty in depictions of Europeans, much less Polynesians), and possessed of a powerful and independent sexuality.

In this radical ethnographic endeavor (admittedly partial, contradictory, and at times even wholly unsuccessful), Gauguin anticipated the stance of the Surrealist author André Breton who wrote fifty years after Gauguin's death: "Surrealism is allied with peoples of color, first because it has sided with them against all forms of imperialism and white brigandage . . . and secondly because of the profound affinities between surrealism and primitive thought." To the Surrea-

lists and to their friend Lévi-Strauss, "primitive" art was the expression of an equilibrium between humans and nature which aboriginal cultures had achieved but which capitalism destroyed. The goal of the Surrealist movement, therefore, as Breton wrote, "was the elaboration of a collective myth appropriate to our time" that could resurrect a primitive balance between nature and society, albeit at a much higher level of technological achievement and global interconnectedness. Gauguin's art and thought, finally—conceived a generation before Freud, Lévi-Strauss, and the Surrealists—lack this progressive notion of an *aufhebung*, or transcendence to a historically higher level. In common with the other Symbolists, Gauguin sought refuge from modernity in a remote and unspoiled land; like them, too, he was frightened by, and yet accepted (at times even revelled in), his own powerlessness and marginality. Unlike them, however, he posited in his art a primitive alternative to the European social and cultural order.

· 16 ·

THE FAILURE AND SUCCESS OF CÉZANNE

SYMBOLISM *IN EXTREMIS*

THE ART OF PAUL GAUGUIN WAS PAINTED ON A canvas as large as the French *imperium*. Enacting the modern roles of tourist and colonialist, Gauguin traveled from Paris to Pont-Aven, Quimper, Arles, Martinique, Papeete, and the Marquesas, seeking consolation for the loss of a bourgeois and masculine prerogative in the metropolis. In so doing, Gauguin, like many avant-gardists before him, was also fleeing modernization and indeed history itself—fleeing, that is, those forces of "universalizing civilization" that left the artist victim to the caprice of the market during a period of economic depression. For the most part, we have seen, Gauguin brought along as baggage on his travels the various hierarchies that generally sustained Europeans of his gender and class. In Tahiti he dreamed of rape (if he did not actually commit it) and he swaggered and patronized, at first, like any colonialist bureaucrat. Yet in the end, it was clear to him (as it was to his Surrealist descendants) that the dynamics of flight and retrospection also propelled an unallayed radicalism and utopianism. In his extreme retreat from metropolitan culture, Classical painting, and mimesis, Gauguin also mapped the contours of a future cultural realm of sensual gratification and human freedom; in his masculinism and primitivism, he charted an expressive terrain more truly androgynous and internationalist than any that had been imagined in Europe before; in his retreat from modernity and partisan politics, he also explored the radical political potential of an autonomous art that intransigently refused the blandishments of a deplored contemporaneity.

Gauguin's art was thus an extremist and a dialectical response to the alienation and despair that wracked the Symbolist generation. Yet there was at least one other achieved artistic response during the *fin de siècle*, equally

vehement in disdaining what Kahn called "the near at hand and the compulsorily contemporaneous," but very different from what has been considered here thus far. Where Gauguin was internationalist in his perspective, Paul Cézanne (1839–1906) was almost parochial in his. He nevertheless created a body of work that, like Gauguin's, announced the modernist conception of art as (in Herbert Marcuse's later words) "the Great Refusal to accept the rules of a game in which the dice are loaded." The game in question is played to enshrine Western progress, power, modernization, and instrumental reason; the Great Refusal is a contrary celebration of traditional culture, erotic surrender, and utopia. These critical values may be detected in the art of Cézanne. For the young Cézanne, painting was a bomb, set to detonate beneath the Ecole, the Academy, and the Salon. Undoubtedly the wild child of Impressionism, Cézanne stimulated critical apoplexies during the 1860's and '70's. Yet he also attained a maturity during which he created a manner of painting and drawing that can be called nothing less than dialectical in its complexity and its critical logic. It was an art of sensual liberation as much as one of formal rigor and it thus laid a foundation for much of the artistic accomplishment of the twentieth century.

PAUL CÉZANNE AND THE END OF NINETEENTH-CENTURY ART

The art and career of Paul Cézanne is the logical endpoint of a book devoted to the critical examination of nineteenth-century art. The reason is simple: no artist was more critical than he himself in exploring both the cognitive and perceptual mechanisms of seeing and representing; indeed, his art reveals more clearly than any before it the inseparability of these two meanings of the word "seeing." Though Cézanne benefited greatly from the artistic insights of Delacroix, Courbet, Manet, and Pissarro, he alone risked the destruction of mimesis in the quest for a manner of representation that was true to both individual apperception and the facts of material reality. To achieve this dialectical seeing, all previous artistic paradigms had to be suspended and a wholly new formal vocabulary devised. The task was daunting, and at times even debilitating. "Cézanne's doubt," as the existentialist philosopher Maurice Merleau-Ponty described it, was a primal uncertainty, the doubt of a first utterance. "I am the primitive of the way that I discovered," Cézanne told Emile Bernard at the end of his life. Yet the new language he spoke was so articulate and compelling that few afterwards could even remember, much less speak, the old.

What therefore emerges as most salient from a survey of Cézanne's art is the aspect of search, invention, discovery, and critical synthesis. Indeed, in the course of his long career, Cézanne changed from a Romantic rebel to a cultural revolutionary. From an artist who, like Delacroix, saw himself in heroic antagonism to a corrupt world, he became an artist who was in his words, "submissive to nature." From an artist who, like Ingres before and the Symbolists after, dreamed of a future based upon the moral verities of the past, he became an artist who devised a means through which a new cultural order could be represented and understood. Yet his artistic revolutionism assumed a form different from any that preceded it. Unlike the work of his much admired Courbet, Cézanne's radical art was not the product of an insurgent content: though artists and critics alike called him "communard," "intransigent," and "anarchist," he mostly eschewed politically charged subject matter. Unlike the painting of his almost equally admired Manet, Cézanne's revolutionary work was not the result of unprecedented esthetic effects: though he was judged incompetent and insolent by most contemporary critics, he understood, respected, and made extensive use of the greatest masterpieces of the past.

The radical newness of Cézanne's paintings was instead a matter of, in Adorno's phrase, their "inherent structure. They are knowledge as nonconceptual objects." The best works by Cézanne, according to this formulation, do not represent the world, they are themselves worlds. "In front of a work by Cézanne," wrote Maurice Denis in 1907, "we think only of the picture; neither the object represented nor the artist's personality holds our attention.... And if at once we say: this is a picture and a classic picture, the word begins to take on a precise meaning, that, namely, of an equilibrium, a reconciliation of the objective and the subjective."

The mature works of Cézanne may then fairly be seen as instances of what the twentieth century has termed "autonomous" creation. These refrain from the expression of

ameliorative social or political solutions in the name of that human "free space" that we saw was only glimpsed by the Impressionists in their years of greatest achievement. The autonomous artwork, as Adorno writes, "is mediated through nothing other than the form of the work itself.... As eminently constructed and produced objects, such works of art ... point to a practice from which they abstain: the creation of a just life." By virtue of their intellectual rigor and sensual desirability, such works exist in silent opposition to a degraded political sphere and a Western society "suffocated in the cultivation of kitsch." Cézanne's art thus becomes the signal instance of that modernist paradigm, the revolutionary artwork that is at the same time apolitical. For this reason, the usual terms of art historical analysis—stylistic sources and influences, literary iconography, biographical references, and critical reception—are stretched beyond their limits in attempts to describe the works produced after about 1885. Formal analysis and dialectics provide the only vocabularies that make any sense for understanding the mature paintings of Cézanne. "A man, a tree, an apple, are not *represented*," wrote the Russian painter Wassily Kandinsky (1866–1944) in "Concerning the Spiritual in Art" (1912), "but used by Cézanne in building up a painterly thing called a 'picture'."

CEZANNE'S DEVELOPMENT: THE QUEST FOR TOTALITY

Cézanne began his career by embracing the cultural revivalism that dominated his native region. Born in 1839 in Aix-en-Provence, he read the vernacular Provençal poetry of Frédéric Mistral (1830–1914), and attended the local Corpus Christi and other religious and secular festivals that flourished during the middle years of the century. In addition, the young Cézanne admired and emulated in early paintings, such as *Sorrow, or Mary Magdalen* (ca. 1867) and *Pastoral Scene* (ca. 354 1870), the work of native Baroque and early nineteenth-century artists, such as the Neoclassical history painter and landscapist François-Marius Granet (1775–1849), in an effort to uphold or revive regional Aixois traditions of religious and landscape art. In fact, it may be argued that Cézanne remained a Provençal artist his whole life; even in his final two decades, after having come to know and share in the fervid, international artistic life of the French capital, Cézanne was drawn back to Aix as to a magnet—its scenery, its architectural monuments, its legends, and traditions. In the last two years before his death, he devoted more time than ever before to the depiction of Mont Sainte-Victoire, site of the ancient Roman victory over an army of invading Teutons and the fabled origin of Aix. He also concentrated upon the theme of bathing, perhaps partially in homage to the Roman *Aquae Sextiae*

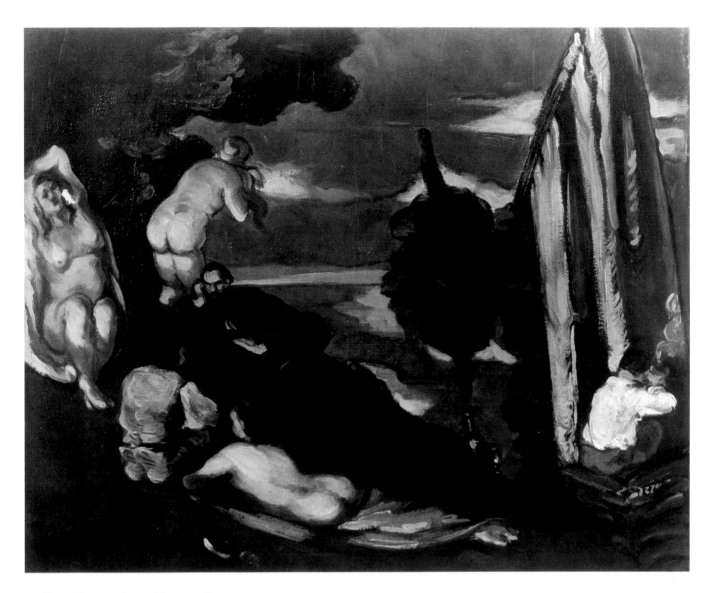

354 PAUL CÉZANNE *Pastoral Scene* ca. 1870. 25¾ × 31¾ (65 × 81)

(Waters of Sextius) that gave the town its name. Cézanne thus began and concluded his career desiring to be the natural product of his beloved land; he would surely have wished it said of him, as the poet Max Buchon did of Courbet, that he "produced his paintings as simply as an apple-tree produced apples."

As a youth, Cézanne roamed the Provençal countryside with his friend Emile Zola, and rhapsodized in French and Latin about the hills, brooks, and clouds he saw, and the panpipes, shepherds, and maidens' love of which he dreamed. But a darker romantic vision also accompanied him on his rambles, and from this the innovative artist emerged. In letters written to Zola in Paris after 1858, Cézanne frequently assumed a tone of Baudelairean irony and spleen in describing his sadistic and misogynist fantasies. In one letter of 1859 to

the future Naturalist writer, Cézanne enclosed a verse allegory entitled "A Terrible Story," which concludes: ". . . and the woman in my arms who had been so pink and rosy suddenly disappeared and turned into a pale cadaver with angular body and rattling bones, and dull empty eyes." This is the Cézanne who painted the deathly *Self-Portrait* (ca. 1861–2), the violent *The Rape* (ca. 1867), the tormented *Pastoral Scene*, and the 356 *Temptation of Saint Antony* (ca. 1870). These works, and others depicting murders, orgies, and an autopsy, are passionate, violent, and expressionistic, invested with the energy and vehemence of an unresolved Oedipal nightmare.

In the *Temptation*, young Paul (prematurely bald) appears in the guise of the tempted and tormented Saint Antony; in *Pastoral Scene*, he sits uncomfortably in the foreground of his own version of Manet's *Déjeuner*; in *A Modern Olympia* (ca. 355

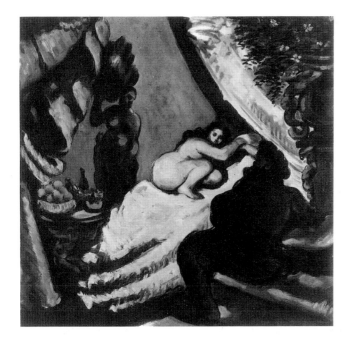

355 PAUL CÉZANNE *A Modern Olympia* ca. 1869–70. 22 × 21⅝ (56 × 55)

356 PAUL CÉZANNE *The Rape* ca. 1867. 35½ × 46 (90.5 × 117)

1869–70), he is a pasha seated stiffly before his concubine. Even the portraits of his father are painted in a high emotional timbre. In the *Portrait of Louis-Auguste Cézanne, Father of the Artist, Reading L'Evénement* (1866), the sitter's torso is awkwardly separated from his crossed legs by the bottom edge of the newspaper slicing across his groin. The erect right arm is similarly cut off from his body by the newspaper, and is set in front of an ominous shadow of gray/orange on the high-backed easy chair. In each of these works, Cézanne demonstrates a willingness to flout moral proprieties and artistic conventions. The violence, eroticism, confessional character, and purposeful awkwardness of these early paintings led observers to characterize them as childish and naive.

Throughout these years, Cézanne repeatedly submitted his works to the Salon with the knowledge that they would never be accepted. He even had the temerity in 1866 to write to the eminent Nieuwerkerke, Superintendent of Fine Arts, demanding a second Salon des Refusés and, in effect, an apology for past injuries. In a reprise of Courbet's words in 1853 to the same Nieuwerkerke, Cézanne wrote: "I am unable to accept the unauthorized judgment of colleagues whom I have not myself appointed to evaluate my work." Thus rejecting the cultural authority of the state, as he did his

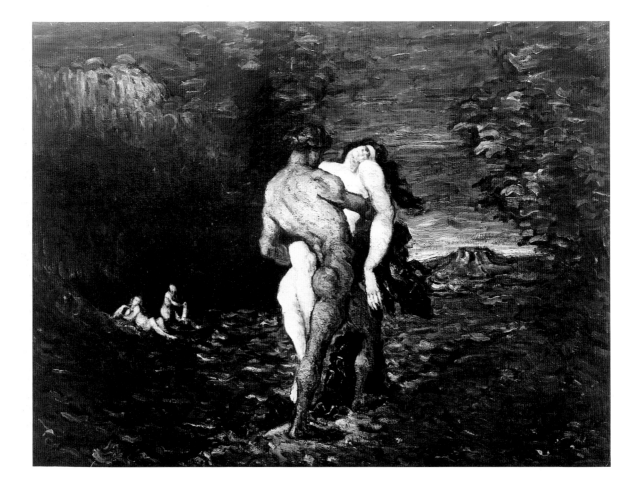

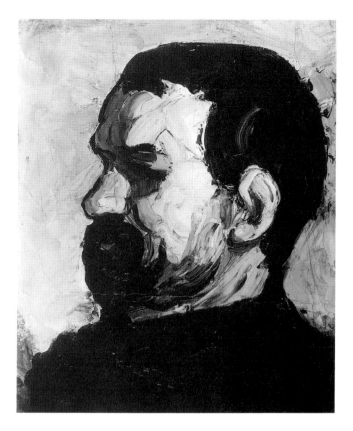

357 PAUL CÉZANNE *Portrait of Uncle Dominique* 1866. 15½ × 12 (39.5 × 30.5)

outlining of nose and brow serves both to establish the contour of the face and to flatten it against the background plane. This quality of pictorial consistency or totality—at once naive and monumental—is unlike anything found in the work of Cézanne's Romantic, Realist, and Impressionist predecessors and foreshadows the achievements of the mature artist.

In *The Rape* (probably representing Pluto's abduction of Persephone), Cézanne focuses equally upon the nude foreground figures, the female attendants in the left middleground, and the truncated Mont Sainte-Victoire in the background. Painted with looping and undulating strokes of paint, the riverbank, water, foliage, mountain, and sky are given nearly equal visual weight, suggesting an all-over two-dimensional structure and balance that act as a counterforce to the emotional depth and expressiveness of the narrative. In other words, even though the picture represents a misogynist dream, its style suggests detachment, abstractness, and objectivity. Even as the young Cézanne indulged his obsessional fears and hatreds of modern woman, he struggled to overcome them in order to re-order vision and design into a single unified procedure.

358 PAUL CÉZANNE *Portrait of the Painter, Achille Emperaire* ca. 1868–70. 78¾ × 48 (200 × 122)

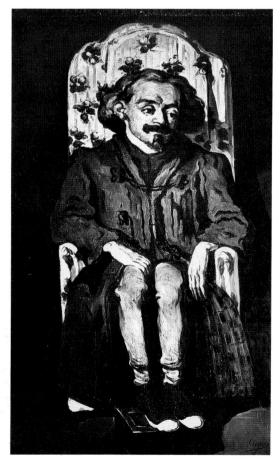

father's career wishes for him (Louis-Auguste would have preferred his son to be a banker or lawyer, like himself), Cézanne became a romantic and an intransigent. Despising the person and rule of Napoleon III, and approving the character and politics of Jacques Vingtras (from Jules Vallé's anarchist novel of the same name), the young artist was a rebel but not yet a revolutionary. Jean-Paul Sartre described the difference: "The revolutionary wants to change the world; he transcends it and moves toward the future, toward an order of values which he himself invents. The rebel is careful to preserve the abuses from which he suffers so that he can go on rebelling against them. He always shows signs of a bad conscience and of something resembling a feeling of guilt. He does not want to destroy or transcend the existing order; he simply wants to rise up against it."

Indications of the future revolutionary temperament are, however, also visible in the early, expressionistic paintings. Their stark contrasts of tonality, shrill juxtapositions of hue, and dense coagulations of paint (often applied with variously shaped palette knives) are new and noteworthy. But what is most important in Cézanne's pictures from before about 1873 is their pictorial clarity and sense of expressive *totality*. All 357 parts of, for example, the *Portrait of Uncle Dominique* (1866) are equally dense, worked, and elaborated. The black

Lawrence Gowing, the art historian and painter, has summarized Cézanne's achievement in works such as *The Rape* and *Portrait of the Painter, Achille Emperaire* (ca. 1868–70) as nothing less than "the invention of *forme* in the French modernist sense—meaning the condition of paint that constitutes a pictorial structure. It is the discovery of an intrinsic structure inherent in the medium and the material." What Gowing refers to as *forme* may be seen, for example, in the tectonic armature created by the insistent verticality of the *Achille Emperaire*: notice the parallels formed by the sides of the chair, the sitter's spindly legs, the pleats in his dressing-gown, the black line running from his red collar to his slippers, and the attenuated Bodoni-style stenciling at the top of the canvas. These parallel lines create a feeling of architectural stability at the same time that they evince a sense of *picturality*—a perception, that is, of the painting as a self-sufficient two-dimensional structure built from vertical and horizontal wooden ribs, covered with canvas, and painted with a viscous colored medium.

The 1867 correspondence of Cézanne's friend A. F. Marion offers some confirmation of the artist's totalizing intentions: "Paul is really very much stronger than [Courbet and Manet]. He is convinced of being able, by a more skillful execution and perception, to admit details while retaining breadth. Thus he would achieve his aims, and his works would become more complete." Fifteen years later, the artist's intention was the same, as Gauguin revealed in a mocking letter to Cézanne's friend Pissarro: "Has M. Césanne [sic] discovered the exact *formula* for a work that would be accepted by everyone? If he should find the recipe for concentrating the full expression of all his sensations into a single and unique procedure, try, I beg you, to get him to talk about it in his sleep by administering one of those mysterious homeopathic drugs and come directly to Paris to share it with us." At the end of his life, Cézanne almost believed he had found his formula; he told Bernard in 1904: "I owe you the truth in painting and I will tell it to you."

CÉZANNE'S ARTISTIC MATURITY

Although Cézanne's quest for artistic totality is visible from the beginning, there can be no question that it changed and grew over the four decades of his career. The paintings of the 1860's and early '70's possess an unprecedented formal consistency and tectonic structure, but they are still dominated by the Baroque drama of chiaroscuro and tonal contrast. Color is not yet fully integrated into their pictorial fabric. In the paintings considered above, color functions primarily to express moods or strong feelings and only partially to indicate mass, volume, depth, and pictorial unity. The "intrinsic structure" of *Uncle Dominique* and *Achille Emperaire* is for the most part the product of paint density, composition, and tonal contrast and not the result of choice of colors or modulation. It is as if the colorless genre of melodrama, as the art historian and curator John Elderfield has written, was fully adequate to express the violent dreams and Oedipal longings of the youthful artist. But as Cézanne gradually attained psychological maturity (perhaps hastened by his liaison, beginning in 1869, with Hortense Fiquet), his artistic vision became richer and more inclusive. As he gradually dismissed from his art the clichéd, adolescent roster of *femmes fatales*, he increasingly explored the dynamics of hue. Impressionism, and especially the art and instruction of Pissarro, would be the most important instrument of Cézanne's totalization of subjective experience and objective reality.

In early 1872, during the bleak dawn following the dark night of the Commune's destruction, Cézanne was living beside Pissarro at Pontoise in the Ile de France, and learning from him the decisive lessons of Impressionism. Cézanne shared with his anarchist friend and mentor a love of landscape and a faith in the healing capacity of rural life. Together they discovered a method for representing their feelings about the plenitude of nature; for Pissarro this meant the depiction of peasant laborers in worked fields, and the creation of textural and coloristic unities of figure and ground. For Cézanne, this method meant the fashioning of a pictorial universe sufficiently complete and nuanced that it could approximate both the motif itself and the powerful and complex sensations he felt before his subject. "I paint as I see, as I feel," he told a critic in 1870, "and I have very strong sensations."

Cézanne used the narrowed tonal range and prismatic hues of Impressionism as a means both of capturing the effects of light and air and of disciplining his sometimes violent and disordered imagination. Indeed, Impressionism, we have seen, was precisely an art of social and psychological distance; it was the artistic expression of a subculture that disdained alienated work and celebrated the implicit freedom of bourgeois and petit-bourgeois leisure. Cézanne accepted Impressionism's principled rejection of instrumentality, but he could not accept its frequent emotional and intellectual shallowness. By the end of the 1870's, he had outstripped his Impressionist teacher by creating works that are both convincing semblances of physical objects and figures and records of the artist's own shifting perceptions over time.

Compared with Pissarro's *Village Near Pontoise* (1873), Cézanne's *House of the Hanged Man, Auvers-sur-Oise* (ca. 1873) possesses an unusually dense and clotted surface. Its color is more uniformly warm than Pissarro's work (note the latter's cool blues alternating with the red roofs in the middle-ground) and its tonality is more even. Unlike his friend and teacher, moreover, Cézanne marks the contours and

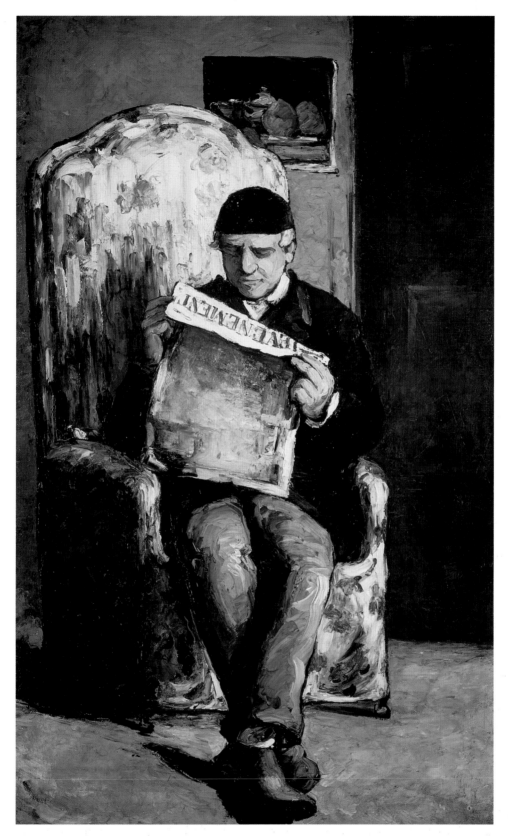

359 PAUL CÉZANNE *Portrait of Louis-Auguste Cézanne, Father of the Artist, Reading L'Evénement* 1866.
78¾ × 47⅛ (200 × 120)

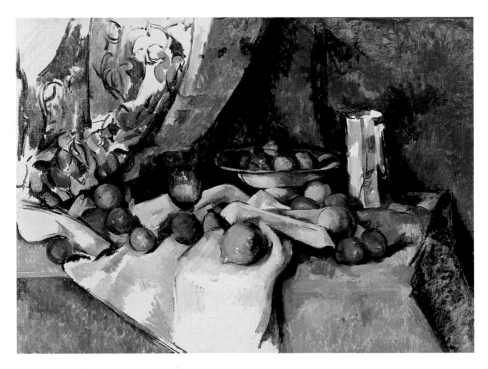

360 PAUL CÉZANNE *Still Life With Apples* ca. 1895–8. 27 × 36½ (68.6 × 92.7)

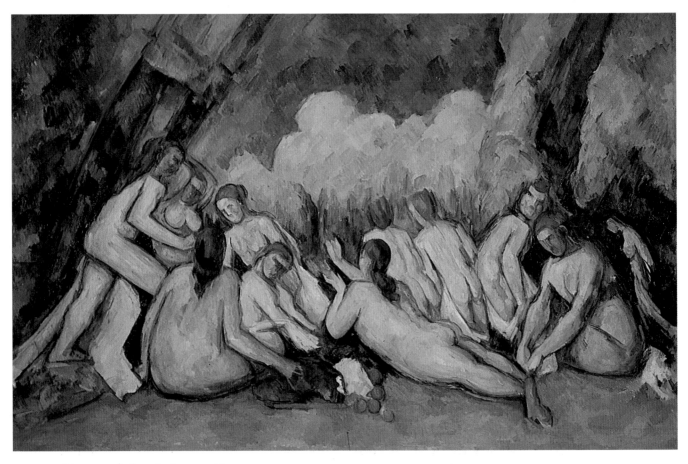

361 PAUL CÉZANNE *The Large Bathers* 1900–06. 67⅞ × 77¼ (172.2 × 196.1)

boundaries of objects with broad lines (compare the treatment of tree-trunks in each), and clearly anchors trees and buildings in the earth. Cézanne's landscape, in sum, suggests a greater planarity and pictorality than Pissarro's, together with a greater mass and solidity.

365   Beside Pissarro's *The Côte des Boeufs at L'Hermitage, Near*
364   *Pontoise* (1877), Cézanne's *L'Estaque* (1876–8) appears balanced and calm. Both works employ divided and multidirectional brushstrokes of brown, green, and blue, but Cézanne's strokes are broader than Pissarro's and manage to evoke the shape, density, and surface texture of the objects they describe. In addition, Cézanne has chosen to highlight and explore, rather than obscure, all the areas in his landscape motif that are physically and visually complex or ambiguous; thus he lavishes attention on the intersection of roof hips and cornices, the convex edges of buildings, the joinings of leaf to branch, the lines where mountains meet the sea, and the places where chimneys (or masts?) break the horizon.

Comparison of these landscapes suggests that while Cézanne may have believed that the energy and ephemerality of Pissarro's Impressionism were appropriate to the depiction of transient atmospheric effects, he found the style to be too unstable, intangible, and inexpressive for the convincing representation of the countryside and its people. But while Cézanne judged Impressionism to be flawed by insubstantiality and emotional remove, he also definitively determined that traditional academic technique, which he thoroughly understood—linear drawing, single-point perspective, Classical anatomy, tonal modeling, and chiaroscuro—was equally flawed by its very procrusteanism; these stolid formal tricks were wholly inadequate to the artist's shifting perceptions of the world as he moved through it, and besides, they were the remnant of an old and discredited order. Thus Cézanne, beginning in the late 1870's, devised an art that employed the faceted, mosaic surface of Impressionism without its evasiveness. Put another way, he marshaled the dynamic, kinesthetic features of Impressionist art, with the architectonic tangibility and expressiveness of his early works. Cézanne wanted monumentality and emotional resolve in his art; he wished, he told Bernard, "to make of Impressionism something solid, like the art in the museums."

THE FAILURE AND SUCCESS OF CÉZANNE

After exhibiting with the Impressionists in their third group exhibition in 1877, Cézanne essentially struck off on his own. Though he kept in occasional contact with members of the group (especially Renoir) he needed no further lessons from them. Nor did he try to exhibit with them; for seven out of the next eight years he tried in vain to show at the Salon, his only

success coming in 1882 when he was admitted as a "pupil" of the charitable juror Antoine Guillemet. His few press notices were as uncomprehending and patronizing as they had been when he first exhibited with the Impressionists nearly a decade earlier; the *Portrait of L. A.* (present whereabouts unknown) was described by the critic of the *Dictionnaire Véron* as "a beginner's work painted at great expense of color." Increasingly melancholic and reclusive, Cézanne was fast fading from public view and becoming legendary. In 1885, Gauguin professed admiration for his art but called him "that misunderstood man, whose nature is essentially mystical . . . he spends whole days on the tops of mountains reading Virgil and gazing at the sky."

At the same time that he was suffering alienation from both avant-garde and academic Paris, Cézanne suffered a number of personal blows that further affected his art. In 1885, an unconsummated passion for a maid from his parent's house at Aix left him angry and confused. The same year, Zola's cruel portrayal of him in *L'Oeuvre* ended the only friendship he ever had. In April 1886, Cézanne grudgingly married Hortense Fiquet (they were already living apart), and six months later attended his father's funeral. This latter event secured him financially but exhausted him emotionally. Convinced by all that had transpired of the futility of human intercourse, and certain that his own death was at hand, Cézanne now worked ceaselessly and with unprecedented dedication. His landscapes, still lifes, and figure paintings progressed apace, and his style quickly achieved the complexity and resolve that a later generation would see as the foundation for its own modern and abstract art.

The twenty years between 1886 and the artist's death in 1906 spanned the careers of Van Gogh, Seurat, Gauguin, and the Symbolists. They witnessed the last Impressionist exhibition (1886), the Eiffel Tower Exposition in Paris (1889), the Dreyfus Affair (1894–1902), the deaths of Zola (1902) and Pissarro (1903), and the exhibition of the Fauves at the Salon d'Automne (1905). None of this had any discernible impact on Cézanne's art; by virtue of his unusual powers of concentration or his paranoia, he devised an autonomous art of extraordinary formal rigor. Generalizations about this art, as Elderfield has observed, are difficult to make because of Cézanne's always different responses to the specific motifs before him, but three basic principles of pictorial invention may be extrapolated through examination of selected works.

1) Holding illusionism at bay—in *Houses in Provence*   366
(1879–82), a perverse humor results from the purposeful avoidance of linear clarity and perspectival exactness. Cézanne lines up the vertical edges of the two largest houses without clarifying their exact spatial locations. He both reveals and obscures the underside of roof eaves and the flat tops of rocks

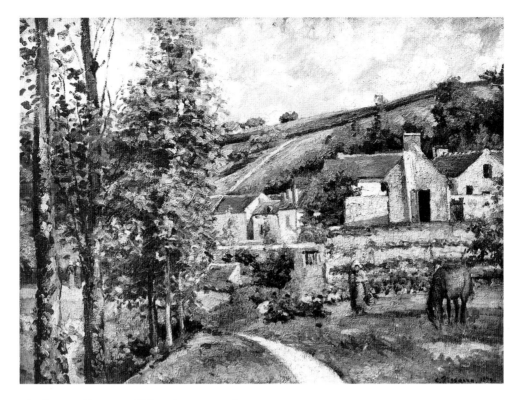

362 CAMILLE PISSARRO *Village Near Pontoise* 1873. $24 \times 31\frac{7}{8}$ (61×81)

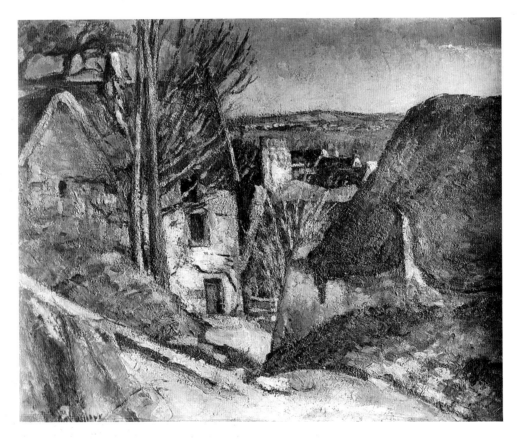

363 PAUL CÉZANNE *House of the Hanged Man, Auvers-sur-Oise* ca. 1873. $21\frac{5}{8} \times 26$ (54.9×66)

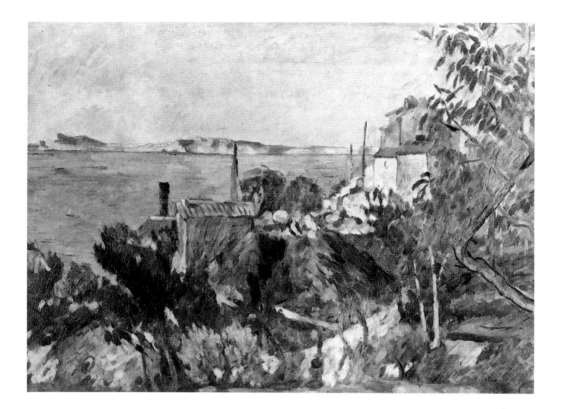

in order to hide the artist's point of view. This game of illusionistic cat-and-mouse helps to preserve the complexity and ambiguity of perception in time and space, and to preserve the integrated surface which is a record of that perception.

2) Use of tectonic facture, or *passage*—in *Mont Sainte-Victoire Seen From Bibémus* (ca. 1898–1900), the brushstroke shape, size, boundary, and direction is independent of the structure and texture of the objects that are represented. This painterly freedom may be considered another example of the resistance to mimesis described above, but in fact a kind of alternative illusionism is involved. The so-called *passage* brushstrokes on the rocks in the middle-ground are like colored gemstone facets, roof shingles or overlapping *affiches*; they are themselves planes that cling to the picture surface yet which constitute the tectonic authenticity of the rock. Once again, the two-dimensional authority of the pictorial support is reconciled with the depth and breadth of nature.

3) A consistent concentration upon the edges of things—in *Still Life With Apples* (ca. 1895–8), the most important parts of the picture are where objects meet—lemon, tablecloth, lime, peach, and goblet; pitcher, tabletop, tablecloth, shadow, peach, apple, peach, tablecloth. At these junctions, colors are juxtaposed and the drama of surface and depth—sensation and understanding—is enacted. For the picture to represent totality, it had to comprise fugitive sensations and unanticipated interactions, not merely independent objects. Colors had to be adjusted across the boundaries of things, and hierarchies between absence and presence eliminated.

364 PAUL CÉZANNE *L'Estaque* ca. 1876. 16¼ × 23¼ (41.9 × 59)

365 CAMILLE PISSARRO *The Côte des Boeufs at L'Hermitage, Near Pontoise* ca. 1873. 45¼ × 34½ (115 × 87.5)

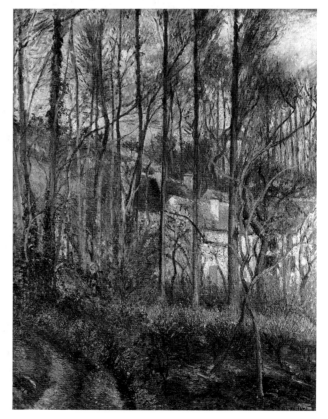

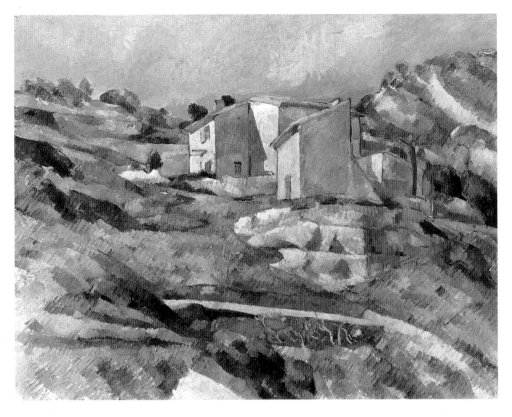

366 PAUL CÉZANNE *Houses in Provence (Vicinity of L'Estaque)* ca. 1879–82. 25½ × 32 (64.7 × 81.2)

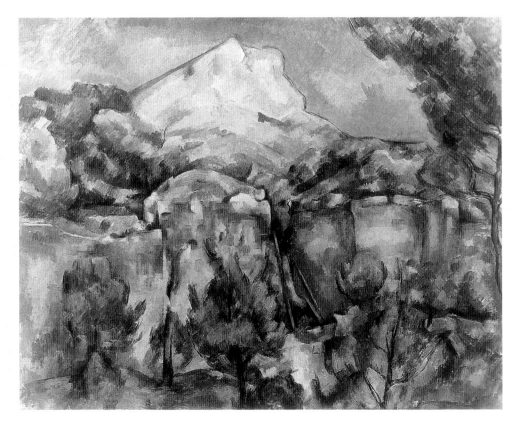

367 PAUL CÉZANNE *Mont Sainte-Victoire Seen From Bibémus* ca. 1898–1900. 25½ × 31½ (65 × 80)

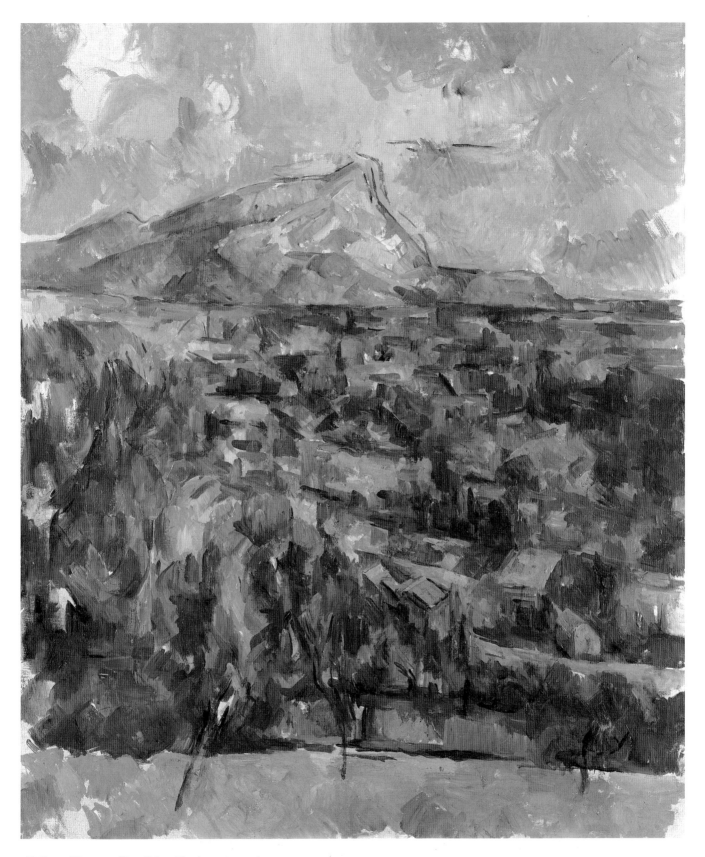

368 **Paul Cézanne** *Mont Sainte-Victoire* ca. 1902–06. 33 × 25⅝ (83.8 × 65)

Physical objects in *Still Life With Apples* are formed from the collision of one color with another. "One should not say model," Cézanne told Bernard, "one should say modulate." What the artist undoubtedly meant was that in order to attend to the depth as well as the surface appearance of things, he must reject traditional modeling with light and dark and instead modulate with warm and cool hues. The *point culminant* of the nearest lemon, for example, is not created by a white highlight but by a subtle array of cooler (receding) greens and yellows against a warmer (advancing) mustard. Indeed, the entire gamut of objects in this monumental painting—fruits, goblet, pitcher, tureen, curtains, table, and cloth—are constituted not by tonal modeling and local color but by color modulation.

Cézanne's art, Merleau-Ponty has written, was paradoxical: "He was pursuing reality without giving up the sensuous surface, with no other guide than the immediate impression of nature, without following the contours, with no outline to enclose the color, with no perspectival or pictorial arrangement. This is Cézanne's suicide: aiming for reality while denying himself the means to attain it." His art was contradictory, as Gauguin described it: "Has Cézanne discovered the prescription for compressing the intense expression of all his sensations into a single and unique procedure?" His art was abstract, as Cézanne himself told Denis: "I wished to copy nature, but I could not. I was only satisfied when I discovered that the sun, for instance, could not be *reproduced*, but that it must be *represented* by something else . . . by color."

Paradoxical, contradictory, and abstract, Cézanne's late paintings might also be called utopian. Though they recall, unlike Ensor's, no fabled past of popular enchantment, and though they imagine, unlike Seurat's, no future of sensual harmony, they are nevertheless themselves dreams of con-
362 cord, cooperation, and totality. In *The Large Bathers* (1900–06), one of three monumental paintings on this subject made in the artist's last half-decade, the boundaries between earth, plant, and human are elided while the autonomy of each is assured. The ten bathers, irregularly outlined in blue (their sex is mostly undetermined), the three large, blue-black trees that strain upward at left and right, and the yellow-brown earth below, share the task of composing the base, sides, and mass of a single great pyramid or mountain, like Mont Sainte-Victoire itself. Yet each of the three elements possess at the same time a purposiveness and formal rigor not present in contemporary works by the Symbolists Munch, Redon, Vrubel, and Hodler. Those

artists expressed a vitalistic longing for the subordination of humans before nature. Cézanne expressed—through a subtle balance of facture, tonality, color, volume, and mass—the desire for the simultaneous independence and cooperation of each.

Mont Sainte-Victoire (1902–06), like the *Large Bathers*, is 368 not only a depiction of a cherished subject—one that recalled the painter's youth amid the hills and waters of Provence—it is also a symphony of color modulation, orchestrated with at once balanced and variegated *passage*. Dozens of tints of blue, gray, and brown, applied with discrete oblong brushstrokes, create an up-and-down and side-to-side jostling; warm browns and yellows and cooler blues and greens instigate a constant shuttling between surface and depth. The mountain peak itself is outlined in blue—once, twice, three times—in order both to record the kinesthesia of the painter's eye, hand, arm, and body and to assert the clarity of that vaunted architecture. Both of these paintings, therefore, one focused on the human and one on the natural—by their unmistakable inscription of the drama of self and environment—express the utopian longing for a reconciliation. That image of concord, which had earlier been dreamed (though somewhat less elementally) by Constable, Courbet, and Van Gogh among others, was one of the most salient critical legacies of the nineteenth century.

"As eminently constructed and produced objects," Adorno writes, "[autonomous artworks] point to a practice from which they abstain: the creation of a just life." To combine perception and apperception, the sensual and the cognitive, the intellectual and the emotional within a single work of art— so Adorno argues—is to betoken a totality that is absent in a world scarred and fragmented by modernization and an exclusive reliance upon reason. Cézanne strove to achieve totality in his art, and in so doing insinuated his criticism of society in the very form of the artwork itself. That formal insinuation—the achievement both of a single artist and of the generations that labored before—may be judged, however, a failure as well as a success. During Cézanne's last years, and especially in the decades that followed, the embedding of criticism in form came more and more to resemble a hibernation of criticism. Indeed, by the time Cézanne was rediscovered by a public familiar with Cubism and abstraction, art and cultural criticism inhabited wholly separate spheres. The story of that fateful segregation cannot be told here; the effort of the present book has been only to show that in the nineteenth century things were different, and that the best art was critical.

CHRONOLOGY

HISTORICAL AND CULTURAL EVENTS

VISUAL ARTS

1780–89

1780   The American War of Independence (begun in 1776) continues. The Gordon Riots in London.

J.-A.-D. Ingres born.

1781   Surrender of the troops of Lord Cornwallis at Yorktown, Virginia, ending the British military effort against the American revolutionists. Immanuel Kant, *Kritik der reinen Vernunft* (Critique of Pure Reason). Jean-Jacques Rousseau, *Confessions*. Lessing dies.

J.-L. David, *Belisarius*. John Singleton Copley, *Death of Major Peirson* (completed 1784).

1782   John Howard urges the reform of Newgate prison, London. Choderlos de Laclos, *Les Liaisons dangereuses* (Dangerous Liaisons).

1783   Treaty of Paris signed, granting recognition and vast lands to the 13 former American colonies. Kant, *Prolegomena* (Prolegomena to Any Future Metaphysics). Mozart, *Idomeneo*. Stendhal born.

1784   Beaumarchais, *Le Mariage de Figaro* (The Marriage of Figaro). Denis Diderot dies.

J.-L. David, *Oath of the Horatii*. Goya, *The Family of the Infante Don Luis*. Sir Joshua Reynolds, *Mrs Siddons as The Tragic Muse*.

1785   Kant, *Grundlegung zur Metaphysik der Sitten* (Foundations of the Metaphysics of Morals). Alessandro Manzoni born.

Benjamin West, *Queen Philippa Intercedes for the Burghers of Calais*.

1786   Death of Prussia's Frederick the Great. Kant, *Metaphysische Anfangsgründe der Naturwissenschaft* (Metaphysical First Principles of Natural Science). Mozart, *Le Nozze de Figaro* (The Marriage of Figaro).

J.-G. Drouais, *Marius at Minturnae*.

1787   Federal Government established in the U.S. The Free African Society is founded in Philadelphia by Richard Allen. J. W. von Goethe, *Egmont*. John Adams, *A Defense of the Constitution of Government of the USA*. Mozart, *Don Giovanni*.

David, *Death of Socrates*. Tischbein, *Goethe on the Ruins in the Roman Campagna*. E.-L. Vigée-Lebrun, *Marie-Antoinette With Her Children*.

1788   Louis XVI summons States-General and recalls Jacques Necker as finance minister. New York federal capital of U.S. Kant, *Kritik der praktischen Vernunft* (Critique of Practical Reason). Arthur Schopenhauer and Byron born.

David, *Love of Paris and Helena*.

1789   The French Revolution begins; storming of the Bastille; feudalism abolished; Declaration of the Rights of Man in France; King and court move from Versailles to Paris. George Washington becomes first U.S. President. William Blake, *Songs of Innocence*.

David, *Lictors Returning to Brutus the Bodies of His Sons*.

1790–99

1790   Louis XVI accepts French constitution. Philadelphia U.S. federal capital. Jews granted civil rights in France. Edmund Burke, *Reflections on the Revolution in France*. Kant, *Kritik der Urteilskraft* (Critique of Judgment). Alphonse de Lamartine born.

1791	Louis XVI arrested at Varennes. Massacre of Champ de Mars. James Boswell, *Life of Johnson*. J. G. von Herder, *Ideen zur Philosophie der Geschichte der Menschheit* (Outlines of a Philosophy on the History of Man, begun 1784). Thomas Paine, *Rights of Man, Part I*. Mozart, *Die Zauberflöte* (The Magic Flute). Death of Mozart.	David, *The Oath of the Tennis Court*. Théodore Géricault born.
1792	Girondist ministry in France; revolutionary Commune estsblished; royal family imprisoned; First Republic proclaimed; trial of Louis XVI; France declares war on Austria, Prussia, and Sardinia. Thomas Paine, *Rights of Man, Part II*. Mary Wollstonecraft, *Vindication of the Rights of Women*. C. J. Rouget de Lisle, *La Marseillaise*. Percy Bysshe Shelley born.	
1793	Louis XVI and Marie Antoinette executed; Reign of Terror; Charlotte Corday murders Marat; Robespierre and St. Just join Committee of Public Safety headed by Danton; worship of God is banned; Holy Roman Empire declares war on France. William Godwin, *The Inquiry Concerning Political Justice*. Kant, *Religion innerhalb der Grenzen der blossen Vernunft* (Religion Within the Limits of Mere Reason).	Louvre, Paris, opens. David, *Death of Marat*. Goya, *The Fire*.
1794	'Feast of Supreme Being' in Paris; Danton and St. Just executed; Legislative Assembly abolishes slavery in French colonies; Robespierre overthrown on 9 Thermidor (July 27). William Blake, *Songs of Experience*. J. G. Fichte, *Grundlage der gesammten Wissenschaftslehre* (The Science of Knowledge). Thomas Paine, *The Age of Reason*.	Goya, *Procession of the Flagellants*. John Trumbull, *The Declaration of Independence*.
1795	Bread riots and White Terror in Paris; establishment of a ruling Directory in France; French occupy Belgium. Friedrich Schelling, *Vom Ich als Princip der Philosophie oder über das Unbedingte im menschlichen Wissen* (Concerning the Self as the Principle of Philosophy or the Absolute in Human Knowledge).	
1796	Napoleon assumes command in Italy. Babeuf's socialist "Conspiracy of Equals" defeated in France. George Washington's "Farewell Address." Spain declares war on Britain. Goethe, *Wilhelm Meisters Lehrjahre* (Wilhelm Meister's Apprentice Years). Schelling, *Das älteste Systemprogram* (System of Philosophy). Friedrich Schlegel, *Versuch über den Begriff des Republikanismus* (Essay on the Concept of Republicanism).	Goya, *The Duchess of Alba*. William Blake, *Newton*. J.-A. Houdon, *George Washington*. Edward Savage, *The Washington Family*. West, *Death on a Pale Horse*.
1797	Napoleon appointed to lead invasion of England. French capture and proclaim Rome a Republic. Battle of Pyramids, Napoleon commands. King Ferdinand IV of Naples takes Rome, French recapture. Samuel Taylor Coleridge, *Kubla Kahn* (published 1816). François René, Vicomte de Chateaubriand, *Essai historique, politique, et moral sur les révolutions anciennes et modernes dans leurs rapports avec la révolution française* (A historical, political and moral study into the effect of ancient and modern revolutions on the French Revolution). Friedrich Hölderlin, *Hyperion*. Kant, *Metaphysik der Sitten* (Metaphysics of Morals). Haydn, "Emperor" Quartet. Franz Schubert born.	A.-L. Girodet, *Portrait of Jean-Baptiste Belley*. Turner, *Millbank, Moon Light*.
1798	Goethe, *Hermann und Dorothea*. Wordsworth and Coleridge, *Lyrical Ballads*. The German literary and esthetic journal *Athenaeum* published in Berlin (until 1800) founded by K. W. F. Schlegel brothers, as the manifesto of the new Romantic movement.	
1799	Napoleon's Parthenopean Republic at Piedmont; Napoleon is made first consul on 18 Brumaire (November 19). Austria declares war on France. Friedrich Schlegel, *Lucinde*. Friedrich	David, *Intervention of the Sabine Women*. Goya, *Los Caprichos*.

1799   Schleiermacher, *Über die Religion* (On Religion, third edn. 1800). Haydn, *The Creation*. Giacomo Leopardi, Alexander Pushkin, and Honoré de Balzac born. Death of George Washington.

1800–09

1800   French army advances on Cairo and Vienna; Napoleon's army conquers Italy. Washington, D.C. new federal capital of U.S. Hölderlin, three odes. Schiller, *Mary Stuart*. Schlegel, *Brief über den Roman* (Letter on the Novel). Lord Macaulay born.

Blake, *The Great Red Dragon and the Woman Clothed With the Sun*. Antonio Canova, *Cupid and Psyche*. David, *Madame Récamier*. Goya, *Portrait of a Woman*.

1801   Union between Ireland and Great Britain. Czar Paul I assassinated, succeeded by Alexander I. English enter Cairo, French troops leave Egypt, recovered by Turks. Slavery reintroduced in French colonies. Hegel and Schelling, *Kritische Journal der Philosophie* (Critical Journal of Philosophy). Schelling, *Ideen zu einer Philosophie der Natur* (Ideas for a Philosophy of Nature). Haydn, *The Seasons*.

David, *Napoleon at the Saint-Bernard Pass*. Goya, *Naked* and *Clothed Maja*, and *Family of Charles IV*. Gros, *Battle of Nazareth*.

1802   Napoleon President of Italian Republic. Wordsworth begins *The Prelude*. Victor Hugo born.

Gérard, *Madame Récamier*. Girodet, *Ossian Receiving the Napoleonic Officers*.

1803   France and Britain renew war. Louisiana Purchase doubles territory of the U.S. Prosper Mérimée born. Choderlos de Laclos and J. G. Herder, theoretician of *Sturm und Drang* (storm and stress), die.

James Barry, *Self-Portrait*. Henry Raeburn, *The Macnab* portrait. Turner, *Calais Pier*.

1804   Napoleon proclaimed Emperor, crowned before Pope Pius VII; Code Napoléon composed and promulgated. Schiller, *William Tell*. Beethoven, "Eroica" symphony. George Sand born. Kant dies.

Gros, *Napoleon in the Plague House at Jaffa*.

1805   Britain, Russia, Sweden, and Austria sign treaty against France. Battle of Trafalgar. Napoleon King of Italy. Peace between Austria and France. William Hazlitt, *An Essay on the Principles of Human Action*. Beethoven, *Fidelio*. Hans Christian Andersen, Giuseppe Mazzini, and Alexis de Tocqueville born. Schiller dies.

Canova, *Tomb of the Archduchess Maria Christina*. Goya, *Doña Isabel Cobos de Procal*. Philipp Otto Runge, *The Hülsenbeck Children*. Turner, *Shipwreck*. Samuel Palmer born.

1806   British occupy Cape of Good Hope. Prussia declares war on France. Napoleon enters Berlin. End of Holy Roman Empire. John Stuart Mill born.

Canova, *Napoleon as Mars*. J. F. Chalgrin begins Arc de Triomphe, Paris. Ingres, *Napoleon on the Imperial Throne*. Bertel Thorvaldsen, *Hebe*.

1807   Prussian and Russian troops fight French forces at Eylau. British parliament forbids slave trade. Wordsworth, *Ode on Intimations of Immortality*. Hegel, *Phänomenologie des Geistes* (Phenomenology of the Mind). Beethoven, "Leonora" overture. Henry Wadsworth Longfellow born.

Canova, *Pauline Borghese as Venus*. David, *The Coronation of Napoleon*. Turner, *Sun Rising in a Mist*.

1808   Act of U.S. Congress forbids importation of slaves from Africa. French army occupies Rome, invades Spain. Napoleon recaptures Madrid after rebellion and Joseph Bonaparte's flight. Goethe, *Faust, Part I*. Charles Fourier, *Théorie des quatre mouvements et des destinées générales* (The Social Destiny of Man). Heinrich Kleist, *Penthesilea*. Beethoven, "Pastoral" symphony. Gérard de Nerval born.

Caspar David Friedrich, *The Cross in the Mountains*. Ingres, *La Grande Baigneuse*. Runge, *Morning*.

1809   Austria and France at war. French take Vienna. Napoleon annexes Papal States. A.W. Schlegel, *Über dramatische Kunst und Literatur* (Lectures on Dramatic Art and Literature, 3 vols., 1809–11). Beethoven, "Emperor" concerto. Nikolai Gogol, Abraham Lincoln, Felix Mendelssohn, Pierre-Joseph Proudhon, and Alfred, Lord Tennyson born.

Friedrich, *Monk by the Sea*.

1810–19

1810 France declares abortions illegal. Goethe, *Zur Farbenlehre* (Theory of Colors). Walter Scott, *The Lady of the Lake*. Mme. de Staël, *De l'Allemagne* (Germany). Kleist, *Über das Marionnettentheater* (On the Marionette Theater). Frédéric Chopin and Robert Schumann born.

Friedrich, *Abbey in the Oak Forest*. Goya begins *The Disasters of War*. J. F. Overbeck founds 'Nazarenes' to revive German religious art.

1811 George III of England insane; Prince of Wales becomes Prince Regent. William Henry Harrison defeats Indians under Tecumseh at Tippecanoe, Indiana. Jane Austen, *Sense and Sensibility*. Théophile Gautier, Franz Liszt, and William Makepeace Thackeray born. Kleist dies.

Ingres, *Jupiter and Thetis*. Thorvaldsen, *Procession of Alexander the Great*.

1812 Napoleon invades Russia, enters Moscow, but retreats with the army greatly diminished. General Malet executed after attempt to end war and reinstate monarch Louis XVIII. British Prime Minister Spencer Percival assassinated in House of Commons. U.S. declares war on Britain. Byron, *Childe Harold's Pilgrimage*. Brothers Grimm, *Kinder- und Hausmärchen* (Fairy Tales). Hegel begins *Wissenschaft der Logik* (Science of Logic, completed 1816). Alexander Herzen and Charles Dickens born.

Canova, *Venus Italica*. Goya, *Portrait of the Duke of Wellington*. Turner, *Snowstorm: Hannibal and His Army Crossing the Alps*.

1813 Prussia and Austria declare war on France. "Battle of the Nations," Leipzig, Napoleon defeated. William of Orange reinstated in Holland, French expelled. Mexico declares independence. Jane Austen, *Pride and Prejudice*. Shelley, *Queen Mab*. Saint-Simon, *De la Réorganisation de la société européenne* (On the Reorganization of European Society). Georg Büchner, Søren Kierkegaard, Giuseppe Verdi, and Richard Wagner born.

Turner, *Frosty Morning*. David Cox, *Treatise on Landscape Painting and Effect in Water Colours*.

1814 Allied armies (Britain, Russia, Austria) enter Paris. Napoleon abdicates, banished to Elba. Louis XVIII takes up throne in Paris. End of Anglo–U.S. "War of 1812". Jane Austen, *Mansfield Park*. Scott, *Waverley*. Wordsworth, *The Excursion*. Mikhail Bakunin, Mikhail Lermontov, and Eugène Viollet-le-Duc born. Fichte dies.

David, *Leonidas at Thermopylae*. Géricault, *The Blacksmith's Signboard*. Goya, *The Uprising of the Second of May 1808* and *The Executions of the Third of May 1808*. Ingres, *Odalisque*. J.-F. Millet born.

1815 Post-Napoleonic creation of Germanic Confederation. Napoleon leaves Elba for France; Louis XVIII flees; "Hundred Days"; Battle of Waterloo; Congress of Vienna marks final defeat of Napoleon. Napoleon abdicates and is exiled to St. Helena; Louis returns and Bourbon dynasty is reestablished. Elizabeth Cady Stanton and Anthony Trollope born.

Goya, *The Junta of the Philippines*. Nash rebuilds Brighton Pavilion in pseudo-oriental style.

1816 Argentina independent. Revival of Luddism in Britain. French naval disaster of the *Medusa*. Saint-Simon edits *L'Industrie* (Industry) until 1818. Jane Austen, *Emma*. Coleridge, *Kubla Khan* (begun 1797). Benjamin Constant, *Adolphe*. Rossini, *Il Barbiere di Siviglia* (The Barber of Seville).

Elgin Marbles bought for British Museum. Canova, *The Three Graces*. Goya, *The Duque de Osuna*.

1817 Beginning of war against Seminole Indians in Georgia and Florida. Byron, *Manfred*. Keats, "Endymion." Hegel, *Enzyklopädie der philosophischen Wissenschaften* (Encyclopedia of the Philosophical Sciences, revised and extended 1827). Henry David Thoreau born.

John Constable, *Flatford Mill*. Pasquale Belli begins building Vatican Museum, Rome.

1818 Border between U.S. and Canada agreed. Chile declares independence from Spain. Jane Austen, *Northanger Abbey*, *Persuasion* (posthumous). Byron, *Don Juan*. Thomas Love Peacock, *Nightmare Abbey*. Mary Shelley, *Frankenstein*. Mme. de Staël, *Considérations sur les principaux événements de la Révolution française* (Thoughts on the Main Events of the French Revolution). Karl Marx and Ivan Turgenev born.

Géricault, *The Bull Market*. Prado Museum, Madrid, founded.

1819	Peterloo Massacre of protestors by British troops in Manchester. U.S. buys Florida from Spain. Keats, "Hyperion" (published 1856). Saint-Simon edits *La Politique*. Schopenhauer, *Die Welt als Wille und Vorstellung* (The World as Will and Idea). Queen Victoria, Prince Albert, Gottfried Keller, Herman Melville, and Walt Whitman born.	Géricault, *The Raft of the Medusa*. John Martin, *The Fall of Babylon*. Turner, *Childe Harold's Pilgrimage*. John Ruskin born.

1820–29

1820	A Spanish revolution leads to constitutional restoration. Duc de Berry assassinated. Missouri Compromise maintains *de jure* slavery in U.S. South. Lamartine, *Méditations poétiques* (Poetic Meditations). Keats, "Ode to a Nightingale." Pushkin, *Ruslan and Ludmila*. Scott, *Ivanhoe, The Monastery, The Abbot*. Shelley, *Prometheus Unbound, The Cenci, Ode to the West Wind*. Washington Irving, *The Sketchbook*. Friedrich Engels and Herbert Spencer born.	George Cruikshank, *Life in London*. Thorvaldsen, *Christ and the Twelve Apostles*.
1821	Greek War of Independence from Ottoman Turks begins. Death of Napoleon. Coronation of George IV of England. Simon Bolívar named President of independent Venezuela. Goethe, *Wilhelm Meisters Wanderjahre* (Wilhelm Meister's Journeyman Years, completed 1829). Shelley, *Adonais*. Hegel, *Grundlinien de Philosophie des Rechts* (Philosophy of Right). Kleist, *Prince Friedrich of Homburg* (posthumous). Thomas de Quincey, *Confessions of an English Opium Eater*. Charles Baudelaire, Fyodor Dostoevsky, Gustave Flaubert, and Nikolae Nekrasov born. Keats dies.	Constable, *The Hay Wain*. Ford Madox Brown born.
1822	Ottoman massacre of Greeks at Chios (Scio). Deciphering of Rosetta Stone by J. F. Champollion. William Hazlitt, *Table Talk*. J.-B. Lamarck, *Histoire des animaux sans vertèbres* (Natural History of Invertebrates). Gregor Mendel, founder of genetics, born.	Canova, *Endymion*. Friedrich, *Woman By the Window*. Eugène Delacroix, *The Bark of Dante*. Canova dies.
1823	Enunciation of Monroe Doctrine. Beethoven, *Missa Solemnis*.	Goya, *A Dog* and *Saturn Devouring His Children*.
1824	Simón Bolívar Emperor of Peru. Beethoven completes Ninth Symphony. Alexandre Dumas (*fils*) born. Byron dies at Missolonghi, Greece; Louis XVIII dies, and brother, Charles X, assumes throne of France.	National Gallery, London, founded. David, *Mars Disarmed by Venus and the Three Graces*. Delacroix, *The Massacre at Scio* [Chios]. Ingres, *Vow of Louis XIII*. J. F. Overbeck, *Christ's Entry into Jerusalem*. Pierre Puvis de Chavannes born. Géricault dies.
1825	Ottoman siege of Missolonghi. Czar Alexander I dies, Nicholas I succeeds. *Diary of Samuel Pepys* published. Hazlitt, *The Spirit of the Age*. Saint-Simon dies.	Constable, *The Leaping Horse*. Samuel Morse, *Portrait of Lafayette*. Palmer, *Rest on the Flight into Egypt*. David dies.
1826	James Fenimore Cooper, *The Last of the Mohicans*. Hazlitt, *The Plain Speaker*. Heinrich Heine, *Buch der Lieder* (Book of Songs).	John James Audubon, *The Birds of America* portfolios. Thomas Cole, *Daniel Boone and His Cabin at Great Osage Lake*. Camille Corot, *The Forum Seen From the Farnese Gardens*. John Martin, *The Deluge*. Gustave Moreau born.
1827	Capitulation of Greek forces on the Acropolis. Manzoni completes *I Promessi Sposi* (The Betrothed, begun 1821). *The Freeman's Journal* begins publication in New York City. Beethoven and Ugo Foscolo die.	Constable, *The Cornfield*. Delacroix, *The Death of Sardanapalus*. Ingres, *The Apotheosis of Homer*. Ary Scheffer, *The Suliot Women*. William Holman Hunt and Arnold Böcklin born.
1828	Duke of Wellington Prime Minister of Britain. Russia declares war on Ottoman Empire. End of Russo-Turkish war. Webster, *An American Dictionary of the English Language*. Schubert, "Unfinished Symphony." Henrik Ibsen, Hippolyte Taine, Leo Tolstoy, and Jules Verne born. Schubert dies.	Delacroix, *Faust*. Dante Gabriel Rossetti born. Goya dies.

1829   Greece achieves independence. Fourier, *Le Nouveau monde industriel et sociétaire* (The New Industrial and Communal World). Rossini, *William Tell*. Schlegel dies.

Turner, *Ulysses Deriding Polyphemus*. John Martin, *The Fall of Ninevah*. John Everett Millais born.

1830–39

1830   July Revolution in France. "Citizen-King" Louis-Philippe becomes limited constitutional monarch. Indian Removal Act signed by President Andrew Jackson. Stendhal, *Le Rouge et le noir* (Scarlet and Black). Tennyson, *Poems, Chiefly Lyrical*. August le Comte, *Cours de philosophie positive* (Treatise on Positive Philosophy, vol. 1). Emily Dickinson, Frédéric Mistral, and Christina Rossetti born. Bolívar and George IV of England die.

End of Nazarene Brotherhood. Corot, *Chartres Cathedral*. Delacroix, *Liberty Leading the People*. Palmer, *Coming From Evening Church and Cornfield in Moonlight with Evening Star*. Camille Pissarro born. Sir Thomas Lawrence dies.

1831   Nat Turner leads Virginia slave revolt. Insurrection of Lyons silk workers. Heine in exile in Paris until 1856. Balzac, *La Peau de chagrin*. Hugo, *Notre-Dame de Paris* (The Hunchback of Notre Dame). Edgar Allen Poe, *Poems*. Pushkin, *Boris Godunov*. Vincenzo Bellini, *La Sonnambula* (The Sleepwalker) and *Norma*. Karl von Clausewitz and Hegel die.

Ando Hiroshige issues his first series of landscape prints, *Famous Places in Edo*. Constable, *Salisbury Cathedral, From the Meadows*. John Martin, *The Fall of Babylon*.

1832   Passage of first Reform Act in Britain, doubling eligible voters. Blackface minstrel T. D. Rice performs "Jim Crow" in Louisville, Kentucky. Goethe, *Faust, Part II* (posthumous). George Sand, *Indiana* and *Valentine*. Tennyson, *The Lady of Shallott*. Clausewitz, *Vom Kriege* (On War, posthumous). Hegel, *Geschichtsphilosophie* (The Philosophy of History, posthumous). Berlioz, *Symphonie Fantastique*. Goethe, Jeremy Bentham, and Scott die.

Constable, *Waterloo Bridge From Whitehall*. Hiroshige publishes series, *Fifty-three Stages of the Tokaido*. Ingres, *M. Louis-François Bertin*. Turner, *Staffa: Fingal's Cave*. Edouard Manet born.

1833   Ferdinand VII of Spain dies, succeeded by a 2 year-old daughter, Isabella II. Abolition of slavery in British colonies decreed. Balzac, *Eugénie Grandet*. Pushkin completes *Yevgeny Onegin* (Eugene Onegin) and first draft of *Medny vsadnik* (The Bronze Horseman). Johannes Brahms born.

Edward Burne-Jones born.

1834   English trade unionists from Tolpuddle transported for sedition. Balzac, *Le Père Goriot* (Old Goriot). Alfred de Musset, *Lorenzaccio*. Pushkin, *Pikovaya dama* (Queen of Spades). Schleiermacher dies.

Honoré Daumier, *Rue Transnonain, April 15, 1834*. Delacroix, *Women of Algiers*. Paul Delaroche, *The Execution of Lady Jane Grey*. Ingres, *Martyrdom of Saint Symphorian*. Edgar Degas, William Morris, and James Abbot McNeill Whistler born.

1835   Whites fight Seminole Indians in new war in Florida. Georg Büchner, *Dantons Tod* (Dantons Death). Théophile Gautier, *Mademoiselle de Maupin*. De Tocqueville, *Democracy in America* (vol. 1; vol. 2, 1840). Donizetti, *Lucia di Lammermoor*. Mark Twain born. Bellini dies.

Constable, *The Valley Farm*. Corot, *Hagar in the Desert*.

1836   Davy Crockett killed at Alamo. Republic of Texas proclaimed. Dickens, *The Pickwick Papers*. Ralph Waldo Emerson, *Nature*. Gogol, *Revizor* (The Government Inspector). Thomas Carlyle, *Sartor Resartus*.

Corot, *Diana Surprised by Actaeon*. François Rude, *The Marseillaise* (*The Departure of the Volunteers of 1792*). Winslow Homer born.

1837   Economic depression in U.S. and Britain. Victoria Queen of England. Capture of Seminole leader Osceola at St. Augustine. Balzac, *Illusions perdues* (Lost Illusions, Parts II and III 1837 and 1839). Carlyle, *The French Revolution*. Algernon Swinburne born. Büchner, Fourier, Leopardi, and Pushkin die.

David d'Angers, Pantheon pediment, Paris. Constable dies.

1838   Publication in London of "People's Charter," demanding universal suffrage. "Trail of Tears" in U.S. moves 14,000 Cherokees from homes in South to West during which 4000 die. Dickens, *Oliver Twist, Nicholas Nickleby*. Rossini, *Benvenuto Cellini*. Henry Brooke Adams born.

National Gallery, London, opened. Christen Kobke, *View of Lake Sortedam*.

1839 Maya culture in Central America examined by John Lloyd. Invention of photography. Stendhal, *La Chartreuse de Parme* (The Charterhouse of Parma). Louis Blanc, *Organisation du travail* (The Organization of Labor). Macaulay begins *History of England.*

                      M. E. Chevreul, *The Principles of Harmony and Contrast of Colors* and *The Application to the Arts.* Paul Cézanne and Alfred Sisley born.

1840–49

1840 Queen Victoria marries Prince Albert. Lermontov, *Geroy nashego vremeni* (A Hero of Our Times). Proudhon, "Qu'est-ce que c'est la propriété?" (What is Property?). Thomas Hardy and Emile Zola born.

                      Corot, *Breton Women at the Well.* Delacroix, *Entry of the Crusaders into Constantinople.* Ingres, *Odalisque with Slave.* John Martin, *The Assuaging of the Waters.* Claude Monet, Odilon Redon, and Auguste Rodin born. Caspar David Friedrich dies.

1841 Britain proclaims sovereignty over Hong Kong in the midst of the Opium War. USS *Creole* slave-ship seized by slaves, who are subsequently freed. Utopian Brook Farm established in Massachusetts. Ralph Waldo Emerson, *Essays: First Series.* Gogol, *Shinel* (The Overcoat). Poe, *The Murders in the Rue Morgue.* Ludwig Feuerbach, *Das Wesen des Christentums* (The Essence of Christianity). Lermontov dies.

                      Berthe Morisot and Auguste Renoir born.

1842 Fugitive Slave Act of 1793 upheld by U.S. Supreme Court. Balzac, *La Comédie humaine* (A Human Comedy) begins to appear. Gogol, *Mërtve dushi* (Dead Souls, Part I). Macaulay, *Lays of Ancient Rome.* Comte, *Cours de philosophie positive* (A Study of Positive Philosophy). Mendelssohn, *A Midsummer Night's Dream.* Verdi, *Nabucco.* William James and Stéphane Mallarmé born. Stendhal and Luigi Cherubini die.

                      David d'Angers, *Victor Hugo.*

1843 Wordsworth becomes English Poet Laureate. Dickens, *A Christmas Carol.* Mérimée, *Carmen.* Tennyson, *Morte d'Arthur.* Carlyle, *Past and Present.* Kierkegaard, *Enten-Eller* (Either/Or, 2 vols.) and *Frygt og Baeven* (Fear and Trembling). William Prescott, *History of the Conquest of Mexico.* Flora Tristan, *L'Union ouvrier* (Union of Workers). Henry James born. Hölderlin dies.

                      Ruskin, *Modern Painters,* vol. 1. Théodore Rousseau, *Under the Birches.* Turner, *Shade and Darkness—The Evening of the Deluge.*

1844 Marx and Engels meet in Paris. Morse demonstrates the 'electric telegraph'. Elizabeth Barrett Browning, *Poems.* Dumas (*père*), *Les Trois Mousquetaires* (The Three Musketeers). Gerard Manley Hopkins, Friedrich Neitzsche, and Paul Verlaine born.

                      Turner, *Rain, Steam, and Speed.* Mary Cassatt, Thomas Eakins, and Henri Rousseau, Le Douanier, born.

1845 Irish famine due to potato crop failure and export of grain to England. Dumas (*père*), *Le Comte de Monte Cristo* (The Count of Monte Cristo). Poe, *The Raven and Other Poems.* Engels, *Die Lage der arbeitenden Klasse in England* (The Condition of the Working Class in England). Margaret Fuller, *Woman in the Nineteenth Century.*

                      Portland vase destroyed and restored. Ingres, *Portrait of Countess Haussonville.*

1846 U.S. declares war on Mexico (to 1848). Free-traders repeal English Corn Law. Proudhon and Marx break relations. Balzac, *La Cousine Bette.* Dostoevsky, *Bedniye lyudi* (Poor Folk). Edward Lear, *Book of Nonsense.* Melville, *Typee.* Berlioz, *Damnation de Faust.* Comte de Lautréamont born. A.W. Schlegel dies.

                      Millet, *Oedipus Unbound.*

1847 U.S. forces take Mexico City. Alexander Herzen leaves Russia and goes into exile in the West. Charlotte Brontë, *Jane Eyre.* Emily Brontë, *Wuthering Heights.* Thackeray, *Vanity Fair.* Alfred de Vigny, *Oeuvres complètes* (Complete Works), 7 vols., begun 1839). Lamartine, *Histoire des Girondins* (History of the Girondists). Marx, *Manifest der Kommunistischen Partei* (The Communist Manifesto). Verdi, *Macbeth.* Wagner, *Tannhäuser.* Thomas Edison and Georges Sorel born. Mendelssohn dies.

                      George Caleb Bingham, *Raftsmen Playing Cards.* Thomas Couture, *Romans of the Decadence.* Rude, *Napoleon Reawakening to Immortality.*

	HISTORICAL AND CULTURAL EVENTS	VISUAL ARTS
1848	Revolution in France, spreads throughout Europe; Louis Napoleon III elected President, establishing Second Republic; Lamartine minister of Foreign Affairs in French provisional government. Revival of British Chartism. Elizabeth Cady Stanton joins in convening the first women's rights meeting in America, the Seneca Falls Convention, in which she presents the women's 'Declaration of Sentiments'. Utopian Oneida Community established in New York. Dumas (*fils*), *La Dame au camélias* (Camille). Elizabeth Gaskell, *Mary Barton*. Chateaubriand, *Mémoires d'outretombe* (Memoires From Beyond the Tomb). Macaulay, *History of England* (vols. 1 and 2). J. S. Mill, *Principles of Political Economy*. Proudhon writes for and edits Paris newspapers (until 1850), including *Le Peuple* and *La Voix du peuple*. Joris-Karl Huysmans born. Chateaubriand dies.	Millet, *The Winnower*. Millais, Rossetti, and Holman Hunt found Pre-Raphaelite Brotherhood. Paul Gauguin born.
1849	Rome declared Republic under Giuseppe Mazzini with support of Giuseppe Garibaldi. French enter Rome and restore Pope Pius IX. National Assembly fails to unify Germany. Marx moves to London. Kierkegaard, *Sygdommen til Doden* (The Sickness unto Death). Proudhon, *Confessions d'un révolutionnaire* (Confessions of a Revolutionary). August Strindberg born. Margaret Fuller, Chopin, and Edgar Allen Poe die.	Ruskin, *The Seven Lamps of Architecture*. Rosa Bonheur, *Plowing in the Nivernais: The Dressing of Vines*. Gustave Courbet, *The Peasants of Flagey Returning From the Fair, After Dinner at Ornans*, and *A Burial at Ornans*. J.-L.-E. Meissonier, *Memory of Civil War (The Barricades)*.

1850–59

1850	King Louis-Philippe of France dies. Michael Faraday publishes his general theory of magnetism. Emerson, *Nature: Addresses and Lectures*. Nathaniel Hawthorne, *The Scarlet Letter*. Tennyson becomes Poet Laureate; *In Memoriam*. Turgenev, *Mesyats v derevne* (A Month in the Country). Engels, *Der deutsche Bauernkrieg* (The Peasant Wars in Germany). Herzen, *S togo berega* (From the Other Shore). Guy de Maupassant born. Balzac and Wordsworth die.	Courbet, *The Stonebreakers*. Goya, *Proverbios* (posthumous). Millais, *Christ in the House of His Parents*. Millet, *The Sower*.
1851	Coup d'état of Louis-Napoleon ends French Second Republic. Sioux land in Iowa and Minnesota surrendered to Federal Government. Great Exhibition, Crystal Palace, London. Hawthorne, *House of Seven Gables*. Melville, *Moby Dick*. Gérard de Nerval, *Voyage en l'Orient* (Journey to the Orient). August Comte, *Système de politique positive* (System of Positive Politics, completed 1854). Proudhon, *Idée générale de la révolution au XIXe siècle* (General Theory of the Revolution of the Nineteenth Century). John Ruskin, *The Stones of Venice* (–1853). Verdi, *Rigoletto*. Wagner, *Opera and Drama*.	Corot, *The Dance of the Nymphs*. Millais, *Ophelia*. Turner dies.
1852	Proclamation of French Second Empire by Napoleon III. Aristide Boucicault invents department store (Bon Marché) in Paris. Dickens, *Bleak House*. Harriet Beecher Stowe, *Uncle Tom's Cabin*. Turgenev, *Zapiski okhotnika* (Sketches from a Hunter's Album). Gogol dies.	F. M. Brown, *Christ Washing Peter's Feet*. Holman Hunt, *The Light of the World*.
1853	U.S.–Mexico boundary settled. Matthew Arnold, *The Scholar Gypsy*. Charlotte Brontë, *Villette*. J. S. Mill, *Principles of Political Economy*. Verdi, *Il Trovatore, La Traviata*. Wagner finishes text of *Ring*.	Bonheur, *The Horse Fair*. Holman Hunt, *The Awakening Conscience*. Vincent Van Gogh born.
1854	Crimean War. Commodore Perry opens Japan to Western trade. Charles Kingsley, *Westward Ho!* Tennyson, "The Charge of the Light Brigade." Thoreau, *Walden*. Viollet-le-Duc, *Dictionnaire raisonné de l'architecture française* (The Complete Dictionary of French Architecture, vol. 1). Oscar Wilde and Arthur Rimbaud born. F. W. J. Schelling dies.	Courbet, *The Meeting (Bonjour, Monsieur Courbet)*. Millet, *The Reaper*. John Martin dies.

1855	Paris Universal Exposition. Hans Christian Andersen, *Mit Livs Eventyr* (The Fairy Tale of My Life). Robert Browning, *Men and Women*. Longfellow, *The Song of Hiawatha*. Nerval, *Aurélia*. Tennyson, *Maud*. Trollope, *The Warden*. Walt Whitman, *Leaves of Grass* (1st edition). Adelbert von Keller, *Der Grüne Heinrich* (Green Heinrich). Kierkegaard and Nerval die.	Courbet, *The Studio of the Painter*, exhibited at Pavilion of Realism at Paris Universal Exposition.
1856	End of Crimean War when Russians capitulate to Austria; Peace Congress in Paris. Nekrasov, *Poet and Citizen*. De Tocqueville, *L'Ancien Régime et la révolution* (The Old Regime and the Revolution). Sigmund Freud born. Heine and Schumann die.	Ingres, *La Source*. John Singer Sargent born.
1857	Dred Scott decision upholds *de jure* slavery in U.S. Baudelaire, *Les Fleurs du mal* (Flowers of Evil). Dickens, *Little Dorrit*. George Eliot, *Scenes from Clerical Life*. Flaubert, *Madame Bovary*. Trollope, *Barchester Towers*. Taine, *Les Philosophes français du XIXe siècle* (French Philosophers of the Nineteenth Century). Verdi, *Simon Boccanegra*. De Musset and Comte die.	National Portrait Gallery, London, opens. "Museum of Ornamental Art" opens in London (future Victoria and Albert Museum). Champfleury, *Réalisme*, manifesto of the Realist movement. Courbet, *The Young Ladies on the Banks of the Seine*. Millet, *The Gleaners*.
1858	Attempt to assassinate Napoleon III. Marx, *Grundrisse* (Sketches). Proudhon, *De la Justice dans la révolution et dans l'église* (Justice in the Revolution and in the Church). Taine, *Essais de critique et d'histoire* (Essays on Criticism and History). Offenbach, *Orphée aux enfers* (Orpheus in the Underworld). Giacomo Puccini born.	William Frith, *Derby Day*. Menzel, *Good Evening, Gentlemen*.
1859	France and Austria begin and end war. France acquires Indo-China. John Brown leads raid on Harper's Ferry, Virginia, in hopes of igniting slave revolt; he is hanged. Baudelaire, "Salon de 1859." Dickens, *A Tale of Two Cities*. George Eliot, *Adam Bede*. Edward Fitzgerald, *Rubáiyát of Omar Khayyám*. Ivan Goncharov, *Oblomov*. Tennyson, *Idylls of the King*. Charles Darwin, *On the Origin of Species by Natural Selection*. Marx, *Zur Kritik der politischen Ökonomie* (Critique of Political Economy). J. S. Mill, *On Liberty*. Charles Gounod, *Faust*. Verdi, *Un Ballo in Maschera* (A Masked Ball). Wagner, *Tristan und Isolde*. Henry Bergson born. I. K. Brunel, de Quincey, Macaulay, und de Tocqueville die.	Manet rejected at the Salon. Corot, *Macbeth*. Millet, *The Angelus*. Whistler, *At the Piano*. Georges Seurat born.

1860–69

1860	Garibaldi proclaims Victor Emmanuel King of Italy. Abraham Lincoln elected President of U.S. Turgenev, *Pervayas lyubov* (First Love) and *Nakanune* (On the Eve). Giuseppe Mazzini, *I Doveri dell'uomo* (The Duties of Man). Anton Chekhov, Jules Laforgue, Hugo Wolf, Claude Debussy, and Gustav Mahler born. Schopenhauer dies.	Jacob Burckhardt, *Die Kultur der Renaissance in Italien* (The Civilization of the Renaissance in Italy). Degas, *Young Spartans Exercising*. Holman Hunt, *Finding of the Savior in the Temple*. Manet, *Spanish Guitar Player*. James Ensor and Walter Sickert born.
1861	Serfdom abolished in Russia. Italy proclaimed kingdom. Civil War in the U.S. (until 1865). Dostoevsky, *Zapiski iz myrtvogo doma* (Memoirs from the House of the Dead, completed 1862). Herzen, *Byloe i dumy* (My Past and Thoughts). Harriet Martineau, *Health, Husbandry and Handicraft*. Sainte-Beuve, *Chateaubriand et son groupe littéraire sous l'empire* (Chateaubriand and his Circle under the Empire).	Manet successful at the Salon; he meets Charles Baudelaire and Edouard Duranty. Pissarro meets Cézanne. Corot, *Orpheus, The Rest*. William Morris founds Morris, Marshall, Faulkner & Co. (later Morris & Co.).
1862	The Battle of Shiloh ends indecisively after 24,000 are killed. Lincoln issues Emancipation Proclamation, freeing slaves. Homestead Act greatly increases settlement of U.S. West. Flaubert, *Salammbô*. Hugo, *Les Misérables*. Christina Rossetti, *Goblin Market*. Turgenev, *Ottsy i deti* (Fathers and Sons). Spencer, *The First Principles*. Count Maurice Maeterlinck born. Thoreau dies.	Frederick Church, *Cotopaxi*. Daumier, *The Third-Class Carriage*. Ingres, *Turkish Bath*. Manet, *Lola de Valence* and *Music in the Tuileries*. Gustav Klimt born.

1863	Navaho and Apache Indians forced to relocate to reservation in New Mexico. French capture Mexico City. Baudelaire, *Le Peintre de la vie moderne* (The Painter of Modern Life). Kingsley, *The Water Babies*. Lincoln, *Gettysburg Address*. J. S. Mill, *Utilitarianism*. Proudhon, *Du Principe fédératif* (Principle of Federation). Viollet-le-Duc, *Entretiens sur l'Architecture* (Interviews on Architecture). Bizet, *Les Pêcheurs de perles* (The Pearl Fishers). D'Annuncio born. Thackeray and Vigny die.	The Salon des Refusés includes works by Cézanne, Guillaumin, Manet, Pissarro and Whistler. Gustave Doré, *Don Quichotte* illustrations. Manet, *Déjeuner sur l'herbe* and *Olympia*. Rossetti, *Beata Beatrix*. Delacroix dies.
1864	The International Working Men's Association (The First International) founded in London. Italy renounces claim to Rome. The right to strike becomes legalized in France. Maximilian proclaimed emperor in Mexico. Dostoevsky, *Zapiski iz podpolya* (Notes from Underground). Chevreul, *Notes sur les couleurs* (Notes on Color).	Manet rejected at the Salon, while Pissarro and Morisot are included. Manet, *The Dead Toreador*. Whistler, *Symphony in White No. II: The Little White Girl*. Henri de Toulouse-Lautrec born.
1865	U.S. Civil War ends (Confederate States surrender) and Lincoln assassinated. Mendel publishes his research on heredity. Matthew Arnold, *Essays in Criticism*. Lewis Carroll, *Alice's Adventures in Wonderland*. John Henry Newman, *Dream of Gerontius*. Francis Parkman, *Pioneers of France in the New World*. Taine, *Nouveaux Essais* (New Essays). Proudhon and Lord Palmerston die.	Manet exhibits *Olympia* at the Salon. Courbet and Monet meet. F. M. Brown, *Work* (begun 1852). Degas, *Woman With Chrysanthemums*. George Innes, *Peace and Plenty*. Moreau, *Orpheus*.
1866	End of Austro-Italian war; Schleswig-Holstein incorporated into Prussia. Former U.S. slaves granted *de jure* civil rights. Dostoevsky, *Prestupleniye i nakazaniye* (Crime and Punishment). Swinburne, *Poems and Ballads*.	Zola publishes book of Salon reviews. Manet meets Zola and Cézanne. Winslow Homer, *Prisoners From the Front*. Monet, *Camille* (*Woman in a Green Dress*).
1867	The French abandon Mexico. Execution of Emperor Maximilian. U.S. purchases Alaska from Russia. Nobel patents dynamite in Sweden, America, and Britain. Ibsen, *Peer Gynt*. Marx, *Das Kapital* (vol. 1). Verdi, *Don Carlos*. Madame Curie born. Baudelaire dies.	Courbet and Manet arrange exhibition at Paris Universal Exposition. Cézanne, *Rape*. Manet, *The Execution of the Emperor Maximilian*. Millais, *Boyhood of Raleigh*. Monet, *Women in the Garden*. Pierre Bonnard born. Ingres dies.
1868	Revolution in Spain. Queen Isabel II flees to France. Gladstone succeeds Disraeli as British Prime Minister. Brahms, *Ein Deutsches Requiem* (A German Requiem). Tchaikovsky, *Symphony No. 1*. Wagner, *Die Meistersinger von Nürnberg*. Stefan George and Maxim Gorky born. Rossini dies.	J.-B. Carpeaux, *The Dance*. Degas, *The Orchestra*. Manet, *Portrait of Emile Zola*. Renoir, *The Skaters*. Edouard Vuillard born.
1869	Heinrich Schliemann begins excavations to locate Troy. Suez Canal opened. Completion of U.S. transcontinental railway. American Women's Suffrage Association founded by Susan B. Anthony. Henry James goes to England. Louisa May Alcott, *Little Women* (1868–9). Dostoevsky, *The Idiot*. Flaubert, *L'Education sentimentale* (A Sentimental Education). Lautréamont, *Les Chants du Maldoror* (The Songs of Maldoror). Tolstoy, *Voyna i mir* (War and Peace). Trollope, *Phineas Finn*. Mark Twain, *The Innocents Abroad*. Verlaine, *Fêtes galantes*. Jules Michelet, *L'Histoire de France* (History of France), *L'Histoire de la révolution française* (History of the French Revolution). J. S. Mill, *The Subjection of Women*. Wagner, *Das Rheingold*. André Gide and Frank Lloyd Wright born.	Café Guerbois becomes the favorite meeting place of the Impressionists. Manet, *A Balcony*. Monet, *La Grenouillère*. Degas, *The Orchestra of the Paris Opera*. Henri Matisse born.

1870–79

1870	Outbreak of Franco-Prussian War and French defeat; Napoleon III capitulates; Third Republic proclaimed in Paris; Prussians begin siege. Italians enter Rome, claiming it capital city. Ratification of 15th Amendment giving voting rights to former slaves. Jules Verne, *Vingt mille lieues sous les mers* (Twenty Thousand Leagues Under the Sea). Wagner, *Die Walküre* (The Valkyries). Dickens, Mérimée, Dumas *père*, Herzen, and Lautréamont die.	Manet joins the National Guard when war breaks out. Cézanne, *The Murder*. Fantin-Latour, *A Studio at Batignolles*. Meissonier, *The Siege of Paris*. Frédéric Bazille is killed in active service.

1871   A Socialist Commune is established in Paris in March and bloodily repressed in May by government forces; Thiers becomes President; Paris under martial law. King William I of Prussia proclaimed Emperor of United Germany. George Eliot, *Middlemarch*. Darwin, *The Descent of Man*. Verdi, *Aïda*. Marcel Proust and John Millington Synge born.

Courbet involved in destruction of Napoleon's Column in the Place Vendôme. Rossetti, *The Dream of Dante*.

1872   Civil War in Spain. Feminist Victoria Woodhull runs for U.S. Presidency. Lewis Carroll, *Through the Looking Glass*. Dostoevsky, *Besy* (The Possessed, or The Devils). Strindberg, *Master Olof*. Nietzsche, *Die Geburt der Tragödie* (The Birth of Tragedy, revised 1878, 1886). Alexander Scriabin born. Gautier and Mazzini die.

Manet sells 29 paintings to Durand-Ruel. Böcklin, *Battle of the Centaurs*. Degas, *A Carriage at the Races*. Millet, *Four Seasons*. Monet, *Impression, Sunrise* and *The Basin at Argenteuil*. Whistler, *The Artist's Mother*.

1873   Financial panic across Europe and North America. Napoleon III dies at Chislehurst, England. Spain proclaimed Republic. Germans leave France. Trollope, *The Eustace Diamonds*. Verne, *Le Tour du monde en 80 jours* (Around the World in 80 Days). J. S. Mill, *Autobiography* (posthumous). Spencer, *The Study of Sociology*. Alfred Jarry born. Mill dies.

Walter Pater, *Studies in the History of the Renaissance*. Degas visits New Orleans. Manet meets Mallarmé. Cézanne, *A Modern Olympia*. Monet, *Autumn Effects, Argenteuil*. Morisot, *The Cradle*.

1874   Schliemann begins excavating Homeric cities in Greece. Disraeli returns as Prime Minister. Hardy, *Far from the Madding Crowd*. Verlaine, *Romances sans paroles* (Songs Without Words). Brahms, *Hungarian Dances*. Mussorgsky, *Boris Godunov*. Verdi, *Requiem*. Wagner, *Der Ring des Nibelungen* completed.

First Impressionist Exhibition, Paris. Pissarro exhibits in this and all other Impressionist exhibitions (1874–86), which he largely organized; Manet refuses to participate. Manet, *Monet Working on his Boat in Argenteuil*. Monet, *The Seine at Argenteuil*. Renoir, *La Loge*.

1875   Trollope, *The Way We Live Now*. Mark Twain, *The Adventures of Tom Sawyer*. Bizet, *Carmen*. Thomas Mann and Rainer Maria Rilke born. Hans Christian Andersen, Bizet, and Manzoni die.

Edmond and Jules de Goncourt publish *L'Art du dix-huitième siècle* (Art of the Eighteenth Century). Caillebotte, *Floorscrapers*. Eakins, *The Gross Clinic*. Menzel, *Iron Rolling Mill*. Monet, *The Red Boat, Argenteuil* and *Poplars Near Argenteuil*. Corot and Millet die.

1876   General Custer and his U.S. cavalry force all killed at the Battle of Little Big Horn by Sioux warriors. Telephone invented in U.S. First Socialist International dissolved. Wagner's Festival Theatre at Bayreuth opens. George Eliot, *Daniel Deronda*. Pérez Galdós, *Doña Perfecta*. Henry James, *Roderick Hudson*. Mallarmé, *L'Après-midi d'un faune* (The Afternoon of a Faun). Nietzsche, *Unzeitgemässe Betrachtungen* (Thoughts out of Season, or Untimely Meditations, begun 1873). Wagner, *Siegfried*. Bakunin and George Sand die.

Second Impressionist Exhibition. Moreau, *Salome*. Renoir, *Le Moulin de la Galette*.

1877   Turkey and Russia at war. Queen Victoria Empress of India. Capture of Nez Perce braves and Chief Joseph in Montana territory. Edison invents phonograph. Flaubert, *Trois Contes* (Three Tales). Henry James, *The American*. Tolstoy, *Anna Karenina*. Trollope, *The American Senator*. Turgenev, *Nov* (Virgin Soil). Zola, *L'Assommoir*. Nekrassov dies.

Third Impressionist Exhibition. Caillebotte, *Paris Street: Rainy Weather*. Cézanne, *Still Life With Apples*. Eakins, *William Rush Carving His Allegorical Figure of the Schuylkill River*. Winslow Homer, *The Cotton Pickers*. Monet, *Gare St. Lazare, Paris* and *Argenteuil, the Bank in Flower*. Rodin, *The Age of Bronze*. Courbet dies.

1878   Russian–Turkish armistice signed. Paris Universal Exposition. Hardy, *The Return of the Native*. Henry James, *The Europeans*. Swinburne, *Poems and Ballads*. Engels, *Anti-Dühring* (including Socialism: Utopian and Scientific).

William Morris publishes *The Decorative Arts*. Whistler sues Ruskin for libel. Cassatt, *The Blue Room*. Degas, *The Rehearsal*. Monet, *Rue Montorgueil Decked Out with Flags*. George Cruikshank dies.

1879   British–Zulu War; peace signed. Edison invents electric light bulb in U.S. French Socialist Party formed. Gustave Charpentier, *La Vie moderne* (Modern Life). Ibsen, *Et Dukkehjem* (A Doll's House). Henry James, *Daisy Miller*. Frege, *Begriffsschrift* (Conceptual Notation). Tchaikovsky, *Eugene Onegin*. Viollet-le-Duc dies.

Fourth Impressionist Exhibition. Bouguereau, *Birth of Venus*. Mary Cassatt, *The Cup of Tea*. Renoir, *Mme. Charpentier and Her Children*. Rodin, *John the Baptist*. Daumier and Couture die.

1880–89

1880   Transvaal declares its independence. Dostoevsky, *Bratya Karamazovy* (The Brothers Karamazov). Maupassant, *Boule de suif* (Ball of Tallow) published in Zola's Naturalist collection *Les Soirées de Médan* (Evenings in Medan). Zola, *Nana*. Henry Brooks Adams, *Democracy*. Nietzsche, *Menschliches Allzumenschliches* (Human, All-too-human, begun 1878). Taine, *La Philosophie de l'art* (The Philosophy of Art). Guillaume Apollinaire, Alexander Blok, and Robert Musil born.

Fifth Impressionist Exhibition. Cézanne, *Château de Médan*. Pissarro, *The Outer Boulevards*. Renoir, *Place Clichy*. Rodin, *The Thinker* and commission of *The Gates of Hell* (completed 1917).

1881   The Boer War begins. Czar Alexander II and U.S. President Garfield assassinated. "Jim Crow" laws passed in Tennessee, furthering segregation. Flaubert, *Bouvard et Pécuchet* (posthumous). Ibsen, *Gengangere* (Ghosts). Henry James, *The Portrait of a Lady*. Maupassant, *La Maison Tellier*. Nietzsche, *Morgenröte* (The Dawn). Dostoevsky dies.

Sixth Impressionist Exhibition. Degas, *Little Dancer Aged Fourteen*. Monet, *Sunshine and Snow*. Renoir, *Luncheon of the Boating Party*. Pablo Picasso born. Samuel Palmer dies.

1882   Susan Brownell Anthony (with Elizabeth Cady Stanton and Matilda Joslyn Gage), *History of Woman Suffrage* (vol. 1, completed 1922). Nietzsche, *Die Fröhliche Wissenschaft* (The Gay Science). Tchaikovsky, "1812 Overture." Wagner, *Parsifal*. Darwin, Disraeli, Emerson, Garibaldi, Longfellow, Trelawny, and Trollope die.

Seventh Impressionist Exhibition. Cézanne, *Self-Portrait*. Manet, *Bar at the Folies-Bergère*. Seurat, *Farm Women at Work*. D. G. Rossetti dies.

1883   Marxist party founded in Russia by Plekhanov and others. Robert Louis Stevenson, *Treasure Island*. Huysmans, *L'Art moderne* (Modern Art). Nietzsche, *Also Sprach Zarathustra* (Thus Spake Zarathustra, completed 1892). Metropolitan Opera House, New York, opens. Léo Delibes, *Lakmé*. Franz Kafka born. Marx, Turgenev, and Wagner die.

Monet settles at Giverny. Durand-Ruel arranges series of one-man exhibition of Monet, Pissarro, Renoir, and Sisley. Cézanne, *Rocky Landscape*. Renoir, *Umbrellas*. Manet and Gustave Doré die.

1884   Huysmans, *A Rebours* (Against the Grain). Ibsen, *Vildanden* (The Wild Duck). Mark Twain, *The Adventures of Huckleberry Finn*. Engels, *Der Ursprung der Familie, des Privateigentums und des Staats* (The Origin of the Family, Private Property, and the State). Frege, *Die Grundlagen der Arithmetik* (The Foundations of Arithmetic).

The Société des Vingt holds its first exhibition. Manet memorial exhibition at the Ecole des Beaux-Arts. Redon, Seurat, and Signac become involved in the new Société des Indépendants. Bartholdi, *Statue of Liberty*. Rodin, *The Burghers of Calais* commissioned. Seurat, *A Bathing Place, Asnières*. Whistler exhibits *Portrait of the Artist's Mother* at Salon.

1885   Belgian Leopold II declares himself sovereign of Congo Free State. Pasteur invents vaccine against rabies. Freud studies under Charcot at the Salpêtrière hospital for nervous diseases in Paris and becomes interested in hysteria and hypnosis. Walter Pater, *Marius the Epicurean*. Zola, *Germinal*. Kropotkin, *Memoirs of a Revolutionist*. Marx, *Das Kapital* (vol. 2, posthumous). J. S. Mill, *Nature, The Utility of Religion*, and *Theism*, 3rd edn. (all posthumous). Victor Hugo dies.

Cézanne, *Mont Sainte-Victoire*. Van Gogh, *The Potato Eaters*. Redon, *Homage to Goya*.

1886   Apache chief Geronimo captured, ending last major U.S.-Indian war. Orléans and Bonaparte families banished from France. Haymarket Massacre of strikers and police in Chicago. Ibsen, *Rosmersholm*. Henry James, *The Bostonians*. Rimbaud, *Les Illuminations*. R. L. Stevenson, *The Strange Case of Dr. Jekyll and Mr. Hyde*. Zola, *L'Oeuvre*. Engels, *Ludwig Feuerbach und der Ausgang der klassischen deutschen Philosophie* (Ludwig Feuerbach and the End of Classical German Philosophy). Marx, *Das Kapital* published in English. Jean Moréas, manifesto of Symbolism in *Le Figaro*. Nietzsche, *Jenseits von Gut und Böse* (Beyond Good and Evil). Liszt dies.

Eighth and last Impressionist Exhibition. Félix Fénéon publishes *Les Impressionnistes en 1886*. Cézanne breaks with Zola after publication of *L'Oeuvre*, and marries Hortense Fiquet. Rodin, *The Kiss*. Seurat, *A Sunday Afternoon on the Island of the Grande Jatte*.

1887   General Boulanger fails coup d'état in Paris. Pérez Galdós, *Fortunata and Jacinta*. Nietzsche, *Zur Genealogie der Moral* (On the Genealogy of Morals). Verdi, *Otello*. Laforgue dies.

Gauguin leaves France for Martinique. Pissarro and Seurat exhibit with Les Vingt in Brussels. Cézanne, *Mont Sainte-Victoire* and *Five Bathers*.

1888	'Kaiser' Wilhelm II becomes Emperor of Germany. Eastman invents paper photographic films and Kodak box camera. Ibsen, *Fruen fra Havet* (The Lady From the Sea). Rudyard Kipling, *Plain Tales from the Hills*. Strindberg, *Miss Julie*. Oscar Wilde, *The Happy Prince, and Other Tales*. Edward Bellamy, *Looking Backward, 2000–1887*. Bergson, *Essai sur les données immédiates de la conscience* (Time and Free Will). George Moore, *Confessions of a Young Man*. Nietzsche, *Ecce Homo* (published 1908), *Nietzsche Contra Wagner*, *Götzendämmerung* (The Twilight of the Idols), and completes notes on *Der Wille zur Macht* (The Will to Power). Ruskin, *Praeteritas*. Mahler, *Symphony No. 1*. Nikolai Rimsky-Korsakov, *Scheherazade*.	Gauguin and Bernard develop principles of Synthetism. Bernard, *Buckwheat Harvesters, Pont-Aven*. Ensor, *The Entry of Christ into Brussels in 1889*. Gauguin, *The Vision After the Sermon*. Van Gogh, *The Night Café at Arles*, *The Sower*, and *The Yellow Chair*. Paul Sérusier, *The Talisman*. Seurat, *The Side Show*.
1889	Abortive attempt to set aside French Republic, the "Boulanger affair." Eiffel Tower opened; more than 30 million people visit the Universal Exposition, Paris. Anatole France, *Thaïs*. Tolstoy, *The Kreuzer Sonata*. Mark Twain, *A Connecticut Yankee in King Arthur's Court*. Sir Arthur Evans begins excavating Knossos. Browning and Chevreul die.	Paris Universal Exposition. The Nabis emerge as a group. The Symbolist *La Revue Blanche* starts publication. Eakins, *The Agnew Clinic*. Gauguin, *Yellow Christ*. Van Gogh, *Landscape with Cypress Tree* and *Starry Night*. Monet, *Oatfields* series.

1890–1900

1890	U.S. Congress passes Sherman Anti-Trust Act. Wounded Knee Massacre of 300 Sioux people by troops of 7th Cavalry, South Dakota. First moving picture in New York. Chekhov begins *Tri Sestry* (Three Sisters). Knut Hamsun, *Sult* (Hunger). Ibsen, *Hedda Gabler*. Wilde, *The Picture of Dorian Gray*. Zola, *La Bête Humaine* (The Beast in Man). J. G. Frazer, *The Golden Bough*. William James, *Principles of Psychology*. Alexander Borodin, *Prince Igor* (posthumous). Fauré, *Requiem*. Tchaikovsky, *Pikovaya dama* (Queen of Spades). Gottfried Keller dies.	Giovanni Morelli's essays on connoisseurship republished as *Kunsthistorische Studien über Italienische Malerei*. William Morris, *News From Nowhere*. Whistler, *The Gentle Art of Making Enemies*. Cézanne, *The Cardplayers*. Monet, *Haystacks* series. Seurat, *Chahut*. Van Gogh dies.
1891	Papal encyclical *Rerum novarum* highlights employer's responsibility to workers. Arthur Conan Doyle publishes the first *Adventures of Sherlock Holmes*. Hardy, *Tess of the D'Urbervilles*. Melville, *Billy Budd* (posthumous). Wedekind, *Frühlings Erwachen: eine Kindertragödie* (Spring Awakening: A Tragedy of Childhood). Henry Brook Adams, *History of the United States of America During the Administration of Jefferson and Madison*. Melville and Rimbaud die.	Gauguin leaves for Tahiti. Van Gogh exhibition at Salon des Indépendants. William Morris founds Kelmscott Press. Cassatt, *The Bath*. Gauguin, *Ia Orana Maria*. Monet, *Poplars* series. Alfred Ryder, *Siegfried and the Rhine Maidens*. Seurat, *The Circus*. Seurat dies.
1892	French encounter colonial resistance in Africa. The Dreyfus affair. Homestead, Pennsylvania, steelworks strike. Ibsen, *Bygmester Solness* (The Master Builder). Maeterlinck, *Pelléas et Mélisande*. Wilde, *Lady Windermere's Fan*. Leoncavallo, *I Pagliacci* (The Clowns). Tchaikovsky, *The Nutcracker*. Tennyson and Whitman die.	Monet, *Rouen Cathedral* series. Toulouse-Lautrec, *At the Moulin Rouge*. Gauguin, *Manao tupapau* (The Specter Watches Her).
1893	Franco-Russian alliance. F. H. Bradley, *Appearance and Reality*. Engelbert Humperdinck, *Hansel and Gretel*. Tchaikovsky, *Symphony No. 6*, "Pathétique." Puccini, *Manon Lescaut*. Verdi, *Falstaff*. Maupassant and Taine die.	Edvard Munch, *The Voice*. Vuillard, *The Workroom*. Ford Madox Brown dies.
1894	Alfred Dreyfus convicted of espionage, increasing antisemitism in France. Nicholas II becomes Czar. Pullman strike in Chicago. Anthony Hope, *The Prisoner of Zenda*. Kipling, *The Jungle Book*. George Bernard Shaw, *Arms and the Man*. Debussy, *L'Après-midi d'un faune* (Afternoon of a Faun). Christina Rossetti and R. L. Stevenson die.	Aubrey Beardsley's designs for Wilde's *Salome*. Degas, *Woman at Her Toilette*. Ferdinand Hodler, *The Chosen One*. Rodin, *Balzac*.
1895	Territory in Southern Africa named Rhodesia to honor British imperialist. Theodor Fontane, *Effi Briest*. Verhaeren, *The Tentacular Cities*. H. G. Wells, *The Time Machine*. W. B. Yeats,	Moreau, *Jupiter and Semele*. Pissarro, *Place du Théâtre Français*. Rodin, *Burghers of Calais*.

1895	*Poems*. Freud and Breuer, *Studien über Hysterie* (Studies on Hysteria). Marx, *Das Kapital* (vol. 3, posthumous). Nietzsche, *Der Antichrist*. E. C. Stanton, *The Woman's Bible*. Tchaikovsky's *Swan Lake* performed. Engels dies.	
1896	U.S. Supreme Court upholds "Jim Crow" laws. Freud introduces the term "psychoanalysis." Chekhov, *Ivanov: Chayka* (The Seagull). Ibsen, *John Gabriel Borkman*. Alfred Jarry, *Ubu Roi*. Bergson, *Matière et mémoire* (Matter and Memory). Puccini, *La Bohème*. Verlaine dies.	Monet, *Mornings of the Seine* series. Millais and William Morris die.
1897	Freud's self-analysis recognizing infantile sexuality and the Oedipus complex. Joseph Conrad, *The Nigger of the Narcissus*. Henry James, *The Spoils of Poynton* and *What Maisie Knew*. Edmond Rostand, *Cyrano de Bergerac*. H. G. Wells, *The Invisible Man*. Brahms and Burckhardt die.	Tolstoy, *What is Art?* Gauguin, *Where Do We Come From? What Are We? Where Are We Going?* Max Klinger, *Christ in Olympus*. Matisse, *Dinner Table*. Pissarro, *Boulevard des Italiens*. Rodin, *Victor Hugo*. Le Douanier Rousseau, *The Sleeping Gypsy*.
1898	U.S. declares war on Spain. Zola publishes "J'Accuse" in *L'Aurore*, forcing new Dreyfus trial. Henry James, *The Turn of the Screw*. Wilde, *The Ballad of Reading Gaol*. Bismarck, Gladstone, and Mallarmé die.	Rodin, *Honoré de Balzac*. Burne-Jones and Moreau die.
1899	Dreyfus exonerated. Right-wing Action Française founded in Paris. Chekhov, *Dyadya Vanya* (Uncle Vanya). Kate Chopin, *The Awakening*. Tolstoy, *Voskrenseniye* (Resurrection). Wilde, *The Importance of Being Earnest*. Freud, *Die Traumdeutung* (The Interpretation of Dreams, published 1900, with final chapter giving first full account of dynamic view of mental processes of the unconscious and of the dominance of the "pleasure principle"). Elgar, *Dream of Gerontius*. Puccini, *Tosca*.	Monet, *The Japanese Bridge* series and begins *Waterlilies* series. Sisley dies.
1900		Cézanne, *Still Life With Onions*. Munch, *The Dance of Life*. Renoir, *The Nude in the Sun*. Toulouse-Lautrec, *La Modiste*.

SELECTED BIBLIOGRAPHY

The works listed below are the authors' sources for each chapter, preceded by those titles common to more than one chapter.

Albert Boime, *The Art of Exclusion: Representing Blacks in the Nineteenth Century*. Washington, D.C. and London, 1990.
Patricia Condon, *In Pursuit of Perfection: The Art of J.-A.-D. Ingres*. Louisville, KY: The J. B. Speed Art Museum, 1984.
The Journal of Eugène Delacroix, ed. Hubert Wellington, trans. Lucy Norton. Oxford, 1951, and Ithaca, 1980.
Félix Fénéon, *Au-delà de l'impressionnisme*, ed. Françoise Cachin. Paris, 1966.
French Painting 1774–1830: The Age of Revolution. Detroit, 1985.
Francis Haskell, *Past and Present in Art and Taste*. New Haven, CT, and London, 1987.
Dorothy Johnson, *Metamorphoses of Jacques-Louis David*. Princeton, 1993.
Patricia Mainardi, *Art and Politics of the Second Empire: The Universal Expositions of 1855 and 1867*. New Haven, CT, and London, 1987.
Linda Nochlin, *The Politics of Vision: Essays on Nineteenth-Century Art and Society*. New York, 1989; London, 1991.
Ellwood C. Parry, *The Image of the Indian and the Black Man in American Art, 1590–1900*. New York, 1974.
John Rewald, *The History of Impressionism*. 4th revised edn., New York and London, 1973.
E. P. Thompson, *The Making of the English Working Class*. London and New York, 1963.
Gabriel P. Weisberg (ed.), *The European Realist Tradition*. Bloomington, IN, 1982.
Raymond Williams, *Culture and Society, 1780–1950*. New York and London, 1958; New York, 1980.

Introduction

Louis Althusser, *For Marx*. London, 1973.
Léonce Bénédite, *Great Painters of the XIXth Century and Their Paintings*. London, 1910.
Walter Benjamin, *Illuminations*, ed. Hannah Arendt. London, 1970; New York, 1978.
Albert Boime, *A Social History of Modern Art*, vol. I. Chicago, 1988.
Norman Bryson, *Tradition and Desire: From David to Delacroix*. Cambridge, 1984.
Lorenz Eitner, *An Outline of 19th Century European Painting*. New York, 1987.
E. J. Hobsbawm, *The Age of Revolution: Europe 1789–1848*. London and New York, 1962.
Max Horkheimer, "Traditional and Critical Theory," in *Critical Sociology*, ed. Paul Connerton. Harmondsworth, 1978.
The Marx-Engels Reader, ed. Robert C. Tucker. New York and London, 1978.
Richard Muther, *The History of Modern Painting*, 4 vols. New York, 1907.
Fritz Novotny, *Painting and Sculpture in Europe, 1780–1880*. Baltimore, 1960; 2nd edn. Harmondsworth, 1970.
Robert Rosenblum and H. W. Janson, *19th-Century Art*. New York, 1984; English edn., *Art of the Nineteenth Century*, London, 1984.

Chapter 1

I want gratefully to acknowledge research by others, published and unpublished, which has informed Chapters 1 and 2: Darcy Grigsby on Gros's *Plague House at Jaffa* and Delacroix's *Liberty*; David O'Brien on Gros's *Battle of Nazareth*; Susan Siegfried likewise on the *Nazareth* painting and on Ingres's *Napoleon on the Imperial Throne*; Ewa Lajer-Burchardt on David's *Sabines*; Stephanie Brown on Girodet and Bruno Chenique on Géricault; Francis Haskell on Sommariva; Nina Athanassoglou-Kallmyer on the imagery of the Greek War of Independence; finally Philippe Bordes and Régis Michel on topics too numerous to mention. *Thomas Crow*.

Philip Conisbee, *Eighteenth-Century French Painting*. Ithaca, 1982.
Thomas Crow, *Painters and Public Life in Eighteenth-Century Paris*. New Haven, CT, and London, 1985.
David Dowd, *Jacques-Louis David: Pageant Master of the Republic*. Lincoln, NE, 1948.
Robert Herbert, *David: Brutus*. Harmondsworth, 1972).
Régis Michel *et al.*, *Aux armes et aux arts! Les arts de la Révolution 1789–1799*. Paris, 1989.
Robert Rosenblum, *Transformations in Late Eighteenth-Century Art*. Princeton, 1967.
Elisabeth Vigée-Lebrun, *Memoirs*, trans. L. Strachey, 1903; New York, 1989.

Chapter 2

Nina Athanassoglou-Kallmyer, *French Images from the Greek War of Independence 1821–1830*. New Haven, CT, and London, 1987.
Eugène Delacroix, *Selected Letters 1813–1863*, ed. and trans. J. Stewart. New York, 1970.
Philippe Grunchec, *Master Drawings by Géricault*. Washington, D.C., 1985.
Régis Michel *et al.*, *Géricault*. Paris, 1992.
Frank Anderson Trapp, *The Attainment of Delacroix*. Baltimore and London, 1971.

Chapter 3

Nigel Glendinning, *Goya and His Critics*. New Haven and London, 1977.
J. Guidol, *Goya*, 4 vols. Barcelona, 1971.
F. D. Klingender, *Goya in the Democratic Tradition*. London and New York, 1968.
Fred Licht (ed.), *Goya in Perspective*. Englewood Cliffs, 1973.
—, *Goya: The Origins of the Modern Temper in Art*. New York, 1979; London, 1980.
The Life and Complete Works of Francisco Goya, with a preface by Enrique Lafuente Ferrari. New York, 1981.
André Malraux, *Saturn: An Essay on Goya*. New York, 1957.
Priscilla E. Muller, *Goya's "Black" Paintings: Truth and Reason in Light and Liberty*. New York, 1984.
Alfonso E. Pérez Sánchez and Eleanor A. Sayre *et al.*, *Goya and the Spirit of Enlightenment*. Boston and New York, 1989.
Eleanor A. Sayre *et al.*, *The Changing Image: Prints by Francisco Goya*. Boston, 1974.

Gwyn A. Williams, *Goya and the Impossible Revolution*. London, 1976.

Chapter 4

John Barrell, *The Political Theory of Painting from Reynolds to Hazlitt*. New Haven, CT, and London, 1986.
David Bindman, *Blake as an Artist*. Oxford, 1977.
Jacob Bronowski, *William Blake and the Age of Revolution*. New York, 1965.
Stewart Crehan, *Blake in Context*. London, 1984.
David V. Erdman, *Blake: Prophet against Empire*. 3rd edn., Princeton, 1977.
Morris Eaves, *William Blake's Theory of Art*. Princeton, 1982.
David Irwin, *English Neoclassical Art*. London, 1966.
Geoffrey Keynes (ed.), *Blake: Complete Writings*. London, 1972.
Eudo C. Mason, *The Mind of Henry Fuseli*. London, 1951.
W. J. T. Mitchell, *Blake's Composite Art*. Princeton, 1978.
Morton D. Paley, *The Apocalyptic Sublime*. New Haven, CT, and London, 1986.
Ronald Paulson, *Representations of Revolution*. New Haven, CT, and London, 1983.
William L. Pressly, *The Life and Art of James Barry*. New Haven, CT, and London, 1981.
Gert Schiff, *Johann Heinrich Fuseli*. Zurich, 1973.
Ruthven Todd, *Tracks in the Snow: Studies in English Art and Science*. London, 1946.

Chapter 5

Malcolm Andrews, *The Search for the Picturesque: Landscape Aesthetics and Tourism in Britain*. Stanford, 1989.
John Barrell, *The Dark Side of the Landscape: The Rural Poor in English Painting, 1730–1840*. Cambridge, 1980.
Ann Bermingham, *Landscape and Ideology: The English Rustic Tradition, 1740–1860*. Berkeley, 1986.
David Bindman, "Samuel Palmer's 'An Address to the Electors of West Kent, 1832' Rediscovered," *Blake Quarterly*, 19 (Fall 1985): 56–68.
Albert Boime, "Turner's *Slave Ship*: The Victims of Empire," *Turner Studies*, 10 (Summer 1990): 34–43.
Stephen Daniels, "Humphry Repton and the Morality of Landscape," in *Valued Environments*, eds. J. R. Gold and J. Burgess. London, 1983.
William Feaver, *The Art of John Martin*. Oxford, 1975.
John Gage, *J. M. W. Turner, 'A Wonderful Range of Mind'*. New Haven, 1987.
Nicholas Green, *The Spectacle of Nature*. Manchester, 1990.
Louis Hawes, *Presence of Nature: British Landscape, 1780–1830*. New Haven, CT, 1982.
James Heffernan, *The Re-Creation of Landscape*. Hanover, 1985.
Andrew Hemingway, *Landscape and Urban Culture in Early Nineteenth-Century Britain*. Cambridge, 1992.
Humphrey Jennings, *Pandaemonium: The Coming of the Machine as Seen by Contemporary Observers, 1660–1886*. New York, 1985.

Jack Lindsay, *J. M. W. Turner, A Critical Biography.* New York, 1966.

Franklin Kelly, *Frederic Edwin Church and the National Landscape.* Washington, D.C., 1988.

Joseph Leo Koerner, *Caspar David Friedrich and the Subject of Landscape.* London and New Haven, CT, 1990.

John McCoubrey, "Time's Railway: Turner and the Great Western," *Turner Studies,* 6 (Summer 1986): 33–9.

Kenneth W. Maddox, "Asher B. Durand's *Progress:* The Advance of Civilization and the Vanishing American," in *The Railroad in American Art,* eds. S. Danly and L. Marx. Cambridge, MA, 1988.

Victor Miesel, "Philipp Otto Runge, Caspar David Friedrich, and Romantic Nationalism," *Yale University Art Gallery Bulletin,* 33 (October 1972): 37–51.

Ellwood C. Parry, *The Art of Thomas Cole.* Newark, 1988.

Ronald Paulson, *Literary Landscape: Turner and Constable.* New Haven, CT, 1982.

William S. Rodner, "Turner's *Dudley:* Continuity, Change, and Adaptability in the Industrial Black Country," *Turner Studies,* 8 (Summer 1988): 32–40.

Michael Rosenthal, *Constable: The Painter and His Landscape,* New Haven, CT, and London, 1983.

Eric Shanes, *Turner's Human Landscape.* London, 1990.

Lindsay Stainton, *British Landscape Watercolours, 1600–1860.* London, 1985.

William Vaughan, *German Romantic Painting.* New Haven, CT, and London, 1980.

Alan Wallach, "Thomas Cole and the Aristocracy," *Arts,* 56 (November 1981): 94–106.

Raymond Williams, *The Country and the City.* London and New York, 1973.

Chapter 6

Janet Catherine Berlo, "Portraits of Dispossession in Plains Indian and Inuit Graphic Arts," *Art Journal,* 49 (Summer 1990): 133–41.

James Clifford, *The Predicament of Culture.* Cambridge, MA, 1988.

E. McClung Fleming, "From Indian Princess to Greek Goddess: The American Image, 1783–1815," *Winterthur Portfolio,* 3 (1967): 37–66.

Kathryn S. Hight, "'Doomed to Perish': George Catlin's Depictions of the Mandan," *Art Journal,* 49 (Summer 1990): 119–24.

Claude Lévi-Strauss, "New York in 1941," *The View from Afar.* New York, 1985.

David M. Lubin, "*Ariadne* and the Indians: Vanderlyn's Neoclassical Princess, Racial Seduction, and the Melodrama of Abandonment," *Smithsonian Studies in American Art,* 3 (Spring 1989): 3–20.

Julie Schimmel, "Inventing the 'Indian,'" in Truettner (ed.), *The West as America.* See below.

Richard Slotkin, *The Fatal Environment: The Myth of the Frontier in the Age of Industrialization, 1800–1890.* New York, 1985.

Pauline Turner Strong, "Captivity in White and Red: Convergent Practice and Colonial Representation on the British-Amerindian Frontier, 1606–1736," in *Crossing Cultures: Essays in the Displacement of Western Civilization,* ed. Dan Segal. Tuscon and London, 1992.

Joyce M. Szabo, "Howling Wolf: A Plains Artist in Transition," *Art Journal,* 44 (Winter 1984): 367–73.

Alan Trachtenberg, *The Incorporation of America: Culture and Society in the Gilded Age.* New York, 1982.

Patricia Trenton and Patrick T. Houlihan, *Native Americans: Five Centuries of Changing Images.* New York, 1989.

William H. Truettner (ed.), *The West as America: Reinterpreting Images of the Frontier, 1820–1920.* Washington, D.C., and London, 1991.

Edwin L. Wade (ed.), *The Arts of the North American Indian: Native Traditions in Evolution.* New York and Tulsa, 1986.

Eric Wolfe, *Europe and the People Without History.* Berkeley, CA, 1982.

Chapter 7

Lerone Bennett, Jr., *Before the Mayflower: A History of Black America, The Classic Account of the Struggles and Triumphs of Black Americans.* 5th edn., Harmondsworth, 1984.

Whitney Chadwick, *Women, Art, and Society.* London and New York, 1990.

David C. Driskell, with catalog notes by Leonard Simon, *Two Centuries of Black American Art.* New York and Los Angeles, 1976.

Lucretia H. Giese, "*Prisoners from the Front:* An American History Painting?" in Simpson, *Winslow Homer.* See below.

Patricia Hills, "Picturing Progress in the Era of Westward Expansion," in Truettner (ed.), *The West as America.* See Ch. 6.

Karen S. Linn, *That Half-Barbaric Twang: The Banjo in American Popular Culture.* Urbana, 1991.

Robert F. Lucid, "Civil War Humor: Anecdotes and Recollections," *Civil War History,* 2, no. 3 (September 1956): 44–6.

Guy C. McElroy, *Facing History: The Black Image in American Art 1710–1940.* San Francisco and Washington, D.C., 1990.

Dewey F. Mosby and Darrel Sewell, *Henry Ossawa Tanner.* Philadelphia Museum of Art, 1991.

Charlotte Streifer Rubinstein, *American Women Artists from the Early Indian Times to the Present.* New York, 1982.

Marc Simpson, *Winslow Homer: Paintings of the Civil War.* San Francisco, 1988.

Peter H. Wood and Karen C. C. Dalton, *Winslow Homer's Images of Blacks: The Civil War and Reconstruction Years.* Austin, TX, 1988.

Howard Zinn, *A People's History of the United States.* New York, 1980.

Chapter 8

Jean-Paul Aron, *Misérable et glorieuse la femme du xixe siècle.* Paris, 1980.

Charles Baudelaire, *Oeuvres complètes,* ed. Claude Pichois. Paris, 1975.

Albert Boime, *Hollow Icons: The Politics of Sculpture in Nineteenth-Century France.* Kent, OH, 1987.

—, *Thomas Couture and the Eclectic Vision.* New Haven, CT, and London, 1980.

Jacques de Caso, *David d'Angers: Sculptural Communication in the Age of Romanticism.* Princeton, 1992.

Thomas Crow, "Modernism and Mass Culture in the Visual Arts," in *Pollock and After: The Critical Debate,* ed. Francis Frascina. New York, 1985.

Terry Eagleton, *The Function of Criticism.* London, 1984.

Peter Fusco and H. W. Janson (eds.), *The Romantics to Rodin.* Los Angeles, 1980.

Susan K. Grogan, *French Socialism and Sexual Difference.* New York, 1992.

Jürgen Habermas, "The Public Sphere: An Encyclopedia Article," *New German Critique,* 3 (Fall 1974): 49–55.

Neil McWilliam, "David d'Angers and the Pantheon Commission: Politics and Public Works under the July Monarchy," *Art History,* 5: 4 (December 1982): 426–46.

Chapter 9

Walter Benjamin, "The Author as Producer," in *Reflections,* ed. Peter Demetz, trans. Edmund Jephcott. New York and London, 1978.

Albert Boime, "Ford Madox Brown, Thomas Carlyle, and Karl Marx: Meaning and the Mystification of Work in the Nineteenth Century," *Arts Magazine* (September 1979): 116–25.

T. J. Clark, *The Absolute Bourgeois: Artists and Politics in France 1848–1851.* London, 1972; New York, 1973.

—, *Image of the People: Gustave Courbet and the 1848 Revolution.* London and New York, 1973.

Gerard Curtis, "Ford Madox Brown's *Work:* An Iconographic Analysis," *The Art Bulletin* (December 1992): 623–36.

Sarah Faunce and Linda Nochlin, *Courbet Reconsidered.* Brooklyn, 1988.

Klaus Herding, *Courbet: To Venture Independence.* New Haven, CT, and London, 1991.

E. D. H. Johnson, "The Making of Ford Madox Brown's *Work,*' in *Victorian Artist in the City,* ed. I. B. Nadel and F. S. Schwarzbach. New York, 1980.

Letters of Gustave Courbet, ed. and trans. Petra tenDoesschate Chu. Chicago and London, 1992.

Linda Nochlin, *Realism.* Harmondsworth and Baltimore, 1971.

Gabriel P. Weisberg, *The Realist Tradition: French Painting and Drawing, 1830–1900.* The Cleveland Museum of Art, 1981.

Chapter 10

Albert Boime, *The Art of the Macchia and the Risorgimento.* Chicago and London, 1993.

Norma Broude, *The Macchiaioli: Italian Painters of the Nineteenth Century.* New Haven, CT, and London, 1987.

Peter H. Feist, *Geschichte der deutschen Kunst: 1760–1848; 1848–1890.* Leipzig, 1986–7.

Gobineau: Selected Political Writings, ed. and introduced by Michael D. Biddiss, London, 1970.

Elizabeth Gilmore Holt, *The Art of All Nations, 1850–73: The Emerging Role of Artists and Critics.* Princeton, 1981.

The Macchiaioli: Painters of Italian Life, 1850–1900. Los Angeles: The Frederick S. Wight Art Gallery, 1986.

Linda Nochlin, *Realism and Tradition in Art: 1848–1900.* Englewood Cliffs, 1966.

Gabriel P. Weisberg, *Beyond Impressionism: The Naturalist Impulse.* New York, 1992.

Chapter 11

Kathleen Adler and Tamar Garb, *Berthe Morisot.* Oxford and Ithaca, 1987.

Carol Armstrong, *Odd Man Out: Readings of the Work and Reputation of Edgar Degas.* Chicago and London, 1991.

Art in the Making: Impressionism. London: National Gallery of Art, 1990.

Walter Benjamin, *Charles Baudelaire: A Lyric Poet in the Era of High Capitalism,* trans. Harry Zohn. London, 1973.

Norma Broude, *Impressionism: A Feminist Reading.* New York, 1991.

— (ed.), *World Impressionism: The International Movement, 1860–1920.* New York, 1990.

T. J. Clark, *The Painting of Modern Life: Paris in the Art of Manet and His Followers.* London and New York, 1985.

Hollis Clayson, *Painted Love: Prostitution in French Art of the Impressionist Era.* New Haven, CT, and London, 1991.

Sander L. Gilman, *Difference and Pathology: Stereotypes of Sexuality, Race, and Madness.* Ithaca and London, 1985.

George Heard Hamilton, *Manet and His Critics.* London, 1954; New York, 1969.

Anne Higonnet, *Berthe Morisot's Images of Women.* Cambridge, MA, and London, 1992.

Hugh Honour, *The Image of the Black in Western Art,* vol. IV. Cambridge, MA, and London, 1989.

Manet: 1832–1883. New York: The Metropolitan Museum of Art, 1983.

Manet: The Execution of Maximilian—Painting, Politics and Censorship. London: National Gallery of Art, 1992.

Charles W. Millard, *The Sculpture of Edgar Degas.* Princeton, 1976.

The New Painting: Impressionism, 1874–1886. The Fine Arts Museums of San Francisco, 1986.
Perspectives on Morisot, ed. and introduced by T. J. Edelstein. New York, 1990.
Daniel Pick, *Faces of Degeneration: A European Disorder, c. 1848–c. 1918.* Cambridge, 1989.
Meyer Schapiro, "The Nature of Abstract Art," *Collected Essays.* New York, 1978.
Anne Wagner, *Jean-Baptiste Carpeaux: Sculptor of the Second Empire.* New Haven, CT, and London, 1986.

Chapter 12

Adelyn Dohme Breeskin, *Mary Cassatt: A Catalogue Raisonné of the Oils, Pastels, Watercolors, and Drawings.* Washington, D.C., 1991.
Michael Fried, *Realism, Writing, Disfiguration: On Thomas Eakins and Stephen Crane.* Chicago, 1987.
William H. Gerdts, *American Impressionism.* New York, 1984.
Lloyd Goodrich, *Thomas Eakins.* 2 vols., Cambridge, MA, 1982.
Gordon Hendricks, *The Life and Work of Thomas Eakins.* New York, 1974.
Patricia Hills (ed.), *John Singer Sargent.* New York, 1986.
Elizabeth Johns, *Thomas Eakins: The Heroism of Modern Life.* Princeton, 1983.
T. J. Jackson Lears, *No Place of Grace: Antimodernism and the Transformation of American Culture, 1880–1920.* New York, 1981.
David M. Lubin, *Act of Portrayal: Eakins, Sargent, James.* New Haven, CT, and London, 1985.
Nancy Mowll Mathews, *Mary Cassatt.* New York, 1989.
— with B. S. Shapiro, *Mary Cassatt: The Color Prints.* New York, 1989.
Stanley Olson, *John Singer Sargent, His Portrait.* New York, 1986.
Richard Ormond, *John Singer Sargent: Paintings, Drawings, Watercolors.* London and New York, 1970.
Griselda Pollock, *Mary Cassatt.* London, 1980.
Alan Trachtenberg, *The Incorporation of America: Culture and Society in the Gilded Age.* New York, 1982.
H. Barbara Weinberg, *The Lure of Paris: Nineteenth-Century American Painters and Their French Teachers.* New York, 1991.
Bryan Jay Wolf, *Romantic Re-Vision: Culture and Consciousness in Nineteenth-Century American Painting and Literature.* Chicago, 1982.

Chapter 13

The Art Institute of Chicago, "The Grande-Jatte at 100," *Museum Studies,* 14: 2 (1989), ed. Susan F. Rossen.
Albert Boime, "Georges Seurat's *Un Dimanche à la Grande-Jatte* and the Scientific Approach to History Painting," *Historienmalerei in Europa* (Mainz am Rhein), 1990, pp. 303–33.
Norma Broude (ed.), *Seurat in Perspective,* Englewood Cliffs, 1978.
Henri Dorra and John Rewald, *Seurat: L'Oeuvre peint, biographie, et catalogue critique.* Paris, 1959.
Erich Franz and Bernd Growe, *Georges Seurat: Drawings.* Boston, 1984.
John Gage, "The Technique of Seurat: A Reappraisal," *The Art Bulletin,* 69: 3 (September 1987): 448–54.
Joan Ungersma Halperin, *Félix Fénéon: Aesthete and Anarchist in Fin-de-Siècle Paris.* New Haven, CT, and London, 1988.
César de Hauke, *Seurat et son œuvre.* 2 vols., Paris, 1961.
Robert Herbert *et al., Georges Seurat, 1859–1891.* New York: The Metropolitan Museum of Art; London: National Gallery, 1991.
Alan Lee, "Seurat and Science," *Art History,* 10: 2 (June 1987): 203–26.

Herbert Marcuse, *Negations: Essays in Critical Theory,* trans. Jeremy T. Shapiro. Boston and London, 1968.
Camille Pissarro, 1830–1903. London: Hayward Gallery, 1981.
John Rewald, *Post-Impressionism: From Van Gogh to Gauguin.* 3rd edn., New York and London, 1978.
Ralph E. Shikes and Paula Harper, *Pissarro: His Life and Work.* New York, 1980.
Jean Sutter (ed.), *The Neo-Impressionists.* New York and London, 1970.
Richard Thomson, *Seurat.* Oxford, 1985.
Toulouse-Lautrec and His Contemporaries: Posters of the Belle Epoque. Los Angeles County Museum of Art, 1985.

Chapter 14

Klaus Berger, *Japonisme in Western Painting from Whistler to Matisse.* Cambridge, MA, 1992.
Albert Boime, "Van Gogh's *Starry Night*: A History of Matter and A Matter of History," *Arts Magazine* (December 1984): 86–103.
The Complete Letters of Vincent Van Gogh, Greenwich, CT, and London, 1979.
J.-B. de la Faille, *The Works of Vincent Van Gogh: His Paintings and Drawings.* 4 vols., Amsterdam and London, 1970.
Jan Hulsker, *The Complete Van Gogh: Paintings, Drawings, Sketches.* New York, 1980.
—, *Vincent and Theo Van Gogh: A Dual Biography.* Ann Arbor, MI, 1985.
Japonisme in Art: An International Symposium, ed. Society for the Study of Japonisme. Tokyo, 1980.
Tsukasa Kodera, "Japan as Primitivistic Utopia: Van Gogh's *Japonisme* Portraits," *Simiolus,* 3: 4 (1984): 189–208.
Griselda Pollock, "Artists, Mythologies and Media: Genius, Madness and Art History," *Screen,* 21: 3 (1980): 57–96.
—, "Stark Encounters: Modern Life and Urban Work in Van Gogh's Drawings of the Hague 1881–3," *Art History,* 6: 3 (September 1983): 330–58.
—, "Van Gogh and the Poor Slaves: Images of Rural Labour as Modern Art," *Art History,* 11: 3 (September 1988): 408–32.
— and Fred Orton, *Vincent Van Gogh: Artist of His Time.* Oxford and New York, 1978.
Odilon Redon, *To Myself: Notes on Life, Art, and Artists,* trans. Mira Jacob and Jeanne L. Wasserman. New York, 1986.
Vincent: Bulletin of the Rijksmuseum Vincent van Gogh, Amsterdam, 1–4 (1970–76).

Chapter 15

The Art of Paul Gauguin, with essays by Richard Brettell *et al.* Washington, D.C., 1988.
Roland Barthes, *Mythologies.* New York, 1977.
Ruth Butler (ed.), *Rodin in Perspective.* Englewood Cliffs, 1980.
Jacques de Caso and Patricia B. Sanders, *Rodin's Sculpture: A Critical Study of the Spreckels Collection.* San Francisco, 1977.
Henri le Chartier, *Tahiti et les colonies françaises de la Polynésie.* Paris, 1887.
Stephen F. Eisenman, "Allegory and Anarchism in James Ensor's *Vision Preceding Futurism,*" *Record of the Art Museum of Princeton University,* 46: 1 (1987): 2–17.
—, *The Temptation of Saint Redon: Biography, Ideology, and Style in the Noirs of Odilon Redon.* Chicago and London, 1992.
— and Oskar Bätschmann, *Ferdinand Hodler: Landscapes.* Zurich, 1987.
Albert E. Elsen, *The Gates of Hell by Auguste Rodin.* Stanford, 1985.
John David Farmer, *Ensor.* New York: Solomon R. Guggenheim Museum, 1976.
Paul Gauguin: 45 Lettres à Vincent, Theo et Jo Van Gogh, ed. Douglas Cooper. Lausanne: Rijksmuseum Vincent Van Gogh, 1983.

Paul Gauguin: Letters to his Wife and Friends, ed. Maurice Malingue, trans. Henry J. Stenning. London, (1948); Cleveland and New York, 1949.
Paul Gauguin, *Noa Noa,* trans. O. F. Theis. New York, (n.d.). See also *Noa Noa: Gauguin's Tahiti,* ed. and with text by N. Wadley. Oxford, 1985.
Reinhold Heller, *Munch: His Life and Work.* London, 1984.
Susan Hiller (ed.), *The Myths of Primitivism.* London, 1991.
E. J. Hobsbawm, *The Age of Empire: 1875–1914.* London, 1987; New York, 1989.
Elizabeth Gilmore Holt (ed.), *The Triumph of Art for the Public: The Emerging Role of Exhibitions and Critics.* New York, 1979.
Michel Hoog, *Paul Gauguin: Life and Work.* New York and London, 1987.
Aline Isdebsky-Pritchard, *The Art of Mikhail Vrubel.* Ann Arbor, MI, 1982.
S. Kaplanova, *Vrubel.* Leningrad, 1975.
Diane Lesko, *James Ensor: The Creative Years.* Princeton and Guildford, 1985.
Claude Lévi-Strauss, *Myth and Meaning.* London, New York, and Toronto, 1978.
Louise Lippincott, *Edvard Munch: Starry Night.* Malibu, 1988.
Leo Lowenthal, "Knut Hamsun," in *The Essential Frankfurt School Reader,* eds. Andrew Arato and Eike Gebhardt. New York, 1977; Oxford, 1978.
Stephen Charles McGough, *James Ensor's "The Entry of Christ into Brussels in 1889".* New York and London, 1985.
Monchoisy [Mativet], *La Nouvelle Cythère.* Paris, 1888.
Colin Newbury, *Tahiti Nui: Change and Survival in French Polynesia, 1767–1945.* Honolulu, 1980.
Douglas L. Oliver, *Ancient Tahitian Society.* Honolulu, 1974.
Fred Orton and Griselda Pollock, "Les Données bretonnantes: la prairie de la représentation," *Art History,* 3: 3 (September 1980): 314–44.
Griselda Pollock, *Avant-Garde Gambits 1888–1893: Gender and the Colour of Art History.* London and New York, 1993.
Abigail Solomon-Godeau, "Going Native," *Art in America* (July 1989): 119–28 and 161.
Anne M. Wagner, "Rodin's Reputation," in *Eroticism and the Body Politic,* ed. Lynn Hunt. Baltimore and London, 1991.

Chapter 16

Theodor W. Adorno, "Commitment," in *The Essential Frankfurt School Reader,* eds. Andrew Arato and Eike Gebhardt. New York, 1977; Oxford, 1978.
Paul Cézanne: *Letters: Revised and Augmented Edition,* ed. John Rewald. New York, 1984.
John Elderfield, "The World Whole: Color in Cézanne," *Arts Magazine,* 52: 8 (April, 1978): 148–53.
Lawrence Gowing *et al., Cézanne: The Early Years 1859–1872.* London: Royal Academy of Arts; New York, 1988.
Mary Louise Krumrine, *Paul Cézanne: The Bathers.* Basle: Kunstmuseum, 1989; New York and London, 1990.
Mary Tompkins Lewis, *Cézanne's Early Imagery.* Berkeley and London, 1989.
Jack Lindsay, *Cézanne: His Life and Art.* London, 1969.
Herbert Marcuse, *Reason and Revolution: Hegel and the Rise of Social Theory.* London, 1955; New York, 1960.
Maurice Merleau-Ponty, *Sense and Non-Sense.* Evanston, IL, 1973.
William Rubin (ed.), *Cézanne: The Late Work.* New York: Museum of Modern Art; London, 1977.
J.-P. Sartre, *Baudelaire.* London, 1964; New York, 1967.
Judith Wechsler (ed.), *Cézanne in Perspective.* Englewood Cliffs, 1975.

LIST OF ILLUSTRATIONS

Measurements are in inches (centimeters in parentheses), height before width before depth, unless otherwise stated.

in 1889 1888. Oil on canvas, 8'6½ × 14'6 (260 × 430.5). Collection of J. Paul Getty Museum, Malibu, CA. **321** *Iston, Pouffamatus, Cracozie, and Transmouff, Famous Persian Physicians Examining the Stools of King Darius after the Battle of Arbela* 1886. Etching, 9⅜ × 7 (23.7 × 17.8). Koninklijk Museum voor Schone Kunsten, Antwerp. **322** *Old Woman With Masks* 1889. Oil on canvas, 21¼ × 18½ (54 × 47). Musée des Beaux-Arts, Ghent. **323** *The Gendarmes* 1892. Oil on canvas, 14 × 21⅝ (35.5 × 55). Museum voor Schone Kunsten, Ostend. **324** *My Portrait in 1960* 1888. Etching, 2¾ × 4¾ (6.9 × 12). Bibliothèque Royale de Belgique, Brussels.

FAVEAU, Félicie de **182** *Christina of Sweden Refusing to Give Mercy to Her Squire Monaldeschi* ca. 1827. Plaster, 15¾ × 22⅞ (40 × 58). Musée des Beaux-Arts, Louviers.

FLANDRIN, Hippolyte-Jean **212** *Napoleon III* 1860–61. Oil on canvas, 83½ × 58 (212 × 147). Musée National du Château, Versailles.

FLAXMAN, John **24** "The Fight for the Body of Patroculus," from *Illustrations to Homer's "Iliad"* 1793. Engraving, 6⅝ × 13 (16.8 × 33.6). **98** "Design for the Monument to British Naval Victories with a Statue of Britannia," 1799. Engraved by William Blake, 8¼ × 5¾ (21 × 14.6). The Trustees of the British Museum, London.

FRIEDRICH, Caspar David **132** *Abbey in the Oak Forest* 1809–10. Oil on canvas, 39½ × 67⅜ (100.4 × 171). Schloss Carlottenburg, Berlin.

FUSELI, Henry **100** *Thor Battering the Midguard Serpent* 1790. Oil on canvas, 51½ × 36¼ (131 × 92). Royal Academy of Arts, London. **103** *The Nightmare* 1790. Oil on canvas, 30 × 24⅞ (76 × 63). Goethe Museum, Frankfurt. **104** *Symplegma (Man and Three Women)* ca. 1810. Watercolor, 7½ × 9⅝ (18.9 × 24.5). By courtesy of the Board of the Trustees of the Victoria and Albert Museum, London.

GAUGUIN, Paul **313** *Green Christ* 1889. Oil on canvas, 36¼ × 28¾ (92 × 73). Musées Royaux des Beaux-Arts de Belgique, Brussels. **314** *Yellow Christ* 1889. Oil on canvas, 36½ × 28¾ (92 × 73). Albright-Knox Art Gallery, Buffalo, NY. General Purchase Fund. **317** *The Seaweed Gatherers* 1889. Oil on canvas, 34¼ × 48½ (87 × 123). Folkwang Museum, Essen. **318** *Bonjour Monsieur Gauguin* 1889. Oil on canvas, 44½ × 36¼ (113 × 92). Národní Galerie, Prague. **319** *Jug in the Form of a Head, Self-Portrait* 1889. Glazed stoneware, height 7½ (19.3). Museum of Decorative Arts, Copenhagen. **320** *Christ in the Garden of Olives* 1889. Oil on canvas, 28¾ × 36¼ (73 × 92). Norton Gallery and School of Art, West Palm Beach, FL. **339** *Manao tupapau (The Specter Watches Her)* 1892. Oil on canvas, 28¾ × 36½ (73 × 92). Albright-Knox Art Gallery, Buffalo, NY. A. Conger Goodyear Collection. **340** *The Meal, or The Bananas* 1891. Oil on canvas, 28¾ × 36½ (73 × 92). Musée d'Orsay, Paris. Photo © R.M.N. **341** *Vahine no te vi (Woman of the Mango)* 1892. Oil on canvas, 28⅝ × 17½ (72.7 × 44.5). Baltimore Museum of Art. The Cone Collection formed by Dr. Claribel Cone and Miss Etta Cone of Baltimore. **351** *Mahana no Atua (Day of the God)* 1894. Oil on canvas, 26⅞ × 36 (68.3 × 91.5). The Art Institute of Chicago. Helen Birch Bartlett Collection, 1926.198. Photo © 1993, The Art Institute of Chicago, All Rights Reserved. **352** *Te Faaturuma (Silence, or To Be Dejected)* 1891. Oil on canvas, 36 × 27 (91.2 × 68.7). Worcester Art Museum, Worcester, MA. **353** *Where Do We Come From? What Are We? Where Are We Going?* 1897. Oil on canvas, 54¾ × 12'3½ (139 × 374.5). Courtesy, Museum of Fine Arts, Boston. Arthur Gordon Tompkins Residuary Fund.

GEORGIN, F., and J.-B. Thiebault **188** *The Apotheosis of Napoleon* 1834. Print, 16 × 23 (40.6 × 58.2). Photo Bibliothèque Nationale, Paris.

GÉRARD, François **23** *Cupid and Psyche* 1798. Oil on canvas, 73¼ × 52 (186 × 132). Musée du Louvre, Paris. **31** *Ossian* 1801. Oil on canvas, 72⅝ × 76½ (184.5 × 194.5). Kunsthalle, Hamburg. Photo © Elke Walford. **56** *Entry of Henri IV into Paris* 1817. Oil on canvas, 16'7⅞ × 31'4¼ (510 × 958). Musée National du Château, Versailles. Photo © R.M.N.

GERICAULT, Théodore **52** *The Charging Light Cavalryman (chasseur)* 1812. Oil on canvas, 11'5½ × 8'8¾ (349 × 266). Musée du Louvre, Paris. Photo Bulloz. **53** *The Wounded Heavy Cavalryman (cuirassier)* 1814. Oil on canvas, 11'9 × 9'7¾ (358 × 294). Musée du Louvre, Paris **58** *Severed Limbs* 1818. Oil on canvas, 20½ × 25⅛ (52 × 64). Musée Fabre, Montpellier. **59** *Despair and Cannibalism on the Raft of the Medusa* 1818. Black pencil, brown ink, heightened with white gouache on beige paper, 11 × 15 (28 × 38). Private collection. **60** *Pity the Sorrows of the Poor Old Man* 1821. Lithograph, 12½ × 14⅞ (31.7 × 37.6). Bibliothèque Nationale, Paris. **61** *Portrait of an Insane Man* 1822–3. Oil on canvas, 24 × 19¾ (61.2 × 50.2). Ghent Museum. Photo A.C.L. **62** *The Raft of the Medusa* 1819. Oil on canvas, 16'1 × 23'6 (490.2 × 716.3). Musée du Louvre, Paris. Photo © R.M.N.

GEROME, Jean-Léon **226** *Reception of the Siamese Ambassadors by Napoleon III and the Empress Eugénie at Fontainebleau, June 27, 1861* 1861–4. Oil on canvas, 50⅜ × 8'6⅜ (128 × 260). Musée National du Château, Versailles. Photo © R.M.N.

GILLRAY, James **105** *Phaeton Alarm'd!* 1808. Engraving, 13 × 14½ (33 × 36.8). The Trustees of the British Museum, London.

GILPIN, William **111**, **112** Plates from *Three Essays: On Picturesque Beauty, On Picturesque Travel, and On Sketching* 1792. Both 6⅛ × 9 (15.5 × 22.5).

GIRODET, Anne-Louise **12** *Pietà* 1789. Oil on canvas, 11' × 92½ (335 × 235). Church of Montesquieu-Volvestre, Haute-Garonne. **13** *The Sleep of Endymion* 1791. Oil on canvas, 19⅜ × 24½ (49 × 62). Musée du Louvre, Paris. **25** *Portrait of Jean-Baptiste Belley* 1797. Oil on canvas, 63 × 45 (160 × 114.3). Musée National du Château, Versailles. Photo © R.M.N. **32** *Ossian Receiving the Napoleonic Officers* 1802. Oil on canvas, 37 × 73½ (93.9 × 186.7). Musée National du Château de Malmaison, Reuil-Maison. Photo Bulloz. **33** *The Deluge* 1806. Oil on canvas, 14'1¾ × 11'2¼ (431 × 341). Musée du Louvre, Paris. **49** *Atala at the Tomb* 1808. Oil on canvas, 77½ × 8'6⅜ (197 × 260). Musée du Louvre, Paris. Photo Bulloz. **51** *The Revolt at Cairo* 1810. Oil on canvas, 11'8⅛ × 16'4⅞ (356 × 500). Musée National du Château, Versailles. Photo © R.M.N.

GIRTIN, Thomas **115** *Kirkstall Abbey* 1800. Watercolor, 12 × 20 (30.5 × 50.8). The Trustees of the British Museum, London. **116** *Somerset House* for "Eidometropolis," 1802. Watercolor, 9⅝ × 21¼ (24.4 × 54). The Trustees of the British Museum, London.

GOGH, Vincent Van **295** *La Berceuse* 1889. Oil on canvas, 36¼ × 28¾ (92 × 73). State Museum Kröller-Müller, Otterlo. **296** *The Artist's Bedroom in Arles* 1888. Oil on canvas, 28¼ × 35½ (79 × 90). Rijksmuseum Vincent van Gogh, Amsterdam. **297** *Carpenter's Workshop and Laundry* 1882. Pencil, ink, and paint on laid paper, 11¼ × 18⅜ (28.5 × 47). State Museum Kröller-Müller, Otterlo. **299** *The Bearers of the Burden* 1881. Pencil and ink on laid paper, 17 × 23⅝ (43 × 60). State Museum Kröller-Müller, Otterlo. **300** *The Potato Eaters* 1885. Oil on canvas, 32¼ × 44⅞ (82 × 114). Rijksmuseum Vincent van Gogh, Amsterdam. **304** *Portrait of Père Tanguy* 1887–8. Oil on canvas, 36¼ × 29½ (92 × 75). Musée Rodin, Paris. Photo © R.M.N. **306** *Yellow House at Arles* 1888. Oil on canvas, 28⅜ × 36 (72 × 91.5). Rijksmuseum Vincent van Gogh, Amsterdam. **307** *The Night Café* 1888. Oil on canvas, 28½ × 36¼ (72.4 × 92). Yale University Art Gallery, New Haven. Bequest of Stephen Carlton Clark, B.A. 1903. **308** *Self-Portrait With Bandaged Ear* 1889. Oil on canvas, 23⅝ × 19¼ (60 × 49). Courtauld Institute Galleries, London. **309** *Joseph Roulin* 1888. Oil on canvas, 32 × 25¾ (81.2 × 65.3). Courtesy, Museum of Fine Arts, Boston. Robert Treat Paine II Bequest. **310** *Eugène Boch* 1888. Oil on canvas, 23⅝ × 17¾ (60 × 45). Musée d'Orsay, Paris. **311** *Starry Night* 1889. Oil on canvas, 29 × 36¼ (73.7 × 92.1). The Museum of Modern Art, New York. Acquired through the Lillie P. Bliss Bequest. **312** *Crows in the Wheatfields* 1890. Oil on canvas, 19⅞ × 39½ (50.5 × 100.3). Rijksmuseum Vincent van Gogh, Amsterdam.

GOYA, Francisco **72** *Caprichos 1* frontispiece, 1799. Etching and aquatint, 8⅝ × 6 (21.9 × 15.2). Biblioteca Nacional, Madrid. **73** *Caprichos 43* "El sueño de la razón produce monstruos" (The sleep of reason produces monsters") 1799. Etching and aquatint, 8½ × 6 (21.6 × 15.2). Biblioteca Nacional, Madrid. **74** *Conde de Floridablanca* 1783. Oil on canvas, 81½ × 42 (207 × 106.7). Banco Urquijo, Madrid. **75** *Charles IV and His Family* 1801. Oil on canvas, 9'2¼ × 11'1¼ (280 × 335.9). Museo del Prado, Madrid. **76** *The Family of the Duque de Osuna* 1788. Oil on canvas, 88⅞ × 68½ (225.7 × 174). Museo del Prado, Madrid. Photo Mas, Barcelona. **77** *Queen María Luisa Wearing a Mantilla* 1799. Oil on canvas, 82¾ × 51⅛ (210 × 130). Patrimonio Nacional, Palacio Real, Madrid. Photo Mas, Barcelona. **78** *Naked Maja* ca. 1798–1805. Oil on canvas, 37⅜ × 74¾ (94.9 × 189.9). Museo del Prado, Madrid. **79** *Clothed Maja* ca. 1798–1805. Oil on canvas, 37⅜ × 74¾ (94.9 × 189.9). Museo del Prado, Madrid. **80** *Courtyard with Lunatics* 1793–4. Oil on canvas, 17¼ × 12⅞ (43.8 × 32.7). Meadows Museum, Dallas. **81** *The Knife Grinder* ca. 1808–12. Oil on canvas, 25⅝ × 19⅝ (65 × 50). Reproduced by courtesy of the Board of Directors of the Budapest Museum of Fine Arts. **82** *The Executions of the Third of May, 1808* 1814. Oil on canvas, 8'8¾ × 11'3⅞ (266 × 344.8). Museo del Prado, Madrid. Photo Mas, Barcelona. **83** *The Witches' Sabbath* 1797–8. Oil on canvas, 17⅜ × 12¼ (44 × 31). Museo Lázaro Galdiano, Madrid. **84** *Caprichos 68* "Linda maestra!" ("A fine teacher") 1799. Etching and aquatint, 8⅜ × 5⅞ (21.3 × 15). Biblioteca Nacional, Madrid. Photo Mas, Barcelona. **85** *Caprichos 50* "Los Chincillas" ("The Chincillas") 1799. Etching and aquatint, 8¼ × 5⅞ (20.8 × 15.1). Biblioteca Nacional, Madrid. **86** *Caprichos 10* "El amor y la muerte" ("Love and Death") 1799. Etching and aquatint, 8½ × 6 (21.8 × 15.3). Biblioteca Nacional, Madrid. **87** *Caprichos 52* "Lo que puede un sastre!" ("What a tailor can achieve!") 1799. Etching and aquatint, 8½ × 6 (21.7 × 15.2). Biblioteca Nacional, Madrid. Photo Mas, Barcelona. **88** *The Uprising of the Second of May, 1808* 1814. Oil on canvas, 8'9 × 11'4⅛ (226.7 × 345.8). Museo del Prado, Madrid. **89** *The Disasters of War 26* "No se puede mirar" ("One can't look") ca. 1810–20. Etching and lavis, 5⅝ × 8¼ (14.4 × 21). Photo Mas, Barcelona. **90** *The Disasters of War 2* "Con razon ó sin ella" ("Whether Right or Wrong") ca. 1810–20. Etching and lavis, 6⅛ × 8 (15.5 × 20.5). **91** *The Disasters of War 79* "Murió la verdad" ("Truth is dead") ca. 1810–20. Etching, 7 × 8⅝ (17.5 × 22). Photo Mas, Barcelona. **92** *The Disasters of War 80* "Si reucitariá?" ("If she were to rise again?") ca. 1810–20. Etching, 7 × 8⅝ (17.5 × 22). Photo Mas, Barcelona. **93** *The Disasters of War 84* "La seguridad de un reo no exige tormento" ("The custody of a criminal does not call for torture") ca. 1810–20. Etching and burin, 4½ × 3⅜ (11.5 × 8.5). Photo Mas, Barcelona. **94** *Saturn Devouring His Children* ca. 1820. Mural transferred to canvas, 57⅛ × 32⅝ (145 × 82.9). Museo del Prado, Madrid.

GRANDVILLE **198** "Apple of the Hesperides and rum ice," from *Un Autre Monde* 1844. Photo Bibliothèque Nationale, Paris.

GROS, Antoine-Jean **39** *The Battle of Nazareth* 1801. Oil on canvas, 53¼ × 76¾ (135 × 195). Musée des Beaux-Arts, Nantes. Photo © Patrick Jean. **40**

Napoleon in the Plague House at Jaffa 1804. Oil on canvas, 17′5½ × 23′7½ (532.1 × 720). Musée du Louvre, Paris. Photo © R.M.N.

GUÉRIN, Pierre-Narcisse **20** *The Return of Marcus Sextus* 1798. Oil on canvas, 85½ × 95½ (217 × 243). Musée du Louvre, Paris. Photo © R.M.N. **48** *Aurora and Cephalus* 1811. Oil on canvas, 8′4¼ × 73¼ (254.5 × 186). Musée du Louvre, Paris. Photo © R.M.N. **55** *Henri de Rochejaquelein* 1817. Oil on canvas, 85 × 56 (216 × 142). Musée Municipal, Cholet.

GUYS, Constantin **234** *The Champs-Elysées* 1855. Oil on paper, 9½ × 16⅜ (24.1 × 41.6). Musée du Petit Palais, Paris. Photo Bulloz.

HARRIET, Fulchran-Jean **19** *Oedipus at Colonus* 1796. Oil on canvas, 61½ × 52⅜ (156 × 133). Private collection. Photo © R.M.N.

HENNEQUIN, Philippe-Auguste **21** *Allegory of 10 August* 1799. Detail. Oil on canvas, 88⅛ × 68⅞ (224 × 175). Musée des Beaux-Arts, Rouen.

HERSENT, Louis **54** *Louis XVI Distributing Alms to the Poor* 1817. Oil on canvas, 70 × 90¼ (178 × 229). Musée Nationale du Château, Versailles. Photo © R.M.N.

HODLER, Ferdinand **336** *The Night* 1891. Oil on canvas, 45⅝ × 9′9¾ (116 × 299). Kunstmuseum, Bern. **337** *The Mönch With Clouds* 1911. Oil on canvas, 25⅜ × 36 (64.5 × 91.5). Private collection. **342** *The Beech Forest* 1885. Oil on canvas, 39¾ × 51½ (101 × 131). Kunstmuseum, Solothurn. **343** *Lake Geneva Seen From Chexbres* 1904. Oil on canvas, 27⅝ × 42½ (70.2 × 108). Collection du Musée des Beaux-Arts, Lausanne. Photo J.C. Ducret. **345** *Valentine in Agony* 1915. Oil on canvas, 23⅞ × 35⅝ (60.5 × 90.5). Oeffentliche Kunstsammlung, Basel.

HOMER, Winslow **161** *Prisoners From the Front* 1866. Oil on canvas, 24 × 38 (60.9 × 96.5). The Metropolitan Museum of Art, New York. Gift of Mrs. Frank B. Porter, 1922 (22.207). Copyright © 1984 By The Metropolitan Museum of Art. **164** *A Bivouac Fire on the Potomac* 1861. Wood engraving, 13¾ × 20 (34.9 × 50.8). Sterling and Francine Clark Art Institute, Williamstown, MA. **165** *Our Jolly Cook* 1863. Lithograph, 13⅞ × 11⅛ (35.2 × 28). Amon Carter Museum, Forth Worth, TX. **166** *The Bright Side* 1865. Oil on canvas, 13¼ × 17½ (33.7 × 44.4). The Fine Arts Museum of San Francisco. Gift of Mr. and Mrs. John D. Rockefeller 3rd, 1979.7.56. **168** *A Visit From the Old Mistress* 1876. Oil on canvas 18 × 24⅛ (45.7 × 61.3). National Museum of American Art, Smithsonian Institution, Washington, D.C. Photo Art Resource, New York.

HOSMER, Harriet **169** *Beatrice Cenci* 1857. Marble, 17⅛ × 41⅛ × 17 (43.8 × 104.7 × 43.1). St. Louis Mercantile Library. **170** *Zenobia in Chains* 1859. Marble, height 49 (124.5). Wadsworth Atheneum, Hartford. Gift of Mrs. Josephine M. J. Dodge.

HUNT, William Holman **200** *The Awakening Conscience* 1853. Oil on canvas, 29½ × 22 (74.9 × 55.8) *excluding frame*. Tate Gallery, London.

INGRES, Jean-August-Dominique **35** *Napoleon on the Imperial Throne* 1806. Oil on canvas, 8′8⅝ × 63 (265.7 × 160). Musée de l'Armée, Palais des Invalides, Paris. **36** *The Ambassadors of Agamemnon Visiting Achilles* 1801. Oil on canvas, 43¼ × 61 (109.9 × 154.9). Ecole nationale supérieure des Beaux-Arts, Paris. **37** *Jupiter and Thetis* 1811. Oil on canvas, 11′4⅝ × 8′5¼ (347 × 257.2). Musée Granet, Aix-en-Provence. **38** *The Turkish Bath* 1862. Oil on canvas, diameter 42½ (108). Musée du Louvre, Paris. **63** *The Apotheosis of Homer* 1827. Oil on canvas, 12′8 × 16′11 (386 × 515.6). Musée du Louvre, Paris. Photo © R.M.N. **68** *The Vow of Louis XIII* 1824. Oil on canvas, 13′9¾ × 8′8⅛ (421 × 264.5). Montauban Cathedral. Photo Bulloz. **70** *Henri IV Playing With His Children* 1817. Oil on canvas, 39 × 49¼ (99.1 × 125). Musée du Petit Palais, Paris. Photo Bulloz. **184** *M. Louis-François Bertin* 1832. Oil on canvas, 46 × 37½ (116.8 × 95.3). Musée du Louvre, Paris. Photo Bulloz. **228** *Oedipus and the Sphinx* 1808. Oil on canvas, 74⅜ × 56⅝ (188.9 × 143.8). Musée du Louvre, Paris.

ISRAELS, Jozef **301** *The Frugal Meal* 1876. Oil on canvas, 35 × 54⅝ (88.9 × 138.7). © Glasgow Museums: Art Gallery and Museum, Kelvingrove.

JOCELYN, Nathaniel **154** *Cinque* 1839. Oil on canvas, 30¼ × 25½ (76.8 × 64.8). New Haven Colony Historical Society. Gift of Dr. Charles B. Purvis, 1898.

JOHNSON, Eastman **158** *Old Kentucky Home (Negro Life in the South)* 1859. Oil on canvas, 36 × 45 (91.4 × 114.3). Courtesy of The New-York Historical Society, New York City. **159** *A Ride for Liberty: The Fugitive Slaves* ca. 1862–3. Oil on board, 22 × 26¼ (55.8 × 66.6). The Brooklyn Museum. Gift of Miss Gwendolyn O. L. Conkling.

JOHNSTON, Frances Benjamin **152** *Class in American History* 1899–1900. Platinum print, 7½ × 9½ (19 × 24.1). The Museum of Modern Art, New York. Gift of Lincoln Kirstein.

KAUFMANN, Theodor **160** *On to Liberty* 1867. Oil on canvas, 36 × 56 (91.4 × 142.2). The Metropolitan Museum of Art, New York. Gift of Erving and Joyce Wolf, 1982. All rights reserved, The Metropolitan Museum of Art.

KING, Charles Bird **142** *Young Omahaw, War Eagle, Little Missouri, and Pawnees* 1822. Oil on canvas, 36⅛ × 28 (91.8 × 71.1). National Museum of American Art, Smithsonian Institution, Washington, D.C. Gift of Miss Helen Barlow. Photo Art Resource, New York. **148** *Keokuk, Sac (Watchful Fox)* 1827. Oil on panel, 17½ × 13¾ (44.4 × 34.9). National Museum of Denmark, Copenhagen.

KRIMMEL, John Lewis **153** *Quilting Frolic* 1813. Oil on canvas, 16⅞ × 22⅜ (42.8 × 56.8). The Henry Francis du Pont Winterthur Museum. Courtesy, Winterthur Museum.

KROHG, Christian **328** *Sick Girl* 1880–81. Oil on canvas, 40¾ × 23¼ (103.5 × 51.4). © Nasjonalgalleriet, Oslo.

LABILLE-GUIARD, Adélaïde **6** *Self-Portrait With Two Pupils* 1785. Oil on canvas, 83 × 59½ (210.8 × 151.1). The Metropolitan Museum of Art, New York. Gift of Julia A. Berwind 1953 (53.225.5). All rights reserved, The Metropolitan Museum of Art.

LANDON, Charles, after Anne-Louise Girodet **50** *Pygmalion and Galatea* from Landon's *Annales du Musée de l'école moderne des Beaux-Arts*, 1819. Engraving, 5⅛ × 3¾ (13 × 9.5).

LEIBL, Wilhelm **219** *Town Politicians* 1877. Oil on canvas, 30 × 38⅛ (76 × 97). Museum Stiftung Oskar Reinhart, Winterthur.

LEUTZE, Emmanuel **141** study for *Westward the Course of Empire Takes its Way (Westward Ho!)* 1861. Oil on canvas, 33¼ × 43⅜ (84.5 × 110.2). National Museum of American Art, Smithsonian Institution, Washington, D.C. Photo Art Resource, New York.

LEWIS, Edmonia **172** *Forever Free* 1867. Marble, 41¼ × 11 × 7 (104.8 × 27.9 × 17.8). Howard University, James A. Porter Gallery of Afro-American Art, Washington, D.C. **173** *Hagar in the Wilderness* 1868. Marble, 52⅝ × 15¼ × 17 (133.6 × 38.8 × 43.4). National Museum of American Art, Smithsonian Institution, Washington, D.C. Photo Art Resource, New York. Gift of Delta Sigma Theta Sorority, Inc. **174** *Old Indian Arrowmaker and His Daughter* 1872. Marble, height 27 (68.6). Carver Museum, Tuskegee Institute, AL.

MANET, Edouard **231** *The Barricade* ca. 1871. Watercolor and gouache, 18⅜ × 13⅛ (46.5 × 33.4). Reproduced by courtesy of the Board of Directors of the Budapest Museum of Fine Arts. **232** *Music in the Tuileries* 1862. Oil on canvas, 30 × 46½ (76 × 118). Reproduced by courtesy of the Trustees, The National Gallery, London. **233** *A Balcony* 1868–9. Oil on canvas, 66½ × 49¼ (169 × 125). Musée d'Orsay, Paris. Photo © R.M.N. **235** *Olympia* 1863. Oil on canvas, 51⅜ × 74⅞ (130.5 × 190). Musée d'Orsay, Paris. Photo © R.M.N. **248** *A Bar at the Folies-Bergère* ca. 1882. Oil on canvas, 37¾ × 51¼ (96 × 130). Courtauld Institute Galleries, London.

MARIS, Jacob **298** *The Bleaching Yard* 1870. Oil on canvas, 16⅛ × 22½ (41 × 57). © Rijksmuseum-Stichting Amsterdam.

MARTIN, John **124** *The Fall of Ninevah* 1829. Mezzotint, 36 × 26¾ (91.4 × 68). The Trustees of the British Museum, London. **125** *The Last Man* ca. 1832. Watercolor, 18¾ × 27¼ (47.6 × 74). Laing Art Gallery, Newcastle-upon-Tyne.

MENZEL, Adolph von **220** *Iron Rolling Mill* 1872–5. Oil on canvas, 60¼ × 99⅝ (153 × 253). Staatliche Museen, Nationalgalerie, Berlin.

MILLAIS, John Everett **199** *Christ in the House of His Parents* 1850. Oil on canvas, 33½ × 54 (85 × 137.2). Tate Gallery, London. **330** *Ophelia* 1851. Oil on canvas, 30 × 40 (76.2 × 101.6). Tate Gallery, London.

MILLET, Jean-Françoise **197** *The Gleaners* 1857. Oil on canvas, 33 × 44 (83.8 × 111.8). Musée du Louvre, Paris. Photo Bulloz. **201** *The Sower* 1850. Oil on canvas, 39¾ × 32½ (101 × 82.5). Courtesy, Museum of Fine Arts, Boston. Shaw Collection.

MONET, Claude **237** *Regatta at Argenteuil* 1872. Oil on canvas, 19 × 29½ (48 × 75). Musée d'Orsay, Paris. **246** *Women in the Garden* 1866–7. Oil on canvas, 8′4 × 81 (255 × 205). Musée d'Orsay, Paris. Photo © R.M.N. **335** *Waterlilies* 1905. Oil on canvas, 35⅛ × 36½ (89.2 × 92.7). Courtesy, Museum of Fine Arts, Boston. Given in memory of Governor Alvan T. Fuller by the Fuller Foundation, 61.959.

MOREAU, Gustave **227** *Oedipus and the Sphinx* 1864. Oil on canvas, 80⅝ × 41 (204.7 × 104.1). The Metropolitan Museum of Art, New York. The Bequest of William H. Herriman, 1921. All rights reserved, The Metropolitan Musem of Art.

MORISOT, Berthe **247** *Laundresses Hanging Out the Wash* 1875. Oil on canvas, 13 × 16 (33 × 40.6). © 1993 National Gallery of Art, Washington, D.C. Collection of Mr. and Mrs. Paul Mellon **249** *The Psyché* 1876. Oil on canvas, 25¼ × 21¼ (64 × 54). Thyssen-Bornemisza Collection, Lugano, Switzerland.

MUNCH, Edvard **327** *Sick Child* 1885–6. Oil on canvas, 47 × 46½ (119.4 × 119). © Nasjonalgalleriet, Oslo. **329** *The Voice* 1893. Oil on canvas, 34½ × 42½ (87.6 × 108). Courtesy, Museum of Fine Arts, Boston. **338** *Madonna* 1895–7. Color lithograph, 23⅞ × 17½ (60.6 × 44.5).

NAST, Thomas **167** *Entrance of the Fifty-fifth Massachusetts (Colored) Regiment into Charleston, South Carolina, February 21, 1865* 1865. Pencil, neutral wash, and oil, heightened with white, on board, 14¼ × 21¼ (36.2 × 53.9). Courtesy, Museum of Fine Arts, Boston. M. and M. Karolik Collection of American Watercolors and Drawings, 1800–75.

PALMER, Samuel **120** *A Hilly Scene* ca. 1826. Watercolor, pen, and tempera, 8⅛ × 5¼ (20.6 × 13.3). Tate Gallery, London.

PAPETY, Dominique **193** *The Dream of Happiness* 1843. Oil on canvas, 12′1¾ × 20′8 (370 × 635). Musée de Compiègne. Photo © R.M.N.

PEYRON, Pierre **2** *The Death of Alcestis* 1785. Oil on canvas, 10′8 × 10′6 (327 × 325). Musée du Louvre, Paris. Photo © R.M.N.

PILOTY, Karl von **218** *Seni Before Wallenstein's Corpse* 1855. Oil on canvas, 10′2¾ × 11′11¾ (312 × 365). Neue Pinakothek, Munich.

PILS, Isidore **204** *The Death of a Sister of Charity* 1850. Oil on canvas, 95 × 10′ (241 × 305). Musée d'Orsay, Paris. Photo © R.M.N.

PISSARRO, Camille **238** *Hoarfrost* 1873. Oil on canvas, 25⅝ × 36⅝ (65 × 93). Musée d'Orsay, Paris. **241** *Edge of the Woods or, Undergrowth in Summer* 1879. Oil on canvas, 49⅝ × 63¾ (126 × 162). The Cleveland Museum of Art. Gift of Hanna Fund. **287** *L'Isle Lacroix, Rouen, Mist* 1888. Oil on canvas, 18¼ × 21⅞ (44 × 55). Pennsylvania Museum of Art. Courtesy of the John G. Johnson Collection, Philadelphia. **362** *Village Near Pontoise* 1873.

INDEX